Health for Life

Teacher's Edition

Authors

Julius B. Richmond
John D. MacArthur Professor of Health Policy
Director, Division of Health Policy Research and Education
Harvard University
Advisor on Child Health Policy
Children's Hospital of Boston
Boston, Massachusetts

Elenore T. Pounds
Health Education Writer
Downers Grove, Illinois

Physical Fitness Author

Charles B. Corbin
Professor, Department of Health and Physical Education
Arizona State University
Tempe, Arizona

Teacher's Edition Contributors

Matthew Bustamante
Bilingual/Cross-Cultural Education Specialist
Bandini Elementary School
Montebello, California

Linda Froschauer
Teacher
Weston Public Schools
Weston, Connecticut

Rosalyn Gantt
Teacher
Midway Elementary School
Cincinnati, Ohio

Jon Hisgen
School Health Coodinator
Pewaukee Public Schools
Pewaukee, Wisconsin

Jeanne Mannings
Teacher
Adamsville Elementary School
Atlanta, Georgia

Candace Purdy
Health Teacher
Maine South High School
Park Ridge, Illinois

Shirley Van Sickle
Health Teacher
DeVeaux Junior High School
Toledo, Ohio

Scott, Foresman and Company
Editorial Offices: Glenview, Illinois

Regional Offices: Sunnyvale, California • Tucker, Georgia • Glenview, Illinois • Oakland, New Jersey • Dallas, Texas

Reading Consultant
Robert A. Pavlik
Professor and Chairperson
Reading-Language Arts Department
Cardinal Stritch College
Milwaukee, Wisconsin

Medical Consultant
Jerry Newton, M.D.
Director, Health Services
San Antonio Independent School District
Clinical Professor, Pediatrics
University of Texas Medical School, San Antonio
San Antonio, Texas

Content Specialists
Dental Health
Mary Banas
Program Specialist
Bureau of Health Education and Audiovisual Services
American Dental Association
Chicago, Illinois

Drug Education
Chwee Lye Chng
Assistant Professor
Division of Health Education
North Texas State University
Denton, Texas

Merita Thompson
Professor
Department of Health Education
Eastern Kentucky University
Richmond, Kentucky

Family Life Education
Linda A. Berne
Professor
Department of Health and Physical Education
The University of North Carolina at Charlotte
Charlotte, North Carolina

Nutrition
Jean Mayer
President
Tufts University
Medford, Massachusetts

Safety and First Aid
Janice Sutkus
Technical Specialist
National Safety Council
Chicago, Illinois

Thinking Skills Consultant
Bert Pearlman
Director, Curriculum Research and Evaluation
Office of the County Superintendent of Schools
Santa Barbara, California

Consultants in Gifted Education
Gail Daud
Teacher in Gifted Education
Spring Shadows Elementary School
Houston, Texas

Peter Loudis
Teacher of Gifted and Talented
Spring Branch Junior High School
Houston, Texas

Consultants in Special Education
Judi Coffey
Educational Consultant
Learning Disabilities Specialist
Jonesboro, Arkansas

Wanda Nottingham-Brooks
Learning Disabilities Teacher
Morrisonville Junior and Senior High School
Morrisonville, Illinois

Cooperative Learning Consultant
Robert E. Slavin
Director, Elementary School Program
Center for Research on Elementary and Middle Schools
Johns Hopkins University
Baltimore, Maryland

Consultant for Multilingual/ Multicultural Education
Jesús Cortez
Professor of Education
Director, Center for Bilingual/ Multicultural Studies
California State University
Chico, California

Reviewers and Contributors
Lourdes Alcorta-Rogover
Educational Consultant
Former Teacher
Miami, Florida

Ruth Ann Althaus
Professor of Public Health
Master of Public Health Program
Illinois Benedictine College
Lisle, Illinois

Bryan Cooke
Professor
Department of Community Health
College of Health and Human Services
University of Northern Colorado
Greeley, Colorado

Bo Fernhall
Director, Fitness and Cardiac Rehabilitation
Department of Physical Education
Northern Illinois University
DeKalb, Illinois

Adele G. Russman
School Counselor
Main Street School
Exeter, New Hampshire

Joan Salmon
School Nurse
Greenwood School Corporation
Greenwood, Indiana

David R. Stronck
Associate Professor of Health Education
Department of Teacher Education
California State University, Hayward
Hayward, California

Martin C. Ushkow, M.D.
Medical Director
Syracuse School District

ISBN: 0-673-29596-6

2345678910VHJ99989796959493929190

Contents

Health for Life

When teaching health,

"Unless a child is alert, healthy, well-fed and fit, you cannot teach that child those subjects traditionally called basics."

J. Michael McGinnis
Former Deputy Assistant
U.S. Secretary for Health

the student is the subject matter.

Scott, Foresman's *Health for Life* provides the components teachers need to teach students how to develop good health for life.

Pupil's Edition	Test Book
Teacher's Edition	Posters
Teacher's Resource Book	Overhead Transparencies
Teacher's Resource File	Big Book (K)
Workbook	Activities Book (K)
Workbook Teacher's Edition	Primary Learning System

Pupil's Edition

Responsibility—to self,

"Health education helps people develop a sense of responsibility for their own health betterment as individuals and as members of families, communities, or governments."

World Health Organization

family, and community.

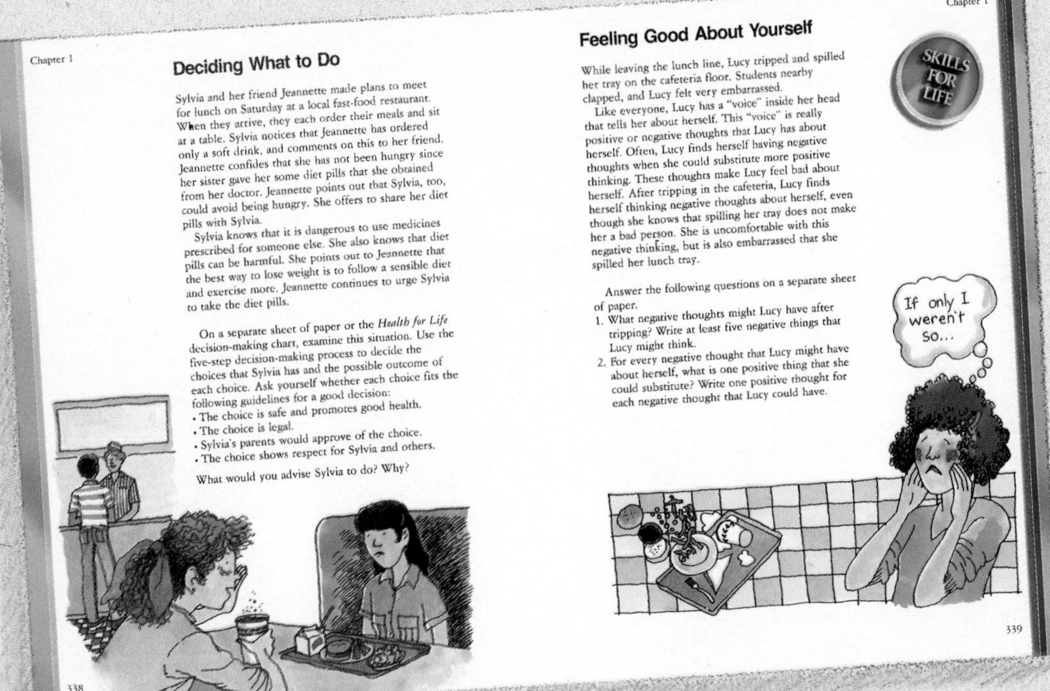

Chapter 1

Deciding What to Do

Sylvia and her friend Jeannette made plans to meet for lunch on Saturday at a local fast-food restaurant. When they arrive, they each order their meals and sit at a table. Sylvia notices that Jeannette has ordered only a soft drink, and comments on this to her friend. Jeannette confides that she has not been hungry since her sister gave her some diet pills that she obtained from her doctor. Jeannette points out that Sylvia, too, could avoid being hungry. She offers to share her diet pills with Sylvia.

Sylvia knows that it is dangerous to use medicines prescribed for someone else. She also knows that diet pills can be harmful. She points out to Jeannette that the best way to lose weight is to follow a sensible diet and exercise more. Jeannette continues to urge Sylvia to take the diet pills.

On a separate sheet of paper or the *Health for Life* decision-making chart, examine this situation. Use the five-step decision-making process to decide the choices that Sylvia has and the possible outcome of each choice. Ask yourself whether each choice fits the following guidelines for a good decision:

- The choice is safe and promotes good health.
- The choice is legal.
- Sylvia's parents would approve of the choice.
- The choice shows respect for Sylvia and others.

What would you advise Sylvia to do? Why?

338

Chapter 1

Feeling Good About Yourself

While leaving the lunch line, Lucy tripped and spilled her tray on the cafeteria floor. Students nearby clapped, and Lucy felt very embarrassed.

Like everyone, Lucy has a "voice" inside her head that tells her about herself. This "voice" is really positive or negative thoughts that Lucy has about herself. Often, Lucy finds herself having negative thoughts when she could substitute more positive thinking. These thoughts make Lucy feel bad about herself. After tripping in the cafeteria, Lucy finds herself thinking negative thoughts about herself, even though she knows that spilling her tray does not make her a bad person. She is uncomfortable with this negative thinking, but is also embarrassed that she spilled her lunch tray.

Answer the following questions on a separate sheet of paper.

1. What negative thoughts might Lucy have after tripping? Write at least five negative things that Lucy might think.
2. For every negative thought that Lucy might have about herself, what is one positive thing that she could substitute? Write one positive thought for each negative thought that Lucy could have.

SKILLS FOR LIFE
If only I weren't so...

339

The ***Skills for Life Handbook*** provides activities for every chapter to help students develop life skills that will help them deal with challenges throughout their lives. These life skills include decision making and communication.

Health at Home

Using Photographs to Examine Your Growth

Photographs of yourself and family members can illustrate many of the topics discussed in this chapter. Compare school photographs of yourself taken over the past several years. Look for physical features that have changed a lot and those that have changed little.

Some pictures, like the one here, might show a family member when he or she was close to your age. You might ask an adult to help you find such a picture. Examine it closely. Notice any resemblance between yourself and the person in the photograph.

Ask adults in your family if they remember when they started their growth spurts. Ask them what changes they experienced. How did they handle the changes of growth?

Reading at Home

The Answer Book About You by Mary Etling and Rose Wyler. Grosset and Dunlap, 1980. Find answers to some questions young people ask about their growth and development.

How You Grow and Change by Dorothy Baldwin and Claire Lister. Bookwright/Watts, 1984. Further explore the changes of growth.

71

The ***Health at Home*** feature provides an opportunity for students to share health information or an activity with their family.

Pupil's Edition

Content

Age-appropriate

Health for Life teaches students what they need and want to know at the time they need and want to know it.

Easy to comprehend

Health for Life makes it easy for students to learn important health concepts through motivating visuals and text and built-in comprehension aids.

- Lesson titles in question form involve students immediately and set the purpose for reading.
- The text answers the question and involves students in learning through a personal and active writing style and purposeful, instructional illustrations.
- Review questions help students assess mastery of the lesson's objective.

4 How Do Your Health Decisions Affect Your Growth?

Your heredity and your endocrine glands are not the only factors that affect your growth. Your health decisions have a strong influence on how you grow. You cannot control the actions of your heredity or your endocrine system. However, you can make decisions that influence your health and growth.

Your heredity sets limits for your growth. The pictures on these two pages show some of the health decisions that affect your growth within those limits. For example, the genes you inherit might set an upper boundary of five feet nine inches (about 175 cm) for your adult height. However, you might not reach this height if you have poor eating habits during your school years. Your body needs the right amounts and the right kinds of food to grow as it should. You can give your body the materials it needs for growth by eating a variety of foods. A good variety includes fruits and vegetables; dairy products; breads and cereals; and meat and fish. Eating too much of one kind of food does not give your body what it needs for proper growth.

Food and rest affect health and growth.

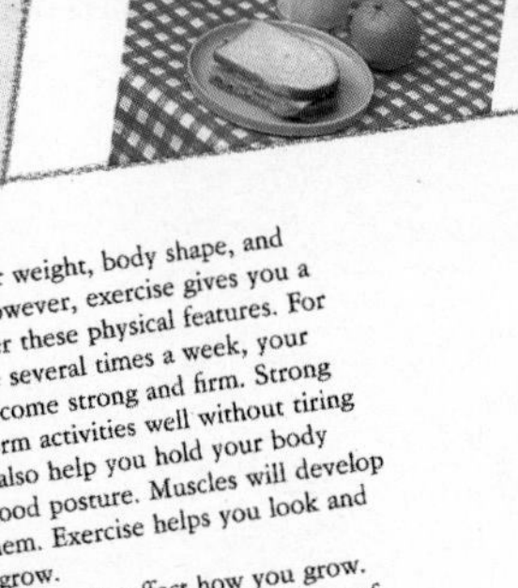

Heredity sets limits for weight, body shape, and muscle development. However, exercise gives you a great deal of control over these physical features. For example, if you exercise several times a week, your muscles are likely to become strong and firm. Strong muscles help you perform activities well without tiring easily. Strong muscles also help you hold your body correctly, giving you good posture. Muscles will develop only if you exercise them. Exercise helps you look and feel your best as you grow.

Your decisions about rest also affect how you grow. Most people your age need about nine to ten hours of sleep each night. While you sleep, your body uses energy from the food you eat to build new cells. Also, your body produces most of your growth hormone while you sleep.

Eating right, exercising, and getting enough sleep are wise decisions you can make to help you grow properly.

Think Back • *Study on your own with Study Guide page 319.*

1. If the upper limit of a girl's inherited adult height is five feet six inches (about 160 cm), will she definitely be that tall as an adult? Explain your answer.
2. What are three decisions you can make that affect your growth?

Exercise affects health and growth.

Application

Health for Life provides many opportunities for students to develop healthy behavior as they apply health concepts to their own lives.

The ***Health Watch Notebook*** provides an activity at the beginning of each chapter to help students look for application of health concepts in the media and the world around them.

at the prices you can afford. The consumer skills you learn now can be used throughout your lifetime.

Health Watch Notebook

Collect magazine and newspaper advertisements and place them in your notebook. Under each ad, explain how it influences the consumer.

1 How Can You Become a Wise Health Consumer?
2 How Can Advertising Influence You as a Consumer?
3 What Should You Consider When Choosing Health Products?
4 How Can You Benefit Most from a Health

Health Activities Workshop

Evaluating Ads and Products

1. Make a collection of ads for health products from newspapers and magazines. Note the advertising methods used to get people to buy. Identify the useful information. Which ads are most appealing? Which of the advertised products would you consider using?

2. Think of as many advertising jingles and slogans as you can. Hum the jingles and read a list of the slogans to some of your classmates. How many products can you and your classmates identify from the jingles and slogans? Evaluate the effectiveness of each jingle and slogan.

3. Design an ad for a health product, as these students are doing. You can choose an existing product or make up one of your own. You might choose toothpaste, shampoo, or another health product that you are familiar with. Decide on a brand name. Draw a logo. Try to make your ad influence people through words and pictures. Share your ad with your classmates. Would they buy your product?

4. Think about a health product you use frequently. Do you know if you are making wise consumer choices about this product? To find out, go to the library and find a consumer publication. Look for information about the product. Be sure that the publication also contains information about competitor's products. Evaluate the different brands. Write down the benefits and drawbacks of each brand. Give reasons why you would choose one brand over another.

268

The ***Health Activities Workshop*** provides opportunities for students to apply what they have learned in the preceding lessons and develop health habits.

Project Keep-Fit is a six-page feature in the fitness chapter that demonstrates an age-appropriate exercise program with a warm-up, workout, cool-down, and sitting exercises.

project keep fit

Project Keep-Fit is an exercise program that can help you improve your physical health and your physical abilities. Be sure to have your teacher help you learn how to do these exercises correctly. Also, it is a good idea to check with your doctor before beginning any exercise program.

The program begins with warm-up exercises to stretch muscles and prepare your body for more vigorous activity. The warm-up exercises can also be used for the cool-down, preparing your body to return to its normal amount of activity. The main part of the program, called the *Workout*, includes exercises that build all parts of fitness.

Warm-Up

Side Stretcher
- Stand with your feet about twelve inches apart. Hold your right hand up over your head.
- Bend as far as you can to the left. Reach as low as you can with your left arm and

Toe Reach
- Sit on the floor with your legs straight. Spread them about three feet apart.
- Bend your body forward over your right leg and reach toward your toes. Reach as far as you can. Try to touch your head to your knee. Keep your leg straight. Hold for six seconds.
- Return to the starting position and repeat over your left leg.
- Return to the starting position and repeat reaching midway between your legs.
- Do five stretches to each side and to the middle.

Jumping Jacks
Do jumping jacks for one minute.

Teacher's Edition

Easy-to-Teach and Flexible

A ***3-step teaching plan*** makes the lessons easy to teach.

1 Motivate
Suggestions for introducing the lesson

2 Teach
Strategies for teaching the lesson

3 Assess
Answers for lesson review questions plus an additional question to develop higher-order thinking skills

A ***teaching options section*** provides added flexibility to your planning.

Teaching Plan

Lesson 1 pages 236–237

Lesson Objective
Explain why good posture is important to good health and how posture can be improved.

Health Vocabulary
Posture

1 Motivate
Introducing the Lesson
Ask students to write a simple explanation of what they think good standing posture involves. Save the papers so that students can compare them, at the end of the lesson, to what they have learned.

2 Teach
Strategies for Pages 236 and 237
• Write the lesson title question on the chalkboard. • Direct students to read page 236 to find the answer. (Good posture keeps bones and muscles in position to support the body without strain. Good posture helps prevent headaches, lower back pains, muscle soreness, and weariness.) • Discuss the drawing on page 236. Be sure students understand the difference between good and poor posture.

posture (pos′chər), the position of the body.

Did You Know?
Scoliosis (skō′lē ō′sis) is a condition in which the spine curves to the side, as shown in this X-ray photograph. Poor posture does not cause scoliosis. However, poor posture is sometimes a symptom of this condition. Scoliosis typically develops between the ages of eight and fifteen. Many schools have screening programs to find and help students who have developed scoliosis.

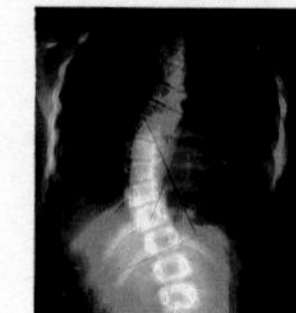

1 Why Is Good Posture Important to Your Health?

Think of the last time you stood in one place for a long period of time. Perhaps you were waiting in line to see a movie, or presenting a report in class. Did you quickly get tired of standing? Did your neck, back, or shoulders begin to ache? Such reactions might mean you could improve your **posture**—the way you hold your body.

The drawing shows how good posture keeps various parts of the body balanced in a straight column. Bones and muscles are in position to support the body weight properly. Now notice what happens when one part of the body, such as the head, moves out of line. Other parts of the body must move out of line to balance the body. This movement puts unnecessary strain on certain bones, muscles, and other body parts. Poor posture can cause headaches, lower back pains, and other muscle soreness.

Good posture helps prevent these aches and pains. Good posture also helps you stand, sit, or move about for long periods of time without getting tired. Then you can perform activities better. In addition, good posture improves the way you look.

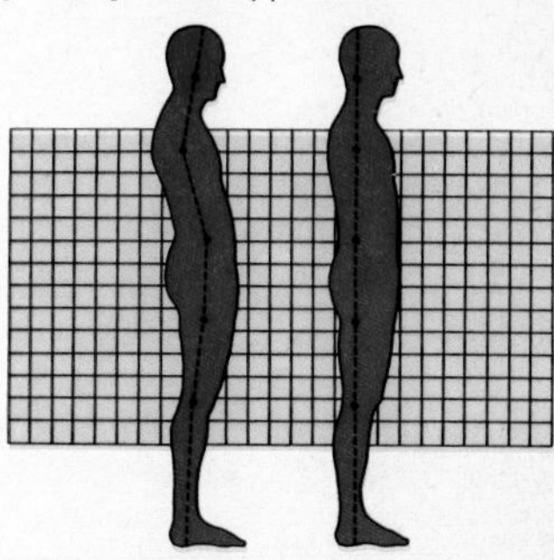

Good posture keeps the body balanced in a straight column.

236

Teaching Options

Health Background
Scoliosis is an abnormal lateral curvature of the spine. This disease affects 8 to 10 percent of young people as they go through their growth spurt. Scoliosis affects girls seven times more often than boys. Ninety percent of the cases have no known cause. During screening tests, an observer looks for such signs as one shoulder blade or hip higher than the other, a hump in the back near the ribcage or waist, or a leaning to one side. Treatment can include traction, casts, bracing, an exercise program, or surgery.

Enrichment
Suggest that students find out more about people for whom good posture is important in their work. (models, athletes, actors, and so on) Encourage students to write short reports on why good posture is important for these people.

Health and Art
Suggest students make health posters showing good posture while sitting or walking. If possible, display the posters on a bulletin board.

Reteaching
If possible, ask the physical education teacher or school nurse to visit the class and demonstrate other exercises that promote good posture.

236 Chapter 8 Lesson 1

Health Background provides helpful background information to expand your knowledge of lesson content.

Enrichment, Reteaching, Health and (other subject), and ***Special Education*** suggestions provide additional ways to help you meet the various needs of your students.

How Can You Improve Your Posture?

Your posture depends greatly upon the rest of your health. Therefore, an important way to improve your posture is to keep your body strong and healthy. Eating a balanced diet and getting plenty of exercise help build the strong bones and muscles needed for good posture. Two simple exercises for improving posture are shown here. Be sure your teacher shows you how to do them correctly. You can also help improve your posture by getting enough sleep at night. If you are rested, you will be less likely to get tired and slouch during the day.

Another way to improve your posture is to practice good posture throughout the day. While sitting, keep your body far back on the chair. When standing or walking, keep your head centered over the rest of your body. Be aware of your posture throughout the day. If you find you are slumping in your chair, make an effort to sit up straight.

The posture you develop now will likely be the posture you have throughout your life. Therefore, developing good, healthy posture is an important part of your daily health practices.

Think Back • *Study on your own with Study Guide page 330.*

1. How is good posture important to good health?
2. How can posture be improved?

237

• Ask what problems bad posture can cause. (strain on bones, muscles, and other body parts; headaches, lower back pain, and muscle soreness) • Discuss scoliosis. Emphasize that poor posture does not cause scoliosis. • Ask students to read page 237 to learn ways to improve posture. (keep body strong and healthy, get enough sleep, practice good posture throughout the day, exercise)

3 Assess

Expanding Student Thinking

Ask students why they think it is important to develop good posture while they are still young. (Good posture is part of healthy growth; bad posture habits are difficult to break as one gets older.)

Thinking Skill When students tell why good posture is important while they are young, they are *interpreting information.*

Answers to Think Back

1. Good posture helps prevent muscle soreness; helps a person stand, sit, or move about without getting tired easily; improves one's ability to perform activities; and improves one's appearance.

2. Posture can be improved by improving other aspects of health such as fitness, diet, and sleep. Posture can also be improved by practicing good posture throughout the day and by doing certain exercises.

Life Skills

Use this worksheet for practice in improving personal health care. This matter may be reproduced from the Teacher's Resource Book and is located on page 29 of the Student's Workbook. Use with Chapter 8: pages 236–255.

Thinking Skill: **By listing personal care activities, students are recalling information. By making a plan to fit these activities into their day, students are organizing information.**

Name ____________________ Life Skills

Use with Chapter 8: pages 236–255.

Making a Plan for Good Health

Personal care is important at all times. You can help keep yourself in good health by practicing good personal care. Make sure you know how to take care of your health every day. List what you can do in each of the areas below.

1. **Good Posture** Keep body strong and healthy, practice it by keeping head centered over body during the day
2. **Good Dental Care** Brush and floss teeth daily, choose food wisely, visit a dentist regularly
3. **Good Skin Care** Wash face and hands several times a day
4. **Good Hair Care** Shampoo hair often, being sure to rinse it well
5. **Relieve Fatigue** Change activity, get rest, food, exercise, or do something enjoyable
6. Make a plan to fit these personal care activities into each day. Write your plan in the space provided on the right.

My Plan for Good Health

Time	Activity
	Answers might vary.
7:30 a.m.	Brush teeth Wash face
8:00 a.m.	Eat healthy Breakfast
4:30 p.m.	Play hockey
9:00 p.m.	Go to sleep

Extension Idea: **Encourage students to evaluate their personal care habits after one week and suggest improvements.** 105

Chapter 8

Reduced copies of blackline masters from the ***Teacher's Resource Book*** appear on pages where they are best used.

Other Features

- ***The Teacher's Health Handbook*** in the front of the Teacher's Edition provides professional articles with helpful information on such topics as teaching about AIDS, reporting child abuse, preventing sexual abuse, and helping students cope with death.
- A 2-page insert before each chapter includes a ***Chapter Planning Guide*** showing what is available with each chapter, a list of resources, and a bulletin board idea.
- Thinking Skills are highlighted where activities and assessment questions develop these skills.

Supplementary Materials

Ancillary Components

- Teacher's Resource Book
  - Project Keep-Fit Exercise Guide
  - Teacher's Resource File Activities
  - Family Letters (English and Spanish)
  - Overhead Transparency Masters
  - Poster Notes
  - Life Skills Worksheets
  - Vocabulary Worksheets
  - Study and Review Worksheets
  - Health and (another subject) Worksheets
- Workbook
  - Repeats TRB worksheets in workbook format
- Workbook Teacher's Edition
- Test Book
- Posters
- Overhead Transparencies
  - Full-color for grades 1–3, 4–6, and 7–8

The various ancillaries accompanying *Health for Life* provide teachers with the flexibility they need to meet the school's health curriculum and the needs of the classroom.

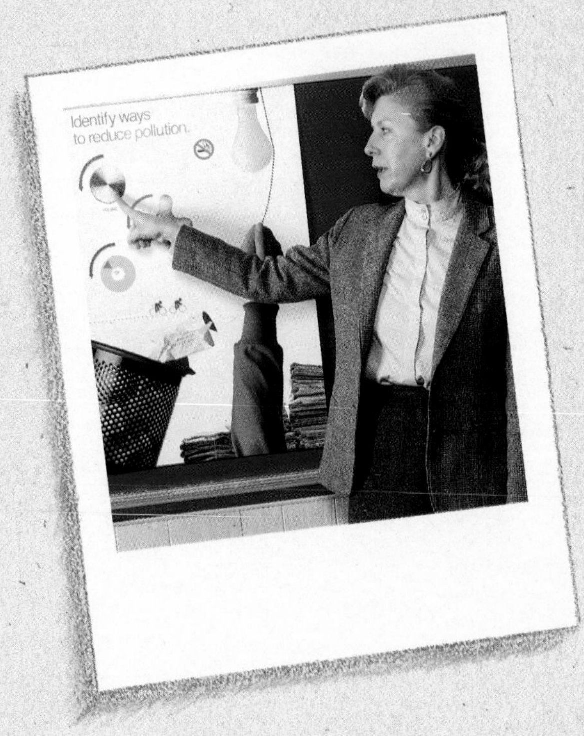

Enrichment

The Poster package provides one colorful teaching poster per chapter.

The ***Teacher's Resource Book*** provides blackline master worksheets for every chapter: Life Skills; Health and (another subject). It also has a Family Letter in English and Spanish for each chapter.

Flexible

Reteaching

The ***Overhead Transparency*** package provides at least one colorful overhead per health strand plus extra overheads on life skills and the body systems.

The ***Teacher's Resource Book*** provides blackline master worksheets for every chapter: Vocabulary; Study and Review.

Name ______________________ Chapter 6 Test B

Multiple Choice Choose the best answer.

1. Drugs that prevent, treat, or cure an illness are called
   a. hallucinogens. b. alcohol.
   c. medicines. d. narcotics.
2. To prepare prescription medicine, a pharmacist follows orders from
   a. a doctor.
   b. the patient.
   c. no one.
   d. a nurse.
3. If a person feels side effects from a medicine, the person should
   a. take more of the medicine.
   b. ignore the side effects.
   c. stop taking the medicine.
   d. take smaller doses.
4. Drug misuse means to
   a. incorrectly use medicine.
   b. take prescription medicine with a doctor's order.
   c. use only your prescription medicines.
   d. follow the information on medicine labels.
5. The intentional use of drugs for reasons other than health is
   a. an overdose. b. drug abuse.
   c. withdrawal. d. drug misuse.
6. A person who is physically dependent on a drug and stops taking it may suffer from
   a. an overdose. b. tolerance.
   c. drug misuse. d. withdrawal.
7. An overdose of a drug is
   a. too much for the body to use.
   b. becoming dependent on the drug.
   c. absorbed by the brain.
   d. a physical need for the drug.
8. Marijuana contains
   a. THC ony. b. over 400 chemicals.
   c. narcotics. d. LSD.
9. When marijuana is smoked, the heartbeat
   a. slows down. b. speeds up.
   c. stays the same. d. stops.
10. A disease in which a person cannot control the use of alcohol is
    a. cirrho... b. alcoholism.
    c. emph... ...bronchitis.
11. Alcohol ... the
    a. bra...
    c. liv...
12. A su... form... lun...
    a. ...
    c. ...
13. ...

Health for Life © Scott, Foresman and Company

Name ______________________ Chapter 6 Test B

Short Answer Complete the chart.

Type of Drug	Description
16. ________	Includes tranquilizers and barbiturates
17. ________	Its use often causes malnutrition; produces dependence quickly
18. ________	Immediate effects are very unpredictable; includes PCP
19. ________	Includes the fumes of glue and paint
20. ________	Causes changes in the senses; includes LSD
21. ________	Speeds up the work of the nervous system
22. ________	Includes cocaine and amphetamines
23. ________	Slows down the work of the nervous system
24. ________	Includes codeine, morphine, and heroin

Short Essay Write your answers in complete sentences.

25. What can a person do to resist pressure from others to use drugs?

26. How are cigarettes a threat to people's health?

52

Health for Life © Scott, Foresman and Company

Assessment

The ***Test Book*** provides two 2-page tests per chapter—Form A and Form B—plus answers.

Health for Life

	Mental Health and Social Health	Body Structure, Function, and Growth	Nutrition
K	• Learning and accomplishments • Taking care of things • Being kind • Talking about feelings • Helping at home	• Body parts • Growing and changing • Keeping clean • Eye care • The heart • Teeth • Things you have learned	• Breakfast • Fruits and vegetables • Foods from plants and animals • Healthy snacks and meals • Trying new foods
1	• Feeling happy • Feeling sad • Feeling angry • Feeling scared • Showing feelings • Talking about feelings • Liking yourself • Helping new students • Healthy mealtimes • Enjoying family walks	• Eyes • Learning and seeing • Ears • Learning and hearing • Hands • Learning and touching • Nose • Learning and smelling • Tongue • Learning and tasting • Food and growing • First teeth	• Food and growing • Food and strength • Food and health • Food and energy • Breakfast foods • Eating good foods • Trying new foods • Healthy snacks
2	• Feelings • Changing feelings • Feelings and other people • Differences in people • Feeling lonely • Making friends • Worried feelings • Showing feelings • Dealing with mistakes • Having fun alone	• Brain and learning • Senses and learning • Nerves • Bones • Joints, muscles, and movement • Heart, lungs, and exercise • Muscles and exercise • Teeth • Sleep and growth	• Food for growth and energy • Four food groups • Healthy meals and snacks • Trying new foods • Shopping for healthy foods
3	• Different feelings • Ways of expressing feelings • Dealing with fear, hurt, and death • Dealing with things going wrong • Getting along with others • Fitness and feeling good	• Cells • Tissues • Muscles • Bones • Brain • Nerves • Senses • Heart • Blood vessels • Lungs • Digestive system • Growth • Parts and kinds of teeth	• Healthy food choices • Food and nutrients • Four food groups • Healthy meals • Eating different vegetables • Healthy snacks • Wise food shopping • Preparing and serving healthy meals
4	• Understanding yourself • Self-image • Feelings and body changes • Dealing with anger • Steps in decision making • Dealing with disagreements • Getting along with others	• Cells to systems • Circulatory system • Digestive system • Respiratory system • Sense organs • Nervous system • Types of teeth • Skin • Eyes and Ears • Growth and growth spurt	• Need for food • Nutrients • Four food groups • Diseases and lack of nutrients • Healthy eating habits • Keeping food from spoiling • Preparing foods safely • Buying foods carefully
5	• Self-image • Improving self-image • Similarities and differences in people • Dealing with problems, anger, shyness, and uncomfortable feelings • Friendships • Learning to relax	• Bones • Muscles • Sense organs • Nervous system • Digestive system • Respiratory system • Circulatory system • Urinary system • Teeth • Cell division • Growth and hormones	• Nutrients • Carbohydrates • Proteins • Vitamins • Minerals • Four food groups • Planning healthy meals • Limiting salt and sugar • Adding fiber • Reducing fat • Healthy snacks • Food labels
6	• Self-image and confidence • Improving self-image • Building good relationships • Anger • Dealing with stress • Setting and reaching goals • Changing feelings • Exercise and mental health	• Endocrine glands and growth • Puberty • Heredity • Chromosomes • Genes • DNA • Gender determination • Trait variation in families • Health decisions and growth • Emotions and growth	• Carbohydrates • Fiber • Proteins • Fats • Vitamins, minerals, water • Four food groups • Limiting sugar, fat, salt, cholesterol • Food processing • Additives • Choosing foods wisely • Labels
7	• Improving mental health • Self-image • Emotional needs • Stress • Solving problems and making decisions • Getting along with others • Communicating • Peer pressure • Families	• Cells • Skeletal and muscular systems • Digestive system • Respiratory system • Circulatory and lymphatic systems • Urinary system • Nervous system • Endocrine system • Heredity • Puberty	• Nutrients • Simple and complex carbohydrates • Saturated and unsaturated fats • Complete proteins • Four food groups • Limiting sugar, salt, cholesterol, fat • Eating disorders • Food shopping
8	• Changing self-image • Decision making • Reaching goals • Career decisions • Effects of stress • Handling stress • Improving relationships • Dealing with peer pressure	• Growth and maturation • Hormones • Ovaries • Testes • Heredity • Chromosomes • Genes • DNA • Circulatory, respiratory, and skeletal systems and exercise • Ears • Eyes	• Nutrition research • Not skipping meals • Calories • Adding starch and fiber • Avoiding excess sugar, sodium, saturated fat, cholesterol • Preserving nutrients • Preventing food-borne illness

Scope and Sequence

Grade	Physical Fitness	Safety and First Aid	Drugs
K	• Exercise • The heart and exercise • Good posture • Safe places to play	• Home safety • Poison safety • Playing safely • Traffic safety • Car and bus safety • Caring for injuries	• Taking medicine
1	• Exercise and play • Different kinds of play • Strong muscles and play • Strong muscles and sitting • Strong muscles and standing • Balance • Walking • Playing and good health	• Eye safety • Crossing streets safely • Playing safely • Safety with matches and fire • Car safety • Getting adult help • Safety and medicines • Safety around strangers • Safety at home	• Learning about medicines • How medicines help • Medicine safety • Feeling better without medicines • Rules for taking medicines • Knowing who should give medicines
2	• Exercising and health • Exercise and the heart • Exercise and the lungs • Exercise and the muscles • Kinds of exercise • Exercising safely • Playing safely • Coordination	• Exercising safely • Safety and medicines • Bicycle safety • Walking safely • Safety around strangers • Safety at school • Safety around animals • Safety at home • First aid for minor injuries	• Medicines and drugs • Medicines prevent and cure illness • Using medicines safely • Tobacco smoke and health • Nicotine • Caffeine and health • Feeling better without medicines
3	• Physical fitness • Some benefits of fitness • Fitness and posture • Agility • Exercise and fitness • Need for exercise • Exercise and building strength • Exercise and stretching • Becoming physically fit	• General safety rules • Car safety • Bicycle safety • Appliance safety • Poison safety • Swimming safety • Fire safety • Medicine safety • Exercising safely • First aid for cuts and bites	• Prescription and over-the-counter medicines • Use of medicines • Rules for medicine safety • Caffeine • Alcohol • Nicotine • Marijuana • Choosing not to use harmful drugs
4	• Benefits of physical fitness • Muscle fitness • Flexibility • Muscle strength and endurance • Posture • Building fitness • Sports skills • Lifetime sports • Playing sports and games	• Pedestrian and bicycle safety • Water safety • Safety when alone • Keeping foods safe • Medicine safety • Dealing with emergencies • First aid for cuts, nosebleeds, burns, and blisters	• OTC and prescription medicines • Using medicines safely • Tobacco • Alcohol • Marijuana • Cocaine • Abuse of household products • Healthy decisions about drugs
5	• Importance of fitness • Health fitness • Skills fitness • Pulse rate • Improving cardiovascular fitness • Improving muscle fitness • Muscular endurance • Flexibility • Planning an exercise program	• Preventing accidents • Pedestrian, car, and bicycle safety • Camping safety • Water safety • Fire safety • Safety when alone • Dealing with emergencies • Choking • Exercising safely	• Medicine safety • Drug misuse and abuse • Tobacco • Alcohol • Depressants • Narcotics • Hallucinogens • Stimulants • Inhalants • Marijuana • Cocaine • Crack • Avoiding drug abuse
6	• Exercise and cardiovascular, respiratory, and muscular systems • Muscular strength, endurance, flexibility • Control of body fatness • Calories • Skills fitness • Setting fitness goals • Exercising safely	• Accident prevention • Traffic safety • Preventing falls, poisonings, electrical shock, and fires • Safety around strangers • Handling emergencies • Choking • Artificial respiration • Burns • Shock	• Medicines • Drug misuse and abuse • Depressants, stimulants, narcotics, hallucinogens, and inhalants • Designer drugs • Steroids • Marijuana • Alcohol • Tobacco • Healthy decisions about drugs
7	• Health and skills fitness • Cardiovascular fitness, muscular strength and endurance, flexibility, body fatness • Parts of skills fitness • FIT principle • Planning fitness program • Safety	• Avoiding unnecessary risks • Bicycle and auto safety • Swimming and boating safety • Storm safety • Bleeding • Poisoning • Shock • Sprains • Fractures • Heat stroke • Frostbite	• Prescription and OTC drugs • Tobacco • Alcohol • Marijuana • Depressants, stimulants, narcotics, hallucinogens, and inhalants • Anabolic steroids • Choosing not to abuse drugs
8	• Benefits of being fit • Parts of fitness • Exercise and the heart, blood vessels, lungs, skeletal muscles, and bones • Exercise and body leanness • Lifetime fitness • Personal fitness program	• Fire safety • Safety with electrical equipment • Motor-vehicle safety • Artificial respiration • Choking • Severe bleeding • Shock • Burns • Natural disasters	• New medicines • Drug abuse • Effects of alcohol, tobacco, and marijuana • Depressants, stimulants, narcotics, hallucinogens, and inhalants • Anabolic steroids • Avoiding drug abuse

Health for Life

Grade	Personal Health Care	Diseases	Consumer Health
K	• Keeping clean • Eye care • Exercise • Bedtime • Posture • Teeth and dental care • Dentist visit • Ways to stay healthy	• Eye care • Teeth care • Coughs and sneezes • Staying well • Doctor • Keeping the community healthy	• Eye care • Safety with poisons • Preparing healthy foods • Visiting the dentist • Medicines
1	• Taking care of eyes • Feeling better without medicine • Taking care of teeth • Sleep • What to do for a cold • Staying well • Washing hands • Visiting the dentist • Visiting the doctor	• Germs • Disease and medicine • Colds • Cavities • Preventing disease • Treating disease	• Safety with medicines • Care of the teeth • Visiting the dentist • Visiting the school nurse • Choosing healthy foods
2	• Staying healthy • Keeping hands and body clean • Brushing and flossing teeth • Cavities • Caring for the eyes • Caring for the ears • Sleep and health • Feeling better without medicines	• Germs and keeping clean • Germs and the teeth • Teeth and cavities • Polio • Sore throats • How germs spread	• Shopping for healthy foods • Deciding about medicines seen on TV • Talking to doctors and nurses about how you feel
3	• Washing hands when preparing food • Visiting the dentist • Cavities • Plaque • Brushing and flossing • Avoiding sticky foods • Avoiding harmful drugs • Becoming physically fit	• Germs and food • Bacteria • Tuberculosis • Strep throat • Vaccines • Viruses • Measles • Mumps • Polio • Spread of diseases • Cavities • Heart disease • Lung cancer • AIDS	• Being a wise food shopper • Visiting a dentist • Choosing products for tooth care wisely • Recognizing different kinds of medicines • Knowing when medicines are not needed
4	• Building physical fitness • Sleep • Tooth care • Gum care • Plaque • Calculus • Skin structure and care • Eye and ear care • Healthy eating habits • Preventing disease	• Bacteria • Viruses • Body fights disease • AIDS • Spreading germs • Food and disease • Heart and lung diseases • Vitamin deficiency diseases • Cancer • Diabetes • Arthritis • Allergies	• Choosing health care products wisely • Learning from labels • Learning from ads • Food shopping • Recognizing OTC medicines in safe containers • Reading medicine labels
5	• Health practices for growth • Caring for the body systems • Ear care • Eye care • Dental care • Choosing health care products • Choosing healthy foods • Improving fitness	• Germs • Food poisoning • Rabies • Typhoid fever and water pollution • Rickets • Tooth decay • Allergies and food choices • Heart disease • Stroke • Bronchitis • Emphysema • Cancer • AIDS	• Choosing health care products wisely • Determining need • Using ads • Product availability • Label information • Considering cost • Using food labels • Using medicine labels
6	• Healthy diet • Controlling body fatness • Achieving fitness goals • Preventing disease • Improving posture • Dental care • Eye and ear care • Skin care • Hair care • Sleep, rest, and recreation • Reducing fatigue	• Bacteria • Viruses • Body defenses • Antibodies • AIDS • Colds • Sinusitis • Influenza • Pneumonia • Controlling disease • Cardiovascular disease • Cancer • Allergies • Cirrhosis	• Choosing foods wisely • Evaluating ads • Health care products • Unit pricing • Net weight • Reading labels • Fads • Health checkup • Hospital care
7	• Sleep • Dental care • Periodontal disease • Malocclusion • Skin and hair care • Acne • Diet improvement • Planning a fitness program • Helping prevent cancer and cardiovascular disease	• Pathogens • Mono • Hepatitis • AIDS • Sexually transmitted diseases • Controlling diseases • Anorexia • Bulimia • Cardiovascular disease • Cancer • Arthritis • Epilepsy • Diabetes	• Food shopping • Labels • Guide for shopping • Clothes shopping • Choosing health care products • Evaluating health care services • Quackery • Patient responsibility • Consumer protection
8	• Handling stress • Maintaining weight in normal range • Building fitness • Skin care • Acne • Good posture • Scoliosis • Dental health • Teeth position • Ear and eye care	• Advances in disease diagnosis • Imaging devices • Advances in surgical procedures • Artificial body parts • Transplant surgery • Understanding mental illness • Disease prevention • AIDS	• Being a skillful consumer • Evaluating ads • Avoiding quackery • Health care services • Paying for health care • Being a wise food shopper • Exercise clothing • Products for skin

Scope and Sequence

	Community and Environmental Health	Family Health	Careers
K	• Taking care of things around you • Caring for the community • Throwing away litter	• Helping at home • Talking over feelings • Bedtime • Safety at home • Car safety • Breakfast • Medicine	• Doctor • Dentist • Community workers
1	• Health workers • School nurse • Dentist • Doctor • Street cleaners • Keeping the neighborhood clean • Keeping school clean • Keeping parks clean	• Showing love • Having healthy mealtimes • Walking with your family • Safety at home • Medicine safety • Helping your family • Keeping parks clean	• School nurse • Dentist • Doctor • Street cleaner
2	• What happens in hospitals • Hospital workers • Ways to help health workers • Keeping a neighborhood clean • Community workers • Making water safe to use	• Talking with your family about feelings, drug safety, and the body • Helping with meals • Exercising with your family • Being quiet or loud • Sharing safety ideas • Talking about hospitals	• Doctor • Dentist • Eye doctor • Ear doctor • Nurse • People who take X-ray pictures • People who keep hospitals clean • Garbage collector • Street cleaner • People who make water safe to use
3	• Medical care • Health department workers • Sanitation workers • Pasteurization • Air pollution and prevention • Water pollution and treatment • Litter • Recycling	• Help with scared, hurt, or sad feelings • Making healthy food choices • Caring for teeth • Being safe at home • Medicine safety • Family fitness • Helping the community	• Dietitian • Dental hygienist • X-ray technologist • Firefighter • Pharmacist and assistant • Hospital workers • Health department worker • Sanitation worker • Public health nurse
4	• Healthy environment • Air pollution • Incinerators • Water pollution • Sewage • Noise pollution • Food safety • Health and recreation • Water-treatment plants • Controlling pollution	• Learning about family differences • Sharing information about health concerns • Sharing safety rules • Eating fewer fatty foods • Sharing ideas about air pollution • Exercising together	• Psychologist • Certified laboratory assistant • Physical education teacher • Lifeguard • Orthodontist • Dental assistant • Chef • Food and drug inspector • Nurse's aide • Sanitarian
5	• Air pollution and health • Protecting air • Water pollution and health • Protecting water • Land use • Landfills • City planning • Controlling disease • Treatment plants • Food inspection	• Getting along well with family • Understanding the heart • Learning about ads • Trying nutritious recipes • Family fitness • Using medicines safely • Being safe alone • Learning about community	• Social worker • Physical or inhalation therapist • Sound technician • Farmer • Fitness leader • Pharmacist • Drug counselor • Firefighter • Forest ranger • Ecologist • Soil scientist
6	• Health department • Hospitals • Volunteer services • Water pollution • Air pollution • Acid rain • Disposal of garbage • Noise pollution • Providing a clean environment • Recreational areas	• Planning study time • Breaking the salt habit • Participating in lifetime activities • Home safety • Drug safety • Detecting plaque • Becoming a careful health consumer • Reducing pollution	• Pediatrician • Geneticist • Recreational therapist • Counselor • Construction inspector • Medical lab worker • Psychiatrist • Dietitian • Sanitary engineer • Landscape architect
7	• Pollution and health • Air pollution • Water pollution • Noise pollution • Controlling diseases • Mental health services • Caring for people with special needs • Protecting the environment	• Kinds of families • How families fulfill needs • Getting along with family • Family customs • Sharing information • Keeping a sleep journal • Family exercise program • Finding health services	• Employment specialist • Speech pathologist • Oral surgeon • EEG technologist • Food technologist • Market researcher • Safety technician • Epidemiologist • Environmental health technician
8	• Local and state health departments • Federal health agencies • Improving world health • Effects of pollution • Environmental protection • Volunteer conservation • Biodegradable products	• Investigating job interests • Reducing stress at home • Improving family relations • Making wise purchases • Healthy lifestyles • Making a home safe • Reducing pollution at home	• Biofeedback technician • Home economist • Physical therapist • Audiologist • Lawyer • Radiologic technologist • EMT • Medical records administrator • Sewage plant operator • Registered nurse

Philosophy of Health for Life

Health for Life seeks to motivate young people to build healthy lifestyles—for today and for the future. A wealth of scientific research indicates that the way we live has a profound effect on our health and that personal health habits have much to do with whether we are healthy or sick. These personal health habits pertain to smoking; to abuse of alcohol and other drugs; to sleep, rest, exercise, and nutrition; to the ability to deal constructively with stress; to willingness to follow safety guides. All these aspects of lifestyle are under an individual's control, and even small changes in lifestyle can bring about substantial reduction in health risks for many individuals. Developing desirable personal health habits requires motivation. Thus, motivation assumes a key role in the program. Many lessons begin with health-related, true-to-life situations, problems, or queries. The aim is to arouse interest, curiosity, and eagerness to read on to learn more. Students are also motivated by the frequent in-text activities. These activities make possible a "doing" as well as a reading approach to learning about health. The activities offer a change of pace as well as an aid to reinforcement of important health knowledge, attitudes, and behavior.

> "*Health for Life* seeks to motivate young people to build healthy lifestyles—for today and for the future."

Health for Life teaches students crucial life skills such as decision making, goal setting, coping, and resisting peer pressure. The activities in the *Skills for Life Handbook* enable students to practice these life skills. The program encourages students to think for themselves and to develop responsibility for their health.

The content of *Health for Life* is accurate, up-to-date, and age-appropriate. Content is based on what young people need to know about health. Content is also based on what young people want to know about health. Much consideration has been given to available research on children's own health interests, concerns, and curiosities at each successive age level. The presence of student-oriented content (content that tells young people what they need and want to know at the time they need and want to know it) further enhances the ability of the program to motivate students toward healthy life-styles.

Julius B. Richmond
John D. MacArthur Professor of Health Policy
Director, Division of Health Policy Research and Education
Harvard University
Advisor on Child Health Policy
Children's Hospital of Boston

Elenore T. Pounds
Health Education Writer
Former Elementary Teacher
Downers Grove, Illinois

Using Health for Life

The Pupil's Edition of *Health for Life* is organized into chapters that function as independent units. You can teach the chapters in any order, and you can choose which chapters you want to fit your curriculum needs and the time schedule. Although each chapter focuses primarily on one of twelve strands, other strands are integrated into the chapters when appropriate. The Scope and Sequence Charts on pages T14–T17 of the Teacher's Edition show how the twelve health strands are covered in your book and others in the series.

To help you decide which chapters or lessons to use, *Health for Life* provides the following items in the Teacher's Edition: The Time Schedule (shown on this page), the Scope and Sequence chart for your book (pages T50–T60), and the Chapter Planning Guide preceding each chapter.

The features listed in the Chapter Planning Guides are described below.

Pupil's Edition

Activities

- *Health Watch Notebook:* a project at the beginning of each chapter in which students find application of health concepts in the media and the world around them
- *Health Activities Workshop:* individual activities following some lessons where students apply what they have learned in a variety of ways

Enrichment

- *Did You Know?:* a margin feature describing interesting facts related to lesson content
- *Health Focus:* a chapter feature focusing on achievements of people in the health field
- *Health at Home:* a chapter feature suggesting an activity on health information for students to share with their families

Assessment

- *Think Back:* review questions at the end of every lesson
- *Chapter Review:* a review of lesson objectives and vocabulary plus fill-in-the-blank, short answers, and essay questions

Independent Study

- *On Your Own:* a margin feature with writing assignments calling for application of health concepts taught in the lessons
- *Study Guide:* study and review questions for every lesson in a special section in the back of the book
- *Skills for Life Handbook:* a special section in the back of the book with activities for each chapter that develop such life skills as decision-making, goal setting, and communication

Teacher's Edition

- *Chapter Planning Guide:* an overview of the chapter and lesson features and supplementary materials and a list of resources
- *Teaching Plan:* a three-step approach to every lesson with suggestions to motivate, teach, and assess students
- *Teaching Options:* a special section for each lesson with a health background and suggestions for enrichment, reteaching, special education, and relating health to another subject

Supplementary Materials

- *Teacher's Resource Book:* blackline masters for every chapter including family letters; overhead transparency masters; and worksheets for study and review, vocabulary, life skills, and health and another subject
- *Workbook:* worksheets from the Teacher's Resource Book in workbook format
- *Test Book:* two forms of a two-page test for every chapter
- *Posters:* one teaching poster per chapter with activities and teaching suggestions on the back
- *Overhead Transparancies:* colorful overheads to help teach about life skills, body systems, and other health topics

Time Schedule*

Chapter	Time	Semester
1 Learning About Yourself	4 weeks	1st
2 Growing and Changing	3 weeks	
3 Choosing Foods for Good Health	4 weeks	
4 Becoming Physically Fit	4 weeks	
5 Safety and First Aid	3 weeks	
6 Drugs: What They Are and What They Do	4 weeks	2nd
7 Fighting Against Disease	4 weeks	
8 Daily Care for Good Health	3 weeks	
9 Your Decisions as a Health Consumer	3 weeks	
10 Working for a Healthy Community	4 weeks	

*Based on an average of teaching 120 minutes each week.

Thinking Skills

Developing Thinking Skills

Health for Life presents students with up-to-date, age-appropriate health information. This information is helpful only if students can use it to guide their actions and to build healthy lifestyles. Thinking Skills are the tools students need in order to apply health information to their lives.

The thinking skills developed in *Health for Life* are listed in the chart on page T21. These skills include skills people use to gather, interpret, and evaluate information. Their classification is based on Bloom's Taxonomy of Educational Objectives. Notice that the basic skills in levels 1 and 2 are necessary for the development of the higher order of thinking skills listed in the third level. For example, students need to collect, recall, interpret, and organize information in order to make a decision.

Both basic and higher order thinking skills can be and should be introduced in grades 1–8. Teachers can encourage the development of all levels of thinking skills by:

- allowing students to draw upon their familiar, concrete experiences to extend their knowledge;
- involving students in learning activities that include hands-on experiences;
- supplying students with direct instruction in specific skills;
- providing extended practice in the use of thinking skills; and
- challenging students with questions and problems that require the use of various thinking skills to solve.

> *"Thinking skills are the tools students need in order to apply health information to their lives."*

An ongoing program for developing thinking skills involves encouraging students to think about these skills and about their own thought processes. Questions can be worded to encourage students to think. Such questions as "What were your specific thoughts as you answered?" help students become more aware of their thinking processes. As students communicate their thoughts, they will learn that people think and reach conclusions in different ways. As students develop self-concepts of themselves as thinkers, they will rely more on their own thinking than on rote memory.

Skills Development in *Health for Life*

Student materials, *Teacher's Edition* margin notes, and Teacher's Notes in the *Teacher's Resource Book* are designed to help develop thinking skills. Throughout the *Health for Life* program, students are given opportunities to develop a variety of thinking skills within the student text. For example, students are taught the five-step decision-making process at many grade levels. Decision making is presented as a way to solve everyday problems. Students are encouraged to improve their communication skills as a way to get along better with others and improve social health. Using the skills of collecting information and judging and evaluating are often encouraged as a part of consumer health involving nutrition, health care products, and health care services.

Pupil's Edition

- In-text questions focus students' thinking while reading.
- Throughout the series, students are asked to interpret information from pictures and charts.
- *On Your Own* (grades 3–8) in lesson margins emphasizes information gathering and communicating skills.
- *Five-step decision-making process* (grades 4–8) allows students to use a hierarchy of thinking skills to make a decision or to solve a problem.
- *Health Activities Workshop* in each chapter allows students to apply newly acquired knowledge to hands-on experiences.

• A *Health Focus* feature in each chapter includes *Talk About It* questions to stimulate an exchange of ideas in discussions.
• *Think Back* questions at end of each lesson extend students' thinking.
• *Chapter Review* questions require the use of a continuum of thinking skills.
• *Skills for Life Handbook* in the back of the textbook motivates students to use a wide range of thinking skills.

Teacher's Edition
• The *Expanding Student Thinking* question in the *Assess* section of each lesson's *Teaching Plan* provides a higher-order assessment question for the lesson.
• *Enrichment, Reteaching,* and *Health and Other Subjects* activities in the *Teaching Options* of the lesson reinforce and extend thinking skills.
• Skills used in Pupil's Edition and Teacher's Edition material are highlighted in heavy italics in the sidenotes.

Ancillary Components
• A *Teacher's Resource Book* contains worksheets designed to help students develop and practice thinking skills and to apply and evaluate health information.
• Posters provide opportunities for students to practice thinking skills.
•*Test Book* contains test questions for each chapter that require students to use both basic and higher-order thinking skills.

Thinking Skills Developed in *Health for Life*

1. Gathering and Recalling Information
- Collecting Information
  - Observing
  - Measuring
- Recalling Information
- Communicating
  - Naming
  - Listing
  - Describing
  - Recording

2. Understanding and Interpreting Information
- Classifying
  - Sequencing (Steps in a Process Following Directions)
  - Grouping According to Categories
- Organizing Information
  - Comparing (Identifying Similarities)
  - Contrasting (Identifying Differences)
  - Summarizing
  - Recognizing Patterns and Relationships
- Interpreting Information
  - Comprehending Meaning
  - Interpreting Pictures, Charts, and Graphs
  - Visualizing
  - Recognizing Main Idea, Supporting Details
  - Restating or Explaining Ideas
  - Recognizing Cause and Effect

3. Applying and Evaluating Information
- Generalizing
- Making Inferences
- Applying Information to New Situations
- Making Analogies
- Drawing Conclusions
- Suggesting Alternatives
- Judging and Evaluating
  - Distinguishing Fact from Opinion, Bias, and Propaganda
  - Ranking Ideas and Information According to Criteria
  - Reconciling Inconsistent Criteria
  - Recognizing Relevant Information and Data
  - Making Decisions

Comprehension and Vocabulary

Improving Reading Comprehension

Reading skills are a vital tool in any learning endeavor. *Health for Life* provides interesting and comprehensible texts to help students learn about health.

Close Relationship Between Text and Illustrations Illustrations and text interact to increase student interest and comprehension of main ideas and important vocabulary in *Health for Life*. These illustrations support or expand topics discussed in the text.

Active Writing Style Action verbs serve as the predicates of most sentences and appear in many lesson titles and picture captions. Use of action verbs stimulates students' visual, auditory, and kinesthetic memories. Regular use of the active voice helps clarify the cause and effect relationships among the concepts and processes of health. A judicious use of *you* appears throughout the lessons of each book. Such language helps students recognize the relevance of the subject matter to their own lives.

Subjects and predicates appear close to one another, usually near the beginning of the sentence. This style helps students quickly grasp the meaning of each sentence. For clear readability, sentences are never continued from one page to the next. Main ideas are completed within each page. Every page begins with a new paragraph.

Organization. The chapters in *Health for Life* are divided into lessons that lend themselves to daily reading assignments. Every lesson opens with a title question. The content of each lesson contains the main ideas and supporting details that answer the title question. Throughout the lesson, in subtitles and in the text, questions serve to focus students' attention as they read.

> "Reading skills are a vital tool in any learning endeavor."

Setting Purposes for Reading. Each chapter opens with a paragraph that acts as an advance organizer, introducing students to the subject matter while capturing their interest with an accompanying photograph. This device taps students' experiential background and helps them make connections to the new information in the chapter. The last paragraph of each chapter opener functions as a structured overview.

Reflecting During Initial Reading Research into textbook comprehension identifies the value of questions within chapters as well as at the end of chapters. In *Health for Life,* questions at the end of lessons check students' comprehension of the major concept of the lesson.

Applying After Reading Each chapter contains one or more *Health Activities Workshops* that offer opportunities for hands-on experiences to reinforce concepts students read about in the lessons. The *Health at Home* feature guides students to share and apply important health information in their homes. Included also in this feature is *Reading at Home,* which identifies sources for supplementary reading students can do independently.

Evaluating After Reading The *Chapter Review* reinforces students' understanding of the main ideas of the chapter. Beginning in Book 3, students are given the opportunity to demonstrate their understanding by writing answers to essay questions.

Introduce *Health for Life* Show your students how the chapters and lessons are organized. Explain how to use the vocabulary and other comprehension features. You may wish to refer students to the page entitled *When You Read This Book* at the front of the student text.

Modeling Health Vocabulary

For students to understand health topics, they need to learn to comprehend the language and vocabulary of health. In the *Pupil's Edition*, the vocabulary words students need to know appear in boldface type the first time they appear. The words are defined in context and, beginning with Book 3, they are listed with the pronunciation and definition in the margin of the page on which they are introduced.

In the *Teacher's Edition*, the first page of each chapter lists all the vocabulary words introduced in the chapter. The first page of each lesson lists the vocabulary words introduced in that lesson. Also included in the *Teacher's Edition* at the beginning of each chapter is a list of words to preteach. These words include vocabulary words introduced in previous chapters and words that may be unfamiliar to some students. General suggestions for introducing new words are found on the first page of each chapter in the *Teacher's Edition* under the heading, *Modeling Health Vocabulary*. Other techniques for introducing new words are described below.

> *"For students to understand health topics, they need to learn to comprehend the language and vocabulary of health."*

Word Association Write one or more new words on the chalkboard. Let students name other words that come to mind when they hear or see each of the words listed.

Word Groups Write a list of new words on the chalkboard. Ask students to group the words into two or more categories based on the words' meanings or associations. Encourage students to think of titles for their word categories.

Word Predictions List new words on the chalkboard. Discuss the words one at a time, asking students to explain what they think each word means. You may also wish to ask them to consider who might use a certain word and when. Let students record the word predictions. When students have completed the chapter, let them compare their predictions with their current understandings of the words.

Word Similarities and Differences Choose new words that have homonyms. List the new words and their homonyms in pairs on the chalkboard. Then write a sentence leaving a blank space for students to insert the correct word from the list.

Features Analysis Some vocabulary words or groups of words lend themselves to the technique of features analysis. You can use this technique to reinforce word meanings as students read or review the chapter. Make a table similar to the one shown below by listing selected words in columns, listing features or characteristics of the word categories in a row, and drawing the lines to form boxes. Direct students to read down the table, marking off features that apply to the given word.

Word Parts Select new words that have prefixes or suffixes. Ask students to identify the prefixes, roots, and suffixes. Discuss the meanings of each part of the word. Ask students to use the word parts as clues for predicting the meanings of the words.

Using the Glossary
At the end of each book in the *Health for Life* series is a *Glossary*. This section lists pronunciation guides and definitions for each word to preteach and for each vocabulary word. Review how to find words in the *Glossary*, and help students use the pronunciation guides.

Dr. Robert A. Pavlik
Professor and Chairperson
Reading-Language Arts Department
Cardinal Stritch College

Features Analysis

Characteristics	**Types of teeth**			
	Incisors	**Cuspids**	**Bicuspids**	**Molars**
Crown	√	√	√	√
Enamel	√	√	√	√
Dentin	√	√	√	√
Pulp	√	√	√	√
Root(s)	√	√	√	√
Sharp point(s)	√	√	√	
Broad top				√
Bite food	√			
Tear food		√		
Crush food			√	
Grind food				√

Cooperative Learning

In cooperative learning, students work in four- to five-member learning teams to help one another master academic knowledge and skills. The goal of cooperative learning is to increase the level of achievement of all students. Research has shown that if students work on teams that are rewarded for the learning of *all* team members, they learn more than do students in traditional classroom settings.

> *"If students work on teams that are rewarded based on the learning of all team members, they learn more than do students in traditional classroom settings."*

Three concepts are essential for cooperative learning to work. First, teams receive rewards (such as an achievement certificate) for the results of the *team's* effort. Second, the success of the team depends on the learning of each team member; therefore, learning must be assessed on an individual basis, for example, by a score obtained on a quiz taken by oneself. In other words, the team cannot "win" because one person on the team knows all the answers while other members have not learned the material. All members of the team must achieve a specified level of competence. This aspect of cooperative learning leads students to help each other learn the required material so that all can do well on a quiz. Third, each student must have the opportunity to be successful. This means that students can help their teams be successful by improving over their past performance. Thus, when developing criteria for team success, be sure to work in a way to credit those who may not get the highest scores, but may show significant improvement over their own previous scores. In this way, all students are challenged to do their best, even if they find a certain subject difficult. This third concept motivates students by rewarding them for doing better than they have in the past (rather than comparing them to others). This approach makes success possible for all students, and increases student enthusiasm and motivation for learning.

Research has shown that cooperative learning techniques have many important by-products in addition to improved achievement by all students. The cooperative learning situation gives students the opportunity to practice life management skills in the areas of social interaction and communication. By setting up teams made of members of diverse abilities and ethnic backgrounds, students learn the important lesson of how to work with and appreciate the contributions of all people. Cooperative learning has proved to be particularly effective in the social integration of students, who, for one reason or an other, seem different to their classmates.

Cooperative learning also seems to improve students' self-esteem. This seems to be due to the positive effect of the cooperative, mutually supportive group experience and to the improvement in learning that usually occurs. Students also develop norms that include a positive attitude toward academic achievement.

Cooperative Learning in *Health for Life*

To use cooperative learning in *Health for Life,* first assign students to four-member learning teams. If the class does not divide evenly by four, a few five-member teams may be assigned. Each team should have one relatively high achiever, one low achiever, and two or three average achievers, and should be mixed in sex and ethnicity. Let students choose

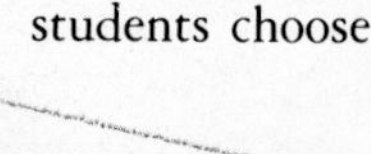

team names and sit together during health periods. You might change team assignments every four to six weeks.

Two principal cooperative learning formats that can be used in *Health for Life* are *Jigsaw* and *STAD* (Student Teams—Achievement Divisions). Brief descriptions of these formats appear on the first page of each chapter and on the Chapter Review. More detailed descriptions follow.

Jigsaw

In *Jigsaw* each team member becomes an "expert" on a unique topic for a chapter. Four topics are suggested in the *Teaching Options* at the beginning of each chapter. Assign topics at random. If a team has five members, two may share a topic.

All students should read the entire chapter, but they should especially be looking for information on their own topics. At the end of the chapter, students from different teams who had the same topic meet in "expert groups" to discuss their topics. You may wish to circulate among the groups to guide their discussion and to see that they are focusing on the right information.

After twenty to thirty minutes, have students return to their teams and take turns presenting what they have learned to their teammates. Finally, all students take a test covering all topics. Teams that average 90% or more on the test may earn attractive Superteam certificates; those that average 80–90% may earn smaller Greatteam certificates. These criteria and rewards may be adjusted to your preferences and circumstances.

STAD

In *STAD* students study together to help one another prepare for individual tests. At the end of each chapter, give students about one class period to work in their learning teams to master the material presented in the Chapter Review. After the teams have had enough time to complete the Chapter Review and study the material, give students individual tests covering the chapter content. Teams may earn certificates or other rewards based on average team scores, as described above. A reminder of the use of *STAD* is given on the second page of each Chapter Review.

You may wish to combine *Jigsaw* and *STAD* by allowing students to study the Chapter Review after they have finished reporting to the team on their topics. By engaging in cooperative learning in the elementary classroom, students become aware of and understand the advantages of such cooperative strategies for future learning endeavors.

Robert E. Slavin
Center for Research on Elementary and Middle Schools
Johns Hopkins University

Limited English Proficient Studen[ts]

Limited English Proficient (LEP) students are students whose first language is not English and and who lack sufficient proficiency in English to do the work at their grade level. Most of these students are intellectually capable of the work and want to succeed in school; however, their difficulties in communication and the resulting problems in school often frustrate the LEP student. Many students have poor self-esteem stemming from these problems. Many have not had good experiences in school. Often, the anticipation of failure leads to anxiety that inhibits learning.

> *"Teachers can provide a comfortable, low-risk, supportive environment in which LEP students will be willing to risk speaking in English."*

The teacher who wants to foster growth and learning for LEP students faces a unique challenge. The goal is to empower students through educational experiences that give them an opportunity to understand the content and improve their language skills in a context that respects language differences and cultural diversity.

There are several general strategies that the teacher can use to help LEP students.

1. Create a classroom environment that reduces anxiety and promotes aliveness, spontaneity, and creativity.
2. Encourage observation.
3. Encourage, but do not force, participation.
4. Realize that the beginning language learner goes through an active listening period called the "silent period"; therefore, do not interpret language silence as lack of interest.
5. Do not isolate the students through excessive special assignments.
6. Be sure LEP students receive critical thinking assignments and creative activities. Avoid assignments that are rote, repetitive, and inhibit language production.
7. Provide assignments that allow students to use pictures (from magazines or drawn) to answer questions or illustrate concepts. Encourage them to label the pictures with the apprrpriate English term.
8. Cultivate peer recognition through activities that team LEP students with native speakers.
9. Build basic language skills by using English in familiar contexts.
10. Develop new content from familiar content. Use examples from the LEP students' cultures; for example, discussions of nutrition can include foods and eating customs from other cultures.
11. Use concrete approaches to new content, such as hands-on materials, gestures, body language, pantomime, role-playing, and visual aids.
12. When speaking, use a slower but natural speech rate, shorter sentences, and repetition; that is, repeat the same concept in several different ways.
13. Give positive feedback to let students know they are on the right track. Do not correct grammatical errors but rather model correct language usage for the students.
14. Monitor students' comprehension frequently and provide reteaching as needed.

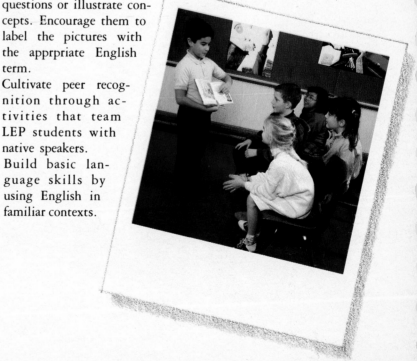

One of the most important things for a teacher to do for LEP students is provide a comfortable, low-risk, supportive environment in which the students will be willing to risk speaking and communicating in English. The *Health for Life* program is particularly suited to this. The mental and social health chapters emphasize the value of all people and cultures and teach life skills, such as self-esteem building, which are particularly helpful to the LEP student. Health education is also based on the needs common to all people—such as the physical needs for food and good hygiene, the social need for good communication skills, and the personal need for self-esteem and ways to cope with stress. Since the LEP students have as much experience in life as the other students, they have as much to contribute. The key is to make them aware of the value of their contributions and to help them develop their language skills so that they can communicate. Showing how the same problem or issue is handled in different cultures is of great value to all students.

Each chapter has features that can be used to help LEP students. Modeling vocabulary with visual aids, gestures, or skits will be of great value. The Cooperative Learning suggestions provide the opportunity for students to work with linguistically more proficient peers and to contribute to the group. Many of the *Health Watch Notebook* and *Health Activities Workshop* suggestions involve the use of pictures. Many of the suggestions in the *Teacher's Edition* for Enrichment, Reteaching, Health and Art, Health and Drama, Special Education, and worksheets in the *Teacher's Resource Book* involve the use of pictures, drama, or models. All of these help the LEP students understand the concepts better. Many also give them the opportunity to interact and communicate with their peers. When asking questions in class, include some that can be answered by pointing to something or pantomime. As students gain fluency, ask them questions that require word answers.

Jesús Cortez
Professor of Education
Director, Center for Bilingual/ Multicultural Studies
California State University, Chico

Special Education Students

The goals of health education include the development of physical, emotional, and social well-being. A classroom environment that fosters patience and understanding can be of great benefit in the realization of these goals.

Just as the special talents and abilities of students vary, so do their special needs. Adapting instructional methods to accommodate these needs can be enjoyable and beneficial for the entire class.

"Just as the special talents and abilities of students vary, so do their special needs."

In the *Teacher's Edition*, a minimum of two suggestions appear in each chapter to help teachers adapt or expand the chapter material to meet the special needs of students with physical handicaps, learning disabilities, hearing impairments, or visual impairments.

The activities are not designed to remediate disabilities, but rather to help special students get the maximum benefit from the lesson. The suggestions are aimed at helping students grasp concepts that will help them understand or appreciate the main point of the lesson.

Following are some suggestions to help teachers structure their classrooms or adapt their teaching methods to accommodate the needs of special students.

Visually Impaired Students

- Seat students near front of the room in good light.
- Provide hands-on experiences, such as working with models or clay.
- Tape-record text material.
- Allow students to complete assignments orally or to tape-record them.
- Assign a student partner.
- Administer tests orally; allow students to respond orally or use a tape recorder.
- Permit students to move about so that they can be as close as possible to charts and other wall displays.
- Do not expect students with special lenses or other magnification devices to read as much material or as quickly as other students.

Hearing-Impaired Students

- Seat students near front of room.
- Write key words and phrases on the chalkboard during discussions.
- Guide students to the correct page during discussions.
- Administer written tests.
- Look at each student when talking to him or her. Talk normally.
- Learn the students' method of communication, such as sign language.
- Assign oral reports as group activities.
- Encourage verbal interaction within students' capabilities.

Physically Handicapped Students

- Adjust the physical environment to fit students' needs.
- Encourage a variety of verbal activities and other opportunities for social interaction.

Learning-Disabled Students

- Avoid seating students in very distracting or stimulating environments.
- Place students in small groups rather than large groups for activities.
- Provide clear, concrete directions.
- Make attractive easy-to-read health materials available.
- Provide a structured environment in which expectations are clear.

All students can benefit from their association with individuals who possess a range of talents and abilities. Students learn to become more patient and understanding of others if they share common interests and work together in an accepting environment.

Judi Coffey
Educational Consultant
Learning Disabilities Specialist

High-Potential Students

Recognizing the unique needs and abilities of high-potential students is the first step toward meeting the challenge of teaching these students. High-potential students may or may not excel in the classroom. They may exhibit desire for challenge in some curriculum areas while remaining unmotivated in other areas. However, most high-potential students show a combination of several of the following traits: unusual ability to grasp and retain information; a high degree of curiosity; advanced insight into casual relationships; highly developed verbal skills; and creativity in one or more areas. Efforts in meeting the needs of high-potential students should be geared toward accomodating these characteristics.

All students, especially high-potential students, need an environment in which they can be intellectually and emotionally comfortable. Allow students time and opportunity to formulate and ask questions. Be ready to admit when you do not have an answer to a student's question. Use such a situation as an opportunity to allow interested students to research possible answers and present them to the class.

High-potential students need to be stimulated to go beyond normal requirements. You can inspire them by providing access to materials or people who can help them focus their interests.

Following are some suggestions for encouraging high-potential students when they study health. Let students explore the different ways health concepts apply to their lives. Give students the opportunity to apply what they have learned in practical ways. Stress active, independent learning. Encourage students to recognize their strengths and strive to meet challenges without demanding perfection from themselves.

High-potential students need to be engaged in activities that are challenging in both content and process. Allowing students to explore areas beyond but related to the curriculum gives them the opportunity to accommodate their varied interests and learning styles. The suggested activities in the *Teacher's Edition* of *Health for Life* encourage students to choose a variety of modes of expression—from writing, to computer programming, to fine arts and music.

Give students with similar interests time to work together on extra activities. However, make sure that the students involved in extra activities adhere to the standards set for the class in understanding health concepts covered. Encourage these students to share with the class what they have learned.

Activities for high-potential students in *Health for Life* help students develop higher-order thinking skills, such as making analogies, drawing conclusions, judging and evaluating, and making decisions. By developing these skills and combining them with the skills of collecting information and communicating, students can become independent learners.

> *"High-potential students need to be stimulated to go beyond normal requirements."*

Evaluating high-potential students calls for flexibility. A variety of evaluation techniques can be used, depending on the activity and on the needs and personality of the student. Some students can proceed independently for a considerable length of time. Other students need frequent feedback for focus or for encouragement. Checklists or rating scales can provide rapid, understandable feedback. For long-term assignments or independent-study projects, a contract with the student can be an invaluable tool for evaluation. Every evaluative process should reflect an effort to help guide each high-potential student toward the discovery and fulfillment of his or her special talents and capabilities.

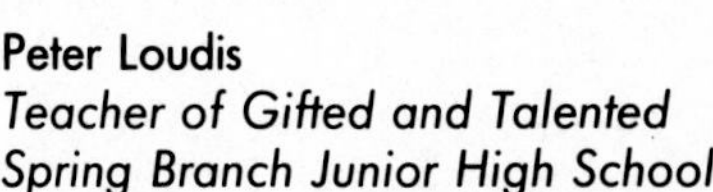
Peter Loudis
Teacher of Gifted and Talented
Spring Branch Junior High School

Physical Fitness

Physical fitness is an essential aspect of health. It includes two parts: health fitness and skills fitness. Exercise is essential for developing both parts of physical fitness. Unlike some factors that affect health, exercise is under each individual's control. Everyone, regardless of ability, can exercise. Students who learn the importance of exercise and who begin to incorporate exercise into their daily activities at a young age will gain health benefits throughout their lives.

> *"Students who learn the importance of exercise and begin to incorporate it into their daily activities will gain benefits throughout their lives."*

Lifetime Fitness

For exercise to become an intrinsic part of daily life, it must be geared to the interests and needs of the individual. The individual should perform exercises at his or her own pace and evaluate his or her unique progress. The fitness program presented in *Health for Life* can help guide students to follow their own paths to lifetime fitness. The program is based on a six-step continuum designed to lead students from dependence toward independence in planning a personal fitness program. In each book the steps are introduced and developed according to the needs and abilities of the students at that age. The steps are as follows: exercising for fun and for sense of competence, achieving fitness, developing fitness vocabulary, recognizing personal fitness patterns, evaluating fitness needs, and planning a fitness program.

Step 1: Exercising for fun and for sense of competence To be motivated to exercise, students must enjoy fitness activities. Throughout the program, exercises are introduced in a manner that helps students have fun while exercising. The exercises help students develop competence in the parts of fitness, and thus help increase their confidence. Students who feel confident about exercising are more likely to exercise in their free time.

Step 2: Achieving fitness The well-planned fitness program in *Health for Life* helps students build all parts of health fitness. The exercises included in the program are safe, appealing, age-appropriate, and easy to teach and learn. As students follow the exercises and begin to achieve fitness, they find that exercise helps them feel their best, look their best, and enjoy life. The positive experience of exercising can help them become interested in learning more about fitness.

Step 3: Developing fitness vocabulary
Students must learn the language of fitness to increase their knowledge of physical fitness. Fitness vocabulary is introduced throughout the series when students are able to comprehend the definitions and to incorporate the concepts into their understanding of fitness.

Step 4: Recognizing personal fitness patterns
As students learn more about exercise and fitness, they will begin to select activities that best suit their interests. To become increasingly independent, students need to learn to select exercises that meet their personal needs and interests.

Step 5: Evaluating fitness needs
Throughout *Health for Life* students are encouraged to exercise at their own pace and to evaluate their own fitness needs as appropriate to their stage of development. Younger students will assess fitness programs based on their enjoyment. Older students are prompted to consider the parts of health and skills fitness they need to improve.

Step 6: Planning a fitness program
Having evaluated their fitness needs, students can plan individualized programs. *Health for Life* gives students the information they need to plan such programs. Students are encouraged

to consider not only their immediate fitness needs but also their projected needs. In this way, students can plan lifetime fitness activities that can help them stay healthy throughout their lives.

Project Keep-Fit

In addition to the fitness information provided in the lessons, each fitness chapter includes an exercise program—*Project Keep-Fit.* At each grade, this program matches the interests and abilities of the students of that age. Each exercise program is developmentally sound and includes a warm-up, a workout, and a cool-down. The program can contribute to fitness and help students enjoy exercising.

One page of *Project Keep-Fit* is devoted to exercises that can be done while students are seated in their chairs. These exercises are well suited for students who are temporarily or permanently limited to a chair. Guidance is given to help handicapped students evaluate their needs and plan activities that will help them improve all parts of health fitness.

Throughout the series, students are encouraged to recognize that many different kinds of activities can contribute to fitness and to exercising on their own. The *Exercise Guide* included in the *Teacher's Resource Book* helps students record their progress and begin to develop independence in meeting their own fitness needs.

With guidance, students can begin to evaluate their interests and fitness needs and can be encouraged to develop personal exercise patterns to meet those needs.

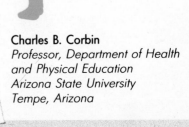

Charles B. Corbin
Professor, Department of Health and Physical Education
Arizona State University
Tempe, Arizona

Teacher's Health Handbook

The *Teacher's Health Handbook* contains a variety of professional articles on topics of concern to health teachers. This reference tool will help you as you prepare to teach *Health for Life* in your classrooms. Some of the articles, such as those on AIDS and life skills, provide additional background information to supplement the text. Other articles provide information on subjects that you may want to teach but are not covered in the pupil edition, such as the prevention of sexual abuse. A number of the articles provide classroom management tips and suggestions for handling difficult situations with students, such as a student whose parent has just died. The *Handbook* concludes with lists of sources of information: books, hotlines, health information sources, and sources for the computer software and audio-visual materials recommended in the *Chapter Planning Guide* at the beginning of each chapter in the *Teacher's Edition.*

Characteristics of 11- to 12-Year-Olds

At ages eleven and twelve, the differences among young people become startlingly apparent.

These youngsters mature physically, socially, and emotionally at different rates. Many girls and a few boys are experiencing the growth spurt and are nearing puberty.

Development of Students Who Have Not Begun the Growth Spurt Sixth grade students who have not yet begun the growth spurt continue their physical development in much the same manner as during the previous year. They become increasingly coordinated and develop good control of the smaller muscles. They are alert, energetic, and like to be busy. They generally are eager to master new skills and to do things well.

Physical Development Before the growth spurt begins, students may experience a slowing down in growth that lasts from six months to a year. Following this period of slow growth is the growth spurt—a period of rapid growth which may last for one or two years or longer. For most girls, this growth spurt begins around age eleven or twelve, although it may occur any time between the ages of eight and fourteen. The growth spurt occurs one or two years later for most boys.

Puberty and the Growth Spurt The growth spurt consists of a rapid gain in both height and weight. In girls, weight gain can be relatively quick and dramatic, with gains of ten to twenty pounds in a year not uncommon. In boys, the weight gain may be more gradual, spanning several years. Many girls in this age group are taller and heavier than many of the boys in the class.

During or immediately after the growth spurt, the stage of sexual maturation, or puberty, begins. The reproductive system matures and secondary sexual characteristics develop. Although students who have completed puberty are physically able to reproduce, they are not emotionally or socially mature enough to handle the responsibilities of parenthood.

In girls, puberty includes widening of the hips, growth and maturation of the breasts, and gain in body fat that gives the body a rounded look. Pubic and underarm hair begins to grow. Oil glands in the skin increase their production of oil. Sweat glands become more active, and changes in chemical composition of sweat occur. The vocal cords lengthen and the voice deepens. The genitals enlarge. The ovaries increase in size and begin to produce hormones, resulting in the onset of the menstrual cycle. Many girls begin menstruating around ages twelve or thirteen. However, it is not uncommon for a girl to begin menstruating as early as age ten or as late as age fifteen.

The average monthly cycle is about twenty-eight days long, though shorter cycles, longer cycles, and cycles of varying lengths are common. Around the middle of the cycle, one of the ovaries releases an egg which travels to the uterus. At the same time, hormones stimulate the thickening of the lining of the uterus. This thickened lining helps nourish the egg if it becomes fertilized. If the egg does not become fertilized, hormone levels change, and in about two weeks the lining of the uterus disintegrates. This event marks the beginning of menstruation. Extra blood, uterine tissue, and the unfertilized egg leave the body in the menstrual flow. Then the monthly cycle, including ovulation and menstruation, begins again.

During the first year of menstruation, a girl's cycle may be irregular. The ovaries may secrete varying amounts of hormones, and ovulation might not occur. However, within a few years, a regular cycle is usually established.

In boys, physical maturation includes broadening of the chest and widening of the shoulders. Hair first appears in the pubic region and under the arms and then on the face, neck, and chest. In the skin, oil and sweat production increases and sweat changes in composition. The vocal cords also lengthen, but the increase in size of the vocal cords is greater for boys than for girls. The genitals and testes enlarge and sperm production begins. Boys tend to experience the changes of puberty at about ages thirteen to fifteen.

The growth and physical changes taking place may drain eleven- and twelve-year-olds of energy. Students may seem tired and easily fatigued. What appears to be laziness may really be the result of the body's need for rest. This tiredness contrasts sharply with the energy of the student who is not experiencing the growth spurt.

The awkwardness that some young people experience while undergoing rapid growth is due to the differing rates of growth of various parts of the body. The hands and feet may grow first. Then the arms and legs lengthen. Later the trunk grows and secondary sexual characteristics develop.

Emotional Development of Sixth-Grade Students Eleven- and twelve-year-olds want to have increased independence, but they are still dependent, to some extent, on adults. One day they may seem to be quite mature; the next day they may behave childishly.

Students who are nearing puberty may sometimes seem difficult to get along with. Their moods may change quickly. They may become critical of adults or be rebellious and refuse to follow adult guidelines about bedtime, cleanliness, and appropriate dress. Letting students express their negative thoughts and feelings can be helpful to them. However, maintaining clear rules and mutual respect is important. Students respond well to adults' faith in their ability to make good decisions. By showing understanding and a sense of humor, adults can help all involved meet the ups and downs of this period.

Social Development of Sixth-Grade Students Sixth-grade students are concerned about whether or not others like them and how others view their actions. They are beginning to try to understand the behavior and feelings of others.

Being a member of a group gives eleven- and twelve-year-olds the feeling of belonging and of being liked by others. However, some students simply are not interested in belonging to a group. If a student has shown the ability to make and maintain friendships even with one or two other people, the lack of a group involvement should not be a cause for concern.

Friendship patterns may shift from those of earlier years. For example, many students who have been close friends up until sixth grade may find themselves drifting apart. Friends may develop different interests as they mature at different rates.

Girls are usually more mature socially than most boys. The girls may become interested in boy-girl relationships before their male classmates do. Helping students understand and accept these differences can spare the students much anxiety and help them adjust to the changes of growth.

Helping Sixth-Grade Students Cope with Changes Sixth-grade students need encouragement to think on their own, to develop independent judgment, and to form and express their opinions. Providing opportunities for students to begin to become independent can help them grow and mature.

Many students this age are eager for information about the growth and changes they anticipate or are experiencing. Information on emotional development during preadolescence and adolescence can help the students better understand and adjust to the mood changes they may experience.

The changes that occur during these years can be stressful to students of all different developmental levels. Some ways to deal with stress include talking problems out, taking a break from a difficult situation, using physical exercise to work off anger, doing something for someone else, prioritizing tasks and taking them one at a time, setting realistic goals, and taking the initiative with friends or activities.

Peer pressure can be a strong force in the lives of sixth-grade students. Students benefit from learning how to say "no" to negative peer pressure. By learning how to respect differences among people, they can avoid exerting or succumbing to peer pressure.

Young adolescents deal with many changes in these years of rapid growth. Emphasis on the excitement of learning new skills, making new friends, and taking on increased responsibilities can help students have positive attitudes toward the growth and maturation they experience during this time.

Teaching Life Management Skills

Today's youth faces problems that are unprecedented in type and magnitude.

Drug abuse, teen pregnancy, AIDS, sexual abuse, depression, and suicide are issues facing all young people. Studies have shown that children with a variety of problems, such as drug abuse, pregnancy, and dropping out of school, have common psychological profiles. These children often have low self-esteem, a high need for social approval, high stress levels, poor coping skills, low assertiveness, and poor decision-making skills. Even children who seem well-adjusted often have low self-esteem and have problems coping with stress, making decisions, and resisting peer pressure.

One way to help all children cope with the stresses and challenges in their lives is to teach them life management skills. These skills fall into seven categories:

- self-esteem building
- goal setting
- decision making
- coping
- social and communication
- peer resistance
- consumer

Learning these skills at a young age will benefit the students throughout their lives.

Preparation For Teaching

Health for Life incorporates the teaching of life skills into every area of the health curriculum. Concepts are presented in the mental and social health chapters. Opportunities to practice the skills are provided mainly in the Skills for Life Handbook, but also appear in the Health Activities Workshops, the Workbooks, and in the Teacher's Resource Books.

The teaching of life skills will be facilitated if the teacher can encourage each student to achieve his or her potential, ask questions, and explore the physical and social environment. The classroom atmosphere should also encourage students to share knowledge, help, and praise.

Help your students see how each skill can be used in a wide variety of situations—in the playground and lunchroom, at home with relatives and friends, during sports activities, at parties, at restaurants and stores, and even when home alone. As often as you can, model these skills for your students. Show them how you use the same life skills.

The Seven Skills

Self-Esteem Building Skills Self-esteem—good feelings about oneself—can be considered the foundation for learning. Children with high self-esteem learn better, and improving a child's self-esteem often results in improved achievement in school. Children with low self-esteem often have a harder time saying "no" when their peers suggest some unhealthy activity, such as smoking. They also tend to experience anxiety and stress that can interfere with learning and social development.

Self-image is the mental picture that one has about oneself. Self-esteem is the positive feelings one has about that self-image. Some students have low self-esteem because of experiences at home, in some cases including psychological and/or physical abuse. In other children, low self-esteem results from physical differences, behavioral problems, learning difficulties, or unknown causes. Even children with generally high self-esteem experience fluctuations in their feelings about themselves. Help raise children's self-esteem by encouraging each child and by teaching self-esteem building skills.

Negative thoughts about oneself (e.g., "I'm so stupid.") and about one's potential (e.g., "I'll never understand this math.") lower self-esteem. Realistic thinking (e.g., "I can learn math!") can help raise self-esteem. Students need to learn how to recognize negative thinking and how to change it to positive, realistic thinking. Hand in hand with high self-esteem is a sense of identity. Students need to learn how they are special and unique.

Goal-Setting Skills Goal-setting can help students build high self-esteem and a sense of identity. Students can use goal-setting skills to overcome weaknesses, build strengths, and get what they want from life. It is important to emphasize both in words and actions that comparing your achievements with someone else's is counterproductive. There will always be someone better and someone worse than you. Therefore, the most useful and satisfying approach is to measure yourself against the goals you set

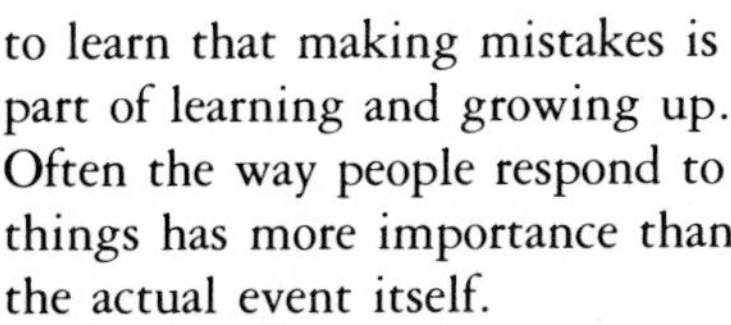

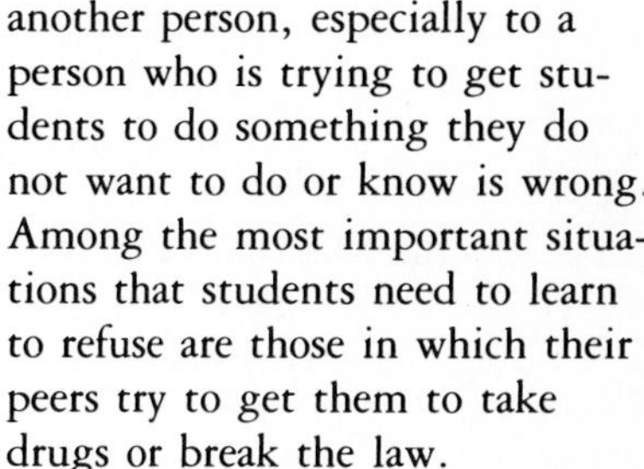

for yourself. Teachers can show students that success comes from discovering what is important to oneself, setting realistic goals, and making a plan for achieving those goals.

Components of goal-setting skills include how to assess your abilities; how to break a large goal into smaller, manageable parts; how to motivate oneself; and how to manage your time.

Decision-Making and Problem-Solving Skills The five-step process of decision-making was designed to help students think carefully about their decisions and the choices available to them. The four guidelines for responsible choices (safe and healthy, legal, acceptable to family, and respectful) were developed to help students realize the need to eliminate those choices that will lead them into trouble.

Problem-solving and decision-making are closely allied. In many situations, the existence of a problem means that a decision must be made. Thus, the five-step approach to decision-making also works for problem-solving.

Coping Skills Teachers can help students cope with unexpected difficulties by teaching them how to deal with emotional responses to events in life and to anxiety and stress. Children also need to learn that making mistakes is part of learning and growing up. Often the way people respond to things has more importance than the actual event itself.

Children need to learn to understand and accept their feelings. In many instances, they also need to learn that they can control their feelings and not let their feelings control them. The immature way to handle feelings is to act them out in negative ways, as for example, hitting a person a child might be angry with. Another unhealthy way to handle emotions is to ignore or repress them. Teachers can encourage students to acknowledge and accept their feelings, even "embarrassing" ones such as fear, but then to think before taking an action.

Social and Communication Skills Social skills include how to choose and make friends; how to be cooperative, considerate, and understanding; how to show respect and sensitivity to other people's feelings; and how to resolve disagreements. Communications skills include how to communicate clearly and avoid misunderstandings, how to listen, and how to understand body language.

Refusal Skills and Peer Resistance Teaching refusal skills gives students a variety of ways to say "no" to another person, especially to a person who is trying to get students to do something they do not want to do or know is wrong. Among the most important situations that students need to learn to refuse are those in which their peers try to get them to take drugs or break the law.

Peer pressure can be positive or negative, but students who get into trouble often have succumbed to negative peer pressure. Students who learn how to say "no" and have a good chance of keeping their friends have gained a valuable skill. (You might also want to discuss how to cope with losing a friend because the student would not do something—such as drugs—with him or her, as well as how to find friends with similar values.) The open discussion of the issues also serves to establish an environment in which it is acceptable to say "no."

Consumer Skills The media are a very powerful influence on students. Advertising is motivated by the drive to sell products, and advertisers often use psychological appeals to the potential consumer. Students are rarely aware of the techniques that advertisers use, but they are frequently taken in by them. Beer producers are among the most influential, for they have equated beer drinking with masculinity, adulthood, acceptance, fun, and rewards.

Teaching students to be aware of the techniques that advertisers use can help students become better consumers and also, perhaps, make them less susceptible to the sales pitches for cigarettes and alcohol and the negative values in many ads.

Linda A. Berne
Professor, Department of Health and Physical Education
The University of North Carolina at Charlotte

Teaching About AIDS

AIDS—acquired immune deficiency syndrome—is a fatal disease for which there is as yet no cure. It is a leading cause of death worldwide. Today the best hope for curbing the spread of AIDS and allaying fears is through education.

Preparation for Teaching

Because teaching about AIDS can be controversial, school districts should develop a comprehensive educational policy and obtain community support before teaching begins. They should involve representatives from the school board, school administration and faculty, students, parents, medical societies, health department, clergy, and civic groups. It would also be beneficial to develop a policy for dealing with cases of AIDS among students or staff.

After establishing an educational policy, the district can develop a curriculum with age-appropriate content and methods. A useful document is "Guidelines for Effective School Health Education to Prevent the Spread of AIDS," developed by the Centers for Disease Control (see Bibliography). The material on AIDS in *Health for Life* has been developed in accordance with those guidelines.

There are two ways to approach teaching about AIDS. The school can provide a program for training current staff. Or, the school can bring in trained AIDS educators to do the teaching. Local health departments and health agencies, such as the American Red Cross, can often provide trained educators.

The school should also consider holding an AIDS education program for parents, ideally before the program for students begins, both to educate parents and to enable them to reinforce the concepts taught in school.

The AIDS Virus

The virus that causes AIDS is known as HIV. It is a fragile virus that dies quickly outside the body and is easily killed by disinfectants, bleach, and heat sterilization. Thus HIV is hard to catch and can be spread only by direct transmission of certain body fluids—blood, semen, and vaginal secretions—from one person to another. HIV can only infect a person who is exposed to infected body fluids.

Certain behaviors can expose a person to these body fluids and thus the possibility of contracting AIDS: (1) intimate sexual contact with an infected person and (2) sharing intravenous drug needles and syringes with an infected person. These behaviors provide the opportunity for HIV to get into the bloodstream.

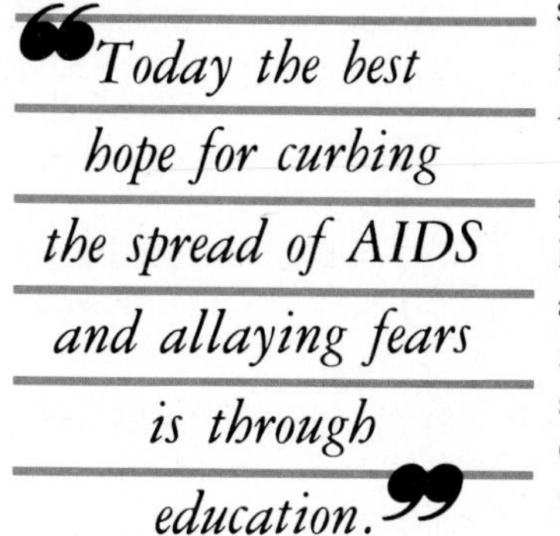

"Today the best
hope for curbing
the spread of AIDS
and allaying fears
is through
education."

Intimate sexual contact includes sexual intercourse and any other behaviors in which a person's sex organs touch or enter the openings of another person's body. Statistics from the Centers for Disease Control show that the greatest number of cases of AIDS is documented to have been acquired by male-to-male sexual contact. However, each year the number of reported cases acquired by male-female contact has steadily increased.

When intravenous drug needles are shared, some blood from one user remains in the needle or syringe. Then infected blood can get injected into another person who uses the needle or syringe. Reused needles for tatooing or ear piercing also can spread the virus.

People can get the AIDS virus in two other, very rare, ways. One is through blood transfusions. However, since 1985, all donated blood in the United States is thoroughly screened for antibodies to HIV. HIV also can spread from an infected pregnant mother to her baby through the placenta during childbirth or in breast milk.

AIDS is not restricted to certain types or races of people or to certain geographic locations. Teenagers, children, and females, as well as males, can become infected. AIDS can spread to anyone by behaviors that expose the person to body fluids infected with the AIDS virus.

It is alarming that for years people can have the AIDS virus and be able to transmit it but show no sign of the disease. Currently, one to two million people are infected with HIV, but many of them do not know it. The only way to know if a person has the AIDS virus is by a special blood test (ELISA or Western Blot tests).

To protect oneself from AIDS, the U.S. Surgeon General recommends: (1) abstaining from sex or having sex only with one uninfected partner, and (2) not sharing intravenous drug needles.

For those who engage in sexual intercourse with persons who are at risk for AIDS or persons whose infection status is unknown, the Surgeon General recommends the use of a latex condom to reduce the likelihood of infection. The condom must be applied properly and used from start to finish for every sexual act. Although a latex condom does not provide 100% protection (because it could leak, break, or slip off), it provides the best protection. Using (with the condom) spermicides that seem active against HIV and other sexually transmitted organisms provides additional protection.

Although elementary school children are unlikely to engage in the risky behaviors, junior high and high school students are more likely to become sexually active and some may engage in intravenous drug use.

Because blood carries the AIDS virus, health care workers who can be exposed to patients' blood must take special precautions. Laboratory workers wear protective gloves and masks, as do many doctors, nurses, dentists, and dental hygienists.

HIV can be found in small amounts in tears, saliva, sweat, urine, and feces, but there is no evidence that the virus is spread by these fluids. According to the Surgeon General, you cannot get AIDS from clothes, toilet seats, swimming pools, mosquitoes, eating utensils, or drinking glasses. You cannot get the AIDS virus from closed mouth kissing, hugging, or touching a person with AIDS. The AIDS virus is not transmitted by sneezes and coughs. Since AIDS is actually difficult to get, there is no need to be afraid of a person with AIDS or the AIDS virus.

How the Virus Causes Disease

HIV causes illness by weakening the body's immune system (the body's natural defense against pathogens). HIV attacks a specific immune system cell called the T-helper cell (a kind of white blood cell). HIV invades the T-helper cell, reproduces itself, then destroys the T-helper cell. The immune system makes antibodies against HIV, but eventually HIV wins out, and destroys so many T-helper cells that the body has difficulty fighting certain diseases.

An infected person might begin to show signs of a disease called AIDS-related complex (ARC). Signs and symptoms of ARC include swollen lymph glands, night sweats, fever, weight loss, diarrhea, fatigue, and lack of resistance to infection. (Note that these are also signs of many other diseases unrelated to AIDS.) These symptoms might come and go or might progress to full-blown AIDS.

As the immune system continues to weaken, people suffering from ARC may develop full-blown AIDS. The symptoms of full-blown AIDS include the symptoms of ARC, but those symptoms occur more often, last longer, and are more severe. The person also develops opportunistic diseases, which are rare diseases that take the "opportunity" of a weakened immune system to attack the body. The two opportunistic diseases commonly affecting AIDS patients are Kaposi's sarcoma (a rare cancer) and *Pneumocystis carinii* pneumonia (a rare form of pneumonia). Many people with AIDS also suffer brain damage. People with full-blown AIDS usually die within one to three years.

Notice that there is a difference between being infected with the AIDS virus and having the disease AIDS (referred to above as "full-blown AIDS"). People who are infected with the AIDS virus may not be sick; they may not even know that they are infected. People with the disease AIDS (full-blown AIDS) have a variety of serious signs and symptoms, for example, fever, weight loss, diarrhea, fatigue, lack of resistance to infection, swollen lymph glands, and one or more opportunistic diseases.

Although no cure has yet been found for AIDS, some treatments can minimize the severity and frequency of symptoms in some people. Scientists around the world are working hard to find a cure and a vaccine.

Linda A. Berne
Professor, Department of Health and Physical Education
The University of North Carolina at Charlotte

Teaching How to Prevent Sexual Abuse

Sexual abuse can leave lasting emotional scars and lead to a destructive cycle of abuse. Rape and date rape are also serious problems. Teachers can help students learn when and how to protect themselves.

Preparation for Teaching Before offering a unit on sexual abuse and rape prevention, a program philosophy and guidelines should be established, with input from teachers, administrators, school nurses, social workers, and parents. The books listed in the Bibliography will be useful. The *Health for Life Teacher's Resource Book* contains age-appropriate teaching materials, including a blackline master and teaching strategies.

Schools should inform parents about what will be taught and how to deal with questions their children may have. An informational session for parents before teaching starts would be useful.

Teachers must understand the subjects of sexual abuse and rape prevention and the surrounding issues, and must feel comfortable teaching them. Training sessions for teachers can be of great benefit. Teachers also need to become familiar with community groups and service agencies that offer support, resources, and information about sexual abuse. Teachers should also know state requirements for detecting and reporting child sexual abuse.

The classroom teacher is perhaps in the best position to discuss these subjects with students because his or her ongoing contact with students facilitates the development of trust. The teacher can organize a presentation with the needs and limitations of particular students in mind. Teachers also have access to other school personnel and community resources to effectively refer students in case any personal trauma is uncovered. (For more information on the signs of sexual child abuse, see page T41, "Recognizing and Reporting Child Abuse.")

"Although it is important to teach students their right not to be touched in uncomfortable ways, it is also important not to frighten them."

While discussing sexual abuse prevention, the teacher should project warmth and objectivity. Although it is important to teach students their right not to be touched in uncomfortable or scary ways, it is also important to not frighten them or make them fearful of adults.

In sixth to eighth graders, sexual development and interest may be beginning. It is especially important to handle delicately the subject of touching and sexual aggression in the context of dating. Emphasize that no one has the right to touch another person without that person's consent, even on a date or in marriage.

Students should feel that they can ask questions about anything. It may be helpful to have a question box for the students to put questions that they do not feel comfortable asking in class. Students may put their names on questions if they wish a personal, private answer from the teacher.

Health Background Child sexual abuse can be defined as sexual involvement imposed upon a child by an adult (or older child). It can include forcing a child to look at the abuser's genitals or forcing the child to undress and expose himself or herself. It may also involve handling of a child's genitals and attempts at or actual penetration of the vagina, anus, or mouth. Incest includes any form of sexual activity between family members, either blood relatives or stepparents or stepchildren.

Most victims are first assaulted during the pre-adolescent years, around ages 8 or 9. Sexual abuse is often characterized by progressive sexual activity over time. The abuser usually uses bribery, threats, or the child's dependency to take advantage of the child and ensure secrecy. Children of either sex may be abused at any age.

Sexual assault involves the use of violence or force. Rape is one type of sexual assault. It is an act of anger and power, not an expression of sexual pleasure. Date rape occurs when a girl's date forces her to engage in sexual behavior against her will. The boy may use physical force, threats, or pressure. Date rape may result from unclear communications between partners.

Most states have laws against statutory rape, which is sexual intercourse with a female who is below legal age, with or without her consent. Legal age, usually from 15 to 18, varies by state.

Linda A. Berne
Professor, Department of Health and Physical Education
The University of North Carolina at Charlotte

Recognizing and Reporting Child Abuse

In every state, teachers and school officials who have reason to suspect a case of child abuse are required to report the case to a specified state agency. Compliance is often motivated by the realization that reporting a case can help prevent further harm to the student. In addition, all states protect from liability all professionals who report, in good faith, any instance of child abuse.

Each state defines child abuse by statute as consisting of one or more of the following elements: nonaccidental physical injury, physical neglect, sexual molestation, or emotional abuse. Your school probably has information about your state's statute. You also might write or call the department in your state responsible for providing services for children and families, such as the Children's Protective Services or the Attorney General's office. Additional information is available from several national organizations (see Health Resources list).

> *"Reassure the student that he or she is no way at fault and that you will get him or her the needed help."*

If a student tells a teacher about an incident of abuse, the teacher should accept the student's report as true. Try not to exhibit shock or anger at the student's recounting. Try to be attentive and offer a supportive, confidential environment in which the student can discuss his or her situation and feelings. Reassure the student that he or she is in no way at fault for the abuse, and that you will get him or her the help needed.

Most abused students are afraid to report abuse. The teacher needs to be aware of signs that may indicate child abuse: repeated, unexplained or inconsistently explained injuries; frequent urinary infections; torn or stained clothing; neglected appearance; regression to infantile behavior; destructive, aggressive, hyperactive, nervous, or disruptive behavior; passive, withdrawn, or noncommunicative behavior; exceptional secrecy; fear of adults or other children; extreme fear of or seductiveness with opposite sex; precocious sexual knowledge or behavior; running away; arriving very early at school and leaving very late; habitual absenteeism or tardiness; sudden drop in school performance; crying without provocation. (Note: some of these can be signs of problems other than abuse.)

A student's artwork or stories can also give subtle or obvious signs that the student has been abused. Show the student's work to a school psychologist, who can help determine whether the suspicions are warranted.

Document any clues suggesting child abuse. Documentation should include any observations about the student's appearance or behavior that may be signs of abuse and the date or dates of these observations. Record the student's explanation for any changes in appearance or behavior. Documentation will be essential for a filed report.

Discuss suspected cases of child abuse with the school nurse, psychologist, social worker, or principal to help determine whether a report should be filed. Other school officials may wish to meet with or observe the student. School policy may dictate that the staff involved make a joint decision about whether or not to file a report.

Reporting child abuse usually involves a phone call to a state agency. Verbal information may be requested to help determine if an emergency exists and if the student's life or health is in immediate danger. A few days later, the agency might request a detailed, written report. The agency will use this information to investigate the case.

To be informed of progress in a case, you may wish to keep in touch with school staff and perhaps with the agency involved. However, agencies are required to keep certain information confidential to protect the rights of the people involved. Even if information is not available, the continued support of the school staff can help both the student and the agency.

Many sources of help are available to students and families with child abuse problems. Some programs include parent support groups, child support groups, telephone hotlines, emergency nurseries or day-care centers, and programs showing students how to recognize and respond to inappropriate behavior. Remember that child abuse occurs in all sectors of society, and that reporting suspected cases ultimately helps both the child and the adult.

Joan Salmon
School Nurse
Greenwood School Corporation

Teaching Safety for Latchkey Children

Latchkey children are children who are left alone, without adult supervision, on a regular basis. About two million to seven million children between the ages of five and thirteen years regularly care for themselves before or after school.

Some studies show that latchkey children can thrive on the experience and benefit from the time they spend on their own. Other studies indicate that these children experience loneliness and isolation and may become depressed and fearful. For any given student, the experience can sometimes be negative, other times positive.

All children can benefit by learning how to be safe at home and how to deal with emergencies. This knowledge can be helpful even when an adult is home, as for example, if the adult suffers an accident.

The teacher can help latchkey students in regard to safety, life skills, nutrition, and schedules. The teacher can also provide help against boredom, and give emotional support.

Safety Discuss ways of being safe when home alone. By keeping the tone of the conversation positive and nonthreatening, you can help decrease fear and anxiety and help the student focus on how to be safe. You may want to discuss the following safety procedures:

- Making emergency phone calls
- Treating simple injuries
- What to do in an emergency, both medical and household
- Practicing home fire drills
- Answering the door or telephone
- Keeping the housekey safe
- Preventing accidents

These topics are dealt with throughout the *Health for Life* series as appropriate for students at each grade level. The series contains activities that students can do at home and gives information that students can share with the family to reinforce safety concepts.

> *"All children can benefit by learning how to be safe at home and how to deal with emergencies."*

Life Skills For students to handle caring for themselves successfully, they need to develop skills such as problem solving, decision making, goal setting, coping, and peer resistance. Throughout the *Health for Life* series, especially in the *Skills for Life Handbook,* these skills are taught in a form and context that students can apply to their situations at home. Learning to care for oneself and overcome one's fears also helps build the student's self-esteem.

Nutrition Latchkey students are usually responsible for fixing snacks and other meals. Teach students how to make healthy snacks and meals. The nutrition chapters in *Health for Life* will help you explain why healthy snacks and meals are important.

Schedules and Boredom Latchkey children often have a lot of unstructured time. All students would benefit from learning to make a schedule for homework, chores, sports, etc. Teachers can also discuss ways to overcome boredom.

Emotional Support Be available to listen if a student wishes to talk about fears, loneliness, or any problems he or she is having when home alone. Also be alert for signs that the child may be having problems with being home alone. Children who frequently are late to school, dress inappropriately for the weather, forget lunch or lunch money, or do not bring homework or required notes from home may be on their own in the morning. Teachers can work with the student, parents, and other school staff to help a student who is experiencing difficulties in being home alone. Teachers can suggest programs before and after school sponsored by community agencies (such as YMCA, YWCA, Scouts) and the schools. Some communities have phone services especially for latchkey students to call when they need help, advice, or simply someone to talk to.

Joan Salmon
School Nurse
Greenwood School Corporation

Helping Students Cope with Family Problems

For some students who come from homes with difficult problems, the school is the only stable, secure environment in their lives. For others, school may be a source of increased stress or become an arena for acting out in response to a difficult home situation. What a teacher may diagnose as a learning dysfunction or a behavioral problem could be an inability to cope with a family problem.

Difficult family situations can help some students learn and mature. Other students may need extra time before they can adjust in a healthy way. A student may exhibit physical, emotional, or behavioral changes in response to a problem in the home. Any sudden change in the student's personality, alertness, attitudes, or habits may indicate a troubling family situation. Serious problems may call for intervention by the school nurse, social worker, or principal.

Some students face difficulties from having to adjust to changes in the family situation or home environment. Divorce is probably the most common situation that changes family structure. Students whose parents divorce may go through a period of confusion, anger, and grief akin to that experienced by one whose parents have died. For this reason, you may wish to refer to "Helping Students Cope with Death" on page T44 for some ideas about such situations.

Be sensitive to the feelings of a student whose parents are divorcing, and give reassurance that, with time, the student will adjust to the changes and feel better. In class discussions, try to avoid portraying only one type of family. In this way you can help all students feel comfortable when talking about families.

Circumstances that bring about new family arrangements can cause anxiety in a student. For example, recently divorced families may have new financial limitations. When a divorce settlement ends in dual custody, the children also may face the emotional stress of adjusting to two different households. If parents remarry, children have to learn to accept new family members and new roles.

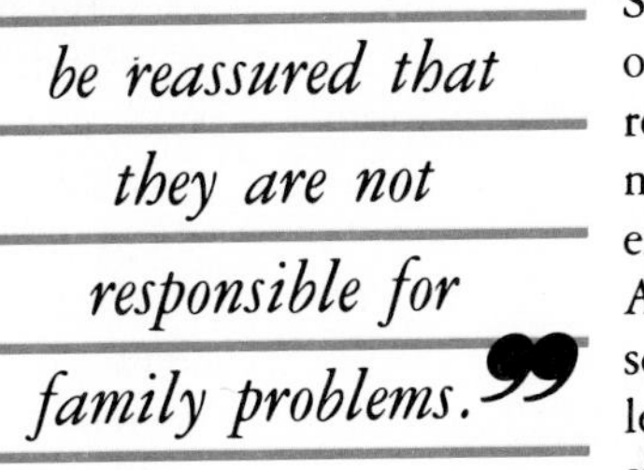
"Students need to be reassured that they are not responsible for family problems."

Foster and adopted children and members of their families need to make the same kinds of adjustments as members of stepfamilies. In addition, foster or adopted children may feel embarrassed if they do not know or have contact with their biological parents. The teacher should be sensitive to the feelings of such students, especially when discussing family traits.

Guide a student to express his or her feelings about changes in family situations. Writing and drawing are both good ways for students to express their feelings. Giving the student an opportunity to talk privately and to express feelings without fear of criticism can also help the student adjust.

Financial hardship is another problem some families face. Though the school can do little to help the student in such a situation, a sensitive teacher can avoid increasing stress on the student. For example, when suggesting that students bring certain materials from home for school projects, be aware that in some families common materials may be, in fact, luxuries. When asking students to bring or wear certain clothing for fitness or other activities, be sensitive to the fact that some students may not own such clothing.

Some students might face the difficult situation of living with an adult who is physically or emotionally abusive or who has an alcohol or drug addiction problem. Such a student may or may not suffer directly from physical neglect, abuse, or emotional stress. Any teacher or school official who learns that a student suffers from neglect or abuse may be legally responsible to report the condition to the proper authorities. "Recognizing and Reporting Child Abuse" (page T41) gives information about legal responsibilities.

Other than reporting abuse or neglect, the school can do little to help in a family situation involving personal or substance abuse. However, it is important for the teacher to be sensitive to the student's feelings and fears. Students may need to be reassured that they are not responsible for family problems.

Joan Salmon
School Nurse
Greenwood School Corporation

Helping Students Cope with Death

When the death of a close relative or friend occurs, a student might have no past experience to help him or her express feelings about death. Healthy emotional development depends on the ability to express feelings and to complete the mourning process.

Recognizing signs of grief is essential for helping a grieving student. Common expressions of grief include shock, anger, guilt, anxiety, fear, regression, sorrow, forgetfulness, and, occasionally, aggression. A lack of interest in schoolwork may also be a sign of grief. Such emotions may be expressed immediately after the death or in the weeks or months that follow. Some students show no obvious signs of grief. Students who do not show their feelings may need as much or more help than students who show obvious signs of grief. A teacher who recognizes signs of grief can help by demonstrating concern and being ready to listen to the student talk about his or her feelings.

> *"Healthy emotional development depends on the ability to express feelings and to complete the mourning process."*

Healthy emotional development depends on the ability to express feelings and to complete the mourning process.

A grieving student might exhibit anger because he or she feels abandoned. The student might also feel guilty. In either case, the student needs to be reassured that his or her feelings are natural. The student may need help in determining how to best release feelings of grief, anger, and other emotions. He or she should be informed that it is acceptable for someone who is grieving to cry, to be quiet, or to talk about memories of the person who died.

Students may need reassurance about adult behavior, especially if the adults seem distracted or inattentive. The student may need to be told that the adult is feeling grief and will probably be able to talk about it when he or she feels a little better.

Students in the middle elementary grades may be puzzled by different religious or cultural customs surrounding death. Students in a class may come from various religious or cultural backgrounds. You may wish to present information about the different customs and rituals of the groups represented within the class. However, avoid contradicting the religious teachings of the home or expressing your personal religious beliefs when presenting such information.

Students of this age understand that death is an inevitable occurrence. They may have specific questions about causes of death. Such information should be presented in a factual but sympathetic manner. Try to avoid euphemisms, which usually serve to confuse rather than reassure students. Do not feel compelled to explain everything at one time. Give students time to think over explanations and come back with additional questions. If students ask the same question several different times, they may need time to comprehend the answer. Try to answer the question the same way each time, with patience and understanding. Let students dominate the discussion and explore questions.

Usually a student works through grief without need of professional guidance. However, occasionally grief becomes so intense as to interfere with the student's development. If, by six months after the death of a significant person in the student's life, the student has not begun to resume his or her normal routine, professional counseling may be needed. If you are aware that a student is experiencing prolonged, intense grief, you may wish to discuss the situation with the principal or social worker.

If a student misses a class due to the death of a close relative or friend, you can use the opportunity to allow classmates to ask questions and express their feelings. You may wish to use this time to discuss how students can express sympathy to someone who is grieving. If a classmate dies, students should be given time to discuss their feelings and fears. Students may want to discuss what they would like to remember about their classmate and plan a special activity or project to do as a remembrance.

The death of a pet can be a very serious experience for a student, for it may be the student's first experience with death. The student may feel a great sense of loss. By discussing the death with the student, you can help him or her handle grief and establish a basis for dealing with other deaths later in life.

Joan Salmon
School Nurse
Greenwood School Corporation

Helping Prevent Suicide

Suicide rates among adolescents have increased 300 percent during the past 25 years. Present indications are that the rates are continuing to rise.

Most suicidal people are ambivalent. They want to live and die at the same time, and may shift back and forth many times before taking any action. This ambivalence means that the opportunity for prevention exists.

Signs of Impending Suicide

The clues that potential suicides give of their intentions are often last-minute cries for help.

- **Talking about death and suicide** More than 60 percent of suicides mention their intentions to others, in statements such as "The world would be better off without me," "I wish I were dead," "You'll be sorry when I'm gone," "I'm going to kill myself."
- **Preoccupation with death and dying** The student may obsessively read or write about death. English and art teachers are often in a position to notice this. The student may also become involved with cults involved with death or violence.
- **Giving away prized possessions** A student might give items to friends or family with comments such as, "I want you to have this. I won't be needing it anymore."

Other Warning Signs

Other behaviors and clues may indicate that a student is very troubled and needs psychological and emotional support.

- **Expressions of hopelessness and loneliness** Comments may include "I can't cope anymore," "Nobody cares about me."
- **Changes in behavior** Behaviors may include withdrawing from friends, family, usual school activities, sudden poor school attendance; mood swings for no apparent reason; increased consumption of alcohol or drugs; increased risk-taking without fear of danger; sudden perkiness and carefree attitude; sudden angry outbursts.
- **Depression** Indicators of depression include crying, never having fun, insomnia, tiredness, inability to concentrate or make decisions, excessive guilt feelings, change in appetite.
- **Stressful situations** Many who attempt suicide have recently experienced the following: death or suicide of someone (not necessarily someone close); divorce of parents; rejection; problems in school, at home, or at work; trouble with the law; sexual problems, including pregnancy; serious or permanent injury.

> *"Most suicidal people are ambivalent. This ambivalence means that the opportunity for prevention exists."*

Myths About Suicide

False statements pertaining to suicide include:

- **People who talk about suicide never actually do it.** Actually, more than 60 percent of suicide attempters/completers tell someone about their plan.
- **If you talk about suicide with a person who seems depressed or has shown some of the warning signs, you might inadvertently cause them to commit suicide.** In fact, ignoring the person increases his or her feelings of isolation and may make suicide more likely.
- **Teaching students about suicide will put the idea in their heads.** In fact, suicide prevention education usually increases communication between students and teachers, making it more likely that students will consult teachers when problems arise. It is especially important to discuss suicide immediately after a death has occurred. Left undiscussed, suicide may appear intriguing, dramatic, romantic, and an accepted way to solve problems.

What Teachers Can Do

First, believe any threat. If a student talks to you about suicide, listen carefully. Stay with the student. Try to comfort him or her. Finally, get help. Do not make the mistake of thinking that you can talk someone out of suicide or that they just need a sympathetic listener. A person planning suicide is too confused to benefit from just talking things out.

For help, contact the school counselor, nurse, principal, local mental health agencies, or suicide hotlines. In an emergency, you can dial 911.

At the beginning of each school year, teachers should review with students the resources available to help students with problems, including depression, anxiety, drug abuse, and thoughts of suicide. The student handbook should list support services and outreach programs. Up-to-date posters indicating support services and hotlines should be hung throughout the school.

Adele G. Russman
School Counselor
Main Street School

Teaching Prevention of Teenage Pregnancy

In the United States, more than one million teenage girls become pregnant each year.

Of these pregnancies, 80 percent are unplanned and unwanted. Thus it is important to teach both teenage girls and boys how to prevent pregnancy.

Preparation for Teaching

Philosophy and curriculum guidelines should be developed with input from teachers, administrators, school nurses, social workers, and parents. The books in the Bibliography will be helpful.

The school can provide its faculty with a training program presented by health educators from local health departments, health agencies, universities, or hospitals. If the teachers feel uncomfortable teaching pregnancy prevention, specially trained community health educators might lead the classroom presentations. Teachers can then act as consultants for follow-up and lead students to other community resources.

For the parents, an informational presentation can clarify what will be taught and suggest how parents can answer their children's questions.

Students in the program should feel there is no question they cannot ask. Details the teachers cannot answer in class can always be answered afterwards or by a community health educator. It may be helpful to have a box in which students can put questions that they do not feel comfortable asking in class.

The most useful way to focus a pregnancy prevention program is to stress self-responsibility and abstinence. Learning self-responsibility gives the student the skills and facts to decide how to take care of his or her own body, health, and ultimately, future.

Health Background on Pregnancy Prevention

The health and social risks of adolescent pregnancy include:

- Suicide—Teenage mothers are seven times more likely to attempt suicide than other adolescents of the same age.
- Miscarriage—from 10 to 25 percent of teenage pregnancies result in spontaneous abortion.
- Malnutrition—The adolescent mother is still physically growing. She may find it difficult to meet her nutritional needs as well as those of a growing fetus.
- Interruption of education—80 percent of girls and 40 percent of boys who become parents by age 17 drop out and never complete high school.
- Child abuse and neglect—Mothers younger than 18 are twice as likely to abuse their children.
- Poverty—75 percent of households headed by women younger than 25 are classified as below the poverty level and rely on governmental assistance.
- Morbidity and mortality—The risk of maternal death due to complications of pregnancy and childbirth is 60 percent higher for mothers younger than 16 than for mothers over 20.
- Perpetuating the teenage pregnancy cycle—80 percent of teenage girls who give birth before age 15 are daughters of teenage mothers; 15 percent of babies born to women younger than 18 are second or third children.

There are many theories as to why teen pregnancy is so widespread. After puberty, the sex drive is a powerful force, and the age of puberty has decreased. Peer pressure to engage in sexual intercourse can be strong. The media, which have a strong influence on teens, often portray people who focus on short-term pleasures without considering long-term consequences or responsibilities. The media also rarely portray pregnancy or disease as possible results of unplanned or unprotected sexual activity. Adolescents may have few positive role models to show the value of abstinence. Teenagers also tend to feel indestructible. They may realize that having sex can lead to unwanted pregnancy, but believe it would never happen to them personally. Often teenagers lack accurate information about reproduction and pregnancy.

Linda A. Berne
Professor, Department of Health and Physical Education
The University of North Carolina at Charlotte

Bibliography

AIDS

"Guidelines for Effective School Health Education to Prevent the Spread of AIDS," in *Morbidity and Mortality Weekly Report,* 37 (1988), and in *Journal of School Health,* v. 58 (1988).

Surgeon General's Report on Acquired Immune Deficiency Syndrome, U.S. Department of Health and Human Services.

Child Abuse Prevention

Erickson E., McEvoy A., and Colucci, N. *Child Abuse and Neglect: A Guidebook for Educators and Community Leaders,* ed 2. Learning Publications, 1984.

Tower, C.C. *Child Abuse and Neglect: A Teacher's Handbook for Detection, Reporting, and Classroom Management.* National Education Association, 1984.

Latchkey Children

For Teachers and Parents

Long, L., and Long, T. *The Handbook for Latchkey Children and Their Parents.* Arbor House, 1983.

Robinson, B. E.; Rowland, H. and Coleman, M. *Latchkey Kids: Unlocking Doors for Children and Their Families.* D.C. Heath, 1986.

For Students and Parents

Gilbert, S. *By Yourself.* Lothrop, Lee & Shepard, 1983.

Kyte, K.S. *In Charge: A Complete Handbook for Kids with Working Parents.* Alfred A. Knopf, 1983.

Teaching Life Management Skills

Bershad, C. and DiMella N. *The Changer and the Changed: A Working Guide to Personal Change.* Management Sciences for Health, 1983.

Borba, M. and others. *Self-Esteem: A Classroom Affair.* Harper & Row, 1982.

Canfield, J. and Wells, H. *100 Ways to Enhance Self-Concept in the Classroom: A Handbook for Teachers and Parents.* Prentice-Hall, 1976.

Johnson, E.W., and McClelland, D.C. *Learning to Achieve.* Scott, Foresman, 1984. (student text and teacher's manual, available at two levels: 3–6 and 6–9.)

Medical Problems

Chronic Illness in the Classroom: Asthma, Cancer, Diabetes, Epilepsy, Skin Disorders, Sickle Cell Anemia, Substance Abuse (videotapes). Charlotte Mecklenburg School, Audiovisual Production, 800 Everett Place, Charlotte, NC 28205; (704) 343-5440

Hobbs, N., and Perrin, J.M., eds. *Issues in the Care of Children with Chronic Illness.* Jossey-Bass, 1985.

Johnson, M.P., Lubker, B.B., and Fowler, M.G. "Teacher Needs Assessment for the Educational Management of Children with Chronic Illnesses." *Journal of School Health,* v. 58 (1988).

Newton, J. *School Health Handbook.* Prentice-Hall, 1984.

School Health: A Guide for Health Professionals. ed. 4. American Academy of Pediatrics, 1987.

Pregnancy Prevention

Berne L.A. *Human Sexuality: A Responsible Approach.* Scott, Foresman, 1988. (student book and teacher's manual)

Burt, J. and Meeks, L. *Education for Sexuality,* ed 3. Saunders College Publishing, 1985.

Kirby D. *Sexuality Education: A Guide to Developing and Implementing Programs.* Network Publications, 1984.

Sexual Abuse Prevention

For Children

Dayee F. *Private Zone: A Book Teaching Children Sexual Assault Prevention Tools.* Charles Franklin Press, 1982.

Fay, J., and Flerchinger B.J. *Top Secret: Sexual Assault Information for Teenagers Only.* King County Rape Relief, 305 South 43rd, Renton, WA, 98055

Freeman, L. *It's My Body: A Book to Teach Children How to Resist Uncomfortable Touch.* Parenting Press, 1984.

Girard. L.W. *My Body Is Private.* Albert Whitman, 1984.

Stringer, G. *Date Rape! Terri and J.R. Talk to Teens.* Network Publications.

Wachter O. *No More Secrets for Me.* Little, Brown, 1983.

For Parents

Fay J. and others. *He Told Me Not to Tell.* King County Rape Relief, 305 South 43rd, Renton, WA 98055.

For Teachers

Berne LA: *Human Sexuality: A Responsible Approach.* Scott, Foresman, 1988. Student text with teacher's manual.

Kempe, R.S., and Henry, C. *The Common Secret: Sexual Abuse of Children and Adolescents.* W.H. Freeman, 1984.

Plummer C.A. *Preventing Sexual Abuse: Activities and Strategies for Those Working with Children and Adolescents.* Learning Publications, 1984.

Suicide Prevention

American Academy of Pediatrics, "Surviving: Coping with Adolescent Depression and Suicide." (brochure), 1985.

Gardner, S. *Teenage Suicide.* Messner, 1985.

Giffin, M.E. and Felsenthal, C.A. *Cry for Help.* Doubleday, 1983.

Giovacchini, P. *The Urge to Die: Why Young People Commit Suicide.* Macmillan, 1981.

Klagsbrun, F. *Too Young to Die: Suicide and Youth.* Houghton Mifflin, 1976.

McCoy, K. *Coping With Teenage Depression: A Parent's Guide.* New American Library, 1982.

Toll-Free Hotlines

AIDS
Centers for Disease Control
National AIDS Hotline
1-800-342-AIDS

Cancer
National Cancer Institute
Cancer Information Service
1-800-638-6694

Child Abuse
Child Abuse Hotline
1-800-422-4453

Diabetes
American Diabetes Association
1-800-232-3472

Drug Abuse
National Institute on Drug Abuse
1-800-662-HELP
Psychiatric Institute of America
1-800-COCAINE

Drug Abuse Prevention
Just Say No Kids Club
1-800-258-2766

Epilepsy
Epilepsy Foundation of America
1-800-332-1000

Hearing Impairment
Better Hearing Institute
1-800-EAR-WELL
National Hearing Aid Hotline
1-800-521-5247

Missing and Runaway Children
Missing Children
1-800-843-5678
Runaways
1-800-231-6946

Product Safety
U.S. Consumer Product Safety Commission
1-800-638-CPSC

Sexually Transmitted Diseases
V. D. Hotline
1-800-227-8922

Stuttering
National Center for Stuttering
1-800-221-2483

Health Resources

Air Pollution Control Association
P.O. Box 2861
Pittsburgh, PA 15230

Alcoholics Anonymous General Services Office
468 Park Avenue South
New York, NY 10003

Al-Anon Family Groups (AAFG)
1372 Broadway
New York, NY 10018-6106

American Alliance for Health, Physical Education, Recreation and Dance
1900 Association Drive
Reston, VA 22091

American Automobile Association
8111 Gatehouse Road
Falls Church, VA 22047

American Cancer Society
19 West 56 Street
New York, NY 10019

American Dental Association
Bureau of Health Education and Audiovisual Services
211 East Chicago Avenue
Chicago, IL 60611

American Diabetes Association
P.O. Box 25757
1660 Duke St.
Alexandria, VA 22313

American Heart Association
7320 Greenville Avenue
Dallas, TX 75231

American Lung Association
1740 Broadway
New York, NY 10019

American Medical Association
535 North Dearborn Street
Chicago, IL 60610

American Red Cross
17th and 12th Sts. NW
Washington, DC 20006

American School Health Association
P.O. Box 708
Kent, OH 44240

Bureau of Community Health Services
Health Services Administration
Parklawn Building
5600 Fishers Lane
Rockville, MD 20857

Centers for Disease Control
Center for Health Promotion and Education
1600 Clifton Road N.E.
Atlanta, GA 30333

Consumer Information Center
Pueblo, CO 81009

Council for Exceptional Children
1920 Association Drive
Reston, VA 22091

Council on Family Health
420 Lexington Avenue
New York, NY 10017

Food and Drug Administration
Office of Consumer Inquiries
Parklawn Building
5600 Fishers Lane
Rockville, MD 20857

Food and Nutrition Information Center
6505 Belcrest Road
Hyattsville, MD 20782

Human Nutrition Information Service
Department of Agriculture
National Agricultural Library Building
Beltsville, MD 20705

National Center for Education in Maternal and Child Health
38th and R Sts. NW
Washington, DC 20057

National Center for the Prevention and Control of Rape
5600 Fishers Lane
Room 6C-12
Rockville, MD 20857

National Center on Child Abuse and Neglect
Office of Child Development
P.O. Box 1182
Washington, DC 20013

National Clearinghouse for Alcohol and Drug Abuse Information
P.O. Box 2345
Rockville, MD 20852

National Clearinghouse for Mental Health Information
National Institute of Mental Health
Parklawn Building
5600 Fishers Lane
Rockville, MD 20857

National Committee for Prevention of Child Abuse
332 S. Michigan Ave., Suite 950
Chicago, IL 60604

National Committee on Youth Suicide
67 Irving Pl.
New York, NY 10003

National Dairy Council
6300 North River Road
Rosemont, IL 60018-4233

National Health Information Clearinghouse
P.O. Box 1133
Washington, DC 20013

National Highway Traffic Safety Administration
U.S. Dept. of Transportation
400 7th St., Room 5130
Washington, DC 20590

National Institute of Child Health and Human Development
Building 31
9000 Rockville Pike
Bethesda, MD 20892

National Safety Council
444 North Michigan Avenue
Chicago, IL 60611

Office of Consumer Affairs
U.S. Department of Health and Human Services
1009 Premier Building
Washington, DC 20201

President's Council on Physical Fitness and Sports
450 5th Street NW
Suite 7103
Washington, DC 20001

U.S. Environmental Protection Agency
401 M St. SW
Washington, DC 20460

School-Age Child Care Project
Wellesley College Center for Research on Women
Wellesley, MA 02181
(provides information on child care policy and technical assistance on establishing child care programs)

Software Sources

Aquarius Software
P.O. Box 128
Indian Rocks Beach, FL 33535

BLS Tutorsystems
5153 W. Woodmill Ste. 18
Wilmington, DE 19808

Cambridge Development Laboratory
1696 Massachusetts Avenue
Cambridge, MA 02138

Control Health Software
18653 Ventura Boulevard #348
Tarzana, CA 91356

DYNACOMP, Inc.
1064 Gravel Road
Webster, NY 14580

Educational Activities, Inc.
P.O. Box 392
Freeport, NY 11520

Educational Images
P.O. Box 3456, West Side Station
Elmira, NY 14905

EPCOT Educational Media
500 South Buena Vista Street
Burbank, CA 91521

HRM Software
175 Tompkins Avenue
Pleasantville, NY 10570

Learning Seed Company
21250 North Andover Road
Kildeer, IL 60047

Marshfilm Enterprises, Inc.
P.O. Box 8082
Shawnee Mission, KS 66208

MCE, Inc.
157 South Kalamazoo Hall, 250
Kalamazoo, MI 49007

M.D. Anderson Hospital
P.O. Box 157
6723 Bertner Avenue
Houston, TX 77030

MECC Distribution Center
3490 Lexington Avenue North
St. Paul, MN 55112-8097

Right On Programs
755 New York Ave.
Huntington, NY 11743

Sunburst Communications, Inc.
39 Washington Avenue
Pleasantville, NY 10570

Synergistic Software
830 North Riverside Drive
Renton, WA 98055

Audio-Visual Sources

Agency for Instructional Technology
Box A
Bloomington, IN 47402

AIMS Media
6901 Woodley Avenue
Van Nuys, CA 91406-4878

Alfred Higgins Productions, Inc.
9100 Sunset Blvd., Suite 100
Los Angeles, CA 90069

All Media Productions
1424 Lake Drive, S. E.
Box K
Grand Rapids, MI 49501

AAHPERD
American Alliance for Health, Physical Education, Recreation, and Dance
1900 Association Drive
Reston, VA 22091

American Automobile Association
8111 Gatehouse Road
Falls Church, VA 22047

American Cancer Society
19 West 56 Street
New York, NY 10019

Barr Films
Box 7878
12801 Schabarum Avenue
Irwindale, CA 91707-7878

BFA Educational Media
Phoenix/BFA Film and Video, Inc.
468 Park Avenue South
New York, NY 10016

Boy Scouts of America
Audio-Visual Division
1325 Walnut Hill Lane
Irving, TX 75038

Britannica
Encyclopedia Britannica Educational Corporation
425 North Michigan Avenue
Chicago, IL 60611

Churchill Films
662 North Robertson Blvd.
Los Angeles, CA 90069-9990

Coronet Films and Video
Coronet/MTI Film and Video
108 Wilmot Road
Deerfield, IL 60015

Creative Learning
P.O. Box 134
Saunderstown, RI 02874

Curriculum Innovations, Inc.
3500 Western Avenue
Highland Park, IL 60035

Demco, Inc.
Box 7488
2120 Fordem Avenue
Madison, WI 53707

Direct Cinema Ltd. Inc.
P.O. Box 69589
Los Angeles, CA 90069

Educational Activities, Inc.
P.O. Box 392
Freeport, NY 11520

Educational Dimensions Corporation
Box 126
Stamford, CT 06904

Educational Record Center
1575 Northside Drive
Building 400 Ste. 400
Atlanta, GA 30318

Educational Frontiers
157 Chambers Street
New York, NY 10003

EXAR Communications
267B McClean Avenue
Staten Island, NY 10305

Film Communicators
Division of Coronet/MTI Film and Video
108 Wilmot Road
Deerfield, IL 60015

Focus Media, Inc.
P.O. Box 865
839 Stewart Avenue
Garden City, NY 11530

Food and Drug Administration
5600 Fishers Lane
Rockville, MD 20857

Good Apple, Inc.
Box 299
Carthage, IL 62321

Guidance Associates, Inc.
Box 3000, Communications Park
90 South Bedford Road
Mount Kisco, NY 10549

Human Relations Media
175 Tompkins Avenue
Pleasantville, NY 10570

International Film Bureau, Inc.
332 South Michigan Avenue
Chicago, IL 60604

J. Weston Walch, Publisher
P.O. Box 658
321 Valley Street
Portland, ME 04104-0658

Johnson Institute
751 Metro Blvd. Ste. 250
Minneapolis, MN 55435

Kimbo Educational
P.O. Box 477
Long Branch, NJ 07740

Knowledge Unlimited
Box 52
Madison, WI 53701

Learning Arts
P.O. Box 179
Wichita, KS 67201

Learning Corporation of America
130 East 59 Street
New York, NY 10022

Learning Tree Filmstrips
Learning Tree Publishing, Inc.
7108 South Alton Way
Englewood, CO 80112

Marshfilm Enterprises, Inc.
P.O. Box 8082
Shawnee Mission, KS 66208

MTI Teleprograms
Coronet/MTI Film and Video
108 Wilmot Road
Deerfield, IL 60015-9925

National Film Board of Canada
1251 Avenue of the Americas
New York, NY 10020

National Geographic Society
Educational Services
17 and M Streets, N.W.
Washington, DC 20036

National Wildlife Federation
1412 16th Street, N.W.
Washington, DC 20036-2266

New Day Films
853 Broadway
New York, NY 10002

Pyramid Film and Video
Box 1048
Santa Monica, CA 90406

SC Communications, Ltd.
629A Mount Pleasant Road
Toronto, Ont., Canada
M4S-2M9

Scholastic Inc.
730 Broadway
New York, NY 10003

Society for Visual Education, Inc.
1345 Diversey Parkway
Chicago, IL 60614

Sunburst Communications, Inc.
39 Washington Avenue
Pleasantville, NY 10570

U.S. Department of Transportation
400 Seventh Street, S.W.
Washington, DC 20590

Walt Disney Educational Media
500 South Buena Vista Street
Burbank, CA 91521

Mental and Social Health

Book 5

Mental Health

Understanding that you are unique: 18
Other people affect self-image: 19
  Working to have friendships: 19
  Working to get along well with members of the family: 19
Personal strengths and good self-image: 20–21
Improving self-image by making certain changes: 22
How you are like other people: 24–25
Learning about personal differences: 26–27
Dealing with uncomfortable feelings: 28–31
  Dealing with anger: 28–29
  Dealing with shy feelings: 30–31
Dealing with problems: 32–33, 35
  Making decisions: 32–33
Dealing with unsolvable problems: 34–35
How people can be good friends: 36–39
  Why people become friends: 37
  Why friends are important: 37
  Why friendships sometimes change: 38
  What makes a good friend: 39
Learning to relax: 43
Effects of feelings on appetite: 154–155

Social Health

How to improve self-image: 19
  Working to have friendships: 19
  Working to get along well with members of the family: 19
Improving self-image by making certain changes: 22
How you are like other people: 24–25
Learning about personal differences: 26–27
Dealing with uncomfortable feelings: 28–31
  Dealing with anger: 28–29
  Dealing with shy feelings: 30–31
How people can be good friends: 36–39
  Why people become friends: 37
  Why friends are important: 37
  Why friendships sometimes change: 38
  What makes a good friend: 39

Book 6

Mental Health

Self-image: 20
Characteristics of a good self-image: 21
  Confidence: 21
  Willingness to try new things: 21
  Learning from mistakes: 21
  Awareness of being unique: 21
Improving self-image: 22–23
  You are special: 22
  Remember your strengths: 22
  Recognize and accept weaknesses: 23
  Expect to make mistakes sometimes: 23
  Accept not getting what you want: 23
Knowing yourself: 24–25
Dealing with stress: 30–35
  Causes of stress: 30
  Harmful effects of too much stress: 31
  Dealing with problems that cause stress: 32–33
  Learning to relax: 34
  Making decisions: 35
How to set and reach goals: 36–41, 42
  Deciding what goals to set: 37
  Discovering what abilities help people set goals: 38–39
Changing emotions and relationships as a person grows: 66–67
Dealing with growth and change by accepting responsibility and communicating: 68–69
Exercise and mental health: 106

Social Health

Accepting differences helps people get along with one another: 21
Getting along better with others: 26–29
  Build good relationships: 26
  Treat people as you want to be treated: 26–27
  Develop good friendships: 27
Dealing with angry feelings: 28–29
Emotions and relationships often change with growth: 66–67
Dealing with growth and change: 68–69
Exercise and social health: 107

Book 7

Mental Health

Mental Health: 20–21
  How people can improve their mental health: 22–25, 34
What helps people feel good about themselves: 24–25
  Self-image: 24
  Goals: 24
Emotional needs people have: 26–29
  Emotions influence behavior: 26
  Dealing with emotional needs: 28–29
How stress affects people: 30–33
  Causes of stress: 30
  Harmful effects of stress: 32–33
  Ways to deal with stress: 32–33
Solving problems and making decisions: 36–39
  Ways people avoid problems: 36
  Working through problems: 38
  Consequences: 38
  Expressing emotions in helpful ways: 43
  Mental health and the growth spurt: 112

Social Health

What feeling right about others means: 46–49
  Why getting along with others is important: 47
  How can you get along with others: 48–49
Communicating effectively: 50–53, 58
  How to communicate better when talking: 50–51, 58
  How to communicate better when listening: 52
  The importance of body language in communication: 53
How peer pressure affects people: 54–57
  Postivie peer pressure: 54
  Negative peer pressure: 55
  Dealing with negative peer pressure: 56–57
How family members relate to each other: 60–62
  Nuclear family: 60
  Single-parent family: 60
  Extended family: 60
  How families fulfill needs: 61
  Getting along better with the family: 62
Family customs: 67

Body Structure, Function, and Growth

Book 5

Body Structure and Function

What the body is made of: 46–47
Functions of the bones: 48–49
Joints and movement: 50–51, 54
Ligaments and tendons: 50
Parts of the bones: 52–53, 54, 69
Cartilage: 53
Functions of the muscles: 56–57, 60
Voluntary and involuntary muscles: 58
Eyes: 72–73, 82, 116
Ears: 74, 83, 111
Skin: 75, 82
Tongue: 76–77, 83
Nose: 76–77
Brain: 78–79
Spinal cord: 80–81
How the nervous system carries messages: 81
Digestive system: 84–87
Digestion: 84–87
  And the mouth and esophagus: 84–85, 87
  And the stomach: 84–85, 87
  And the small intestine: 86–87
  And the large intestine: 86–87
Breathing and the lungs: 88–93
  How the nose helps in breathing: 88
  How muscles help in breathing: 92
  Air and the lungs: 90–91
  Exchange of oxygen and carbon dioxide: 88, 90–91
Circulatory system: 94–99, 102
  Heart: 94–95, 105
  Blood vessels: 96–97
  Blood: 98–99
Urinary system and liquid waste: 100
  Kidneys and waste removal: 100
  Bladder and urine storage: 100
Makeup of teeth: 118–119
  Enamel: 118
  Cementum: 118
  Dentin: 119
  Pulp: 119

Growth and Development

Body growth and cell division: 46–47, 54
Cartilage and bone growth: 53
Helping muscles develop: 59, 172–173, 176–183
How the body grows: 62–65
  Hormones: 62
  Pituitary gland: 62
Growth spurt: 63
Differences in ways people grow: 64–65

Book 6

Structure and Function

How endocrine glands affect growth: 54–55
  Hormones: 54
  Pituitary gland: 54–55
  Testes: 55
  Sperm cells: 55
  Ovaries: 55
  Egg cells: 55
  Puberty: 55
How the body uses nutrients: 76–81
How exercise affects the cardiovascular and respiratory systems: 108–109
Exercise and muscles: 110–111
Uses of body fat: 112
Calories and body function: 114–115
Major body shapes: 121
Structure of respiratory system: 210
Structure of sinuses: 212
Structure of tonsils: 215
Structure of skin: 244–245

Growth and Development

How different parts of the body grow: 52–73
Growth and body proportions: 53, 73
How heredity affects growth: 56–61, 62
What determines heredity: 57
  Chromosomes: 57
  DNA: 57
  Genes: 57
How chromosomes pass from parent to child: 58
What determines whether a person is a boy or a girl: 59
Why individuals in a family differ: 60–61, 70
How health decisions can affect growth: 64–65
Emotions and relationships often change as a person grows: 66–67
Dealing with growth and changes: 68–69

Book 7

Body Structure and Function

Body cells: 70–71
Skeletal system: 72–73, 79
  Enables body movement: 72
  Protects body organs: 72
  Gives support: 72
Muscular system: 74–75, 79
  Skeletal muscles: 74–75
  Smooth muscles: 75
  Cardiac muscles: 75
How the digestive system changes food: 76–78, 79
How digested food is absorbed: 78
  Villi: 78
Respiratory system: 80–81, 89
How breathing takes place: 82–83
Circulatory system: 84–87, 88
How blood circulates throughout the body: 84–85
Parts of blood: 86
Lymphatic system: 87
Urinary system: 90–91
Nervous system: 92–96
  Senses: 92
  Cerebrum: 92–93
  Cerebellum: 93
The brain and automatic functions of the body: 94
  Brain stem: 94
Functions of the spinal cord: 94–95
  Sensory nerve cells: 94–95
  Motor nerve cells: 94–95
  Reflexes: 94–95, 97
Nerve cells transmit messages: 96
Endocrine system: 98–101
  Endocrine glands: 98–101
  Pituitary gland: 98–99
  Thyroid gland: 98–99
  Parathyroid gland: 98–99
  Pancreas: 99–100
  Adrenal glands: 99–100
  Reproductive glands: 99, 101
  Ovaries: 101
  Testes: 101

Growth and Development

Pituitary gland and growth: 98
Reproductive glands: 101
How the body grows and changes: 108–113
  Growth spurt: 108–109
Heredity affects growth: 110–111, 120
  Chromosome: 110
  Gene: 110
  DNA: 110
Puberty: 112–113

Nutrition

Book 5	Book 6	Book 7
Kinds of foods the body needs: 134–135 Nutrients: 134 Carbohydrates: 135 Proteins: 135 Vitamins: 135 Minerals: 135 Basic four food groups: 136–137, 140, 146 Planning healthy meals: 138–139, 140 Goals for healthy eating: 142–143 Limit salt in the diet: 142 Add fiber to diet: 142 Eat less fat: 143 Limit sugar in the diet: 143 Choosing healthy snacks: 144–146, 147 Limiting candy and soft drinks: 145 Why tea and coffee are harmful: 145 Using the basic four food groups to guide snack food selection: 146 Using food labels to help choose foods: 148–149, 150 Effects of feelings on appetite: 154–155 Trying nutritious recipes: 159	Effect of nutritional decisions on growth potential: 64–65 Why people need food: 76–81 Nutrients: 76 Carbohydrates and the body: 77 Fiber: 77 Fats and the body: 78 Proteins and the body: 79 Vitamins, minerals, and water and the body: 80–81 A healthy diet: 82–87, 88–89 Getting the nutrients the body needs: 82–85 Using the basic four food groups: 82–85 Limiting certain foods: 86–87 Sugar: 86 Fat: 86 Cholesterol: 86–87 Salt: 87, 103 How food processing affects the quality of food: 90–95 Food processing: 90 Drying and freeze-drying of food: 91 Canning and freezing of food: 92 Nutrition and processed foods: 93 Food and additives: 94 Fortified or enriched food: 94 Preservatives: 94 Cooking foods in nutritious ways: 95 How to be a wise food consumer: 96–98, 99 Learning from food labels: 97, 99 Choosing foods wisely in a restaurant: 98 Nutrition and control of body fatness: 112–115 Nutrition and prevention of disease: 221, 223, 228–229 Nutrition and fatigue: 250	Need for different nutrients: 134–139 How carbohydrates contribute to health: 134 Simple carbohydrates: 134 Complex carbohydrates: 135 Importance of fats: 136 Saturated fats: 136 Unsaturated fats: 136 Importance of proteins: 137 Amino acids: 137 Complete protein foods: 137 Incomplete protein foods: 137 How vitamins help keep you healthy: 138–139 How minerals help keep you healthy: 138–139 Importance of water to health: 139 Getting the needed nutrients: 140–143 Basic four food groups: 140–141 Using the four food groups to plan meals: 142–143 Limiting sugar, salt, cholesterol, and fats: 146–148, 149 Eating disorders: 154–155 Anorexia nervosa: 154 Bulimia: 154 Overeating: 155 How to become a wise food shopper: 156–159 What can be learned from food labels: 156 Unit pricing: 157 Additional food shopping tips: 158–159 Inproving your diet: 163

Physical Fitness

Book 5

Book 6

Book 7

Safety and First Aid

Book 5

Safety
Safety and exercising: 175, 179
Using medicines safely: 192, 194, 223
Preventing accidents: 226–239
Preventing traffic accidents: 228–232, 233
- Be a safe pedestrian: 228
- Be a safe passenger in a car: 229
- Follow rules for safe bicycling: 229, 232, 233
- Make sure bicycle is safe to ride: 230–231, 233

Preventing outdoor accidents: 234
- Use campfires safely: 235
- Hike safely: 236–237, 244
- Avoid poisonous plants and animals: 237

Preventing water accidents: 238–239
- Dive only into deep water: 238
- Use a personal flotation device: 238
- Use H.E.L.P.: 238

What to do in case of a fire: 240–243, 244
- Fires in large buildings: 242
- Clothing fires: 242

Being safe when you are home alone: 253
Using safety gear to protect ears: 109

First aid
First-aid kit: 244
What to do in an emergency: 246–249
- Dealing with choking: 246–247

Book 6

Safety
Preventing accidents: 142–143
Traffic safety rules: 143
Acting safely at home: 144–149, 150
- Preventing falls: 144, 150
- Preventing poisonings: 145, 150
- Preventing electrical shock: 146
- Preventing fires: 147, 165

Safety around strangers: 148–149
- When home alone: 148
- While outside: 149

First Aid
How to be prepared for emergencies: 152–155
- How to get help quickly: 152–153
- How to be prepared for a fire emergency: 154–155
- Items needed to deal with home emergencies: 155

How to help in a medical emergency: 156–161
- Follow first-aid procedures: 156, 162
- First aid for choking: 157
- Artificial respiration: 158–159
- Care for burns: 160
- Care for shock: 161

Book 7

Safety
Exercising safely: 190–193
Help prevent accidents: 230–233
- Learn and follow safety rules: 230
- Do not take unnecessary risks: 231
- Be careful: 231

Bicycle safety rules: 232
Automobile safety rules: 233
Safety while swimming or boating: 234–236
- How to be a safe swimmer: 234–235, 236
- Safety rules for boaters: 235
- Drownproofing: 236

Precautions during a storm: 238–239, 251

First Aid
First-aid techniques for life-threatening emergencies: 240–245, 246–247
- Stopped breathing and artificial respiration: 240–241
- Cardiopulmonary resuscitation (CPR): 241
- Choking: 242–243
- Severe bleeding and direct pressure: 244
- Poisoning: 244
- Shock: 245

First-aid technique for other emergencies: 248
- Fracture: 248
- Splint: 248
- Sprain: 249
- Overexposure to heat and cold: 250
- Heat exhaustion: 250
- Heatstroke: 250
- Frostbite: 251
- Hypothermia: 251

Making a safety plan: 255

Drugs

Book 5

Book 6

Book 7

Personal Health Care

Book 5	Book 6	Book 7
Providing for healthy bone growth: 53 Ways to help muscles develop: 59, 172–173, 176–183 Caring for the nervous system: 81 Caring for the digestive system: 86 Caring for the respiratory system: 92 Caring for the circulatory system: 99 Caring for the ears: 108–110 Caring for the eyes: 112–113 Recognizing vision problems: 114–115, 116 Farsighted: 114–115 Nearsighted: 114–115 Astigmatism: 114–115 Caring for the teeth: 118–119 Brushing and flossing: 118–119 Regular dental checkups: 120 Choosing health care products wisely: 122–127, 131 Determining the need for a product: 122 Finding out about available products: 123, 131 Using label information to help make wise choices: 124–125 Considering the cost of various products: 126 Asking for professional advice: 127 Goals for healthy eating: 142–143 Limit salt in the diet: 142 Add fiber to the diet: 142 Eat less fat: 143 Limit sugar in the diet: 143 Choosing healthy snacks: 144–146, 147 How to improve cardiovascular fitness: 168–169, 170 How to improve muscular fitness: 172–173 Strength: 172 Muscular endurance: 172 Flexibility: 173 Some safety rules for medicine use: 194–195 Dealing with minor health problems without medicines: 196 Using medicines correctly: 197 Making wise decisions about tobacco and alcohol: 210–211 How to avoid drug abuse: 216–219 Using medicines safely at home: 223 Preventing traffic accidents: 228–232, 233 Preventing outdoor accidents: 234 Preventing water accidents: 238–239	Dealing with stress: 30–35 Dealing with problems that cause stress: 32–33 Learning to relax: 34 Making decisions that help with stress: 35 How health decisions affect growth: 64–65 Getting the nutrients the body needs: 82–85 Using the basic four food groups: 82–85 Limiting certain foods: 86–87 Sugar: 86 Fat: 86 Cholesterol: 86–87 Salt: 87 Controlling body fatness: 114–115 Calorie consumption: 114 Regular exercise: 114 How to set fitness goals: 120–125 Determine needs, interests, and abilities: 120–121 Determine current level of health fitness: 122–123 Determine current level of skills fitness: 124–125 Achieving fitness goals: 126–129 Determine amount of physical activity needed: 128 Exercise safely: 128–129 Acting safely at home: 144–149 Helping prevent cardiovascular diseases and cancer: 221, 223 Dealing with allergies: 227 How a healthy lifestyle can help prevent disease: 228–229 Why good posture is important to health: 236–237 Ways to improve posture: 237 Taking care of the teeth: 238–241, 246 Causes of most dental problems: 238–239, 246, 255 Plaque: 238, 255 Tooth decay: 238–239 Gum disease: 239 How brushing and flossing help prevent dental problems: 240–241, 255 Care of eyes and ears: 242–243 Vision problems: 242–243 Hearing problems: 243 Why people should take care of their skin and hair: 244–245, 246 Why sleep, rest, and recreation are important: 248–251 Reducing fatigue: 250–251	Importance of sleep: 114–118, 119 Why sleep is needed: 114–115 How much sleep is needed: 115 What happens during sleep: 116–117 REM sleep: 117 Dreams: 117 Care of the teeth: 122–125 Causes of dental problems: 122 Plaque: 122 Calculus: 122 Periodontal disease: 122 Brushing and flossing helps teeth and gums: 123 Other ways to keep teeth healthy: 124 Fluoride: 124 Sealants: 124 Braces and dental problems: 124–125 Malocclusion: 124–125 Care of the skin and hair: 126–127 Dealing with skin problems: 127 Keeping a sleep journal: 131 Using the basic four food groups to plan meals: 142–143 Limiting sugar, salt, cholesterol, and fats: 146–148 Improving your diet: 163 Learning how to plan your own fitness program: 188 Helping keep yourself well: 264 How to help prevent cardiovascular diseases: 270 Helping prevent cancer: 275 Preventing cardiovascular diseases: 287

Disease

Book 5

Communicable Disease

Noncommunicable Disease

Book 6

Communicable Disease

Noncommunicable Diseases

Book 7

Communicable Disease

Noncommunicable Diseases

Consumer Health

Book 5	Book 6	Book 7
Choosing health products wisely: 122–127, 131 Determining the need for a product: 122 Finding out about available products: 123, 131 Using advertising to make choices: 123 Using label information to help make wise choices: 124–125 Considering the cost of various products: 127 Using food labels to help choose foods: 148–149, 150	How to be a wise food consumer: 96–98, 99 Learning from food labels: 97, 99 Choosing foods wisely in a restaurant: 98 Becoming a wise health consumer: 258–261, 283 Guidelines for careful shopping: 259 How advertising influences consumers: 262–267 Jingles, logos, and packaging: 264–265 Evaluating ads: 266–267, 268 What to consider when choosing health products: 270–274, 275 Unit price: 271, 275, 283 Net weight: 271, 275, 283 How reading labels makes people better consumers: 272–273, 283 Fads: 274 How people can benefit the most from a health checkup: 276–279 What happens during a health checkup: 278–279	How to become a wise food shopper: 156–159 What can be learned from food labels: 156 Unit pricing: 157 Additional food shopping tips: 158–159 Basic guides for shoppers: 200–203 Careful thinking that wise shoppers use: 200 Investigating that wise shoppers do: 202 Shopping wisely for clothes: 204–207 How to care for clothing you buy: 206 Choosing clothes wisely: 204–205, 207 Being a wise consumer of health care products: 208–211 Choosing dental care products: 208 Choosing hair care products: 209 Choosing skin care products: 210 Being a wise consumer of health care service: 212–215 Evaluating health care services: 212 Detecting quackery: 213, 216 Being a responsible patient: 214–215 Protection for the consumer: 218–221 Manufacturers help protect the consumer: 218 Federal agencies help protect the consumer: 219 Private organizations help protect the consumer: 220–221, 224 How consumers can help protect themselves: 222–223 Finding health care services in your community: 227

Community and Environmental Health

Book 5

Community Health

Sources of air pollution: 256–257
Air pollution and health: 257
How communities protect the air: 258–259, 270
Why clean water is a community health concern: 260–263
Sources of water pollution: 260–261
Water pollution and health: 262–263
How communities protect their water supply: 262–263
Why the careful use of land is a community health concern: 264–265
Ways to use the land carefully: 266–269, 270
- Recycling: 266
- Landfill: 266
- City planning: 267

Controlling the spread of disease: 272–275
- With vaccines: 272
- With sewage-treatment plants: 262–263
- With water-treatment plants: 262–263
- With voluntary health agencies: 272, 275

Environmental Health

Causes of air pollution: 256–257
Air pollution and health: 257
Helping protect the air: 258–259, 270
- Car pools and riding public transportation: 258
- Scrubbers on factory smokestacks: 258
- Using solar energy: 259

Why water becomes polluted: 260–261
- Addition of sewage to the water supply: 260
- Addition of toxic wastes to the water supply: 261

Water pollution and health: 262
Protecting the water supply: 262–263, 270
Damaging the land: 264–265
Using the land carefully: 266–269, 270

Book 6

Community Health

Health services people provide for the community: 286–291
- Health departments and the community: 286–287
- Hospitals and the community: 288–290
- Volunteers and the community: 291

Disposing of garbage more safely: 298–299
- Sanitary landfill: 298
- Recycling: 298

Discovering how the community fights pollution: 300–301
How a community reduces noise: 302–303
Recreational areas and opportunities provided by a community: 304–307
Helping keep a community healthy: 308–309, 310

Environmental Health

Health services provided by a community: 286–291
- Protection against disease: 287
- Hospital care: 288–290
- Volunteer work: 291

How people help provide a clean environment: 292–297
Sewage: 292
How treatment plants improve a community's water supply: 293
Dangers of ground-water pollution: 294
Problems caused by air pollution: 295
Effects of acid rain: 296
Reducing air pollution: 297
Disposal of garbage: 298–299
- Sanitary landfill: 298
- Recycling: 298
- Incineration: 299

Reducing noise pollution: 302–303
Reducing pollution at home: 313

Book 7

Community Health

Centers for Disease Control: 282–283
Air pollution and the community: 320, 334
- Causes of most air pollution: 320
- Air pollution and health: 321–322
- How air pollution can be reduced: 322–323

Water pollution and the community: 324–334
- Different kinds of water pollution and health: 324–325
- How water pollution can be dealt with: 326–327

Noise pollution and the community: 328, 334
- How noise affects human health: 328
- How loud noise can be reduced: 329

How communities deal with other health problems: 330
- Kinds of health agencies that help a community: 330
- How disease in a community can be controlled: 331, 334
- Mental health services available in a community: 332
- How communities care for people with special needs: 333

How people can contribute to community health: 336–337
Protecting the environment: 338
Using products again and again: 341

Environmental Health

Centers for Disease Control: 282–283
How air pollution affects the environment: 320–323, 334
- Causes of most air pollution: 320
- Air pollution and health: 321–322
- How air pollution can be reduced: 322–323

Water pollution: 324–327, 334
- Water pollution and health: 324–325
- How water pollution can be dealt with: 326–327

Noise pollution: 328–329, 334
- How noise affects human health: 328
- How noise pollution can be reduced: 329

Protecting the environment: 338
Recycling products: 341

Family Health

Book 5	Book 6	Book 7
Working to get along well with other members of the family to improve self-image: 19 Observing the different parts of a bone: 69 Understanding the heart: 105 Learning about advertising: 131 Trying nutritious recipes: 159 Family fitness: 189 Using medicines safely at home: 223 Being safe when home alone: 253 Learning about your community: 279	Building good relationships with family and friends: 26–27 Planning your study time: 47 How family members can help you deal with growth and change: 68–69 Using photographs to examine your growth: 73 Breaking the salt habit: 103 Participating in lifetime activities: 139 Acting safely at home: 144–149, 150 Planning and practicing fire drills: 165 Checking the home for drug safety: 197 Controlling the spread of disease germs: 233 Using the "Green Detective" to find plaque: 255 Becoming a careful health consumer: 283 Reducing pollution at home: 313	Expressing emotions: 43 How family members relate to each other: 60–62 How families fulfill needs: 61 Getting along with the family: 62 Family customs: 67 Sharing information about body systems: 105 Keeping a sleep journal: 131 Improving your diet: 163 Family exercise program: 197 Finding health care services in your community: 227 Making a safety plan: 255 Preventing cardiovascular diseases: 287 Analyzing alcohol and tobacco advertisements: 317 Using products again and again: 341

Careers

Book 5	Book 6	Book 7
Musician: 27 Social worker: 35 X-ray technologist: 55 Physical therapist: 61 Sound technician: 83 Sound effects technician: 83 Inhalation therapist: 93 Doctor: 108, 127, 193, 195 Audiologist: 111 Optician: 117 Dentist: 120, 127 Farmer: 141, 267 Food scientist: 151 Sports medicine doctor: 171 Fitness leader: 177 Pharmacist: 193, 197 Drug counselor: 211 Helicopter firefighter: 245 Forest ranger: 245 Ecologist: 271 Soil scientist: 271	Counselor and psychiatrist: 43 Pediatrician: 53 Geneticist: 63 Chef and dietitian: 89 Activity specialist: 119 Recreational therapist: 119 Camp counselor: 119 Playground leader: 119 Construction inspector: 151 Building inspector: 151 Mechanical inspector: 151 Doctor: 173 Pharmaceutical plant worker: 191 Chemist: 191 Medical technologist: 217 Medical laboratory technician: 217 Medical laboratory assistant: 217 Dentist: 243 Hairstylist: 247 Dancer: 247 Advertising copywriter: 269 Comparison shopper: 275 Epidemiologist: 286 Sanitarian: 286 Public health nurse: 287 Sanitary engineer: 300 Landscape architect: 301	Personnel worker: 35 Speech pathologist: 59 Family counselor: 59, 332 Occupational therapist: 79 Respiratory therapist: 89, 335 EEG technologist: 121 Dentist: 121, 123–124, 212 Orthodontist: 125 Restaurant worker: 145 Food technologist: 149 Sports broadcaster: 189 Physical education instructor: 189 Dental hygienist: 212 Nurse: 212 Paramedic: 212 Pharmacist: 212, 290 Psychiatrist and clinical psychologist: 212 Public health nurse: 212, 335 Consumer safety inspector: 217 Marketing research worker: 217 Occupational safety technician: 237 Police officer: 247 Family physician: 265, 290–291 Epidemiologist: 281 Drug rehabilitation counselor: 311, 332 Environmental health technician: 335

Health for Life

Authors
Julius B. Richmond
John D. MacArthur Professor of Health Policy
Director, Division of Health Policy Research and Education
Harvard University
Advisor on Child Health Policy
Children's Hospital of Boston
Boston, Massachusetts

Elenore T. Pounds
Health Education Writer
Downers Grove, Illinois

Physical Fitness Author
Charles B. Corbin
Professor, Department of Health and Physical Education
Arizona State University
Tempe, Arizona

Scott, Foresman and Company
Editorial Offices: Glenview, Illinois

Regional Offices: Sunnyvale, California • Tucker, Georgia • Glenview, Illinois • Oakland, New Jersey • Dallas, Texas

Authors

Julius B. Richmond, M.D., is the John D. MacArthur Professor of Health Policy and the Director of the Division of Health Policy Research and Education at Harvard University. He also is Advisor on Child Health Policy at the Children's Hospital of Boston. Dr. Richmond served as Surgeon General for the U.S. Public Health Service and as Assistant Secretary for Health from 1977–1981. Trained as a pediatrician, Dr. Richmond joined the faculty of the Harvard Medical School in 1971. He was professor of child psychiatry and human development before being appointed Surgeon General.

Elenore T. Pounds, M.A., is a health education writer and lecturer. A former elementary teacher, she served as directing editor of the Health and Personal Development Program. She is co-author of *Health and Growth, You and Your Health,* and other health publications.

Charles B. Corbin, Ph.D., is professor and coordinator of graduate studies in the Department of Health and Physical Education at Arizona State University. A former elementary physical education teacher, he previously served as professor and head of graduate studies in the Department of Health, Physical Education, and Recreation at Kansas State University. Dr. Corbin is the author of many research and professional publications, especially in the area of lifetime fitness.

ISBN: 0-673-29586-9

12345678910VHJ9998979695949392919089

Consultants

Reading
Robert A. Pavlik, Ed.D.
Professor and Chairperson
Reading–Language Arts Department
Cardinal Stritch College
Milwaukee, Wisconsin

Medical
Jerry Newton, M.D.
Director, Health Services
San Antonio Independent School Dist.
Clinical Professor, Pediatrics
University of Texas Medical School, San Antonio
San Antonio, Texas

Design
Design direction by Norman Perman
Graphic Designer and Art Consultant

Cover photograph by Michael Mauney

Acknowledgments
The dental health information contained in Chapter 8 is considered by the American Dental Association to be in accord with current scientific knowledge, 1986.

For further acknowledgments, see page 384.

Content Specialists

Dental Health
Mary Banas
Program Specialist
Bureau of Health Education and Audiovisual Services
American Dental Association
Chicago, Illinois

Drug Education
Chwee Lye Chng
Assistant Professor
Division of Health Education
North Texas State University
Denton, Texas

Merita Thompson
Professor
Department of Health Education
Eastern Kentucky University
Richmond, Kentucky

Family Life Education
Linda Berne
Professor
Department of Health and Physical Education
The University of North Carolina
Charlotte, North Carolina

Nutrition
Jean Mayer
President
Tufts University
Medford, Massachusetts

Safety and First Aid
Janice Sutkus
Technical Specialist
National Safety Council
Chicago, Illinois

Reviewers and Contributors

Lourdes Alcorta-Rogover
Educational Consultant
Former Teacher
Miami, Florida

Ruth Ann Althaus
Professor of Public Health
Master of Public Health Program
Illinois Benedictine College
Lisle, Illinois

Matthew Bustamante
Bilingual/Cross-Cultural Education Specialist
Bandini Elementary School
Montebello, California

Judi Coffey
Educational Consultant
Learning Disabilities Specialist
Jonesboro, Arkansas

Bryan Cooke
Professor
Department of Community Health
College of Health and Human Services
University of Northern Colorado
Greeley, Colorado

Gail Daud
Teacher in Gifted Education
Spring Shadows Elementary School
Houston, Texas

Bo Fernhall
Director, Fitness and Cardiac Rehabilitation
Department of Physical Education
Northern Illinois University
DeKalb, Illinois

Linda Froschauer
Teacher
Weston Public Schools
Weston, Connecticut

Rosalyn Gantt
Teacher
Midway Elementary School
Cincinnati, Ohio

Jon Hisgen
School Health Coordinator
Pewaukee Public Schools
Pewaukee, Wisconsin

Peter Loudis
Teacher of Gifted and Talented
Spring Branch Junior High School
Houston, Texas

Jeanne Mannings
Teacher
Adamsville Elementary School
Atlanta, Georgia

Wanda Nottingham-Brooks
Learning Disabilities Teacher
Morrisonville Junior and Senior High School
Morrisonville, Illinois

Bert Pearlman
Director, Curriculum Research and Evaluation
Office of the County Superintendent of Schools
Santa Barbara, California

Candace Purdy
Health Teacher
Maine South High School
Park Ridge, Illinois

Joan Salmon
School Nurse
Greenwood School Corporation
Greenwood, Indiana

Jean Clark Shuemake
Teacher
Urban Park Elementary School
Dallas, Texas

Betty Smith
Teacher of Talented and Gifted
Kiest/Urban Park Elementary School
Dallas, Texas

David R. Stronck
Associate Professor of Health Education
Department of Teacher Education
California State University, Hayward
Hayward, California

Terry Thompson
Teacher
Bowie Elementary School
Lubbock, Texas

Shirley Van Sickle
Health Teacher
DeVeaux Junior High School
Toledo, Ohio

Learning About Yourself 18

Growing and Changing 48

Choosing Foods for Good Health 74

Chapter 4 Becoming Physically Fit 104

9

Chapter 6

Drugs: What They Are and What They Do 166

Fighting Against Disease 198

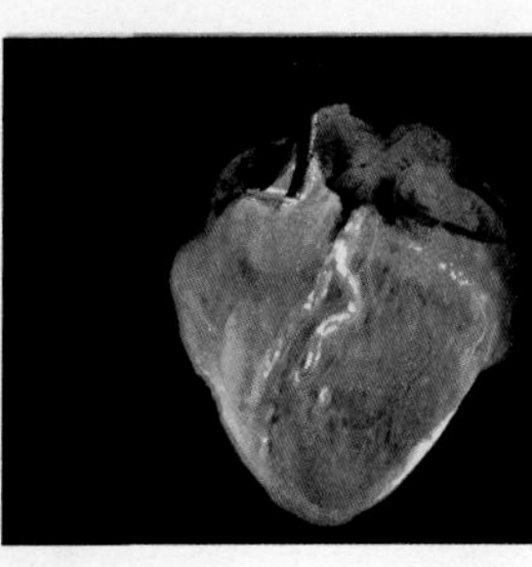

Chapter 8 Daily Care for Good Health 234

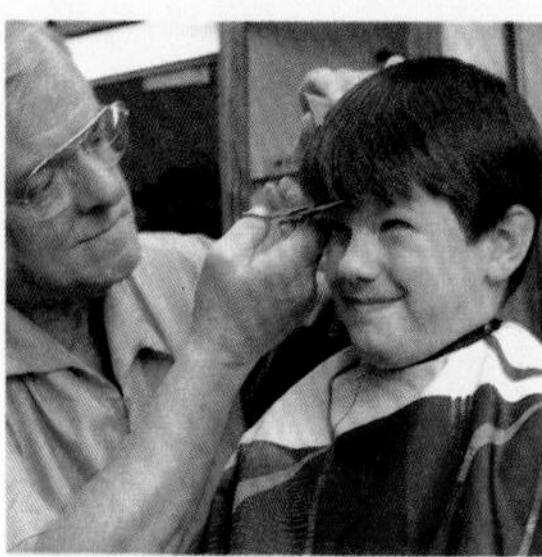

Chapter 9 Your Decisions as a Health Consumer 256

Chapter 10 Working for a Healthy Community 284

Why Learn About Health

"When you have your health, you have just about everything." You might have heard this saying before. What does it mean to you? Most people agree that good health is one of the most important qualities a person could have. When you are healthy, you can enjoy life more fully, whether at school, work, or play. You not only feel and look your best, but you can think more clearly and get along better with others.

In the past, being healthy meant not being sick. Today, people are becoming aware of a more complete idea of health. This idea includes physical, mental, and social health. *Physical health* is the condition of your body. *Mental health* includes how you feel about yourself and how you handle problems. *Social health* involves the way you handle your relationships.

Good health is the responsibility of every person. Today more than ever, people can take control of their health. Because you are making more and more of your own health decisions, learning about health is very important. Decisions such as what to eat, whether or not to exercise, and how to treat others are part of daily life. To make the wisest decisions, you need sound, accurate information. Then you need to know how to use this information. Finally, you need to develop *skills for life*—skills that help you deal with events in your life in positive and healthful ways. Scott, Foresman's *Health for Life* provides all these tools, but it is up to you to use them. Make good health a part of your day and a part of your life, now and in the future.

Teaching Plan

Applying Reading Skills

Use this page to introduce your students to the basic lesson format of *Health for Life.* The features of a typical lesson page are highlighted. By following the simple five-step procedure, students will understand how lessons are organized to facilitate learning of concepts and vocabulary.

1. Lesson titles and subheads, stated in question form, focus on the topic of the lesson. They specify what information the students should search for. The title can serve as an informal pretest.

2. Visual images can help communicate lesson concepts. Illustrations have been carefully selected to serve as teaching tools. Discuss with the students what is happening in each picture. Encourage students to use the pictures to help them answer the title and subhead questions. You might use the following technique to help focus students' attention on the visual aid. Ask students to make a mask to cover the page and to cut a hole in the mask large enough to show the picture but not the caption. Discuss with students what is shown in the picture. Identify the action shown and who is doing the action.

3. As students begin reading the lesson, they will already have some idea of what to search for. Use the lesson title and subhead questions to focus attention on the key points. Reading should be purposeful.

4. Vocabulary words are highlighted in boldface type the first time they appear. The pronunciations and definitions of vocabulary words are in the margins of the page where the words first appear. As students read the words in context, encourage them to learn and use these new terms. The **Glossary** at the end of the textbook lists all boldface words and their definitions for review and reference.

5. The final step involves applying the new concepts. Encourage students to apply the new information in answering the questions at the end of the lesson.

When You Read This Book

1. Read the question.

2. Look at the pictures.

3. Find the answers.

4. Learn the health words.

sanitary landfill, an area of land where garbage is buried in such a way as to minimize water pollution, air pollution, and the spread of disease.

recycling, changing a waste product so that it can be used again.

3 How Can People Dispose of Garbage More Safely?

Disposing of garbage is a major problem for many large cities. Garbage has to go somewhere. In the past, "somewhere" was usually a street, river, or open dump on the edge of town. These methods of garbage disposal were extremely unhealthy. The garbage attracted rats and other animals that carried diseases. The trash was often burned at the dump, but this burning caused much air pollution.

Today many communities dispose of garbage in ways that pollute as little as possible. One way is by using a **sanitary landfill.** Bulldozers smash the garbage together, as shown. Then a tractor covers the garbage with a layer of dirt. The next day, another layer of garbage is compacted and covered with dirt. This process is repeated with each day's garbage. Sanitary landfills reduce some kinds of pollution, but they must be checked constantly for leaks. Some landfills leak dangerous chemicals into the soil and groundwater. Another problem with sanitary landfills is that they use up a lot of land, and many communities are running out of land for them.

Another way to deal with the garbage problem is by **recycling**—changing waste products so they can be used again. The glass bottles in the picture, for example, will be separated according to their color. The glass will be crushed, melted, and made into new bottles. Paper, aluminum, and rubber are some other materials that can be recycled.

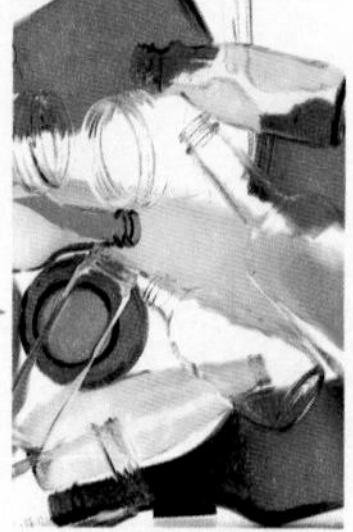

Glass can be recycled.

How is garbage buried at a sanitary landfill?

298

16

Some communities burn garbage in large furnaces called incinerators. Trucks empty the garbage into a huge pit, like the one shown. A crane lifts the garbage and drops it down a chute that leads to an incinerator. Many incinerators have scrubbers or other devices to remove many of the materials from the smoke.

Disposing of wastes without polluting improves the quality of life in a community. Clean water, air, and land provide what a community needs for good health.

Did You Know?
Some hospitals and large apartment buildings in Sweden use one of the most advanced garbage-disposal systems in the world. Trash is dumped into chutes and is sucked through a vacuum-powered pipeline to a central incinerator. The heat from the burning garbage generates electricity, warms buildings, and melts ice on roads during the winter.

Think Back • *Study on your own with Study Guide page 335.*

1. What are the advantages and disadvantages of using sanitary landfills to dispose of garbage?
2. How does recycling and incineration help communities deal with garbage disposal?

5. Use what you learned.

Some communities burn garbage in large incinerators.

299

Pupil Edition	Activities	Enrichment	Assessment	Independent Study
Chapter 1 Learning About Yourself, pp. 18–47	Health Watch Notebook, p. 18	Health Focus, p. 44 Health at Home, p. 45	Chapter 1 Review, pp. 46–47	Study Guide, pp. 316–317 Skills for Life Handbook, pp. 338–340
Lesson 1 What Is Self-Image? pp. 20–23	Health Activities Workshop, pp. 24–25		Think Back, p. 23	On Your Own, p. 21 Study Guide, p. 316
Lesson 2 How Can You Get Along Better With Others? pp. 26–29			Think Back, p. 29	On Your Own, pp. 27, 29 Study Guide, p. 316
Lesson 3 How Can You Deal With Stress? pp. 30–35		Did You Know? p. 31, 34	Think Back, p. 35	Study Guide, p. 317
Lesson 4 How Can You Set and Reach Goals? pp. 36–41	Health Activities Workshop, pp. 42–43		Think Back, p. 41	On Your Own, p. 38 Study Guide, p. 317

Teacher Resources

Kaplan, Leslie S. *Coping with Peer Pressure.* Rosen, 1983. Describes adolescence and tells why adolescents give in to peer pressure. Includes a chapter on peer pressure as it relates to gifted and learning-disabled students.

Saunders, Antoinette, and Remsberg, Bonnie. *The Stress-Proof Child.* Holt, 1984. Includes a bibliography of children's books, advice on recognizing physical and emotional signs of stress, and exercises to alleviate stress.

Schultz, Edward W., and Heuchert, Charles M. *Childhood Stress and the School Experience.* Human Science Press, 1983. Describes what stress is, what school stress is, and how to help children learn to manage stressful school situations while learning coping skills.

Audio-Visual Resources

See page T43 for addresses of Audio-Visual Sources.

Before using any audio-visual materials, preview them for appropriateness for your students.

Friends: How They Help . . . How They Hurt, Sunburst Communications, Inc., filmstrips with cassettes. Examines the meaning of friendship by looking at how to make friends, how to cope when friends change, and what to do when friends become a problem.

If You Knew How I Feel: Brad's Learning Disability, Centron Educational Films, film or video, 17 minutes. Teaches students the importance of being sensitive to the feelings of others.

Life Actions Cause Stress, Britannica, filmstrips with cassettes. Teaches students how to alleviate or manage stress by letting students work through simulated case studies involving stress.

Pardon Me for Living, Learning Corp. of America, film, 30 minutes. Tells the story of school friendships and the typical dynamics in which sixth-graders are likely to engage.

Computer Software

Feeling Better, DYNACOMP. Helps children reduce feelings of anger, depression, and anxiety by teaching them about the nature of feelings and emotions.

	Teacher's Edition	Teacher's Resource Book	Test Book
Enrichment	Suggestions for each lesson: L. 1—pp. 20, 22 L. 2—pp. 26, 28 L. 3—pp. 30, 32, 34 L. 4—pp. 36, 38, 40	Family Letter, p. 17 * Life Skills, p. 21 * Health and Art, p. 24	
Reteaching	Suggestions for each lesson: L. 1—pp. 20, 22 L. 2—pp. 26, 28 L. 3—pp. 30, 32, 34 L. 4—pp. 36, 38, 40	Transparency Masters, pp. 19-20 * Vocabulary, p. 22 * Study and Review, p. 23	
Assessment	Expanding Student Thinking: one assessment question per lesson that develops higher-order thinking skills—pp. 25, 29, 35, 41		Chapter 1 Test, Form A, pp. 9-10 Chapter 1 Test, Form B, pp. 11-12

* Also available in Workbook format (Student Edition and Teacher's Edition)

Chapter 1 Poster

A set of posters is available in a separate package. It provides a teaching poster for every chapter, including discussion and activity suggestions on the back. The poster for Chapter 1 is titled "What long-term goals do you have?"

Overhead Transparencies

A set of color overhead transparencies is available for Grade 6. You may wish to use Transparencies 1, 2, and 4 to help teach decision-making, coping with stress, and goal setting.

Bulletin Board

Cut out magazine pictures of a variety of people who look like they feel good about themselves. Ask students to list some characteristics of people who feel good about themselves.

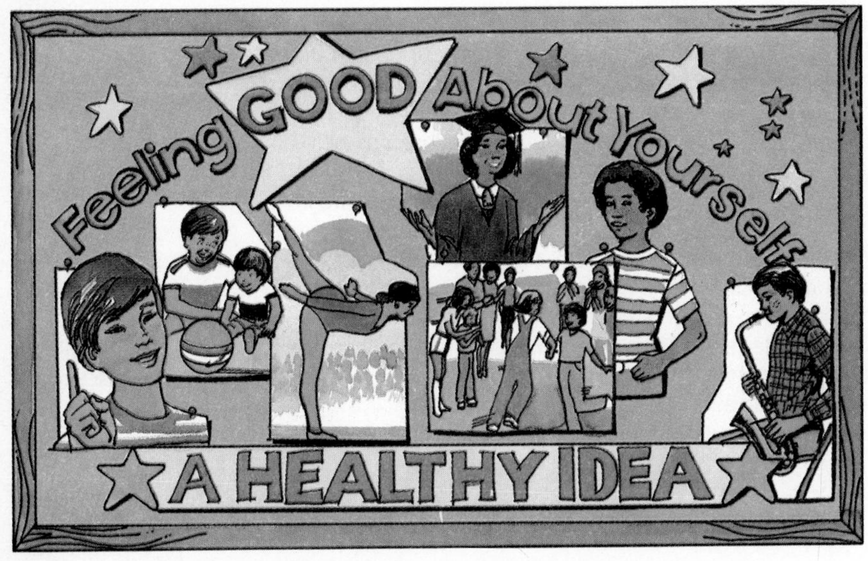

Teaching Plan

Chapter 1 pages 18–47

Chapter Main Idea
People can learn how to stay mentally and socially healthy

Chapter Goals
- Appreciate the importance of getting along with others.
- Take responsibility for improving one's own mental health.
- Deal with stress in healthy ways.
- Use the decision-making process to work through problems.
- Express attitudes toward self that show a positive self-image.

Lifetime Goal
Take steps to improve one's self-image now and in the future.

Health Vocabulary
Attitude, goal, relationship, self-image, stress

Words to Preteach
Ability, characteristic, confidence, long-term goal, realistic, responsibility, self-confidence, short-term goal

Chapter 1

Learning About Yourself

The people in the picture have a goal. Can you guess what it is? For two days, the mountaineers have been climbing the slopes of Mt. Rainier. They are willing to put up with hardships such as blistering wind and exhaustion because their goal is important to them. You probably have goals too. They might not include climbing Mt. Rainier, but each of your goals is just as important to you.

This chapter discusses goals and how to reach them. The chapter will also help you understand more about yourself and your relationships with others. Useful suggestions will show how you can work to improve yourself throughout your lifetime.

Health Watch Notebook

Think of a time when you accomplished a goal that was important to you. Write a paragraph in your notebook describing how it felt to achieve something that you had worked hard for.

1 What Is Self-Image?
2 How Can You Get Along Better with Others?
3 How Can You Deal with Stress?
4 How Can You Set and Reach Goals?

18

Teaching Options

Modeling Health Vocabulary
Use this technique to introduce new words as you teach each lesson in this chapter. First, introduce the word. Present the word in two sentences that serve to clearly define the word. One sentence you might use to introduce the word *goal* is the following: *Shannon's goal this year is to improve in math.* Either read the sentences to the students or write them on the chalkboard. Ask the students to generate two meaningful sentences using the word. Additional successful techniques for introducing new words can be found on page T23.

Cooperative Learning
Jigsaw Format (See page T24.)
Assign the following topics at random to your cooperative learning teams.

Topic A: Describe characteristics of a good self-image. Name ways a self-image can be improved.
Topic B: Explain how having good relationships helps a person build a good self-image.
Topic C: Explain ways a person can cope with stress.
Topic D: Explain how a person can set and reach goals.

Have students search for information on their topic as they read the chapter. Then let all students with the same topic meet in an expert group to discuss the information. When students return to their teams, they may take turns presenting their topics to the team. Then give students a test covering all topics to complete individually (Chapter 1 test A or B in the Test Book). Award Superteam certificates to teams whose average test scores exceed 90%, and Greatteam certificates to teams whose average test scores exceed 80%.

Introducing the Chapter

Ask students to look at the picture and read page 18. Discuss the main goal of the mountaineers. (reaching the summit) Ask students why it is important that the mountaineers get along with each other. (Communication and cooperation are important to the success of the expedition.) Finally ask students to write a brief paragraph about how they think the mountaineers will feel about themselves when they reach their goal. You may wish to send the Family Letter home at this time. You may want to assign Study Guide pages 316–317 for students to use independently as they read the lessons. The Study Guide can also be used as an extra chapter review. You might want to assign the activities in the Skills for Life Handbook on pages 338–340. See teaching strategies for the Handbook on pages 336–337.

Strategies for Health Watch Notebook

Encourage students to read their paragraphs to the class. Help students understand that feelings accompanying the achievement of a goal are feelings of positive self-image. Ask students if they can think of ways to add a new, harder goal to the goal they have achieved.

Family Letter

Use the Family Letter (English or Spanish version) to introduce the subject matter of the chapter to the family and to suggest a way the family can become involved in the student's learning experience. This master may be reproduced from the Teacher's Resource Book.

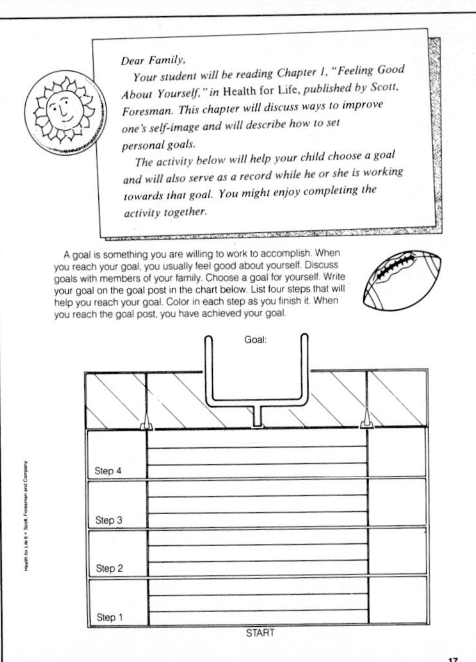

Dear Family,

Your student will be reading Chapter 1, "Feeling Good About Yourself," in Health for Life, *published by Scott, Foresman. This chapter will discuss ways to improve one's self-image and will describe how to set personal goals.*

The activity below will help your child choose a goal and will also serve as a record while he or she is working towards that goal. You might enjoy completing the activity together.

A goal is something you are willing to work to accomplish. When you reach your goal, you usually feel good about yourself. Discuss goals with members of your family. Choose a goal for yourself. Write your goal on the goal post in the chart below. List four steps that will help you reach your goal. Color in each step as you finish it. When you reach the goal post, you have achieved your goal.

Goal:

Step 4

Step 3

Step 2

Step 1

START

17

For High-Potential Students

Ask students to suggest a favorite TV or book character they might like to meet. Then ask them to write dialogue for an imaginary first meeting with that character. Encourage students to include dialogue that reflects an understanding of ways to build good relationships.

Teaching Plan

Lesson 1 pages 20–23

Lesson Objective
Describe the characteristics of a good self-image and list some attitudes that can help improve a self-image.

Health Vocabulary
Attitude, self-image

1 Motivate

Introducing the Lesson
Let students volunteer to share their feelings about the start of a new school year. Encourage students to name things they look forward to at school. Point out that many students start the school year with new hopes and plans. Ask volunteers to suggest what some hopes and plans might be. (improving grades, joining clubs, doing well in sports events, making new friends) Direct students to make a list of things they would like to accomplish this year in school. Suggest that they keep the list in a folder throughout the year as a reminder and a record to compare with their actual accomplishments.

self-image, the way a person feels about himself or herself.

1 What Is Self-Image?

The young people here are ready to start a new year at school. Like you, they have some special hopes and plans. They want to do as well as they can in their schoolwork. Some want to succeed in other ways. For example, some students might want to join school clubs or sports teams. Others might want to write for the school paper. Still others, especially the newcomers, want to make new friends.

A good **self-image** can help these people do many of the things they want to do. A good self-image can help you too. A self-image is the way a person feels about himself or herself. If you have a good self-image, you generally feel good about yourself.

Teaching Options

Health Background

A person who exhibits a positive self-image also exhibits self-esteem. Attitudes that formulate a person's self-image begin to develop at an early age. A strong self-image depends upon an individual's recognition of personal strengths as well as weaknesses.

Enrichment
Encourage students to find out about people who overcame physical hardship to accomplish a goal. Students should report on how a good self-image helped the person accomplish his or her goal.

Health and Language Arts
Ask students to write a story about a person with a good self-image and a person with a poor self-image.

Reteaching
Direct students to sit in pairs. Ask each pair of students to take turns interviewing each other to find out specific things that could be done to improve self-image. Let students report their information to the entire class.

Special Education
Encourage all students to develop a list of their strong points and a list of weaker points which they could improve. Help learning-disabled students think of positive traits they exhibit at home and with friends, as well as in school.

What Are Some Characteristics of a Person with a Good Self-Image?

If you have a good self-image, you have confidence in what you can do. You are willing to try something new. You do not avoid new activities just because you might not do well. You try not to let your mistakes get you down. Instead, you remember that everyone makes mistakes at times and that you can learn from mistakes.

If you have a good self-image, you also recognize that you are a very special person. In fact, you are unique. Nobody in all the world is just like you. Recognizing that you are unique helps you understand that all people are different. You are not just like others, and you do not expect others to be just like you. Accepting differences in people helps you get along with others better.

> ***On Your Own***
> How might a person with a poor self-image feel about himself or herself? Write your ideas on a sheet of paper.

2 Teach

Strategies for Pages 20 and 21

- Direct students to read pages 20 and 21 to find out about self-image.
- Encourage students to name activities they would like to try some day. (Accept all reasonable answers.)
- Ask students how a good self-image can help a person do things. (Answers should include the idea that a strong self-image makes a person feel good about himself or herself.)
- Discuss why a person with a strong self-image is willing to try new things. (has confidence, is not afraid to make mistakes, and so on) • Ask students why it is important for a person to recognize that he or she is unique. (It helps a person appreciate the differences in others and get along well with others.)

Using On Your Own

Accept all answers that show an understanding of the feelings associated with a poor self-image.
Thinking Skill When students explain how a person with a poor self-image might feel, they are *generalizing*.

Life Skills

Use this worksheet for practice in understanding the effects of laughter. This master may be reproduced from the Teacher's Resource Book and also is located on page 1 of the Student's Workbook. Use with Chapter 1: pages 20–23.

Thinking Skill: By answering questions and writing a story, students are interpreting information and communicating information.

Name ______________________ Life Skills

Use with Chapter 1: pages 20–23.

Learning About Laughter

Part I. Read the paragraph and answer the questions.

Did you know that laughter is good for you? Doctors sometimes ask sick people to think of something funny. Laughing can make them feel better. Laughter also helps people who are sad or feeling a lot of unpleasant stress. Laughter can help people forget their problems. A good laugh makes the muscles in the heart, stomach, and chest work harder than usual. Laughing wakes up the whole body. Many people say that laughter is the best medicine in the world. So, the next time you are feeling bad, laugh! You might feel better.

1. Which body parts work harder than usual when you laugh?
   The muscles in the chest, stomach, and heart work harder than usual.
2. Why might a doctor ask sick people to laugh?
   Laughing might help sick people to feel healthier.
3. How can laughter help when a person is unhappy?
   Laughter might help a person forget his or her problems.
4. What people, shows, or books make you laugh?
   Answers will vary depending on the likes and dislikes of each student.

Part II. Think about the funniest situation that has ever happened to you or a member of your family. Write about the situation on another piece of paper. Describe how you felt when you laughed.

Extension Idea: Suggest that students write one or two humorous poems or limericks. 21

Teaching Plan

Lesson 1 continued

2 Teach

Strategies for Pages 22 and 23

• Direct students to read pages 22 and 23 to find out how a person can improve his or her self-image. • Ask students how the person in the picture on page 22 is developing a better self-image. (doing something that she is good at) • Ask students why a person should do things he or she can do well. (so the person can feel good about himself or herself) • Encourage students to name ways to deal with weaknesses. (improve on weaknesses, concentrate on strengths, appreciate the fact that each person is different) • Point out the importance of recognizing that each person is unique and irreplaceable. • Discuss characteristics that make each person in the classroom unique. (Encourage students to list accomplishments as well as physical characteristics and emotional traits.) • Ask a volunteer to describe a healthy attitude toward mistakes. (learn from them, forgive yourself) • Discuss healthy ways to deal with disappointment. (Accept all reasonable answers.)

attitude (at′ə tüd), a way of thinking about a particular idea, situation, or person.

How Can You Make Your Self-Image Better?

Your self-image does not have to stay the same. You can change it. If you have a poor self-image, you can work to make it good. If your self-image is already good, you can make it even better.

The following suggestions can help you improve your self-image. They are examples of good **attitudes**—ways of thinking—about yourself. You might recognize some of them as attitudes you already have. Others you might want to try to develop.

• Keep in mind that you are a special person. Nobody else has exactly the same combination of interests, abilities, problems, and feelings that you have. Nobody can take your place in the world because nobody else is exactly like you. You are an important person.

• Think about what you can do well. Everyone has some strengths. These strengths are different in different people. You might be good in a certain subject in school. Perhaps you are good in a certain sport, in singing or playing an instrument, or in building models. One of your strengths might be getting along well with people and helping others when you can. What do you think the person in the picture is good at? What do you do well?

Being able to take care of animals is one of this girl's strengths.

22

Teaching Options

Anecdote

One way parents can help children develop self-esteem is to give unconditional acceptance. Children who have grown up in an environment of acceptance usually develop high self-esteem, a realistic self-concept, and feelings of self-respect. (Haber, Audrey and Runyon, Richard. *Psychology of Adjustment.* The Dorsey Press, 1984.)

Enrichment

Ask each student to write a letter of encouragement to a relative, friend, or fellow student. Ask students to tell the person what he or she does well, and why the student appreciates that person.

Health and Art

Direct students to draw or cut out pictures of things they like. Suggest that students also cut out letters that spell their name or nickname. Encourage students to make collages out of the pictures and letters.

Reteaching

Ask students to act out ways a person could benefit from making a mistake. Encourage students to tell what a person could learn from the mistake. (Students might want to act out some of their own experiences.) Respect the right of students not to participate.

• Recognize and accept your weaknesses, but do not think about them too much. If you think more about your strengths, you will have enough self-confidence to help overcome your weaknesses, if you wish.
• Expect to make mistakes sometimes. You, like all people, will make mistakes throughout your life. When you make a mistake, learn from it. Try to figure out why you made the mistake so that you do not make the same one again. Understand that nobody is perfect. Making mistakes is part of life.
• Realize that you will not always get what you want. Everyone has disappointments. The way you react to those disappointments can either improve or hurt your self-image. For example, the two people shown here each worked very hard on a poster for a contest, but neither won a prize. They are both unhappy, but which person do you think is reacting in a way that is helpful to her self-image? Why do you think so?

Think Back • *Study on your own with Study Guide page 316.*
1. What is self-image?
2. What are three qualities of a person with a good self-image?
3. What attitudes can help make a self-image better?

Which student has the healthier attitude?

That does it! I'm just no good. If I were good, I would have won. I'm not going to enter any more stupid contests.
Oh well, I'll try again next time. I had fun making my poster and I know it's good. But now that I've seen the winning ones, I think I can do better another time.

• Ask students which person in the picture on page 23 is dealing with disappointment in a positive way. (the girl who is learning from disappointment and is willing to try again)

3 Assess

Expanding Student Thinking

Ask students to analyze advertisements to find out how advertisers appeal to a person's self-image. (Answers should indicate that some advertisers promise that their products or services will make people feel or look better, give people what they deserve, or provide mistake-proof results.)

Thinking Skill When students analyze advertisements, they are *making analogies*.

Answers to Think Back

1. Self-image is the way a person feels about himself or herself.
2. A person with a good self-image has confidence, is not afraid to make mistakes, and understands that he or she is unique.
3. A person's self-image can be improved by focusing on what he or she does well; congratulating himself or herself for being special; and by realizing that he or she will not always get what is wanted.

Health and Art

Use this worksheet for practice in reinforcing self-image through art. This master may be reproduced from the Teacher's Resource Book and also is located on page 4 of the Student's Workbook. Use with Chapter 1: pages 20–23.

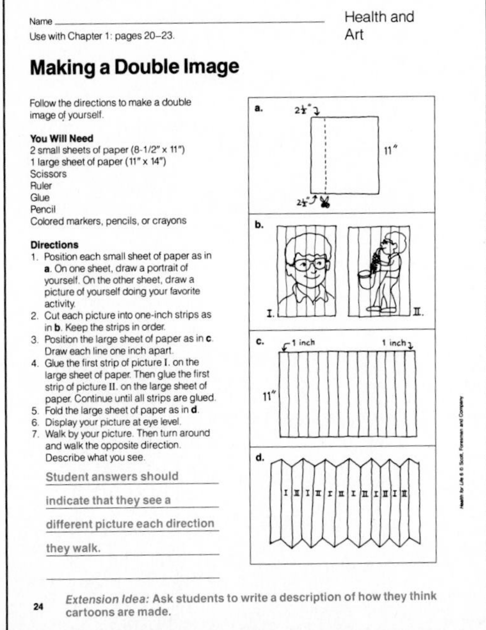
Name ______________________ Health and Art
Use with Chapter 1: pages 20–23.

Making a Double Image

Follow the directions to make a double image of yourself.

You Will Need
2 small sheets of paper (8-1/2" x 11")
1 large sheet of paper (11" x 14")
Scissors
Ruler
Glue
Pencil
Colored markers, pencils, or crayons

Directions
1. Position each small sheet of paper as in **a**. On one sheet, draw a portrait of yourself. On the other sheet, draw a picture of yourself doing your favorite activity.
2. Cut each picture into one-inch strips as in **b**. Keep the strips in order.
3. Position the large sheet of paper as in **c**. Draw each line one inch apart.
4. Glue the first strip of picture I. on the large sheet of paper. Then glue the first strip of picture II. on the large sheet of paper. Continue until all strips are glued.
5. Fold the large sheet of paper as in **d**.
6. Display your picture at eye level.
7. Walk by your picture. Then turn around and walk the opposite direction. Describe what you see.

Student answers should indicate that they see a different picture each direction they walk.

24 *Extension Idea:* Ask students to write a description of how they think cartoons are made.

Activity Plan

Health Activities Workshop pages 24–25

Activity 1 Strategies
Keep in mind that some students will have difficulty with this activity because they do not have a good self-image or do not have many friends, especially if they are new to the community. Encourage new students to list friends from their old community. Accept all answers that students write about themselves.

Thinking Skills By answering the questions about themselves, students are *organizing information* and *communicating.*

Activity 2 Strategies
You might want to coordinate this activity with a language arts or creative writing exercise. You might suggest that students do the activity as an acrostic—writing their names vertically and using each letter in the names as the first letter of a phrase or sentence.

Thinking Skills By writing poetry about themselves, students are *suggesting alternatives* and *communicating.*

Health Activities Workshop

Getting to Know Yourself

1. Like many people your age, you are probably beginning to ask some important questions about yourself. To answer some of these questions, write a newspaper article about yourself. Answer the questions below as you write your article. The picture shows an example of how your article might look.

- Who am I?
- What am I good at?
- What would I like to be better at?
- What do I care most about?
- What is a problem for me?
- Who are my friends?

2. In addition to or instead of the article in Activity 1, write a poem about yourself. The poem might describe your feelings right now, how you generally feel about things, or what you would like to do in the coming year.

24

3. Write down the names of three or four people you admire most. Then, after each name, list the qualities of the person that make you admire him or her. Underline the qualities on the lists that you would like to have. Put a star next to the qualities you think you already have.

4. Make a poster that shows you are a special person. You might want to use a photograph of yourself in the poster.

5. Many different people, organizations, and events have probably influenced your ideas and feelings to help form the person you are. On a sheet of paper, write as many of these sources as you can think of. Some sources might include your family, a scouting troop, and television shows.

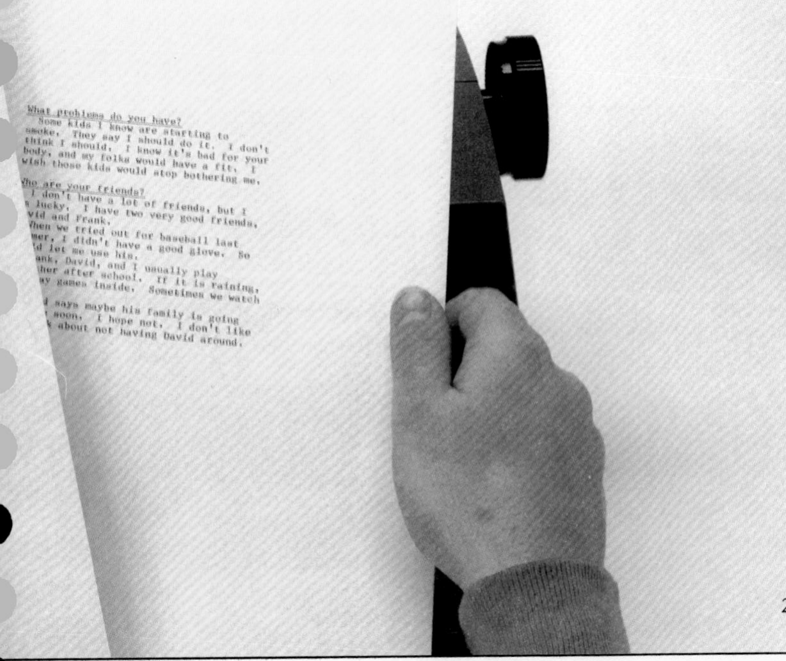

Activity 3 Strategies
Accept all answers the students can explain. Qualities students admire could include personality traits, special talents or abilities, physical characteristics such as a nice smile, or organizational and reasoning skills.
Thinking Skill By listing people's positive qualities, students are *classifying*.

Activity 4 Strategies
Supply magazines for students who would like to cut out pictures to use on their posters. You might suggest that students emphasize their uniqueness by displaying photographs of themselves along with pictures of other people. Students might also like to draw pictures of activities they enjoy doing.
Thinking Skills By making a poster that shows how they are special, students are *generalizing* and *communicating*.

Activity 5 Strategies
You might want to introduce the word *values*—what a person thinks is important in life. As an extension of this activity, lead a discussion on how each source influences the students' values, and which sources they feel are positive and which are sometimes negative.
Thinking Skill By thinking about sources that influence their values, students are *drawing conclusions*.

Teaching Plan

Lesson 2 pages 26–29

Lesson Objective
Explain some ways to build a good self-image and good relationships, and explain why having good relationships with family and friends is important for health.

Health Vocabulary
Relationship

1 Motivate

Introducing the Lesson
Encourage students to name reasons why some people have an easy time making friends and others do not. (Accept all answers the students can explain.)

2 Teach

Strategies for Pages 26 and 27
• Direct students to read pages 26 and 27 to find out how to build good relationships. • Ask students why building good relationships is an important part of having a good self-image. (It helps a person feel accepted and valued.) • Encourage students to look at the pictures on pages 26 and 27 and discuss each kind of relationship shown.

relationship
(ri lā′shən ship), a connection or condition that exists between two or more people.

2 How Can You Get Along Better with Others?

The pictures on these two pages show different kinds of **relationships**—connections between persons or groups. You have different relationships with different people. You have one kind of relationship with your friends and another kind with your teacher. You have different relationships with different family members. Which picture shows a family relationship? a student–teacher relationship?

Building good relationships is an important part of having a good self-image. Getting along with other people helps you feel accepted and valued. Then you feel better about yourself.

What Does Getting Along with Others Mean?

Getting along with others does not mean that you always agree with other people. You do not always have to do what other people do, especially if you think what they are doing is wrong. Getting along with others means that you listen to other people and try to understand how they feel. You do not always try to get other people to do what you want to do. Getting along with others also means that you treat them the way you would like them to treat you.

What four relationships do these pictures show?

26

Teaching Options

Health Background

Attitudes and interests can affect a relationship that is being established, or change existing relationships. Personality traits, a sense of self-acceptance, treating others fairly, and knowing what to look for in a friend are some factors that influence the formation and longevity of a friendship.

Enrichment

Direct students to find out about occupations that require people to work with others. Encourage students to suggest how such jobs could improve a person's self-image.

Health and Drama

Ask students to create and perform a play about how to build friendships. Suggest that students include characters who have good self-images and are likable, and characters who have poor self-images and do not get along well with others. Let students analyze which characters succeed in building friendships, and why.

Reteaching

Ask students to write a paragraph describing how they could improve their relationship with one member of their family. Then have the students tell how that could improve their self-image.

Most people will treat you in some of the same ways you treat them. How do you want to be treated by other people? Do you want to be pushed around and made fun of, or do you want to be liked and treated with respect? If you want to be treated with respect, you have to treat others that way. What are some ways to show respect for members of your family? for friends? for other people you know?

Why Are Friendships Important?

Friendships are very important relationships. You can talk with friends about problems. You can spend time together working on activities you enjoy. People become friends for different reasons. You and your friends probably share some of the same interests. You enjoy some of the same activities. You might have other friends who do not share many of your interests, but they might share some of your attitudes toward certain things.

You cannot be friends with everyone. However, getting along with people who are not your friends is also important. Most people have a few close friends they spend time with, but they are also friendly toward other people who are not their close friends.

On Your Own

Three months after Phil started at his new school, another new boy, Doug, joined his class. Phil remembered how lonely and shy he had felt on his first day in the new school three months before, so he sat with Doug during lunch. A few days later, one of Phil's friends was having trouble with a math lesson. Phil offered to help him after school.

Why is Phil the kind of person others might want for a friend? How might the way Phil treats other people affect his own self-image? Write your answers on a sheet of paper.

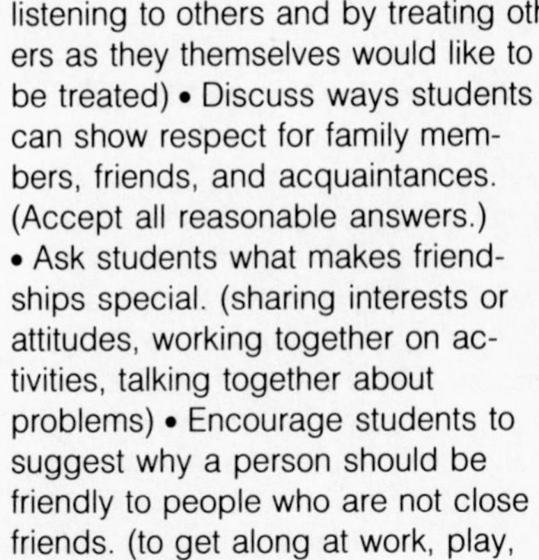

• Encourage students to tell how people can get along with others. (by listening to others and by treating others as they themselves would like to be treated) • Discuss ways students can show respect for family members, friends, and acquaintances. (Accept all reasonable answers.)
• Ask students what makes friendships special. (sharing interests or attitudes, working together on activities, talking together about problems) • Encourage students to suggest why a person should be friendly to people who are not close friends. (to get along at work, play, and school)

Using On Your Own

Phil shows genuine concern for other people's feelings and well-being. By treating other people well, he is more likely to be treated with respect, thus strengthening his own self-image. Also, Phil probably feels good about being able to help others.

Thinking Skill By telling why Phil might be likable and have a good self-image, students are *drawing conclusions*.

Teaching Plan

Lesson 2 continued

2 Teach

Strategies for Pages 28 and 29

• Direct students to read pages 28 and 29 to find out ways to deal with anger. • Encourage students to explain why people usually get angry. (because they feel that they or others have been treated unfairly) • Discuss reasons why a person needs to let feelings out in a healthy way. (to get along with people, to avoid locking up feelings inside) • Encourage students to tell what a person should do with his or her anger. (get rid of the anger; solve the problem that caused the anger) • Direct students to look at the pictures on pages 28 and 29 and name some ways to get rid of anger. (work off angry feelings by exercising; talk with someone about your feelings) • Ask students how talking can help. (Talking with someone can give another person the chance to help solve the problem; talking helps relieve some angry feelings.)
• Encourage students to explain how Marie handled her anger (worked it off; talked to a friend) and how she handled the problem that made her angry (by talking with her sister).

What Can Help When You Are Angry?

Marie was almost ready for school. She went to her closet to get her favorite sweater. The sweater was not there. "Rita did it again!" she shouted. Marie slammed the closet door. She ran to the head of the stairs and called down. "Mom, Rita took my sweater again. Tell her to give it back."

"She's already gone, Marie. Wear something else."

Marie was furious. She thought, "It's just not fair. I never borrow Rita's clothes without asking first. Just wait till I see her this afternoon."

Feeling angry at times, even at people you care about, is part of life. Most people feel angry when they think they have been treated unfairly, or when they see someone else being treated unfairly. Learning to deal with your anger will help you get along better with other people. However, keeping angry feelings locked up inside yourself will make you feel unhappy. You need to get the feelings out in a healthy way.

The first step in dealing with anger is to admit that you are angry. Then you need to get rid of the angry feelings so that you can deal with the problem that made you angry. You are more likely to solve problems when you are not upset. Finally, you need to try to solve the problem that made you angry.

Marie walked to school to help work off her angry feelings.

28

Teaching Options

Anecdote

In a personality test conducted by Mary Biaggio of the University of Idaho, college students who were more easily angered were more narrow-minded, less tolerant, less perceptive about others, and less socially responsible than their peers. (Carey, John. "Better Temper That Temper." *Newsweek*. January 3, 1983, page 43.)

Enrichment

Encourage interested students to make posters about positive ways to deal with anger at a friend or family member. Have the students make up a title or caption for the poster that describes why dealing with this anger is important. Display the posters in the classroom.

Health and Reading

Suggest that students find examples in fiction of people who have to deal with anger. Direct students to analyze whether the character deals with anger in a healthy way.

Reteaching

Direct students to list ways in which exercise can sometimes help a person deal with anger.

Taking your mind off your feelings for a while can often help you get rid of anger. You might work on a hobby, visit a friend, listen to music, or read a book.

You could try being physically active to get rid of your anger. Ride your bike, take a walk, or do some other kind of physical activity. You work off your angry feelings as you exercise. After a while, you probably will be able to think more calmly about the situation that made you angry.

If you are very angry or if your angry feelings stay with you for a long time, you might want to talk about your feelings with someone you trust. You could talk with a family member, a friend, or a teacher. Talking about a problem can help you get your feelings into the open. Then you might be better able to deal with those feelings. The person you talk with might also suggest ways to solve the problem that made you angry. Look at the pictures to see how Marie dealt with her anger.

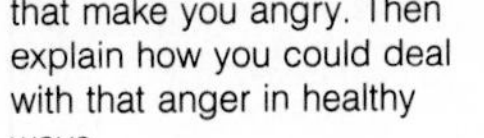

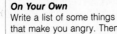

On Your Own
Write a list of some things that make you angry. Then explain how you could deal with that anger in healthy ways.

Think Back • *Study on your own with Study Guide page 316.*

1. How can a person get along better with others?
2. Why are friendships and family relationships important for health?
3. What are some helpful ways to deal with anger?

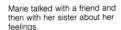

Marie talked with a friend and then with her sister about her feelings.

29

Using On Your Own

Accept all answers that describe healthy ways to deal with unfair, frustrating, or unreasonable situations.
Thinking Skill By thinking of healthy ways to deal with anger, students are *suggesting alternatives.*

3 Assess

Expanding Student Thinking

Ask students to suggest reasons that holding anger inside might not be good for a person. (An angry person might have difficulty working, doing school assignments, or getting along with others. Staying angry for a long time might cause a person to be unhealthy emotionally or physically.)
Thinking Skills By telling why keeping anger inside might not be good for a person, students are *interpreting information* and *generalizing.*

Answers to Think Back

1. A person can get along with others by listening to others, trying to understand how others feel, and by treating others the same way he or she would like to be treated.
2. Friendships and family relationships are important because people need to feel liked and accepted. When people feel that way, they feel better about themselves.
3. Admitting that the anger exists, being physically active, and talking with someone about troubled feelings are ways to deal with anger.

Teaching Plan

Lesson 3 pages 30–35

Lesson Objective
Describe some of the causes and effects of stress, and list ways to deal with stress, including the process of making wise decisions.

Health Vocabulary
Stress

1 Motivate

Introducing the Lesson
Ask volunteers to name situations at school that cause stress. Encourage students to explain how they deal with the stressful situations they have described.

stress, the body's physical and mental reactions to demanding situations.

What is causing Steve's stress?

3 How Can You Deal with Stress?

Steve has a science test next Friday. He has promised to sell twenty tickets for the Boy Scout Jamboree, and so far he has not sold one. His friend Ryan keeps urging him to sign up for basketball at school. At the moment his room is a mess and his mother is annoyed about it. On top of all this Steve knows his father is thinking of taking a new job in another town. His family might have to move.

How do you think Steve is feeling? He is worried about the test. He wishes he had never promised to sell so many tickets. He does not really want to play basketball, but he does not want to tell that to Ryan. Steve's messy room makes him feel uncomfortable now that he really looks at it. Also, he is concerned about the possibility of moving to another town.

These many troublesome feelings cause Steve to feel tense. His head hurts and his stomach is a little upset. He is experiencing **stress**—his body's reactions to the demands he is facing. Stress prepares the body to deal with difficult situations. Sometimes stress can be helpful. When a person is faced with danger, stress gets the body ready to face the danger or to get away from it quickly.

What Causes Stress?

You might think that only upsetting or dangerous events cause stress, but this is not true. Even events you might think of as fun can cause stress. The people on the roller coaster are feeling stress. Getting ready to go on a vacation might cause stress. Any exciting event or situation, such as taking a test, watching an exciting sports event, or arguing with other family members can cause changes in your body that you feel as stress.

Change can also cause stress. Such changes include moving to a different town or school and changes in your family, such as a birth, death, divorce, or illness. Your body reacts to these changes by producing certain chemicals. Even being tired, thirsty, or hungry causes stress. Your body reacts to these situations by signaling you to sleep, drink, or eat.

Teaching Options

Health Background

High levels of stress, especially over long periods of time, seem to be associated with certain diseases. Diseases that are sometimes stress-related include ulcers, asthma, migraine headaches, backaches, and allergies.

Enrichment
Encourage students to find out about the changes that occur in the body as a result of stress.

Health and Science
Show students how to take a pulse by lightly pressing the forefinger and middle finger of one hand against the other wrist right below the thumb. Ask students to find their average pulse rate (While sitting, count pulse for one minute. Do this three times. Add the three pulse rates together and divide by three.) Ask students to take their pulse periodically throughout the day. Suggest that students make a graph of the results.

Reteaching
Ask students to make a chart that shows some of the causes of stress. Tell students to also include a list of activities they enjoy that are relaxing.

What Are Some Harmful Effects of Too Much Stress?

A certain amount of stress cannot be avoided and is not harmful to you. In fact, some amount of stress helps you do your best and is often pleasant. Too much stress, however, can harm your health. Stress affects different people in different ways. Some common effects of stress include headache, sleeplessness, and upset stomach. Feeling nervous, getting angry easily, losing an appetite, or eating too much are other effects of stress.

Sometimes people who are under too much stress begin to have problems with their friends and families. They might become short-tempered. They might have trouble with their schoolwork or jobs. These reactions to stress cause even more stress.

Did You Know?
Whether stress comes from something pleasant or from something unpleasant, the following physical changes occur:
- Special endocrine glands, the adrenals, send the chemical adrenaline into the blood.
- The pupils of the eyes get larger.
- Body temperature rises.
- Breathing becomes faster.
- More blood is sent to the brain, heart, and large muscles.
- The liver sends stored sugar into the blood.

Some causes of stress are fun.

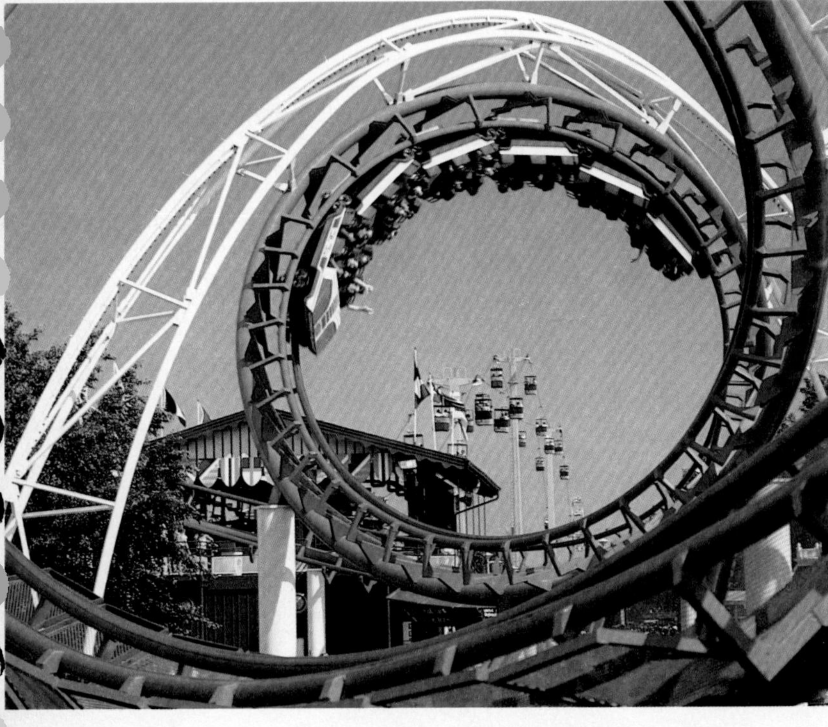

2 Teach

Strategies for Pages 30 and 31

• Direct students to read pages 30 and 31 to learn about the causes and effects of stress. • Ask students when stress might be helpful. (when a person is faced with danger) • Direct students to look at the picture on page 30 and tell how stress can make a person feel. (tense, upset, nervous) • Discuss some stressful situations that are fun. (Answers might include riding roller coasters, getting ready for a vacation, or watching an exciting game.) • Encourage students to name other situations that can cause stress. (arguing, taking tests, feeling hunger or fatigue) • Ask students to name harmful effects of too much stress. (headache, sleeplessness, nervousness, change in appetite) • Discuss how inappropriate reactions to stress can cause more stress. (Answers might include the ideas that grouchiness or inattention to responsibilities can cause problems in getting along with others.)

Teaching Plan

Lesson 3 continued

2 Teach

Strategies for Pages 32 and 33

• Direct students to read pages 32 and 33 to find out how to deal with problems that cause stress. • Encourage students to describe the first step in dealing with stress. (realize that you are upset) • Ask students to list three questions that help a person deal with stress. (Students should list the questions on page 32.) • Direct students to look at the picture on page 32 and tell what problem Steve can solve right away. (cleaning his room) • Discuss why it helps to do something about the most immediate problem. (reduces the number of things to worry about and shows that you can do something about your problems) • Ask students how Steve can solve the problem of Ryan wanting him to play basketball. (decide to tell Ryan about his own wishes and then act on his decision) • Encourage students to explain how studying a little each day can reduce the stress of taking an exam. (makes a person more prepared, gives a person more control over results)

What is Steve doing to relieve his stress?

How Can You Deal with Problems That Cause Stress?

Remember how upset and tense Steve was? Perhaps you have felt like Steve at times. Most people feel upset by stress every now and then. You can deal with stress in several healthy ways.

The first step is to realize that you are upset. Thin about the problems that are bothering you. Then answer these questions.

- Which problems can I do something about now?
- Which problems can wait a while?
- Which problems cannot be changed?

Instead of just worrying and feeling under stress, you are now ready to take action.

When several problems are bothering you, working on one at a time can be helpful. Pick one problem to work on and do something about it right away. Ignor the other troubles for a while. Look back at Steve's problems. What is one thing he can do something about right away?

He should probably clean his room first. If he does that, he can get rid of two problems—the mess in his room and his mother's anger. Also, the physical work of cleaning his room can help get rid of some of his upset feelings.

Which problem could Steve work on next? After he cleans his room, he might start selling the Jamboree tickets to his neighbors. Selling the tickets will probably be less stressful than worrying about them.

Anecdote

The Chinese character for crisis is a combination of two characters—one representing danger and the other representing opportunity.

Enrichment

Direct interested students to interview classmates to find out what situations cause sixth-graders the most stress. Encourage students to report their findings to the class.

Health and Language Arts

Ask students to find a magazine or newspaper article about a famous athlete or performer who experiences stress before performing. Encourage students to report on how that person deals with stress successfully.

Reteaching

Encourage students to think of several situations, similar to Steve's, that a person must deal with. Then ask students to explain how the person could deal with those situations in healthy ways.

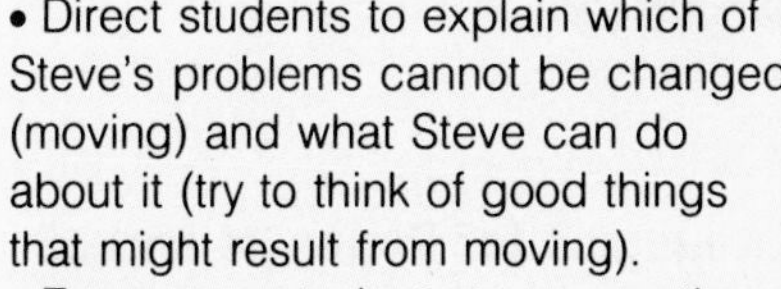

Steve's worry list is getting shorter. Now he can deal with the problem of basketball. Steve can decide to tell Ryan how he feels, instead of putting it off and worrying about it. He can call Ryan and politely tell him that he really does not want to spend his free time playing basketball. Thus, Steve can change this stressful situation by making a decision and then acting on it.

Steve might not be able to get rid of all his nervousness about the science test. However, he can study a little bit each day to prepare himself for it. Each time he studies, he can review what he studied last. Then he can study a little more. Studying and reviewing a little at a time can be more helpful than trying to study everything at the last minute. Just knowing that he is working to prepare himself for the test might help lessen Steve's stress.

Steve has one problem he really cannot change. If his father takes the job in a different town, the family will move. Steve can try to stop thinking about the move so much. He can also try to change his feelings about it. He can remind himself that he will be able to make new friends, explore new places, and do different things in a new town. He can also write to his present friends from time to time.

In dealing with problems, keep in mind that all problems cannot be solved. Some, like Steve's moving, must be accepted. When you are able to accept problems, they often seem less important. What other kinds of problems might need to be accepted?

• Direct students to explain which of Steve's problems cannot be changed (moving) and what Steve can do about it (try to think of good things that might result from moving).
• Encourage students to name other stressful situations that they cannot change. (Answers might include death and divorce.) • Ask students how a person can deal with stressful situations that cannot be changed. (by changing one's attitude)

Teaching Plan

Lesson 3 continued

2 Teach

Strategies for Pages 34 and 35

• Direct students to read page 34 to learn about ways to relax. • Encourage students to name things a person can do to relax. (work on a hobby, do physical exercises or breathing exercises, listen to music) • Ask students how a person can get help with problems too big to deal with alone. (ask friends or family for help; talk about the problems) • Direct students to read page 35 to find out about decision-making steps that can help ease stress. • Ask students how making a decision can help a person get rid of stress. (A person must decide on a solution before acting on it.) • Ask students why a person should list both good and bad results for each choice. (to consider the possible effects of decisions and make the best decision) • Direct students to read the guidelines for good choices and discuss why they help in making good decisions. (Good decisions are based on choices that are safe, legal, acceptable to others, and show respect for oneself and others.)

Did You Know?
Various stress-related health problems such as high blood pressure, ulcers, and headaches sometimes can be controlled through the use of biofeedback. This technique allows a patient to use monitoring equipment to discover how that person's body reacts when stressed. With practice, the patient can learn to control those reactions and control the effects of stress.

How Can You Learn to Relax?

One way to help get rid of stress is to relax. You can teach yourself to relax in several ways.

The picture shows a simple exercise that will help you relax. Sit or lie in a comfortable position. Breathe out as completely as you can. Then breathe in through your nose as deeply as you can. Hold your breath while you count to four in your mind. Next, breathe out through your mouth while you count to eight in your mind. Do this exercise three or four times. You will be surprised how much calmer you will feel. Your heart will slow down and you should feel relaxed. This exercise is very helpful because you can do it almost anywhere.

Playing sports or doing any other kind of physical exercise you enjoy can help you relax. Working on a hobby is also a way to relax. Some people listen to music when they want to relax and get their minds off their problems. Getting your mind off a problem is not the same as avoiding a problem. Taking time off from thinking about a problem can often help you deal with it in a helpful way later.

Sometimes you cannot deal with a problem on your own. You might want to ask for help at such a time. Talk about your feelings with someone you trust. Sharing your feelings will often help you feel more relaxed. Also, a friend or family member might suggest ways to deal with your problem.

Breathing exercises can help you relax.

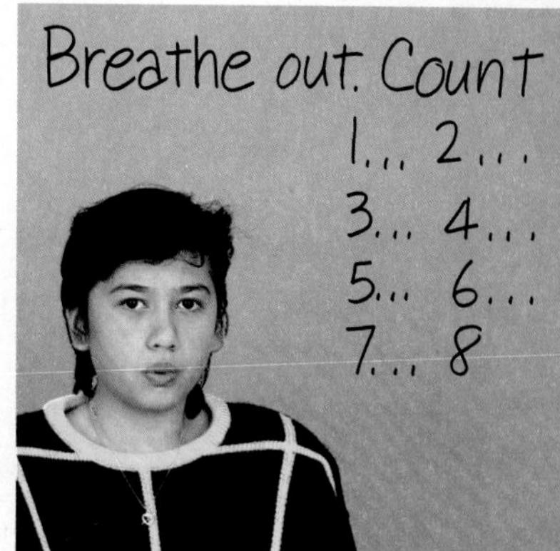

34

Teaching Options

Enrichment

Direct students to think of a character in a book or movie who had to make an important decision. Encourage students to analyze the decision the character made.

Health and Language Arts

Ask interested students to write a few paragraphs about a difficult decision they had to make and what the results of the decision were.

Reteaching

Encourage students to think of daily situations in which a person could use the decision-making model. List the situations on the chalkboard.

Special Education

Help learning-disabled students identify school-related causes of stress for them. Then help these students identify ways they can deal with this stress.

How Can Making Decisions Help You Deal with Stress?

Dealing with stress often includes making a decision. You need to decide how to deal with the situation that is causing stress. Then you need to carry out your decision. Many people have trouble making decisions and then carrying them out.

You can follow five steps to help yourself make decisions and then follow through on them.

Step 1. Realize that a decision is needed. If you are feeling stress, you need to do something about it.
Step 2. List the possible choices. Think of all the ways to deal with the problem that is bothering you. Remember that some problems, such as Steve's worry about moving, cannot be solved and must instead be accepted. You might want to list accepting the problem as a possible choice of dealing with it.
Step 3. List the possible results of each choice. You might think of several ways to deal with your problem. Now think about the good and bad results that might happen from each choice. For each choice, ask yourself if it fits the guidelines on the right. You can eliminate choices that do not fit the guidelines.
Step 4. Decide which choice is best. After you think about the possible results of each choice, you will probably find that one choice stands out as the best one to follow.
Step 5. Judge your decision. After you decide which choice is best, try it. Then judge your choice to see if it worked. Sometimes your choice will not work out the way you want it to. If your first choice for dealing with a problem does not help, try another choice. Remember that you might just have to accept the problem since things often do not work out exactly as you would like.

Guidelines for Responsible Choices

- The choice should be safe and promote health.
- The choice should be legal and follow the rules of school and community.
- The choice would be acceptable to parents and other family members.
- The choice shows respect for self and others.

Think Back • *Study on your own with Study Guide page 317.*

1. What causes stress?
2. How might stress affect the body? a person's actions?
3. What are some ways to deal with stress?
4. What are five steps for making a decision?

3 Assess

Expanding Student Thinking

Direct students to write a brief description of a person in a stressful situation. Tell what the person should do to deal with his or her problem. (Accept answers that reflect an understanding of ways to deal with stress and use decision-making techniques.)

Thinking Skills When students describe stressful situations and ways to deal with them, they are *interpreting information* and *generalizing*.

Answers to Think Back

1. Stress can be caused by any demanding situation.
2. Stress can affect the body by causing headache, upset stomach, and changes in appetite. It can affect actions by causing people to act nervous or angry; eat too little or too much; have trouble with schoolwork or jobs; and have problems with family and friends.
3. Deal with one problem at a time, accept problems that cannot be changed, learn to relax, and learn decision-making steps.
4. Realize that a decision needs to be made; list possible choices; list possible results of each choice; decide which choice is best; judge the decision.

Overhead Transparency Master

Use this blackline master to make a labeled overhead transparency or to make an unlabeled student worksheet. This blackline master may be reproduced from the Teacher's Resource Book.

Chapter 1
Text page 35

Five Steps of Decision Making

Step 1. Realize that a decision is needed.
If you are feeling stress, you need to do something about it.

Step 2. List the possible choices.
Think of all the ways to deal with the problem that is bothering you. Remember that some problems, such as Steve's worry about moving, cannot be solved and must instead by accepted. You might want to list accepting the problem as a possible choice of dealing with it.

Step 3. List the possible results of each choice.
You might think of several ways to deal with your problem. Now think about the good and bad results that might happen from each choice. For example, Steve would need to consider that his friend Ryan might be angry with him for not signing up for basketball.

Step 4. Decide which choice is best.
After you think about the possible results of each choice, you will probably find that one choice stands out as the best one to follow.

Step 5. Judge your decision.
After you decide which choice is best, try it. Then judge your choice to see if it worked. Sometimes your choice will not work out the way you want it to. If your first choice for dealing with a problem does not help, try another choice. Remember that you might just have to accept the problem, since things often do not work out exactly as you would like.

19

Teaching Plan

Lesson 4 pages 36–41

Lesson Objective
Make a list of guidelines to follow that can help a person set and reach goals. Describe how setting goals can affect a person's self-confidence.

Health Vocabulary
Goal

1 Motivate

Introducing the Lesson
Ask students to recall a time when they wanted to learn a new sport or game. Encourage students to tell how they learned the new activity and how they became good at it.

2 Teach

Strategies for Pages 36 and 37
• Direct students to read pages 36 and 37 to learn about the kinds of goals that are healthy to set.
• Encourage a volunteer to define a goal. (something someone wants and is willing to work for) • Ask students to name some short-term goals a person might have. (to clean a room, do well in a game, get a good grade on a test)

goal (gōl), something a person wants to do or achieve.

4 How Can You Set and Reach Goals?

Michael wanted to invite three of his friends to his home for lunch on Saturday afternoon. Before he invited his friends, he asked his mother if they could come over and use the kitchen. Michael told her he would shop for the food. He also told her he and his friends would do all the cooking, and they would clean up the kitchen after lunch. His mother agreed.

Michael and his friends had a great time. Michael's mother was happy too. Michael had set a **goal** for himself and reached it. A goal is something a person wants and is willing to work for. Michael worked to reach his goal of having his friends over for a lunch that they made. He felt good about himself.

People have different goals. Some people have goals about schoolwork or sports. Some have goals that involve hobbies, jobs, pets, or other people. Some goals might take a long time to reach. They are long-term goals. Others might be short-term goals. They take a short time to reach. For example, doing well on a certain test is a short-term goal. Improving grades in general is a long-term goal.

Michael set a goal, worked for it, and reached it.

36

Teaching Options

Health Background

Setting, modifying, and attaining goals is a continuous process throughout a person's life. In order to be well-adjusted, a person must set realistic goals and be willing to modify them on the basis of constraints and opportunities. Pursuing long-term goals involves being tolerant, delaying gratification, and dealing with feelings of stress or resentment caused by sacrifices made during the goal-setting process. Although striving for a goal can be stressful, it also gives direction and purpose to an individual's life.

Enrichment
Ask students to make up stories about a person who sets an unrealistic goal. The students could write their stories or tell them to the class. Ask students how the person might feel about him or herself about setting such a goal. (tense, nervous, anxious) Direct other class members to change the stories so that the characters are no longer unrealistic about their goals. Then discuss how the person's feelings might change. (more confident, relaxed)

Reteaching
Direct students to list some realistic goals for their class to achieve during the school year. Write the goals on the chalkboard.

Health and Social Studies
Direct students to find out how national economic goals are set in other countries. Students might want to research economic goals in Zimbabwe, Spain, Japan, or other countries. Encourage students to report their findings to the class.

What Kinds of Goals Should You Set for Yourself?

People who are good at setting and reaching goals make sure several things are true about the goals.

First, a goal must be good for the person who sets it—you. How was Michael's goal good for him?

Second, the goal should be reachable in ways that are not harmful to others. For example, a person might set a goal of completing a coin collection. The person might decide to take coins from a friend's collection without the friend knowing about it. In reaching his or her goal, the person is harming someone else. What would be a responsible way for the person to reach the goal of completing a coin collection?

Finally, the goal should be realistic. A realistic goal is not too hard and not too easy. A realistic goal takes hard work and, sometimes, a little luck. A goal that is too easy takes no work at all. A goal that is too hard might be impossible to reach and require a great amount of luck. Each student shown here has set a goal of completing a science project in two weeks. Which student has set a goal that is too easy? Which student has set a goal that might be too hard? Which one has set a realistic goal?

Whose goal is the most realistic?

I'm really interested in volcanoes. If I read more about them, I could make a volcano model and a big chart about recent eruptions.

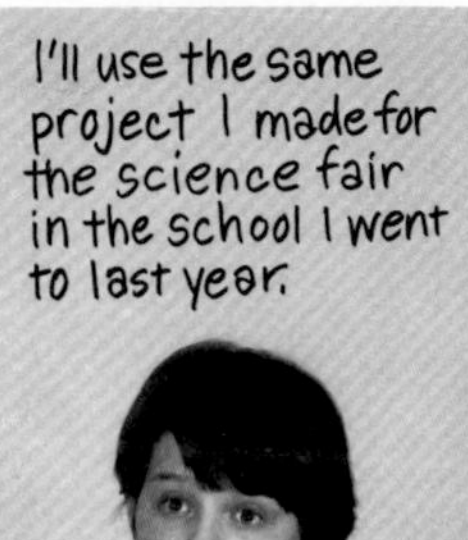

I'll use the same project I made for the science fair in the school I went to last year.

I don't know anything about lasers, but I'll hurry and learn all about them for my project.

37

• Encourage students to suggest some long-term goals a person might have. (to improve grades, get along better with friends, improve a certain skill) • Discuss three standards a person can use to judge whether a goal is a good one. (The goal should be good for the individual, reachable without hurting others, and realistic.) • Encourage students to explain why Michael's goal was good for him. (It presented a challenge, was reachable, and provided an opportunity to have fun.) • Ask students what makes a goal realistic. (It is not too hard and not too easy. It requires hard work and perhaps a little luck.) • Direct students to look at the picture on page 37 and suggest which student has set a realistic goal. (The first student has set a goal that is challenging and reachable. The second student's goal is too easy, and the third student's goal might be too hard.) • Ask students why completing the laser project is not a good goal. (This student does not know enough about lasers and probably cannot complete the project in time.) • Encourage students to tell how the student with last year's project could set a good goal. (The student could expand on the project.)

Teaching Plan

Lesson 4 continued

2 Teach

Strategies for Pages 38 and 39

• Direct students to read pages 38 and 39 to find out how a person can set better goals by knowing his or her abilities. • Encourage students to name the first step in setting a goal. (deciding what to work toward) • Ask students why a person should think about his or her abilities. (to help the person decide what to work toward; to help set realistic goals) • Direct students to look at the picture on pages 38 and 39 and explain what the people pictured are good at. • Ask students to name things they are good at. • Encourage students to describe how they feel when they do activities they can do well. • Discuss some of the advantages of knowing what you are good at. (self-confidence, ability to share skills)

On Your Own

Think of some goals you might like to reach. List your ideas on a sheet of paper. Now think about your abilities. Think of as many of your abilities as you can. List your abilities on another sheet of paper. Compare your lists. Which of your abilities might help you reach some of your goals?

How Can Knowing Your Abilities Help You Set Goals?

The first step in setting a goal is deciding what you want to work toward. To make this decision, you need to think about your abilities—the things you do well.

Knowing what your abilities are can help you decide what to work toward. For example, a person who is good in art might decide to make a drawing for a student art show. A person who is a fast runner might decide to try to make the school track team. Both of these people have set realistic goals. They have abilities that will help them reach their goals.

Think about what you do well. You might be good at math, science, reading, or some other subject. You might be good at more than one subject. You might do well in a sport or in several sports. You might have a good singing voice or play the piano well. Perhaps you are good at caring for pets or farm animals. You might have responsibilities at home that you perform well, such as taking care of the yard or helping to care for younger children. You might have the ability to talk with, listen to, and help other people. What abilities do each of the people shown on these two pages have?

What abilities do these people have?

38

Teaching Options

Anecdote

Most psychologists believe that people are motivated in three major ways—to seek pleasure, to avoid pain, and to realize their potential.

Enrichment

Encourage students to interview people in the community who have set and reached interesting or unusual goals. Ask the people to describe how reaching their goals made them feel about themselves. Encourage students to share their information with the class.

Health and Language Arts

Ask students to find and read a biography about a musician, athlete, politician, explorer, doctor, or other person who overcame obstacles to reach a goal. (Examples include Helen Keller, Charles R. Drew, Abraham Lincoln, Sir Edmund Hillary, and the Wright brothers.) Ask students to give an oral report to the class.

Reteaching

Direct students to make a list of abilities they would like to develop and goals for developing these abilities. Let students keep a journal of their progress in improving these abilities. Respect the right of students not to share their lists or journals.

Knowing you are good at something gives you self-confidence. If you know you have an ability, you know you have a good chance of reaching your goal by working toward it. After you have reached a few goals, you will have even more self-confidence. You might then decide to try new activities. If you try new activities, you might find you have abilities you did not even know about. For example, suppose you have been playing ping-pong for a couple of years and are good at it. You might decide to try tennis. After a while, you might find that you could do fairly well at tennis too. Then you might set a goal of playing in a local tournament.

No two people have exactly the same abilities, so no two people are likely to set exactly the same goals in life. You do not have to set exactly the same goals as your friends. You and your friends might have some goals in common, but you will probably have many others that are different.

Using On Your Own
Encourage students to work with friends to discover some of their abilities. Suggest that volunteers share their goals with the class.

Thinking Skills By making a list of goals and abilities and determining which abilities would help in reaching goals, students are *classifying* and *judging and evaluating*.

Teaching Plan

Lesson 4 continued

2 Teach

Strategies for Pages 40 and 41

• Direct students to read pages 40 and 41 to find out about ways to reach goals. • Encourage students to name the most important step in reaching a goal. (having a plan) • Ask students what should be included in a plan. (several small tasks that can be completed, such as practice, study, discussion) • Discuss why a person should check his or her progress. (to find out whether the plan is working; to get encouragement)
• Discuss the questions a person can ask to find out how to change his or her plan. (Answers should relate to the questions listed on page 40.)
• Ask students how thinking of goals he or she has reached in the past can help a person succeed. (gives a person self-confidence; helps a person think about the reward of finishing) • Encourage students to tell why it helps to think of how good it feels to succeed. (It reminds a person that the work has a purpose.) • Ask students why a goal should be divided into smaller parts. (so that there is the reward of achieving small goals along the way to the larger goal)

How Can You Reach Your Goals?

Once you choose a goal to work toward, you can make a plan telling how you will reach your goal. Your plan should include a list of all the tasks you will have to do to reach your goal. List the tasks in order from first to last. Also list any problems you think you might have in reaching your goal. Then list ways to solve the problems. Think about any help you might need from other people.

Suppose, for example, that your goal is to memorize the part of a character for your school play. Your plan will include several tasks. First, you will need to read the part over several times. Then you will need to figure out how much of the part you need to learn each week in order to have the whole part memorized in time for the rehearsals of the play. You will have to study the part over and over. You might ask someone to watch the script and correct you when you make mistakes.

Once you make your plan, you can begin working on the tasks you listed. Check your progress from time to time. This step is important in reaching any goal you set. When you see that your plan is working, you will be encouraged to keep trying.

Sometimes when you check your progress, you might find that your plan is not working. Then you can change your plan and work toward your goal in a different way. After you have carried out your plan, you might want to ask yourself these questions.

- Did I reach my goal?
- Was my goal good for me and not harmful to others?
- Was my goal realistic—not too hard, not too easy?
- What did I do well in working toward my goal?
- What could I have done better?
- What did I do in working toward this goal that could help me reach future goals?

You might not reach every goal you set. However, you should not feel too badly about failing once in a while. Everybody has disappointments, but most people will reach many of their goals. You are a special person with abilities that can help you reach many goals.

Teaching Options

Enrichment

Encourage students to think of goals they might want to achieve over the course of the school year. Suggest that students develop time lines that divide the goal into smaller tasks to be achieved over time.

Health and Drama

Encourage interested students to write the dialogue for a skit in which someone is helping a friend who is discouraged about a goal.

Reteaching

Ask students to explain how they could learn to shoot a basketball by breaking the skill into smaller parts. (Students might discuss developing speed, hand position, stance, eye contact, and release of the ball.)

What Can Help If You Become Discouraged About a Goal?

As you work toward a goal, you might become tired or discouraged. Most people have these feelings at times. The chart shows several ways to keep working toward your goal in spite of these feelings.

Think about goals you have reached in the past. Kim wanted to learn to play the clarinet. When she got tired of practicing, she thought about how much she enjoyed playing the piano. Her years of practicing piano had been worth the work.

Think about how good you will feel if you succeed. Jim wanted to write a poem good enough to be published in the school newspaper. He thought about how proud he would be to have his friends and family see his poem in the papers.

Divide the goal into smaller parts. Calvin wanted to earn enough money to buy a new twelve-speed bicycle. He knew he would have to work for a long time to get enough money. He set smaller goals of how much money he wanted to earn each month.

Promise yourself a reward for working toward your goal for a certain amount of time. Carla decided to clean up her room. She promised herself she would stop after an hour and listen to music for fifteen minutes.

Set special times to work on your goal. Janet wanted to make a new dress. She decided to work on the dress every night between 7:30 and 8:30.

Think Back • *Study on your own with Study Guide page 317.*

1. What three things should be true about your goals?
2. What is a realistic goal?
3. How can setting goals build self-confidence?
4. What should a plan for reaching a goal include?
5. What can help if a person becomes discouraged about a goal?

3 Assess

Expanding Student Thinking

Direct students to write down a long-term goal a person might have. Then ask students to explain how a person might reach that goal. (Accept answers that show an understanding of how goals are reached.)

Thinking Skills When students explain how a person might reach a goal, they are *communicating* and *suggesting alternatives*.

Answers to Think Back

1. The goal should be good for you. It should be reachable in ways that are not harmful to others, and it should be realistic.
2. A realistic goal is one that is not too hard or too easy to reach.
3. Setting goals helps a person think about his or her abilities. Thinking about things you are good at builds self-confidence and makes reaching the goal more likely.
4. A plan should include a list of tasks necessary to reach the goal, any problems anticipated in reaching the goal, and solutions to the problems.
5. If a person becomes discouraged, he or she can think about goals reached in the past; think about how it will feel to succeed; divide the goal into smaller parts; promise himself or herself a reward for working at the goal for a certain amount of time; and set up special times to work toward the goal.

Activity Plan

Health Activities Workshop pages 42–43

Activity 1 Strategies
Display the reports on the bulletin board and discuss each goal presented in the reports. Ask if any students have goals similar to those of the people they wrote about.
Thinking Skills By reporting about the goals of famous people, students are *collecting information* and *communicating*.

Activity 2 Strategies
Answers should refer to jobs the person had to do to earn money for the bike.
Thinking Skill By describing how a person might have reached a particular goal, students are *suggesting alternatives*.

Activity 3 Strategies
Possible interviewees include other students, parents, teachers, the principal, and neighbors.
Thinking Skills By interviewing people about their goals, students are *collecting information* and *communicating*.

Activity 4 Strategies
When interviewing classmates about possible career choices, students should try to find out about their interviewees' likes, dislikes, interests, and abilities.
Thinking Skills By interviewing classmates about careers, students are *collecting information* and *communicating*.

Health Activities Workshop

Thinking More About Goals

1. Write a report about a real person who is famous for having set and reached a goal. Such a person might be a scientist, a doctor, an athlete, or an inventor. You can find information about such people in books, encyclopedias, magazines, or newspapers.

2. The picture shows that a young person has just reached a goal of being able to buy a bicycle. Describe what the person might have done to reach that goal.

3. Interview a person you know who has set and reached an important goal. The person could be either young or an adult. Ask the person these questions.

- What goals have you reached?
- How did you feel when you reached your goals?
- What new goals are you working toward?

Looking at Careers

4. "What would you like to be when you grow up?" You have probably heard this question before. Perhaps you have asked it to yourself. Working at a particular career is a major goal and accomplishment in many people's lives. However, deciding on a career and planning how to train for it can be confusing. A **counselor** can help young people make such decisions.

A counselor at a high school might help students try to match their abilities and interests with possible career choices. Often the counselor helps students meet with people who are in various fields of work. These people tell students about their work. To be effective, a counselor keeps up with information about jobs of many kinds and the training needed for each kind of job. A counselor usually has four to six years of college education.

Imagine that you are a counselor. Ask a classmate to act as a student who is meeting with you to discuss career choices. Conduct an interview with the student to find out what possible careers might interest him or her.

For more information write to the American Association for Counseling and Development, 5999 Stevenson Ave., Alexandria, VA 22304.

5. Sometimes people have emotional problems that remain troublesome for a long time, such as not being able to deal with stress. Often, friends, family, or a family physician can help solve these problems. In some cases, a **psychiatrist** might be the most helpful.

A psychiatrist is a medical doctor (M.D.) who has additional training in preventing, finding the cause of, and treating emotional problems. Many people think a psychiatrist is concerned only with people who have serious mental illnesses. This is not true. Today, psychiatrists work to build people's self-confidence and improve self-images. They try to prevent people's problems from growing into serious ones.

A psychiatrist first checks to see that disease, injury, or infection is not the cause of a person's problems. Then the psychiatrist works with the person to learn how he or she thinks, feels, and behaves. To be helpful, a psychiatrist needs to know how the person feels about himself or herself, and how the person gets along with others and treats others.

A career closely related to a psychiatrist's is that of a psychologist. Look in an encyclopedia or other library book to find how these careers are alike and how they are different.

For more information write to the American Psychological Association, Educational Affairs Office, 1200 17th Street NW, Washington, DC 20036.

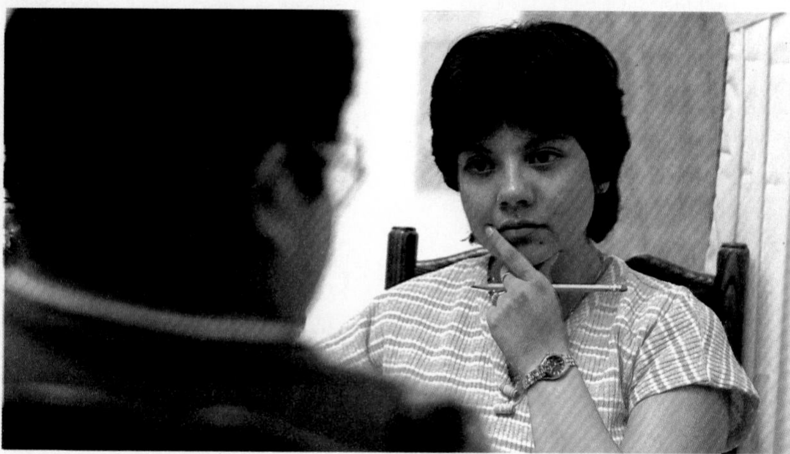

Activity 5 Strategies
Although both careers deal with human relations and emotional and mental problems, a psychologist does not have a medical degree and generally deals with less severe problems than a psychiatrist does.
Thinking Skill By comparing and contrasting careers, students are *organizing information.*

Health Focus page 44

Discussion

Encourage volunteers to describe times they got so involved in a book, television program, or movie that they did not hear someone talking to them. Explain that getting very involved in a project helps a person develop concentration. Point out that when Jasmine Lin concentrated on playing, she was no longer nervous. Encourage students to name some other advantages of being able to concentrate. (keeps a person's mind on the goal instead of the stresses that might be experienced while attaining that goal; helps a person stick with goals)

Answers to Talk About It

1. She won a contest that involved hundreds of other young musicians.
Thinking Skill By telling how Jasmine Lin got a chance to play with the Chicago Symphony, students are *recalling informaton.*

2. Accept answers that show an understanding of how to set realistic goals.
Thinking Skill By listing old goals they have met, and new goals they would like to set, students are *classifying.*

Health Focus

Jasmine Lin Solos with the Chicago Symphony

The curtain rises. On stage the world-famous Chicago Symphony Orchestra begins tuning. As the lights dim, a hush falls over the crowd. The conductor emerges from a side curtain and strides to center stage. Following him is the soloist, twelve-year-old Jasmine Lin. The crowd begins to applaud. As the conductor raises his arms, Jasmine takes up her violin. The music is about to begin.

How did Jasmine come to solo for such a famous symphony at such a young age? She entered a contest with hundreds of other young musicians—and won. Her prize was money for continued music lessons and the honor of playing with the Chicago Symphony Orchestra.

How do you think you would feel about performing in front of a large audience? Like Jasmine, you would probably feel nervous at first. However, once she began playing, Jasmine says she was able to concentrate on the music. She very much enjoyed playing with the orchestra and learning about music from the orchestra members and the conductor.

Encouraged by her success, Jasmine has set new goals. She plans to try to win other music contests. Practicing every day, she says, will help her meet her goals. Listening to others play violin, studying music, and playing duets with her friends also help Jasmine become a better musician.

Setting and meeting goals is something Jasmine does very well. Her advice: Whatever you choose to do, stick with it. Keep working on it every day. With determination, you will likely succeed and feel proud.

Talk About It

1. How did Jasmine Lin get a chance to play with the Chicago Symphony Orchestra?
2. What are some goals for yourself that you have set and met? What are some goals you would like to set now?

44

Teaching Options

Vocabulary

Use this worksheet for practice in reviewing chapter vocabulary words. This master may be reproduced from the Teacher's Resource Book and also is located on page 2 of the Student's Workbook. Use with Chapter 1: pages 18–47.

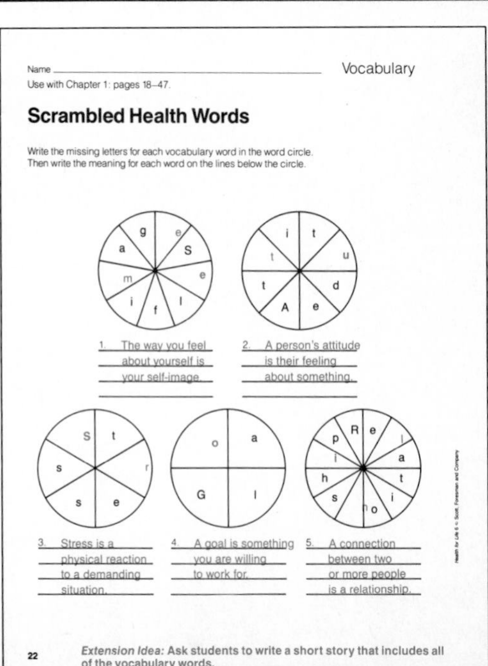

Name ______________________ Vocabulary
Use with Chapter 1: pages 18–47.

Scrambled Health Words

Write the missing letters for each vocabulary word in the word circle. Then write the meaning for each word on the lines below the circle.

1. The way you feel about yourself is your self-image.
2. A person's attitude is their feeling about something.
3. Stress is a physical reaction to a demanding situation.
4. A goal is something you are willing to work for.
5. A connection between two or more people is a relationship.

22

Extension Idea: **Ask students to write a short story that includes all of the vocabulary words.**

Health at Home

Planning Your Study Time

Getting good grades is a goal set by many people your age. To reach this goal, you need time to study. You can plan your study time at home. Begin by answering the following questions about how you study now.

- Do you study every day?
- Do you study at the same time every day?
- Do you do other things while you study, such as watch television, eat, or listen to music?
- Do you take breaks from studying?

You now have enough information to decide whether or not you already plan your study time well. Here are some ideas that can help you improve your study habits.

- Study at the same time every day. You might want to do all your studying at once, or do some work before dinner and the rest right after dinner.
- Try to find a quiet, well-lighted place to study where you will not be bothered by others.
- Do not do anything else while you study.
- Take a break once in a while.
- Review your work in the morning for a few minutes before leaving for school.

You could share these ideas with your family. Other students in your family might want to try to improve their own study habits. Family members who are not students could become more aware of your need for good study habits, and they might be willing to help you work toward this goal.

Reading at Home

Participate in a Group by Judith E. Greenberg and Helen H. Carey. Watts, 1983. Learn how to be a part of a group and how to get along with others.

Secrets of a Small Brother by Richard J. Margolis. Macmillan, 1984. Explore through poems the relationship of two brothers.

Moods and Emotions by Ruth Shannon Odor. Child's World, 1980. Discover the positive and negative feelings people have and ways to recognize those feelings in ourselves.

45

Health at Home
page 45

Strategies
Encourage students to compare the effectiveness of their old study habits with the effectiveness of using the tips on page 47. Suggest that students make a note of the amount of time they spend studying, the number of interruptions, and their grades on tests and assignments. Students might wish to place a list of good study habits in a work area at home to share with the family.

More Reading at Home
Moods and Emotions (Grades 3–6)

Participate in a Group (Grades 5–8)

Secrets of a Small Brother (Grades 2–6)

Naylor, Phyllis Reynolds. *Getting Along with Your Friends.* Abingdon, 1980. Uses a self-help approach to help children learn how to make and get along with friends. (Grades 3–6)

Study and Review
Use this worksheet for practice in reviewing the steps to good decision making. This master may be reproduced from the Teacher's Resource Book and also is located on page 3 of the Student's Workbook. Use with Chapter 1: pages 18–47.

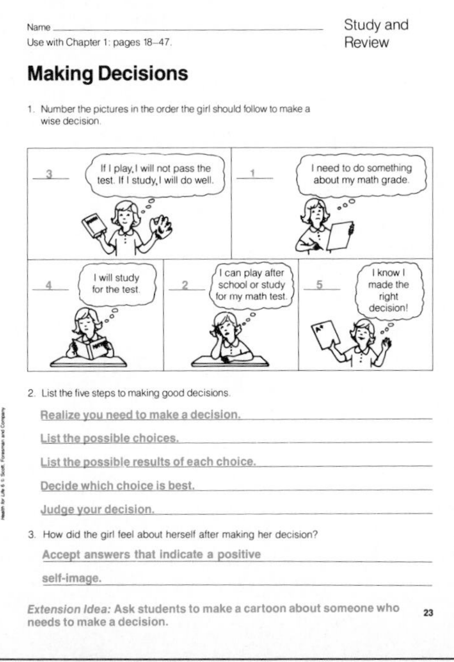

Name ____________ Study and Review

Use with Chapter 1: pages 18–47.

Making Decisions

1. Number the pictures in the order the girl should follow to make a wise decision.

2. List the five steps to making good decisions.

Realize you need to make a decision.

List the possible choices.

List the possible results of each choice.

Decide which choice is best.

Judge your decision.

3. How did the girl feel about herself after making her decision?

Accept answers that indicate a positive self-image.

Extension Idea: Ask students to make a cartoon about someone who needs to make a decision.

23

Chapter 1 Review

pages 46–47

Answers to Reviewing Lesson Objectives

Use this section for guided study or for oral review. Objective numbers match lesson numbers.

1. Students should list characteristics described on page 21 and attitudes on pages 22–23.

2. A person can build good relationships by listening to people, trying to understand how others feel, and by treating others the way they would like to be treated. Good relationships with family and friends are important because they strengthen a person's self-image by making a person feel valued and accepted. Friendships give a person someone with whom to share interests, activities, and attitudes.

3. Stress can be caused by any demanding or exciting situation. Excess stress can cause headaches, stomachaches, change in appetite, nervousness, anger, and problems at school or work. A person can deal with stress by relaxing and using the steps on page 32.

4. Goals that a person sets should be reachable, not harmful to others, and realistic in terms of the person's abilities. In reaching a goal, a person should plan well, get the right amount of help, and keep himself or herself motivated using the tips listed on page 41. Setting goals can improve a person's self-confidence by helping the person to focus on his or her strengths and abilities.

Answers to Checking Health Vocabulary

Use the vocabulary check as a review or as a test.

1. e
2. d
3. a
4. c
5. b
6.–16. Answers will vary but should reflect students' understanding of the meaning of the words as used in the text.

Chapter 1 Review

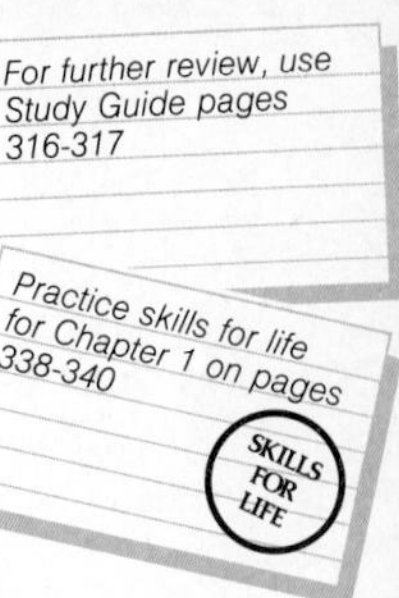

For further review, use Study Guide pages 316-317
Practice skills for life for Chapter 1 on pages 338-340
SKILLS FOR LIFE

Reviewing Lesson Objectives

1. Describe the characteristics of a good self-image. List some attitudes that help improve self-image. (pages 20–23)
2. Explain some ways to build good relationships. Explain why having good relationships with family and friends is important. (pages 26–29)
3. Describe some causes and effects of stress. List some ways of dealing with stress. (pages 30–35)
4. Make a list of guidelines to follow that can help a person set and reach goals. Describe how setting goals can affect a person's self-confidence. (pages 36–41)

Checking Health Vocabulary

Number your paper from 1–5. Match each definition in Column I with the correct word in Column II.

Column I

1. the body's physical and mental reactions to demanding situations
2. the way a person feels about himself or herself
3. a way of thinking about a particular idea, situation, or individual
4. a connection or condition that exists between two or more people
5. something a person wants to do or achieve

Column II

a. attitude
b. goal
c. relationship
d. self-image
e. stress

Number your paper from 6–8. Next to each number write one or two sentences using that word to explain how a person could improve his or her self-image.

6. confidence
7. mistakes
8. unique

Number your paper from 9–16. Next to each number write a sentence about goals using the word or words.

9. short-term goal
10. long-term goal
11. realistic goal
12. abilities
13. plan
14. discouraged
15. reward
16. change

46

Chapter 1 Tests Use Test A or Test B to assess students' mastery of the health concepts in Chapter 1. These tests are located on pages 9–16 in the Test Book.

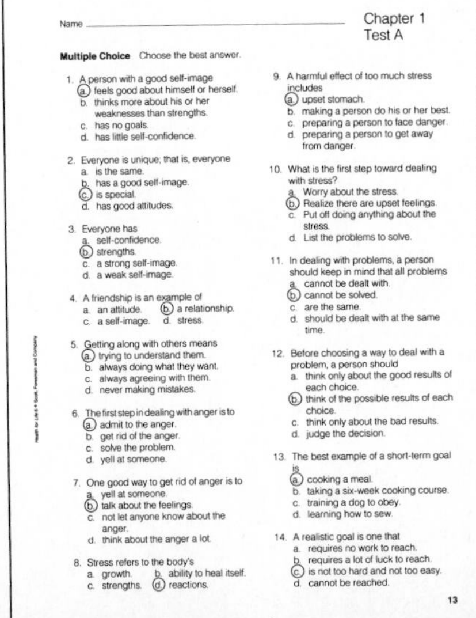

Name ______________________ Chapter 1 Test A

Multiple Choice Choose the best answer.

1. A person with a good self-image
   (a.) feels good about himself or herself.
   b. thinks more about his or her weaknesses than strengths.
   c. has no goals.
   d. has little self-confidence.
2. Everyone is unique; that is, everyone
   a. is the same.
   b. has a good self-image.
   (c.) is special.
   d. has good attitudes.
3. Everyone has
   a. self-confidence.
   (b.) strengths.
   c. a strong self-image.
   d. a weak self-image.
4. A friendship is an example of
   a. an attitude. (b.) a relationship.
   c. a self-image. d. stress.
5. Getting along with others means
   (a.) trying to understand them.
   b. always doing what they want.
   c. always agreeing with them.
   d. never making mistakes.
6. The first step in dealing with anger is to
   (a.) admit to the anger.
   b. get rid of the anger.
   c. solve the problem.
   d. yell at someone.
7. One good way to get rid of anger is to
   a. yell at someone.
   (b.) talk about the feelings.
   c. not let anyone know about the anger.
   d. think about the anger a lot.
8. Stress refers to the body's
   a. growth. b. ability to heal itself.
   c. strengths. (d.) reactions.
9. A harmful effect of too much stress includes
   (a.) upset stomach.
   b. making a person do his or her best.
   c. preparing a person to face danger.
   d. preparing a person to get away from danger.
10. What is the first step toward dealing with stress?
    a. Worry about the stress.
    (b.) Realize there are upset feelings.
    c. Put off doing anything about the stress.
    d. List the problems to solve.
11. In dealing with problems, a person should keep in mind that all problems
    a. cannot be dealt with.
    (b.) cannot be solved.
    c. are the same.
    d. should be dealt with at the same time.
12. Before choosing a way to deal with a problem, a person should
    a. think only about the good results of each choice.
    (b.) think of the possible results of each choice.
    c. think only about the bad results.
    d. judge the decision.
13. The best example of a short-term goal is
    (a.) cooking a meal.
    b. taking a six-week cooking course.
    c. training a dog to obey.
    d. learning how to sew.
14. A realistic goal is one that
    a. requires no work to reach.
    b. requires a lot of luck to reach.
    (c.) is not too hard and not too easy.
    d. cannot be reached.

13

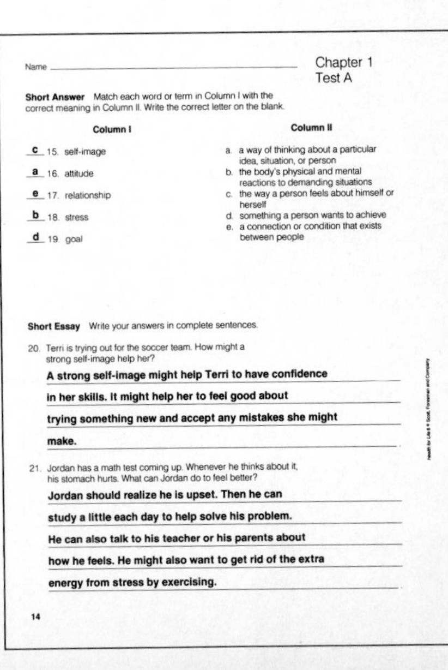

Name ______________________ Chapter 1 Test A

Short Answer Match each word or term in Column I with the correct meaning in Column II. Write the correct letter on the blank.

Column I

__c__ 15. self-image
__a__ 16. attitude
__e__ 17. relationship
__b__ 18. stress
__d__ 19. goal

Column II

a. a way of thinking about a particular idea, situation, or person
b. the body's physical and mental reactions to demanding situations
c. the way a person feels about himself or herself
d. something a person wants to achieve
e. a connection or condition that exists between people

Short Essay Write your answers in complete sentences.

20. Terri is trying out for the soccer team. How might a strong self-image help her?
    A strong self-image might help Terri to have confidence in her skills. It might help her to feel good about trying something new and accept any mistakes she might make.
21. Jordan has a math test coming up. Whenever he thinks about it, his stomach hurts. What can Jordan do to feel better?
    Jordan should realize he is upset. Then he can study a little each day to help solve his problem. He can also talk to his teacher or his parents about how he feels. He might also want to get rid of the extra energy from stress by exercising.

14

Reviewing Health Ideas

Number your paper from 1–15. Next to each number write the word that best completes the sentence.

1. A person who feels good about himself or herself probably has a good ____.
2. A person with a good self-image knows he or she can ____ from mistakes.
3. You are ____, that is, nobody in the world is exactly like you.
4. Everyone has certain ____ and weaknesses.
5. A person has a different ____ with each member of his/her family.
6. A person who wants to be treated with respect should treat others with ____.
7. Keeping ____ feelings locked up inside is not a healthy idea.
8. The first step in dealing with anger is to ____ that you are angry.
9. Stress prepares a person's body to ____ with difficult situations.
10. In dealing with problems, a person should realize that all problems cannot be ____.
11. Learning to relax is one way to help get rid of ____.
12. One exercise that could help a person relax involves ____ in and out deeply.
13. After making a major decision about something, a person should ____ the decision to see if it was really the best one.
14. A ____ goal is not too hard and not too easy.
15. Reaching goals helps build a person's ____.

Understanding Health Ideas

Number your paper from 16–27. Next to each number write the word or words that best answer the question.

16. What is a person's self-image?
17. Why should a person try to figure out why he or she made a certain mistake?
18. What is a relationship?
19. What do friends usually have in common?
20. After admitting that you are angry, what is the next step in dealing with anger in healthy ways?
21. What might a person do to get rid of angry feelings?
22. What is stress?
23. How can stress be helpful?
24. What is one harmful effect of stress?
25. What is the first step in the five-step decision-making process?
26. What are short-term goals?
27. What should be included in a plan for reaching a goal?

Thinking Critically

Write the answers on your paper. Use complete sentences.

1. How would you describe a person with a good self-image?
2. Suppose a friend of yours is very angry about something. How could you help your friend deal with his or her anger?
3. Suppose two friends each invite you to sleep overnight at their houses for the same night. How would you deal with this problem? Use the five steps for making a decision discussed in the chapter.

Answers to Reviewing Health Ideas

1. self-image
2. learn
3. unique
4. strengths
5. relationship
6. respect
7. angry
8. admit
9. deal
10. solved
11. stress
12. breathing
13. judge
14. realistic
15. self-confidence

Answers to Understanding Health Ideas

16. the way a person feels about himself or herself
17. to learn from the mistake and not make the same one again
18. a connection between two or more people
19. interests
20. getting rid of the angry feelings
21. get busy by doing something else and being physically active
22. the body's reaction to demanding situations
23. by preparing the body to deal with difficult situations
24. headache, sleeplessness, upset stomach, loss of appetite
25. realize a decision is needed
26. goals that take a short time to reach
27. a list of tasks, possible problems, solutions for reaching the goal

Answers to Thinking Critically

1. Answers will vary but should include some of the ideas and characteristics found on page 21.
Thinking Skills By describing a person with a good self-image, students are *interpreting information* and *generalizing*.
2. Students might suggest getting the person to admit anger and then helping the person get rid of the angry feelings by talking, exercising, or working on a hobby.
Thinking Skills By listing ways to help a friend deal with angry feelings, students are *interpreting information* and *suggesting alternatives*.
3. Answers will vary, but the process should include the five steps discussed on page 35. Make sure students judge their decisions.
Thinking Skills By using the five-step decision-making process, students are *judging and evaluating* and *making decisions*.

Cooperative Learning Use the STAD Format described on page T24 to have four- to five-member teams study Chapter 1 Review together before completing Chapter 1 Test.

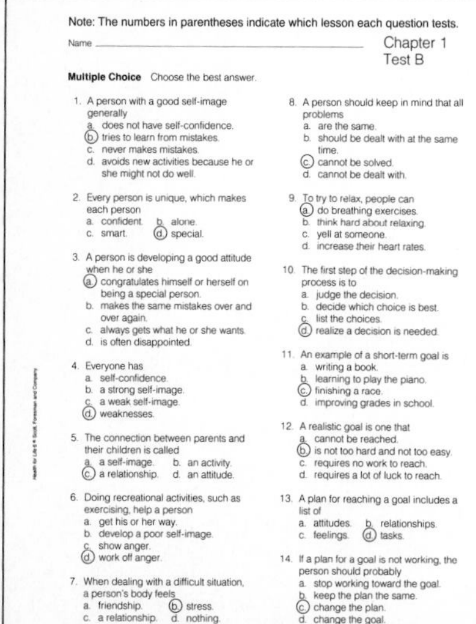

Note: The numbers in parentheses indicate which lesson each question tests.

Name ____________ Chapter 1 Test B

Multiple Choice Choose the best answer.

1. A person with a good self-image generally
   a. does not have self-confidence.
   (b.) tries to learn from mistakes.
   c. never makes mistakes.
   d. avoids new activities because he or she might not do well.
2. Every person is unique, which makes each person
   a. confident. b. alone. c. smart. (d.) special.
3. A person is developing a good attitude when he or she
   (a.) congratulates himself or herself on being a special person.
   b. makes the same mistakes over and over again.
   c. always gets what he or she wants.
   d. is often disappointed.
4. Everyone has
   a. self-confidence.
   b. a strong self-image.
   c. a weak self-image.
   (d.) weaknesses.
5. The connection between parents and their children is called
   a. a self-image. b. an activity. (c.) a relationship. d. an attitude.
6. Doing recreational activities, such as exercising, help a person
   a. get his or her way.
   b. develop a poor self-image.
   c. show anger.
   (d.) work off anger.
7. When dealing with a difficult situation, a person's body feels
   a. friendship. (b.) stress. c. a relationship. d. nothing.
8. A person should keep in mind that all problems
   a. are the same.
   b. should be dealt with at the same time.
   (c.) cannot be solved.
   d. cannot be dealt with.
9. To try to relax, people can
   (a.) do breathing exercises.
   b. think hard about relaxing.
   c. yell at someone.
   d. increase their heart rates.
10. The first step of the decision-making process is to
   a. judge the decision.
   b. decide which choice is best.
   c. list the choices.
   (d.) realize a decision is needed.
11. An example of a short-term goal is
   a. writing a book.
   b. learning to play the piano.
   (c.) finishing a race.
   d. improving grades in school.
12. A realistic goal is one that
   a. cannot be reached.
   (b.) is not too hard and not too easy.
   c. requires no work to reach.
   d. requires a lot of luck to reach.
13. A plan for reaching a goal includes a list of
   a. attitudes. b. relationships. c. feelings. (d.) tasks.
14. If a plan for a goal is not working, the person should probably
   a. stop working toward the goal.
   b. keep the plan the same.
   (c.) change the plan.
   d. change the goal.

15

Name ____________ Chapter 1 Test B

Short Answer Match each word or term in Column I with the correct meaning in Column II. Write the correct letter on the blank.

Column I	Column II
c 15. self-image	a. a way of thinking about a particular idea, situation, or person
a 16. attitude	b. the body's physical and mental reactions to demanding situations
e 17. relationship	c. the way a person feels about himself or herself
b 18. stress	d. something a person wants to achieve
d 19. goal	e. a connection or condition that exists between people

Short Essay Write your answers in complete sentences.

20. Jack practiced for weeks before trying out for football, but he was not chosen to be on the team. How might Jack use this experience to make his self-image stronger?
Jack could congratulate himself for trying something new. He might think about what he does well, accept his weaknesses, and realize that he will not always get what he wants.

21. Why might it be difficult to be friends with everyone one knows?
People must get to know each other before they can become friends. Also, people become friends because they share interests, enjoy the same activities, or share attitudes. Not everyone can share these things.

16

CHAPTER 2 PLANNING GUIDE Pupil Edition

Pupil Edition	Activities	Enrichment	Assessment	Independent Study
Chapter 2 Growing and Changing, pp. 48-73	Health Watch Notebook, p. 48	Health Focus, p. 70 Health at Home, p. 71	Chapter 2 Review, pp. 72-73	Study Guide, pp. 318-319 Skills for Life Handbook, pp. 341-343
Lesson 1 How Are You Growing? pp. 50-52	Health Activities Workshop, p. 53		Think Back, p. 52	Study Guide, p. 318
Lesson 2 How Do Your Endocrine Glands Affect Your Growth? pp. 54-55		Did You Know? p. 54	Think Back, p. 55	Study Guide, p. 318
Lesson 3 How Does Heredity Affect Your Growth? pp. 56-61	Health Activities Workshop, pp. 62-63	Did You Know? pp. 56, 60	Think Back, p. 61	Study Guide, p. 318
Lesson 4 How Do Your Health Decisions Affect Your Growth? pp. 64-65			Think Back, p. 65	Study Guide, p. 319
Lesson 5 How Might Your Emotions and Relationships Change as You Grow? pp. 66-67			Think Back, p. 67	On Your Own, p. 67 Study Guide, p. 319
Lesson 6 How Can You Deal with Growth and Change? pp. 68-69			Think Back, p. 69	Study Guide, p. 319

Teacher Resources

Brandreth, Cyles. *This Is Your Body.* Regent House, 1981. Explores the uniqueness of the human body and growth.

Means, Richard K. *Teaching Health Today.* J. Weston Walch, 1984. Presents a wide variety of techniques for teaching health, including growth and development.

Audio-Visual Resources

See page T43 for addresses of Audio-Visual Sources.

Before using any audio-visual materials, preview them for appropriateness for your students.

The Human Body, National Geographic Society, filmstrip with cassettes. Explains how the endocrine system works and how human life begins and develops.

The Human Endocrine System, Britannica, filmstrip with cassette. Explains the functions of the endocrine system and how it affects the body and health.

The Miracle of Reproduction, 2nd ed., AIMS Media, film or video, 15 minutes. Teaches about the beginning of life and the development of an unborn baby.

The Triangle of Health, Walt Disney, filmstrips with cassettes or records. Teaches students how to develop and maintain their physical, mental, and social well-being.

Computer Software

Heredity Dog. HRM Software. Investigates the principles of heredity.

	Teacher's Edition	Teacher's Resource Book	Test Book
Enrichment	Suggestions for each lesson: L. 1—pp. 50, 52 L. 2—p. 54 L. 3—pp. 56, 58, 60 L. 4—p. 64 L. 5—p. 66 L. 6—p. 68	Family Letter, p. 29 * Life Skills, p. 33 * Health and Mathematics, p. 36	
Reteaching	Suggestions for each lesson: L. 1—pp. 50, 52 L. 2—p. 54 L. 3—pp. 56, 58, 60 L. 4—p. 64 L. 5—p. 66 L. 6—p. 68	Transparency Masters, pp. 31-32 * Vocabulary, p. 34 * Study and Review, p. 35	
Assessment	Expanding Student Thinking: one assessment question per lesson that develops higher-order thinking skills—pp. 52, 55, 61, 65, 67, 69		Chapter 2 Test, Form A, pp. 17-18 Chapter 2 Test, Form B, pp. 19-20

* Also available in Workbook format (Student Edition and Teacher's Edition)

Chapter 2 Poster
A set of posters is available in a separate package. It provides a teaching poster for every chapter, including discussion and activity suggestions on the back. The poster for Chapter 2 is titled "How will you change as you grow?"

Overhead Transparencies
A set of color overhead transparencies is available for Grade 6. You may wish to use Transparencies 1 and 4 to help teach about making good decisions and ways to cope with stress during growth.

Bulletin Board
Draw or cut out shapes or pictures that represent growth and change in people and other living things. Discuss the characteristics of the different stages of growth.

Teaching Plan

Chapter 2 pages 48–73

Chapter Main Idea
Many factors, such as heredity and health decisions, affect the physical, emotional, and social changes of growth.

Chapter Goals
- Accept and appreciate individual differences in growth patterns.
- Express curiosity about heredity.
- Maintain healthy family relationships while developing new friendships outside the family.
- Demonstrate a desire to improve the ability to deal with growth and change.

Lifetime Goal
Make efforts to deal in healthy ways with the physical and emotional changes experienced through life.

Health Vocabulary
Chromosome, DNA, egg cell, endocrine gland, gene, growth spurt, heredity, hormone, ovaries, pituitary gland, puberty, sperm cell, testes

Words to Preteach
Nucleus organ, reproduce, reproductive cell, reproductive gland, self-image, trait

Chapter **2**

Growing and Changing

"Were my feet really ever that small?" You might ask this question if you saw the shoes you wore when you were a baby. You have grown and changed much since then. As the picture suggests, you will grow and change more.

This chapter discusses changes of growth you might be experiencing now or will likely experience in the next few years. You will explore what causes these changes and how you can deal with them as you continue to grow.

Health Watch Notebook

In your notebook, make a family tree, recording the heights of your relatives. Write a paragraph explaining how heredity affects growth.

Teaching Options

Modeling Health Vocabulary
Use this technique to introduce new words as you teach each lesson in this chapter. First, introduce the word. Present the word in two sentences that serve to clearly define the word. One sentence you might use to introduce the term *growth spurt* is the following: *Jack grew more than six inches taller during his growth spurt.* Either read the sentences to the students or write them on the chalkboard. Ask the students to generate two meaningful sentences using the word. Additional successful techniques for introducing new words can be found on page T23.

Cooperative Learning
Jigsaw Format (See page T24.)
Assign the following topics at random to your cooperative learning teams.
Topic A: Explain what happens during the growth spurt.
Topic B: What are the three ways in which heredity determines the growth spurt?
Topic C: How do eating right, exercising, and getting enough sleep help you to grow properly?
Topic D: Explain how a person can set and reach goals.
Have students search for information on their topic as they read the chapter. Then let all students with the same topic meet in an expert group to discuss the information. When students return to their teams, they may take turns presenting their topics to the team. Then give students a test covering all topics to complete individually (Chapter 2 Test A or B in the Test Book). Award Superteam certificates to teams whose average test scores exceed 90%, and Greatteam certificates to teams whose average test scores exceed 80%.

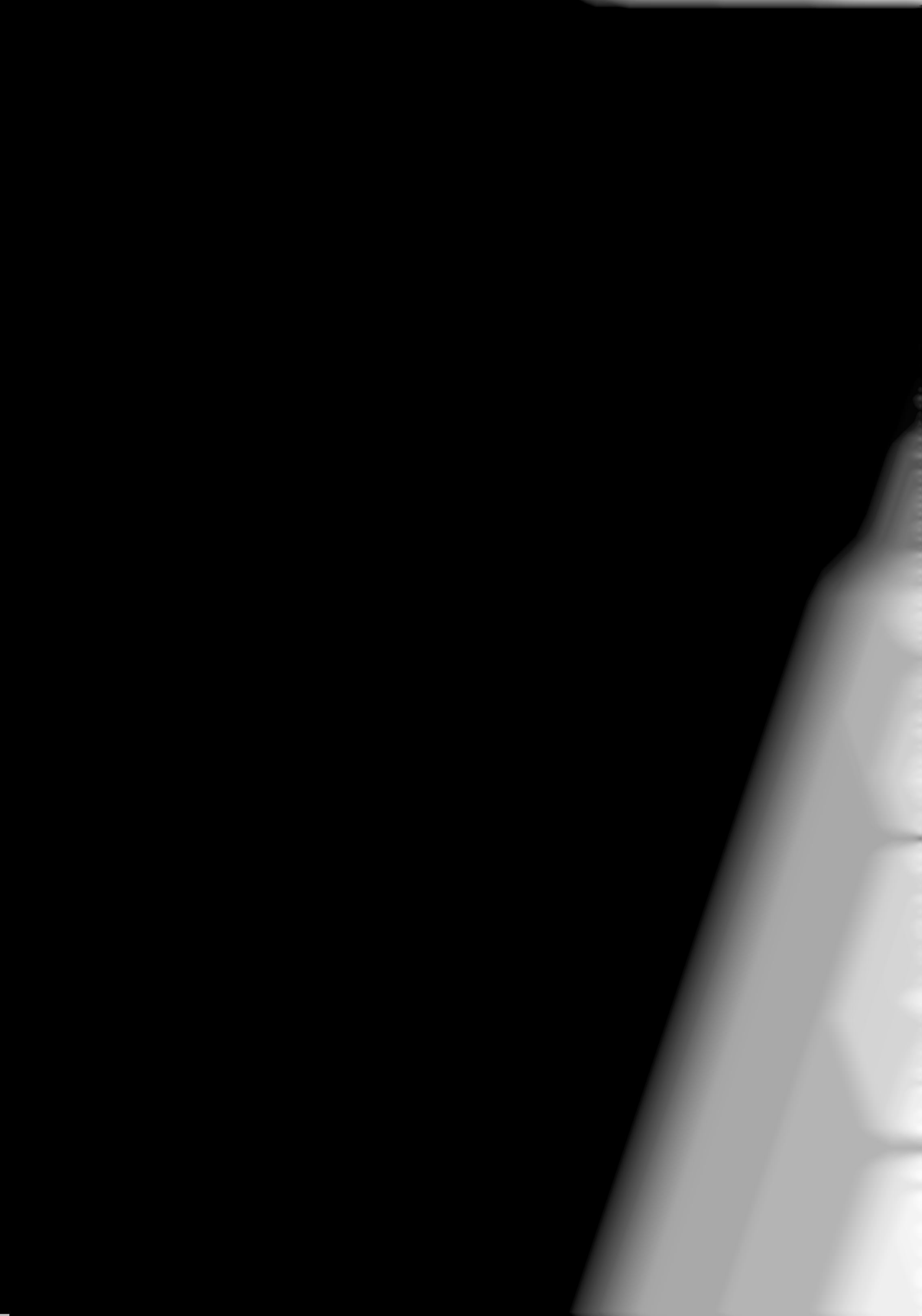

Teaching Plan

Lesson 1 pages 50–52

Lesson Objective
List the physical changes that occur during the growth spurt.

Health Vocabulary
Growth spurt

1 Motivate

Introducing the Lesson
Direct students to look at the picture on pages 50 and 51. Ask students to explain why they think the students in the picture are or are not all about the same age. Discuss the wide range of body sizes that exist for people of every age group. You might want to use some nonhuman examples to point out the variety of size that exists among the same organisms. A field of corn or a lawn, for example, upon close inspection, reveals stalks or blades of many different heights and widths.

1 How Are You Growing?

The picture shows students making scenery for their class play. The picture also gives a clue about the different ways people grow. All the students shown are about the same age. However, they have grown in different ways and are not all the same size. Some students might have grown several inches during the last year. Others might have grown one inch (2.5 cm) last year but will grow two inches this year. Still others might grow only a half-inch over the next two years, then suddenly grow three inches the following year.

These different growth patterns mean that every classroom has students of different heights. You and your classmates have different growth patterns too. Your own growth pattern is just one of the many things that makes you special.

Each person has a different growth pattern.

50

Teaching Options

Health Background

Most children experience a period of rapid growth, or a growth spurt, between nine and fifteen years of age. During this time boys can grow as much as four to twelve inches (10 to 30 cm). Girls' height gains are somewhat less than this. Growth spurts cause the body to use energy more rapidly; therefore, the body requires more food and rest. Research indicates that children have more difficulty studying, concentrating, or withstanding stress during the growth spurt period.

Enrichment
Ask students to investigate curvature of the spine, or scoliosis, that sometimes occurs during the growth spurt. Let a student write to the National Scoliosis Foundation (93 Concord Avenue, Belmont, MA 06178) for information on early detection of the disease. You might want to invite a nurse to class to explain the procedure for detecting scoliosis.

Health and Language Arts
Ask students to write a story describing the feelings of a young person who is growing rapidly, or who is not growing when his or her friends are.

Reteaching
Ask students to bring in old pictures of themselves for display. Discuss ways in which the students have grown since the pictures were taken. You might want to bring in pictures of yourself and join in the discussion.

Special Education
Learning-disabled students who have trouble writing down their thoughts should be allowed to communicate orally what the growth spurt means to them. This communication can take place individually or with a small group of students.

Your body has been growing and changing since before you were born. Old photographs of you would show gains in height and weight over the years. Sometime between the ages of nine and fifteen, however, you will start to grow more quickly. This stage of rapid growth is called a **growth spurt.** It lasts about two to three years. During this time, you might grow as much as five inches (12.5 cm) in a year. You might also gain ten or fifteen pounds (7 kg) in a year. These few extra pounds are a part of growing and do not make a person overweight.

Individuals differ in the age when their growth spurts begin. Girls generally begin their growth spurts at an earlier age than boys. Most girls experience rapid gains in height and weight sometime between the ages of nine and thirteen. Most of this growth usually occurs at age twelve or thirteen. Boys usually begin their growth spurts between the ages of eleven and fifteen. Most of their growth occurs at age fourteen or fifteen. Because of the timing of the growth spurts, many nine- to eleven-year-old boys are shorter than girls their own age. The boys usually catch up later during their own growth spurts.

growth spurt, a period of rapid growth. A growth spurt usually begins between the ages of nine and fifteen.

2 Teach

Strategies for Pages 50 and 51

• Direct students to read page 50 to find out how the young people in the picture have been growing. • Discuss growth patterns and traits that make a person special. (hair color, eye color, and so on) • Help students list some of the changes that occur during the growth spurt. (sudden gains in weight and height) Emphasize that weight gains are normal during the growth spurt. • Ask students to explain how the timing of the growth spurt differs between boys and girls. (Girls generally begin their growth spurts earlier than boys.)

Health and Mathematics

Use this worksheet for practice in averaging numbers. This master may be reproduced from the Teacher's Resource Book and also is located on page 8 of the Student's Workbook. Use with Chapter 2: pages 50–52.

Name ______________________

Use with Chapter 2: pages 50–52.

Health and Mathematics

Average Height and Weight

Use the picture below to help you do each calculation.

To determine the students' average height:
Add all of the heights together.
Divide your answer by the number of students.

To determine the students' average weight:
Add all of the weights together.
Divide your answer by the number of students.

Student	Height	Weight
A	63"(160 cm)	100 lbs. (45 kg)
B	68"(173 cm)	135 lbs. (61 kg)
C	54"(137 cm)	59 lbs. (26 kg)
D	57"(145 cm)	74 lbs. (33 kg)
E	61"(155 cm)	96 lbs. (43 kg)
F	54"(137 cm)	70 lbs. (31 kg)
G	51"(129 cm)	54 lbs. (24 kg)
H	66"(168 cm)	130 lbs. (58 kg)

A B C D E F G H

1. What is the average height of the boys? 60½" (154 cm)
2. What is the average weight of the boys? 92 lbs (41 kg)
3. Are any of the boys average height? No
4. What is the average height of the girls? 58" (147 cm)
5. What is the average weight of the girls? 88 lbs (39 kg)
6. Are any of the girls average weight? No
7. What is the average height of all the students? 59¼" (150 cm)
8. What is the average weight of the students? 89¾ lbs (40 kg)
9. Are any of the students of average height or weight? No
10. Record the heights and weights of the students. What is the average height and weight?

Heights: Answers depend on classroom population. **Average height =** ______

Weights: ______________ **Average weight =** ______

36 *Extension Idea:* Tell the class to collect data from their own class or from another class to find the class's average height and weight.

Teaching Plan

Lesson 1 continued

2 Teach

Strategies for Page 52

• Direct students to read page 52 to find out about body growth. • Direct students to look at the cartoon and discuss why a person is often awkward during a growth spurt. (because changes happen quickly.)

3 Assess

Expanding Student Thinking

Ask students to explain why many nine-to eleven-year old boys are shorter than girls the same age. (Boys usually begin their growth spurts at a later age than girls.)

Thinking Skill Students are *interpreting information.*

Answers to Think Back

1. The body grows rapidly in height and weight during the growth spurt.

2. Girls usually begin their growth spurts earlier than boys. (girls: ages nine to thirteen; boys: ages eleven to fifteen)

3. The feet and hands often grow faster than the legs, arms, and rest of the body.

How Do Different Parts of Your Body Grow?

During the growth spurt, each part of your body grows rapidly toward its adult size. However, this growth does not take place evenly. Different parts of your body grow at different rates. They reach adult size at different times. For example, feet, hands, arms, and legs often grow fastest. They can reach their full adult size before the rest of the body.

The cartoon exaggerates uneven growth. This growth might make a person feel awkward. You might feel as though your legs or arms are too long for your body. Keep in mind that the rest of your body will catch up as your growth continues.

Your growth spurt might have begun in fourth grade, or it might not begin until high school. The timing of your growth spurt will not affect your adult size. However, knowing what to expect during the growth spurt can help you deal with the changes of growth.

Think Back • *Study on your own with Study Guide page 318.*

1. What happens to the body during the growth spurt?
2. How is the timing of the growth spurt usually different between girls and boys?
3. What is an example of uneven growth during the growth spurt?

Different body parts grow at different rates.

Teaching Options

Anecdote

Babies grow very quickly in the first two years of life, gaining an average of ten inches (25 cm) in the first year and five inches (12.5 cm) in the second year. In the third and fourth years, children tend to grow an average of three to four inches (7.5 to 10 cm) per year. From ages five to nine, the rate slows down to an average of two to three inches (5 to 7.5 cm) per year.

Enrichment

Discuss with students some specific ways in which the unevenness of growth patterns can affect daily activities. Some examples might include knocking objects over accidentally, fumbling a ball, and making unusually long strides while walking.

Health and Art

Ask students to examine examples of cartoons. Suggest that students examine editorial cartoons in newspapers as well as cartoon characters on TV and in comics. Point out that many cartoon characters have exaggerated body parts or body proportions.

Reteaching

Ask students to write a paragraph explaining why a person who is not good at sports at age twelve might be better at sports by the time he or she is sixteen years old.

Health Activities Workshop

Thinking About Growing

1. As you grow, your body proportions change. Different parts of the body become larger or smaller in comparison to the rest of the body. You can investigate this comparison. For each person shown below, measure the length of the head and compare it to the total body length. How does this comparison change as a person grows?

2. Write a poem about growth. The poem might describe what happens as a person grows, or it might describe some of your feelings about growing.

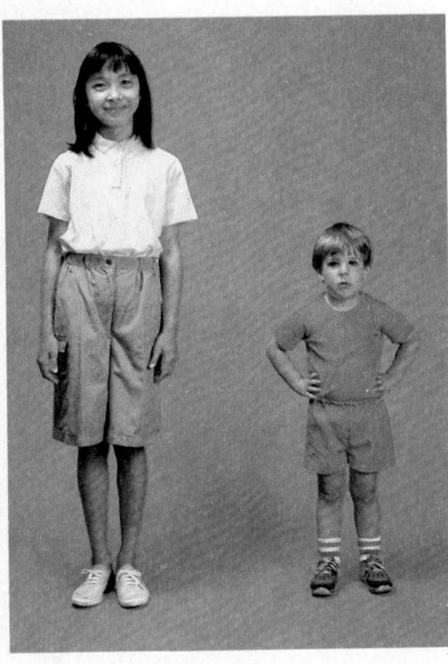

Looking at Careers

3. You have read about some changes that occur during growth. The proper, healthy growth of people your age is a major concern of a **pediatrician.** A pediatrician is a physician who specializes in the care of young people—from infants to teenagers.

A person who wants to be a pediatrician, or any other kind of physician, must attend school for seven to nine years after high school. This education includes three or four years of college, four years of medical school, and at least one year that combines classroom instruction with actual medical practice in hospitals and clinics. Many physicians train for an additional three years to become specialists, such as pediatricians.

Make a list of various kinds of physicians, including pediatricians. You might want to look up "Physicians" in an encyclopedia to find a list. Write what each kind of physician does.

For more information write to the American Academy of Pediatrics, 141 Northwest Point Road, Elk Grove Village, IL 60007.

Activity Plan

Health Activities Workshop page 53

Activity 1 Strategies

Students might also want to measure and compare their own head and body lengths. For very young children the head is usually one-fourth the length of the body. For older children the head is usually one-sixth or one-seventh the length of the body. For adults the head is usually about one-eighth the length of the body.

Thinking Skills By comparing head lengths to total body lengths, students are *interpreting* and *organizing information.*

Activity 2 Strategies

Encourage students to read their poems to the class. You might suggest that students decorate or illustrate their poems. The class poems can be gathered into a booklet. Poems on appropriate health topics could be added to the booklet throughout the year.

Thinking Skill By writing poems about growth, students are *suggesting alternatives.*

Activity 3 Strategies

Ask students what they think they might like about being a pediatrician. Ask what they would dislike. If possible, invite a pediatrician to visit the class to discuss some of the topics presented in the chapter. Discuss with students the medical problems with which various kinds of physicians might deal. A partial list of various kinds of physicians includes: anesthesiologist—administers anesthetics; cardiologist—treats heart disorders; dermatologist—treats skin disorders; ophthalmologist—treats eye diseases; orthopedist—treats diseases of the bones and joints; otolaryngologist—treats ear, nose, and throat diseases; radiologist—uses X rays to diagnose and treat disease.

Thinking Skill By finding out what different kinds of physicians do, students are *collecting information.*

Teaching Plan

Lesson 2 pages 54–55

Lesson Objective
Describe the physical changes caused by the hormones of the pituitary and reproductive glands.

Health Vocabulary
Egg cell, endocrine gland, hormone, ovaries, pituitary gland, puberty, sperm cell, testes

1 Motivate
Introducing the Lesson
Discuss with students the meaning of the word *team.* (A group of individuals working together for a common goal.) Help students name organs of the body that might be called a team. (Answers might include the circulatory system, made up of the heart, arteries, and veins; or the respiratory system, made up of the nose, mouth, windpipe, and lungs.) Explain that another group of organs called the endocrine glands works as a team to control the body's growth and development.

endocrine (en′dō krən) **gland,** an organ that produces chemicals and releases them directly into the blood.

hormone (hôr′mōn), a chemical, made by an endocrine gland, that affects how body cells work.

pituitary (pə tü′ ə ter′ē) **gland,** the endocrine gland that makes growth hormone and other hormones that control the activities of other endocrine glands.

Did You Know?
A condition known as pituitary dwarfism occurs when the pituitary gland produces too little growth hormone. People with this condition seldom grow taller than thirty-five to forty inches (90-100 cm). Scientists have recently learned how to produce growth hormone in the laboratory. The use of this artificial growth hormone will help to reduce the effects of pituitary dwarfism. Up to now, the supply of growth hormone was limited because it had to be taken from pituitary glands.

2 How Do Your Endocrine Glands Affect Your Growth?

You have learned that your body grows rapidly during the growth spurt. What causes this rapid growth? Part of the answer lies within a few tiny organs in your body.

Your growth is directed by a team of organs—the **endocrine glands.** The drawings show the location of some of these glands. The endocrine glands make chemicals called **hormones.** The hormones are released into the blood and carried to cells throughout your body. The hormones control how some parts of your body work. For example, some hormones cause your body to grow in height and weight. Other hormones cause other changes of growth.

The **pituitary gland** affects your growth more than any other gland. The pituitary gland is located at the base of your brain and is about the size of a pea. This tiny gland produces many kinds of hormones. One of these is growth hormone, which directs bone and muscle growth. Your growth spurt begins when your pituitary gland starts making a certain amount of growth hormone. When the pituitary gland stops making so much of this hormone, your growth stops, and you have reached your adult height.

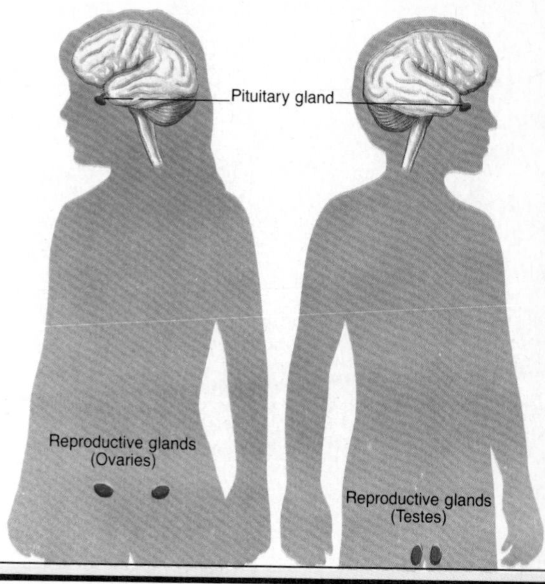

How do these endocrine glands affect growth?

Teaching Options

Health Background
A gland is an organ that separates substances from the blood, changes the substances, and secretes them for use in the body. Endocrine glands are glands from which secretions (hormones) pass directly into the bloodstream or lymph instead of into a duct.

Both male and female sex hormones affect growth centers in the bones, gradually bringing bone growth to a halt. For this reason children who go through puberty early might temporarily be the tallest in the class, but those who go through puberty later might outgrow them.

Enrichment
Ask interested students to find out about other hormones produced by the pituitary gland. Let them report their findings to the class.

Health and Art
Let students make posters showing the location of the pituitary gland and the parts of the body it controls. Some students might wish to show the location of various glands on an outline of the body.

Reteaching
Let students make a chart indicating the effect of the pituitary gland on other parts of the body.

The pituitary produces hormones that control the actions of many other glands. For example, the pituitary gland releases hormones that cause the reproductive glands to become more active. As the reproductive glands become more active, many important changes occur inside and outside the body.

Inside the body the testes in boys begin producing **sperm cells.** The ovaries in girls begin developing **egg cells.** The sperm and eggs are reproductive cells. The development of these cells gives a male or female the ability to reproduce, or have children.

As the testes and ovaries become more active, they begin making hormones of their own. These hormones cause the body to develop several adultlike features. For example, notice in the drawings how the body develops a more adultlike shape. Other changes include a deepening of the voice and the growth of body hair.

The time of life when these body changes take place is called **puberty.** Like the growth spurt, puberty begins at different ages for different people. Puberty usually begins in girls between the ages of eleven and fifteen. The changes of puberty usually begin in boys between the ages of twelve and sixteen.

Think Back • *Study on your own with Study Guide page 318.*

1. How does the pituitary gland affect growth?
2. What are the reproductive glands called in boys? in girls?
3. What changes occur as the reproductive glands become active?

testes (tes′tēz′) *sing.* **testis** (tes′ tis′) male reproductive glands.

sperm (spėrm) **cell,** the male reproductive cell.

ovaries (ō′vər ēz), female reproductive glands.

egg cell, the female reproductive cell.

puberty (pyü′bər tē), a period of time when the body develops more adultlike qualities, including the ability to reproduce.

The body changes shape during puberty.

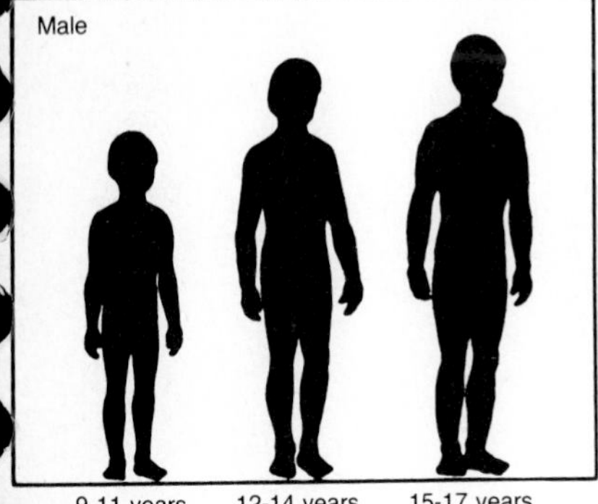

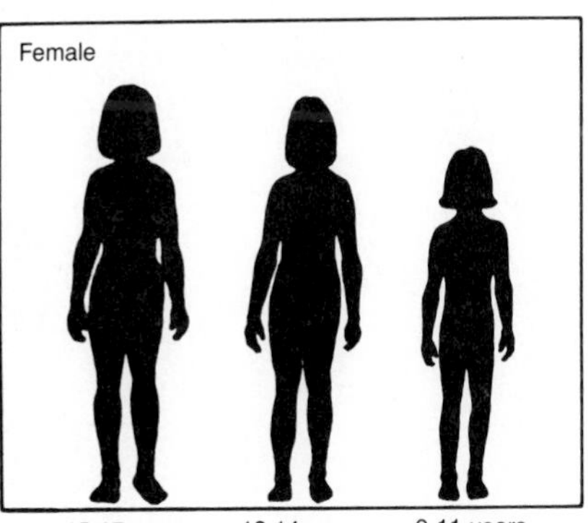

55

2 Teach

Strategies for Pages 54 and 55

• Direct students to read page 54 to find out about endocrine glands and hormones. • Ask students to locate and name the endocrine glands shown in the drawings on page 54. • Discuss the ***Did You Know?*** with students. Explain, that in order to be effective, the chemical mentioned must be given during the normal growth period. • Direct students to read page 55 to find out another important function of the pituitary gland.

3 Assess

Expanding Student Thinking

Ask students why the pituitary gland is sometimes called the *master gland.* (because it produces hormones that tell other glands what to do)

Thinking Skill When students explain why the pituitary gland is sometimes called the master gland, they are *drawing conclusions.*

Answers to Think Back

1. The pituitary gland makes hormones that direct bone and muscle growth. This gland also makes hormones that direct the other glands.
2. The reproductive glands are the testes in boys and ovaries in girls.
3. Changes include a deepening of the voice, new hair growth, more adultlike body shape, and the ability to reproduce.

Overhead Transparency Master

Use this blackline master to make a labeled overhead transparency or to make an unlabeled student worksheet. This blackline master may be reproduced from the Teacher's Resource Book.

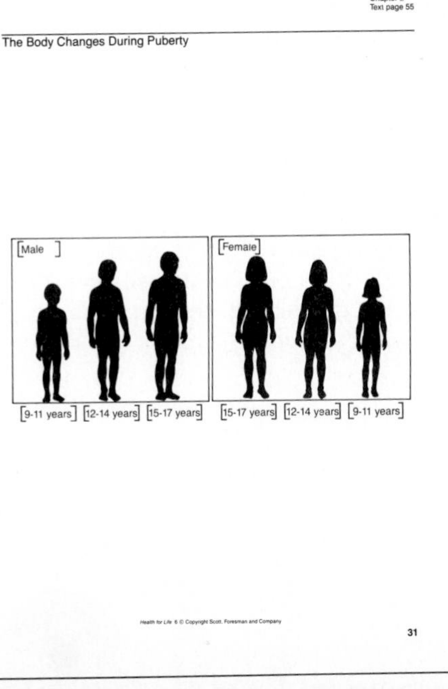
Chapter 2
Text page 55

The Body Changes During Puberty

31

Teaching Plan

Lesson 3 pages 56–61

Lesson Objective
Explain how heredity influences growth patterns and other inherited traits.

Health Vocabulary
Chromosome, DNA, gene, heredity

1 Motivate

Introducing the Lesson
Ask volunteers to suggest ways in which they are like their parents. (Answers might include same color hair, same color eyes, or similar nose.) Help students understand that these traits are inherited. If you have students who are adopted, you might show pictures of famous people and their parents or their children and ask how these parents and children are similar.

heredity (hə red′ə tē), the passing of traits from parents to children.

Did You Know?
Scientists estimate that each human body cell contains between two and three million genes.

3 How Does Heredity Affect Your Growth?

Chris noticed something interesting as his father and uncles were posing for a picture at the family reunion. They were all tall men. In fact, Chris was one of the tallest boys in his class. When he asked his father why most of the males in the family were tall, his father replied, "I guess it's our heredity."

What did Chris's father mean when he spoke about heredity? **Heredity** is defined as the passing on of certain traits from parents to their children. Some inherited traits are eye color, nose shape, the time the growth spurt begins, and adult height. Your mother and father shared in giving you inherited traits.

Shaded figures in Chris's family tree show the ancestors who were taller than the average height. Notice that this trait is more common on the father's side of the family. The trait of being tall was passed on from one generation to the next. Chances are that Chris will also be taller than the average adult male.

The trait of tallness has passed from one generation to the next.

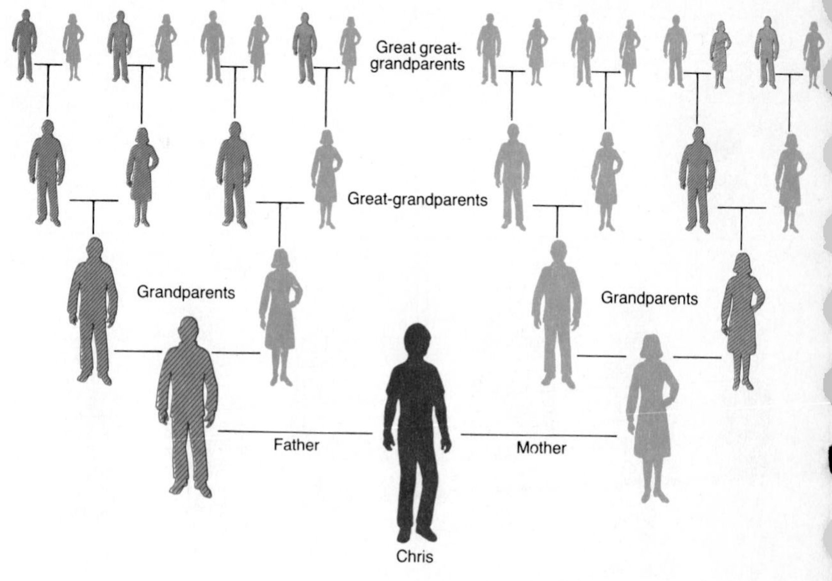

56

Teaching Options

Health Background

Heredity is one factor that determines when the growth spurt begins and ends and how fast the individual will grow during the growth spurt.

Each person inherits genes for every inherited trait. For some traits the genes from one parent might be stronger than the genes from the other. The stronger genes are dominant. The weaker genes are recessive. The presence of a dominant gene will reveal itself in the child's characteristics. The recessive gene will only reveal itself if both parents contribute recessive genes.

Enrichment

Ask students to look in encyclopedias or books on scientific breakthroughs to find out about the discovery of DNA. Let them share their findings with the class.

Health and Art

Ask students to find out more about the parts of a body cell. Let students draw a body cell, labeling the parts and identifying their functions.

Reteaching

Help students make a model of a body cell. Fill a clear-plastic bag (the cell membrane) with gelatin. Use a plum or grape for the nucleus. Other fruits or parts of fruits can be used to stand for other structures in a cell.

What Determines Your Heredity?

The material that determines your heredity is found deep within the body cells. Almost every cell in your body has a central part called a nucleus. The nucleus controls the cell's activities.

Inside the nucleus are strands of matter called **chromosomes.** Each chromosome is made of a chemical substance known as **DNA.** The drawing shows that the structure of DNA looks like a spiraling ladder. The chemical structure of the DNA determines your inherited traits and your heredity. The portion of DNA that affects only one trait is a **gene.** The genes on your chromosomes are a combination of the genes from your mother and father.

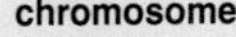

chromosome (krō′mə sōm), a strand of matter in the nucleus of a cell that contains the information for a person's heredity.

DNA, a chemical substance that makes up chromosomes and determines inherited traits.

gene (jēn), a small part of a chromosome that influences a specific inherited trait.

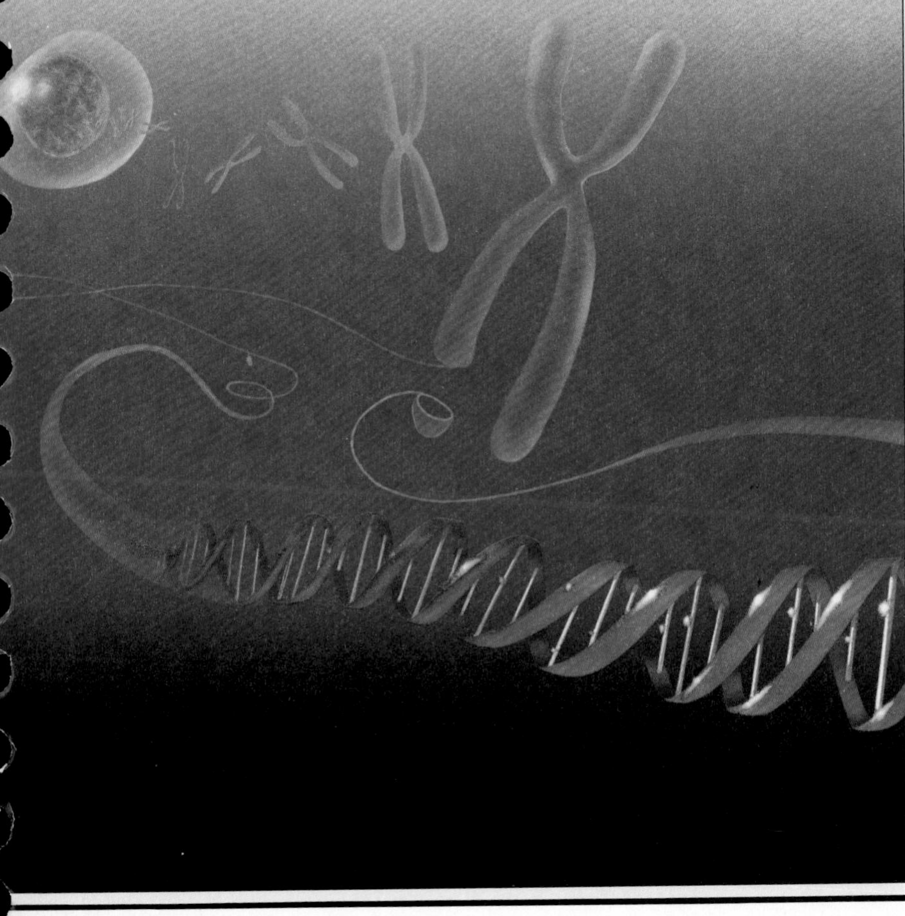

2 Teach

Strategies for Pages 56 and 57

• Direct students to read page 56 to find out what heredity is and how it affects growth. • Discuss the illustration of Chris's family tree. • Some students might want to draw their own family trees for a trait such as eye color, hair color, or height. • Encourage students to explain what a genealogist does. (tries to put together family trees that go back several generations) • Ask what sources a genealogist might use to obtain such information. (birth, death, and marriage certificates; wills, letters, and other written records)
• Review the structure of a body cell and the function of the nucleus.
• Then ask students to read page 57 to learn more about heredity. • Write the terms *chromosome, DNA,* and *gene* on the chalkboard. Be sure students understand the meanings of these terms.

Teaching Plan

Lesson 3 continued

2 Teach

Strategies for Pages 58 and 59

• Direct students to read page 58 to find out how reproductive cells and other cells divide. • Ask students to compare cell division of body cells with that of reproductive cells. (When body cells begin to divide, the chromosomes in the nucleus make exact copies of themselves. The cell then divides just once, so that each new cell has the same number of chromosomes as the original. When reproductive cells divide, the chromosomes usually exchange portions of their DNA. The cell divides twice, although the chromosomes do not make copies of themselves prior to the second division. Therefore, each of the four resulting egg or sperm cells has only half the number of chromosomes as the original cell.)

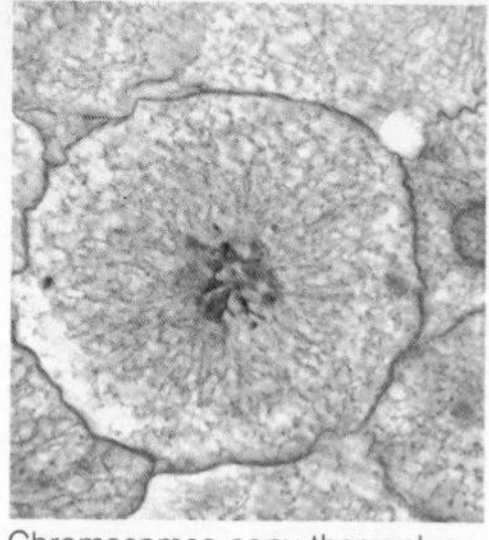
Chromosomes copy themselves and thicken.

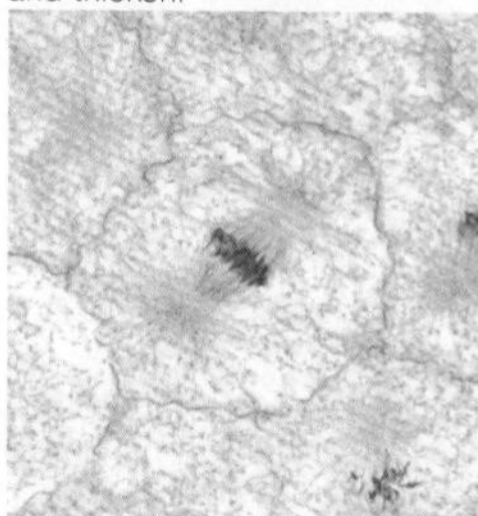
Chromosomes line up.

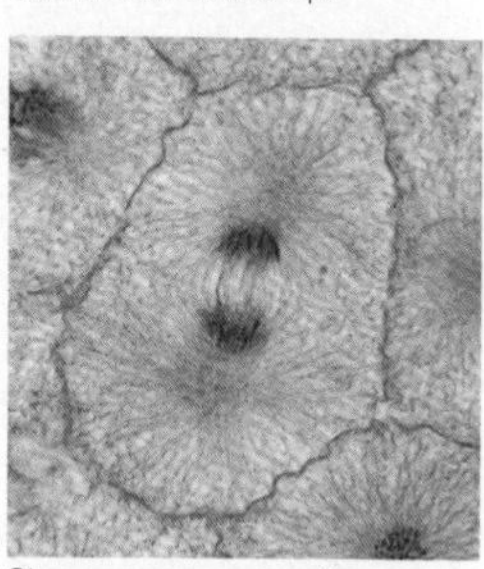
Chromosomes separate.

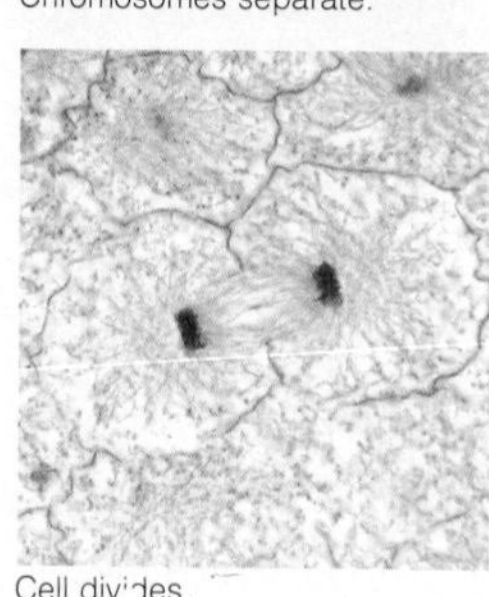
Cell divides.

How Do Chromosomes Pass from Parent to Child?

Almost every cell in your body has forty-six chromosomes. When a cell grows to a certain point, it divides, as shown in the pictures. First, the chromosomes make exact copies of themselves. The chromosomes thicken and the boundary of the nucleus begins to break down. Then, the chromosomes line up in the center of the cell. Next, the copies separate and move to opposite sides of the cell. Finally, the cell divides. Each new cell has forty-six chromosomes like those that were in the original cell.

A reproductive cell, however, grows and divides in a more complicated way than other cells. After the chromosomes make copies of themselves, the reproductive cell divides. Then, each of the two new cells divides again, resulting in four cells, as the drawing shows. This second division takes place without the chromosomes making copies of themselves. Therefore, each of the four sperm or egg cells has only twenty-three chromosomes.

When an egg and sperm cell unite, the twenty-three chromosomes in the sperm cell join the twenty-three chromosomes in the egg cell. The egg now contains forty-six chromosomes and is called a fertilized egg.

This fertilized egg divides and eventually develops into a baby whose cells have forty-six chromosomes. Half of the baby's chromosomes come from the mother, and half of the chromosomes come from the father. These chromosomes contain the information for the child's inherited traits.

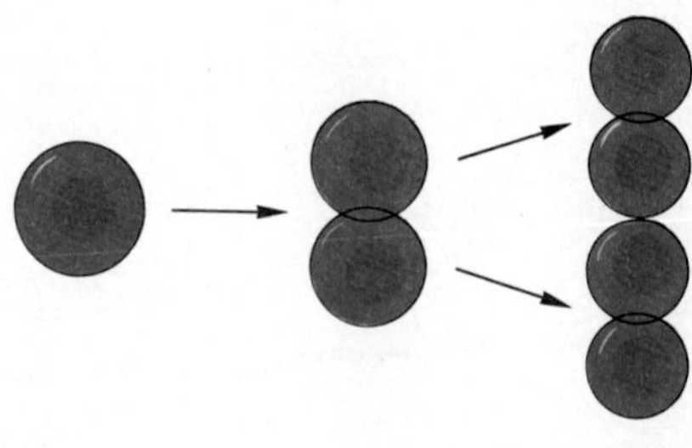
How is the division of a reproductive cell different from other cells?

58

Teaching Options

Anecdote

The DNA of all four billion people alive today could fit on a teaspoon and would weigh less than one twenty-fifth of an ounce (about 1 g). (Bodanis, David. *The Body Book*. Little, Brown, 1984.)

Enrichment

Ask students to use the library to learn about dominant and recessive traits. Guide them to use this information to understand how two brown-eyed parents can produce a blue-eyed child.

Health and Science

Ask students to survey the class to compare the frequency of the following traits: ability or inability to roll the tongue, attached or unattached earlobes, widow's peak or no widow's peak, freckles or no freckles. Let them chart the results. (The ability to roll the tongue, unattached earlobes, a widow's peak, and freckles are dominant traits and, therefore, more frequent.)

Reteaching

Ask students to draw the steps in cell division of a body cell and of a reproductive cell. Tell the students they need to show only two or three chromosomes.

What Determines Whether a Person Is a Boy or a Girl?

The pictures below show the chromosomes from a boy and a girl. To make these pictures, chromosomes from the skin cells of two people were photographed under a microscope. Then, each picture was cut up, and the chromosomes were arranged into twenty-three pairs for each person. Notice the last pair in each picture. These chromosomes are the sex chromosomes. They determine the person's sex. In a female, both sex chromosomes are called X chromosomes. In a male, one sex chromosome is an X and the other is a Y.

An unfertilized egg cell or a sperm cell carries only one chromosome from each of the twenty-three pairs shown in the pictures. Therefore, each egg or sperm cell has only one sex chromosome. The sex chromosome in an egg cell is always an X. The sex chromosome in a sperm cell can be an X or a Y.

The drawing to the right shows what happens if a sperm with an X chromosome unites with an egg cell. The sex chromosomes of the offspring will be XX, and the baby will be a girl. If a sperm with a Y chromosome unites with an egg cell, the sex chromosomes will be XY. The baby will be a boy.

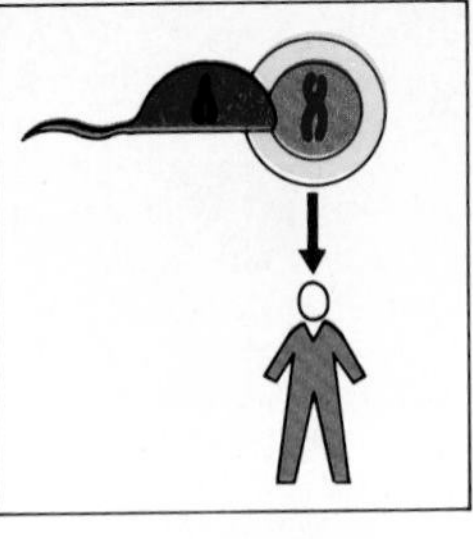

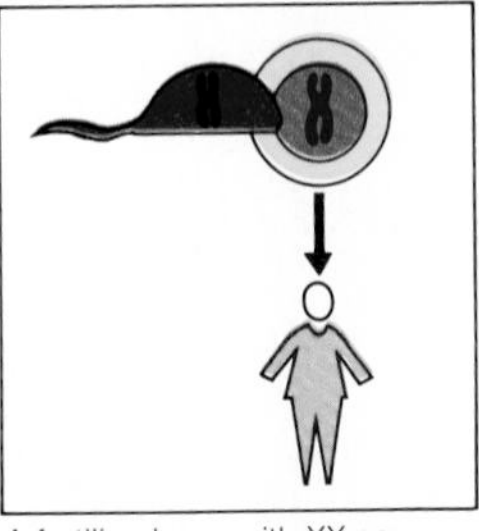

A fertilized egg with XX sex chromosomes will develop into a girl.

A fertilized egg with XY sex chromosomes will develop into a boy.

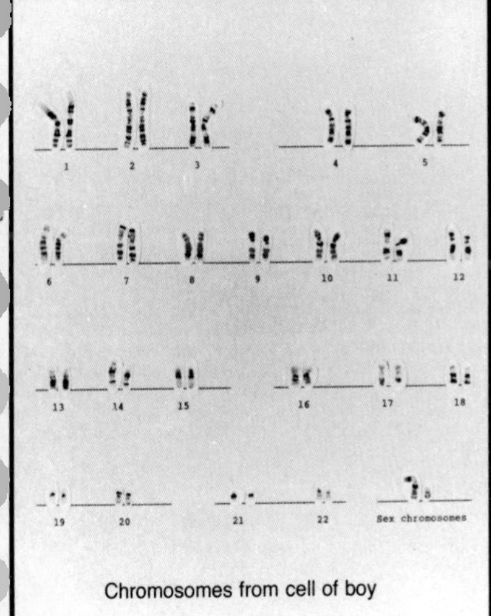

Chromosomes from cell of boy

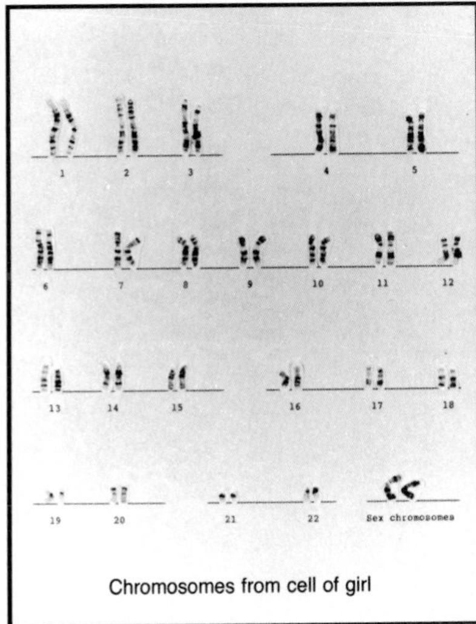

Chromosomes from cell of girl

59

• Guide students to understand that sperm and egg cells have only twenty-three chromosomes each, instead of forty-six. When the sperm and egg join, the fertilized egg cell has the full number of chromosomes. Be sure students understand the difference between a fertilized and an unfertilized egg cell. • Explain that, although half the child's chromosomes come from the mother and half come from the father, the expression of those traits is not always half and half. In other words, a child might resemble one parent more than the other. • Ask students to read page 59 to find out how the sex of a child is determined. • Discuss the illustrations. Ask students which sex cell determines whether a person will be a boy or a girl. Students should understand that the male sex cell (sperm) carries the determining chromosome.

Teaching Plan

Lesson 3 continued

2 Teach

Strategies for Pages 60 and 61

• Direct students to study the picture on page 60 and point out ways in which the three sisters are alike and ways they are different. • Discuss which traits the children seem to have inherited from their father and which from their mother. • Direct students to read page 60 to find out why children in a family differ in various ways.
• Lead students to understand that the thousands of genes on each chromosome mean that many combinations of genes are possible.
• Direct students to read page 61 to learn three ways heredity affects growth patterns. • Ask students to describe how heredity affects growth patterns. (Heredity influences when the growth spurt begins, how fast a person grows, and when the growth spurt ends.)

Did You Know?
Identical twins are the few people who do inherit the same genes from their parents. Identical twins grow from the same fertilized egg cell. In some special way, the fertilized egg separates into two parts, forming two separate, but identical, babies.

Why Do Individuals in a Family Differ?

Different sex chromosomes explain why some people in a family are male and some are female. Yet, even people of the same sex are very different from each other. Why do the sisters in the picture have different traits even though their chromosomes and genes came from the same parents?

Teaching Options

Enrichment

Before assigning this activity, consider the sensitivities of students who are adopted or of a race different from most members of the class.

Ask volunteers to bring to class at least three photographs of past or present family members. Collect and shuffle the photographs. Then help the class sort the photographs into families. Use the photographs to decide whether members of each family inherited the same traits.

Special Education

For learning-disabled students who need a concrete experience, try to have a model of a cell available for students to see and touch.

Reteaching

Ask students to bring in baby pictures of themselves. Post the pictures with a number next to each. Encourage students to try to identify the pictures by matching traits such as shape of eye, nose, mouth, and ear.

The growth and division of reproductive cells gives each reproductive cell a different set of chromosomes. Every child in a family received forty-six chromosomes from the parents, but not the *same* forty-six chromosomes. Each child is likely to have different inherited traits because each child received different chromosomes with different DNA and genes.

How Does Heredity Affect Growth Patterns?

Heredity affects growth patterns in three major ways. First, heredity determines when the growth spurt begins. Certain genes direct the pituitary gland to begin producing more growth hormone. Second, heredity influences how fast a person grows during the growth spurt. Third, heredity helps determine when the growth spurt stops. Genes direct the pituitary gland to stop producing so much growth hormone. At this point, a person has reached full adult height and weight. A person's weight will probably continue to change, but the height will stay the same throughout most of his or her adult life.

The series of pictures shows two brothers at various stages of growth. They have inherited some similar genes, but they did not inherit *all* the same genes. Different heredities gave each of them a different growth pattern. Notice how their heights differed as they grew.

Your growth pattern is part of the heredity that makes you a special person.

Think Back • *Study on your own with Study Guide page 318.*

1. How do a sperm and an egg cell provide a person's inherited traits?
2. Why do children in a family have different inherited traits?
3. In what three ways does heredity affect growth patterns?

Different heredities gave these brothers different growth patterns.

3 Assess

Expanding Student Thinking

Show students a photograph of a parent and child. Ask students to write a paragraph explaining what traits the child inherited from the parent. (Answers will vary depending on characteristics shown in the photographs.)

Thinking Skill When students write the paragraph they are *interpreting information.*

Answers to Think Back

1. A sperm and egg cell each carry twenty-three chromosomes. When the sperm and egg unite, a cell with forty-six chromosomes forms. These forty-six chromosomes determine the inherited traits of the baby that develops from the cell.

2. Each child received different chromosomes and genes from the parents.

3. Heredity affects growth patterns by influencing when the growth spurt begins, how fast a person grows during the growth spurt, and when the growth spurt ends.

Activity Plan

Health Activities Workshop pages 62–63

Activity 1 Strategies

Identical twins develop from a single fertilized egg. The egg grows into a mass of cells that splits in two. The two cell masses have the same genes. Fraternal twins develop from two eggs that were fertilized by different sperm. Therefore, the two developing cell masses have different genes, as do most other offspring. Point out that identical twins are always of the same sex. Students might be interested in finding out more about studies that have been made of the influence of heredity and environment on identical twins. Encourage these students to look for magazine articles on this subject and share their findings with the class.

Thinking Skills By finding out how identical and fraternal twins differ, students are *collecting* and *organizing information.*

Activity 2 Strategies

Students might point out similar skin tones, mouth and nose shape, and hair color. You might want to bring in other pictures of famous paintings of families and have students repeat the activity with each painting.

Thinking Skill When students observe the details in the picture, they are *interpreting information.*

Health Activities Workshop

Investigating Heredity and Growth

1. Use a life science text or an encyclopedia to find out how identical twins differ from fraternal twins.

2. The picture shows a famous painting by the French artist Pierre Renoir. What are some traits that the child seems to have inherited from her mother?

Pierre Auguste Renoir, On The Terrace, 1881, oil on canvas, 39⅜" by 31½", Mr. and Mrs. Lewis L. Coburn Memorial Collection 33.455.

62

Looking at Careers

3. A **geneticist** is a scientist who studies the inheritance and traits of living things. Some geneticists experiment with the genetic makeup of certain plants and animals to develop breeds, or types, that better serve human needs. For example, a plant geneticist might try to develop a type of corn that has better flavor or that can resist disease better. Other geneticists develop different breeds of farm animals, such as cattle or chickens, that grow more quickly or produce better meat. Medical geneticists work to prevent inherited diseases. They try to discover how certain substances affect human genes.

Like all scientists, a geneticist usually has at least seven years of college education.

Use an encyclopedia or a library book about genetics to find out how a plant geneticist develops different kinds of plants. What fruits and vegetables available today are the result of the work of geneticists?

For more information write to the American Society of Human Genetics, St. Christopher's Hospital for Children, 2600 N. Lawrence St., Philadelphia, PA 19133.

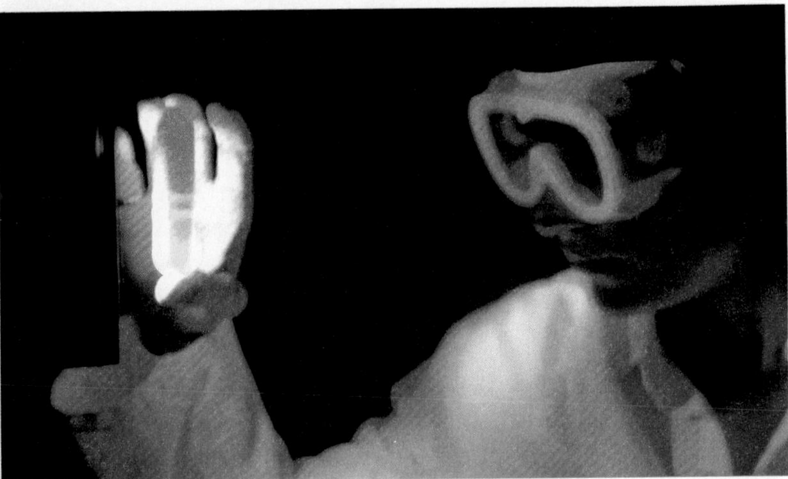

Activity 3 Strategies
Answers should refer to how a geneticist cross-pollinates plants by transferring the pollen from one plant to another. Virtually all kinds of fruits and vegetables available in a supermarket are varieties that have been developed through knowledge of genetics.
Thinking Skill When students find out about the work of geneticists they are *collecting information.*

Teaching Plan

Lesson 4 pages 64–65

Lesson Objective
Give examples of health decisions that affect growth, and explain the importance of sleep, rest, and physical activity.

1 Motivate

Introducing the Lesson
Remind students of the importance of heredity in determining growth patterns. Ask students to think of other factors that might influence growth. (nutrition, exercise, and general health)

2 Teach

Strategies for Pages 64 and 65
• Direct students to read page 64 to find out how diet can affect growth.
• Ask students to describe a healthy breakfast, lunch, and dinner for a growing body. (Answers should include a variety of foods from the four food groups and a limited number of sweet or fatty foods.) • Direct students to read page 65 to find out how health decisions affect a person's weight, body shape, and muscle development.

4 How Do Your Health Decisions Affect Your Growth?

Your heredity and your endocrine glands are not the only factors that affect your growth. Your health decisions have a strong influence on how you grow. You cannot control the actions of your heredity or your endocrine system. However, you can make decisions that influence your health and growth.

Your heredity sets limits for your growth. The pictures on these two pages show some of the health decisions that affect your growth within those limits. For example, the genes you inherit might set an upper boundary of five feet nine inches (about 175 cm) for your adult height. However, you might not reach this height if you have poor eating habits during your school years. Your body needs the right amounts and the right kinds of food to grow as it should. You can give your body the materials it needs for growth by eating a variety of foods. A good variety includes fruits and vegetables; dairy products; breads and cereals; and meat and fish. Eating too much of one kind of food does not give your body what it needs for proper growth.

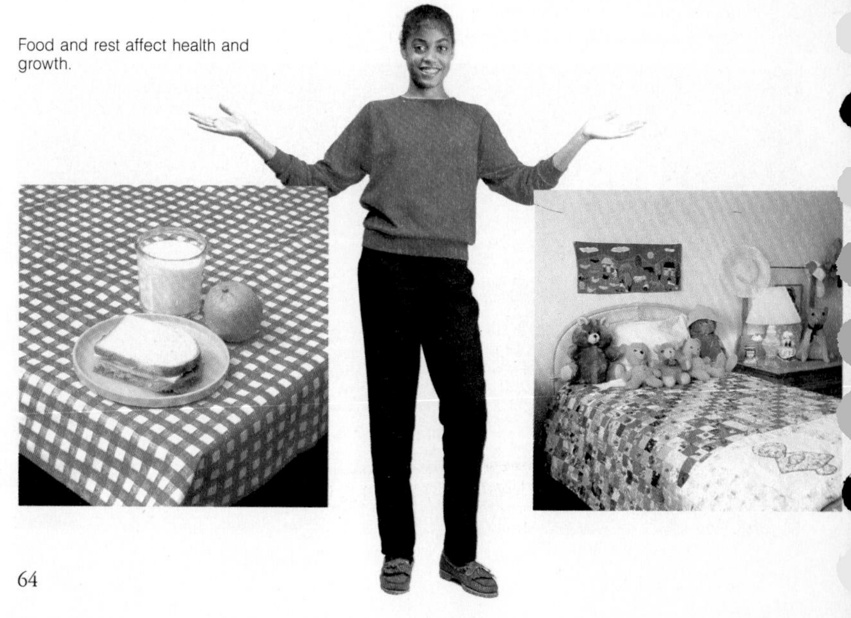

Food and rest affect health and growth.

64

Teaching Options

Health Background

Nutrients in food are an important part of growth because they provide the body with fuel for energy; materials for building, repairing, and maintaining the body's tissues and organs; and help for the body to perform its functions. An improper or unbalanced diet can lead to vitamin or mineral deficiencies, heart and circulatory diseases, or malnutrition. Malnutrition can hinder mental development, cause the body to be deformed, or lead to a variety of diseases.

Enrichment

Discuss with students why eating proper food and getting adequate sleep and exercise are necessary for healthy bodies.

Health and Language Arts

Ask students to suggest physical features that might be inherited from parents. (hair color, eye color, facial features) Let students write a story describing how a certain child is like and unlike his or her parents.

Reteaching

Ask students to write a paragraph on the time they spend each twenty-four hours on sleep, rest, and physical activity. Ask them to tell whether they think the time spent on each activity is adequate to keep them healthy.

Heredity sets limits for weight, body shape, and muscle development. However, exercise gives you a great deal of control over these physical features. For example, if you exercise several times a week, your muscles are likely to become strong and firm. Strong muscles help you perform activities well without tiring easily. Strong muscles also help you hold your body correctly, giving you good posture. Muscles will develop only if you exercise them. Exercise helps you look and feel your best as you grow.

Your decisions about rest also affect how you grow. Most people your age need about nine to ten hours of sleep each night. While you sleep, your body uses energy from the food you eat to build new cells. Also, your body produces most of your growth hormone while you sleep.

Eating right, exercising, and getting enough sleep are wise decisions you can make to help you grow properly.

Think Back • *Study on your own with Study Guide page 319.*

1. If the upper limit of a girl's inherited adult height is five feet six inches (about 160 cm), will she definitely be that tall as an adult? Explain your answer.
2. What are three decisions you can make that affect your growth?

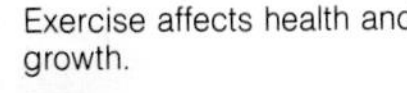

Exercise affects health and growth.

• Ask students to explain why it is important to get adequate rest during the growth years. (New cells are built and growth hormone is produced during sleep.) • Emphasize that the purpose of making wise health decisions is not simply to grow as tall as possible but to allow the body to grow and develop its potential in as healthy a way as possible. You may wish to refer students to Chapter 8 for more information about posture and about sleep.

3 Assess

Expanding Student Thinking

Ask students to explain how both heredity and health decisions affect growth. (Heredity sets the limits for potential height, weight, body shape, and muscle development. Wise health decisions help maximize genetic potential.)

Thinking Skill By explaining how heredity and health decisions affect growth, students are *organizing information.*

Answers to Think Back

1. No, her health decisions might prevent her from reaching that height.

2. Decisions about such topics as eating habits, exercise, posture, rest, and drugs affect growth.

Teaching Plan

Lesson 5 pages 66–67

Lesson Objective
Describe situations that show how emotions and relationships change during growth.

1 Motivate

Introducing the Lesson
Let students volunteer to share concerns they feel about growing up. (not growing at the same rate as others, feeling clumsy, voice cracking, changing friendships, changing moods) Then discuss positive aspects of growing up. (more freedom, new abilities; new, positive experiences; new friends) Be sensitive to the fact that some students might not wish to express their feelings.

2 Teach

Strategies for Pages 66 and 67
• Direct students to read page 66 to learn how their physical growth might lead to emotional changes. • Let students volunteer to relate experiences involving sudden changes in mood. Discuss how these sudden changes might be unpleasant for the person experiencing them and for the person's friends or family.

5 How Might Your Emotions and Relationships Change As You Grow?

Jan had never worried about her appearance before. This year, however, she has noticed some changes that make her feel uncomfortable about the way she looks. Her legs have grown three inches (7.5 cm) since last year. Her feet have grown much larger too, and she sometimes feels clumsy when she walks or runs. She wishes she was not so different from others in her class.

Jan's feelings about her growth show how physical changes can lead to emotional changes. Changes in height and weight might make you worry about your appearance. You might worry more about what others think of you. You might not be happy about the way you are growing because it makes you look different from your friends. Your worries could make you suddenly feel angry at times. Your mood might switch unexpectedly between happy and sad several times a day. Such emotional changes are bothersome, but they are a normal part of growing up.

Carla, Terri and Melissa are in the same class and have been close friends all year. They usually spend their Saturday mornings together.

One day Carla told her friends that her parents bought a piano and she wanted to learn how to play. Saturday morning was the only time she could take lessons.

Between lessons and practicing, Carla spent much less time with her friends.

Teaching Options

Health Background

Emotions become stronger during the growth spurt and during puberty. Emotional changes and concerns about self-image become evident. Many of these concerns stem from the way adolescents view their physical growth. Since they are growing at different rates, adolescents tend to worry about their physical differences. They are often critical of their appearance and worry about their unpredictable emotions during the growth spurt and puberty. During this time of change, adolescents often find security in a peer group.

Enrichment

Let students write short stories illustrating positive responses to changing friendships and relationships within the family.

Health and Math

Help students make histograms showing how much time each day they spend with peers (not including school), with family, and by themselves (not including sleep)

Reteaching

Some students might be interested in keeping a private diary recording their moods and feelings over the course of a few days. Such an exercise can help students sort and reflect upon their feelings and possibly come to healthy conclusions about problems. Remind students that emotional changes are a normal part of growing up.

Changing relationships is another normal part of growing up. Your relationships might change in two main ways as you grow. First, friendships with people your own age will likely become more and more important. Your relationship with your family can remain strong, but you might want to spend more time with your friends than ever before.

Second, some of your friendships might change as you develop new interests. The example pictured on these two pages shows one way new interests can change friendships and lead to new friendships.

Think Back • *Study on your own with Study Guide page 319.*

1. What emotional changes might occur as a person goes through the growth spurt and puberty?
2. In what two ways might relationships change as a person grows up?

On Your Own
If you were Melissa or Terri, would you have been angry with Carla after she decided to take piano lessons? Give a reason for your answer and explain in a paragraph. Think of a time when one of your friendships began, ended, or changed in some other way. Describe what caused the friendship to begin, end, or change.

Carla found out that Debbie, a girl from another class, was also taking piano lessons.

Debbie's family did not have a piano at home, so Carla often invited her over to practice. They quickly became good friends.

Carla, Terri, and Melissa still spend time together, but Carla's new interest in music has changed their friendships. Her new interest has also led to a new friendship.

• Ask the students to read page 67 to find out how a person's relationships might change during the growth years.

Using On Your Own

Some students might feel that Carla needs to devote time to her new interest or that Carla deserted her friends. Answers will vary widely.
Thinking Skills By putting themselves in someone's place and by thinking about their friendships, students are *suggesting alternatives* and *drawing conclusions.*

3 Assess

Expanding Student Thinking

Ask students to suggest positive ways to deal with changing friendships. (accepting the fact that this is normal, saving time for old friends, realizing that old friends will develop new interests and friends too; being patient, explaining your feelings to family or friends)
Thinking Skill When students think of positive ways to deal with changing friendships, they are *suggesting alternatives.*

Answers to Think Back

1. Emotional changes might include worrying more, moodiness, and generally experiencing stronger emotions.
2. Friendships with people your own age become more important, and new friendships are made as interests change.

Life Skills

Use this worksheet for practice in drawing conclusions. This worksheet is located on page 5 of the Student's Workbook. Use with Chapter 2: pages 66–67.

Thinking Skill: When students suggest alternatives they are using creative thinking.

Name ______________________ Life Skills

Use with Chapter 2: pages 48–73.

Solving Problems

Read the story and answer the questions.

Sara earned a weekly allowance by helping her parents around the house. She often felt that she did not have enough money to go shopping or to a movie with her friends. Sara asked her parents for a larger allowance. Her mother said that Sara's allowance was as much as the family could afford.

Sara decided to try and earn some money on her own. She asked the neighbors if they needed any help around their homes. One neighbor, Dr. Smith, said that he would pay Sara to walk his dogs and water his plants. After two weeks, Dr. Smith told Sara she was doing a great job. Sara felt good about earning some money herself. She was able to go out with her friends more often. Also, Sara was able to save some money.

1. How do you think Sara felt after she talked with her parents?
   Answers will vary. Students will probably indicate that Sara felt angry and frustrated; that her parents did not understand.
2. How did Sara feel about herself after she got the job?
   Students should indicate that Sara probably felt proud of herself and her ability to do something about her problem.
3. What kinds of inexpensive activities could Sara do with her friends?
   Answers might include: doing volunteer work, jogging or other forms of exercise, school clubs, simple art and craft projects.
4. What other jobs might Sara do to earn extra money?
   Answers might include: babysitting, yard work, or paper route.

Extension Idea: Ask students to write a continuation of Sara's story that tells how she used the money that she saved.

33

Teaching Plan

Lesson 6 pages 68–69

Lesson Objective
Describe ways to build a positive self-image while growing and changing; explain the role that relationships with family and friends plays in this process.

1 Motivate

Introducing the Lesson
Discuss with students positive ways that they can deal with frustration and anger. (taking deep breaths, trying to calm down before acting or responding, talking it over with a friend, being patient, thinking quiet thoughts)

2 Teach

Strategies for Pages 68 and 69
• Discuss what is meant by a good self-image. (self-confidence, feeling good about yourself, accepting the way you are) • Direct students to read page 68 to find out the advantages of a good self-image. • Encourage students to suggest ways of building a good self-image. • Ask students to read page 69 to learn helpful ways to deal with growing and changing.

6 How Can You Deal with Growth and Change?

As you grow and change, you will probably have many new, interesting, and exciting experiences. At times, however, the changes of growth can be troubling. You might feel uncomfortable about your appearance or feel afraid to make new friends. You can deal with these and other feelings in several ways.

Developing a good self-image is one way to help yourself enjoy your growth. If you have a good self-image, you will have greater confidence in yourself and feel good about yourself as you grow and change.

Accepting responsibility helps you develop a strong self-image. As you grow, you will have more freedoms and privileges. New responsibilities come with these privileges. For example, you become responsible for your own safety when you go places by yourself. If your family lets you visit friends after school, you become responsible for being home on time.

Other responsibilities might include watching a younger brother or sister or doing household chores. The boy shown here was babysitting for his younger sister. His friends wanted him to go with them to the park, but he said he would meet them later. He was responsible for his sister until their mother got home. He thought of his babysitting job as a chance to prove he was trustworthy. Accepting his responsibility made him feel proud and built greater confidence in himself.

Accepting responsibility helps build confidence.

Teaching Options

Health Background

Relaxation can help students deal with the stresses of growing up. When a person relaxes, the brain sends a message to the muscles to rest and loosen up. Other nerves send messages to the heart to beat slower, to the lungs to breathe slower, and to the digestive system to work harder so that energy can be put into building new cells and replacing old ones.

Enrichment
Ask students to discuss new privileges they might have as they grow older. Then discuss the responsibilities that come with these privileges. Ask students how they feel about getting new responsibilities. Then ask how their handling of these responsibilities might affect their relationship with family members.

Health and Art
Invite students to use magazine photographs to make a collage showing people communicating with one another. They might entitle their collages "Communication Is the Key."

Reteaching
Ask students to write a one-page paper about ways self-image can be improved. Include relationships with family and friends in the paper. Suggest that they review Chapter 1 before beginning their papers.

Explaining how you feel is another helpful way to deal with concerns about growth. You might want to talk to someone about your feelings, as this girl is doing. A friend, parent, older sister or brother, or other relative can give the understanding and advice that you need. However, friends and relatives can help you only if you let them. Tell them how you feel and accept their help when they ask, "What's wrong?"

You and your friends will experience many of the same physical and emotional changes even though you will all grow in different ways and at different times. Having patience with the way you and others are growing will be helpful as you grow and change. If you feel as though your body is changing too quickly, remember that your growth will eventually slow down. If you are worried because your friends are changing faster than you, remember that you will have your growth spurt sooner or later. Your own pattern of growth and change is one of the things that makes you a special person.

Explaining how you feel helps you deal with concerns during growth.

Think Back • *Study on your own with Study Guide page 319.*

1. How can accepting responsibility help a person feel good about himself or herself?
2. How can a person's family help him or her deal with the feelings of growth?
3. What does the phrase "having patience with your growth" mean?

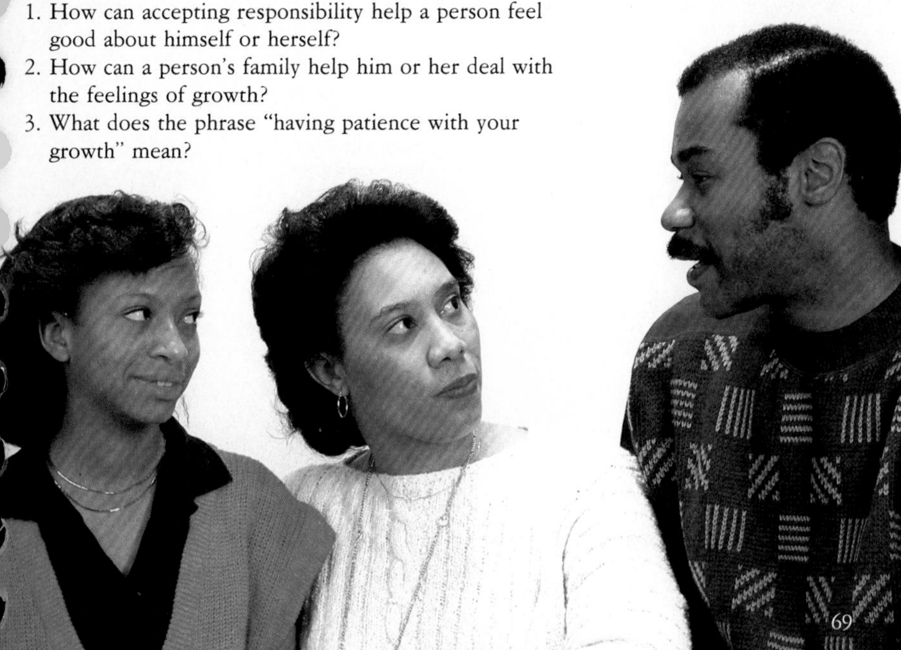

• Discuss ways that family and friends can help students deal with the stress of growing up. Ask students to explain some ways that students can help themselves. (Accept all reasonable answers.)

3 Assess

Expanding Student Thinking

Ask students to list positive ways of dealing with growth and change. (accepting responsibility, developing a good self-image, explaining how you feel, having patience with your growth)

Thinking Skill By listing positive ways of dealing with growth and change, students are *suggesting alternatives*.

Answers to Think Back

1. By accepting responsibility, a person can develop a good self-image and feel good about his or her growth.

2. Family members can provide understanding and advice in dealing with the students' feelings about growth.

3. Having patience with growth means realizing that rapid growth and change in the body will eventually take place and that these rapid changes will eventually slow down.

Teaching Plan

Health Focus page 70

Discussion

After students have read page 70, discuss the preliminary results of Dr. Bouchard's study. (The study shows some of the effects of heredity on behavior.) Ask students to explain why the fact that the twins were raised in separate households is important to the study. (Since the twins' heredity is identical, but their surroundings are different, scientists can find out if a certain trait is caused mainly by heredity or by a person's surroundings.)

Answers to Talk About It

1. He is trying to find out if a certain trait is caused mainly by heredity or by a person's surroundings.
Thinking Skills When students describe Dr. Bouchard's study, they are *recalling information.*
2. Answers might express the idea that shared traits of twins raised in different environments would strongly indicate that the traits are related to heredity rather than the environment.
Thinking Skill When students describe how twin research could help determine the causes of certain traits, they are *drawing conclusions.*

Health Focus

Identical Twins and Scientific Research

No two people grow in exactly the same way, but some people come very close. Identical twins, such as those shown here, have the same genes. Therefore, they have the same inherited traits. Besides looking alike, identical twins often share similar interests, abilities, and growth patterns.

Because identical twins have identical genes, they are very important as subjects in research studies. By observing twins, scientists can find out if a certain trait is caused mainly by heredity or by a person's surroundings. This type of research is especially valuable if twins have been raised in separate households.

Such a study is being conducted now by Dr. Thomas Bouchard at the University of Minnesota. His study involves thirty-three pairs of identical twins and fourteen pairs of nonidentical twins. Each of these twins has been raised apart. Dr. Bouchard has found that identical twins often show similar behavior even though they had different experiences and were brought up in different ways.

Twin studies are helping scientists find out more about the effects that heredity and environment have on personality, mental skills, and diseases such as cancer and heart disease.

Talk About It

1. Why are identical twins important subjects in research studies?
2. How could twin research help determine what causes a certain trait?

Teaching Options

Vocabulary

Use this worksheet for practice in reviewing chapter vocabulary words. This master may be reproduced from the Teacher's Resource Book and also is located on page 6 of the Student's Workbook. Use with Chapter 2: pages 48–73

Name ______________________ Vocabulary

Use with Chapter 2: pages 48–73.

Growth Puzzle

Mark each statement **True** or **False**. Then shade in the squares on the grid that contain the numbers of the true statements. You will find an important word from Chapter 2.

Statements

True ______ 1. A growth spurt is a period of rapid growth that occurs between the ages of nine to fifteen.

False ______ 2. The organ that produces chemicals and releases them directly into the brain is the endocrine gland.

True ______ 3. A hormone is a chemical that affects how body cells work.

True ______ 4. The hormones that control the activities of endocrine glands are produced by the pituitary gland.

False ______ 5. The testes are hormones produced by the male during puberty.

True ______ 6. The male reproductive cell is known as the sperm cell.

False ______ 7. The ovaries are female hormones produced during puberty.

True ______ 8. The reproductive cell produced by the female is known as the egg cell.

False ______ 9. Puberty is the period of time just before the body develops the ability to reproduce.

False ______ 10. During heredity, the body develops more adultlike qualities.

True ______ 11. Chromosomes contain the information for a person's heredity.

True ______ 12. The chemical substance that determines inherited traits and that makes up chromosomes is known as DNA.

True ______ 13. A gene is a small part of a chromosome that influences a specific inherited trait.

1	7	2	13
11	5	9	4
8	3	6	6
3	7	5	8
12	9	10	4
2	9	5	7
12	1	3	1
3	2	7	5
6	8	4	12
11	5	10	9
13	1	8	4
7	5	2	7
4	11	3	2
3	7	10	6
12	6	3	7
1	9	11	5
12	7	2	11
5	10	9	2
3	6	4	12
1	7	9	5
8	3	8	4
12	9	2	10
1	6	11	8
9	5	7	2
12	8	6	10
1	7	9	3
4	5	2	11
3	8	4	7
9	5	2	9
7	1	5	2
2	3	9	7
5	4	10	2
7	8	2	9
9	2	10	5
1	11	4	9
7	12	7	5
5	6	9	10
7	8	2	5
10	5	7	2
1	9	4	7
10	3	7	9
7	6	5	2
5	8	2	7

Write and define the hidden word:

Heredity—the passing of traits from parents to children.

34 *Extension Idea:* Direct students to write a true statement using the hidden word.

Using Photographs to Examine Your Growth

Photographs of yourself and family members can illustrate many of the topics discussed in this chapter. Compare school photographs of yourself taken over the past several years. Look for physical features that have changed a lot and those that have changed little.

Some pictures, like the one here, might show a family member when he or she was close to your age. You might ask an adult to help you find such a picture. Examine it closely. Notice any resemblance between yourself and the person in the photograph.

Ask adults in your family if they remember when they started their growth spurts. Ask them what changes they experienced. How did they handle the changes of growth?

Reading at Home

The Answer Book About You by Mary Etling and Rose Wyler. Grosset and Dunlap, 1980. Find answers to some questions young people ask about their growth and development.

How You Grow and Change by Dorothy Baldwin and Claire Lister. Bookwright/Watts, 1984. Further explore the changes of growth.

Health at Home

page 71

Strategies

If several photographs of the students over the last several years are available, ask students to describe their growth over those years. Do the photographs show any signs of spurts? Has the growth been steady? If students have a family photograph available, ask them to list some of the traits their family members share. Review with students some of the visible changes that accompany the growth spurt. (increased height and weight, new hair growth, more adultlike body shape) Remind students to handle family photographs with care.

More Reading at Home

The Answer Book About You (Grades 5-8)

How You Grow and Change (Grades 4-6)

Simon, Nissa. *Don't Worry, You're Normal.* T.Y. Crowell, 1982. Discusses topics such as nutrition, skin, sleep, emotions, and sexual development. (Grades 6 and up)

Study and Review

Use this worksheet for practice in reviewing growing and changing. This master may be reproduced from the Teacher's Resource Book and also is located on page 7 of the Student's Workbook. Use with Chapter 2: pages 48-73.

Name ______________________ Study and Review

Use with Chapter 2: pages 48–73.

Reviewing Growing and Changing

1. Identify the parts on the diagram.

2. When does the growth spurt occur?

Between the ages of 9–15

3. What three factors affect growth?

Heredity, endocrine glands, health decisions

4. Identify the sex of the offspring with the following sex chromosomes.

X X → XX a. Female

X Y → XY b. Male

5. At what ages in boys and in girls does puberty begin?

In boys, 13–16; in girls, 11–14

6. What are three ways the body changes during puberty?

Hair grows on different parts of the body, body develops more adult shape, voice deepens

7. How might emotions change during puberty?

Answers should include new, stronger emotions and the need to be with friends.

8. How can accepting responsibility help develop a strong self-concept?

Responsibility is an opportunity to do something well, which makes you feel good about yourself.

9. How do physical fitness, nutrition, and drugs affect growth?

Answers should tell the importance of physical fitness and good nutrition and harmful effects of drugs.

Extension Idea: **Ask students to describe how their responsibilities have changed since birth.** 35

Chapter 2 Review

pages 72–73

Answers to Reviewing Lesson Objectives

Use this section for guided study or for oral review. Objective numbers match lesson numbers.

1. Changes include a rapid growth in height and weight and uneven growth of different parts of the body.

2. Hormones of the pituitary gland cause the changes of the growth spurt. Hormones of the reproductive glands cause the development of sperm and egg cells, the development of a more adultlike body shape, hair growth, and a deepening voice.

3. Heredity influences growth patterns and other traits by providing genes from parents. Genes determine inherited traits.

4. Decisions about food, exercise, posture, and rest affect growth. Adequate sleep aids body growth, and physical activity improves strength and posture.

5. The first situation should show how a person begins to suddenly worry about aspects of his or her growth, or how a person's moods change suddenly during the day. The second situation should show how friends become more and more important, or how friendships change.

6. A person can develop a positive self-image during changes of growth by accepting responsibility, communicating with family and friends, and having patience with the timing of growth.

Answers to Checking Health Vocabulary

Use the vocabulary check as a review or as a test.

1. m
2. i
3. a
4. g
5. e
6. j
7. c
8. l
9. d
10. f
11. h
12. k
13. b

Chapter 2 Review

For further review, use Study Guide pages 318-319

Practice skills for life for Chapter 2 on pages 341-343

SKILLS FOR LIFE

Reviewing Lesson Objectives

1. List the physical changes that occur during the growth spurt. (pages 50-52)
2. Describe the physical changes caused by the hormones of the pituitary gland and reproductive glands. (pages 54-55)
3. Explain how heredity influences growth patterns and other inherited traits. (pages 56-61)
4. Give examples of health decisions that affect growth and describe the need to care for the body with adequate sleep, rest, and physical activity. (pages 64–65)
5. Describe situations that show how emotions and relationships change during growth. (pages 66-67)
6. Describe ways to build a positive self-image while growing and changing; describe the role that relationships with family and friends plays in this process. (pages 68–69)

Checking Health Vocabulary

Number your paper from 1-13. Match each definition in Column I with the correct word or words in Column II.

Column I

1. the male reproductive glands
2. the female reproductive glands
3. a strand of matter in a cell's nucleus that contains DNA
4. the passing of traits from parents to children
5. the small part of a chromosome that affects only one trait
6. the endocrine gland that makes growth hormone
7. a female reproductive cell
8. a male reproductive cell
9. a general name for an organ that produces chemicals and releases them directly into the blood
10. the period of rapid growth usually between the ages of nine and fifteen
11. a chemical made by an endocrine gland
12. the period of time when the body develops the ability to reproduce
13. the substance that makes up chromosomes

Column II

a. chromosome
b. DNA
c. egg cell
d. endocrine gland
e. gene
f. growth spurt
g. heredity
h. hormone
i. ovaries
j. pituitary gland
k. puberty
l. sperm cell
m. testes

72

Chapter 2 Tests Use Test A or Test B to assess students' mastery of the health concepts in Chapter 2. These tests are located on pages 17–24 in the Test Book.

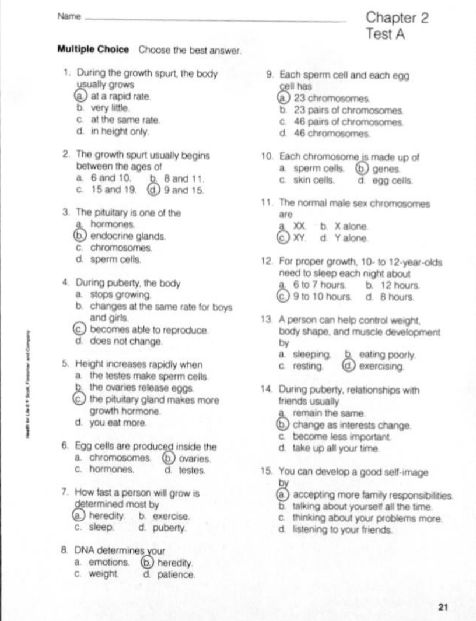

Name ______________________ Chapter 2 Test A

Multiple Choice Choose the best answer.

1. During the growth spurt, the body usually grows
   (a) at a rapid rate. b. very little. c. at the same rate. d. in height only.
2. The growth spurt usually begins between the ages of
   a. 6 and 10. b. 8 and 11. c. 15 and 19. (d) 9 and 15.
3. The pituitary is one of the
   a. hormones. (b) endocrine glands. c. chromosomes. d. sperm cells.
4. During puberty, the body
   a. stops growing. b. changes at the same rate for boys and girls. (c) becomes able to reproduce. d. does not change.
5. Height increases rapidly when
   a. the testes make sperm cells. b. the ovaries release eggs. (c) the pituitary gland makes more growth hormone. d. you eat more.
6. Egg cells are produced inside the
   a. chromosomes. (b) ovaries. c. hormones. d. testes.
7. How fast a person will grow is determined most by
   (a) heredity. b. exercise. c. sleep. d. puberty.
8. DNA determines your
   a. emotions. (b) heredity. c. weight. d. patience.
9. Each sperm cell and each egg cell has
   (a) 23 chromosomes. b. 23 pairs of chromosomes. c. 46 pairs of chromosomes. d. 46 chromosomes.
10. Each chromosome is made up of
    a. sperm cells. (b) genes. c. skin cells. d. egg cells.
11. The normal male sex chromosomes are
    a. XX. b. X alone. (c) XY. d. Y alone.
12. For proper growth, 10- to 12-year-olds need to sleep each night about
    a. 6 to 7 hours. b. 12 hours. (c) 9 to 10 hours. d. 8 hours.
13. A person can help control weight, body shape, and muscle development by
    a. sleeping. b. eating poorly. c. resting. (d) exercising.
14. During puberty, relationships with friends usually
    a. remain the same. (b) change as interests change. c. become less important. d. take up all your time.
15. You can develop a good self-image by
    (a) accepting more family responsibilities. b. talking about yourself all the time. c. thinking about your problems more. d. listening to your friends.

21

Name ______________________ Chapter 2 Test A

Short Answer Match each term in Column I with the correct definition in Column II.

Column I

f 16. hormones
a 17. ovaries
c 18. testes
d 19. sperm cell
b 20. egg cell
g 21. gene
e 22. chromosomes

Column II

a. the female reproductive glands
b. the female reproductive cell
c. the male reproductive glands
d. the male reproductive cell
e. the matter in cell's nucleus containing information for inherited traits
f. the chemicals made by endocrine glands that affect how body cells work
g. the small part of a chromosome that affects only one trait

Short Essay Write your answers in complete sentences.

23. What causes the growth spurt?
    Some endocrine glands affect growth. Endocrine glands release chemicals called hormones into your body. One gland, the pituitary, produces a hormone that starts the growth spurt.
24. Jack and John are brothers with the same parents. How can one have brown hair and one have black hair?
    Each child receives a different set of 46 chromosomes from his or her parents. Jack and John inherited some similar genes. However, children in one family do not inherit the same genes.
25. Why do some people feel uncomfortable about their growth?
    Answers will vary but might refer to the unevenness of the growth of different body parts, the timing of the growth spurt and puberty, unexpected emotional changes, and changing relationships.

22

Reviewing Health Ideas

Number your paper from 1-15. Next to each number write the word that best completes the sentence.

1. During the growth spurt the body grows more ____ than usual.
2. Girls usually experience their growth spurt ____ than boys.
3. During the growth spurt, growth takes place at ____ rates.
4. Growth is directed by a team of organs called the ____ glands.
5. The ____ gland affects growth more than any other gland.
6. A person's ____ can help him or her deal with changes by giving understanding and advice.
7. Eye color and nose shape are examples of inherited ____.
8. Before a body cell divides, the ____ copy themselves.
9. A ____ egg has 23 chromosomes from the egg cell and 23 chromosomes from the sperm cell.
10. If a sperm cell with an X chromosome unites with an egg cell, the offspring will be a ____.
11. Except for identical twins, every child in a family receives 46 chromosomes from the parents but not the ____ 46 chromosomes.
12. A person's heredity sets ____ for his or her growth.
13. Physical changes can lead to ____ changes.
14. People can have greater confidence in themselves if they develop a good ____.
15. ____ gives you control over your weight, body shape, and muscle development.

Understanding Health Ideas

Number your paper from 16-25. Next to each number write the word or words that best answer the question.

16. Between what ages does the growth spurt usually start?
17. What parts of the body usually grow fastest during the growth spurt?
18. What endocrine gland releases hormones that cause the reproductive glands to become more active?
19. What is the period of time called when the body develops adultlike qualities and is able to reproduce?
20. What chemical substance determines a person's heredity?
21. How many chromosomes are in each reproductive cell?
22. How does heredity help determine when the growth spurt begins?
23. What kinds of foods make up a healthy variety of foods for proper growth?
24. How many hours of sleep do eleven- to twelve-year-olds generally need each night?
25. What can a person develop by accepting responsibility?

Thinking Critically

Write the answers on your paper. Use complete sentences.

1. Identical twins have the same genes and, therefore, the same inherited traits. How then might identical twins grow in different ways?
2. Suppose a friend of yours is feeling uncomfortable about the changes of growth. What could you say to help your friend feel better?

Answers to Reviewing Health Ideas

1. rapidly
2. earlier
3. different
4. endocrine
5. pituitary
6. family members
7. traits
8. chromosomes
9. fertilized
10. girl
11. same
12. limits
13. emotional
14. self-image
15. exercise

Answers to Understanding Health Ideas

16. between the ages of nine and fifteen
17. feet, hands, arms, and legs
18. pituitary gland
19. puberty
20. DNA
21. 23 chromosomes
22. controls production of growth hormone by pituitary gland
23. fruits and vegetables, dairy products, breads and cereals, meat, poultry, and fish
24. about nine to ten
25. a good self-image

Answers to Thinking Critically

1. Answers should point to other factors besides heredity that influence a person's physical and emotional growth. Such factors could include nutrition, exercise, rest, and a person's life experiences.
Thinking Skills When students explain how identical twins grow in different ways, they are *drawing conclusions.*
2. Suggestions should include telling the person that everyone is different but eventually everyone follows a similar general pattern of growth, including the growth spurt and puberty.
Thinking Skill When students suggest what to tell a friend who is uncomfortable about growth, they are *interpreting information.*

Cooperative Learning Use the STAD Format described on page T24 to have four- to five-member teams study Chapter 2 Review together before completing Chapter 2 Test.

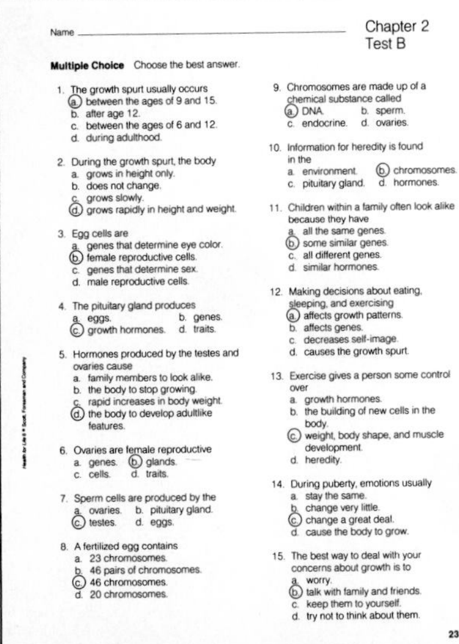

Name ______ Chapter 2 Test B

Multiple Choice Choose the best answer.

1. The growth spurt usually occurs
   (a.) between the ages of 9 and 15.
   b. after age 12.
   c. between the ages of 6 and 12.
   d. during adulthood.
2. During the growth spurt, the body
   a. grows in height only.
   b. does not change.
   c. grows slowly.
   (d.) grows rapidly in height and weight.
3. Egg cells are
   a. genes that determine eye color.
   (b.) female reproductive cells.
   c. genes that determine sex.
   d. male reproductive cells.
4. The pituitary gland produces
   a. eggs. b. genes.
   (c.) growth hormones. d. traits.
5. Hormones produced by the testes and ovaries cause
   a. family members to look alike.
   b. the body to stop growing.
   c. rapid increases in body weight.
   (d.) the body to develop adultlike features.
6. Ovaries are female reproductive
   a. genes. (b.) glands.
   c. cells. d. traits.
7. Sperm cells are produced by the
   a. ovaries. b. pituitary gland.
   (c.) testes. d. eggs.
8. A fertilized egg contains
   a. 23 chromosomes.
   b. 46 pairs of chromosomes.
   (c.) 46 chromosomes.
   d. 20 chromosomes.
9. Chromosomes are made up of a chemical substance called
   (a.) DNA. b. sperm.
   c. endocrine. d. ovaries.
10. Information for heredity is found in the
   a. environment. (b.) chromosomes.
   c. pituitary gland. d. hormones.
11. Children within a family often look alike because they have
   a. all the same genes.
   (b.) some similar genes.
   c. all different genes.
   d. similar hormones.
12. Making decisions about eating, sleeping, and exercising
   (a.) affects growth patterns.
   b. affects genes.
   c. decreases self-image.
   d. causes the growth spurt.
13. Exercise gives a person some control over
   a. growth hormones.
   b. the building of new cells in the body.
   (c.) weight, body shape, and muscle development.
   d. heredity.
14. During puberty, emotions usually
   a. stay the same.
   b. change very little.
   (c.) change a great deal.
   d. cause the body to grow.
15. The best way to deal with your concerns about growth is to
   a. worry.
   (b.) talk with family and friends.
   c. keep them to yourself.
   d. try not to think about them.

23

Name ______ Chapter 2 Test B

Short Answer Match each term in Column I with the correct definition in Column II.

Column I	Column II
a 16. growth spurt	a. rapid growth between ages 9 and 15
c 17. puberty	b. passing of traits between parents and children
g 18. endocrine gland	c. period when body develops the ability to reproduce
e 19. hormone	d. organ that makes growth hormone
d 20. pituitary gland	e. chemical made by an endocrine gland
b 21. heredity	f. portion of DNA that affects only one specific trait
f 22. gene	g. any gland that produces chemicals and releases them into the blood

Short Essay Write your answers in complete sentences.

23. What changes occur during puberty?
   During puberty, a person develops more adultlike features including an adult shape, a deeper voice, and more body hair. Reproductive organs become more active. The testes begin making sperm cells and the ovaries begin developing egg cells.
24. How can eating affect growth patterns?
   If a person does not eat properly, he or she might not reach his or her growth limit. The body needs a variety of healthy foods to grow as it should.
25. How can a good self-image make it easier to deal with the changes of growth?
   A person with a good self-image will probably feel less uncomfortable about the physical changes of growth. The person will have more confidence and feel good about changes in appearance.

24

CHAPTER 3 PLANNING GUIDE Pupil Edition

Pupil Edition	Activities	Enrichment	Assessment	Independent Study
Chapter 3 Choosing Foods for Good Health, pp. 74–103	Health Watch Notebook, p. 74	Health Focus, p. 100 Health at Home, p. 101	Chapter 3 Review, pp. 102–103	Study Guide, pp. 320–321 Skills for Life Handbook, pp. 344–346
Lesson 1 Why Do You Need Food? pp. 76–81		Did You Know? p. 80	Think Back, p. 81	Study Guide, p. 320
Lesson 2 What Is a Healthy Diet? pp. 82–87	Health Activities Workshop, pp. 88–89	Did You Know? p. 82	Think Back, p. 87	On Your Own, p. 85 Study Guide, p. 320
Lesson 3 How Does Food Processing Affect the Quality of Food? pp. 90–95		Did You Know? p. 94	Think Back, p. 95	On Your Own, p. 93 Study Guide, p. 321
Lesson 4 How Can You Be a Wise Food Consumer? pp. 96–98	Health Activities Workshop, p. 99		Think Back, p. 98	On Your Own, p. 97 Study Guide, p. 321

Teacher Resources

Brody, Jane. *Jane Brody's Nutrition Book.* W. W. Norton, 1981. Covers, in detail, every aspect of nutrition, from the basic science of essential nutrients, to the ins and outs of food labels.

Friday, Sandra K., and Hurwitz, Heidi S. *The Food Sleuth Handbook.* Atheneum, 1982. Offers a shopping and cooking guide with easy and appealing ways to win people over to more nutritious, yet reasonable, changes in eating habits.

Null, Gary. *Gary Null's Nutrition Sourcebook for the 80s.* Macmillan, 1983. Provides a comprehensive nutrient and Calorie guide to thousands of common foods.

Audio-Visual Resources

See page T43 for addresses of Audio-Visual Sources.

Before using any audio-visual materials, preview them for appropriateness for your students.

Build a Better Bag Lunch, Alfred Higgins, film, 18 minutes. Offers suggestions for a variety of bag lunches, and describes the proper handling and packaging of foods.

Foods, Fads, and Fallacies, Walt Disney, filmstrips with cassettes. Explores such issues as advertising, food processing, food additives, and more.

Nutrition: Some Food for Thought, Centron Educational Films, film or video, 15 minutes. Provides information to help students make food selections which will ensure that they have an adequate nutrient intake.

Computer Software

Food Facts Fun, Scott Foresman. Uses a game format to teach about foods and their nutrients, the four food groups, and healthy diets.

Internal Journey, EPCOT Educational Media. Traces the process of food digestion and absorption in the human body.

Supplementary Materials

	Teacher's Edition	Teacher's Resource Book	Test Book
Enrichment	Suggestions for each lesson: L. 1—pp. 76, 78, 80 L. 2—pp. 82, 84, 86 L. 3—pp. 90, 92, 94 L. 4—pp. 96, 98	Family Letter, p. 41 * Life Skills, p. 45 * Health and Reading, p. 48	
Reteaching	Suggestions for each lesson: L. 1—pp. 76, 78, 80 L. 2—pp. 82, 84, 86 L. 3—pp. 90, 92, 94 L. 4—pp. 96, 98	Transparency Masters, pp. 43-44 * Vocabulary, p. 46 * Study and Review, p. 47	
Assessment	Expanding Student Thinking: one assessment question per lesson that develops higher-order thinking skills—pp. 81, 87, 95, 98		Chapter 3 Test, Form A, pp. 25-26 Chapter 3 Test, Form B, pp. 27-28

* Also available in Workbook format (Student Edition and Teacher's Edition)

Chapter 3 Poster
A set of posters is available in a separate package. It provides a teaching poster for every chapter, including discussion and activity suggestions on the back. The poster for Chapter 3 is titled "How can you use these to prepare a healthy meal?"

Overhead Transparencies
A set of color overhead transparencies is available for Grade 6. You may wish to use Transparencies 16 and 20 to help teach about the four food groups and reading product labels.

Advance Preparation
You will need to prepare materials in advance for the following activities from the Health Activities Workshop.
Activity 2, page 88 Supply magazines, posterboard, and glue.
Activity 1, page 99 Ask students to save labels from a variety of food products.

Bulletin Board
Cut out magazine pictures of a variety of healthy foods from each of the four food groups. Ask students to cut out pictures of healthy foods that they enjoy, and to add these pictures to the appropriate group on the bulletin board.

Teaching Plan

Chapter 3 pages 74–103

Chapter Main Idea
Knowledge of nutrition and consumerism is necessary to make healthy food choices.

Chapter Goals
- Express knowledge of and interest in planning nutritious meals.
- Use nutritional and other information on food labels to make wise, healthy consumer choices.

Lifetime Goal
Choose nutritious food to promote good health throughout life.

Health Vocabulary
Additive, carbohydrates, cholesterol, fats, fiber, food processing, minerals, nutrient, preservative, proteins, vitamins

Words to Preteach
Bacteria, diet, dietitian, energy, enriched, food consumer, fortified, nutritious, rickets, scurvy, sodium

Chapter 3

Choosing Foods for Good Health

Unless you have just eaten, the food in the picture might look tempting. In this case, however, looks are deceiving—the food in the picture is fake! This dish is an artistic creation of wax, plastic, rubber, and paint made in a Japanese factory. Restaurant owners in Japan often display these delicious-looking works of art in their windows. Such illustrated menus help tourists choose foods in restaurants.

To choose healthy foods you need to know more than just how food looks. This chapter provides information to help you choose the foods you need for a lifetime of good health.

Health Watch Notebook

Think of a question you have about good nutrition. Find articles in newspapers or magazines to answer your question. Place the article in your notebook, and write a paragraph explaining how the information can be helpful to you and others.

Teaching Options

Modeling Health Vocabulary
Use this technique to introduce new words as you teach each lesson in this chapter. First, introduce the word. Present the word in two sentences that serve to clearly define the word. One sentence you might use to introduce the word *fiber* is the following: *Fiber is an essential part of a healthy diet.* Either read the sentences to the students or write them on the chalkboard. Ask the students to generate two meaningful sentences using the word. Additional successful techniques for introducing new words can be found on page T23.

Cooperative Learning
Jigsaw Format (See page T24.)
Assign the following topics at random to your cooperative learning teams.

Topic A: Name the six major nutrients and tell how each helps keep the body healthy.
Topic B: Describe a healthy diet.
Topic C: Describe some foods that should be limited in the diet and tell why they should be limited.
Topic D: How can food labels help a person shop wisely?

Have students search for information on their topic as they read the chapter. Then let all students with the same topic meet in an expert group to discuss the information. When students return to their teams, they may take turns presenting their topics to the team. Then give students a test covering all topics to complete individually (Chapter 3 Test A or B in the Test Book). Award Superteam certificates to teams whose average test scores exceed 90%, and Greatteam certificates to teams whose average test scores exceed 80%.

Introducing the Chapter

Ask students to study the picture. Encourage them to describe the food and suggest how it might taste. Then ask students to read page 74 to find out about the food in the picture. Be sure that students understand that food's appearance has little or nothing to do with its nutritional value. Ask students to identify some sayings about food that they have heard, such as "An apple a day keeps the doctor away," "peaches and cream complexion," "that's baloney," and so on. You might wish to write the sayings on the chalkboard and add to the list as you teach the chapter. Discuss how the sayings might have originated. You may wish to send the Family Letter home at this time. You may want to assign Study Guide pages 320–321 for students to use independently as they read the lessons. The Study Guide can also be used as an extra chapter review. You might want to assign the activities in the Skills for Life Handbook on pages 344–346.

Strategies for Health Watch Notebook

Ask students to share their questions and a summary of their answers with the rest of the class. As each student answers, write the question and the student's answers on the chalkboard. Then ask the class if they can contribute other answers to the question.

Family Letter

Use the Family Letter (English or Spanish version) to introduce the subject matter of the chapter to the family and to suggest a way the family can become involved in the student's learning experience. This master may be reproduced from the Teacher's Resource Book.

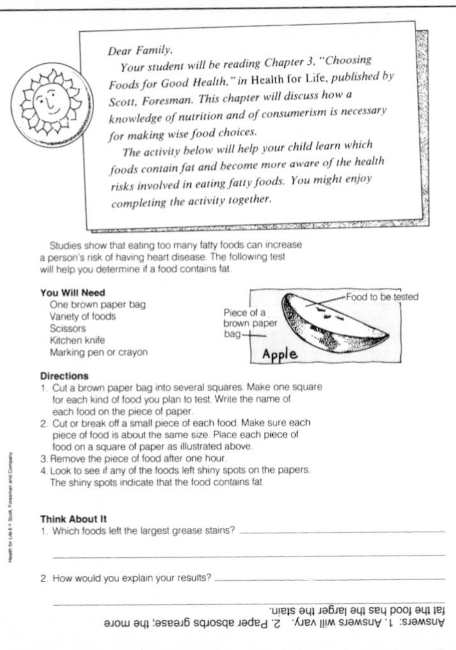

Dear Family,

Your student will be reading Chapter 3, "Choosing Foods for Good Health," in Health for Life, *published by Scott, Foresman. This chapter will discuss how a knowledge of nutrition and of consumerism is necessary for making wise food choices.*

The activity below will help your child learn which foods contain fat and become more aware of the health risks involved in eating fatty foods. You might enjoy completing the activity together.

Studies show that eating too many fatty foods can increase a person's risk of having heart disease. The following test will help you determine if a food contains fat.

You Will Need

One brown paper bag
Variety of foods
Scissors
Kitchen knife
Marking pen or crayon

Directions

1. Cut a brown paper bag into several squares. Make one square for each kind of food you plan to test. Write the name of each food on the piece of paper.
2. Cut or break off a small piece of each food. Make sure each piece of food is about the same size. Place each piece of food on a square of paper as illustrated above.
3. Remove the piece of food after one hour.
4. Look to see if any of the foods left shiny spots on the papers. The shiny spots indicate that the food contains fat.

Think About It

1. Which foods left the largest grease stains? ____________
2. How would you explain your results? ____________

Answers: 1. Answers will vary. 2. Paper absorbs grease; the more fat the food has the larger the stain.

41

For High-Potential Students

Obtain nutrition charts from cookbooks or other resource books and nutrition information panels from packages of processed foods. Help students use the information to construct a chart that shows how the nutritional content of various foods changes according to the ways the foods are processed. Charts should show the differences in the amounts of nutrients contained in various foods and their RDA percentages. Let students determine which is the most nutritious form of each food.

Teaching Plan

Lesson 1 pages 76–81

Lesson Objective
State that food provides nutrients, list the six kinds of nutrients and explain how getting the proper amount of each nutrient helps the body to function.

Health Vocabulary
Carbohydrates, fats, fiber, minerals, nutrient, proteins, vitamins

1 Motivate

Introducing the Lesson
Ask students how long they think a person could live without food. (about two months if liquids are available) Tell students that this lesson will help explain why people need food.

nutrient (nü′trē ənt), a substance found in food that your body needs to stay healthy.

1 Why Do You Need Food?

All the people in the picture are performing activities that require a lot of energy. Where do people get all that energy? They do not absorb it from the sun. They do not soak it up from water. They do not breathe it in from the air. People get their energy from the food they eat.

Food contains certain substances—**nutrients**—that your body needs to stay healthy. Some nutrients give you energy to run, jump, walk, talk, write, and even breathe. Other nutrients help build and repair your body cells. Still others help keep the systems of your body working properly. The six major kinds of nutrients are carbohydrates, fats, proteins, vitamins, minerals, and water. Your body needs some of each kind every day.

Where do people get their energy?

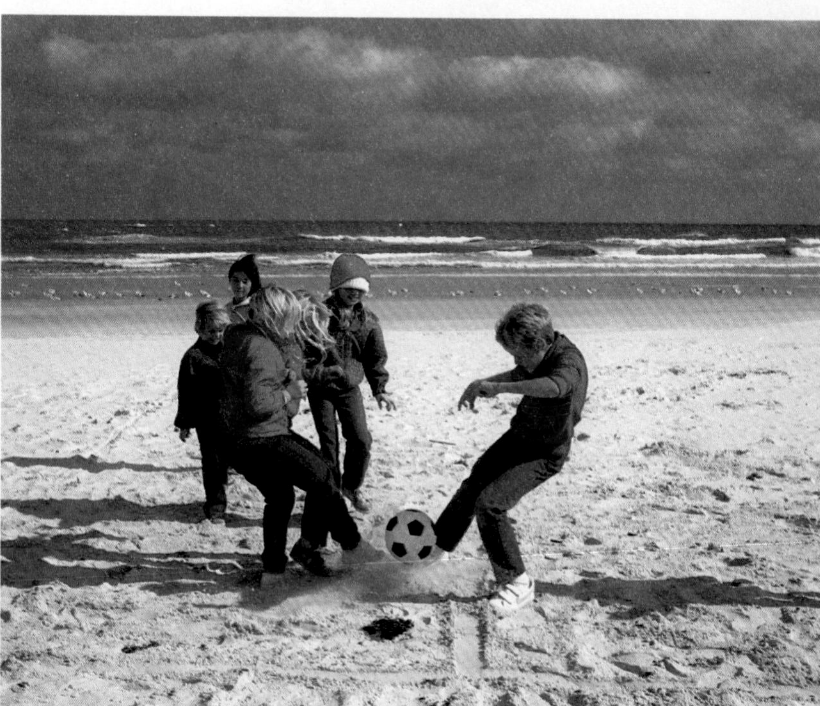

76

Teaching Options

Health Background
Proteins build and repair body tissues, make antibodies, and produce hormones that regulate the body's processes. Vitamins and minerals also help regulate body processes. They assist in blood clotting and strengthen bones and skeletal muscles. Carbohydrates consist primarily of starches and sugars, which provide energy that fuels the body. Fats are another major source of energy. Fats aid digestion and carry certain vitamins throughout the body.

Enrichment
Ask interested students to use nutrition books to find out the sources of bran, the benefits of eating bran, and how to add additional bran to the diet. (Bran comes from the seed coats of cereal grains.)

Health and Social Studies
Let students do library research to determine which countries are major sugar producers. Explain that they should look for information on the production of sugar cane and sugar beets. Tell students to mark the major sugar-producing countries on a world map.

Reteaching
Ask students to name several foods they think contain starch. Let students work in groups of three or four. Provide each group with a small quantity of diluted iodine and samples of foods that students identified as containing starch. *CAUTION: Iodine is poisonous.* Explain that a drop of iodine will turn purple or dark blue when placed on foods containing starch. Let students test the food samples and compare their findings with the list they generated.

The picture shows the most important nutrient. You could live for some weeks without food, but you can survive only a few days without water. Water carries other nutrients to your body cells and carries wastes away from the cells. Wastes are carried out of the body by the urinary system. Water in perspiration also helps cool your body.

The most familiar way to get water is to drink it from a glass. Experts recommend drinking 6–8 glasses of fluid each day. You also get this nutrient in other beverages, fruits, and soups. In fact, most foods contain a great deal of water.

Think Back • *Study on your own with Study Guide page 320.*

1. What does food contain that keeps the body healthy?
2. What are the six kinds of nutrients and what is a function of each?
3. How does fiber help your body?
4. How can you be sure you are getting vitamins and minerals you need in your diet?

Why is water an important nutrient?

3 Assess

Expanding Student Thinking

Ask students to select a food that they think satisfies the most nutritional needs. Let them explain their choice. (Answers should indicate an understanding that one food can satisfy more than one nutritional need. Point out that no single food satisfies *all* of a person's nutritional needs.)

Thinking Skill By determining which food best satisfies nutritional needs, students are *drawing conclusions*.

Answers to Think Back

1. Food contains nutrients.

2. Carbohydrates provide energy; fats provide energy and carry vitamins to body cells; proteins help build, repair, and replace cells; vitamins keep the body working properly; minerals build healthy teeth, bones, muscles, and blood cells; and water carries nutrients to and wastes away from cells.

3. Fiber helps food and wastes pass through the body.

4. Eating a variety of foods should give you all the vitamins and minerals you need.

Overhead Transparency Master

Use this blackline master to make a labeled overhead transparency or to make an unlabeled student worksheet. This blackline master may be reproduced from the Teacher's Resource Book.

Chapter 3
Text page 80

Sources and Functions of Vitamins

Vitamin	Food sources	How it helps your body
A	Whole milk; egg yolk; butter; margarine; liver; green and yellow vegetables	[Aids in preventing eye disorders Helps form and maintain healthy skin, hair, and mucous membranes]
B group B_1 Thiamin	[Meats, especially pork and liver; vegetables; nuts; milk; whole-grain breads and cereals]	Helps release energy from foods Helps nerves function Keeps digestive tract healthy
[B_2 Riboflavin]	Meats, especially liver; eggs; cheese; green, leafy vegetables; whole-grain breads	Helps body use carbohydrates, fats, and proteins to release energy Keeps skin, eyes, and nerves healthy
Niacin	Whole-grain breads and cereals; meat; fish; poultry; legumes	[Helps produce energy from carbohydrates Helps maintain all body tissues]
[C]	Citrus fruits; berries; tomatoes; green, leafy vegetables; green peppers; potatoes	Helps heal wounds Necessary for healthy teeth and gums Helps resist infection
D	[Milk; fish-liver oil; liver]	Helps build strong teeth and bones

43

Teaching Plan

Lesson 2 pages 82–87

Lesson Objective
Describe what a healthy diet should include, and identify the basic four food groups.

Health Vocabulary
Cholesterol

1 Motivate

Introducing the Lesson
Before beginning this lesson, ask students to write down everything they can remember eating the day before, including snacks. Point out that most people do not really think about what they eat. Explain that this lesson will help students take a more critical look at what they eat and what the food they eat does for their bodies.

2 What Is a Healthy Diet?

Did You Know?
Partly because of better diets during infancy and early childhood, people are taller today than ever before. Since the beginning of this century, the average height of men and women in the United States has increased by about four inches (10 cm).

The variety of food in a modern supermarket was not available to people in the early 1900s. The fresh foods sold in grocery stores at that time came from local farmers. Today, thanks largely to air travel and refrigerated train cars, supermarkets sell a variety of fresh fruits and vegetables, such as those shown here, all year round. Not only are more different foods available now, but people know more about choosing foods to stay healthy. For example, nutrition experts have taught people a great deal about a healthy diet for infants and young people.

A healthy diet includes a variety of foods every day. No single kind of food has all the nutrients you need. Therefore, you need to eat a variety of foods to give your body a variety of nutrients.

How Can You Make Sure You Get the Nutrients You Need?

Today a food guide is available that helps people choose foods for a healthy diet. The food guide on the next page includes the basic four food groups. What are they? How many servings are needed daily from each group? You can get all the nutrients you need by eating foods from the basic four food groups in the amounts suggested every day.

Today you can choose from a great variety of fresh foods.

82

Teaching Options

Health Background

A healthy diet provides enough food to balance the amount of energy used each day. Energy is measured in Calories. Foods high in Calories provide more energy than foods low in Calories. For mild activity, girls eleven to fourteen need about 2,300 Calories a day, boys eleven to fourteen need about 2,800 Calories a day.

Evidence seems to link cholesterol intake with heart disease. In societies in which people do not consume much cholesterol in their diets, such as Japan, the rate of heart disease is very low.

Enrichment

Invite students to make extensive lists of the foods included in each of the four food groups. For example, lists for the fruit-vegetable group might include a variety of interesting and exotic selections from around the world. You might make composite lists on the chalkboard.

Ask students to interview people from other countries to learn about foods they eat that differ from American foods, but are still nutritious. If such people are not available, suggest that students consult ethnic cookbooks such as the Time-Life series, which is found in many libraries.

Reteaching

Direct students to make a chart of the food groups and list foods in each group they enjoy eating.

Health and Social Studies

Encourage interested students to choose a country and explore the kinds of foods popular in that country. Then the students can make a lunch or dinner menu that includes food from that country. If you wish, you might arrange a "Foods from Around the World" week in which students bring to class or prepare the meals in their international menus.

	Food Group	Main Nutrients Provided
	**Vegetable-fruit** Four servings a day	Carbohydrates Vitamins A, C, and riboflavin (B_2) Minerals, especially calcium and iron Water
	**Bread-cereal** Four servings a day	Carbohydrates Vitamins, especially the B group vitamins Minerals, especially phosphorus and iron
	**Milk-cheese** Three servings a day for children Four servings a day for teenagers Two servings a day for adults	Fats Proteins Vitamins, especially D and riboflavin (B_2) Minerals, especially calcium and phosphorus Water
	**Meat-poultry-fish-bean** Two servings a day	Fats Proteins Vitamins, especially the B group vitamins Minerals, especially phosphorus and iron

2 Teach

Strategies for Pages 82 and 83

• Write the lesson title question on the chalkboard. • Direct students to read page 82 to learn what a healthy diet is. (foods from all four food groups in the amounts suggested) • Explain that a healthy diet improves the way people look, feel, act, and perform mental and physical activities. • Ask why a person should eat a variety of foods. (No single food supplies all the needed nutrients.) • Let students examine the food guide on page 83. • Review the names of the four groups and the number of servings needed daily from each group. (milk-cheese group—three servings; meat-fish-poultry-bean group—two servings; fruit-vegetable group—four servings; bread-cereal group—four servings) • Discuss the effect of nutrition on growth. Explain that each individual is born with inherited growth patterns that predetermine his or her maximum height but that food and exercise help determine whether or not that maximum height will be reached.

Teaching Plan

Lesson 2 continued

2 Teach

Strategies for Pages 84 and 85

• Tell students to read pages 84 and 85 to learn how to use the food guide. • Ask students to look at the picture and tell which group each of the foods shown belongs to. List the food groups and foods on the chalkboard. Ask students to discuss why they think the family has or has not chosen a healthy meal. • Ask students to select foods from the picture and suggest possible substitutes for them.

The food guide can be used to plan meals to suit everyone's taste.

How Can You Use the Food Guide?

The food guide on page 83 is a very flexible one. Different families can use it to plan very different daily menus. Yet each of the menus can provide enough foods from the basic four food groups. For example, one person might have cold cereal for breakfast, two slices of bread during lunch, and spaghetti for supper. These foods make up four servings from the bread-cereal group. Another person's four servings might come from eating hot cereal for breakfast, rice during lunch and supper, and blueberry muffins for a snack.

84

Teaching Options

Anecdote

The ancient Egyptians may have been the first people to make candy. They did not have sugar, so they made their candy with honey, figs, and dates. (Otfinoski, Steven. *Know Power.* Waldman Publishing, 1981.)

Enrichment

Encourage students to make posters with the theme "Variety is the key to healthy meals." Students might want to draw healthy meals and a variety of foods on their poster.

Health and Social Studies

People living in different parts of the United States eat different types of foods. Ask students to find out what some of the regional American foods are. Cookbooks and newspapers are good sources of information. (Some examples are: South—grits, greens; Southwest—chilies, tortillas, refried beans; Northeast—seafood.) Ask students to try to determine why certain foods are eaten in those areas.

Reteaching

Ask students to remember what they had for breakfast. Ask volunteers to explain how they decided to eat what they did. (Some eat whatever is prepared for them, many fix their own breakfast of something convenient, and others may not eat breakfast at all.) Review the importance of eating a nutritious breakfast.

Variety is the key to healthy meals. Below is one example of a family's food choices for one day. Notice the variety of foods included. Has this family chosen enough foods from each of the four food groups? What changes might you or your family make in this menu to suit your own tastes?

Notice that you do not need to choose foods from each group as part of every meal. Just include the suggested servings in each group sometime during the day. You can do this in regular meals or in snacks.

On Your Own
Use the food guide shown on page 83 to plan meals and snacks for one day. Choose a variety of foods you would enjoy eating and that would give you the right kind and amount of nutrients.

Using On Your Own
Answers will vary but should show an understanding of the need to choose the proper number of servings from each of the four food groups.
Thinking Skills By planning nutritious meals and snacks for one day, students are *interpreting information* and *classifying*.

Teaching Plan

Lesson 2 continued

2 Teach

Strategies for Pages 86 and 87

• Ask students to name their favorite foods or snacks. List these on the chalkboard. • Direct students to read page 86 to learn about the effects of eating too much sugar, fat, and cholesterol. • Ask students to use the chart on page 86 to determine the sugar content of the foods listed on the chalkboard. • Point out that sugar provides a surge of energy about a half hour after it is eaten. When that wears off, more sugar must be eaten for another surge. The energy that is not used is stored as fat. Explain that a balanced diet is healthier because it provides constant energy rather than surges. • Call on students to explain why people should limit fats and cholesterol in their diets. (Eating too many fatty foods can lead to overweight and diseases of the heart and blood vessels. Eating too much cholesterol can also lead to diseases of the heart and blood vessels.) • Direct students to read page 87 to learn how too much salt can harm the body. (can lead to high blood pressure)

Amounts of Sugar in Sweet Foods

Food	Serving size	Teaspoons of sugar
Chocolate bar	1 ounce	7
Chewing gum	1 stick	½
Chocolate cake with icing	1 piece	15
Angel food cake	1 piece	6
Brownie	1 piece	3
Ice Cream	½ cup	5-6
Sherbet	½ cup	6-8
Apple pie	1 piece	12
Sweetened soda pop	12 ounces	6-9
Maple syrup	1 tablespoon	2½

What Kinds of Foods Do You Need to Limit?

Nutrition experts think people need to cut down on foods that contain a lot of sugar, fat, cholesterol, and salt. Frequently eating foods with large amounts of these substances can lead to health problems.

Too much sugar, for example, can cause tooth decay and help make a person overweight. Some foods contain added sugar for a sweeter taste. The chart shows the amount of sugar added to some common desserts and snack foods. You might be surprised by some of the information in the chart. For example, an average-sized chocolate bar contains seven teaspoonfuls of sugar. Most sweetened breakfast cereals are one half sugar.

Instead of eating a lot of these foods, people could try to eat more fresh fruits and vegetables. Fruits and vegetables contain small amounts of natural sugar, but they also provide many other nutrients needed for good health.

Many foods high in added sugar, such as chocolate and ice cream, are also high in fats. A diet that includes a lot of fats can eventually lead to overweight and diseases of the heart and blood vessels. People should try to limit such fatty foods as bacon, lunch meats, potato chips, and fried foods.

86

Teaching Options

Enrichment

Let students conduct research to find out more about Calories—what a Calorie is, how many Calories students their age should consume each day, how Calorie contents in foods are determined, and the Calorie content of some of the foods they commonly eat. (Most fast food restaurants will provide on request complete nutritional information about the foods they serve.)

Health and Home Economics

Ask students to notice, the next time they go to the store, which food items have low-salt substitutes. Encourage students to list these and compare their lists in class.

Reteaching

Encourage students to prepare an uncommon healthy snack. Explain that they can combine anything from the four food groups to make up their snack. It should be nutritious, low in sugar, fats, and salt, and something people will like to eat as a snack. You might want to have students prepare a sample of their snack and share it with the class.

Too much **cholesterol** also can lead to diseases of the heart and blood vessels. This fatlike substance is made naturally in the body and is part of many foods that come from animals. Egg yolks and beef liver are some foods that contain high amounts of cholesterol. Some people should limit the amount of cholesterol in their diet. You might want to discuss this topic further with a doctor.

Salt contains minerals necessary for good health. Enough salt occurs naturally in most foods to satisfy your body's needs. However, many foods, such as bacon, soups, and potato chips, contain added salt. Many people add more salt to food while cooking. Then they add even more salt at the dinner table. Some studies show that too much salt in a person's diet might lead to high blood pressure. You can cut down on salt by not adding salt to foods during cooking or at the table. Also, you might want to look for low-salt products, similar to those shown, the next time you go shopping with your family.

cholesterol (kə les′tə rol′), a fatlike substance that is made naturally in the body and is present in foods from animal sources.

Think Back • *Study on your own with Study Guide page 320.*

1. What should a healthy diet include?
2. How can you be sure your meals provide all the nutrients you need?
3. What are the names of the basic four food groups?
4. What foods should people limit in their diets?

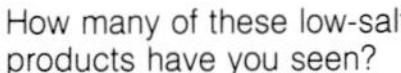

How many of these low-salt products have you seen?

• Ask students to look at the picture and identify low-salt foods that are available as substitutes for food products that are usually high in salt.
• Point out that high blood pressure is common only in countries where people eat a lot of salt. • Explain that a healthy diet provides the right amounts of food, as well as the right kinds of food. • Emphasize that nutrition problems that show up in later years usually are caused by bad nutrition habits begun during childhood.

3 Assess

Expanding Student Thinking

Give students a list of healthy foods. Ask them to identify the food group each belongs to. (Answers will depend on the foods chosen.)

Thinking Skill By putting foods into the proper groups, students are *classifying.*

Answers to Think Back

1. A healthy diet should include a variety of foods from the four food groups.

2. Choosing the correct number of daily servings from the basic four food groups assures you of getting the nutrients you need.

3. The basic four food groups are fruit-vegetable, bread-cereal, milk-cheese, and meat-fish-poultry-bean.

4. Sugar, fat, and salt should be limited in the diet. Some people need to limit cholesterol.

Activity Plan

Health Activities Workshop pages 88–89

Materials
Activity 2 magazines, posterboard, glue

Activity 1 Strategies
If students have difficulty identifying a variety of cooking methods because of lack of experience, suggest that they think about the ways in which manufacturers have prepackaged convenience foods that are sold in grocery stores. Students might also want to ask for suggestions from a parent or other person at home who does the cooking. Encourage students to consider different ways to prepare the same foods for breakfast, lunch, and dinner.
Thinking Skill By listing different ways to prepare foods, students are *suggesting alternatives*.

Activity 2 Strategies
Students might include drawings of foods for which they cannot find photographs. Suggest that students select foods they like to eat and that will provide a balanced diet.
Thinking Skill By placing foods in the correct food groups, students are *classifying*.

Activity 3 Strategies
You might want to provide the ingredients for students to make this snack in class. Discuss in which food group each of the ingredients belongs. Encourage students to create their own nutritious snacks and to share a sample with the class.
Thinking Skills By explaining why a snack is nutritious, students are *classifying* and *interpreting information*.

Activity 4 Strategies
You might want to provide cookbooks for use in the classroom. Some students might develop a dinner menu by interviewing the person who cooks in their household. Discuss the different foods served in various countries and why people eat them.
Thinking Skills By preparing a menu of dishes from other countries and categorizing the foods by food groups, students are *collecting information* and *classifying*.

Health Activities Workshop

Discovering More About Foods for Good Health

1. To add variety to meals, people often serve the same food in different ways. For example, potatoes might be baked, mashed, boiled, or served in soup. List some different ways that each of the following foods might be served: apples, carrots, ground beef, chicken. If you wish, list some other foods and the different ways each can be served.

2. Cut out pictures of food from magazines. Classify the pictures into each of the basic four food groups.

Then glue the pictures on posterboard and write the name of the correct food group under each set of pictures. Also write the number of servings from each group that you need to include in your diet each day.

3. Copy the following recipe for No-Bake Peanut Butter Logs and try making them at home if you can. Why do you think this snack is nutritious?

1 cup powdered milk
1/3 cup honey
1 cup peanut butter
2 tablespoons toasted wheat germ
1/2 cup sesame seeds

Mix all the ingredients together in a bowl, except for the sesame seeds. Shape the mixture into tiny logs and roll them in sesame seeds, as shown. Place the logs on wax paper and refrigerate before eating.

4. Visit the library to find a cookbook of recipes from other countries. Use the cookbook to plan a dinner. The meal might include an appetizer, soup, salad, main course, and dessert. On a sheet of paper, list all the foods included in the meal. Then, classify the foods into the basic four food groups. Also include the name of the country where these foods are popular.

Looking at Careers

5. Think of a person whose career deals with food. Many people would quickly think of a **chef.** Chefs prepare food in restaurants, hotels, schools, airports, hospitals, and factory cafeterias. Besides preparing the food, some chefs might plan the menu, direct the work of the kitchen staff, create new dishes, and buy food supplies.

Many chefs start their careers as kitchen helpers. They learn their skills on the job and eventually become assistant chefs and then chefs. They can also attend special classes at a college or cooking school.

Use a book about restaurants to find out the many different kinds of chefs employed in a large restaurant.

For more information write to the Culinary Institute of America, P.O. Box 53, Hyde Park, NY 12538.

6. In a hospital, the patients' meals are planned by a **dietitian.** A dietitian is an expert on how the body uses nutrients and what nutrients are necessary for good health. Dietitians use their knowledge to plan healthy and tasty meals that meet the special needs of patients in a hospital or nursing home. Dietitians might also work with chefs to plan meals for schools and restaurants.

To become a dietitian, a person must study food science and nutrition in college for four years. After college many dietitians enter an internship program that combines job experience with classroom work.

On a sheet of paper, describe what you might like about this career. What might you not like about it? You might want to keep a folder with information about many careers related to health. Include in this folder your likes and dislikes about the careers.

For more information write to the American Dietetic Association, 430 N. Michigan Ave., Chicago, IL 60611.

Activity 5 Strategies

Students can also interview the person or persons who usually cook at home to find out how they learned to cook. Ask interested students to interview chefs in restaurants in their community. Ask some students to interview chefs in fast food restaurants to determine how their role differs from that of chefs in other types of restaurants.

Thinking Skill By determining the various roles of chefs, students are *collecting information.*

Activity 6 Strategies

You might invite a home economics teacher to speak to your class about the course work and on-the-job training necessary to become a chef or dietitian. Encourage students to write to the address on page 89 for more information.

Thinking Skill By considering the benefits of a career as a chef or dietitian, students are *judging and evaluating.*

Teaching Plan

Lesson 3 pages 90–95

Lesson Objective
List four ways of processing food; explain how each method affects the quality of food and how a person can choose foods processed the healthiest ways.

Health Vocabulary
Additive, food processing, preservative

1 Motivate

Introducing the Lesson
Direct students to look at the photograph of the store on page 90. Ask them how the store shown is different from modern supermarkets. Explain that many differences also exist in the types of food available to people now.

2 Teach

Strategies for Pages 90 and 91
• Write the lesson title question on the chalkboard. • Let students read page 90 to learn how types of foods sold have changed over the years. • Call on a volunteer to define food processing. (the changing of food before it is eaten)

food processing, the changing of food before it is eaten.

A basic food, such as potatoes, comes in many forms.

3 How Does Food Processing Affect the Quality of Food?

Notice the old-fashioned grocery store in the picture. A hunded years ago most grocery stores were about the size of a large living room. Today, many large supermarkets cover an area the size of a football field!

Grocery stores are larger today partly because of the greater variety of foods available. People have discovered how to use basic foods to make new food products. Potatoes are a good example. Years ago people could buy only whole, raw potatoes. Today you can buy potatoes that have been cut, cooked, canned, frozen, and dried to make the products shown here.

Most items in a grocery store come from foods that have been changed in some way. The changing of food before it is eaten is called **food processing.** You process food at home whenever you wash, cut, mix, or cook it. Food processing also takes place at factories. Food might be dried, canned, frozen, partially cooked, or mixed with other substances before it reaches the supermarket. To make the healthiest food choices, you need to know how various processing methods affect the quality of food.

How does this store compare with a modern supermarket?

Teaching Options

Health Background

The Food and Drug Administration (FDA) continually monitors and regulates the use of additives. The Generally Recognized as Safe (GRAS) list was developed in 1958, and listed 675 additives considered safe to use. Since then, certain additives, cyclamates and red dye #2 among them, have been taken off the list after being linked to cancer.

Enrichment
Freeze-dried foods are available from many sources, including outdoor equipment and backpacker supply firms. Encourage interested students to write for catalogs and information about freeze-dried foods. You might want to obtain some of these foods for the class to taste. Volunteers might write to the National Aeronautic and Space Administration, Houston, Texas, for information about how astronauts use freeze-dried food.

Health and Social Studies
Encourage students to talk to a grandparent or other older individual about what foods available today were not available when the older person was a child.

Reteaching
To demonstrate how fruits are dried, you could show your students how to make raisins. Provide a box lined with foil and a handful of grapes cut in half, with the seeds removed. Tell students to scatter the grapes in the bottom of the box and place the box under a light. Dry the grapes until they become raisins. If the students plan to taste the raisins, they should cover the boxes with cheesecloth to keep out insects and dirt. They should also rinse the raisins in water before eating them.

How Do Drying and Freeze-Drying Affect Food?

Drying and freeze-drying are two methods of food processing that preserve foods, or keep foods from spoiling. Drying removes most of the water from foods. Without water, bacteria cannot grow on the food and spoil it. Raisins, dry cereals, pudding mixes, and macaroni are some dried foods. The process of freeze-drying removes water from food while the food is frozen.

Drying and freeze-drying reduce the size and weight of food. These processes make food easier to transport and store. Dried foods are especially convenient for space travel and backpacking. The hikers shown here enjoy the taste and nutrition of a freeze-dried fruit snack without worrying about the fruit spoiling or weighing down their backpacks.

Some freeze-dried foods are convenient as well as nutritious.

• Explain to students that advances in transportation are a major factor, along with food processing, responsible for today's wide variety of foods. • Ask students to name different methods of food processing used by manufacturers. (drying, canning, freezing, partial cooking, mixing with other food substances) • Be sure students understand the timesaving benefits of food processing. • Tell students to read page 91 to learn about drying and freeze-drying. Discuss why drying and freeze-drying keep foods from spoiling. (These processes remove most of the water from food; bacteria need water in order to grow on food and spoil it.) • Call on volunteers to identify foods they have at home that ar dried. (Answers might include coffee, tea, nuts, beans, herbs, spices, raisins, figs, dates, prunes, dry cereals, and pasta.) • Students may also be interested in learning about food processing methods used to prepare foods to be eaten in space. • Because scientists did not know what the problems of eating in a zero-gravity environment might be, early astronauts ate puréed concoctions out of toothpaste tubes. As a result of advances in food processing, especially freeze-drying and irradiation, and experience in eating in space, astronauts can now choose from more than one hundred different items including shrimp, steaks, and au gratin vegetables.

Teaching Plan

Lesson 3 continued

2 Teach

Strategies for Pages 92 and 93

• Direct students to read page 92 to learn about canning and freezing. • Discuss the reasons why people purchase canned and frozen foods. (can be stored for long periods of time, can be prepared quickly) • Ask students who have participated in home canning or freezing to tell the class about their experiences. Invite these students to bring samples to show to the class. • Let the students read page 93. • Discuss disadvantages of processed foods. (loss of nutrients, some have high salt content, most do not taste as good as fresh foods) Make sure students understand that even fresh foods lose nutrients if they are stored too long. Suggest that students look at the picture on page 93 and tell which type of corn the girl should choose. (the fresh corn, if it has not been in the store too long; otherwise the frozen corn might be more nutritious)

Workers separating sliced peaches at a food factory.

What are some advantages of canning your own food?

How Do Canning and Freezing Affect Food?

Many people enjoy canning and freezing their own food, as shown below. Perhaps you have helped can tomatoes or freeze green beans and sweet peppers. Canning and freezing not only preserve food but also shorten the time needed to prepare the food before eating it.

Canned food refers to food in jars and bottles as well as in cans. The containers are sealed airtight to prevent bacteria from entering them. Freezing foods also prevents bacterial growth because bacteria cannot live at such low temperatures.

Most of the canned and frozen foods in a store were partially or completely cooked at a factory. The picture to the left shows part of the canning process at a factory. Here, fresh fruits and vegetables are washed, cut, canned, cooked, and labeled before leaving the factory. Such foods are convenient to use because they can be stored for a long time and they do not take long to prepare at home.

92

Teaching Options

Anecdote

Peanut butter was invented in 1890 by a doctor who wanted a nutritious food high in protein.

Enrichment

Ask students to look in a supermarket for foods that can be purchased in many forms. (For example, cherries can be purchased fresh, canned, frozen, and freeze-dried.) Ask students to evaluate the different forms as to nutrition, cost, and additives.

Encourage interested students to interview older people concerning how food preparations, storage, and quality have changed during their lifetimes. Let the students report their findings to the class.

Invite the produce manager from a local supermarket to speak to the class. Ask the manager to explain how to tell fresh, top-quality produce from stale, inferior produce.

Reteaching

Ask students to select one fruit or vegetable and give several examples of how it might be processed and sold.

Health and Social Studies

Let students conduct library research to find out how foods were preserved for storage before refrigeration and freezing were available.

Encourage interested students to use library sources to find out how the canning process was invented.

How Nutritious Are Processed Foods?

Food processing methods are helpful because they preserve foods and make foods convenient to carry, store, and cook. However, foods lose some of their nutrients during processing. Also, many processed foods are high in salt. Most people think processed foods do not taste as good as fresh foods. For these reasons, many people choose fresh foods whenever possible.

The girl in the picture has a decision to make. She was asked to buy corn for supper, but she has to choose among canned, frozen, and fresh corn. She might make her choice based on the price and preparation time of each product. Which product should she choose if she wants the most nutrients?

Many people would pick the fresh corn-on-the-cob as the most nutritious—the best for health. Many fresh foods do have more nutrients than processed foods. However, fresh foods start to lose nutrients from the time they are picked. Therefore, the shorter the time between picking a food and eating it, the more nutritious that food is. Frozen foods keep almost all their nutrients unless they have been completely precooked. Precooking also removes nutrients from canned foods. In addition, some nutrients in canned foods leak out into the water that is packed in the can.

Now can you tell which product the girl should choose? If the corn-on-the-cob has been grown locally and has not been in the store very long, it is probably the most nutritious. The frozen corn would be the next most nutritious.

On Your Own
Frozen corn is more nutritious than canned corn, but it is also usually more expensive. Suppose a can of corn costs 49 cents and a bag of frozen corn costs 89 cents. Both products have the same amount of corn. Write a paragraph explaining which product you would buy and the reasons for your choice.

Which food item is the most nutritious?

FROZEN CORN

Using On Your Own
Be sure that students understand that the bag and the can are each assumed to contain the same amount of corn by weight. You might want to discuss the ways canned corn can be used compared to the uses for frozen corn. Point out that how food is to be used often determines which form is selected.

Thinking Skills By choosing which product to buy and giving reasons for their choice, students are *judging and evaluating* and *making decisions.*

Teaching Plan

Lesson 3 continued

2 Teach

Strategies for Pages 94 and 95

• Write the lesson title question on the chalkboard. • Tell students to read page 94 to learn about food additives. • Discuss with students the meaning of the word *additive.* (any substance added to a food for a particular purpose) • Ask students to think about all the items they can recall seeing listed on food packages that are considered additives. (Accept all reasonable answers.) • Call on students to read the chart on page 94. Discuss each additive. • Call on volunteers to name the various functions of additives. (add taste, color, texture, or nutrients to a food or keep it from spoiling) • Explain that the FDA regulates the use of additives in the United States. • Direct students to read page 95 to learn about the effects of cooking on nutrients.
• Explain that vegetables lose the least amount of nutrients when they are cooked in a covered pan in a small amount of water for the shortest time possible. Whenever possible, fruits and vegetables should be cooked whole and in their skins for greater nutritional value.

additive (ad′ə tiv), any substance added to food for a particular purpose.

preservative (pri zėr′və tiv), an additive that helps keep food from spoiling.

Did You Know?
Some chemical additives made in laboratories are exact copies of natural substances. For example, beta carotene—the orange coloring in carrots—is made in laboratories and used as a food coloring.

What Substances Are Added to Food During Processing?

You might have seen the words *fortified* or *enriched* on cartons of milk and packages of flour, bread, or cereal. A fortified or enriched food has nutrients added to it. Milk is fortified with vitamin D. Some breads are enriched with a variety of vitamins and minerals.

Any substance added to food for a particular purpose is an **additive.** Pepper and other spices are additives you might use at home to add flavor. Many processed foods contain additives to help preserve them. These additives are **preservatives.** Without preservatives, many foods would spoil before people could use them. Other additives add taste, color, texture, or nutrients to food. The chart shows some additives and tells why they are added to food.

People who work for the Food and Drug Administration (FDA) study and test additives to try to make sure they are safe to use. If the FDA finds an additive to be harmful, the FDA will limit or stop the use of that additive. Even though the additives used today are not thought to be harmful, many people prefer foods with few or no additives.

Functions of Additives

Type of additive	Why it is used
Acids	To control sourness and prevent discoloration
Colorings	To make food look more appetizing
Emulsifiers	To keep substances mixed so product has a uniform texture
Flavorings	To add or bring out flavor
Nutrients	To improve nutritional value
Preservatives	To prevent foods from spoiling

94

Teaching Options

Enrichment

Ask a volunteer to write to the Federal Food and Drug Administration, Washington, DC 20204, and ask for a list of additives identified as unsafe.

Health and Science

Demonstrate how preservatives affect foods. Provide zip closure plastic bags and bakery bread and prepackaged white bread exposed to the air for a few hours. Put a slice of bread in each bag; sprinkle water on each slice; seal and label the bags; and place them in a warm, dark place. Let students observe the bags daily to detemine on which slice of bread mold grows first. *CAUTION: Never open the bags as some students may be allergic to mold.*

Reteaching

Ask students to make a poster that tells why frying food is not a nutritious way to prepare food.

Special Education

Bring in examples of a food in its fresh and processed forms to show to learning-disabled students. Let students note differences between the products.

How Can You Cook Foods in Nutritious Ways?

Cooking food is one way you and your family process food at home. The way you cook food affects the amount of fat, vitamins, and other nutrients that you get. For example, foods lose some of their nutrients when they are overcooked. Fresh vegetables that are cooked until soft have lost much of their vitamins. Vegetables should be cooked just enough to make them tender, yet firm. Another healthy idea is to eat some vegetables raw, since raw vegetables keep most of their nutrients.

Frying foods in butter, oil, or some other fat adds that fat to the foods. Frying in fat also takes some nutrients out. Baking, broiling, steaming, roasting, boiling, and stir-frying provide alternatives to frying. The baked chicken shown here has kept most of its nutrients. It is less fatty than fried chicken. The liquid in the pan came from the chicken itself, not from additional cooking fats.

Think Back • *Study on your own with Study Guide page 321.*

1. What is the difference between processed potatoes and fresh potatoes?
2. How is food processing helpful?
3. Why do some people try to limit processed foods?
4. What are two nutritious ways to cook food?

Baked chicken has less fat than fried chicken.

Source for Did You Know?

Brody, Jane. *Jane Brody's Nutrition Book.* Norton, 1981.

3 Assess

Expanding Student Thinking

Ask students to explain the processing corn goes through from the time it is picked until it is served. Students may describe any of the processing methods discussed, including preparation that takes place at home.

Thinking Skills By identifying the steps in processing corn, students are *interpreting information* and *classifying.*

Answers to Think Back

1. Processed potatoes have been cut, cooked, canned, frozen, dried or changed in some other way before being sold. Fresh potatoes are whole, raw, unchanged potatoes.

2. Food processing helps preserve food and makes it more convenient to store or cook. It can also improve taste, color, and texture.

3. Many people try to limit processed foods because they think these foods might not be as nutritious or tasty as unprocessed foods.

4. Food can be cooked nutritiously by not overcooking and by choosing cooking methods other than frying in substances containing fat.

Life Skills

Use this worksheet for practice in reading food labels to discover and compare nutritional content. This worksheet is located on page 9 of the Student's Workbook. Use with Chapter 3: pages 96–99.

Thinking Skill: By comparing nutrition information on labels, students are organizing information.

Name ______________________ Life Skills

Use with Chapter 3: pages 96–99.

Reading Nutrition Labels

Use the information on the labels to answer the questions.

DRY CEREAL

	1 oz.
CALORIES	120
PROTEIN	5g
CARBOHYDRATES	19g
FAT	2g
SODIUM	180mg
POTASSIUM	120mg

PERCENTAGE OF U.S. RECOMMENDED DAILY ALLOWANCE (U.S. RDA)

	1 oz.
PROTEIN	10
VITAMIN A	*
VITAMIN C	*
THIAMIN	25
RIBOFLAVIN	25
NIACIN	25
CALCIUM	6
IRON	45
VITAMIN D	*
PHOSPHORUS	10

*CONTAINS LESS THAN 2% OF U.S. RDA OF THESE NUTRIENTS

GOLDEN SEEDLESS RAISINS

NUTRITION INFORMATION

Serving Size	½ cup
Servings per Container	5
Calories	250
Protein	3 grams
Carbohydrates	66 grams
Fat	0

PERCENTAGE OF U.S. RECOMMENDED DAILY ALLOWANCE (U.S. RDA) FOR 1/2 CUP SERVINGS

Protein	4	Calcium	4
Vitamin A	4	Iron	6
Vitamin C	*	Phosphorus	6
Thamin	0	Magnesium	6
Riboflavin	2	Copper	10
Niacin	2		

*CONTAINS LESS THAN 2% of U.S. RDA FOR THIS NUTRIENT

GREEN PEAS

NUTRITION INFORMATION PER SERVING

Serving Size	3.3 oz.
Servings per Container	9⅔
Calories	80
Protein	5 grams
Carbohydrates	13 grams
Fat	0
Sodium	95 milligrams

PERCENTAGE OF U.S. RECOMMENDED DAILY ALLOWANCES (U.S. RDA)

Protein	8	Riboflavin	6
Vitamin A	15	Niacin	10
Vitamin C	30	Calcium	2
Thaimin	20	Iron	8

PLAIN YOGURT

NUTRITION INFORMATION

Serving Size	8 oz
Servings per Container	4
Calories	150
Carbohydrates	17 grams
Protein	12 grams
Fat	4 grams

PERCENTAGE OF U.S. RECOMMENDED DAILY ALLOWANCES (U.S. RDA)

Protein	30	Niacin	*
Vitamin A	2	Calcium	40
Vitamin C	*	Iron	*
Thamin	4	Vitamin B12	20
Riboflavin	30	Phosphorus	35

*CONTAINS LESS THAN 2% OF U.S. RDA OF THESE NUTRIENTS

1. Which food has the most protein in one serving? Plain yogurt
2. Which food has the most fat in one serving? Plain yogurt
3. Which has the most carbohydrates in one serving? Golden seedless raisins
4. Which food has the most sodium in one serving? Dry cereal
5. Which food has the most calcium and phosphorus in one serving? Plain yogurt
6. Iron and copper help give you healthy red blood cells. Which food provides both of these nutrients? Golden seedless raisins
7. Which is the best source for iron alone? Dry cereal
8. What percentage of the RDA for vitamin C do green peas contain? 30 percent
9. Vitamin A helps keep the skin and eyes healthy. Which food has the most vitamin A in one serving? Green peas

Extension Idea: Ask students to choose one of the above products and draw the rest of the label.

45

Teaching Plan

Lesson 4 pages 96–98

Lesson Objective
State that a wise food consumer reads and compares food labels, and explain what important information is on food labels. Tell how to make wise food choices when away from home.

1 Motivate

Introducing the Lesson
Ask students to explain how they can tell what is in a food package. (by reading the label) Ask them to recall other kinds of information they have seen on labels. (name of manufacturer, weight of contents, ingredients, nutritional content, Calories per serving, directions for cooking, storage information, date by which food should be purchased or used) Write their answers on the chalkboard and add to the list as you teach Lesson 4.

Food labels have a lot of useful information

4 How Can You Be a Wise Food Consumer?

Lisa poured the milk and sat down to eat her breakfast cereal. She read the back and sides of the cereal box while she ate. Lisa suddenly raised her eyebrows in surprise. On the side panel she read that one serving of the cereal contains fifteen grams of sugar. She knew that fifteen grams is about the same as four teaspoons of sugar! Lisa made two decisions: to start eating unsweetened cereals and to read food labels more often.

Reading food labels is part of being a wise food consumer—someone who consumes, or uses, food. Most foods in a supermarket come in some sort of a container with a label. People often notice the variety of colors, designs, and product names on these labels. However, many people do not bother reading the rest of the information on labels. A wise food consumer reads and compares labels to find products with the best nutrition possible at the best price.

What Can Food Labels Tell You?

Food labels are like maps. They can tell you a lot if you know how to read them. Notice the labels on the food containers below. Each label has a list of ingredients. The ingredients must be listed in order by weight so that the main ingredients are at the top of the list.

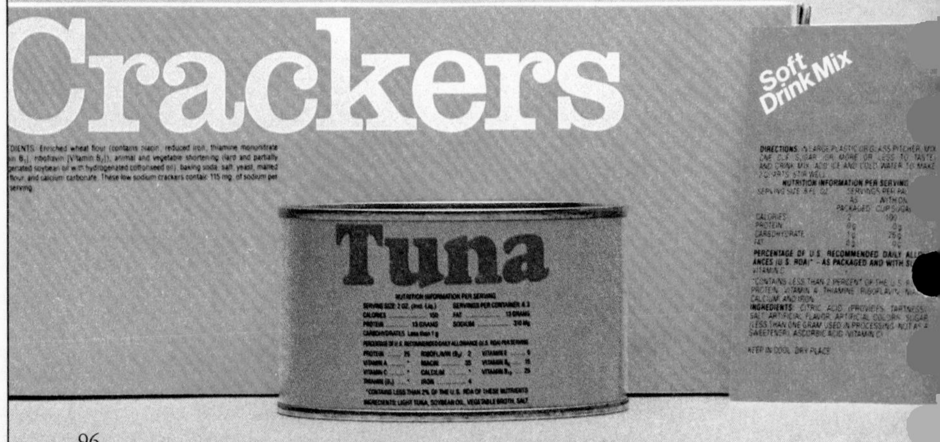

96

Teaching Options

Health Background

Reading food labels and noting ingredients, net weights, costs, dates, and nutritional values are some ways consumers can make wise food choices. Some categories of food are not required to have ingredients' lists (mayonnaise, ice cream, cheese for example), but must conform to certain standards.

Enrichment

Point out that mayonnaise, ice cream, and cheese do not require an ingredients panel on their packages. Encourage interested students to determine the contents of one of these products. They can do this by writing to the manufacturer or to the Food and Drug Administration, Washington, DC 20204.

Health and Art

Discuss packaging and how if influences purchases. Explain to students that manufacturers use color, package shape, brand name, slogans, and illustrations to get attention and encourage purchases. Let students design a package for a favorite food that will attract consumers' attention.

Reteaching

Ask students to bring in food labels from cereal, canned tomatoes, or canned or dehydrated soup containers. Group students in teams of three or four and give each group labels from the same product made by several different manufacturers. Tell them to compare the labels and list the differences in what the manufacturers include on the labels. Discuss how comparing the labels of similar products can help the students be wise food consumers.

For example, notice that the first two ingredients on the red box of cereal are rolled oats and sugar. Therefore, the box of cereal contains more oats, by weight, than sugar. What else, besides tunafish, is in the can of tuna shown on page 96?

Some labels also contain nutrition information. This information includes the amount of protein, vitamins, minerals, and other nutrients in each serving. The amount of fat, salt, and cholesterol might also be part of the nutrition information. Such information is especially important to consumers who are trying to limit the fat, salt, or cholesterol they eat. Notice the vitamins that are contained in the crackers shown on page 96. On several items you might notice the letters RDA. What do they mean?

The next time you go to the store, look for other information on food labels, such as the weight, date, name of manufacturer, and storage information. With a little practice, you can use food labels to become a better consumer.

On Your Own
Analyze one of the food labels on these two pages. Write the product name on a sheet of paper. Then answer the following questions. What is the ingredient in the largest amount? the lowest? What other information is given on the label? Which food group or groups does the food product belong to? What kinds of nutrients does it have?

2 Teach

Strategies for Pages 96 to 98

• Direct students to read page 96 to learn ways to be a wise food consumer. • Discuss the types of products on which they can recall seeing a list of ingredients on the label. (most prepackaged foods) • Let students read page 97 to learn about food labeling. • Ask students what types of information are found on food labels. (ingredients, nutritional information, weight, date, name of manufacturer, storage information, product guarantee) • Discuss how this informaiton is useful. (Answers should indicate an awareness of the connection between packaged food label information and a healthy diet.) • Explain to students that "net weight" means the weight of the food without the weight of the packaging. • Allow students to read page 98 to learn how to be a wise food consumer in a restaurant. • Ask students which foods on the menu shown they would avoid in order to limit fat. (onion rings, fried fish, fried chicken, fried hamburger, whole milk, chocolate cake, and pie with ice cream) • Ask which they would avoid to limit sugar. (soda pop, chocolate cake, and pie with ice cream) • Students may enjoy discussing the various types of restaurants in which they have eaten and how the menus and foods differed.

Teaching Plan

Lesson 4 continued

3 Assess

Expanding Student Thinking

Ask students to list three foods people might want to limit when ordering from a restaurant menu and why people may need to restrict intake of those particular foods. (Salt can lead to high blood pressure and heart problems; sugar can lead to tooth decay and overweight; fats can cause heart disease, overweight, and blood vessel disease.)

Thinking Skill Students are *interpreting information.*

Answers to Think Back

1. A wise food consumer reads and compares food labels to make the best possible choices.
2. The box of cereal contains most sugar by weight because ingredients are listed in order by weight.
3. Nutritional information might include the amount of nutrients in each serving and the amount of fat, salt, and cholesterol.
4. A wise consumer generally chooses foods low in fats, sugar, or salt. A person can also order smaller portions or take excess food home to avoid overeating.

How Can You Be a Wise Food Consumer in a Restaurant?

You have already learned in this chapter how to make healthy food choices in the supermarket and at home. Making healthy choices is important when eating in restaurants too. Some restaurant meals are high in fats, sugar, and salt. By choosing carefully, you can order a healthy meal.

Suppose you are at a restaurant, and a waiter gives you a menu like the one below. Which foods on the menu would you avoid if you want to limit fatty foods in your diet? Which foods would you avoid if you want to limit sweet foods in your diet?

When eating at a restaurant, you do not need to feel shy about ordering small portions or taking leftover food home. Some people tend to overeat at restaurants. Eating out can be a convenient and pleasant experience. You can use your knowledge about nutrition to make it a healthy experience too.

Think Back • *Study on your own with Study Guide page 321.*

1. What does a wise food consumer do to make the best possible food choices?
2. The first four ingredients on a certain box of cereal are sugar, oats, barley, and yeast. What does the box of cereal contain most, by weight? How do you know?
3. What kind of nutritional information might appear on a food label?
4. What healthy food choices can a wise food consumer make while eating at a restaurant?

Which foods would you choose for a healthy, good-tasting meal?

Appetizers: batter-fried onion rings; vegetable soup; raw vegetable platter with yogurt dip

Dinners: broiled fish; batter-fried fish; baked chicken; fried chicken; broiled steak; fried hamburger; beans, rice, and cheese casserole

Beverages: low-fat milk; whole milk; soda; orange juice; coffee; tea

Desserts: chocolate cake; fruit pie with ice cream; fresh fruit cup; yogurt with fresh blueberries

98

Teaching Options

Anecdote

In 1902 the first fully automated restaurant opened in Philadelphia. Foods were displayed behind little windows and customers served themselves by inserting coins to open the windows so they could get the food. These restaurants became known as "Automats."

Enrichment

Let students design and prepare a menu that helps customers make healthy eating choices. The menus should include three different lunches or dinners all of which provide healthy foods and a balanced diet.

You might want to ask a local restaurant or industrial cafeteria to arrange a special tour of its food storage and preparation areas.

Health and Social Studies

Direct students to research restaurants serving various ethnic foods. They may want to visit the restaurants and look at the menus, telephone for information, or use the library's resources.

Reteaching

Provide menus from several local restaurants for students to analyze. Give each group of three or four students a different menu. Ask them to determine which foods should not be ordered if a customer is on a fat-restricted diet, a low-salt diet, or a sugar-free diet. Let each team report its results to the class. The menus can also be used to gain practice in using the basic four food groups to choose healthy meals in a restaurant.

Health Activities Workshop

Investigating Food Labels

1. Bring to class a label from an empty food can, box, or jar from home. Then answer each of the following questions about the product:

- Which ingredient does this product contain the most of, by weight?
- What is the product's net weight—the weight of the product without the packaging?
- What vitamins does this product contain?
- Where would you write to send complaints or compliments about this product?

Using the information on the label, write at least five questions of your own. Exchange the list and labels with a classmate, and try to answer each other's questions.

2. Play an ingredients game. At home, write down the ingredients of several food products. At school, list the ingredients of each product on one side of the chalkboard. List the food products on the other side of the chalkboard in any order, as shown. See if your classmates can match each product with its list of ingredients.

3. Design your own food label. Use your imagination and what you have learned in this chapter to make the label both attractive and useful for consumers. If you wish, tape your label onto a can, jar, or box. You might design a label for a familiar brand name or make up your own brand name.

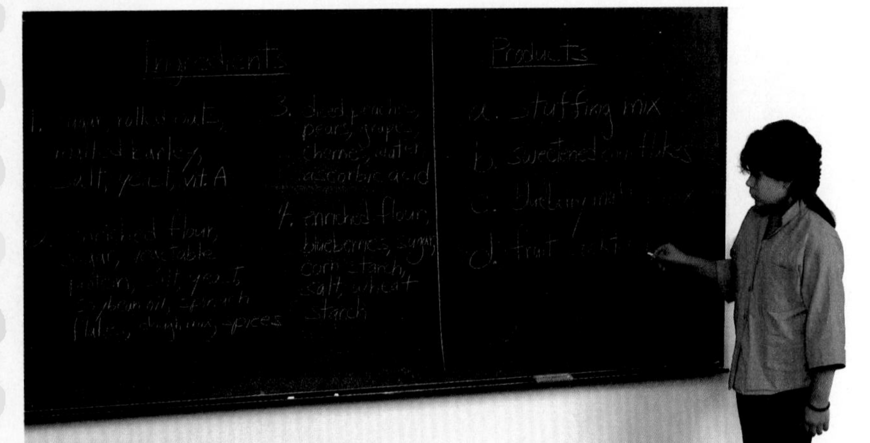

Health Activities Workshop page 99

Materials
Activity 1 labels from a variety of food products

Activity 1 Strategies
You might want to include some labels from generic foods. Additional questions might involve the size of a serving, the number of calories per serving, amount of protein, amount of carbohydrates, mineral content, directions for cooking, directions for storage, and date by which the product should be purchased. Point out that students may not be able to answer all of each other's questions because some food labels provide more information than others. Discuss those questions that cannot be answered. Encourage students to write to manufacturers to suggest ways to improve the information on a label or to explain why a particular label provides good information.
Thinking Skills By formulating and answering questions about information on food labels, students are *collecting* and *interpreting information.*

Activity 2 Strategies
You might want to have students work in groups. Students could bring the labels to school and put them on the bulletin board with the lists of ingredients covered. Ingredients' lists can be posted elsewhere on the board. The board with labels and lists can be used to play a matching game.
Thinking Skills By matching products and ingredients, students are *collecting information* and *classifying.*

Activity 3 Strategies
Encourage students to make their designs eye-catching. Point out that many products have slogans or designs on their labels that help consumers quickly identify and remember the product. Students should determine which label information to include based on what they have learned.
Thinking Skills By designing a food product label, students are *organizing information* and *suggesting alternatives.*

Health Focus page 100

Discussion

Point out that British sailors became known as "limeys" because lemons and limes were included on British naval vessels to prevent scurvy. Sailors ate fresh fruit or fruit juice because no method then existed for preserving fruit without losing vitamin C. Today, people can get vitamin C by drinking juice or eating canned, frozen, or fresh fruit.

Suggest that interested students conduct library research to identify other diseases that are controllable through diet. One such disease, *beriberi*, damages the nerves and heart.

Answers to Talk About It

1. Dr. James Lind is important because he discovered that scurvy could be prevented by including lemons and limes in the diet.
Thinking Skill Students are *recalling information*.
2. Answers should point to a lack of nutrients caused by a lack of variety in the diet.
Thinking Skills Students are *interpreting information* and *drawing conclusions*.

Health Focus

An Important Discovery About Disease and Diet

In the early 1700s, sailors in the British Navy led a very dangerous life. Fierce battles and raging storms at sea claimed many lives. Perhaps the greatest hazard of naval life, however, was a disease called *scurvy* (skėr′vē). On long voyages, scurvy often caused sore gums, a loss of teeth, bleeding within the body, and death. In fact, during wartime more British sailors died of scurvy than of battle wounds.

Then in the mid-1700s, a physician named James Lind studied this disease. He thought that scurvy might be related to the sailors' diets, which consisted only of salted beef and biscuits. Dr. Lind found that eating lemons prevented and cured scurvy. The painting shows Dr. Lind giving lemon juice to a sailor suffering from this disease. Lemon juice was included in the sailors' diets, and scurvy disappeared from the British Navy practically overnight.

Dr. Lind knew that something in the juice of lemons prevented scurvy. That "something" was later discovered to be vitamin C. Today scurvy is rare in the United States because most people include fruits and other sources of vitamin C in their diets.

The discovery of the cure for scurvy shows the importance of a varied diet. Eating a variety of foods helps provide the vitamins needed for good health.

Talk About It

1. Why is Dr. James Lind an important person in medical history?
2. Besides getting scurvy, what other kinds of food-related problems might have developed by eating a diet consisting only of salted beef and biscuits?

100

Teaching Options

Health Background

Around 1900, Christiaan Eijkman, a Dutch scientist, studied *beriberi* in Indonesia. The diets of the people there consisted mainly of rice. Dr. Eijkman found that people who ate polished rice—rice with the thin outer covering removed—developed beriberi. People who ate unpolished, or whole, rice did not get the disease. Dr. Eijkman thought that the covering of rice contained a substance that prevented beriberi. That substance was later identified as vitamin B_1. Beriberi is still common in some countries.

Vocabulary

Use this worksheet for practice in reviewing chapter vocabulary words. This master may be reproduced from the Teacher's Resource Book and also is located on page 10 of the Student's Workbook. Use with Chapter 3: pages 74–103.

Name ______________________ Vocabulary
Use with Chapter 3: pages 74–103.

Nutrition Wordsearch

Find and circle eleven nutrition terms in the wordsearch.
List each term and its meaning in the space below.

A C A R B O H Y D R A T E S F A A T S O E M A N C A R B O T A H Y D R V T
Z F D A Q B O O K R L V G E N P R E S E R V A T I V E L L O V D N T S I M
L O D L U F T A U Z I O E R L L R X O N O M P R O C E M B A Q U I R F T I
M O E S A T E Y M T V I T R N E T O C G O R I N E S T F S C R M F L I A N
O P R E S E R V I O A N U T R I E N T O F S L N V O T R A O C A I B E M E
T C S O F O O D P R O C E S S I N G A E L H G D E O B C A T L G B R L I T
H R H A F O D E N C T N A D I M N D P R I O A V N R N E S H S A E T I N A
A O E L M A M L P A R I B C I S U D T I O N P M P L A N K I T O R V N S L
U S J L I M O T T P A G L A P A K C H O L E S T E R O L I N O T S A U L M
B K O X Y C O O D E P H S N O N T T F I B A C H O L A D S O N G R E T P I

	Term	Meaning
1.	ADDITIVE	Substance added to food for a particular purpose
2.	CARBOHYDRATES	Group of nutrients that includes sugar, starch, and fiber
3.	CHOLESTEROL	A fatlike substance found in foods from animal sources
4.	FATS	Nutrients that provide energy and carry certain vitamins
5.	FIBER	A carbohydrate that helps move food and wastes through the body
6.	FOOD PROCESSING	The changing of food before it is eaten
7.	MINERALS	Nutrients needed for healthy teeth, bones, and muscles
8.	NUTRIENT	Substance found in food that the body needs to stay healthy
9.	PRESERVATIVE	An additive that helps keep food from spoiling
10.	PROTEINS	Nutrients that build, repair, and maintain body cells
11.	VITAMINS	Nutrients needed in small amounts to keep the body healthy.

46 *Extension Idea:* Use each of the terms to describe a healthy diet.

Breaking the Salt Habit

Eating too much salt over a long period of time can lead to high blood pressure in some people. Your body does need some salt—about a tenth of a teaspoon each day. The average American, however, consumes two or four teaspoons every day!

Many food products you buy at the store contain added salt. You can become aware of which products contain salt by examining the labels of foods in your kitchen or pantry. Look also for the word *sodium,* the chemical symbol Na, and any term that includes *sodium.*

With so many products containing salt, you might think it is impossible to avoid too much salt. However, the tips below can help you and your family break the salt habit. You might want to share these tips with your family.

- Cut down on extremely salty foods. These foods include potato chips and other snack chips, pretzels, salted peanuts, olives, pickles, and lunch meats.
- Try to reduce the amount of salt added to food while cooking.
- Borrow a low-salt cookbook from the library. Many recipes use herbs and spices rather than salt to add flavor to food. Ask if you can plan a meal or help cook a meal from a low-salt cookbook.
- Taste before adding salt to anything you eat. Better yet, remove the saltshaker from the table altogether.

Reading at Home

Junk Food—What It is, What It Does by Judith S. Seixas. Greenwillow, 1984. Find out what junk food is, how it affects you, and what you can do about it.

Stuffin' Muffin: Muffin Pan Cooking for Kids by Strom Scherie. Young People's Pr. Mar., 1982. Have fun cooking meals from this very special cookbook.

Health at Home

page 101

Strategies

Point out to students that canned vegetables usually contain more salt than frozen or fresh vegetables. Explain that one way to eliminate some of the salt from canned vegetables is to rinse them in clear water before cooking them. Be sure students understand that salt intake can best be limited by purchasing fresh or frozen vegetables. You might want to ask students to bring their lists to class. Appoint a group to tabulate the information from all the students' lists and to determine which items commonly purchased are highest in salt content. Let the group report the findings to the class. Students may want to reproduce this "salt alert sheet" to share with their parents. Invite the school nurse or dietitian to your class to discuss the most recent findings about salt in diets.

More Reading at Home

Junk Food—What It Is, What It Does (Grades 5-8)

Stuffin' Muffin: Muffin Pan Cooking for Kids (Grades 4-6)

George, Jean Craighead. *The Wild, Wild Cookbook.* T. Y. Crowell, 1982. A field guide for finding, harvesting, and cooking wild plants. (Grades 5-8)

Study and Review

Use this worksheet for practice in studying and reviewing basic nutrition. This master may be reproduced from the Teacher's Resource Book and also is located on page 11 of the Student's Workbook. Use with Chapter 3: pages 74-103.

Name ____________________ Study and Review

Use with Chapter 3: pages 74–103.

Nutrition Review

Part I. Complete the chart.

Nutrient Group	What the nutrient does for the body	Sources of nutrient
1. Carbohydrates	2. Provide the body with energy	Milk, honey, fruits, vegetables, and grain
Fats	3. Provide energy; carry vitamins to cells	4. Butter, meat, oil, and margarine
5. Proteins	Build, repair, and replace cells	6. Meat, fish, beans, peas, and eggs
Vitamins	7. Keep body working properly	8. Meat, fish, milk, fruits and vegetables
9. Minerals	10. Keep body working properly	Meat, fish, milk, fruits, and vegetables
11. Water	Carries other nutrients to and from cells Helps cool body	12. Beverages, fruits, and soup

Part II. Answer the questions.

1. What is a nutrient? A substance the body needs to stay healthy
2. Why should you eat a variety of food? To get all of the nutrients you need for good health
3. What is food processing? A way of preparing food for storage or consumption
4. What are two methods of processing food? Freeze-drying; canning
5. What are the four food groups? Meat-poultry-fish-bean, Bread-cereal, Fruit-vegetable, Milk-cheese

***Extension Idea:* Ask students to list ways to limit fats, salt, and sugar in their diets.**

47

Review Plan

Chapter 3 Review

pages 102–103

Answers to Reviewing Lesson Objectives

Use this section for guided study or for oral review. Objective numbers match lesson numbers.

1. Carbohydrates—provide energy, some help move food and wastes through the body; fats—supply energy and certain vitamins to body cells; proteins—build, repair, and replace cells and provide energy; vitamins—keep the body working properly; minerals—help give people healthy teeth, bones, muscles, and blood cells; water—carries nutrients to cells and wastes from cells, helps cool the body.

2. A healthy diet should include a variety of foods. It should include the correct number of servings from each of the four food groups every day. The basic four food groups and suggested daily servings from each are the milk-cheese group—3, meat-fish-poultry-bean group—2, fruit-vegetable group—4, and bread-cereal group—4.

3. Drying and freeze-drying preserve food and reduce the size and weight of food. Canning and freezing preserve food and reduce cooking time. Some nutrients are lost from food during the canning process. The various methods of processing foods also affect the taste. Reading labels and cooking to preserve nutrients are healthy ways to choose foods.

4. Labels often tell what ingredients a product contains; amounts of nutrients the product contains; amounts of sugar, fats, salt, and cholesterol in the product; product weight, and date of manufacture. This information can help people choose foods that are nutritious and that do not have large amounts of substances they want to limit in their diets. It can also help people make wise food choices at restaurants.

Answers to Checking Health Vocabulary

Use the vocabulary check as a review or as a test.

1. h **5.** j **9.** d
2. k **6.** b **10.** g
3. e **7.** a **11.** i
4. f **8.** c

Chapter 3 Review

Reviewing Lesson Objectives

1. List the six kinds of nutrients and explain how getting the proper amount of each nutrient helps the body to function. (pages 76–81)
2. Describe what a healthy diet should include. List the basic four food groups and the suggested servings from each group. (pages 82–87)
3. List four ways of processing food. Explain how each method affects the quality of food and how a person can choose foods processed the healthiest ways. (pages 90–95)
4. Explain what important information is on food labels. Tell how to make wise food choices when away from home. (pages 96–98)

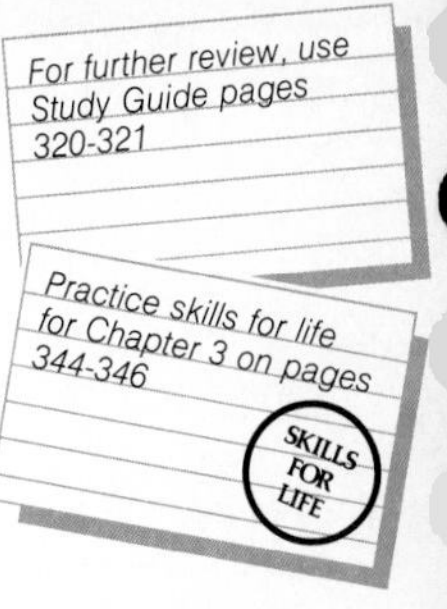

For further review, use Study Guide pages 320-321
Practice skills for life for Chapter 3 on pages 344-346
SKILLS FOR LIFE

Checking Health Vocabulary

Number your paper from 1–11. Match each definition in Column I with the correct word or words in Column II.

Column I

1. a substance found in food that the body needs to stay healthy
2. a group of nutrients needed in small amounts to keep the body working properly; examples include A and D
3. a carbohydrate that helps move food and wastes through the body
4. the changing of food before it is eaten
5. the group of nutrients that builds, repairs, and maintains body cells
6. the group of nutrients that includes sugar, starch, and fiber
7. any substance added to food for a particular purpose
8. a fatlike substance that is made naturally in the body and is present in foods from animal sources
9. a group of nutrients that provides energy and carries certain vitamins through the body
10. a group of nutrients needed to provide healthy teeth, bones, muscles, and blood cells
11. an additive that helps keep food from spoiling

Column II

a. additive
b. carbohydrates
c. cholesterol
d. fats
e. fiber
f. food processing
g. minerals
h. nutrient
i. preservative
j. proteins
k. vitamins

Chapter 3 Tests Use Test A or Test B to assess students' mastery of the health concepts in Chapter 3. These tests are located on pages 25–32 in the Test Book.

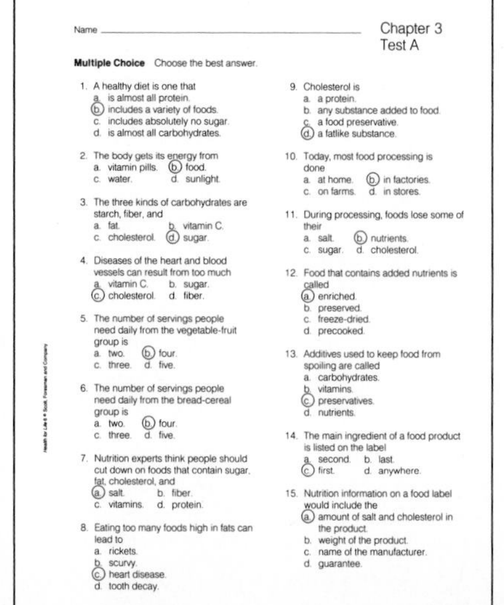

Name ______________________ Chapter 3 Test A

Multiple Choice Choose the best answer.

1. A healthy diet is one that
 a. is almost all protein.
 (b.) includes a variety of foods.
 c. includes absolutely no sugar.
 d. is almost all carbohydrates.
2. The body gets its energy from
 a. vitamin pills. (b.) food.
 c. water. d. sunlight.
3. The three kinds of carbohydrates are starch, fiber, and
 a. fat. b. vitamin C.
 c. cholesterol. (d.) sugar.
4. Diseases of the heart and blood vessels can result from too much
 a. vitamin C. b. sugar.
 (c.) cholesterol. d. fiber.
5. The number of servings people need daily from the vegetable-fruit group is
 a. two. (b.) four.
 c. three. d. five.
6. The number of servings people need daily from the bread-cereal group is
 a. two. (b.) four.
 c. three. d. five.
7. Nutrition experts think people should cut down on foods that contain sugar, fat, cholesterol, and
 (a.) salt. b. fiber.
 c. vitamins. d. protein.
8. Eating too many foods high in fats can lead to
 a. rickets.
 b. scurvy.
 (c.) heart disease.
 d. tooth decay.
9. Cholesterol is
 a. a protein.
 b. any substance added to food.
 c. a food preservative.
 (d.) a fatlike substance.
10. Today, most food processing is done
 a. at home. (b.) in factories.
 c. on farms. d. in stores.
11. During processing, foods lose some of their
 a. salt. (b.) nutrients.
 c. sugar. d. cholesterol.
12. Food that contains added nutrients is called
 (a.) enriched.
 b. preserved.
 c. freeze-dried.
 d. precooked.
13. Additives used to keep food from spoiling are called
 a. carbohydrates.
 b. vitamins.
 (c.) preservatives.
 d. nutrients.
14. The main ingredient of a food product is listed on the label
 a. second. b. last.
 (c.) first. d. anywhere.
15. Nutrition information on a food label would include the
 (a.) amount of salt and cholesterol in the product.
 b. weight of the product.
 c. name of the manufacturer.
 d. guarantee.

Health for Life 6 © Scott, Foresman and Company

29

Name ______________________ Chapter 3 Test A

Short Answer Match each term in Column I with the correct definition in Column II. Write the correct letter on the blank.

Column I

c 16. nutrient
e 17. proteins
g 18. minerals
a 19. vitamins
b 20. fiber
h 21. fats
f 22. additives
d 23. food processing

Column II

a. nutrients needed in small amounts to keep body working properly
b. a carbohydrate that helps move food and wastes through the body
c. a substance in food that body needs to stay healthy
d. the changing of food before it is eaten
e. nutrients that build, repair, and maintain body cells
f. any substance added to food for a particular purpose
g. nutrients that provide healthy teeth, bones, muscles, and blood cells
h. nutrients that provide energy and carry certain vitamins through the body

Short Essay Write your answers in complete sentences.

24. Why are food additives used?
Food additives are added to foods for many reasons. Some help preserve food. Others add nutrients. Many additives add color, texture, or flavor.

25. Describe three reasons to read labels on the products you might buy at a grocery store.
Answers will vary, may include: to check for sugar content, salt content, amount of fat and cholesterol, additives, preservatives, date, weight, or guarantee.

Health for Life 6 © Scott, Foresman and Company

30

Reviewing Health Ideas

Number your paper from 1–15. Next to each number write the word or words that best complete the sentence.

1. The carbohydrate that helps move food and wastes through the body is ____.
2. Potatoes, rice, macaroni, and bread are all good sources of ____, a kind of carbohydrate.
3. Like carbohydrates, ____ are a group of nutrients that supply energy.
4. Nutrition experts recommend that people choose ____ sources as well as animal sources of protein.
5. Minerals that help build strong bones include ____ and phosphorus.
6. A healthy diet includes a ____ of foods every day.
7. A person should have two servings from the ____ group every day.
8. A person should eat ____ servings each day from the fruit-vegetable group.
9. Nutrition experts think people should limit foods that contain much sugar, fat, cholesterol, and ____.
10. Drying and freeze-drying removes water from food so that ____ cannot grow in it.
11. Some ____ in canned foods leak out into the water packed in the can.
12. Food that has nutrients added to it would have the word fortified or ____ on its package.
13. Fresh vegetables lose much of their vitamins if they are cooked until ____.
14. A wise food consumer reads and ____ food labels.
15. Ingredients are listed in order by ____.

Understanding Health Ideas

Number your paper from 16–25. Next to each number write the word or words that best answer the question.

16. What are the six major groups of nutrients?
17. What nutrients do experts think should make up half of your diet?
18. How can a person best be sure of getting all the vitamins and minerals he or she needs?
19. What are the basic four food groups and the recommended daily servings from each group?
20. What health problem can too much fat and cholesterol in the diet cause?
21. What health problem might too much salt in the diet cause?
22. What are four common methods of food processing?
23. Why are additives used in food?
24. Which government organization studies and tests additives?
25. How can you make wise choices in a restaurant?
26. What are some alternative cooking methods to frying?
27. What is a food consumer?
28. What information can be found on a food label?

Thinking Critically

Write the answers on your paper. Use complete sentences.

1. Why are vitamin pills probably unnecessary if someone has a balanced diet?
2. Suppose you had a glass of milk, half a grapefruit, two slices of toast, and a soft-boiled egg for breakfast. List foods for the rest of the day that would provide a healthy daily diet.

103

Answers to Reviewing Health Ideas

1. fiber
2. starch
3. fats
4. vegetable
5. calcium
6. variety
7. meat-fish-poultry-bean
8. four
9. salt
10. bacteria
11. nutrients
12. enriched
13. soft
14. compares
15. weight

Answers to Understanding Health Ideas

16. carbohydrates, fats, protein, vitamins, minerals, and water
17. carbohydrates
18. by eating a variety of foods each day
19. milk-cheese—3, meat-fish-poultry-bean—2, fruit-vegatable—4, and bread-cereal—4
20. overweight and diseases of the heart and blood vessels
21. high blood pressure
22. drying, freeze-drying, canning, and freezing
23. to preserve food or to add taste, color, texture, or nutrients
24. Food and Drug Administration
25. by avoiding fatty foods, ordering small portions, taking leftovers home, and limiting sweet foods.
26. baking, broiling, steaming, roasting, boiling, and stir-frying
27. a person who uses food
28. a list of ingredients, nutrition information, weight, dates, name of manufacturer, storage information, and guarantees

Answers to Thinking Critically

1. A balanced diet naturally contains a variety of vitamins in the right amounts. Supplementary vitamin pills are probably unnecessary.
Thinking Skills Students are *drawing conclusions.*
2. Answers should include foods that provide the right number of servings from the basic four food groups shown on page 83.
Thinking Skills Students are *suggesting alternatives.*

Cooperative Learning Use the STAD Format described on page T24 to have four- to five-member teams study Chapter 3 Review together before completing Chapter 3 Test.

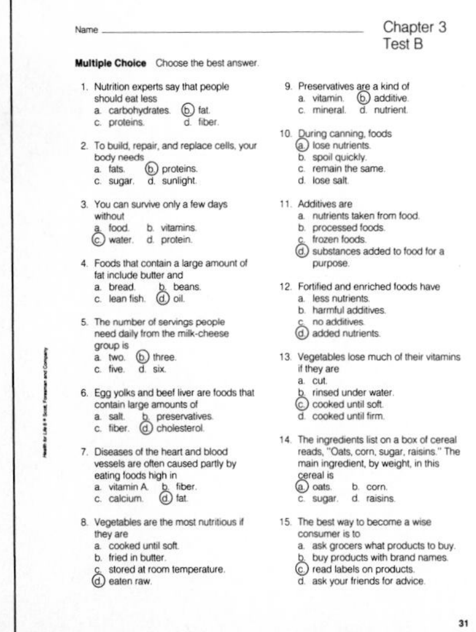
Name ____________ Chapter 3 Test B

Multiple Choice Choose the best answer.

1. Nutrition experts say that people should eat less
   a. carbohydrates. (b.) fat. c. proteins. d. fiber.
2. To build, repair, and replace cells, your body needs
   a. fats. (b.) proteins. c. sugar. d. sunlight.
3. You can survive only a few days without
   a. food. b. vitamins. (c.) water. d. protein.
4. Foods that contain a large amount of fat include butter and
   a. bread. b. beans. c. lean fish. (d.) oil.
5. The number of servings people need daily from the milk-cheese group is
   a. two. (b.) three. c. five. d. six.
6. Egg yolks and beef liver are foods that contain large amounts of
   a. salt. b. preservatives. c. fiber. (d.) cholesterol.
7. Diseases of the heart and blood vessels are often caused partly by eating foods high in
   a. vitamin A. b. fiber. c. calcium. (d.) fat.
8. Vegetables are the most nutritious if they are
   a. cooked until soft. b. fried in butter. c. stored at room temperature. (d.) eaten raw.
9. Preservatives are a kind of
   a. vitamin. (b.) additive. c. mineral. d. nutrient.
10. During canning, foods
    (a.) lose nutrients. b. spoil quickly. c. remain the same. d. lose salt.
11. Additives are
    a. nutrients taken from food. b. processed foods. c. frozen foods. (d.) substances added to food for a purpose.
12. Fortified and enriched foods have
    a. less nutrients. b. harmful additives. c. no additives. (d.) added nutrients.
13. Vegetables lose much of their vitamins if they are
    a. cut. b. rinsed under water. (c.) cooked until soft. d. cooked until firm.
14. The ingredients list on a box of cereal reads, "Oats, corn, sugar, raisins." The main ingredient, by weight, in this cereal is
    (a.) oats. b. corn. c. sugar. d. raisins.
15. The best way to become a wise consumer is to
    a. ask grocers what products to buy. b. buy products with brand names. (c.) read labels on products. d. ask your friends for advice.

31

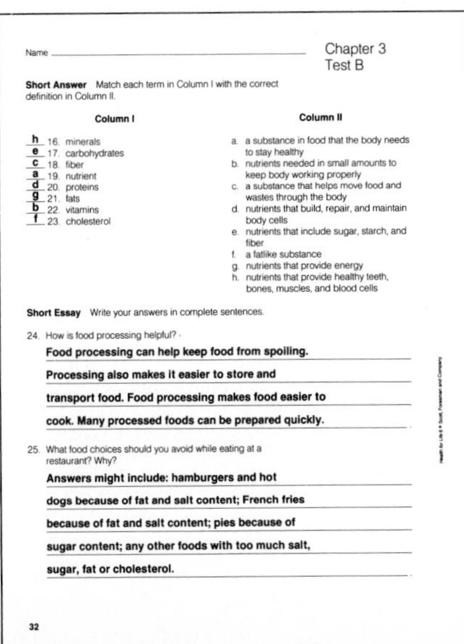
Name ____________ Chapter 3 Test B

Short Answer Match each term in Column I with the correct definition in Column II.

Column I	Column II
h 16. minerals	a. a substance in food that the body needs to stay healthy
e 17. carbohydrates	b. nutrients needed in small amounts to keep body working properly
c 18. fiber	c. a substance that helps move food and wastes through the body
a 19. nutrient	d. nutrients that build, repair, and maintain body cells
d 20. proteins	e. nutrients that include sugar, starch, and fiber
g 21. fats	f. a fatlike substance
b 22. vitamins	g. nutrients that provide energy
f 23. cholesterol	h. nutrients that provide healthy teeth, bones, muscles, and blood cells

Short Essay Write your answers in complete sentences.

24. How is food processing helpful?
    Food processing can help keep food from spoiling. Processing also makes it easier to store and transport food. Food processing makes food easier to cook. Many processed foods can be prepared quickly.
25. What food choices should you avoid while eating at a restaurant? Why?
    Answers might include: hamburgers and hot dogs because of fat and salt content; French fries because of fat and salt content; pies because of sugar content; any other foods with too much salt, sugar, fat or cholesterol.

32

CHAPTER 4 PLANNING GUIDE Pupil Edition

Pupil Edition	Activities	Enrichment	Assessment	Independent Study
Chapter 4 Becoming Phyically Fit, pp. 104–139	Health Watch Notebook, p. 104 Project Keep-Fit, pp. 130–135	Health Focus, p. 136 Health at Home, p. 137	Chapter 4 Review, pp. 138–139	Study Guide, pp. 322–323 Skills for Life Handbook, pp. 347–349
Lesson 1 How Does Exercise Improve Health? pp. 106–111			Think Back, p. 111	On Your Own, p. 111 Study Guide, p. 322
Lesson 2 How Does Exercise Help Control Body Fatness? pp. 112–115		Did You Know? pp. 112, 115	Think Back, p. 115	Study Guide, p. 322
Lesson 3 What Is Skills Fitness? pp. 116–117	Health Activities Workshop, pp. 118–119		Think Back, p. 117	Study Guide, p. 322
Lesson 4 How Can You Set Good Fitness Goals? pp. 120–125			Think Back, p. 125	On Your Own, p. 120 Study Guide, p. 323
Lesson 5 How Can You Achieve Your Fitness Goals? pp. 126–129			Think Back, p. 129	On Your Own, p. 126 Study Guide, p. 323

Teacher Resources

Alter, Judy. *Surviving Exercise.* Houghton Mifflin, 1983. Contains "readying exercises" for any activity, and includes a safe, complete warm-up and cool-down program.

Corbin, Charles S., and Lindsey, Ruth. *Fitness for Life.* Scott, Foresman, 1983. Teaches students how to solve their own fitness and exercise problems so they can maintain fitness throughout life.

Lyttle, Richard B. *The Games They Played: Sports in History.* Atheneum, 1982. Describes how ancient sports evolved into the games we play today.

Siegel, Alice, and McLoone, Margo. *It's a Girl's Game Too.* Holt, 1980. Includes a brief history of various sports, and gives helpful hints for girls who play sports.

Audio-Visual Resources

See page T43 for addresses of Audio-Visual Sources.

Before using any audio-visual materials, preview them for appropriateness for your students.

Exercise Workshop, Educational Activities, Inc., cassettes or records. Provides body stretching exercises designed to increase body tone, flexibility, and knowledge of various muscle groups.

Fitness for Living, Walt Disney, filmstrips with cassettes. Conveys the importance of starting on the road to physical fitness early, and encourages students to take responsibility for their own fitness. Endorsed by the President's Council on Physical Fitness.

The Human Body: What Can Go Wrong? Series II, Focus Media, Inc., filmstrips with cassettes. Describes ailments and injuries which may occur during exercise or other physical activities.

Why Exercise? AIMS Media, film or video, 14 minutes. Shows how exercise increases strength and endurance, and improves flexibility.

Computer Software

Heartlab, Educational Activities, Inc. Provides students with an opportunity to observe the heart in action (through simulation). Instructs students on how to take a pulse reading before and after exercising, to measure how the heart responds to work.

	Teacher's Edition	Teacher's Resource Book	Test Book
Enrichment	Suggestions for each lesson: L. 1—pp. 106, 108, 110 L. 2—pp. 112, 114 L. 3—p. 116 L. 4—pp. 120, 122, 124 L. 5—pp. 126, 128	Family Letter, p. 53 * Life Skills, p. 57 * Health and Mathematics, p. 60	
Reteaching	Suggestions for each lesson: L. 1—pp. 106, 108, 110 L. 2—pp. 112, 114 L. 3—p. 116 L. 4—pp. 120, 122, 124 L. 5—pp. 126, 128	Transparency Masters, pp. 55-56 * Vocabulary, p. 58 * Study and Review, p. 59	
Assessment	Expanding Student Thinking: one assessment question per lesson that develops higher-order thinking skills—pp. 111, 115, 117, 125, 129		Chapter 4 Test, Form A, pp. 33-34 Chapter 4 Test, Form B, pp. 35-36

* Also available in Workbook format (Student Edition and Teacher's Edition)

Chapter 4 Poster

A set of posters is available in a separate package. It provides a teaching poster for every chapter, including discussion and activity suggestions on the back. The poster for Chapter 4 is titled "Which physical activities have you tried?"

Overhead Transparencies

A set of color overhead transparencies is available for Grade 6. You may wish to use Transparencies 2, 5, and 12 to help teach about the respiratory system, goal setting, and ways to exercise safely.

Advance Preparation

You will need to prepare materials in advance for the following activities from the Health Activities Workshop.
Activity 1, page 118 Provide several meter sticks or yard sticks.
Activity 3, page 118 Provide posterboard and magazines that could be cut up for posters.

Bulletin Board

Encourage students to draw or cut out magazine pictures of people having fun while exercising. Use these pictures to make a colorful bulletin board. Ask students to talk about the fun they have while exercising.

Teaching Plan

Chapter 4 pages 104–139

Chapter Main Idea
Developing and achieving physical fitness goals can contribute to a healthy lifestyle.

Chapter Goals
- Express a desire to achieve personal physical fitness.
- Appreciate the need to exercise safely.

Lifetime Goal
Understand that fitness can be achieved and maintained throughout life.

Health Vocabulary
Agility, Calorie, cardiovascular system, coordination, flexibility, muscular endurance, physical fitness, respiratory system

Words to Preteach
Artery, blood vessels, calipers, carbon dioxide, diabetes, heart disease, high blood pressure, nutrients, oxygen

Chapter 4

Becoming Physically Fit

"We did it!" The feelings of joy and accomplishment are obvious in those words and this picture. Whether participating in a sporting event or doing daily activities, being physically fit helps you perform your very best.

This chapter explains how exercise and physical fitness can help you have a healthy life. You will learn how you can become physically fit and have fun doing it. The chapter includes several exercises you might do. Through proper exercise, you will discover how to stay fit throughout your life.

Health Watch Notebook

In your notebook, write three fitness goals that you would like to achieve. As you read the chapter, note ways in which you can meet your goals. Keep track of your progress as you develop a personal fitness plan.

104

Teaching Options

Modeling Health Vocabulary
Use this technique to introduce new words as you teach each lesson in this chapter. First, introduce the word. Present the word in two sentences that serve to clearly define the word. One sentence you might use to introduce the term *physical fitness* is the following: *A person can build physical fitness by exercising regularly.* Either read the sentences to the students or write them on the chalkboard. Ask the students to generate two meaningful sentences using the word. Additional successful techniques for introducing new words can be found on page T23.

Cooperative Learning
Jigsaw Format (See page T24).
Assign the following topics at random to your cooperative learning teams.
Topic A: Explain how exercise helps a person become physically fit.
Topic B: Describe how a person can control his or her body fatness.
Topic C: Name the six parts of skills fitness and define each one.
Topic D: What are some rules to remember when setting up a fitness plan?
Have students search for information on their topic as they read the chapter. Then let all students with the same topic meet in an expert group to discuss the information. When students return to their teams, they may take turns presenting their topics to the team. Then give students a test covering all topics to complete individually (Chapter 4 test A or B in the Test Book). Award Superteam certificates to teams whose average test scores exceed 90%, and Greatteam certificates to teams whose average test scores exceed 80%.

Introducing the Chapter

Encourage students to discuss their daily physical activities by asking them what activities they enjoy. (Answers might include playing games, riding bicycles, and sports.) Ask students how they think these activities help keep their bodies fit. Tell students that they would probably benefit from a planned daily exercise program. Explain that even students who exercise regularly may not be doing all the different types of exercises their bodies need. When students try exercises from this chapter, supervise them carefully. The general strategies for Project Keep-Fit on page 130 need to be followed for all exercise programs. You may wish to send the Family Letter home at this time. You may want to assign Study Guide pages 322–323 for students to use independently as they read the lessons. The Study Guide can also be used as an extra chapter review. You might want to assign the activities in the Skills for Life Handbook on pages 347–349.

Strategies for Health Watch Notebook

Help students decide on their fitness goals by outlining for them the six fitness skills as described on pages 116 and 117. Students may want to consider their favorite activities in deciding on fitness goals.

Family Letter

Use the Family Letter (English or Spanish version) to introduce the subject matter of the chapter to the family and to suggest a way the family can become involved in the student's learning experience. This master may be reproduced from the Teacher's Resource Book.

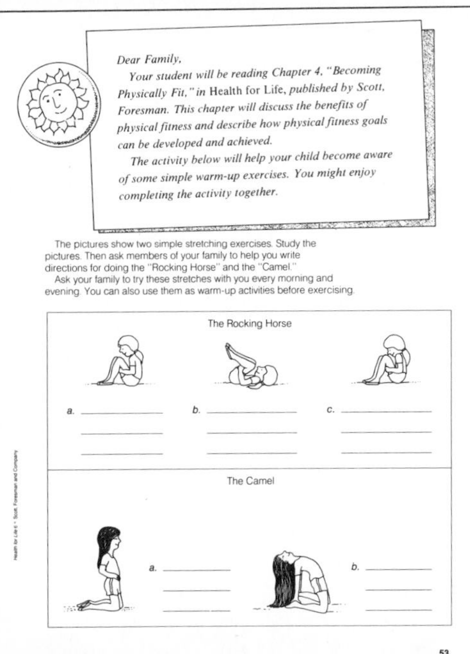

Dear Family,

Your student will be reading Chapter 4, "Becoming Physically Fit," in Health for Life, *published by Scott, Foresman. This chapter will discuss the benefits of physical fitness and describe how physical fitness goals can be developed and achieved.*

The activity below will help your child become aware of some simple warm-up exercises. You might enjoy completing the activity together.

The pictures show two simple stretching exercises. Study the pictures. Then ask members of your family to help you write directions for doing the "Rocking Horse" and the "Camel."

Ask your family to try these stretches with you every morning and evening. You can also use them as warm-up activities before exercising.

The Rocking Horse

a. ______

b. ______

c. ______

The Camel

a. ______

b. ______

53

For High-Potential Students

Encourage interested students to identify health and skills fitness goals that they feel are most important to their age group. Students should then design a series of exercise machines and activities that could be used to reach their health and fitness goals. Students might refer to a book of cartoons by Rube Goldberg for ideas.

Teaching Plan

Lesson 1 pages 106–111

Lesson Objective
Explain how exercise helps improve mental health, social health, and physical health. Recognize the role that regular, vigorous physical activity plays in promoting a positive self-concept and a healthy body.

Health Vocabulary
Cardiovascular system, flexibility, muscular endurance, physical fitness, respiratory system

1 Motivate

Introducing the Lesson
Ask students what kind of exercise they get. (Answers might include bicycling, running, and swimming.) Ask them to describe how they feel when they are exercising. (Answers will vary depending on the activity but might include happy, excited, tired.)

1 How Does Exercise Improve Health?

After a good night's sleep and a campfire breakfast, Allison was ready for a morning hike with the rest of her scout troop. In the afternoon the girls went canoeing around the lake. After dinner Allison helped organize a softball game. Exercise is important to Allison. It helps her enjoy an active, healthy life. Most people enjoy doing some kind of exercise. What kinds of exercise do you like to do?

What Areas of Health Can Exercise Improve?

You probably know that exercise can improve physical health. You might be surprised to learn that exercise can also improve mental health. Relieving stress is one important way exercise can improve mental health. If you are worried or angry, physical activity can help you feel calmer and more relaxed.

Exercise can also improve your mental health by helping you feel good about yourself. Regular exercise can help you look your best. You feel good about yourself when you know you look the best you can. Physical activity also helps build strong, fit muscles that help you have good posture. Having good posture helps you look and feel your best.

Exercise can help you feel good about yourself by giving you a feeling of accomplishment. The girls in the picture have run the entire length of the beach for the first time. How does that help them feel good about themselves?

How does exercise help people enjoy life?

106

Teaching Options

Health Background
Cardiovascular fitness refers to the fitness of the cardiovascular and respiratory systems—the heart, blood, blood vessels, and lungs. This type of fitness is perhaps the most important in terms of physical health benefits. Studies show that people with good cardiovascular fitness have less heart disease and are less likely to die from heart attacks than people with poor cardiovascular fitness.

Enrichment
If possible, invite a doctor or physical therapist to visit the class to explain how exercise is often used to help people recover or decrease debilitation from certain illnesses.

Health and Language Arts
Ask students to write a paragraph describing how a physically fit person might look, feel, and act. (Accept paragraphs that reflect student understanding of the information on pages 106 and 107.

Reteaching
Direct students to observe a team sport played by other students during recess or after school. Encourage students to look for examples of communication and cooperation during the game. Such observations can also be made while watching a professional sporting event on television. Let students report their findings to the class.

Exercise can also improve your social health. The students in the picture have found that taking part in exercise is a good way to meet people and make friends. Such team sports as volleyball and basketball help people learn to communicate and cooperate. These skills can help you get along well with other people all through your life.

The area of health most affected by exercise is physical health. Exercise improves your **physical fitness.** If you are physically fit, you do not get tired easily during exercise. Your body parts work at their best. You are also less likely to develop certain diseases. Exercise helps you look, feel, and be as healthy as you can be.

physical fitness, the ability to exercise, play, and work without tiring easily and without a high risk of injury.

What social skills are being developed here?

2 Teach

Strategies for Pages 106 and 107

• Write the lesson title on the chalkboard. • Then ask students to read pages 106 and 107 to learn some benefits of exercise. • Discuss how exercise helps improve physical health. (helps people build strong muscles and resist disease, improves posture) • Ask students to list ways exercise improves mental health. (helps people feel more relaxed and feel good about themselves, improves appearance) Emphasize that when people feel stress, anger, or worry, exercise can help them relax.

• Discuss how exercise helps a person's social health. (Participating in group activities is a good way to meet people, make new friends, and learn to communicate and cooperate.) Point out that these skills are important throughout life. • Ask what physical fitness is. (The ability to exercise, work, or play without tiring or getting injured easily.) Emphasize that a person does not need to be an athlete to be physically fit. • Be sure students understand that exercise is what most improves a person's physical fitness.

Teaching Plan

Lesson 1 continued

2 Teach

Strategies for Pages 108 and 109

• Write the term *cardiovascular system* on the chalkboard. • Then ask students to read page 108 and the first paragraph of page 109 to learn how exercise affects the cardiovascular system. • Be sure they understand that the cardiovascular system carries oxygen and nutrients to cells and carries wastes away from the cells. • Ask students to point out which heart in the picture on page 108 is stronger. (The one pumping more blood.)
• Discuss how exercise can affect the cardiovascular system. (Exercise makes the heart stronger. A fit heart can supply the extra blood muscles need when they are working hard. Exercise also helps keep the blood vessels free of fatty material and helps develop an extra branching of arteries in the heart.) • Ask the students what activities they would enjoy more if their muscles did not tire easily. (Answers will vary but might include strenuous sports or activities.)
• Ask a volunteer to read the last three paragraphs on page 109 to find out what happens when a person breathes.

cardiovascular (kär′dē ō vas′kyə lər) **system,** the body system made up of the heart, blood, and blood vessels. This system moves oxygen and nutrients to body cells and removes cell wastes.

How Can Exercise Affect Your Cardiovascular System?

Many parts of your body work together as body systems. Your heart, blood, and blood vessels make up your **cardiovascular system.** This system takes oxygen and nutrients to your cells and carries carbon dioxide and other wastes away from your cells. Exercise that involves all parts of your body can improve the way your cardiovascular system works.

For example, exercise can make your heart stronger. Notice in the drawings that a strong, fit heart pumps more blood with each beat. A strong heart beats less often and rests longer between beats. This extra rest helps the heart stay strong, just as the right amount of sleep helps you stay healthy.

Your blood takes oxygen to your muscles and carries carbon dioxide and other wastes away from them. When you exercise hard, your muscles use more oxygen and make more wastes. Muscles become tired and cannot work if they do not get enough oxygen and if the wastes are not removed. A fit heart is able to supply the extra blood your muscles need when they are exercising. What activities would you enjoy more and be better at if your muscles did not tire quickly?

The heart pumps blood through blood vessels called arteries. Sometimes fatty material builds up on the inside walls of an artery. If too much fatty material builds up over the years, the flow of blood through the artery might become slower or might even stop. Regular exercise helps keep your arteries clear of fatty material.

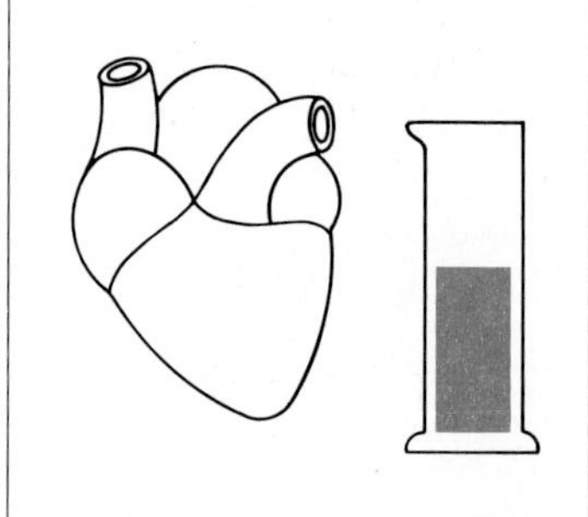

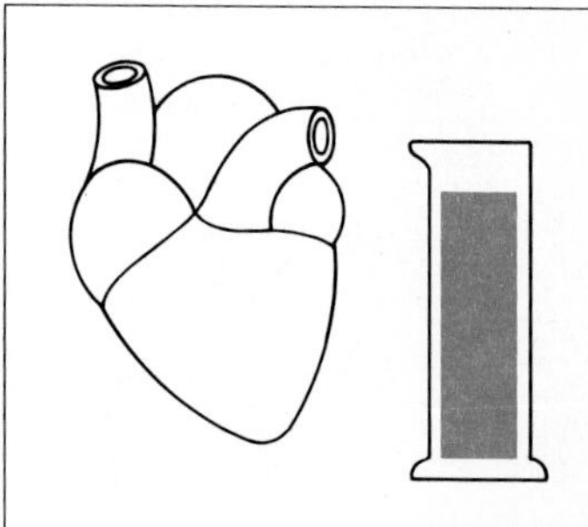

The heart of a more active person pumps more blood with each beat.

108

Teaching Options

Anecdote

When a person engages regularly in exercise that makes the heart beat faster, the muscle that makes up the left ventricle of the heart becomes stronger. Then the heart can pump out more blood per beat. This process is called increased stroke volume and is important in endurance activities.

Enrichment

Encourage interested students to find pictures in an anatomy text showing how the exchange of oxygen and carbon dioxide takes place in the alveoli—the tiny air sacs in the lungs. Then let them make diagrams or posters showing this process.

Health and Science

Let interested students find out about some of the machines used to measure fitness of the heart and lungs. These machines include the treadmill, the EKG, and oxygen analyzers.

Reteaching

Suggest that students write a paragraph explaining how muscle movement causes air to move into and out of the lungs.

Look carefully at the two hearts below. The heart on the right has a richer network of blood vessels than the other heart. People who exercise regularly often develop more branching of the arteries in the heart. This richer network of arteries helps to carry more oxygen to the heart.

respiratory (res′pər ə tôr′ē) **system,** the body system that includes the nose, air passages, and lungs. This system helps bring oxygen to the body and remove carbon dioxide from the body.

How Can Exercise Affect Your Respiratory System?

Your **respiratory system** works with your cardiovascular system. Your nose, air passages, and lungs make up your respiratory system. Air flows into your lungs when you breathe in. In the lungs, oxygen from the air passes into your bloodstream, and carbon dioxide passes from your bloodstream into the air. The carbon dioxide leaves your body when you breathe out.

As the drawings to the right show, muscles move your chest up and out when you breathe in. This action makes your chest cavity larger. Air moves into your lungs, and they expand to fill up the extra space in your chest. When you breathe out, the muscles contract. Your chest cavity gets smaller and moves air out of your lungs.

The muscles that move your chest become stronger when you exercise regularly. Stronger muscles make the chest cavity larger when you breathe in. Therefore, you can take in more oxygen and get rid of more carbon dioxide with each breath. You breathe more deeply and less often, so you get the air you need with less effort. You can exercise longer and harder without getting out of breath.

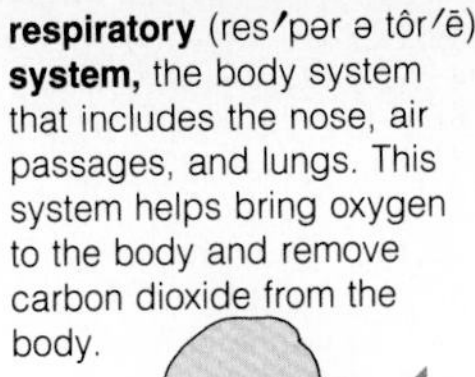

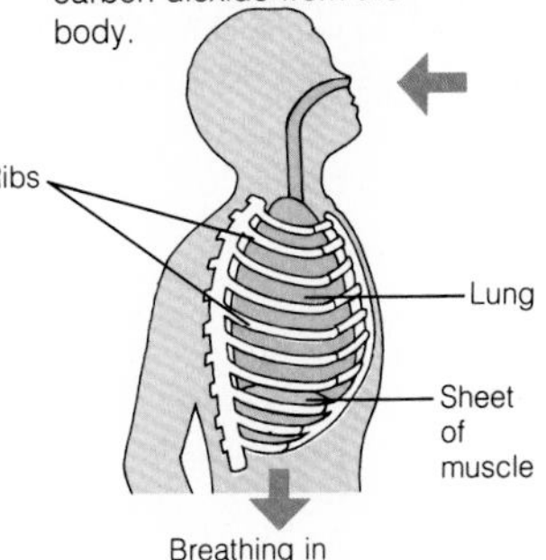

Breathing in

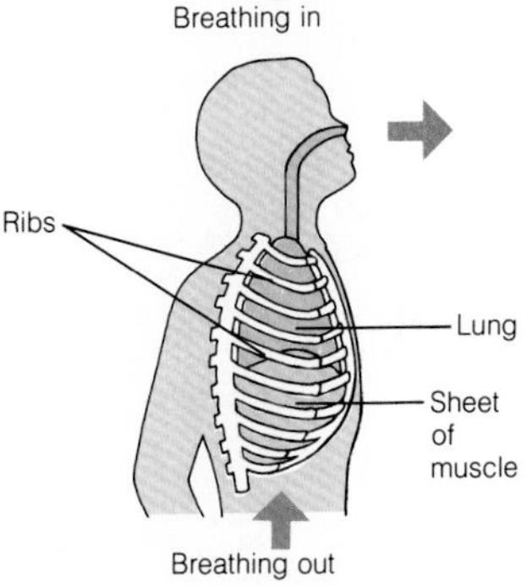

Breathing out

The heart of a more active person often has a richer network of arteries.

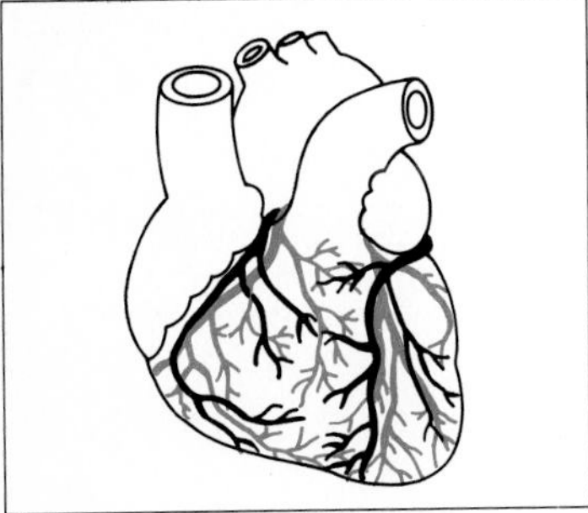

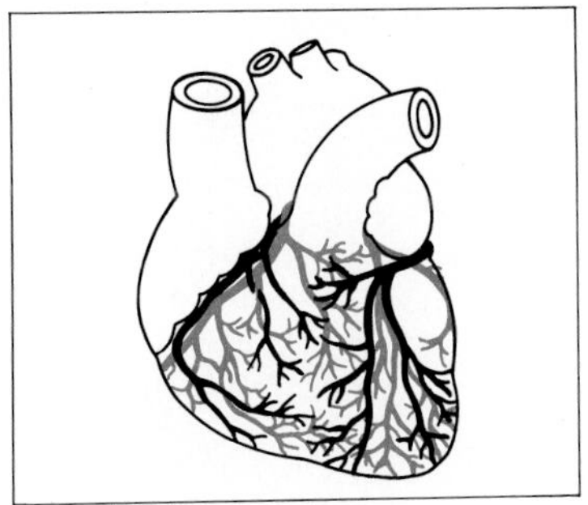

• Direct students' attention to the pictures of the chest cavity on page 109 and discuss how air is inhaled and exhaled. • Guide students to understand that the chest cavity enlarges when a person takes in air, and becomes smaller when a person exhales. • Discuss how exercise affects the respiratory system. (Exercise makes the muscles that move the chest stronger. With strong muscles a person can breathe more deeply and take in more air with less effort. This means a person can exercise longer and harder without getting out of breath.) • Help students understand the functions of the cardiovascular and respiratory systems. Point out that the two systems work together to supply the body with needed substances, such as oxygen, and get rid of wastes, such as carbon dioxide.

Teaching Plan

Lesson 1 continued

2 Teach

Strategies for Pages 110 and 111

• Write the terms *muscular strength, flexibility,* and *muscular endurance* on the chalkboard. Ask students to explain their meaning. (Muscular strength is the ability of muscles to move more weight than usual. Flexibility is the ability to move joints fully and easily. Muscular endurance is the ability of muscles to work for long periods without tiring.) • Then ask students to read pages 110 and 111 to understand how exercise improves the muscles. • Call on volunteers to read the captions on page 110 and discuss what other kinds of jobs require these types of fitness.

Using On Your Own

Responses might include the following: muscular strength—sit-ups, push-ups, lifting weights, and gymnastics; flexibility—stretching, dancing, and gymnastics; muscular endurance—carrying books, jogging, swimming, and hiking.

Thinking Skill Students are *classifying.*

flexibility (flek′sə bil′ə tē), the ability to move the joints fully and to move body parts easily.

muscular endurance (en dyür′əns), the ability of muscles to work for long periods of time without getting tired.

How Does Exercise Improve Your Muscles?

You have more than six hundred muscles in your body. Large muscles in your thighs help you stand and run. Tiny muscles in your skin raise hairs and cause goosebumps to form when you are cold. Exercise cannot make you grow more muscles, but regular exercise does improve your muscles in the three ways shown here.

Athletes do stretching exercises like this one to build **flexibility.** Flexible muscles allow your body parts to move fully and easily without causing injury.

Exercises that cause your muscles to lift more than they normally do make your muscles stronger. This gymnast needs a lot of muscular strength to lift his body to this position.

110

Teaching Options

Enrichment

Ask interested students to find out how increased strength, flexibility, and endurance might help a cross-country skier.

Health and Science

Encourage students to use a science book to find out about the three types of muscles: skeletal, smooth, and cardiac.

Reteaching

If possible, suggest students visit a local high school, a YWCA, or a YMCA to observe and learn about fitness machines that help improve strength and flexibility.

Muscles that have strength, flexibility, and endurance are not easily injured and do not become sore easily. Muscles that have strength, flexibility, and endurance can help a person perform certain activities better. Which sports and jobs could you perform better if you had good strength? good flexibility? good muscular endurance?

Cardiovascular fitness, muscular strength, flexibility, and muscular endurance are parts of physical fitness. These parts of fitness are called health fitness because they help you have good health and resist certain diseases.

On Your Own
Besides the activities shown here, list or describe two other activities that you think improve muscular strength, flexibility, and muscular endurance.

Think Back • *Study on your own with Study Guide page 322.*

1. How can regular exercise improve mental and social health?
2. How can regular exercise improve the cardiovascular system? the respiratory system?
3. In what three ways can exercise improve muscles?

Activities that make your muscles work for longer periods of time than normal build **muscular endurance.** Muscles with endurance can exercise for a long time without tiring. These bicyclists have trained their muscles to keep working through the entire race.

111

3 Assess

Expanding Student Thinking

Ask students to explain how poor cardiovascular fitness might affect a person who has good muscular endurance. (The muscles can work for a long time, but the heart cannot supply them with enough blood. The muscles do not get enough oxygen and the wastes they produce are removed too slowly. The person will be out of breath and the muscles tire quickly because of the lack of oxygen and the buildup of wastes.)

Thinking Skill Students are *organizing information.*

Answers to Think Back

1. Regular exercise can help improve mental health by relieving stress, by improving self-image, and by providing a feeling of accomplishment. Exercise can improve social health by developing cooperation and communication skills.

2. Regular activity improves the cardiovascular system by strengthening the heart so that it beats more slowly, pumps more blood per beat, and rests longer between beats. Blood vessels are less likely to have buildup of fatty deposits. The network of blood vessels in the heart can become richer. Regular exercise improves the respiratory system by strengthening the chest muscles so that breathing is more efficient.

3. by building strength, flexibility, and endurance

Teaching Plan

Lesson 2 pages 112–115

Lesson Objective
Describe the benefits of having the proper amount of body fat, and explain how regular, vigorous physical exercise can help control body fatness.

Health Vocabulary
Calorie

1 Motivate

Introducing the Lesson
Explain that having some body fat is important to good health. Ask students to guess what percentage of their body weight should be fat to maintain good health. List students' guesses on the chalkboard. Point out that a person their age should have between 10 and 15 percent of the body weight as fat, to maintain good health. Explain that though body fatness is important, preoccupation with body fatness can lead to eating disorders, which can cause serious illness.

body fatness, the amount of a person's weight that is body fat.

Did You Know?
In spite of what you might hear in ads, there is no "quick and easy" safe way to reduce body fat. The best way involves a combination of exercise and eating the right foods.

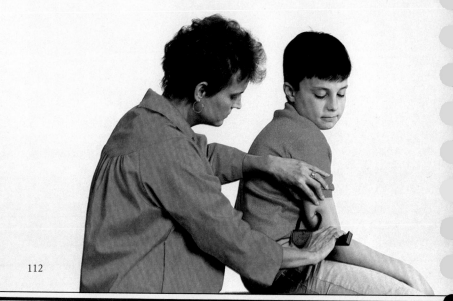

2 How Does Exercise Help Control Body Fatness?

Your body is made up of many different kinds of tissue. Two kinds of tissue are muscle and bone. Another is fat. The amount of a person's weight that is body fat is called **body fatness.** Body fatness is another part of health fitness.

Many people think body fat is something bad. However, a certain amount of fat is important to your health. Fat stores certain vitamins, such as A, D, E, and K. Fat helps keep your body warm during cold weather. Fat cushions and protects your organs from injury when your body is bumped. A certain amount of fat helps give your body its shape. Also, body fat stores energy. In fact, that is exactly what fat is—stored energy. The body uses stored fat to provide energy if it cannot get enough energy from foods.

About half of your body fat surrounds your organs and muscles. The other half is found under your skin. A doctor is doing a skinfold test on the boy in the picture. A tool called a caliper is used to measure the thickness of a fold of skin and fat on the boy's arm. The measurement tells the doctor how much body fat the boy has.

A skinfold test can measure body fatness.

112

Teaching Options

Health Background
Since muscles weigh more than fat, some muscular people may have a relatively high body weight and not have too much body fat. People can also have a low body weight and still have too much body fat. Being overfat is a more serious problem than being overweight because an overfat person has more fat than is healthy. Very low amounts of body fat in females may result in abnormal menstrual functioning.

Enrichment
Ask students to think about the relationship between body fatness and body weight. Discuss whether a person with a high body weight necessarily has too much body fat. (Students should recognize that people with high body weight do not necessarily have too much body fat, they may have large bones or large muscles.)

Health and Mathematics
Encourage students to use the information in the chart on page 113 to make bar graphs showing the percentage of fat in a 120-pound (about 55.5-kg) woman and a 160-pound (about 72.5-kg) man.

Reteaching
Ask students to write a paragraph explaining the dangers to health of having too little body fat.

How Much Body Fat Does a Person Need?

Having some fat is important to good health. However, too little or too much fat can cause problems. Without enough fat, the body does not have enough stored energy and cannot work properly. People who try to lose weight sometimes lose too much body fat. Losing too much fat can be harmful. Without enough stored energy, muscle tissue might begin to break down to give the body the energy it needs. A person who loses too much weight can become very weak and develop serious diseases.

Having too much fat can also be unhealthy. Too much fat can keep a person from being able to work and play actively. A person who has too much fat usually gets tired more quickly than someone who is lean. Adults who have too much fat are more likely to develop heart disease, high blood pressure, and diabetes than other adults.

The amount of body fat a person your age needs is about 10 to 15 percent of his or her total body weight. This amount will probably change as you grow older. Boys and girls both develop more muscle as they grow older, but a healthy girl usually needs to have more body fat than a healthy boy. This combination of muscle and fat helps people look their best. The picture shows the average amounts of fat and other tissues in a physically fit man and woman.

What percentage of a physically fit person's body is fat?

2 Teach

Strategies for Pages 112 and 113

• Discuss how body fat is important to the body. • Discuss how body fat is important to health. (stores, vitamins such as A, D, E, and K; provides and stores energy; keeps the body warm; protects organs; helps give the body shape) • Direct the students to look at the picture and ask them to identify the calipers. (tool used to measure body fat) • Suggest that students read page 113 to find out how much body fat a person needs. • Discuss with students what problems are caused by not having enough body fat. (The body does not have enough stored energy and cannot work properly. Muscle tissue might begin to break down. Serious illness can develop.) • Point out that a person with too much body fat may tire easily and may not be able to work and play actively. • Ask students to name diseases for which adults are at higher risk if they have too much body fat. (heart disease, high blood pressure, or diabetes) • Discuss with students the amount of body fat a person their age needs. (10–15 percent of total body weight) • Point out that to be healthy, women usually need to have a slightly higher percentage of body fat than men. • Direct the students' attention to the chart and point out the percentage of fat found in various body tissues.

Teaching Plan

Lesson 2 continued

2 Teach

Strategies for Pages 114 and 115

• Write the word *Calorie* on the chalkboard. Be sure students understand that a Calorie is a unit used not only to measure how much energy a food can produce in the body, but also how much energy the body uses during an activity. • Then ask the students to read page 114 to learn how a person can control body fatness.

• Be sure students understand that if a person takes in more energy in the form of food than the body uses up, the body gains fat and weight; if a person uses up more energy than he or she takes in, the body uses energy stored in body fat and the person loses fat and weight. Be sensitive to the feelings of underweight and overweight students. • Ask what can be done to prevent too much body fat. (exercise, eating healthy food)

• Guide students to understand that some foods are high in Calories and low in nutrients. • Review the Calorie chart on page 115. Emphasize the fact that the number of Calories used during an activity depends on how long the activity is done and on the person's weight.

Calorie (kal′ər ē), a unit used to measure the amount of energy a food can produce in the body and the amount of energy the body uses during activity.

How Can You Control Body Fatness?

The best way to control body fatness is to balance the amount of energy you take into your body with the amount of energy your body uses. Your body gets energy from the food you eat. The energy in food is measured in units called **Calories.** The number of Calories you need depends partly on how active you are. If you are a very active person, you need more energy and more food than someone who is less active. Most people your age need to take in between two thousand and three thousand Calories every day. However, individuals differ in the amount of Calories they need.

If you take in more Calories than you use, your body stores the energy in the form of body fat. You gain weight. If your body uses more Calories than you take in, your body begins to use up stored energy—body fat. You lose weight. When the number of Calories you use is the same as the number of Calories you eat, your weight stays the same.

Regular exercise can help prevent a person from gaining too much body fat. Regular exercise increases the amount of Calories that a person uses. Eating the right kinds and amounts of food is important too. Foods such as candy, cake, and potato chips are high in Calories but have very few nutrients. The sensible way to take in the right amount of Calories and nutrients you need is to choose foods from the basic four food groups in the daily food guide shown in Chapter 3.

The Calorie and activity chart on the next page shows how many Calories certain activities use in fifteen minutes. Notice that the number of Calories used depends partly on how long the activity is done without stopping. The number of Calories used also depends on a person's weight—the greater the body weight, the more Calories used.

The chart shows that jogging and bicycling are good activities to use up extra Calories. These activities can be done for a long time without stopping. Therefore, more Calories are used. What other activities on the chart can be done for a long time without stopping?

Teaching Options

Anecdote

Exercise is important in losing excess body fat. A person who walks fifteen minutes a day for a year without changing eating habits will lose five to six pounds (about 2 to 3 kg) of fat.

Enrichment

Discuss with students why a person of higher body weight will use up more Calories doing the same 15-minute exercise than will a person of lower body weight.

Health and Mathematics

Direct students to choose the two activities from the chart that they would enjoy the most. Then ask them to calculate the number of Calories they would use if they did each activity for thirty minutes three times a week.

Reteaching

Suggest the students make drawings showing two ways to control body fat. Students should write captions for their drawings.

Think Back • *Study on your own with Study Guide page 322.*

1. Why is a certain amount of body fat important for good health?
2. What is the best way to control the amount of body fat?
3. How does exercise help control the amount of body fat?

Did You Know?
Scientists have found that young people with too much body fat often do not eat much more than young people who do not have too much body fat. However, the young people with too much body fat are usually much less active than the young people with less body fat.

Calories Used in Fifteen Minutes of Certain Activities

Activity	Calories Used in 15 Minutes by Persons Weighing			
	65 pounds	*75 pounds*	*85 pounds*	*95 pounds*
badminton (recreation)	38	42	48	56
basketball (half-court)	33	37	42	48
basketball (full-court, moderate)	47	53	59	69
bicycling (level ground, 5½ miles per hour)	34	38	42	49
bicycling (level ground, 13 miles per hour)	72	81	91	105
dance, modern (moderate)	28	32	35	41
football (moderate)	34	38	43	49
hiking (with 40-pound pack, 3 miles per hour)	46	52	58	67
horseback riding (walk)	23	25	28	32
jogging (5½ miles per hour, 11 minutes to jog a mile)	72	81	91	105
jogging (7 miles per hour, 8½ minutes to jog a mile)	94	106	118	137
skating, ice (moderate)	38	44	48	56
skiing, cross-country (5 miles per hour)	78	89	99	114
soccer (moderate)	60	68	76	87
swimming (pleasure, 25 yards in 1 minute)	41	46	51	59
swimming (crawl, 50 yards in 1 minute)	71	80	90	104
walking (2 miles per hour)	23	26	30	35

• Remind students of the importance of a balanced diet. Caution students not to start any diet without the permission of a responsible adult and advice of a physician.

3 Assess

Expanding Student Thinking

Ask students to describe what could happen to a person who took in more Calories daily than he or she used up. Tell the students to include health problems that could develop over a long period of time. (Answers will vary but might include overweight, tiredness, strain on the heart and lungs, fatty tissue buildup in the blood vessels, possible heart disease or diabetes.)

Thinking Skill Students are *drawing conclusions.*

Answers to Think Back

1. Body fat provides the body with stored energy, helps give the body its shape, cushions and protects internal organs, stores certain vitamins, and helps keep the body warm in cold weather.

2. The best way to control the amount of body fatness is to combine a healthy diet with regular exercise. The body must use up the Calories it takes in each day.

3. Exercise can help control the amount of body fatness by increasing the number of Calories being used by the body.

Health and Mathematics

Use this worksheet for practice in laying out a jogging course. This master may be reproduced from the Teacher's Resource Book and is located on page 16 of the Student's Workbook. Use with Chapter 4: pages 112–115.

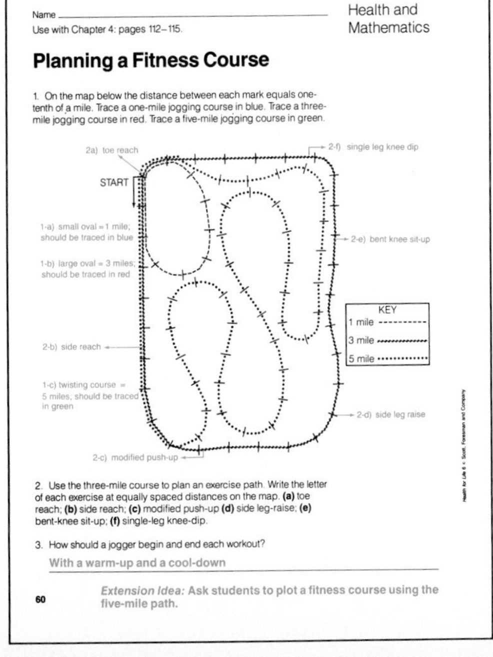

Name ______

Use with Chapter 4: pages 112–115.

Health and Mathematics

Planning a Fitness Course

1. On the map below the distance between each mark equals one-tenth of a mile. Trace a one-mile jogging course in blue. Trace a three-mile jogging course in red. Trace a five-mile jogging course in green.

2. Use the three-mile course to plan an exercise path. Write the letter of each exercise at equally spaced distances on the map. **(a)** toe reach; **(b)** side reach; **(c)** modified push-up **(d)** side leg-raise; **(e)** bent-knee sit-up; **(f)** single-leg knee-dip.

3. How should a jogger begin and end each workout?
With a warm-up and a cool-down

60

Extension Idea: Ask students to plot a fitness course using the five-mile path.

Teaching Plan

Lesson 3 pages 116–117

Lesson Objective
Explain what skills fitness is, and list the six parts of skills fitness.

Health Vocabulary
Agility, coordination

1 Motivate

Introducing the Lesson
Encourage volunteers to share experiences of improving at an activity through practice. Then ask students what types of skills they think are involved in the game of softball (running, hitting, throwing, and changing directions quickly) or some other sport or activity. Discuss how these skills might be improved through practice.

2 Teach

Strategies for Pages 116 and 117
• Call on a volunteer to read the first paragraph on page 116. • Be sure students understand that skills fitness is the ability to perform well in activities that require certain skills. • Call on volunteers to read the captions for the pictures on pages 116 and 117.

agility (ə jil′ə tē), the ability to change the position of the body quickly and to control body movements.

coordination (kō ôrd′n ā′shən), the ability to use the senses together with body parts or to use two or more body parts together.

3 What Is Skills Fitness?

Cardiovascular fitness, muscular strength, muscular endurance, flexibility, and body fatness make up the five parts of health fitness. All of these parts of fitness can be improved by regular exercise. Physical fitness also includes skills fitness, the ability to perform well in activities that require certain skills. Exercise can improve your skills fitness in ways that will help you all through your life.

Agility is the ability to change your body position quickly and to control the movement of your whole body. Agility is important in sports such as soccer and gymnastics and in jobs such as construction work.

Balance is the ability to stay upright while standing or moving. Balance is an important skill in skiing, skating, and most sports. What jobs do you think would be better performed with good balance?

Coordination is the ability to use your senses, such as sight, together with your body parts or to use two or more body parts together. People with good hand-eye or foot-eye coordination are good in hitting and kicking games such as soccer and ping pong. For what other sports would coordination be important? Why is coordination important for surgeons and typists?

116

Teaching Options

Health Background

People with good skills fitness may be more active than those with poorer skills fitness. However, skills fitness does not directly affect health. Different people have different strengths and weaknesses in skills fitness. People should realize that they can enjoy many sports and have good health fitness even if they do not excel in a particular skills fitness area.

Enrichment

Direct students to choose an activity they would like to learn or improve at. Encourage them to practice the skills used in the activity and to keep a diary of their progress.

Health and Art

Divide the class into six groups. Assign one of the six parts of skills fitness to each group. Then ask each group to make a collage of pictures or drawings showing people performing activities that require that particular part of skills fitness. Remind students that sports activities are not the only activities requiring skills fitness. Many work activities could also be shown.

Reteaching

Ask students to list sports or games they enjoy. Discuss which parts of skills fitness would enhance performance in each activity.

Special Education

Help learning-disabled students identify ways that each part of skills fitness helps them in their everyday life. (For example: *agility* helps them catch a falling object; *coordination* helps them play a musical instrument; *speed* helps them run to catch a bus; *reaction time* helps them make a fast start in a race; *balance* helps them ride a bicycle; and *power* helps them swing a bat.)

What Are the Parts of Skills Fitness?

Skills fitness has six parts. Each of these parts is useful in many different sports and jobs. Think about activities that involve each part of skills fitness as you read the descriptions of skills fitness on these two pages.

Think Back • *Study on your own with Study Guide page 322.*

1. How is skills fitness different from health fitness?
2. What are the six parts of skills fitness?

Power is the ability to quickly do activities that require strength. This part of skills fitness involves both strength and quickness. Power is important in sports such as swimming and football and in jobs such as household moving and ranching.

Reaction time is the amount of time it takes you to start moving once you observe the need to move. Good reaction time helps people who enjoy fencing or karate to avoid fast attacks. Good reaction time is important for many people who work on factory assembly lines.

Speed is the ability to perform a movement or cover a distance in a short period of time. Speed is important in running and skating and for many factory jobs.

• As each part of skills fitness is mentioned you may wish to write the part of skills fitness on the chalkboard. (agility, balance, coordination, power, reaction time, and speed) • Ask students what jobs would be aided by good balance. (Students might mention construction worker, acrobat, window washer, ballet dancer.) • Discuss what sports would be helped by good coordination. (Students might mention tennis, softball, rugby, hockey, skiing.) • Discuss ways in which power is important in sports such as swimming and football and jobs such as household moving and ranching.

3 Assess

Expanding Student Thinking

Ask students to define and give examples of the difference between power and muscular strength. (Power is the ability to use muscular strength quickly as in discus-throwing or shot-put; muscular strength is the ability to move muscles with force regardless of the time involved.)

Thinking Skill Students are *interpreting information.*

Answers to Think Back

1. Skills fitness is the ability to perform specific physical tasks. Health fitness is concerned with physical wellness.

2. The six parts of skills fitness are agility, balance, coordination, power, reaction time, and speed.

Activity Plan

Health Activities Workshop pages 118–119

Materials
Activity 1 several meter sticks or yard sticks
Activity 3 materials for making posters

Activity 1 Strategies
You may wish to make three bar graphs showing how many centimeters or inches the stick fell before the student grabbed it. The graphs will show the range in reaction time and the improvement after three trials. Be sure not to record students' names on the graph.
Thinking Skill By doing the reaction time test, students are *collecting information.*

Activity 2 Strategies
If you have students whose weight is not on the chart, ask them to estimate the Calories used based on the increments for the weights listed. Students can use the chart on page 115 to figure out how long it would take to use up Calories from a given snack when doing other activities. Use the chart to help students estimate the number of Calories they might use in fifteen minutes of walking and jogging. (Answers will vary depending on the individual's weight.) Students should recognize that some people may avoid certain snacks because the snacks contain too many Calories for the amount of exercise the people do, and they don't want to gain weight.)
Thinking Skills By comparing exercise time with Calorie intake, students are *organizing* and *interpreting information.*

Activity 3 Strategies
Suggest the students use various designs for their posters. Designs might involve slogans, magazine pictures, key words drawn in a significant way, or an ad for a fitness event.
Thinking Skills When students make posters about exercising, they are *organizing information* and *communicating.*

Health Activities Workshop

Examining Some Parts of Fitness

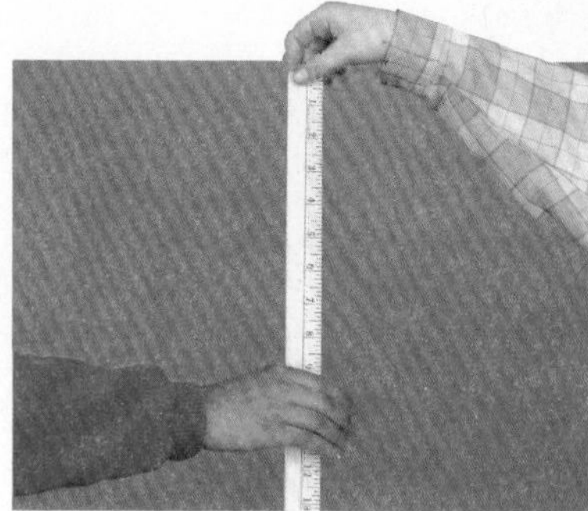

1. You can use a yardstick to test your reaction time. Ask a partner to hold the top of the stick with the thumb and first finger. Hold your thumb and fingers on either side of the stick, as shown, but do not touch it.

Your partner should drop the stick without warning you. Try to catch it between your thumb and fingers as quickly as possible. Do this test three times. Record how many inches slip through your hand before you catch the stick each time. Then switch places with your partner.

2. Choose a food high in Calories from those listed in the first chart. Write down the name of the food, the serving size, and the number of Calories in the food. Look at the second chart. Find the weight closest to your own. Use the column that gives your weight to complete this activity.

How long would you have to walk to use up the Calories in the food you chose? How long would you have to jog? Why might some people avoid this food as a snack? Try this activity with other foods from the first chart.

3. Make a poster that you think would effectively urge someone to exercise for fitness.

Calories Provided by Certain Foods

Food/Serving Size	Calories
apple, 1 medium	80
gelatin, flavored, 1 cup	140
orange, 1 medium	70
pretzels, 10 sticks	230
carrot, 1 medium	30
cookies, chocolate chip, 3	165
chocolate candy, 1 ounce	150
ice cream, 1 cup	260
celery, 1 stalk	7
cola, carbonated, 12 ounces	140
French fries, 1 average serving	300
cupcake, chocolate cake with icing, 1	170

Calories Used in 15 Minutes by

Persons Weighing	75	85	95 *(pounds)*
Activity			
walking	26	30	35
jogging	81	91	105

118

Looking at Careers

Some large companies provide exercise classes and other kinds of physical recreation for employees. These companies often hire **activity specialists.** The specialist tests employees for physical fitness and helps plan their fitness goals. Then the specialist can set up fitness programs that help people meet their goals.

A **recreational therapist** uses knowledge of physical fitness to help handicapped children. A recreational therapist works with a child's doctor. Together they plan activities that improve the fitness of the child. These activities might include sports, games or dance.

Activity specialists and recreational therapists might work in hospitals, schools, nursing homes, sports centers, and company buildings. To become an activity specialist or recreational therapist, you must finish high school and four years of college.

Many other kinds of jobs are available in the fields of fitness and recreation. Some positions, such as **camp counselor** and **playground leader,** can be filled by people still in high school or college. The camp counselors shown here are also guides and organizers.

You might visit your local park district or community center to find out more about these kinds of jobs. Talk to the people about any special skills and abilities needed. People often like to share information about their jobs.

For more information write to the National Recreation and Park Association, 1601 North Kent Street, Arlington, VA 22209.

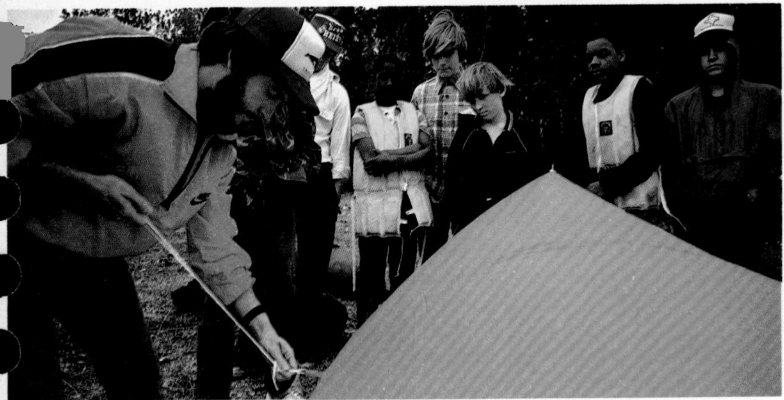

Activity 4 Strategies
Nursing homes and rehabilitation centers are places that might employ activity specialists and recreational therapists. You may wish to contact a local nursing home or rehabilitation center to arrange for a tour of the facility or for a demonstration by an activity specialist or recreational therapist. You might instead wish to invite an activity specialist or recreational therapist to visit the classroom.

Thinking Skills When students learn more about a career as a recreational therapist, recreational specialist, camp counselor, or playground leader, they are *collecting information* and *communicating.*

Teaching Plan

Lesson 4 pages 120–125

Lesson Objective
List factors that need consideration before setting fitness goals.

1 Motivate

Introducing the Lesson
Discuss health fitness and its importance to everyone. Review the six parts of skills fitness. (agility, balance, coordination, power, reaction time, and speed)

2 Teach

Strategies for Pages 120 and 121
• Ask students to read pages 120 and 121 to find out what a person should consider before setting fitness goals. • Discuss reasons people want to be physically fit. (achieve good health, feel good about themselves, interest in certain sports or jobs)
• Point out that planning a fitness program includes understanding individual needs, abilities, and interests.
• Ask students to look at the pictures on page 120 and tell which parts of health and skills fitness the construction worker and the gymnast need. (Accept all reasonable answers.)

On Your Own
Choose two sports from the following list. Write the name of each sport at the top of a sheet of paper. Then list the parts of skills fitness a person interested in each sport would need to develop. Finally, explain how each part of skills fitness would help the person perform that sport.

basketball	auto racing
football	bicycling
gymnastics	golf
ice skating	hiking
rodeo event	ping-pong
running	soccer
softball	swimming
tennis	volleyball

4 How Can You Set Good Fitness Goals?

Some people think only athletes need to be physically fit, but this idea is not true. Physical fitness is important for everybody. Being physically fit helps you look and feel your best. Being physically fit is one of the most important goals you can set for yourself. Setting fitness goals can help you build fitness, and you can have fun doing it.

You can help decide what your fitness goals should be by determining your needs, interests, and abilities. Deciding how fit you are right now can also help you set your fitness goals.

What Are Your Needs, Interests, and Abilities?

People want to be physically fit for different reasons. Most people want to be fit in order to have good health and to feel good about themselves. They can reach these goals by working to improve each of the five parts of health fitness. Some people want to be fit because they are interested in certain sports. These people might need to develop all six parts of skills fitness.

Many people need extra ability in certain parts of health and skills fitness. Which parts of health and skills fitness does the construction worker especially need? Which parts does the gymnast especially need?

These people especially need certain parts of fitness.

120

Teaching Options

Health Background
Students do not usually think in terms of goals when performing physical activities. However, the activities they perform do help them achieve the goal of good health. The planning and attaining of fitness goals can contribute to both feeling and looking good. Setting good fitness goals is an important first step toward taking responsibility for personal health.

Enrichment
Ask students to list factors besides heredity and body type that can affect a person's ability to perform well in a particular sport. (skills fitness, health fitness, practice, size, effort, willingness, and ability to communicate)

Health and Language Arts
Direct interested students to find information on the training programs or exercises famous athletes use. Ask students to analyze how these activities help them build health fitness and skills fitness. Encourage students to report their findings to the class.

Reteaching
Ask students to write a paragraph explaining what should be considered before setting fitness goals and why. (Answers should include the main ideas on pages 120 and 121.)

Understanding your abilities can help you decide what your fitness goals should be. The kind of body you have helps determine some of your abilities. Everyone is born with a certain kind of body. Notice the three main adult body types in the pictures.

Some people are naturally more muscular than others. Such people might have greater strength. They can also build their muscles more easily than other people.

Some people have thin body types. Such people have a harder time building large muscles. However, they can develop good muscular endurance and cardiovascular fitness as easily as other people.

Some people have a body type that makes it easy for them to gain body fat. These people can stay lean, build muscle, and do well in many sports, but it might take extra effort.

Your body type and natural abilities make it easier to improve some parts of fitness, but harder to improve other parts. You can work to improve the parts of fitness that are more difficult for you. A little more effort often makes up for a lack of ability.

Different people have different body types.

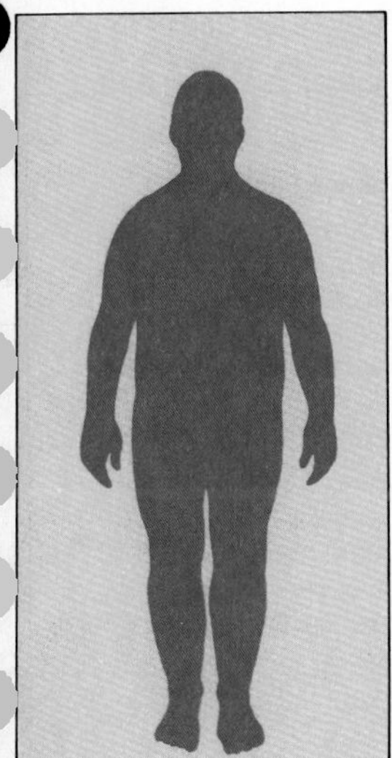

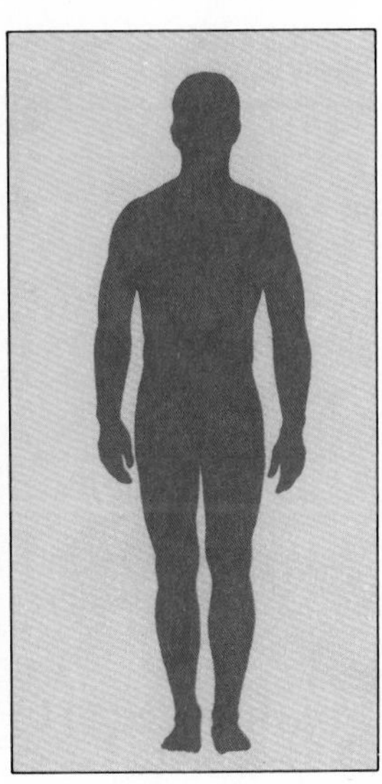

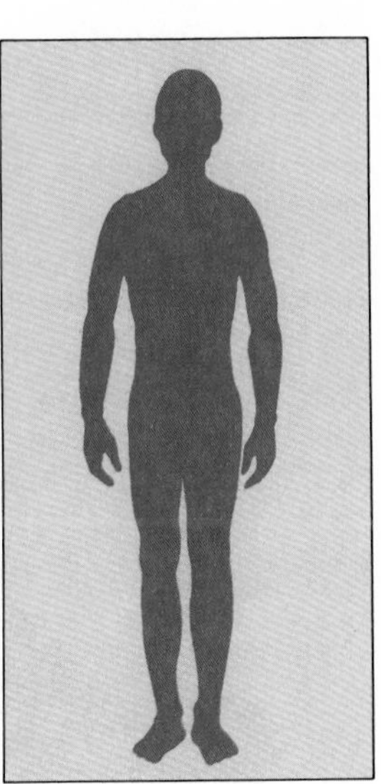

• Discuss the three body types in the picture on page 121. • Point out that heredity affects various physical characteristics, including body type. Explain that having a certain body type should not discourage a person from going into any sport that he or she is interested in. Note that building health fitness and skills fitness can help almost anyone participate in any sport.
• Explain to students that at their age it might be difficult to determine body type because height, weight, and body shape change so rapidly during puberty. Be sensitive to feelings of self-consciousness in students and avoid discussion that might hurt the self-image of individuals.

Using On Your Own
Before assigning the activity, review with students the parts of skills fitness on pages 116 and 117.
Thinking Skills By explaining the aspects of skills fitness necessary for various sports, students are *interpreting information* and *drawing conclusions*.

Teaching Plan

Lesson 4 continued

2 Teach

Strategies for Pages 122 and 123

• Direct students to read the first paragraph of page 122. Then review the parts of health fitness tested in the activities. (cardiovascular fitness, muscular strength, muscular endurance, and flexibility) Explain to students that the activities are not complete tests of fitness but, instead, give an indication of what the different parts of health fitness entail. If a student has any medical problems that excuse him or her from physical education class, do not allow that student to do the following activities. Tell the students that in determining a fitness program they should know their level of health fitness. • Before beginning the activities, be sure students know how to find and measure their pulse. Direct them to the picture on page 123 to help them locate the pulse point. Ask students to calculate their resting pulse by counting the number of beats they feel in 10 seconds and multiplying this number by 6. Explain that this number is the resting pulse, measured in beats per minute. • Call on a volunteer to read the explanation of in-place running.

What Kind of Health Fitness Do You Have?

Before you can set good fitness goals, you need to determine which parts of physical fitness you are strong in and which parts you need extra work in.

Try the activities on these two pages. As you perform each one, think about what part of health fitness it measures and how that part of health fitness is different from the others. These activities will help you understand more about each part of health fitness and show you what parts you might need to improve.

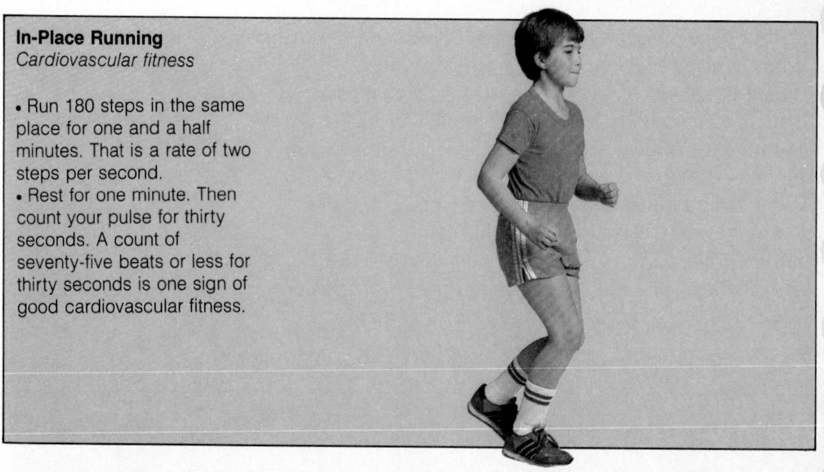

In-Place Running
Cardiovascular fitness

• Run 180 steps in the same place for one and a half minutes. That is a rate of two steps per second.
• Rest for one minute. Then count your pulse for thirty seconds. A count of seventy-five beats or less for thirty seconds is one sign of good cardiovascular fitness.

Push-Up
Strength

• Face the floor and support your body on your hands and feet.
• Keep your body straight as you lower yourself until your nose touches the floor.
• Push with your arms to return your body to the starting position. Keep your body straight as you push up.
• Try to do five push-ups.

Bent Knee Push-Up

• Lie face down with your hands on the floor next to your shoulder and your knees and feet on the floor.
• Keep your body straight as you push the upper part of your body off the floor.
• Keeping your knees and feet on the floor, lower your body until your nose or chest touches the floor.
• Try to do five bent knee push-ups.

122

Teaching Options

Anecdote

On a flight from New Orleans to New York, the pilot heard a steady thumping sound in the plane. After checking the instrument panel thoroughly, the pilot did not find anything wrong. After twenty minutes, the thumping stopped. On landing in New York, a flight attendant informed the pilot that one of the passengers had locked himself in the forward lavatory and jogged in place for twenty minutes. (Gilmore, Clarence Percy. *Exercising for Fitness.* Time-Life, 1981.)

Enrichment

Ask students to think of other tests they might use to learn about their cardiovascular fitness, muscular strength, muscular endurance, and flexibility. Students may wish to illustrate tests with pictures. EE 1D

Health and Social Studies

Ask interested students to do research and make a list of the inventions over the last one-hundred years that have reduced physical activity for many people living in the United States. Tell students to list the specific activity affected by each invention. (For example, automobiles reduced the amount of walking and horseback riding; electricity and gas reduced the need to chop and carry wood.

Reteaching

Ask students to write a paragraph explaining why finding out about their levels in different areas of physical fitness could be helpful in determining their fitness goals. (Accept any answers students can explain.) EE 1D

Special Education

Let orthopedically handicapped students design tests to help them assess their fitness levels. Students should design a test for each of the following parts of health fitness: cardiovascular fitness, muscular strength, muscular endurance, and flexibility. Ask students to list any equipment or assistance they might need to take their test.

While getting an idea of your health fitness, you will find it helpful to measure your pulse. Your pulse is caused by the rush of blood into the arteries after each beat of your heart. To check your pulse, place your index and middle fingers of one hand on the wrist just below the thumb of the other hand. Notice this position in the picture. Press gently and you should feel your pulse.

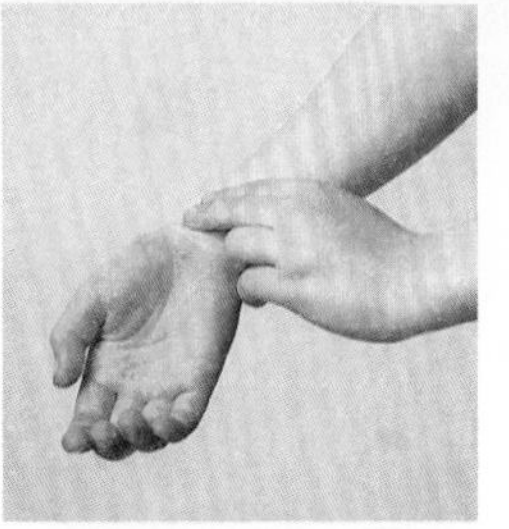

Two-Minute Jump
Muscular endurance

- Put your hands behind your head. Bend your knees slightly.
- Place your right foot in front of a line on the floor. Place your left foot behind the line.
- Jump in place, switching your feet so that you land with your left foot in front of the line and your right foot behind it.
- Try to jump 240 times in two minutes. That is a rate of two jumps every second.

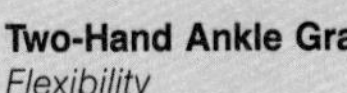

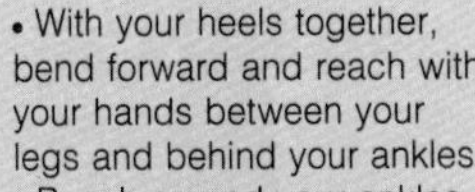

Two-Hand Ankle Grab
Flexibility

- With your heels together, bend forward and reach with your hands between your legs and behind your ankles.
- Reach around your ankles and clasp your hands in front of your ankles. Interlock your hands for at least the full length of your fingers.
- Hold for a count of five while keeping your feet still.

• Let students do the activity while you time them. You may wish to start out running with the class to set the correct pace for them. After the students have run for 1½ minutes and rested for 30 seconds, ask them to count their pulse and record it on a sheet of paper. Explain that a count of 75 beats for 30 seconds is a sign of good cardiovascular fitness. • Tell students that this information and information from the other activities is for their personal use only. • Call on two volunteers to demonstrate the two ways to do a push-up. Be sure students keep their bodies straight as they do the exercise. Tell them to avoid arching the back. Encourage students to do as many push-ups as they can up to five. Ask the students to indicate on paper how well they did. • Use masking tape or chalk to make lines on the floor for the two-minute jump described on page 123. • Ask a student to read the description of the exercise. Let a volunteer demonstrate the exercise before students begin. Warn students to bend their knees when they land. • Ask students to do the exercise and record the results. Call on a student to read the description of the two-hand ankle grab. Ask a volunteer to demonstrate the activity before students begin. Let the students do the activity and record how they did.

Teaching Plan

Lesson 4 continued

2 Teach

Strategies for Pages 124 and 125

• For the activities on pages 124 and 125 you will need the following: chalk or masking tape, two or more volleyballs or basketballs, and stopwatches or a clock with a second hand. You may wish to have students do these activities in a gymnasium or other large area. The class could do one activity at a time, or you could set up stations for each activity in different parts of the room and let students rotate from station to station. Tell students in advance to wear clothes suitable for exercise. • Ask a volunteer to read the first paragraph on page 124 aloud. • Explain that the following activities will help the students determine their level of skills fitness. Discuss how each person has different strengths and weaknesses in regards to skills fitness. Remind students that no matter what their level of skills fitness, they can achieve good physical fitness. • For each activity, call on a volunteer to read the directions while another volunteer demonstrates the activity.

What Kind of Skills Fitness Do You Have?

You can do some simple activities to help you understand more about the parts of skills fitness and to find out what parts of skills fitness you might want to improve. Try each activity on these two pages. As you perform each one, think about how the part of skills fitness the activity measures is different from other parts of skills fitness.

Line Jump
Agility

• Balance on your right foot on a line drawn on the floor or ground, or made with tape.
• Jump so that your left foot lands to the right of the line.
• Jump to the left side of the line, landing on your right foot.
• Jump again, landing on the line with your left foot.
• Practice once. Then see if you can do the activity two out of three times without losing your balance.

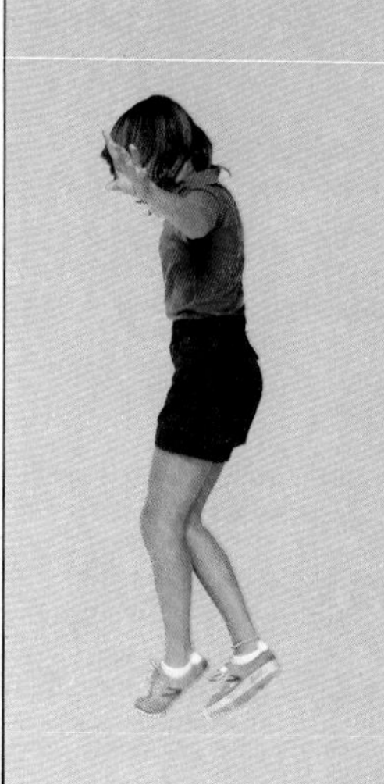

Backward Hop
Balance

• Hop backward on one foot for five hops with your eyes closed. Do not allow your other foot to touch the ground.
• Stop after the last hop and hold your balance for three seconds.
• Try this activity twice. Then repeat it while hopping on the other foot.

Double Ball Bounce
Coordination

• Hold a volleyball or basketball in each hand.
• Starting at the same time with each hand, bounce both balls at the same time. Bounce the balls at least knee high.
• Bounce both balls three times in a row without losing control of either ball.
• Try this activity three times.

124

Teaching Options

Enrichment

Ask students to list ways that improving certain parts of skills fitness can help them do specific everyday activities better. (Accept any reasonable answers.)

Health and Dance

Let students combine some or all of the activities in the skills assessment test into a dance routine. Students should set their routines to music. Ask students to teach their routines to each other.

Reteaching

The directions for most of the tests on pages 124 and 125 suggest that students practice the activities before taking the test. Let students discuss why practice is an important part of improving skills fitness.

Think Back • *Study on your own with Study Guide page 323.*

1. How can your interests and needs help you set good fitness goals?
2. How can determining your abilities help you set good fitness goals?

Standing Long Jump
Power

- Make a line on the floor with chalk or with masking tape. Lie down on the floor so that your feet are even with the line. Then ask a partner to make another line by your head so that the two lines represent the length of your body.
- Stand with your toes at the edge of one line.
- Swing your arms forward and try to jump beyond the second line. You should not run or hop before jumping.
- Try this activity twice.

Tube Catch
Reaction time

- For this activity, roll a sheet of paper to make a paper tube. Keep the tube together with tape.
- Lay the tube on a table or desk so that slightly less than half of the tube extends over the edge.
- Tap the tube so that it flips off the table or desk. Try to catch the tube before it hits the floor.
- See how many times you can catch the tube out of five tries.

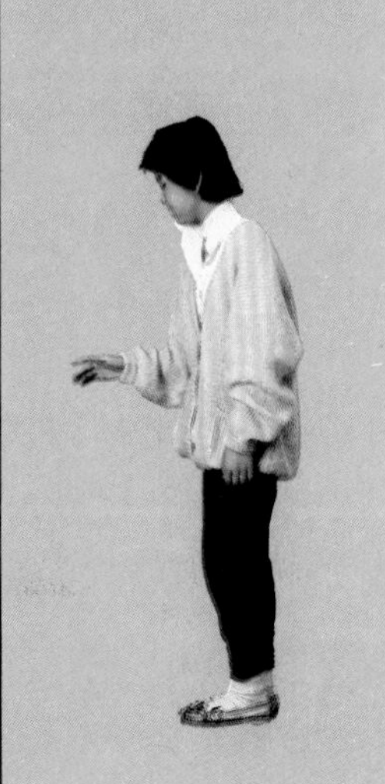

Run In Place
Speed

- Stand with your feet about shoulder width apart.
- When a partner says "Go," run in place as fast as you can for ten seconds. As you run in place, count the number of times each foot touches the ground. Your partner should watch the clock or have a watch with a second hand.
- Try this activity twice.

Make sure everyone understands how to do each activity correctly before beginning and that they follow the directions accurately. For activities involving jumping and hopping, remind students to bend their knees as they land. Caution students to be especially careful when doing the tube catch so that other students in the area are not injured.

3 Assess

Expanding Student Thinking

Encourage students to write fitness goals for themselves based on their needs, abilities, interests, and present levels of fitness. Ask them to explain the goals they chose.

Thinking Skill By choosing and explaining fitness goals, students are *judging* and *evaluating.*

Answers to Think Back

1. Interests and needs help determine the parts of fitness a person needs to build. Students might give an example to show how interests and needs help a person set fitness goals.

2. Knowing their abilities can help people determine in which parts of physical fitness and skills fitness they have already attained a degree of proficiency and in which parts they need extra work. People can also set goals that will take advantage of their natural abilities.

Life Skills

Use this worksheet for practice in analyzing a fitness program. This master may be reproduced from the Teacher's Resource Book and is located on page 13 of the Student's Workbook. Use with Chapter 4: pages 126–129.

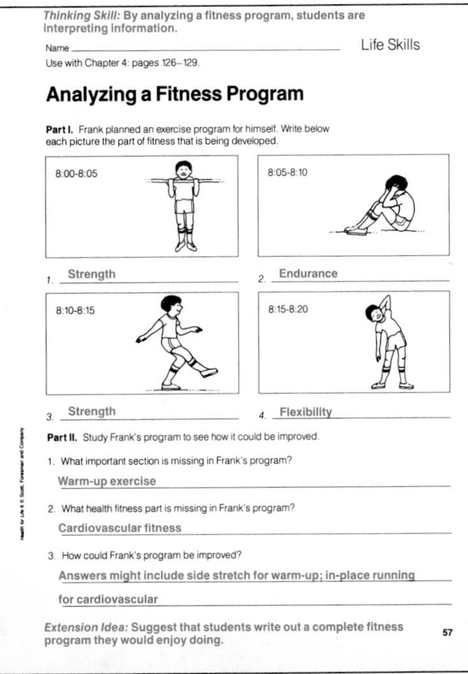

Thinking Skill: By analyzing a fitness program, students are interpreting information.

Name ______________ Life Skills

Use with Chapter 4: pages 126–129.

Analyzing a Fitness Program

Part I. Frank planned an exercise program for himself. Write below each picture the part of fitness that is being developed.

8:00-8:05 — 1. Strength

8:05-8:10 — 2. Endurance

8:10-8:15 — 3. Strength

8:15-8:20 — 4. Flexibility

Part II. Study Frank's program to see how it could be improved.

1. What important section is missing in Frank's program?
   Warm-up exercise
2. What health fitness part is missing in Frank's program?
   Cardiovascular fitness
3. How could Frank's program be improved?
   Answers might include side stretch for warm-up; in-place running for cardiovascular

Extension Idea: Suggest that students write out a complete fitness program they would enjoy doing.

57

Teaching Plan

Lesson 5 pages 126–129

Lesson Objective
Explain how a person can achieve fitness goals.

1 Motivate

Introducing the Lesson
Ask students to think about times they have had a feeling of accomplishment. Encourage students to realize that setting and achieving fitness goals can produce this sense of accomplishment.

2 Teach

Strategies for Pages 126 and 127
• Direct students to read pages 126 and 127 to find out what kinds of activities can help them achieve their fitness goals. • Discuss the activities listed in the charts. Help students identify activities that develop each part of health fitness and activities that develop each part of skills fitness. • Encourage students to decide which areas of fitness they need to develop and to choose three activities that will help meet those goals. • Explain that exercises can be used in combination with games and sports to develop some parts of fitness.

On Your Own
On a sheet of paper, make a list of the sports in the charts that could be done alone. Make another list of the sports that are team sports. Then, make a third list of the sports in the charts that could be played only during certain times of the year.

5 How Can You Achieve Your Fitness Goals?

Remember that special feeling of accomplishment you had when you first learned to ride a bicycle? You had set a goal. You worked very hard. You probably took a few tumbles, but you finally achieved your goal—and you had fun doing it.

You can earn that same sense of accomplishment by achieving your physical fitness goals. Setting fitness goals can be fairly easy. Achieving those goals takes time, but it can be done—and it can be fun!

The charts on these two pages list many sports activities that can help you achieve your fitness goals. Notice which areas of fitness each activity improves. Once you have set goals to improve certain areas of fitness, try activities that will strengthen those areas.

Skill-Related Benefits of Sports Activities

Activity	Improves balance	Improves coordination	Improves reaction time	Improves agility	Improves power	Improves speed
Badminton	Fair	Excellent	Good	Good	Fair	Good
Baseball	Good	Excellent	Excellent	Good	Excellent	Good
Basketball	Good	Excellent	Excellent	Excellent	Excellent	Good
Bicycling	Excellent	Fair	Fair	____	____	Fair
Bowling	Good	Excellent	____	Fair	Fair	Fair
Canoeing	Good	Good	Fair	____	Good	____
Dance, Aerobic	Fair	Good	Fair	Good	____	____
Dance, Ballet	Excellent	Excellent	Fair	Excellent	Good	____
Football	Good	Good	Excellent	Excellent	Excellent	Excellent
Gymnastics	Excellent	Excellent	Good	Excellent	Excellent	Fair
Jogging	Fair	Fair	____	____	____	____
Racquetball; Handball	Fair	Excellent	Good	Excellent	Fair	Good
Skating, Ice	Excellent	Good	Fair	Good	Fair	Good
Skating, Roller	Excellent	Good	____	Good	Fair	Good
Skiing, Cross-Country	Fair	Excellent	____	Good	Excellent	Fair
Soccer	Fair	Excellent	Good	Excellent	Good	Good
Softball	Fair	Excellent	Excellent	Good	Good	Good
Swimming	Fair	Good	____	Good	Fair	____
Tennis	Fair	Excellent	Good	Good	Good	Good
Volleyball	Fair	Excellent	Good	Good	Fair	Fair
Walking	Fair	Fair	____	____	____	____

Teaching Options

Health Background

To improve cardiovascular fitness a person should exercise continuously for thirty minutes at least three times per week, bringing the heart rate to the target rate (about 75 percent of the maximum heart rate, which is 220 minus the person's age) for at least fifteen minutes of that time. Increasing muscular endurance requires gradually increasing the length of time a muscle is exercised. Exercises that improve cardiovascular fitness can also improve endurance for the muscles exercised.

Enrichment

Let interested students find out what clubs or organizations in the community offer physical fitness or sports programs for young people. Ask the students to share their findings with the class.

Health and Drama

Ask students to pantomime some of the activities listed in the chart. Encourage students to move in such a way as to emphasize one of the fitness skills used in that activity. Let the other students try to identify the fitness skill being portrayed.

Reteaching

Divide the class into two groups and ask each group to plan a specific fitness program using the information on charts on pages 126 and 127. One program should be designed to improve health fitness and the other to improve skills fitness.

Notice that some activities are not very helpful for improving certain parts of fitness. For example, swimming does not do much to improve reaction time, as shown by the dash in the *reaction time* column for swimming. However, swimming is a good or excellent activity for improving other parts of skills and health fitness. You should not stop doing an enjoyable activity just because it does not improve a certain part of fitness. Instead, try to include additional activities that can help you achieve your fitness goals.

Health-Related Benefits of Sports Activities

Activity	Develops cardiovascular fitness	Develops muscular strength	Develops muscular endurance	Develops flexibility	Helps control fatness
Badminton	Fair	—	Fair	Fair	Fair
Baseball	—	—	—	—	—
Basketball (half court)	Fair	—	Fair	—	Fair
Bicycling	Excellent	Fair	Good	—	Excellent
Bowling	—	—	—	—	—
Canoeing	Fair	Fair	Good	—	Fair
Dance, Aerobic	Excellent	Fair	Good	Good	Excellent
Dance, Ballet	Good	Good	Good	Excellent	Good
Football	Fair	Good	Good	—	Fair
Gymnastics	Fair	Excellent	Excellent	Excellent	Fair
Jogging	Excellent	—	Good	—	Excellent
Racquetball; Handball	Good-Excellent	—	Good	—	Good-Excellent
Skating, Ice	Fair-Good	—	Good	—	Fair-Good
Skating, Roller	Fair-Good	—	Fair	—	Fair-Good
Skiing, Cross-Country	Excellent	Fair	Good	—	Excellent
Soccer	Excellent	Fair	Good	Fair	Excellent
Softball	—	—	—	—	—
Swimming	Excellent	Fair	Good	Fair	Excellent
Tennis	Fair-Good	—	Fair	—	Fair-Good
Volleyball	Fair	Fair	—	—	Fair
Walking	Good	—	Fair	—	Good

Using On Your Own

You may wish to help students get started by pointing out sports that fit each of the three categories. Students might mention that swimming is an individual sport, basketball is a team sport, and cross-country skiing is a seasonal sport.

Thinking Skill When students figure out which sports can be done alone, which sports are team sports, and which can only be played during certain times of the year, they are *classifying*.

Overhead Transparency Master

Use this blackline master to make a labeled overhead transparency or to make an unlabeled student worksheet. This blackline master may be reproduced from the Teacher's Resource Book.

Chapter 4
Text page 126

Benefits of Sports Activities

Skill-Related Benefits of Sports Activities

Activity	Improves balance	Improves coordination	Improves reaction time	Improves agility	Improves power	Improves speed
Badminton	Fair	Excellent	Good	Good	Fair	Good
Baseball	Good	Excellent	Excellent	Good	Excellent	Good
Basketball	Good	Excellent	Excellent	Excellent	Excellent	Good
Bicycling	Excellent	Fair	Fair	—	—	Fair
Bowling	Good	Excellent	—	Fair	Fair	Fair
Canoeing	Good	Good	Fair	—	Good	—
Dance, Aerobic	Fair	Good	Fair	Good	—	—
Dance, Ballet	Excellent	Excellent	Fair	Excellent	Good	—
Football	Good	Good	Excellent	Excellent	Excellent	Excellent
Gymnastics	Excellent	Excellent	Good	Excellent	Excellent	Fair
Jogging	Fair	Fair	—	—	—	—
Racquetball; Handball	Fair	Excellent	Good	Excellent	Fair	Good
Skating, Ice	Excellent	Good	Fair	Good	Fair	Good
Skating, Roller	Excellent	Good	—	Good	Fair	Good
Skiing, Cross-Country	Fair	Excellent	—	Good	Excellent	Fair
Soccer	Fair	Excellent	Good	Excellent	Good	Good
Softball	Fair	Excellent	Excellent	Good	Good	Good
Swimming	Fair	Good	—	Good	Fair	—
Tennis	Fair	Excellent	Good	Good	Good	Good
Volleyball	Fair	Excellent	Good	Good	Fair	Fair
Walking	Fair	Fair	—	—	—	—

55

Teaching Plan

Lesson 5 continued

2 Teach

Strategies for Pages 128 and 129

• Ask students to read the first paragraph on page 128. • Discuss with students how much exercise a person their age needs to maintain fitness. (at least three times a week) • Ask students how fast the heart should beat when they exercise. (135 to 155 beats per minute) Discuss how long they should exercise with the heart beating at this rate (at least 15 minutes) Point out that making the heart pump at a rate of 135 to 155 beats per minute helps build cardiovascular fitness. • Suggest students read pages 128 and 129 to find out how to exercise safely. • Discuss with students why they should warm up before exercising. (to stretch muscles; to prepare the muscles and the heart for more active exercise; to help avoid injuries) • Discuss the danger of unsafe equipment. (It can cause serious injuries.) • Discuss the importance of being fit before taking part in a particular sport. (Although sports can build fitness, a certain amount of fitness is necessary to help prevent injury while playing a sport.)

How Much Physical Activity Do You Need?

Fitness experts suggest that you exercise at least three times a week to build and maintain fitness. You should exercise hard enough to make your heart beat at a rate of 135 to 155 beats per minute. You need to keep your heart beating at this rate for at least fifteen minutes at a time. Your heart is a muscle. Making your muscles work harder than usual makes them stronger. Making your heart work harder for at least fifteen minutes will build cardiovascular fitness. You can check your pulse to keep track of how hard your heart is working while you exercise.

How Can You Exercise Safely?

You need to follow a few safety guidelines as you exercise to meet your fitness goals. These guidelines will help you avoid injuries and soreness.

• **Warm up before you exercise.** You should warm up your muscles with gentle exercises before you do more active exercises. The side stretch, toe reach, and jumping jack described on page 130 are good warm-up exercises. They stretch muscles and help prevent muscle injuries. Slow walking or slow jogging are other good warm-up exercises that stretch muscles and get your heart ready for more active exercises.

Comfortable clothing allows free movement during exercise.

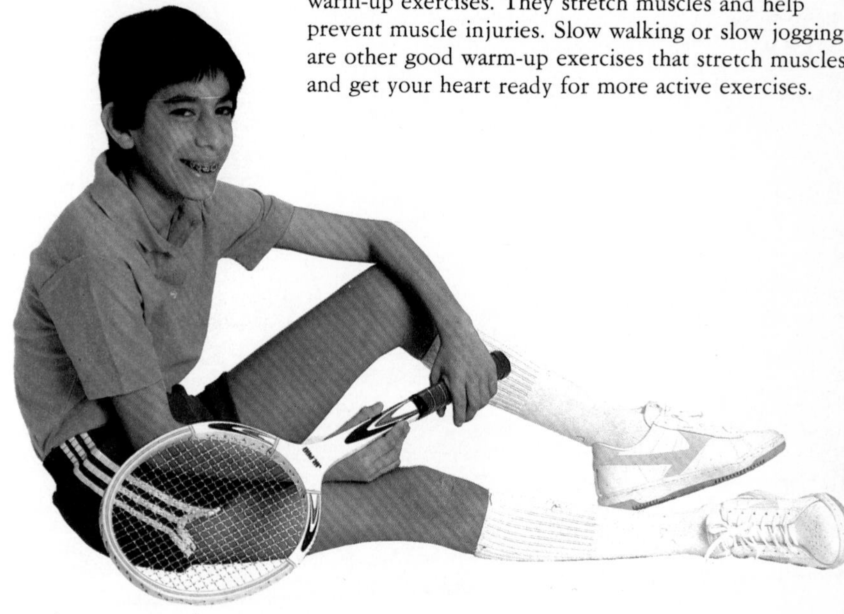

128

Teaching Options

Anecdote

In 1980, Terry Fox ran halfway across Canada to raise money to fight cancer. He ran 3,339 miles (about 5,372 km), from St. John's, Newfoundland, to Thunder Bay, Ontario. Fox had had one leg amputated due to cancer several years before his run. Terry Fox received the Order of Canada, the highest honor a Canadian civilian can achieve, for his courageous run. Fox died on June 28, 1981.

Enrichment

If possible, ask a physical education teacher to lead the class in some warm-up and cool-down exercises.

Let students choose an activity that promotes cardiovascular fitness and muscular strength and endurance. Then suggest they write a paragraph on specific ways the activity provides these benefits. Let students refer to the chart on page 127 for information.

Health and Science

Encourage interested students to find out more about what causes muscle tiredness, muscle soreness, and muscle injuries. Suggest that students report their findings to the class.

Reteaching

Ask students to explain the six guidelines listed in this lesson for safe exercise. You might wish to choose a sport such as ice skating or bicycling and ask the students to apply each of the guidelines to the sport.

• **Dress properly for exercise.** How is the boy in the picture dressed correctly for active exercise? He is wearing comfortable exercise shoes that support and protect his feet. His clothes are loose enough to allow free movement.

• **Use safe equipment and exercise in a safe place.** Make sure any exercise equipment you use is in good condition. Unsafe equipment, such as a cracked baseball bat or a bicycle that is too large for its driver, can cause serious injuries. Also make sure that the area you plan to exercise in is safe. Joggers should run in a smooth area free of holes. Bicycle drivers should use safe bicycle paths. If your community has no bicycle paths, ride in an area that is known to be safe.

• **Make sure you are fit for a sport before you take part in it.** Sports can build good fitness, but you need to have a certain amount of fitness to attempt certain sports. A few weeks of exercising can help you build fitness for a sport.

• **Cool down after you exercise.** A complete exercise routine always includes cooling down with gentle exercises after you finish more active exercise. Cooling down helps prevent soreness and helps you slowly lower your heart rate back to normal. The same exercises used for warming up are good for cooling down.

• **Gradually increase the amount of exercise you do.** If you have not exercised for a long time, you need to start slowly. As you continue, you can gradually build up the amount of exercise you do. For example, you might exercise two times during the first week. Then you can gradually build up to exercising five times every week. Starting slowly and increasing gradually helps prevent injuries.

Think Back • *Study on your own with Study Guide page 323.*

1. What kind of activities should a person choose when achieving fitness goals?
2. How often should a person exercise to build and maintain fitness?
3. What are six guidelines for exercising safely?

• Let students discuss the importance of cooling down after exercising.
• Explain that cooling down helps prevent muscle soreness. • Ask students to explain why a person should increase gradually the amount of exercise he or she does. (Gradual increase helps develop fitness and decreases the chance of injury.)

3 Assess

Expanding Student Thinking

Ask students whether the same exercise could be used by a person who wants to improve flexibility and coordination and by a person who wants to improve power and muscular endurance. (Answers will vary but should demonstrate the understanding that, in general, different exercises can build different skills areas.
Thinking Skills Students are *interpreting* and *organizing information.*

Answers to Think Back

1. To achieve fitness goals, a person should choose exercises that improve the parts of fitness that are part of the chosen goals.
2. A person should exercise at least three times a week.
3. Six guidelines for safe exercise are: warm up first; dress properly; use safe equipment and a safe location; make sure you are fit enough for a particular sport; cool down after exercising; gradually increase exercise time.

Teaching Plan

Project Keep-Fit

pages 130–135

General Strategies

Supervise the students carefully to be sure they are exercising correctly. Emphasize to students the importance of working at their own pace. Before beginning an exercise program, check students' health records to find out if any students have medical problems that would limit their ability to do the exercises safely. Some students will need to check with their doctor before doing Project Keep-Fit or any exercise program. Students who complain of nausea, dizziness, cramps, pain, or extreme exhaustion should stop exercising and go to the nurse. An adult in the student's family should be notified of any of the above reactions.

Be sure all students understand how to do the exercises correctly and that they follow the directions accurately. Encourage students to bring or wear soft-soled, flat shoes on the days you plan to practice the exercises.

The exercises can be done as part of an exercise circuit. To set up an exercise circuit, arrange to use a large, open area, such as a gymnasium, an athletic field, a track, or a jogging path. Make signs with the names of each of the exercises. Place the signs along a circular route in the order in which the exercises are listed. If an outdoor area large enough for an exercise circuit is not available, students can do the exercises in a cleared area in the classroom.

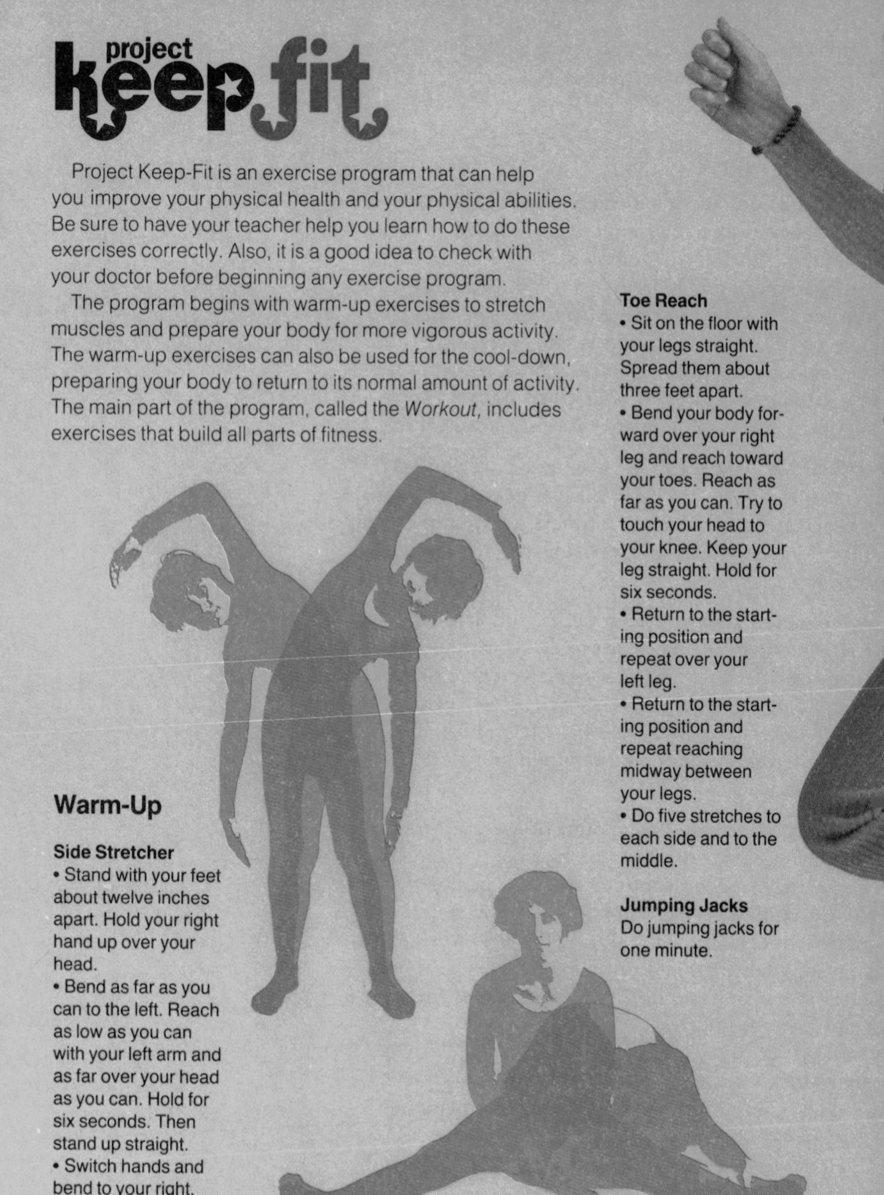

project keep fit

Project Keep-Fit is an exercise program that can help you improve your physical health and your physical abilities. Be sure to have your teacher help you learn how to do these exercises correctly. Also, it is a good idea to check with your doctor before beginning any exercise program.

The program begins with warm-up exercises to stretch muscles and prepare your body for more vigorous activity. The warm-up exercises can also be used for the cool-down, preparing your body to return to its normal amount of activity. The main part of the program, called the *Workout*, includes exercises that build all parts of fitness.

Warm-Up

Side Stretcher
- Stand with your feet about twelve inches apart. Hold your right hand up over your head.
- Bend as far as you can to the left. Reach as low as you can with your left arm and as far over your head as you can. Hold for six seconds. Then stand up straight.
- Switch hands and bend to your right.
- Do five stretches to each side.

Toe Reach
- Sit on the floor with your legs straight. Spread them about three feet apart.
- Bend your body forward over your right leg and reach toward your toes. Reach as far as you can. Try to touch your head to your knee. Keep your leg straight. Hold for six seconds.
- Return to the starting position and repeat over your left leg.
- Return to the starting position and repeat reaching midway between your legs.
- Do five stretches to each side and to the middle.

Jumping Jacks
Do jumping jacks for one minute.

130

Strategies for Page 130

Ask students to read page 130. Discuss the purpose of the warm-up, the workout, and the cool-down. Encourage students to name activities that could make up these parts of an exercise program.

Let students read the directions and study the picture of the **side stretcher.** Warn the students not to lean forward or bounce as they do the side stretcher. Bouncing movements can injure the muscles. Ask students to stand with the legs about a foot apart and try the exercise. Encourage students to hold the stretch for a count of ten. Then ask them to repeat the side stretcher to the opposite side. Let students repeat the exercise, doing up to three stretches to each side. Discuss with students how this exercise builds flexibility in the muscles along the sides of the trunk, the upper arm, and legs.

Encourage students to look at the picture of the **toe reach** and read the directions for the exercise. Allow students to move to an area where they will have enough room to sit with the legs apart in the straddle position. Tell students to keep their legs straight as they reach forward. Warn them not to make bouncing or jerking movements while doing this exercise. Let them try the exercise, encouraging them to hold each stretch for a count of ten. Encourage students to do three stretches to each side and to the middle. Ask students to discuss how the muscles in the legs, arms, shoulders, and lower back feel after they do the toe reach.

Ask students to prepare for the **jumping jacks.** Tell them to move to an area where they have enough room to hold their arms straight out to the sides. Direct them to stand straight with their feet together and their arms down at their sides. Tell students to jump up in the air, spreading their feet apart, and swinging their arms out to the side and then upward, clapping their hands above the head. Then tell them to jump again, returning the arms and legs to the starting position. Encourage students to do jumping jacks for as long as they can for up to two minutes. Discuss why jumping jacks are a good warm-up exercise.

Workout

To help you experience the fun of becoming fit, the exercises for the workout of Project Keep-Fit have been developed into an exercise circuit, as the map shows. A circuit adds variety to your exercise. You might think of other ways to arrange the activities into a circuit, depending on the kind of space you have.

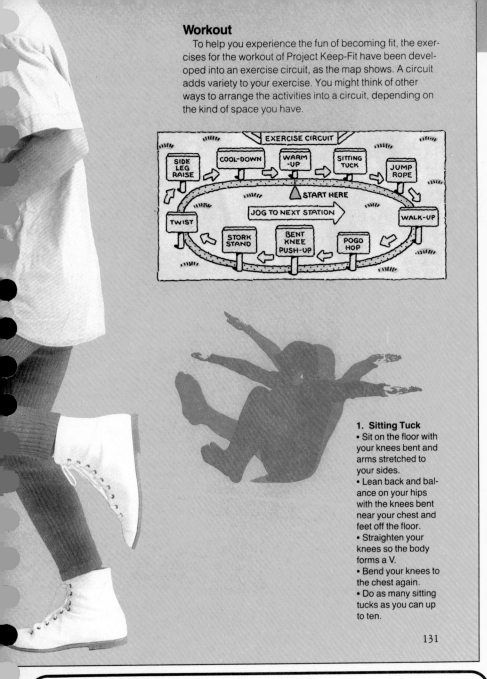

1. Sitting Tuck

- Sit on the floor with your knees bent and arms stretched to your sides.
- Lean back and balance on your hips with the knees bent near your chest and feet off the floor.
- Straighten your knees so the body forms a V.
- Bend your knees to the chest again.
- Do as many sitting tucks as you can up to ten.

131

General Strategies

Be sure all students know how to do the exercises before they begin the exercise circuit. Refer them to the pictures and instructions on pages 131 to 134. You could ask a volunteer to demonstrate the exercises and let students practice before they use the exercise circuit.

To avoid congestion, direct students to start at different stations of the exercise circuit. Signal when students should move on the next station. Remind students not to hold their breath but to breathe normally while exercising.

Encourage students to keep moving throughout the exercise period. Ask them to jog from one station to the next. If some students complete an exercise before time to go to the next station, tell them to jog in place until you signal them to move on. Remind students that the circuit is not a race, but a way to improve parts of fitness and make fitness enjoyable.

Strategies for Page 131

Ask students to read page 131 and look at the map of the exercise circuit. Let students list some benefits of an exercise circuit. Guide students to understand that using an exercise circuit helps provide a period of continuous exercise. Discuss how continuous exercise can help build cardiovascular fitness.

Ask students to review the direction for the **sitting tuck.** Tell them to make sure to keep the back straight as they do the exercise. Guide students to understand that doing the sitting tuck helps strengthen and improve endurance of the abdominal muscles.

Project Keep-Fit Exercise Guide

Use this worksheet to guide students as they practice the Project Keep-Fit exercises at home. The worksheet is located in the Teacher's Resource Book.

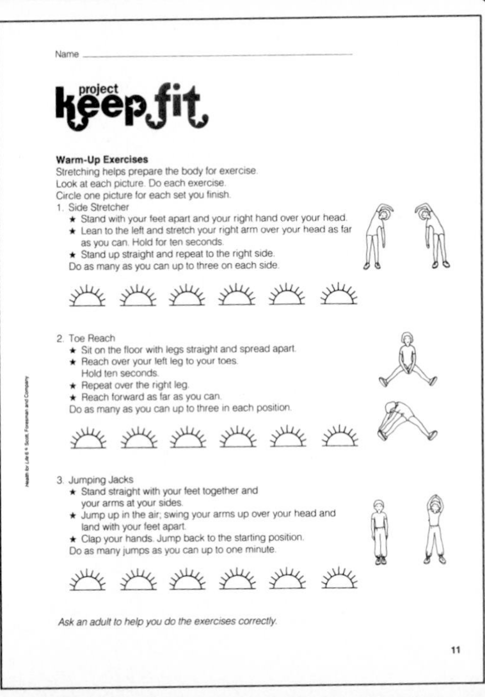

Name ______________________

project keep fit

Warm-Up Exercises

Stretching helps prepare the body for exercise.
Look at each picture. Do each exercise.
Circle one picture for each set you finish.

1. Side Stretcher
   - ★ Stand with your feet apart and your right hand over your head.
   - ★ Lean to the left and stretch your right arm over your head as far as you can. Hold for ten seconds.
   - ★ Stand up straight and repeat to the right side.

   Do as many as you can up to three on each side.

2. Toe Reach
   - ★ Sit on the floor with legs straight and spread apart.
   - ★ Reach over your left leg to your toes. Hold ten seconds.
   - ★ Repeat over the right leg.
   - ★ Reach forward as far as you can.

   Do as many as you can up to three in each position.

3. Jumping Jacks
   - ★ Stand straight with your feet together and your arms at your sides.
   - ★ Jump up in the air; swing your arms up over your head and land with your feet apart.
   - ★ Clap your hands. Jump back to the starting position.

   Do as many jumps as you can up to one minute.

Ask an adult to help you do the exercises correctly.

11

Project Keep-Fit continued

Strategies for Page 132

Read the instructions for **jumping rope** to the students. Provide students with a commercial jump rope or other suitable rope to use as a jump rope. Be sure students have enough space to swing the rope without interference. Tell students to bend their knees as they land. Encourage them to jump rope in place for fifty jumps. Discuss how jumping rope can build muscular endurance in the legs and can build cardiovascular fitness if done long enough.

Encourage students to review the instructions for the **walk up.** Tell students to keep the legs straight and to avoid arching the back as they do this exercise. Ask them to repeat the exercise fifteen times. As a variation, when students have brought their feet as close to their hands as they can, tell them to walk the hands forward to the starting position and repeat the exercise. Students should notice that this exercise builds strength and flexibility of the arm, leg, and hip muscles.

Make sure that students understand how to do the **pogo hop.** Tell students to avoid pulling forward on the head. Such pulling can strain the neck muscles. Remind students to bend their knees as they land. Encourage them to try to do fifty pogo hops. Help them understand that this exercise can build muscular endurance in the legs and cardiovascular fitness, if done long enough.

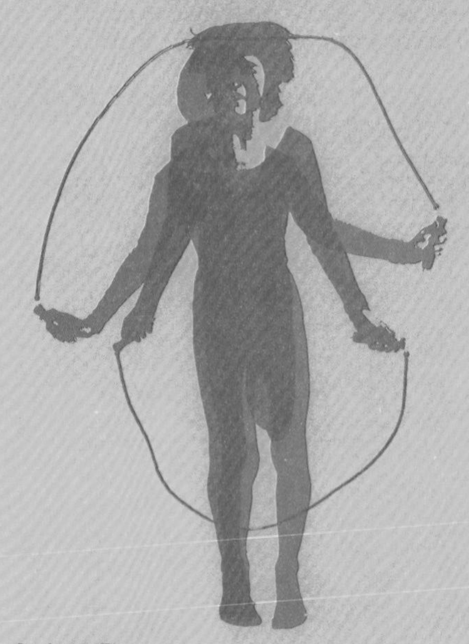

4. Pogo Hop
- Lock your hands behind your head and place your right leg forward and your left leg back.
- Jump in the air, changing positions of your legs so that when you land your left leg is forward and your right leg is back.
- Do as many pogo hops as you can for up to two minutes.

2. Jump Rope
- Jump rope in place.
- Do as many jumps as you can for up to two minutes.

3. Walk-Up
- Support your body with your arms and feet in a push-up position.
- Slowly bring your feet forward as if walking toward your hands, but do not move your hands. Walk forward as far as you can.
- Walk your feet slowly back to where you started.
- Do as many walk-ups as you can up to fifteen.

132

Project Keep-Fit Exercise Guide

Use this worksheet to guide students as they practice the Project Keep-Fit exercises at home. The worksheet is located in the Teacher's Resource Book.

Name ______________________

project keep fit

Workout Exercises

Look at each picture. Do each exercise.
Circle one picture for each set you do.

1. Sitting Tuck
   - ★ Sit on the floor with knees bent and arms straight.
   - ★ Lean back, balance on your hips, knees bent near your chest and feet flat on the floor.
   - ★ Straighten your knees so your body forms a **V.**

   Do as many as you can up to fifteen.
2. Jump Rope
   - ★ Jump rope in place.
   - ★ Land with your knees bent.

   Jump for as long as you can up to two minutes.
3. Walk-Up
   - ★ Lie on the floor with arms straight. Hold your body in a push-up position.
   - ★ Slowly walk your feet forward toward your hands.
   - ★ Do not move your hands.
   - ★ Walk your feet slowly back to the starting position.

   Do as many as you can up to fifteen.
4. Pogo Hop
   - ★ Stand with knees slightly bent and rest your hands on your shoulders.
   - ★ Put your right leg forward and your left leg back.
   - ★ Jump up and move left leg forward and right leg back.

   Continue hopping for as long as you can up to two minutes.

Ask an adult to help you do the exercises correctly.

12

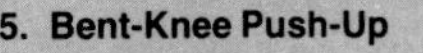

5. Bent-Knee Push-Up

• Lie on your stomach with the palms of your hands on the floor next to your shoulders.
• Keep your knees touching the floor while you push the upper part of your body off the floor.
• Lower your body to the starting position.
• Do as many push-ups as you can up to fifteen.

6. Stork Stand

• Stand with your arms out to the sides.
• Lean forward on one foot, lifting your other leg up behind you. Hold the position for a count of ten.
• Repeat standing on the other foot.
• Do this activity three times for each foot.

Strategies for Page 133

Make sure students know how to do the **bent-knee push-up.** Warn students to keep the back straight throughout the exercise. However, students who have great difficulty doing this exercise should be allowed to make the exercise easier by bringing their knees closer to their hands and elevating the hips. Tell students to do as many push-ups as they can up to fifteen. Guide students to understand that this exercise can help build strength in the muscles of the arms and shoulders.

Let students read the instructions for the **stork stand.** Remind students to keep the back straight and the head up as they do the exercise. Ask them to try to repeat the exercise three times on each leg. Encourage students to notice how the stork stand helps them improve their balance, a part of skills fitness.

Project Keep-Fit Exercise Guide

Use this worksheet to guide students as they practice the Project Keep-Fit exercises at home. The worksheet is located in the Teacher's Resource Book.

Name ______________________

project keep fit

Workout Exercises (continued)

5. Bent-Knee Push-Up
★ Lie on your stomach with hands next to your shoulders.
★ Push up; keep your back straight and knees on the floor.
Do as many as you can up to fifteen.

6. Stork Stand
★ Stand on your left foot and lean forward.
★ Hold arms out to the side and lift right leg behind you.
★ Hold ten seconds, then repeat with the other leg.
Do as many as you can up to three with each foot.

7. Twist
★ Stand with your arms straight out to your sides.
★ Twist your body to the left and hold for ten seconds.
★ Repeat to the right and do as many as you can up to three.

8. Side Leg-Raise
★ Lie on your right side with your head resting on your arm.
★ Lift your left leg as high as you can.
★ Repeat with right leg. Keep legs straight.
Do as many as you can up to fifteen with each leg.

Ask an adult to help you do the exercises correctly.

13

Project Keep-Fit continued

Strategies for Page 134

Review the instructions for the **twist** with the students. Warn them not to lean forward or make jerking movements as they do this exercise. Tell students to keep the back straight as they twist. Encourage students to hold the stretch for a count of ten. Ask them to try to do three twists to each side. Discuss how this exercise builds flexibility of the upper body and trunk.

Let students read the instructions for the **side leg-raise.** Tell students not to lean forward or backward when doing this exercise. Remind students to lift the leg so that it remains aligned with the other leg, which is on the floor. They should avoid bringing the leg forward or backward as they raise it. Encourage students to do fifteen leg-raises on each side. Discuss how this exercise builds muscular strength and endurance of the leg, hip, and buttock muscles.

When students have completed the exercises, encourage them to cool down by repeating the warm-up exercises on page 130. They should do slow cardiovascular exercise first, such as slow jumping jacks, followed by stretching. Discuss with the students how the cool-down helps the body. (prepares it to return to a normal amount of activity) Let students evaluate the exercise program as to whether it was too hard, too easy, or just right. Encourage students to adjust the program according to individual needs. You may wish to ask students to repeat the exercise circuit regularly for a few weeks. Encourage them to gradually increase the number of times they do each exercise. Let them discuss any improvements they notice in health and skills fitness. Students should recognize that, with regular repetition, such parts of fitness as muscular strength, endurance, and cardiovascular fitness, will improve.

Talk about different places that could be used for an exercise circuit. You may wish to encourage students to consider setting up an exercise circuit at or near their homes.

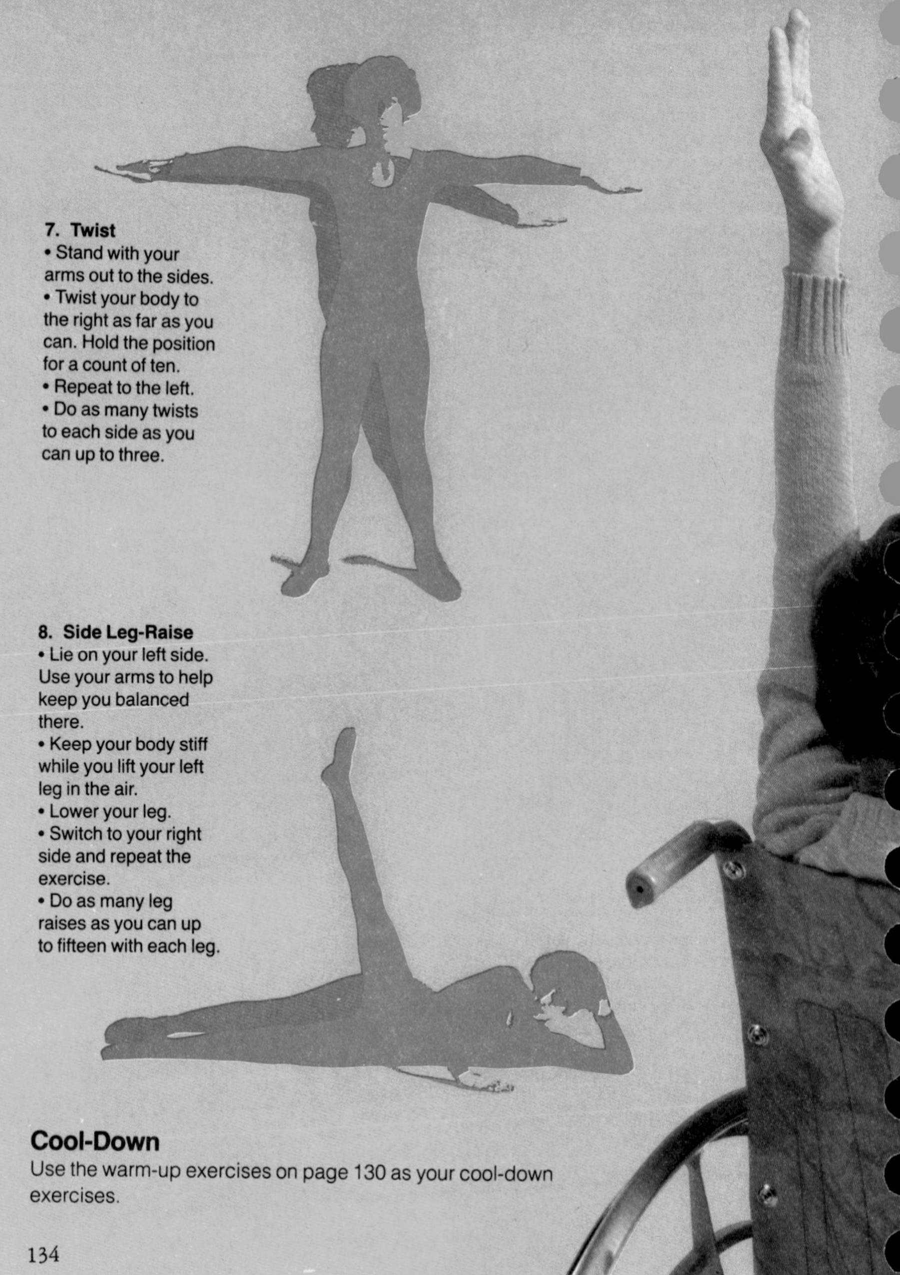

7. Twist
• Stand with your arms out to the sides.
• Twist your body to the right as far as you can. Hold the position for a count of ten.
• Repeat to the left.
• Do as many twists to each side as you can up to three.
8. Side Leg-Raise
• Lie on your left side. Use your arms to help keep you balanced there.
• Keep your body stiff while you lift your left leg in the air.
• Lower your leg.
• Switch to your right side and repeat the exercise.
• Do as many leg raises as you can up to fifteen with each leg.
Cool-Down
Use the warm-up exercises on page 130 as your cool-down exercises.
134

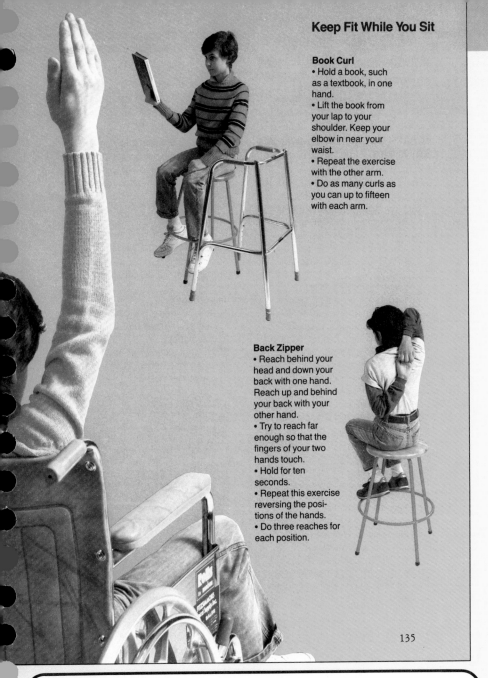

Keep Fit While You Sit

Book Curl

- Hold a book, such as a textbook, in one hand.
- Lift the book from your lap to your shoulder. Keep your elbow in near your waist.
- Repeat the exercise with the other arm.
- Do as many curls as you can up to fifteen with each arm.

Back Zipper

- Reach behind your head and down your back with one hand. Reach up and behind your back with your other hand.
- Try to reach far enough so that the fingers of your two hands touch.
- Hold for ten seconds.
- Repeat this exercise reversing the positions of the hands.
- Do three reaches for each position.

135

General Strategies

These exercises are good for students who want to exercise at their desks. They are also well suited for students who are temporarily or permanently limited to a chair. For example, a student who has limited mobility due to a leg injury might benefit from these exercises. However, before recommending these exercises to any student with a physical limitation, be sure to consult with the student's parents, guardian, or physician to find out if the student's movements or activities need to be restricted in any way.

Strategies for Page 135

Ask students to discuss how these exercises might be useful to people who are confined to wheelchairs, people with leg injuries, or people who spend a large amount of time sitting.

Encourage students to read the directions for the **book curl.** Ask students to use a hardbound book for this exercise. You might also substitute canned foods, plastic milk bottles filled with various amounts of water, or small dumbbells for weights. Tell students to raise and lower the weights slowly. Inform them that lowering the weight is as important as lifting it for building arm strength. Let students who have trouble doing the book curl use a lighter-weight object. As arm strength increases, a heavier object can be substituted. Encourage students to do fifteen book curls with each arm. Guide students to realize that this exercise builds muscular strength and endurance of the arms.

Let students read the directions for the **back zipper** and study the picture. Encourage students to try the exercise. Some students may not be able to touch hands in both positions. Tell such students to reach as far as they can and hold the stretch. Encourage students to stretch for six to ten seconds. Encourage them to repeat the back zipper three times for each of the two hand positions. Point out that this exercise builds flexibility of the arms, shoulders, and upper back.

Project Keep-Fit Exercise Guide

Use this worksheet to guide students as they practice the Project Keep-Fit exercises at home. The worksheet is located in the Teacher's Resource Book.

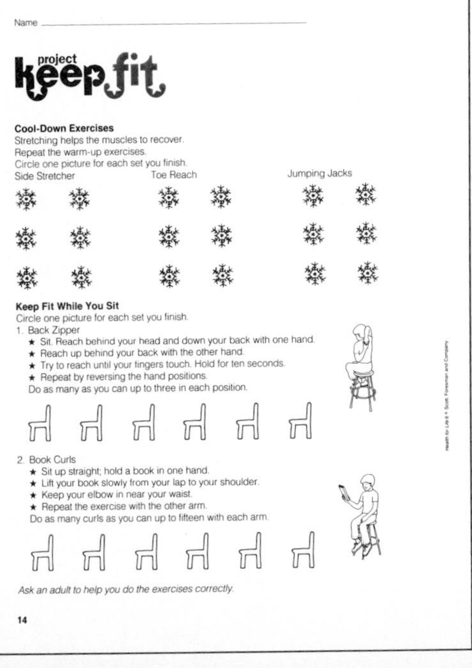

Name ______

project keep fit

Cool-Down Exercises

Stretching helps the muscles to recover.
Repeat the warm-up exercises.
Circle one picture for each set you finish.

Side Stretcher | Toe Reach | Jumping Jacks

Keep Fit While You Sit

Circle one picture for each set you finish.

1. Back Zipper
   - ★ Sit. Reach behind your head and down your back with one hand.
   - ★ Reach up behind your back with the other hand.
   - ★ Try to reach until your fingers touch. Hold for ten seconds.
   - ★ Repeat by reversing the hand positions.

   Do as many as you can up to three in each position.

2. Book Curls
   - ★ Sit up straight; hold a book in one hand.
   - ★ Lift your book slowly from your lap to your shoulder.
   - ★ Keep your elbow in near your waist.
   - ★ Repeat the exercise with the other arm.

   Do as many curls as you can up to fifteen with each arm.

Ask an adult to help you do the exercises correctly.

14

Teaching Plan

Health Focus page 136

Discussion

Let students share any experiences they have had canoeing, camping, or hiking. Ask them what aspects of physical fitness help a person more fully enjoy each of these activities. (muscular endurance, balance, coordination, and power) Discuss what other types of skills are particularly important for canoeing. (Students might mention good judgment, good communication skills, ability to work with others.)

Answers to Talk About It

1. Being physically fit enabled the students to canoe and put up tents under rough conditions and still enjoy the trip.
Thinking Skill Students are *recalling information.*

2. Accept any reasonable answers that the students can explain. Being in good shape would be helpful on almost any vacation involving walking, hiking, swimming, or other fitness activities. Physical fitness is also an advantage in emergency situations such as having to walk far for help.
Thinking Skills Students are *interpreting information* and *classifying.*

Fitness Counts on Everglades Adventure

You can probably think of many ways that being physically fit contributes to health. You might not realize that fitness can also contribute to enjoyment of a vacation. The students from East Haddam, Connecticut, can tell you fitness was an extremely important part of their vacation.

One winter, twelve students from Connecticut took a guided cruise through the Florida Everglades. Why would they need to be physically fit for such a trip? This cruise was made in canoes that the students paddled themselves for two weeks!

During the two weeks the students had many adventures. They paddled through the quiet marshes and peaceful woodlands of the Florida coast. Here they saw many animals they had never seen before. Large storks perched on the tops of trees. Alligators peered at them from fallen logs. Porpoises swam playfully beside them.

However, not everything about the trip was peaceful. On the first day of canoeing the students battled fierce winds and waves. With the rough weather, progress was slowed to a snail's pace. Then it took the students several hours to put up their tents. The winds were so strong the tents kept blowing over.

Because the students were physically fit, they were able to enjoy the canoe trip despite the weather. Before they left Connecticut, each person passed a fitness test. Each one had to run several miles and show that he or she could swim and canoe well. Being physically fit allowed the students to paddle through the Everglades with ease on peaceful days and handle the hardships during the more difficult days.

Talk About It

1. How did being physically fit help the students on their trip through the Everglades?
2. On what other types of vacations would it be helpful to be in good physical shape?

Teaching Options

Vocabulary

Use this worksheet for practice in reviewing chapter vocabulary words. This master may be reproduced from the Teacher's Resource Book and is located on page 14 of the Student's Workbook. Use with Chapter 4: pages 104–139.

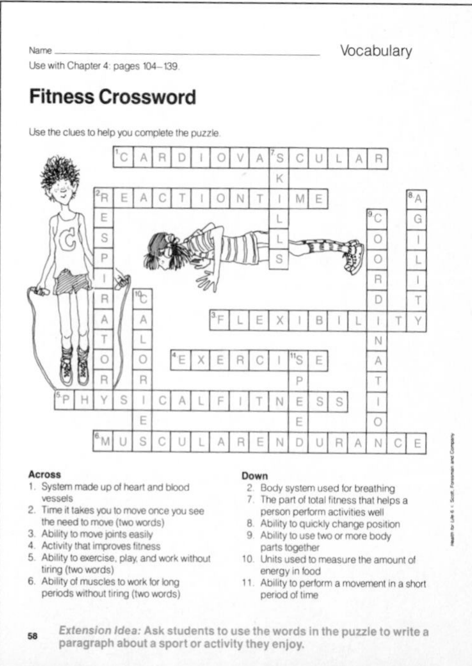

Name ____________________ Vocabulary

Use with Chapter 4: pages 104–139.

Fitness Crossword

Use the clues to help you complete the puzzle.

Across
1. System made up of heart and blood vessels
2. Time it takes you to move once you see the need to move (two words)
3. Ability to move joints easily
4. Activity that improves fitness
5. Ability to exercise, play, and work without tiring (two words)
6. Ability of muscles to work for long periods without tiring (two words)

Down
2. Body system used for breathing
7. The part of total fitness that helps a person perform activities well
8. Ability to quickly change position
9. Ability to use two or more body parts together
10. Units used to measure the amount of energy in food
11. Ability to perform a movement in a short period of time

58 *Extension Idea:* **Ask students to use the words in the puzzle to write a paragraph about a sport or activity they enjoy.**

Participating in Lifetime Activities

Many games and sports can be enjoyed by people of all ages. These games are called lifetime activities. Unlike many sports, these activities can be done all through your life. Badminton, golf, jump rope, cross-country skiing, bicycling, skin diving, running, tennis, skating, dancing, swimming, and walking are just a few of the lifetime activities you can enjoy.

These activities can be a good way for a family to spend time together because people of all ages can participate. Also, many of the activities do not need costly equipment or large groups of players. A person does not have to be highly skilled to enjoy these activities.

Help your family plan a fitness break. You might play indoors with a sponge ball or have a jump rope contest. Ask members of your family to go bicycling or play badminton on a Saturday afternoon. Your family could take a walk together after dinner. What activities might your family enjoy doing together?

Lifetime activities can help your family become interested in physical fitness and maintain fitness all through life.

Reading at Home

The New Physical Fitness by Richard Lyttle. Watts, 1981. Learn to take care of your body through exercise and diet.

Your Muscles and Ways to Exercise Them by Margaret Cosgrove. Dodd, Mead, 1980. Read about the effects of exercise on muscles.

Health at Home
page 137

Strategies
Let volunteers share what lifetime activities their parents or older relatives in their families enjoy. Discuss which of these activities younger members of the family are learning. Ask students to discuss whether children tend to take up the sports or other physical activities, such as hiking or camping, that their parents enjoy.

Ask the students to think about how their family can build or maintain physical fitness. Suggest that they explore games and activities that the family could do together to be more physically fit.

More Reading at Home
The New Physical Fitness (Grades 6–7)

Your Muscles and Ways to Exercise Them (Grades 5–6)

Liptak, Karen. *Aerobics Basics.* Prentice-Hall, 1983. Provides step-by-step instruction for a variety of aerobic exercises. (Grades 3–6)

Study and Review
Use this worksheet for practice in identifying the parts of fitness. This master may be reproduced from the Teacher's Resource Book and is located on page 15 of the Student's Workbook. Use with Chapter 4: pages 104–139.

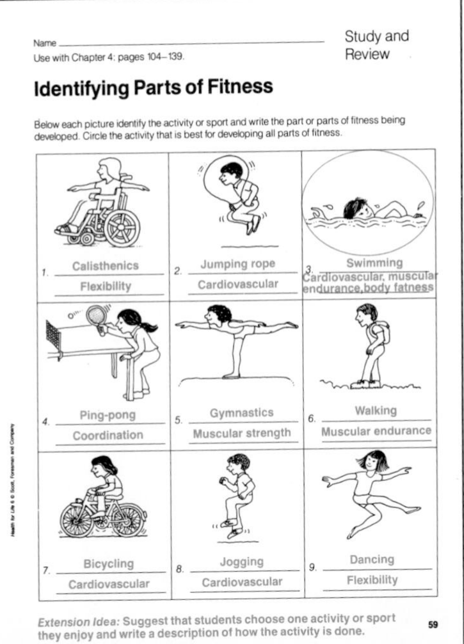

Name ______________________ Study and Review
Use with Chapter 4: pages 104–139.

Identifying Parts of Fitness

Below each picture identify the activity or sport and write the part or parts of fitness being developed. Circle the activity that is best for developing all parts of fitness.

1. Calisthenics Flexibility	2. Jumping rope Cardiovascular	3. Swimming Cardiovascular, muscular endurance, body fatness
4. Ping-pong Coordination	5. Gymnastics Muscular strength	6. Walking Muscular endurance
7. Bicycling Cardiovascular	8. Jogging Cardiovascular	9. Dancing Flexibility

Extension Idea: Suggest that students choose one activity or sport they enjoy and write a description of how the activity is done.

59

Chapter 4 Review

pages 138–139

Answers to Reviewing Lesson Objectives

Use this section for guided study or for oral review. Objective numbers match lesson numbers.

1. Exercise promotes a positive self-concept by relieving stress, helping a person look his or her best, encouraging new friendships, and developing communication and cooperation skills. Exercise promotes a healthy body by improving a person's cardiovascular fitness and muscular strength, flexibility, and muscular endurance.

2. The right amount of body fat is important to health because fat stores vitamins and energy that the body needs. Fat also gives the body shape, helps keep the body warm, and protects organs from injury. However, having too much body fat can help contribute to health problems. Exercise helps control body fatness by using up Calories.

3. Skills fitness is the ability to perform well in activities that require certain skills. The parts of skills fitness are agility, balance, coordination, power, reaction time, and speed.

4. A person should determine his or her needs, interests, abilities, and present fitness.

5. A person can achieve fitness goals by choosing activities that develop the parts of fitness that are desired, by exercising the proper amount and length of time, and by exercising safely.

Answers to Checking Health Vocabulary

Use the vocabulary check as a review or as a test.

1. g
2. f
3. h
4. b
5. a
6. c
7. e
8. d
9–20. Answers will vary but should reflect students' understanding of the meaning of the words as used in the text.

Chapter 4 Review

For further review, use Study Guide pages 322-323
Practice skills for life for Chapter 4 on pages 347-349
SKILLS FOR LIFE

Reviewing Lesson Objectives

1. Recognize the role that regular, vigorous activity plays in promoting a positive self-concept and healthy body. (pages 106–111)
2. Explain how the right amount of body fat is important to health. Explain how regular, vigorous activity can help control body fatness. (pages 112–115)
3. Explain what skills fitness is. List the six parts of skills fitness. (pages 116–117)
4. Explain how interests, needs, and abilities help a person set fitness goals. (pages 120–125)
5. Explain how a person can achieve fitness goals. (pages 126–129)

Checking Health Vocabulary

Number your paper from 1–8. Match each definition in Column I with the correct word or words in Column II.

Column I

1. the ability to exercise without tiring easily and without a high risk of injury
2. the ability of muscles to exercise for a long time without tiring
3. the body system that includes the air passages and lungs
4. a unit used to measure the energy in food and the energy used in activity
5. the ability to change body position quickly and to control the movement of the whole body
6. the body system made of the heart, blood, and blood vessels
7. the ability to move the body parts fully and easily
8. the ability to use the senses with the body parts or to use two or more body parts together

Column II

a. agility
b. Calorie
c. cardiovascular system
d. coordination
e. flexibility
f. muscular endurance
g. physical fitness
h. respiratory system

Number your paper from 9–20. Next to each number write a sentence using that part of fitness.

9. cardiovascular fitness
10. muscular strength
11. flexibility
12. muscular endurance
13. body fatness
14. agility
15. balance
16. coordination
17. power
18. reaction time
19. speed
20. skills fitness

138

Chapter 4 Tests Use Test A or Test B to assess students' mastery of the health concepts in Chapter 4. These tests are located on pages 33–40 in the Test Book.

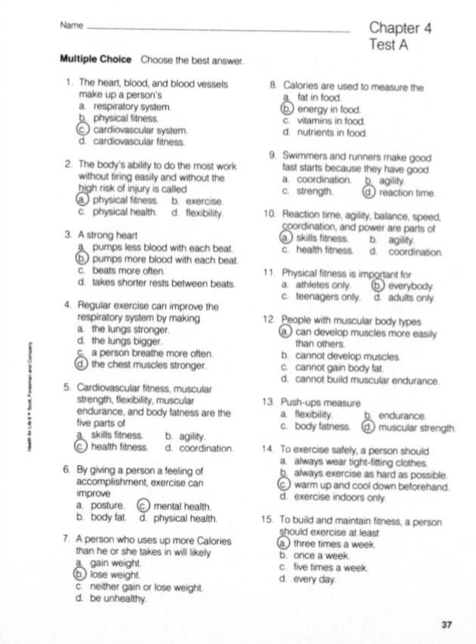

Name ______________ Chapter 4 Test A

Multiple Choice Choose the best answer.

1. The heart, blood, and blood vessels make up a person's
   a. respiratory system.
   b. physical fitness.
   c. cardiovascular system.
   d. cardiovascular fitness.
2. The body's ability to do the most work without tiring easily and without the high risk of injury is called
   a. physical fitness. b. exercise.
   c. physical health. d. flexibility.
3. A strong heart
   a. pumps less blood with each beat.
   b. pumps more blood with each beat.
   c. beats more often.
   d. takes shorter rests between beats.
4. Regular exercise can improve the respiratory system by making
   a. the lungs stronger.
   d. the lungs bigger.
   c. a person breathe more often.
   d. the chest muscles stronger.
5. Cardiovascular fitness, muscular strength, flexibility, muscular endurance, and body fatness are the five parts of
   a. skills fitness. b. agility.
   c. health fitness. d. coordination.
6. By giving a person a feeling of accomplishment, exercise can improve
   a. posture. c. mental health.
   b. body fat. d. physical health.
7. A person who uses up more Calories than he or she takes in will likely
   a. gain weight.
   b. lose weight.
   c. neither gain or lose weight.
   d. be unhealthy.
8. Calories are used to measure the
   a. fat in food.
   b. energy in food.
   c. vitamins in food.
   d. nutrients in food.
9. Swimmers and runners make good fast starts because they have good
   a. coordination. b. agility.
   c. strength. d. reaction time.
10. Reaction time, agility, balance, speed, coordination, and power are parts of
    a. skills fitness. b. agility.
    c. health fitness. d. coordination.
11. Physical fitness is important for
    a. athletes only. b. everybody.
    c. teenagers only. d. adults only.
12. People with muscular body types
    a. can develop muscles more easily than others.
    b. cannot develop muscles.
    c. cannot gain body fat.
    d. cannot build muscular endurance.
13. Push-ups measure
    a. flexibility. b. endurance.
    c. body fatness. d. muscular strength.
14. To exercise safely, a person should
    a. always wear tight-fitting clothes.
    b. always exercise as hard as possible.
    c. warm up and cool down beforehand.
    d. exercise indoors only.
15. To build and maintain fitness, a person should exercise at least
    a. three times a week.
    b. once a week.
    c. five times a week.
    d. every day.

37

Name ______________ Chapter 4 Test A

Short Answer Match each meaning in Column I with the correct word or words in Column II. Write the correct letter on the blank.

Column I

__e__ 16. the body system that includes the nose, air passages, and lungs
__c__ 17. the body system made up of the heart, blood, and blood vessels
__d__ 18. the ability to exercise, play, and work without tiring easily and without a high risk of injury
__a__ 19. the ability of muscles to work for long periods of time without getting tired
__b__ 20. the ability to move the joints fully and to move body parts easily

Column II

a. muscular endurance
b. flexibility
c. cardiovascular system
d. physical fitness
e. respiratory system

Short Essay Write your answers in complete sentences.

21. Jane weighs more than Mary. Both people run every day for 15 minutes. Why does Jane lose more weight than Mary?
    The number of Calories a person uses while exercising depends on how long the person exercises and how much the person weighs. Jane loses more weight because more Calories are used by people who weigh more.
22. Why are the same exercises used to warm up and cool down?
    To warm up before exercise and to cool down after exercise, you need to do gentle, stretching exercises. These kinds of exercises can slowly get you ready to exercise and slowly bring your body down to its normal activity level.

38

Reviewing Health Ideas

Number your paper from 1–14. Next to each number write the word that best completes the sentence.

1. ____ can improve mental health by relieving stress.
2. A stronger heart pumps ____ blood with each beat than a weaker heart.
3. People who exercise regularly often develop more branching of the ____ in the heart.
4. Stronger chest muscles let a person take in more oxygen and get rid of more carbon ____ with each breath.
5. Stretching exercises make the muscles more ____.
6. Fat is stored ____.
7. About half of a person's fat is under the ____.
8. A person who uses up more Calories than he or she takes in will likely ____ weight.
9. Cardiovascular fitness, muscular strength, flexibility, muscular endurance, and body fatness are parts of ____ fitness.
10. Being able to meet a ping-pong ball with a paddle is a result of good hand-eye ____.
11. The tube catch can be used to test the part of skills fitness called ____.
12. People need to exercise at least ____ times a week to build and maintain fitness.
13. Before beginning highly active exercise, a person should do ____ exercises.
14. Cooling down after active exercise helps to slowly lower the heart ____ back to normal.

Understanding Health Ideas

Number your paper from 15–22. Next to each number write the word or words that best answer the question.

15. What skills important to social health can people learn while playing team sports?
16. What happens to muscles if they do not get enough oxygen and do not have wastes taken away?
17. What kind of tissue can break down if a person does not have enough body fat?
18. If a person eats food that contains 2,500 Calories and uses up 2,000 Calories, what happens to the other 500 Calories?
19. What part of skills fitness involves covering a certain distance in a short period of time?
20. What three things should a person determine before setting fitness goals?
21. What should people do if they enjoy an activity that does not improve a part of fitness that they want to improve?
22. How fast should the heart beat during exercise to build and maintain fitness?

Thinking Critically

Write the answers on your paper. Use complete sentences.

1. For each part of skills fitness write the name of a sport, job, or daily activity that requires that part. Explain why the part of skills fitness is important to the activity.
2. What advice would you give to someone who wanted to become physically fit?

139

Answers to Reviewing Health Ideas

1. exercise
2. more
3. arteries
4. dioxide
5. flexible
6. energy
7. skin
8. lose
9. health
10. coordination
11. reaction time
12. three
13. warm-up
14. rate

Answers to Understanding Health Ideas

15. communication and cooperation
16. tire and cannot work
17. muscle
18. stored as fat
19. speed
20. individual needs, interests, and abilities
21. include other activities
22. between 135 and 155 beats per minute

Answers to Thinking Critically

1. Answers will vary but students should explain why that activity requires the particular skill.
Thinking Skills When students explain why certain parts of skills fitness are required in certain activities, they are *classifying* and *generalizing*.
2. Answers might include advice about setting specific fitness goals and choosing activities to meet those goals. Answers might also discuss safety measures to take while exercising.
Thinking Skills When students make suggestions for people who want to become physically fit, they are *suggesting alternatives*.

Cooperative Learning Use the STAD Format described on page T24 to have four- to five-member teams study Chapter 4 Review together before completing Chapter 4 Test.

Name ____________________ Chapter 4 Test B

Multiple Choice Choose the best answer.

1. Relieving stress is one way that exercise can improve
   a. posture. (b) mental health. c. body fat. d. physical health.
2. The cardiovascular system is made up of the
   a. muscles. b. oxygen and wastes. c. lungs and air passages. (d) heart, blood, and blood vessels.
3. Regular exercise can help prevent
   a. an increase in the number of arteries in the heart. b. the heart from beating too slowly. (c) the buildup of fatty material inside arteries. d. an increase of oxygen to the heart.
4. Energy is stored in the body's
   a. bones. b. muscles. (c) fat. d. lungs.
5. The amount of body fat on a healthy eleven- or twelve-year-old should be
   a. none. b. 1 percent of total body weight. (c) 10 to 15 percent of total body weight. d. 25 percent of total body weight.
6. A person who takes in more Calories than are used stores the extra Calories as
   a. blood. b. heat. c. muscle. (d) body fat.
7. Having agility is most important in
   (a) gymnastics. b. running. c. softball. d. farming.
8. Hitting a baseball with a bat is a result of good hand-eye
   a. agility. b. balance. c. power. (d) coordination.
9. Agility, balance, coordination, power, reaction time, and speed are parts of
   (a) skills fitness. b. muscular endurance. c. flexibility. d. muscular strength.
10. People who naturally have thinner bodies
    a. cannot build muscles. (b) can develop good muscular endurance. c. cannot build physical fitness. d. can build large muscles easily.
11. When people run in place and then check their pulse, they are measuring their
    a. strength. b. flexibility. (c) cardiovascular fitness. d. muscular endurance.
12. The Tube Catch activity measures
    a. speed. b. power. (c) reaction time. d. balance.
13. To build and maintain fitness, people should exercise at least
    a. once a week. b. five times a week. c. twice a week. (d) three times a week.
14. During exercise, a person's heart should beat each minute at a rate of
    a. 100. (b) 135 to 155. c. 100 to 120. d. 125 to 130.
15. Right before exercising, a person should
    (a) warm up. b. eat. c. cool down. d. run fast.

39

Name ____________________ Chapter 4 Test B

Short Answer Match each meaning in Column I with the correct word or words in Column II. Write the correct letter on the blank.

Column I	Column II
c 16. the ability to stay upright while standing or moving	a. reaction time
e 17. the ability to change your body position quickly and to control the movement of your whole body	b. speed
d 18. the ability to quickly do activities that require strength	c. balance
b 19. the ability to perform a movement or cover a distance in a short period of time	d. power
a 20. the amount of time it takes you to start moving once you see the need to move	e. agility

Short Essay Write your answers in complete sentences.

21. While Steve was on a diet, his doctor said that he lost too much body fat. Now Steve feels tired and cannot exercise. Why?
    Steve feels tired because body fat is important to a person's health. Body fat is stored energy. When you lose too much body fat, you can become very weak and sick.
22. Why is it important for a person to exercise regularly?
    Regular exercise helps build cardiovascular fitness, improving your health. Your body gets more oxygen and gets rid of wastes better.

40

Pupil Edition	Activities	Enrichment	Assessment	Independent Study
Chapter 5 Safety and First Aid, pp. 140–165	Health Watch Notebook, p. 140	Health Focus, p. 162 Health at Home, p. 163	Chapter 5 Review, pp. 164–165	Study Guide, pp. 324–325 Skills for Life Handbook, pp. 350–352
Lesson 1 How Can You Prevent Accidents? pp. 142–143		Did You Know? p. 143	Think Back, p. 143	Study Guide, p. 324
Lesson 2 How Can You Act Safely at Home? pp. 144–149	Health Activities Workshop, pp. 150–151		Think Back, p. 149	On Your Own, p. 149 Study Guide, p. 324
Lesson 3 How Can You Be Prepared for Emergencies? pp. 152–155			Think Back, p. 155	On Your Own, p. 153 Study Guide, p. 325
Lesson 4 How Can You Help in a Medical Emergency? pp. 156–161		Did You Know? pp. 157, 159	Think Back, p. 161	Study Guide, p. 325

Teacher Resources

The American Medical Association Family Medical Guide. American Medical Association, 1982. Contains information about safety procedures and first-aid treatment.

Arnold, Charles G., ed. *Aquatic Safety and Lifesaving Program,* YMCA, 1979. Explains how to be safe in the water, and what to do if someone needs help.

Basic Bicycling. AAHPERD, 1982. Presents informative tips on bicycle riding and maintenance.

Standard First-Aid and Personal Safety. American National Red Cross, Doubleday, 1979. Provides tips and techniques for giving first aid until professional medical help arrives.

Audio-Visual Resources

See page T43 for addresses of Audio-Visual Sources.

Before using any audio-visual materials, preview them for appropriateness for your students.

Bicycling Visual Skills, American Automobile Association, film, 13 minutes. Teaches children how the rules of the road apply to both bicycle and car drivers.

Fire Safety: Flammable Liquids, AIMS Media, film or video, 14 minutes. Explains the physical properties of flammable and combustible liquids, and tells how to handle such liquids.

First Aid for Young People, BFA Educational Media, film or video, 15 minutes. Demonstrates the latest American Red Cross procedures for first aid.

The Heimlich Maneuver: How to Save a Choking Victim, 2nd ed., AIMS Media, film or video, 17 minutes. Demonstrates the Heimlich Maneuver and teaches how people can use it to help someone who is choking.

Thinking About School Bus Safety, American Automobile Association, film, 8 minutes. Uses peer interaction to present proper and safe bus behavior.

Computer Software

Babysitter's Manual, Control Health Software. Teaches babysitters about accident prevention and safety, and explains how to seek aid if an injury occurs.

	Teacher's Edition	Teacher's Resource Book	Test Book
Enrichment	Suggestions for each lesson: L. 1—p. 142 L. 2—pp. 144, 146, 148 L. 3—pp. 152, 154 L. 4—pp. 156, 158, 160	Family Letter, p. 65 * Life Skills, p. 69 * Health and Language Arts, p. 72	
Reteaching	Suggestions for each lesson: L. 1—p. 142 L. 2—pp. 144, 146, 148 L. 3—pp. 152, 154 L. 4—pp. 156, 158, 160	Transparency Masters, pp. 67–68 * Vocabulary, p. 70 * Study and Review, p. 71	
Assessment	Expanding Student Thinking: one assessment question per lesson that develops higher-order thinking skills—pp. 143, 149, 155, 161		Chapter 5 Test, Form A, pp. 41–42 Chapter 5 Test, Form B, pp. 43–44

* Also available in Workbook format (Student Edition and Teacher's Edition)

Chapter 5 Poster
A set of posters is available in a separate package. It provides a teaching poster for every chapter, including discussion and activity suggestions on the back. The poster for Chapter 5 is titled "Find the safety practices."

Overhead Transparencies
A set of color overhead transparencies is available for Grade 6. You may wish to use Transparency 14 to help teach first aid for choking.

Advance Preparation
You will need to prepare materials in advance for the following activity from the Health Activities Workshop.
Activity 4, page 151 Supply newspapers, magazines, and encyclopedias.

Bulletin Board
Encourage volunteers to draw various rooms in a home. Each drawing should show ways that the room is safe. Use these rooms to make a house on the bulletin board. Ask other students to find and explain the ways the home is safe.

In what ways is this home safe?

Teaching Plan

Chapter 5 pages 140–165

Chapter Main Idea
Applying safety rules to daily life and acquiring skills in basic first aid help in the prevention and treatment of accidents.

Chapter Goals
- Recognize that accident prevention is desirable behavior.
- Avoid unnecessary risks in daily situations.
- Become better prepared for emergencies.
- Express an interest in acquiring further knowledge and skills by inquiring about first-aid classes.

Lifetime Goal
Incorporate safety practices and first-aid skills into a healthy lifestyle.

Health Vocabulary
Artificial respiration, emergency, first aid, poison, shock

Words to Preteach
Abdomen, circulation, unnecessary risk

Chapter 5

Safety and First Aid

What do all the hats in the picture have in common? They are all worn by people who are concerned with safety or first aid—for themselves and for others. Where might you see each kind of hat being worn?

This chapter shows how you can make safety a part of your everyday life. You will learn how to prevent accidents. The chapter also discusses ways that you can help someone, and perhaps save someone's life, during an emergency. Practicing safety and developing first-aid skills is an important part of your future health.

Health Watch Notebook

Look through newspapers or magazines for an article about an accident. Paste the article in your notebook. Write a paragraph describing what caused the accident, what its consequences were, and how the accident could have been prevented.

1 How Can You Prevent Accidents?
2 How Can You Act Safely at Home?
3 How Can You Be Prepared for Emergencies?
4 How Can You Help in a Medical Emergency?

140

Teaching Options

Modeling Health Vocabulary
Use this technique to introduce new words as you teach each lesson in this chapter. First, introduce the word. Present the word in two sentences that serve to clearly define the word. One sentence you might use to introduce the word *poison* is: *Many household cleaners contain poison.* Either read the sentences to the students or write them on the chalkboard. Ask the students to generate two meaningful sentences using the word. Additional successful techniques for introducing new words can be found on page T23.

Cooperative Learning
Jigsaw Format (See page T24.)
Assign the following topics at random to your cooperative learning teams.
Topic A: Name ways to prevent accidents at home, crossing streets, and riding in a car.
Topic B: What actions should be taken during a fire emergency?
Topic C: What first aid measures should be taken when a person is choking, burned, or in shock?
Topic D: What is artificial respiration and when is it used?
Have students search for information on their topic as they read the chapter. Then let all students with the same topic meet in an expert group to discuss the information. When students return to their teams, they may take turns presenting their topics to the team. Then give students a test covering all topics to complete individually (Chapter 5 test A or B in the Test Book). Award Superteam certificates to teams whose average test scores exceed 90%, and Greatteam certificates to teams whose average test scores exceed 80%.

Introducing the Chapter

Ask students to look at the picture and tell what the hats have in common. Then ask students to read page 140 to find the answer to the question. (The hats are worn by people who are concerned with safety or first aid.) Let students suggest where each hat might be worn. You may wish to send the Family Letter home at this time. You may want to assign Study Guide pages 324–325 for students to use independently as they read the lessons. The Study Guide can also be used as an extra chapter review. You might want to assign the activities in the Skills for Life Handbook on pages 350–352.

Strategies for Health Watch Notebook

Before assigning this activity, you may wish to ask students to name locations where accidents occur. (the home, the workplace, the highway, and so on) Then divide students into teams and have members of each team look for written accounts of a different type of accident.

Family Letter

Use the Family Letter (English or Spanish version) to introduce the subject matter of the chapter to the family and to suggest a way the family can become involved in the student's learning experience. This master may be reproduced from the Teacher's Resource Book.

Dear Family,

Your student will be reading Chapter 5, "Safety and First Aid," in Health for Life, *published by Scott, Foresman. This chapter will discuss ways to prevent accidents and ways to treat victims of accidents.*

The activity below will help your child learn how to handle emergencies. You might enjoy completing the activity together.

What would you do if someone in your family had a bad fall? Do you know who to call and how to help?

Thinking about what to do in case of an emergency can help you be prepared. Talk with your family about what to do in case of a fire, or if someone swallows something poisonous. Make an emergency list of **Who to Call** and **What to Do.** You might want to keep this list near the telephone.

The ______________ Family Emergency List

Who to Call

1. ______________ 4. ______________ 7. Fire: ______________

2. ______________ 5. ______________ 8. Police: ______________

3. ______________ 6. ______________ 9. Doctor: ______________

What to Do

Fire ______________

Bad Fall ______________

Poisoning ______________

65

For High-Potential Students

Ask students to list a few common accidents that can occur in the home. Then show students examples of cartoons by Rube Goldberg. Let students make drawings of their own Rube Goldberg-type machines that could aid in home safety. For example, they might draw a smoke alarm, a child-proof safety cap, or an emergency telephone number dialer.

Teaching Plan

Lesson 1 pages 142–143

Lesson Objective
Describe several ways to avoid unnecessary risks, thereby avoiding traffic and other accidents.

1 Motivate

Introducing the Lesson
Ask students to name some school rules. Then encourage students to speculate about what school would be like without rules. Help them understand that many school rules help prevent accidents.

2 Teach

Strategies for Pages 142 and 143
• Ask students to read page 142 to learn about ways to prevent accidents. • Be sure students understand the difference between necessary and unnecessary risks. Almost any action, such as crossing a street, involves some risk. However, crossing a street against a red light is an unnecessary risk. • Ask students to read page 143 to find out how to help prevent traffic accidents. • Ask students to tell what the people in the pictures are doing to prevent accidents.

POOL RULES
- SHOWER BEFORE ENTERING POOL.
- CAPS MUST BE WORN BY ALL SWIMMERS.
- ONLY QUALIFIED SWIMMERS MAY SWIM IN THE DEEP END.
- NO ROUGH PLAY.
- ONLY ONE PERSON ON THE DIVING BOARD.
- NO RUNNING.

1 How Can You Prevent Accidents?

"Accidents do not just happen; they are caused." This statement means that people usually cause accidents by taking unnecessary risks. Swimming in an off-limits area and playing around railroad cars are two unnecessary risks that could lead to accidents. You can prevent many accidents by avoiding unnecessary risks.

How is the girl in the picture avoiding unnecessary risks? She is picking up some clothes and other items that are on the stairs. Think about the accidents that could occur if those items were left on the stairs.

Following safety rules can also prevent accidents. Safety rules, such as those shown here, often appear at a swimming pool. Sometimes you might feel that such rules prevent you from having fun. Remember that the purpose of safety rules is to protect you and others from harm. Imagine what would happen if students were allowed to run in school halls. Think about how dangerous swimming would be without a lifeguard.

How is this person avoiding unnecessary risks?

142

Teaching Options

Health Background

Most accidents can be prevented. Although many activities are risky, certain precautions reduce those risks. Precautions for avoiding traffic accidents include obeying traffic regulations and making sure that all bicycle equipment is working properly. Precautions in the home include locking up poisonous products, lighting stairways adequately, and storing sharp tools properly. Fire prevention involves keeping flammable materials away from a stove, replacing worn-out wiring, and using caution when working with matches or appliances.

Enrichment

Encourage students to find out about the use of air bags for automobile safety. Ask students to list some of the arguments for and against the use of air bags.

Tell students to refer to automobile and consumer magazines to list the ten safest types of cars. Suggest that students find out what factors safe cars have in common.

Health and Language Arts

Suggest that students write advertisements or put on skits that stress the importance of safety features in automobiles.

Reteaching

Discuss whether your state has a seat-belt law and ask students to list arguments for and against such a law.

Ask students to suggest types of accidents that might occur if schools had no playground rules.

What Are Some Traffic Safety Rules?

The people in these pictures are avoiding unnecessary risks and accidents by following traffic rules. Notice that the girl is going to cross the street at a crosswalk. She is also watching for traffic. Being careful around traffic is one way to avoid accidents.

The teenager in the picture is avoiding unnecessary risks by taking a training class for his all terrain vehicle. He knows that his new vehicle can be fun, but very dangerous. Taking a training class can help him become a safe driver.

The girl in the car is avoiding unnecessary risks by wearing a safety belt. How is the bicycle rider avoiding unnecessary risks and helping prevent injuries?

Think Back • *Study on your own with Study Guide page 324.*

1. In general, how can accidents be prevented?
2. How could someone avoid unnecessary risks while climbing stairs?
3. What are three ways people can prevent traffic accidents?

> **Did You Know?**
> Most motor-vehicle injuries and deaths occur when people are thrown against the windshield, dashboard, or some other object. More than half of these deaths could be prevented if people in motor vehicles wore safety belts all of the time.

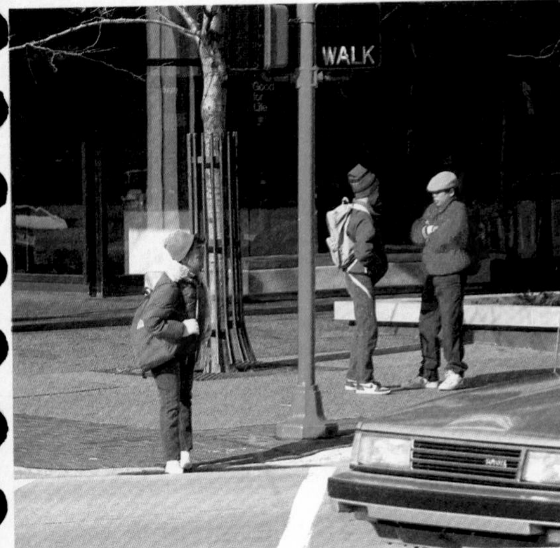

How are the people in these pictures avoiding unnecessary risks?

Source for Did You Know?
National Highway Traffic Safety Administration

3 Assess

Expanding Student Thinking

Ask students to think of safety rules for driving a bicycle, taking a shower or bath, and turning on a fan. (driving a bicycle: not riding two on a bicycle, riding with both hands on the handlebars, obeying traffic safety rules, paying attention to traffic; taking a shower or bath: having a nonskid surface or rubber bath mat on the bottom of the tub or shower stall, not using radios or other electric appliances near the bathtub; turning on a fan: keeping hands away from the blades)

Thinking Skill By thinking of ways to prevent accidents, students are *generalizing*.

Answers to Think Back

1. Accidents can be prevented by avoiding unnecessary risks.

2. Unnecessary risks on stairs can be avoided by not running, by holding the handrail, and by keeping stairs free of objects.

3. Answers might include watching for traffic, crossing a street at a crosswalk, taking traffic safety classes, wearing safety belts, sitting in car seats, wearing bicycle helmets, and using proper hand signals.

Life Skills

Use this worksheet for practice in identifying and designing car safety features. This master may be reproduced from the Teacher's Resource Book and is located on page 17 of the Student's Workbook. Use with Chapter 5: pages 142–143.

Thinking Skill: When students design car safety features, they are suggesting alternatives.

Name ______________________ Life Skills

Use with Chapter 5: pages 142–143.

Designing Car Safety Features

Part I. Draw the safety equipment listed below on the car. Use a red marker, pencil, or crayon. Describe how each item increases the safety of the car.

1. Safety belt Answers might include holding passengers in seat.
2. Windshield wiper Answers might include increasing visibility.
3. Rear window defogger Answers might include increasing visibility.
4. Front and rear bumper Answers might include absorbing impact.

Part II. Design three new items to increase the car's safety. Draw, in blue, your new items on the car. Describe each item on the lines below.

1. Answers will vary.
2. Answers will vary.
3. Answers will vary.

Extension Idea: Suggest that students list ways motorists can increase vehicle safety.

69

Teaching Plan

Lesson 2 pages 144–149

Lesson Objective
Describe safety precautions that could prevent falls, poisonings, electric shock, fires, and other potential accidents at home.

Health Vocabulary
Poison

1 Motivate

Introducing the Lesson
Write the following list on the chalkboard: at school, on an airplane, at home, at a beach, at a playground, on a bicycle. Then take an informal survey to see where students think accidents are most likely to occur. Review the results at the end of the lesson.

Safety Rules to Prevent Falls

- Keep floors clean and dry.
- Use nonskid mats in showers, bathtubs, and on the bathroom floor.
- Use a sturdy ladder when reaching into high cabinets.
- Keep all stairways and halls brightly lit.
- Keep stairways and halls free of objects, such as books and toys.
- Keep electrical cords away from doorways and hallways.
- Fasten rugs and carpeting securely to the floor.
- Keep outdoor walks and stairs free of ice and snow.

2 How Can You Act Safely at Home?

What comes to mind when you hear the word *accident*? Many people think of automobile crashes and accidents that happen away from home. A large number of accidents, however, occur inside the home. Falls, fires, and other accidents often occur because of unnecessary risks at home.

How Can You Prevent Falls?

You have probably fallen at one time or another. You might have slipped on a wet floor or tripped on a stair. Falls are the most common type of accident in the home. Most falls result in minor bumps and bruises, but some falls can be very serious.

By knowing the most common causes of falls, you can take actions to prevent them. For example, a rug on a slippery floor can lead to dangerous falls. The people in the picture are helping to prevent this kind of accident. They are putting rubber backing on the rug to keep it in place when people walk on it. The chart lists several other safety rules to prevent falls. Try to practice these rules at home.

Rubber backing keeps the rug in place.

144

Teaching Options

Health Background

Most home accidents are caused by neglect and carelessness. Doors, stairs, floors, hallways, kitchens, and bathrooms should be checked for such hazards as improper lighting, obstacles, slippery floors, and combustible materials. Most fires start in the kitchen, living room, or bedrooms and are due to faulty heating systems, stove fires, smoking in bed, and faulty electrical wiring. Most electrical outlets can cause injuries ranging from minor shock to major tissue damage and death.

Enrichment
If possible, invite a representative from the local poison control center to speak to the class about the ways the center serves the community.

Health and Social Studies
Ask students to find out what the National Safety Council (NSC) is, what it does, and when it was founded. (The NSC is a nonprofit organization that promotes safety and occupational health, supports accident prevention laws, and produces and distributes educational literature about safety. It was founded in 1913.)

Reteaching
Ask students to make a list of possible safety hazards in a home. Then let students exchange lists. Challenge students to suggest ways to correct all the hazards on the lists they receive.

ow Can You Prevent Poisonings?

A **poison** is a substance that is harmful if it gets side the body. When you think of poisons, you might imagine bubbly potions in a laboratory, or a rattlesnake's venom. Actually, such common items as eaning fluids, bleaches, detergents, and paint thinner are poisons. They can cause severe illness or death if hey get into the body. Even the fumes of these ubstances can be poisonous. Medicines also can poison you if they are not used properly.

The labels of some poisons carry the familiar skull nd crossbones or other warning signs. The labels also explain how to use the products safely.

Many poisonings happen to young children. They cannot read the warning signs on labels and will put almost any substance into their mouths. Therefore, all oisons and medicines should be kept out of reach of small children. Many people store their household leaners on high shelves so that young children cannot each them. Some people lock these materials in a cabinet. The picture shows a kind of lock that helps revent small children from opening the cabinet oors. The lock can be released only by pushing down on the white bar. The chart lists other ways to revent poisonings.

poison, a substance that is harmful if it gets inside the body.

Safety Rules to Prevent Poisonings

- Label poisons clearly, and keep them out of the reach of young children.
- Store poison in its original container so it will not be mistaken for something else.
- Read labels carefully before taking medicines or using household products.
- Store medicines and household products out of reach of young children.
- Check medicines from time to time and properly dispose of all old medicines.
- Properly dispose of all empty containers that have held poisons or medicines.

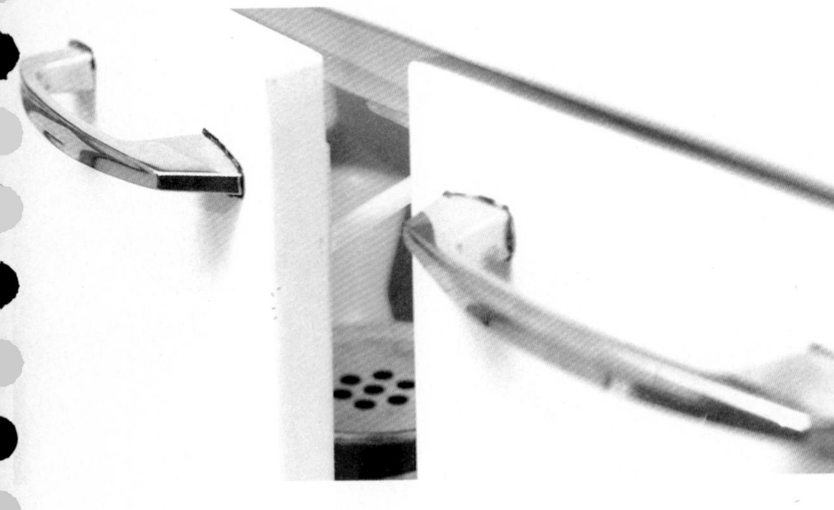

2 Teach

Strategies for Pages 144 and 145

• Ask students to read the lesson title question. Briefly discuss possible answers. Then let students read page 144 to learn about preventing falls.
• Call on students to read aloud the safety rules listed. • Instruct students to read page 145 to learn about preventing poisonings. • Ask a student to define poison. (a substance that is harmful if it gets into the body) Tell students that the warning on product labels usually lists dangerous ingredients and harmful effects of the poisons the product contains. • Ask students why they think poisonings are more common among young children than among older children and adults. (Young children cannot read warnings on labels; they might think the contents are food or candy.)
• Discuss each of the safety rules listed. • Ask students to find out the telephone number of the community's poison control center. (The number should be listed in the front pages of the local telephone directory.)

Teaching Plan

Lesson 2 continued

2 Teach

Strategies for Pages 146 and 147

• Ask students to read page 146 to learn about preventing electric shocks. • Ask what can cause electric shock. (using plugs or outlets improperly and using appliances when a person is wet or near water) • Ask a student to explain how safety plugs can prevent shocks. (They keep young children from sticking small objects or their fingers into outlets.)
• Ask why using electrical appliances near water is dangerous. (Electricity passes through water easily.)
• Discuss each safety rule listed on page 146.

Safety Rules to Prevent Electric Shock

- Do not touch the metal prongs of a plug when putting it into an outlet.
- Do not plug too many appliances into the same outlet.
- Use safety plugs to cover unused outlets.
- Do not allow electrical appliances to get near water or use them when you are wet.
- Do not use an appliance if its cord is damaged.
- Tell an adult if you see a damaged cord, wire, or electrical appliance.

How Can You Prevent Electric Shocks?

When you walk across a carpet and then touch a metal object, you often get a slight electric shock. This shock is not harmful. Other electric shocks, however, can be strong enough to kill a person. You can prevent electric shocks by practicing the rules shown to the left.

Many electric shocks occur when someone uses plugs and outlets improperly. When you put a plug into an outlet, be careful not to touch the metal prongs on the plug. Also, do not plug too many appliances into the same outlet. Such an overload can cause a fire. Unused outlets should be covered so that young children cannot stick tiny objects into them.

Electricity flows through water easily. Therefore, you should never touch a radio, hair dryer, or other electrical appliance when any part of your body is wet. Also, never allow these appliances near water.

Plastic or rubber coatings on wires protect a person from electric shocks. Sometimes these coatings can become cracked and worn. If you see any damaged wires, tell an adult immediately.

How are these people helping to prevent a fire?

146

Teaching Options

Anecdote

A large number of fatal accidents occur in the home. Each year in the United States, about 12,000 deaths result from falls, about 3,000 deaths result from poisoning, about 4,600 deaths result from fire, and about 1,000 deaths result from electric shock. (National Safety Council, 1983.)

Enrichment

Ask students to bring to school newspaper articles about local building fires in which the cause of the fire is given. Discuss the articles with students and help them to see that in most cases the fires were preventable.

Health and Social Studies

Encourage interested students to research the famous electical experiment that Benjamin Franklin performed during a storm. Ask the students to find out why Benjamin Franklin was very lucky he lived to tell about it.

Reteaching

Ask students to prepare safety posters for their homes. The posters should deal with conditions that might cause electric shocks and fires. Then ask students to conduct inspections of their homes to discover possible safety hazards. Students might want to discuss with their families what they have learned about home safety and how they can make their homes safer.

Special Education

Learning-disabled students will benefit from concrete examples of the safety items discussed in the lesson. You might let students examine safety plugs, a smoke detector, and a safety latch for cabinet doors.

How Can You Prevent Fires?

The picture shows several ways of preventing another common type of home accident—fires. Notice the people putting a screen around the fireplace. The screen prevents sparks and small pieces of burning wood from falling into the living room. The boy is moving the magazines away from the fireplace in case some sparks get through the screen. The woman is disconnecting a plug so that the outlet is not overloaded.

Now look at the people in the kitchen. The man is putting the matches in an upper cabinet out of reach of the young child. Meanwhile, the girl is dampening the burnt-out match to make sure it cannot start a fire when she throws it away. The chart lists other ways to avoid risks that could lead to a fire.

Unlike a fall or poisoning, a fire often harms more than one person. If you live in an apartment building, a fire in your apartment can spread throughout the entire building. You protect your family and your neighbors, as well as yourself, whenever you do something to prevent a fire.

Safety Rules to Prevent Fires

- Install smoke detectors.
- Handle matches carefully.
- Dispose of used matches properly.
- Keep matches and other fire sources away from young children.
- Keep flammable materials away from the stove and other heat sources.
- Throw out flammable materials, such as newspapers, cardboard boxes, and old rags.
- Keep electrical wiring in good working order by replacing damaged cords, cracked plugs, and loose connections.
- Never overload an outlet.
- Turn off space heaters before leaving a room or going to bed.

- Ask students to read page 147 to find out ways to prevent fires.
- Explain that some apartment buildings have fire walls or fire doors that help keep a fire within the apartment in which it starts. The fire wall or fire door can help prevent the fire from spreading throughout the entire building. • Ask students to point out the safety precautions shown in the drawing. Discuss the safety rules and encourage students to give examples of how each rule could help prevent a fire.

Health and Language Arts

Use this worksheet for practice in remembering safety rules. This master may be reproduced from the Teacher's Resource Book and is located on page 20 of the Student's Workbook. Use with Chapter 5: pages 142–149.

Name ______________________

Use with Chapter 5: pages 142–149.

Health and Language Arts

Safety Acrostic

An acrostic is a poem or series of sentences in which certain letters, usually the first in each line, form a message. Make your own safety acrostic by writing the letters of your first name, last name, or a safety word as shown below. Then use each letter to start a sentence about safety.

Safety Rules to Prevent Electric Shock

D amaged cord means do not use it.
E mpty sockets should be covered by safety plugs.
N ever use electrical appliances near water.
I nspect appliance cords.
S ockets should not be touched.
E lectric outlets should not be overloaded with plugs.

Answers might include: looking through a window or a peephole to see who is at the door; never opening the door to a stranger; not letting a stranger know that you are home alone; staying several feet away from a car if answering a motorist's questions, or telling the motorist to ask an adult; and never entering a stranger's car.

Extension Idea: Challenge students to write safety sentences for each letter of the alphabet.

Lesson 2 continued

2 Teach

Strategies for Pages 148 and 149

• Ask students what they would do if they were home alone and someone knocked on the door. If a student responds "I would open the door," guide students to realize that this is an unnecessary risk. • Ask students to read pages 148 and 149 to learn about acting safely when home alone. • Discuss with students the dangers of allowing a stranger inside when parents are not home or of letting a stranger know that a young person is home alone. • Discuss with students what they should do if a stranger in a car asks for directions. (Tell the stranger to ask an adult or to inquire at a service station. As an alternative, the student could give the directions but stand several feet away from the car.)

Using On Your Own

Answers will vary. Some students might not realize that a door chain can easily be broken from the outside if the chain is all that prevents the door from being opened. The chain can be cut or can be broken by suddenly pushing against the open door.

How Can You Act Safely When You Are Home Alone?

Sometimes you might be home alone. Perhaps you get home from school before the rest of your family comes home. You might stay home on a Saturday morning while your family goes shopping. Preventing accidents at home is especially important when you are alone because help might not be available right away if an accident occurs.

Knowing how to act safely toward strangers is also important while you are alone. Suppose you were home alone and heard a knock at the door. Would you open the door right away? To be safe, you should first find out who is on the other side of the door. You could look out a window or look through a peephole, as shown. If the caller is a stranger, do not open the door. Instead, ask "Who is it?" through the closed door.

You should never let a stranger know you are home alone. If the stranger asks to see your father, for example, you might say that he cannot come to the door right now and ask the caller to come back later. This safety rule also applies to strangers who call on the telephone.

When someone calls at the door, find out who is there.

148

Teaching Options

Enrichment

Invite a law enforcement officer or a representative from a missing children's organization to speak to the class about what students can do when a stranger tries to approach them.

Health and Art

Direct students to make posters that suggest ways to act safely around strangers. Try to have the posters displayed in school hallways or other places where children in other classes can see them.

Reteaching

Let students write a paragraph telling how they would respond if a stranger called and asked for their parents when their parents were not home.

Sometimes you might meet a stranger while outside. For example, someone in a car might ask you for directions. You do not have to give the directions. You can tell the stranger to ask an adult or go to a nearby service station. If you choose to give directions, stay several feet away from the car, as these girls are doing. The chart lists other safety rules you should follow when dealing with strangers.

You probably think of your home as a place of safety and protection. You have seen, however, that many daily activities, such as climbing the stairs or using a household cleaner, can involve a certain amount of risk. By avoiding the unnecessary risks, you can help keep your home safe for yourself and your family.

Think Back • *Study on your own with Study Guide page 324.*

1. What are three ways to help prevent a fall?
2. What are three ways to help prevent poisonings?
3. What are three ways to prevent electric shock?
4. What is the safe way to dispose of used matches?
5. What should someone do if he or she is home alone and a stranger knocks at the door?

How are these people acting safely toward a stranger?

On Your Own
Some people have small chains on the doors to their homes. These chains allow someone to open the door a few inches to see the person outside. On a sheet of paper, explain why it would not be safe to open a door to a stranger even if the door was chained.

Safety Rules of Acting Toward Strangers

- When someone knocks at the door or rings the doorbell, look through a window or peep hole to see who it is.
- Never open the door to a stranger.
- Do not let a stranger know that you are home alone.
- If a motorist asks you directions, stay several feet from the car. Remember, you can tell the motorist to ask an adult.
- Never enter a stranger's car.

149

Such chains, by themselves, are not adequate protection.
Thinking Skill By evaluating the safety of door chains as protection, students are *judging and evaluating.*

3 Assess

Expanding Student Thinking

Ask students to list safety features that could be found in a home or at school. Features might include fire doors, fire extinguishers, smoke detectors, safety goggles, safety chains and door locks, a list of emergency phone numbers, nonskid mats, and safety plugs for electric outlets.
Thinking Skill By identifying safety features, students are *organizing information.*

Answers to Think Back

1. Answers can include any three ways that are listed in the table on page 144.
2. Answers can include any three ways that are listed in the table on page 145.
3. Answers can include any three ways that are listed in the table on page 146.
4. To dispose of matches safely, rinse them under water before throwing them away.
5. The person should not let the stranger in and should not let the stranger know he or she is home alone.

Activity Plan

Health Activities Workshop pages 150–151

Materials
Activity 4 Newspapers, magazines, encyclopedias

Activity 1 Strategies
Shovels, and other implements, such as rakes, can be very dangerous if left lying about. People can trip and fall on them. Children might play with them and injure themselves. Stepping on the end of a shovel or rake can cause the handle to flip up and cause injury.
Thinking Skill When students describe accidents that can be caused by leaving a shovel or rake lying on the ground, they are *drawing conclusions.*

Activity 2 Stragtegies
You might want to bring to class some products or labels that display the skull and crossbones. You might also obtain poison control stickers, such as the Mr. Yuk symbol, to show to students or to give to students for use at home.
Thinking Skills By designing a warning sign for poisons, students are *communicating* and *suggesting alternatives.*

Activity 3 Strategies
Ask students to list daily activities they are involved in and the type of accidents—such as falls, shocks, fire, poisonings, and other injuries—that could result if they are not cautious. You might ask the students to do this activity in a group.
Thinking Skills As students write down daily activities, accidents that could occur, and ways of avoiding unnecessary risks, they are *suggesting alternatives* and *drawing conclusions.*

Health Activities Workshop

Exploring Ways to Practice Safety

1. The boy in the picture is picking up a shovel from the sidewalk. Write the different kinds of accidents that could result if the shovel were left on the sidewalk or if a rake were left on the lawn.

2. The skull and crossbones and the Mr. Yuk symbol are two warning signs of poisons. Design your own warning sign for poisons. Give the sign a name.

3. Think of ways you can avoid unnecessary risks and prevent accidents in your daily activities. For example, first write down a common activity, such as washing before school. Then write what kinds of accidents could occur during that activity. Finally, list several ways to avoid the unnecessary risks that could cause those accidents. In this example, you could list using nonskid mats on the bathroom floor and wiping up any water on the floor to avoid falls.

150

4. Draw a picture or find one in a newspaper or magazine that shows a person with a high-risk job. You might look for a firefighter, test pilot, race car driver, police officer, tree trimmer, or football player. Glue or tape the picture onto a sheet of paper. Then, write a paragraph describing the risks of the job and how that person avoids unnecessary risks while on the job. You might need to use an encyclopedia or other book to get your information.

Looking at Careers

5. When your house or apartment was built, one or more construction inspectors probably looked at it. These people check buildings, bridges, roads, dams, and other structures to make sure they are safe for people to use. Different kinds of inspectors check for different things.

Building inspectors check the plans of a building before construction begins. During construction, the inspectors check the foundation, materials, and building methods. **Electrical inspectors** examine the wiring, lighting, and other electrical parts. A building with unsafe or incorrect wiring can be a fire hazard. **Mechanical inspectors** inspect the plumbing, including septic tanks, sewer systems, and heating systems.

Construction inspectors must be at least high school graduates. Many inspectors also have studied architecture or engineering in college.

You can discover a career you might like by making a list of your interests and the things you care about. For example, if you enjoy building models and working outside and you care about people's safety, you might like to be a construction inspector. Make up a list of your interests. Keep the list in a folder and add to it as your interests change.

To find out more about construction inspectors, write to the International Conference of Building Officials, 5360 South Workman Mill Rd., Whittier, CA 90601.

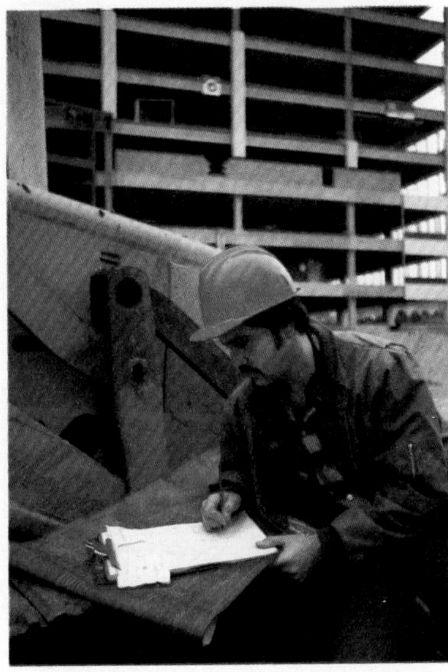

Activity 4 Strategies

Help the students with their research as needed. When they have completed the project, explain to them that accidents also occur in what are considered low-risk jobs. Ask students to think of conditions in office buildings and stores that might lead to accidents.

Thinking Skills By describing how the person in the picture avoids unnecessary risks, students are *interpreting information* and *drawing conclusions*.

Activity 5 Strategies

Encourage students to include in their list of interests both their school interests and things they like to do outside of school. Be sure students understand that many careers relate to nonacademic interests. You might want to invite a construction inspector to speak to the class.

Thinking Skills When students list their interests and find out about a career, they are *collecting* and *organizing information.*

Teaching Plan

Lesson 3 pages 152–155

Lesson Objective
List the kinds of telephone numbers and other items that help in preparing for an emergency and explain why each item is important.

Health Vocabulary
Emergency

1 Motivate

Introducing the Lesson
Read a newspaper or magazine article describing an emergency situation and help students identify what people on the scene could do in response to such a situation.

emergency, a sudden need for quick action.

3 How Can You Be Prepared for Emergencies?

Notice the picture of the fire station. A firefighter checks face masks, gas tanks, fire extinguishers, and other special gear on the vehicle. He makes sure everything is ready for use. The proper knowledge, skills, and equipment make this firefighter well prepared for an emergency.

An **emergency** is a sudden need for quick action. No one can predict exactly how he or she will react in an emergency. However, by being prepared, you have the best chance of reacting correctly and safely. For example, your school's fire drill procedure can prepare you for a fire emergency.

How Can You Get Help Quickly?

One way to be prepared for all kinds of emergencies is to know how to get help. For most emergencies, help is only a telephone call away. Knowing who to call and what to say might save someone's life.

Firefighters are well prepared for an emergency.

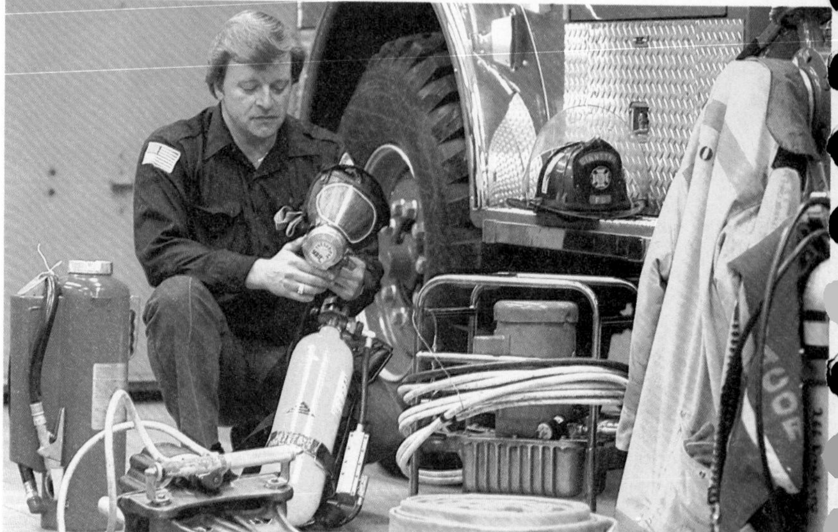

152

Teaching Options

Health Background

Serious emergencies include severe bleeding, loss of breathing, poisoning, burns, and shock. Knowing the correct emergency numbers to call and providing correct information are vitally important. When reporting a poisoning emergency, the caller should tell how the poisoning occurred (by ingestion, inhalation, or skin contact) and the type of poison involved. Callers sometimes are given first-aid instructions.

Enrichment
Ask students to find out more about one of the following occupations: paramedic, firefighter, police officer, emergency room doctor or nurse, poison-control center worker. Stress should be placed on how people with these jobs deal with emergencies.

Health and Drama
Prepare several slips of paper, each containing information describing an emergency situation. Let volunteers take a slip of paper and act out making an emergency telephone call to deal with the situation described.

Reteaching
Ask students to write a paragraph telling what kinds of emergency numbers could be kept near a phone and what types of information should be given in an emergency situation.

The police department, fire department, doctor's office, hospital, and poison control center are some places you can call in an emergency. The telephone numbers of these places should be listed near the telephone, as shown. This list should also include numbers of several nearby friends and numbers where family members can be reached at work.

If you need emergency help and you do not have the right telephone number nearby, you can dial 0 for operator. He or she will get you help. Many communities use 911 as a special emergency number. Find out if your community has such a number.

When you call for help, you need to give certain information. For most emergencies, the person you call will need to know *what* the emergency is and *where* it is. Also, the person will likely need your name and address. He or she might ask you questions about the emergency. Try to stay calm so you can answer the questions clearly. Be sure you do not hang up the telephone until you have given all the needed information.

On Your Own
Make a list of emergency numbers for your own home. You might want to make a smaller list to tape to the telephone receiver. This list could include the police and fire department numbers.

What telephone numbers should be listed in case of an emergency?

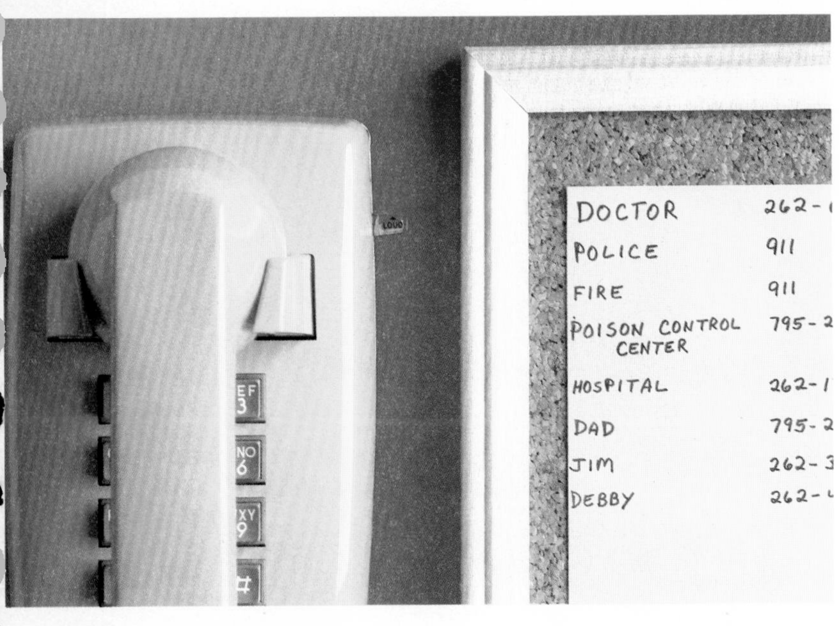

DOCTOR 262-
POLICE 911
FIRE 911
POISON CONTROL CENTER 795-2
HOSPITAL 262-1
DAD 795-2
JIM 262-3
DEBBY 262-

2 Teach

Strategies for Pages 152 and 153

• Ask students to read pages 152 and 153 to learn how to get help in an emergency. • Call on students to name places one might need to call in an emergency. (police department, fire department, doctor, hospital, poison control center, family members, friends) • Discuss with students what information they should give during an emergency call. (what the emergency is, where it is, and the caller's name and address) Make sure students understand that they should stay on the phone until the person on the other end has finished asking questions. • Ask students to find out if their community has an emergency 911 number. Stress that such numbers are to be used only in case of an emergency. Tying up an emergency line for other reasons could prevent someone from getting needed emergency help.

Using On Your Own

If you cannot locate enough telephone directories, write the necessary emergency numbers on the chalkboard and instruct students to complete the lists at home. Tell students to include their last name and address on the list so that a person who does not live there could give the information in an emergency.

Thinking Skills When students make their emergency lists, they are *collecting* and *organizing information.*

Teaching Plan

Lesson 3 continued

2 Teach

Strategies for Pages 154 and 155

• Direct students to read pages 154 and 155 to learn how to prepare for fire emergencies. • Discuss with students the items needed at home to protect against and fight fires. (smoke detectors, a fire extinguisher, an emergency escape ladder) Then discuss other items that are helpful in case of any emergency. (battery-operated radio, flashlight, candles, matches, first-aid kit) • Encourage students to explain why an emergency radio should be operated on batteries. (In case the electricity fails, the radio can be used to get information about an emergency such as a tornado or hurricane.) • Discuss the four basic classes of fire extinguishers. Explain that each class indicates the kind of fire for which the extinguisher is designed. Class A is for burnable materials such as paper and wood, class B is for paint or oil fires, class C is for electrical fires, and class D is for burnable metal fires. • Explain to students that a smoke alarm senses the presence of smoke and sounds an alarm.

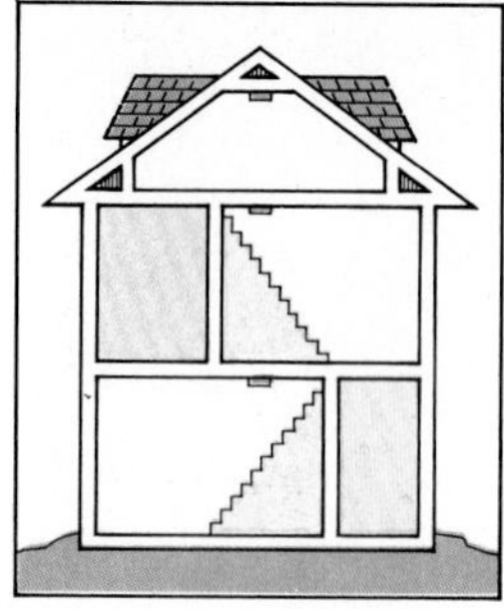

Why should a building have several smoke alarms?

How Can You Be Prepared for Fire Emergencies?

Fire drills help prepare you for fire emergencies at school. You can prepare for fire emergencies at home too. The woman shown to the left is increasing her family's chances of surviving a major fire. She is installing a smoke alarm. A smoke alarm makes a loud, shrill noise when smoke reaches it. The drawing shows that a smoke alarm should be installed in several places throughout a home or other building. With the proper equipment, people are alerted to a fire no matter where it starts.

What would you do if you saw a small fire in a trash can at home? This kind of emergency might require the use of a fire extinguisher. Every household should have at least one fire extinguisher to put out small fires. You need to know where the extinguisher is located and how to use it before an emergency occurs. By being prepared, you would not have to waste precious seconds looking for the extinguisher and learning how to use it.

How would these items be helpful during an emergency?

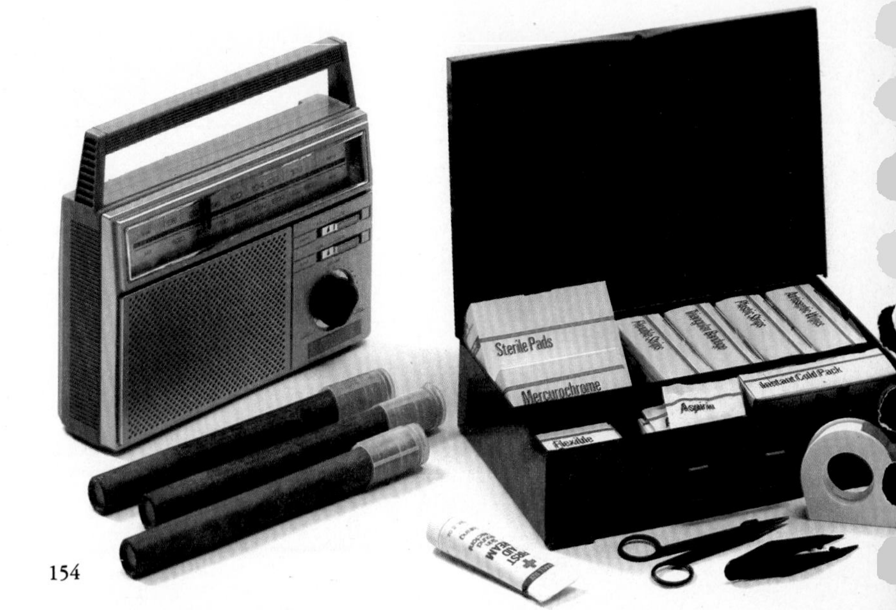

154

Teaching Options

Anecdote

A person who becomes involved in an accident or emergency immediately after it occurs is called the first responder. Good Samaritan laws protect first responders from legal liability for rendering emergency care or failing to arrange for further medical treatment.

Enrichment

Ask students to determine what classes of fire extinguishers their school has and where the fire extinguishers are located.

Health and Language Arts

Ask students to write a letter to an insurance company that sells homeowner's insurance. Students should ask how insurance rates might change after smoke alarms are installed in a home.

Reteaching

Bring a fire extinguisher to class. Ask students to read the information on the extinguisher's canister and tags. Discuss the various types of information such as directions for use, kinds of fires the extinguisher puts out, inspection approvals, and directions for refilling.

Some home fires are too large to be put out with a small fire extinguisher. If a large fire occurs, leave the building immediately. Have two or three escape routes already planned. You can practice these escape routes by having fire drills, just as you do at school. Once you are safely out of the building, call for help from a neighbor's house.

What Items Should a Home Have for Any Emergency?

A fire extinguisher is one item your family should have in case of an emergency. The picture shows other items you might need. A battery-operated radio, a flashlight, and candles and matches will be useful if the electricity goes out. An emergency escape ladder, as shown here, can help you safely leave a building. The first-aid kit can help you and your family treat minor medical emergencies. The kit shown here includes bandages, gauze, cotton, scissors, tweezers, and an antiseptic to treat small wounds. Be sure to read the directions on the items in the first-aid kit. If you know how to use emergency supplies, you will be prepared if you need to use them.

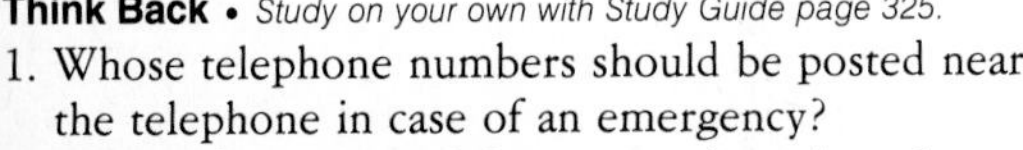

Think Back • *Study on your own with Study Guide page 325.*

1. Whose telephone numbers should be posted near the telephone in case of an emergency?
2. What information might you need to give when calling for emergency help?
3. How can you prepare for fire emergencies at home?
4. What are some emergency items every home should try to have?

3 Assess

Expanding Student Thinking

Ask students to name ways in which police officers are prepared for an emergency. (Students might mention that police officers are trained in first aid and other emergency procedures, carry first-aid kits and police equipment, carry a two-way radio, and often travel with a partner.)

Thinking Skill By naming ways in which police officers are prepared for an emergency, students are *generalizing*.

Answers to Think Back

1. Emergency numbers should include those of the fire department, police department, hospital, doctor's office, poison control center, several close neighbors, and parents' workplaces.

2. When calling for emergency help give your name, address, and telephone number; the nature of the emergency; and when and where the emergency occurred.

3. Prepare for fire emergencies at home by installing smoke alarms and having fire extinguishers you know how to use. Some students might also mention practice fire drills at home.

4. Every home should have a fire extinguisher, smoke alarms, a battery-operated radio, flashlight, emergency ladder, extra batteries, candles, matches, and a first-aid kit.

Teaching Plan

Lesson 4 pages 156–161

Lesson Objective
Explain the general guidelines for administering first aid in case of choking, stopped breathing, burns, and shock.

Health Vocabulary
Artificial respiration, first aid, shock

1 Motivate

Introducing the Lesson
Ask students to name situations that they consider medical emergencies. Then ask what they think could be done in such situations before a doctor or a paramedic arrives.

2 Teach

Strategies for Pages 156 and 157
• Write the lesson title question on the chalkboard. • Let students read page 156 to learn about basic first-aid procedures. • Call on students to name the four basic rules that cover emergencies. (Stay calm, send for help as quickly as possible, do not move an injured person unless absolutely necessary, and do not do more than you know how to do properly.)

first aid, immediate medical care given to someone who is injured or suddenly ill.

4 How Can You Help in a Medical Emergency?

Some emergencies involve people who are injured or ill. A person might be choking on a piece of food. A hot iron might fall on someone's arm. Such emergencies require immediate medical attention—**first aid.** Different emergencies require different kinds of first aid. However, certain rules apply for all kinds of emergencies and first aid.

Giving first aid requires clear thinking and correct, quick actions. Therefore, the first thing you need to do is stay calm. Second, send for help as quickly as possible. If no one else is near, go for help only after the person is out of immediate danger. For example, a person who has stopped breathing will need your immediate attention. Tell someone else to call for help while you start first aid. Third, do not move an injured person unless you must, such as moving someone away from a burning building. Moving the person often makes the injury worse.

Finally, do not do more than you know how to do. The information in this lesson shows only some basic ways to perform first aid. In order to be trained properly, people in the picture are attending a first-aid class. First-aid classes teach people how to develop the knowledge and skills that might one day save a person's life.

First-aid classes teach first aid thoroughly.

156

Teaching Options

Health Background

First-aid procedures must be learned before one can assist with such medical emergencies as choking, stopped breathing, burns, and shock. First-aid courses are often available from the Red Cross, the YMCA and YWCA, community colleges, hospitals, and clinics.

Enrichment
Obtain a first-aid kit from the school nurse or the physical-education department. Let students explain how each of the items in the kit might be used to give first aid.

Health and Science
Ask students to find out how the first-aid technique pictured on page 157 helps remove food from the throat. (The procedure forces air out of the throat, which causes the lodged food to come out also.) The Heimlich maneuver forces air out of the throat because of the quick thrusts given to the diaphragm. Ask students to use library sources to find out where the diaphragm is and what its function is in the body.

Reteaching
Ask students to draw a diagram of the respiratory system to show where a piece of food or other object might be lodged when a person is choking. Students might need to refer to an encyclopedia.

How Can You Help Someone Who Is Choking?

Choking occurs when a piece of food or other object blocks air from moving through the windpipe. A person who is choking usually tries to cough up the object. Do not interfere as long as the person can cough or speak. However, you must start first aid if the person cannot cough, speak, or breathe. If someone else is nearby, ask them to call for help. The following pictures show the first aid you can give to someone who is choking.

Did You Know?
Suppose you are alone and begin to choke. You can perform first aid on yourself by leaning forward and thrusting your abdomen against the back of a chair.

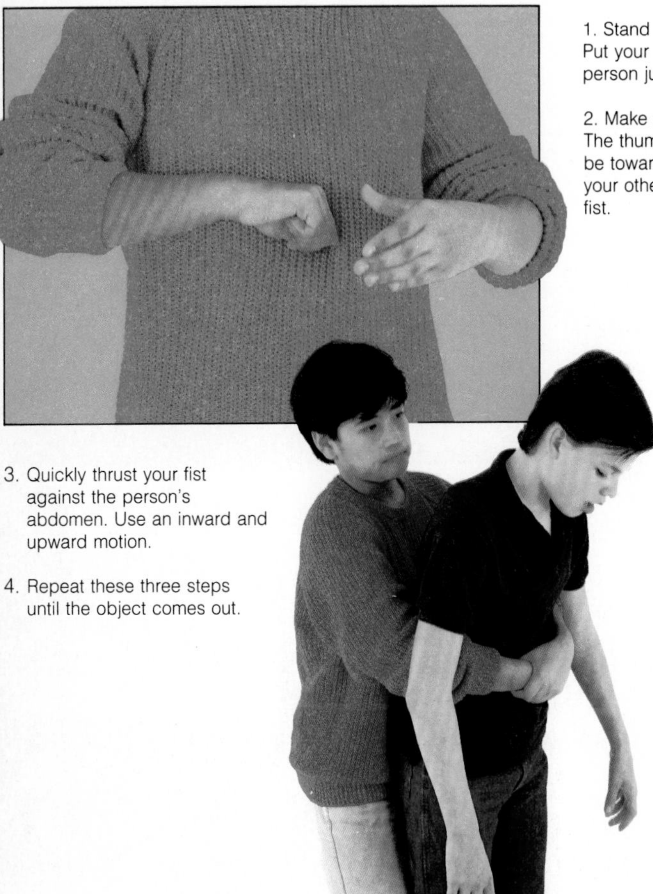

1. Stand behind the person. Put your arms around the person just above the navel.

2. Make a fist with one hand. The thumb of the fist should be toward the person. Wrap your other hand around the fist.

3. Quickly thrust your fist against the person's abdomen. Use an inward and upward motion.

4. Repeat these three steps until the object comes out.

• Suggest that students read page 157 to learn how to help someone who is choking. Ask students how they can tell if someone is choking. (The person cannot cough, speak, or breathe.) Ask a volunteer to tell how a person can help someone who is choking. (He or she can stand behind the person, place the arms around the person's waist above the navel, clench the fists, with thumbs toward the victim, and give quick upward and inward thrusts.) • Point out to students that this procedure is called abdominal thrusts or the Heimlich maneuver. • Ask students to demonstrate on a doll or model the procedure for helping a person who is choking. *CAUTION: Improper application of the Heimlich maneuver can result in severe damage to internal organs. Do not let students use an actual subject.* Point out that sometimes people must perform this procedure on themselves. Tell students that this procedure is described in the ***Did You Know?*** on page 157.

Teaching Plan

Lesson 4 continued

2 Teach

Strategies for Pages 158 and 159

• Write the term *artificial respiration* on the chalkboard. Ask the students to try to determine the meaning of the term by examining the meanings of the two separate words. (*Artificial* means "not natural" and *respiration* means "breathing." Artificial respiration means "breathing by other than natural means.") • Direct students to read page 158. • Ask what types of accidents might cause stopped breathing. (choking, near drowning, poisoning) • Ask students what kinds of workers they think would be required to know how to perform artificial respiration. (Answers might include firefighting, lifeguards, doctors, nurses, and paramedics.) • Call on students to read each of the steps on pages 158 and 159 while the rest of the class examines the pictures.

artificial respiration (är′tə fish′əl res′pə rā′shən), a method of first aid that forces air into the lungs.

How Can You Help Someone Who Has Stopped Breathing?

Choking, poisoning, or a near drowning can all cause a person to stop breathing. First aid for stopped breathing includes **artificial respiration**—a method of forcing air into the lungs. Starting artificial respiration right away is very important. Most people suffer brain damage or die after only four to six minutes without oxygen. The pictures and captions on these two pages show how to perform artificial respiration.

1. Find out if the person is conscious. Gently shake the shoulder and ask loudly, "Are you OK?" If you do not get an answer, send someone for medical help if you can. Then begin artificial respiration.

2. Place the person on his or her back. Put one hand on the person's forehead. Open the air passage by gently lifting the chin up with your fingers. Remove any food or other material in the person's mouth.

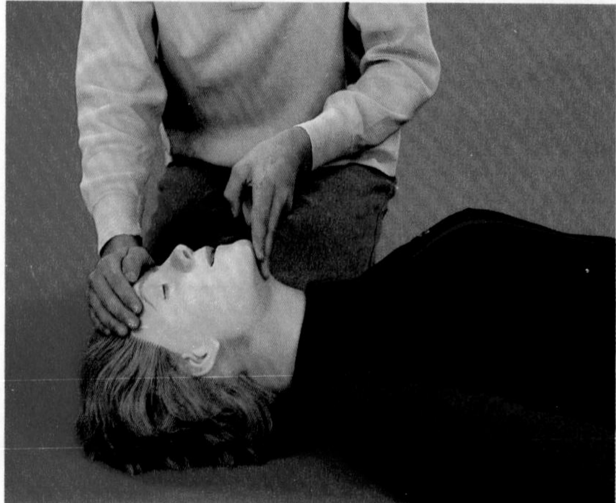

3. Place your cheek and ear close to the person's mouth and nose. Look at the chest to see if it rises and falls. Listen and feel for air to be exhaled for three to five seconds.

158

Teaching Options

Anecdote

More than three thousand Americans choke to death each year. Preventing such deaths was a major concern of Dr. Henry Heimlich, who in 1974 developed the idea that a powerful thrust to the abdomen, forcing air up the windpipe, could expel any foreign object.

Enrichment

Invite a paramedic to the class to explain emergency first-aid procedures and to demonstrate some of the steps involved.

Health and Language Arts

Ask students to read a book or magazine article about someone who saved a life by using CPR or artificial respiration or about someone whose life was saved by one of these first-aid procedures. Such articles are common in *Child Life* and *Boy's Life*. Students can report to the class on what they read.

Reteaching

Ask students to list the steps in administering artificial respiration (without referring to the textbook) and to draw pictures to show how the procedure is performed. Supply a large doll or a dummy for students to use to practice artificial respiration.

Special Education

If a mannequin, such as the one shown in the pictures, is available, allow visually impaired students to pracice and demonstrate their ability to perform artificial respiration. Point out that the steps require simple motor skills rather than any visual abilities.

Some situations, such as a heart attack, can cause a person's heartbeat as well as breathing to stop. First aid for such cases includes cardiopulmonary resuscitation (CPR). In giving CPR, a person applies rhythmic pressure on the chest to force the blood to circulate. A person should use CPR only if he or she has been trained to do so.

Did You Know?
Park districts, hospitals, the YMCA, the National Red Cross, scouting groups, and other organizations sometimes offer first-aid classes. They also might offer classes that teach CPR.

4. If the person is still not breathing, keep the airway open and pinch the nostrils closed. Keep one hand under the chin for support. Then, seal your mouth tightly over the person's mouth and give two full breaths. As you give the breaths, you should be able to see the person's chest rise.

5. Look, listen, and feel again for breathing. If the person is still not breathing, give one breath every five seconds for anyone over eight years old. Continue giving the breaths until the person breathes without assistance or until help arrives. For children under eight years old, give one breath every four seconds. For infants, give one puff of air every three seconds.

6. If the person is still unconscious but breathing on his or her own, continue to maintain the open airway.

- Explain to students that cardiopulmonary resuscitation (CPR) is a procedure for helping people whose heartbeat and breathing have both stopped. It consists of compressing the heart to push blood throughout the body while, at the same time, giving the person artificial respiration. The heart is compressed by pressing down on the breastbone. Explain to students that review classes are given for people who have taken basic first aid and CPR because continuing to practice these skills is important. Doctors and nurses usually take refresher training in CPR each year.

Teaching Plan

Lesson 4 continued

2 Teach

Strategies for Pages 160 and 161

• Ask students to read page 160. • Call on students to read aloud the information in the chart. • Discuss the chart in detail to make sure students understand the different types of burns and how to treat them. • Direct students to read page 161 to find out how to help a person who is in shock. • Discuss with students the meaning of shock. (inadequate blood circulation which causes body functions to slow down) • Call on students to list symptoms of shock. (cold, moist, clammy skin; nausea or vomiting; faintness or loss of consciousness; confusion, trembling, or nervousness; rapid, shallow breathing; rapid, weak pulse; and unusual thirst) • Ask students what first-aid measures should be taken. (Lay the person down, keep him or her warm, raise the legs—except when legs, head, or chest are injured—and secure help as quickly as possible.)

How Can You Help Someone Who Has a Burn?

You have probably experienced a minor burn at some time in your life. Perhaps you touched a dish that just came out of a hot oven. You might have relieved the pain by running cool water over your fingers. Applying cool water is one of the correct ways to give first aid for a minor, first-degree burn.

The chart shows the correct ways to give first aid for all kinds of burns. Notice that for first-degree and second-degree burns, the general treatment is to apply cool water and to cover the burn with a sterile cloth or bandage. Third-degree burns are more serious and require the immediate attention of medical professionals. A third-degree burn should be covered with a sterile dressing until help arrives.

First Aid for Burns

Signs	Type of burn	Treatment
Redness Mild pain and swelling Unbroken skin	First-degree: Injures only the outside layer of skin. Possible causes are sunburn, brief contact with hot objects, and hot water or steam.	Immediately run cool water over the injured area or put the injured area in cool water until the pain stops. Do not use ice directly on a burn. Gently pat the skin dry. Cover the skin with a bandage called a sterile dressing. Do not apply ointments, sprays, or home remedies.
Redness More skin damage Blisters Swelling (lasts several days)	Second-degree: Injures layers of skin beneath the surface. Possible causes are deep sunburn, hot liquids, and flash burn from gasoline.	Follow the treatment for a first-degree burn. Do not break the blisters. Do not apply an ointment, spray, or home remedy. Take off the dressing if the pain returns. Put a clean cloth wrung out in cool water over the area. When the pain stops, carefully dry the area and cover with a new dressing. Get medical help quickly.
Charred or white appearance. Complete loss of all skin layers. Little pain because nerve endings have all been destroyed	Third-degree: Destroys all layers of skin. Possible causes are fire, electricity, and prolonged contact with hot substances.	Cover the burn with a sterile dressing or clean cloth. Get medical help quickly. Be ready to begin artificial respiration if breathing stops. Do not remove any clothes stuck to the injured area. Do not apply any treatment to the burn itself.

Note: A victim's burns might include a combination of degrees. Be sure to look at all injured areas.

160

Teaching Options

Enrichment

Let several students demonstrate first aid for stopped breathing, choking, burns, and shock. Let other students pose as victims. The remaining students can evaluate the performances of those giving first aid.

Reteaching

Ask each student to write on a piece of paper one step in the first-aid procedure for dealing with either choking, stopped breathing, burns, or shock. Collect the papers. Then let each student pick one and decide to which first-aid procedure the step belongs.

How Can You Help Someone Who Is in Shock?

Shock occurs when the heart, lungs, brain, and other organs do not get enough blood. The body functions slow down. Any kind of accident or severe illness can cause a person to go into shock. This condition is often more serious than the injury or illness that caused the shock. Common signs of shock include cold, damp skin; nausea; faintness; trembling; rapid breathing; rapid, weak pulse; and unusual thirst.

First aid for shock includes laying the person down and keeping the person warm, as shown. Unless the person has a leg, chest, or head injury, you should raise the legs to improve circulation of the blood. First aid also includes sending someone for help. If no one is nearby, you should get help yourself after the person is lying down and covered.

People in a serious accident should be treated for shock even if the signs of shock do not appear. Early treatment can help prevent the person from going into shock later.

shock, a condition that occurs when the body fails to circulate blood adequately, causing body functions to slow down.

Think Back • *Study on your own with Study Guide page 325.*

1. What should a person remember when giving any kind of first aid?
2. What is the first-aid procedure for choking?
3. What are the steps of artificial respiration?
4. How does first aid for a first-degree burn differ from first aid for a third-degree burn?
5. How should someone treat a person for shock?

What is the proper first aid for shock?

3 Assess

Expanding Student Thinking

Ask students to imagine that a paramedic has arrived at the scene of an accident where two people have cuts and bruises and another person has stopped breathing. Instruct students to outline the order in which the paramedic would treat these medical problems. (The paramedic would first treat the person who has stopped breathing. When the person begins breathing again, the paramedic would treat all victims for shock, and would then treat cuts.)

Thinking Skill Students are *organizing information.*

Answers to Think Back

1. Stay calm, send for help as quickly as possible, do not move the victim unless absolutely necessary, and do not attempt more than you are trained to do.

2. Stand behind the choking victim and thrust a fist against the abdomen. If choking continues, repeat the procedure.

3. Answers should include the steps to take, as listed on pages 158 and 159.

4. First aid for a third-degree burn does not include applying cool water to the burn, but does include getting medical help quickly.

5. Keep the person covered and lying down. Raise the legs unless the person has a leg or chest or head injury. Send for help.

Overhead Transparency Master

Use this blackline master to make a labeled overhead transparency or to make an unlabeled student worksheet. This blackline master may be reproduced from the Teacher's Resource Book.

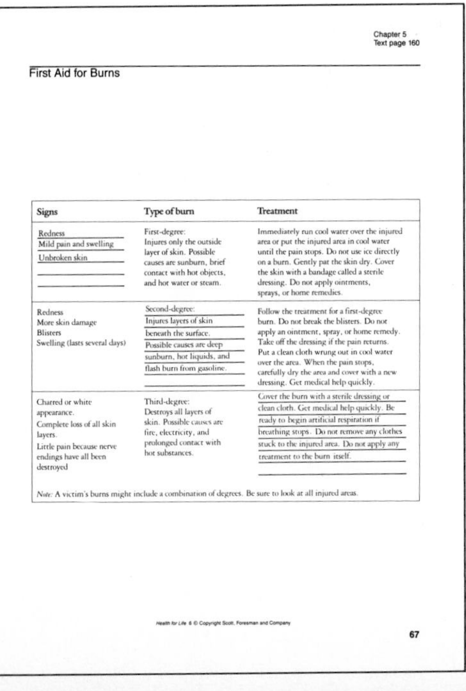

Chapter 5
Text page 160

First Aid for Burns

Signs	Type of burn	Treatment
Redness Mild pain and swelling Unbroken skin	First-degree: Injures only the outside layer of skin. Possible causes are sunburn, brief contact with hot objects, and hot water or steam.	Immediately run cool water over the injured area or put the injured area in cool water until the pain stops. Do not use ice directly on a burn. Gently pat the skin dry. Cover the skin with a bandage called a sterile dressing. Do not apply ointments, sprays, or home remedies.
Redness More skin damage Blisters Swelling (lasts several days)	Second-degree: Injures layers of skin beneath the surface. Possible causes are deep sunburn, hot liquids, and flash burn from gasoline.	Follow the treatment for a first-degree burn. Do not break the blisters. Do not apply an ointment, spray, or home remedy. Take off the dressing if the pain returns. Put a clean cloth wrung out in cool water over the area. When the pain stops, carefully dry the area and cover with a new dressing. Get medical help quickly.
Charred or white appearance. Complete loss of all skin layers. Little pain because nerve endings have all been destroyed	Third-degree: Destroys all layers of skin. Possible causes are fire, electricity, and prolonged contact with hot substances.	Cover the burn with a sterile dressing or clean cloth. Get medical help quickly. Be ready to begin artificial respiration if breathing stops. Do not remove any clothes stuck to the injured area. Do not apply any treatment to the burn itself.

Note: A victim's burns might include a combination of degrees. Be sure to look at all injured areas.

67

Teaching Plan

Health Focus page 162

Discussion

Make sure students understand that if Leslie had not had proper training, she could not have saved her mother's life. Cardiopulmonary resuscitation should only be used by people who are trained in the procedure. Ask students to describe any examples they know of where a person saved another person's life because he or she had first-aid training and remained calm in an emergency.

Answers to Talk About It

1. Leslie remained calm in the emergency and gave her mother cardiopulmonary resuscitation and artificial respiration.

Thinking Skill By explaining how Leslie's training helped her mother, students are *recalling information.*

2. Students' responses about how they would react to an accident will vary. Remaining calm and knowing the proper first aid to perform might help students react correctly to an emergency situation.

Thinking Skill When students suggest what could help them react correctly in an emergency, they are *drawing conclusions*.

Health Focus

Leslie's First Aid Saves Her Mother's Life

When Leslie Maack was learning about first aid in her sixth-grade health class, she never thought she would use it so soon. Just two weeks later, however, Leslie performed first aid that saved her mother's life.

Leslie awoke one night to find her mother lying on the bedroom floor. A blood vessel in her brain had ruptured. She was not breathing, and her heart had stopped beating. Leslie's older sister and grandmother were stunned, but Leslie knew exactly what to do. She immediately started giving her mother artificial respiration and CPR—a kind of first aid that circulates the blood artificially.

For five minutes, Leslie performed this first aid and kept her mother alive. An ambulance arrived shortly and took her mother to the hospital.

Leslie's successful experience at CPR made her the star of her health class. The class had studied first aid for victims of stopped breathing, choking, drowning, and other kinds of accidents. The students had been able to practice artificial respiration and CPR on a Red Cross manikin.

Besides learning the correct procedures for first aid, the class had also learned how to react to an emergency. Leslie's knowledge of first aid would not have done much good if she had panicked when she saw her mother lying on the floor. Fortunately, she remained calm and started first aid immediately. Leslie's ability to manage a life-threatening situation shows the importance of learning first aid.

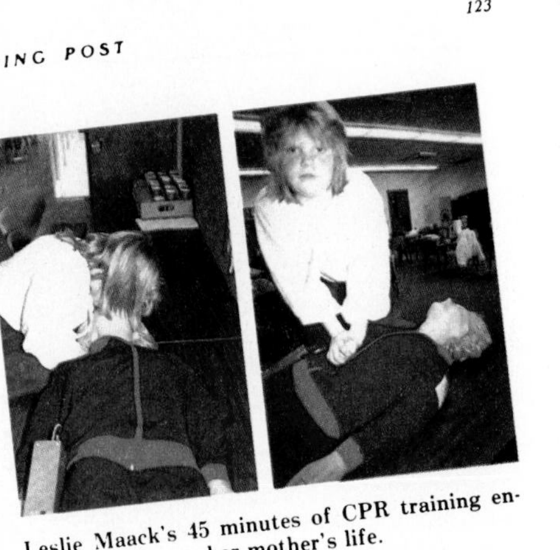
123

...ING POST

Leslie Maack's 45 minutes of CPR training enabled her to save her mother's life.

Leslie Maack, 11, awoke at 2 a.m. to see her mother lying on the bedroom floor, blue, breathless and without a heartbeat. Before she gave herself a chance ... the cardio-pulmonary rescue ... before.

Talk About It

1. What are two ways in which Leslie's training helped her save her mother?
2. How do you think you would react to an emergency like the one described here? What might help you react correctly?

Teaching Options

Vocabulary

Use this worksheet for practice in reviewing chapter vocabulary words. This master may be reproduced from the Teacher's Resource Book and is located on page 18 of the Student's Workbook. Use with Chapter 5: pages 140–165.

Name ____________________ Vocabulary

Use with Chapter 5: pages 140–165.

Hidden Safety Message

Use the clues to help you fill in the blanks. Then discover the hidden message spelled out by the letters in the boxes.

1. [S] H O C K
2. [A] C C I D E N T S
3. A R T I [F] I C I A L R E S P I R A T I O N
4. S M O K [E] D E T E C T O R
5. [T] E L E P H O N E
6. E M E R G E N C [Y]
7. R [I] S K
8. [S] T R A N G E R
9. [F] I R E D R I L L
10. F I R E E X T [I] N G U I S H E R
11. F I [R] S T A I D
12. P O I [S] O N
13. I N S P E C [T] O R

Clues

1. A condition in which the body fails to adequately circulate blood
2. Following safety rules is one way to avoid ____.
3. A first-aid method that forces air into the lungs
4. This warns you of a fire
5. Using this is often the best way to get help in an emergency
6. A sudden need for quick action
7. Taking an unnecessary ____ can lead to an accident.
8. Someone you do not know
9. Useful for putting out small fires
10. Practice for a fire emergency
11. Immediate medical care given to someone who is injured
12. A substance that is harmful if it gets inside the body
13. A person who checks the safety of buildings

70

Extension Idea: **Suggest that students write a short home-safety guide using the vocabulary words in the puzzle.**

Planning and Practicing Fire Drills

You probably have three or four fire drills a year at school. Do you have any fire drills at home? People often panic during a fire and get confused about how they should act and where they should go. Home fire drills, like the one shown here, will help you and your family react correctly if a real emergency occurs.

Decide on two escape routes, if possible, from the building. Decide where your family should meet outside. By meeting outside, you can find out if everyone is safe.

Practice your escape routes several times a year. Be sure to practice during the day and at night. Follow the escape routes as quickly as possible, but remember these safety rules.

- Walk quickly down the stairs.
- Keep a flashlight next to each bed for night fire drills.
- Keep all doorways and hallways clear of objects so that you do not fall during the fire drill.
- Practice crawling close to the floor to avoid dangerous smoke and vapors.

Reading at Home

By Yourself by Sara Gilbert. Lothrop, 1983. Learn about how to deal with being home alone and how to handle various emergency situations.

Fractures, Dis-Lo-Ca-Tions, and Sprains by Alan E. Nourse. Watts, 1978. Find out what each of these injuries is and how to take care of them.

In Charge—A Complete Handbook for Kids with Working Parents by Kathy S. Kyte. Knopf, 1983. Discover how it is possible to take care of yourself and deal with a possible crisis while your parents are at work.

163

Health at Home

page 163

Strategies

Before students read page 165, let them suggest what they think families should do when conducting fire drills at home. (Accept all reasonable answers.) List their answers on the chalkboard. After students have read page 165, discuss the safety rules found there and compare them with the chalkboard list. Review your school's floor plan and escape routes with students. Students might wish to bring their home escape routes to class to compare them with other students' escape routes.

More Reading at Home

By Yourself (Grades 4–6)

Fractures, Dis-Lo-Ca-Tions, and Sprains (Grades 4–5)

In Charge—A Complete Handbook for Kids with Working Parents (Grades 4–6)

Chaback, Elaine, and Fortunato, Pat. *The Official Kids' Survival Kit: How to Do Things on Your Own.* Little, Brown, 1981. Alphabetical entries give practical advice for coping with everyday situations as well as handling accidents and common emergencies. (Grades 4–6)

Study and Review

Use this worksheet for practice in reviewing first-aid procedures. This master may be reproduced from the Teacher's Resource Book and is located on page 19 of the Student's Workbook. Use with Chapter 5: pages 140–165.

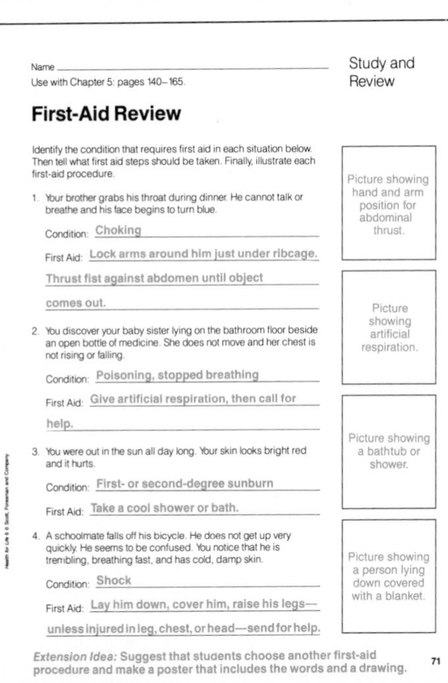

Name ______________________

Use with Chapter 5: pages 140–165.

Study and Review

First-Aid Review

Identify the condition that requires first aid in each situation below. Then tell what first aid steps should be taken. Finally, illustrate each first-aid procedure.

1. Your brother grabs his throat during dinner. He cannot talk or breathe and his face begins to turn blue.
   Condition: Choking
   First Aid: Lock arms around him just under ribcage. Thrust fist against abdomen until object comes out.

   Picture showing hand and arm position for abdominal thrust.

2. You discover your baby sister lying on the bathroom floor beside an open bottle of medicine. She does not move and her chest is not rising or falling.
   Condition: Poisoning, stopped breathing
   First Aid: Give artificial respiration, then call for help.

   Picture showing artificial respiration.

3. You were out in the sun all day long. Your skin looks bright red and it hurts.
   Condition: First- or second-degree sunburn
   First Aid: Take a cool shower or bath.

   Picture showing a bathtub or shower.

4. A schoolmate falls off his bicycle. He does not get up very quickly. He seems to be confused. You notice that he is trembling, breathing fast, and has cold, damp skin.
   Condition: Shock
   First Aid: Lay him down, cover him, raise his legs—unless injured in leg, chest, or head—send for help.

   Picture showing a person lying down covered with a blanket.

Extension Idea: Suggest that students choose another first-aid procedure and make a poster that includes the words and a drawing.

71

Review Plan

Chapter 5 Review

pages 164–165

Answers to Reviewing Lesson Objectives

Use this section for guided study or for oral review. Objective numbers match lesson numbers.

1. A person can avoid unnecessary risks and prevent accidents by obeying safety rules, crossing at crosswalks, wearing safety belts, and using proper hand signals while driving a bicycle.

2. Students should list some of the safety precautions found in the charts about preventing falls (page 144), poisonings (page 145), electric shocks (page 146), and fires (page 147). Students should also list safety rules telling how to act toward strangers (page 149).

3. Emergency numbers include those of the police department, fire department, doctor's office, hospital, and poison control center, as well as numbers of nearby friends and work numbers of family members. Emergency items include fire extinguishers, battery-operated radios, extra batteries, flashlights, candles, matches, and a first-aid kit. In addition, smoke alarms, emergency escape ladders, and a floor plan of the home or building showing marked escape routes are helpful in emergencies.

4. Students should list the first-aid guidelines found in the charts and pictures on page 157 (choking), pages 158 and 159 (stopped breathing), page 160 (burns), and page 161 (shock).

Answers to Checking Health Vocabulary

Use the vocabulary check as a review or as a test.

1. e
2. a
3. d
4. c
5. b
6.–16. Answers will vary but should reflect students' understanding of the meaning of the words as used in the text.

Chapter 5 Review

Reviewing Lesson Objectives

1. Describe several ways to avoid unnecessary risks and accidents, including traffic accidents. (pages 142–143)
2. Describe several safety precautions that can prevent falls, poisonings, electric shocks, fires, and other possible dangerous situations at home. (pages 144–149)
3. List the kinds of telephone numbers and other items that help in preparing for an emergency. (pages 152–155)
4. Explain the guidelines for giving first aid for choking, stopped breathing, burns, and shock. (pages 156–161)

For further review, use Study Guide pages 324-325

Practice skills for life for Chapter 5 on pages 350-352

SKILLS FOR LIFE

Checking Health Vocabulary

Number your paper from 1–5. Match each definition in Column I with the correct word or words in Column II.

Column I

1. a condition that occurs when the body fails to circulate blood adequately
2. a method of first aid that forces air into the lungs
3. a substance that is harmful if it gets inside the body
4. immediate medical care given to someone who is injured or suddenly ill
5. a sudden need for quick action

Column II

a. artificial respiration
b. emergency
c. first aid
d. poison
e. shock

Number your paper from 6–8. Next to each number write a sentence describing the kind of burn listed below.

6. first-degree burn
7. second-degree burn
8. third-degree burn

Number your paper from 9–16. Next to each number write a sentence using each word or words.

9. unnecessary risk
10. safety belt
11. accident
12. crosswalk
13. electric shock
14. stranger
15. smoke alarm
16. first-aid kit

164

Chapter 5 Tests Use Test A or Test B to assess students' mastery of the health concepts in Chapter 5. These tests are located on pages 41–48 in the Test Book.

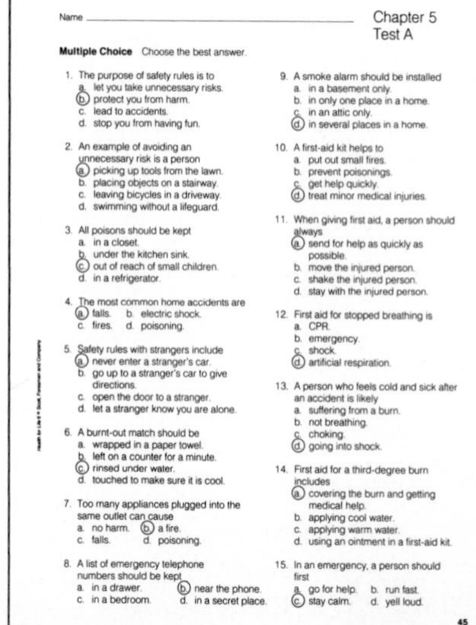

Name ____________ Chapter 5 Test A

Multiple Choice Choose the best answer.

1. The purpose of safety rules is to
   a. let you take unnecessary risks.
   (b) protect you from harm.
   c. lead to accidents.
   d. stop you from having fun.
2. An example of avoiding an unnecessary risk is a person
   (a) picking up tools from the lawn.
   b. placing objects on a stairway.
   c. leaving bicycles in a driveway.
   d. swimming without a lifeguard.
3. All poisons should be kept
   a. in a closet.
   b. under the kitchen sink.
   (c) out of reach of small children.
   d. in a refrigerator.
4. The most common home accidents are
   (a) falls. b. electric shock.
   c. fires. d. poisoning.
5. Safety rules with strangers include
   (a) never enter a stranger's car.
   b. go up to a stranger's car to give directions.
   c. open the door to a stranger.
   d. let a stranger know you are alone.
6. A burnt-out match should be
   a. wrapped in a paper towel.
   b. left on a counter for a minute.
   (c) rinsed under water.
   d. touched to make sure it is cool.
7. Too many appliances plugged into the same outlet can cause
   a. no harm. (b) a fire.
   c. falls. d. poisoning.
8. A list of emergency telephone numbers should be kept
   a. in a drawer. (b) near the phone.
   c. in a bedroom. d. in a secret place.
9. A smoke alarm should be installed
   a. in a basement only.
   b. in only one place in a home.
   c. in an attic only.
   (d) in several places in a home.
10. A first-aid kit helps to
    a. put out small fires.
    b. prevent poisonings.
    c. get help quickly.
    (d) treat minor medical injuries.
11. When giving first aid, a person should always
    (a) send for help as quickly as possible.
    b. move the injured person.
    c. shake the injured person.
    d. stay with the injured person.
12. First aid for stopped breathing is
    a. CPR.
    b. emergency.
    c. shock.
    (d) artificial respiration.
13. A person who feels cold and sick after an accident is likely
    a. suffering from a burn.
    b. not breathing.
    c. choking.
    (d) going into shock.
14. First aid for a third-degree burn includes
    (a) covering the burn and getting medical help.
    b. applying cool water.
    c. applying warm water.
    d. using an ointment in a first-aid kit.
15. In an emergency, a person should first
    a. go for help. b. run fast.
    (c) stay calm. d. yell loud.

45

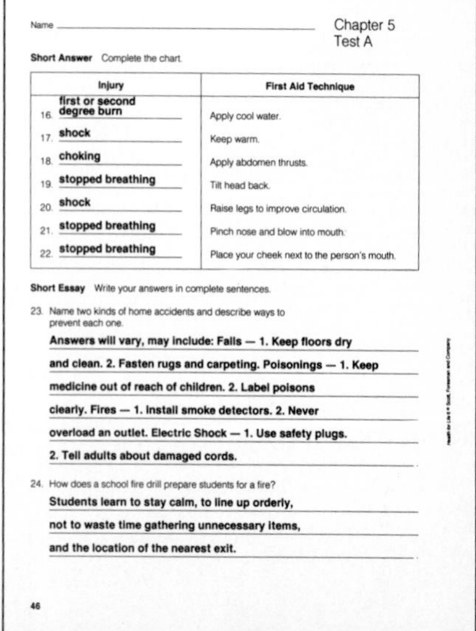

Name ____________ Chapter 5 Test A

Short Answer Complete the chart.

Injury	First Aid Technique
16. **first or second degree burn**	Apply cool water.
17. **shock**	Keep warm.
18. **choking**	Apply abdomen thrusts.
19. **stopped breathing**	Tilt head back.
20. **shock**	Raise legs to improve circulation.
21. **stopped breathing**	Pinch nose and blow into mouth.
22. **stopped breathing**	Place your cheek next to the person's mouth.

Short Essay Write your answers in complete sentences.

23. Name two kinds of home accidents and describe ways to prevent each one.
    Answers will vary, may include: Falls — 1. Keep floors dry and clean. 2. Fasten rugs and carpeting. Poisonings — 1. Keep medicine out of reach of children. 2. Label poisons clearly. Fires — 1. Install smoke detectors. 2. Never overload an outlet. Electric Shock — 1. Use safety plugs. 2. Tell adults about damaged cords.
24. How does a school fire drill prepare students for a fire?
    Students learn to stay calm, to line up orderly, not to waste time gathering unnecessary items, and the location of the nearest exit.

46

Reviewing Health Ideas

Number your paper from 1–15. Next to each number write the word or words that best completes the sentence.

1. You can avoid unnecessary risks while riding in a car by wearing a ____ ____.
2. Picking up objects left on a stairway is one way of avoiding ____.
3. Falls are the most common type of accident at ____.
4. Cleaning fluids and medicines can be ____, and should be kept out of the reach of young children.
5. Unused outlets should be ____ in some way if children are around.
6. You should never let a stranger know you are home ____.
7. A list of emergency telephone numbers is most useful if it is near the ____.
8. Every household should have at least one fire ____.
9. During any emergency, it is important to stay ____.
10. During an emergency, you should send for ____ as soon as possible.
11. Start first aid immediately if a choking person cannot cough, ____, or breathe.
12. First aid for choking includes thrusting a fist against the ____.
13. During artificial respiration, you open the air passage by pulling the ____ up and tilting the head back.
14. While breathing into a person's mouth during artificial respiration, you should keep the person's ____ closed.
15. A ____-degree burn can be treated by running cool water over the burn.

Understanding Health Ideas

Number your paper from 16–25. Next to each number write the word or words that best answer the question.

16. What is one way a person can avoid unnecessary risks on a bicycle?
17. What should a person do before throwing away a burnt-out match?
18. If you are home alone and someone knocks at the door, what should you do first?
19. What should you do if you are giving directions to a motorist?
20. Who should you call if you need the police, but do not have the telephone number?
21. What information will a person need if you call for emergency help?
22. What items should a home have for any emergency?
23. After opening the air passage, what should you check before continuing artificial respiration?
24. What kind of burn should be covered and treated further only by a medical professional?
25. What should people in serious accidents always be treated for?

Thinking Critically

Write the answers on your paper. Use complete sentences.

1. Write a paragraph in response to the following statement: "Safety rules only stop me from having fun."
2. For each situation, explain the correct way to respond.
   a. A motorist asks you to come near the car to give directions.
   b. The child you are babysitting for has just swallowed cleaning fluid.

Cooperative Learning Use the STAD Format described on page T24 to have four- to five-member teams study Chapter 5 Review together before completing Chapter 5 Test.

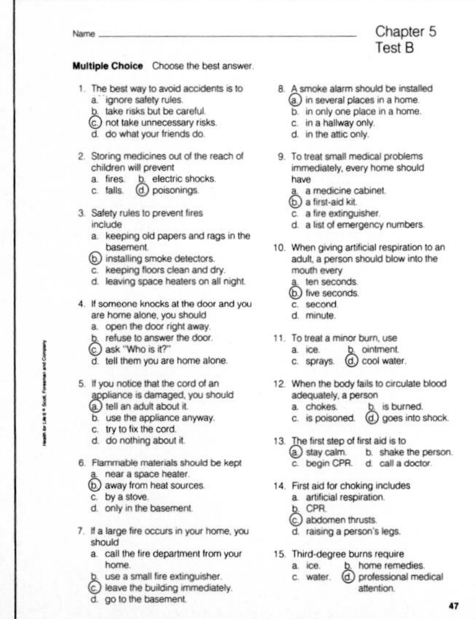

Name ____________________ Chapter 5 Test B

Multiple Choice Choose the best answer.

1. The best way to avoid accidents is to
   a. ignore safety rules.
   b. take risks but be careful.
   (c.) not take unnecessary risks.
   d. do what your friends do.
2. Storing medicines out of the reach of children will prevent
   a. fires. b. electric shocks.
   c. falls. (d.) poisonings.
3. Safety rules to prevent fires include
   a. keeping old papers and rags in the basement.
   (b.) installing smoke detectors.
   c. keeping floors clean and dry.
   d. leaving space heaters on all night.
4. If someone knocks at the door and you are home alone, you should
   a. open the door right away.
   b. refuse to answer the door.
   (c.) ask "Who is it?"
   d. tell them you are home alone.
5. If you notice that the cord of an appliance is damaged, you should
   (a.) tell an adult about it.
   b. use the appliance anyway.
   c. try to fix the cord.
   d. do nothing about it.
6. Flammable materials should be kept
   a. near a space heater.
   (b.) away from heat sources.
   c. by a stove.
   d. only in the basement.
7. If a large fire occurs in your home, you should
   a. call the fire department from your home.
   b. use a small fire extinguisher.
   (c.) leave the building immediately.
   d. go to the basement.
8. A smoke alarm should be installed
   (a.) in several places in a home.
   b. in only one place in a home.
   c. in a hallway only.
   d. in the attic only.
9. To treat small medical problems immediately, every home should have
   a. a medicine cabinet.
   (b.) a first-aid kit.
   c. a fire extinguisher.
   d. a list of emergency numbers.
10. When giving artificial respiration to an adult, a person should blow into the mouth every
    a. ten seconds.
    (b.) five seconds.
    c. second.
    d. minute.
11. To treat a minor burn, use
    a. ice. b. ointment.
    c. sprays. (d.) cool water.
12. When the body fails to circulate blood adequately, a person
    a. chokes. b. is burned.
    c. is poisoned. (d.) goes into shock.
13. The first step of first aid is to
    (a.) stay calm. b. shake the person.
    c. begin CPR. d. call a doctor.
14. First aid for choking includes
    a. artificial respiration.
    b. CPR.
    (c.) abdomen thrusts.
    d. raising a person's legs.
15. Third-degree burns require
    a. ice. b. home remedies.
    c. water. (d.) professional medical attention.

47

Name ____________________ Chapter 5 Test B

Short Answer Complete the chart.

Observe This Home Safety Rule	To Prevent This Kind of Accident
Keep floors clean and dry.	16. **fall**
Install smoke alarms.	17. **fire**
Keep medicines out of children's reach.	18. **poisoning**
Do not use electrical appliances near water.	19. **electric shock**
Keep outdoor walks free of ice.	20. **fall**
Properly dispose of all old medicine.	21. **poisoning**
Rinse matches before throwing them away.	22. **fire**

Short Essay Write your answers in complete sentences.

23. What three safety rules would you make for a swimming pool? Explain why.
    Answers will vary, may include: Do not run because you could fall on the slippery floor; Do not swim without a lifeguard because you could drown; Do not push people into the water because they could hurt themselves.
24. You are hiking with a friend and she falls and twists her ankle. Her ankle hurts too much to walk, and she asks you to help her walk. What should you do?
    First, you should stay calm. Second, you should not try to move her or help her walk. Third, you should go for help immediately. Also, you should not try to perform any first aid that you are not sure about.

48

Answers to Reviewing Health Ideas

1. safety belt
2. falls
3. home
4. poisons
5. covered
6. alone
7. telephone
8. extinguisher
9. calm
10. help
11. speak
12. abdomen
13. neck
14. nostrils
15. first

Answers to Understanding Health Ideas

16. by wearing a helmet or using proper hand signals
17. rinse it under water
18. find out who is at the door before opening it
19. stay several feet away from the car and motorist
20. the operator or an emergency number such as 911
21. what the emergency is, where it is, the person's name and address
22. battery-operated radio, flashlight, candles and matches, fire extinguisher, first-aid kit, and an escape ladder.
23. if the person is breathing
24. third-degree burn
25. shock

Answers to Thinking Critically

1. Answers should indicate that the purpose of safety is not to prevent fun but to prevent accidents. Responses should show that students understand that activities can be fun within limits set by safety rules.

Thinking Skills By writing about safety rules, students are *generalizing.*

2. a. Do not approach the car. Directions can be given from a distance. Students might suggest that the motorist ask an adult for directions.

b. Stay calm and call the poison control center or hospital. Information about the kind of substance swallowed will be needed, so the container should be available.

Thinking Skills By explaining ways to respond to potentially dangerous situations, students are *suggesting alternatives.*

CHAPTER 6 PLANNING GUIDE Pupil Edition

Pupil Edition	Activities	Enrichment	Assessment	Independent Study
Chapter 6 Drugs: What They Are and What They Do, pp. 166–197	Health Watch Notebook, p. 166	Health Focus, p. 194 Health at Home, p. 195	Chapter 6 Review, pp. 196–197	Study Guide, pp. 326–327 Skills for Life Handbook, pp. 353–355
Lesson 1 What are Drugs? pp. 168–169		Did You Know? p. 169	Think Back, p. 169	Study Guide, p. 326
Lesson 2 What Are Medicines and How Do People Use Them Safely? pp. 170–173		Did You Know? p. 172	Think Back, p. 173	Study Guide, p. 326
Lesson 3 What Are the Dangers of Drug Abuse? pp. 174–179		Did You Know? p. 176	Think Back, p. 179	Study Guide, p. 326
Lesson 4 How Does Marijuana Affect Health? pp. 180–181			Think Back, p. 181	Study Guide, p. 327
Lesson 5 How Does Alcohol Affect Health? pp. 182–185			Think Back, p. 185	On Your Own, p. 182 Study Guide, p. 327
Lesson 6 How Does Tobacco Affect Health? pp. 186–189	Health Activities Workshop, pp. 190–191	Did You Know? p. 186	Think Back, p. 189	On Your Own, p. 187 Study Guide, p. 327
Lesson 7 How Can People Make Healthy Decisions About Drugs? pp. 192–193			Think Back, p. 193	Study Guide, p. 327

Teacher Resources

Ausubel, David P. *What Every Well-Informed Person Should Know About Drug Addiction,* Nelson-Hall, 1980. Provides information about various drugs and the effects of drug addiction.

Handbook of Nonprescription Drugs. American Pharmaceutical Association, 1982. Contains descriptions of many over-the-counter drugs. (Written for pharmacists, but usable by lay people.)

Tessler, Diane Jane. *Drugs, Kids, and Schools.* Scott, Foresman, 1980. Provides activities to help teachers work constructively with kids who use drugs, or who may be considering the use of drugs.

Audio-Visual Resources

See page T43 for addresses of Audio-Visual Sources.

Before using any audio-visual materials, preview them for appropriateness for your students.

Alcohol and Children, Educational Activities Inc., filmstrip with cassette. Provides an introduction to alcohol education, and illustrates the social, medical, and personal problems that have arisen from the misuse of alcoholic beverages.

Drugs and Children, Educational Activities, Inc., filmstrips with cassettes. Looks at drugs available today, how they are tested, and how medicines can be used correctly.

Health Decisions: Drugs, Alcohol and Smoking, Learning Tree Filmstrips, filmstrips with cassettes. Examines the legal aspects and negative consequences of using drugs, alcohol, or cigarettes.

Marijuana Alert! BFA Educational Media, film or video, 20 minutes. Explores the harmful effects of marijuana on human physiology.

Smoking and Children, Educational Activities, Inc., filmstrip with cassette. Examines the health hazards associated with the use of tobacco.

Computer Software

The Smoking Decision, Sunburst Communications, Inc. Uses decision-making situations to help students form opinions about the use of cigarettes.

	Teacher's Edition	Teacher's Resource Book	Test Book
Enrichment	Suggestions for each lesson: L. 1—p. 168 L. 2—pp. 170, 172 L. 3—pp. 174, 176, 178 L. 4—p. 180 L. 5—pp. 182, 184 L. 6—pp. 186, 188 L. 7—p. 192	Family Letter, p. 77 * Life Skills, p. 81 * Health and Art, p. 84	
Reteaching	Suggestions for each lesson: L. 1—p. 168 L. 2—pp. 170, 172 L. 3—pp. 174, 176, 178 L. 4—p. 180 L. 5—pp. 182, 184 L. 6—pp. 186, 188 L. 7—p. 192	Transparency Masters, pp. 79-80 * Vocabulary, p. 82 * Study and Review, p. 83	
Assessment	Expanding Student Thinking: one assessment question per lesson that develops higher-order thinking skills—pp. 169, 173, 179, 181, 185, 189, 193		Chapter 6 Test, Form A, pp. 49-50 Chapter 6 Test, Form B, pp. 51-52

* Also available in Workbook format (Student Edition and Teacher's Edition)

Chapter 6 Poster
A set of posters is available in a separate package. It provides a teaching poster for every chapter, including discussion and activity suggestions on the back. The poster for Chapter 6 is titled "What can you drink instead of alcohol?"

Overhead Transparencies
A set of color overhead transparencies is available for Grade 6. You may wish to use Transparencies 3 and 17 to help teach about ways to say no and the effects of drugs.

Advance Preparation
You will need to prepare materials in advance for the following activities from the Health Activities Workshop.
Activity 1, page 190 Provide information about the cost of a pack of cigarettes.
Activity 3, page 190 Ask students to collect newspaper and magazine clippings about automobile accidents.

Bulletin Board
Encourage students to draw posters that show different ways to say no to drugs and posters that show alternatives to drugs. Display these posters on the bulletin board.

Teaching Plan

Chapter 6 pages 166–197

Chapter Main Idea
Misuse and abuse of drugs can have harmful effects on the body.

Chapter Goals
- Appreciate the importance of using medicines safely.
- Demonstrate an understanding of the dangers of drug abuse.
- Use the decision-making process to make the most healthy decisions about drugs.
- Assume responsibility for saying no to drugs.

Lifetime Goal
Appreciate the importance of choosing not to use drugs as a means of leading a healthy life.

Health Vocabulary
Alcoholism, cirrhosis, dependence, depressant, drug, drug abuse, drug misuse, hallucinogen, inhalant, narcotic, overdose, over-the-counter medicine, prescription medicine, stimulant, tolerance, withdrawal

Chapter 6

Drugs: What They Are and What They Do

The old-fashioned medicine containers in the picture might be interesting to look at, but the medicines they once contained often were not safe. This chapter describes the safe use of medicines and the harmful effects of using illegal drugs. You will also learn the dangers of other substances, such as alcohol and tobacco. In addition, the chapter suggests ways to resist trying drugs—an important choice for a healthy life.

Health Watch Notebook

Look through magazines or newspapers for an article describing how drug use has affected society. Place the article in your notebook. Write a paragraph describing how the drug user, as well as others, was harmed.

1 What Are Drugs?
2 What Are Medicines and How Do People Use Them Safely?
3 What Are the Dangers of Drug Abuse?
4 How Does Marijuana Affect Health?
5 How Does Alcohol Affect Health?
6 How Does Tobacco Affect Health?
7 How Can People Make Healthy Decisions About Drugs?

166

Teaching Options

Modeling Health Vocabulary
Use this technique to introduce new words as you teach each lesson in this chapter. First, introduce the word. Present the word in two sentences that serve to clearly define the word. One sentence you might use to define the word *tolerance* is the following: *A person who takes a drug repeatedly might develop a tolerance to that drug.* Either read the sentences to the students or write them on the chalkboard. Ask the students to generate two meaningful sentences using the word. Additional successful techniques for introducing new words can be found on page T23.

Cooperative Learning
Jigsaw Format (See page T24.)
Assign the following topics at random to your cooperative learning teams.

Topic A: Describe the difference between legal and illegal drugs and give examples of each.
Topic B: Describe the difference between prescription and OTC drugs and tell how each can be used safely.
Topic C: Explain how drug abuse harms a person and society.
Topic D: Describe the actions of stimulants, depressants, narcotics, hallucinogens, and tobacco.

Have students search for information on their topic as they read the chapter. Then let all students with the same topic meet in an expert group to discuss the information. When students return to their teams, they may take turns presenting their topics to the team. Then give students a test covering all topics to complete individually (Chapter 6 test A or B in the Test Book). Award Superteam certificates to teams whose average test scores exceed 90%, and Greatteam certificates to teams whose average test scores exceed 80%.

Words to Preteach

Alcohol, amphetamine, barbiturate, carbon monoxide, chewing tobacco, chronic bronchitis, cocaine, emphysema, mainstream smoke, marijuana, medicine, nicotine, second-hand smoke, side effects, sidestream smoke, snuff, tar, tranquilizer

Introducing the Chapter

Direct the students to look at the picture. Ask students why the medicines were sometimes more harmful than helpful. (They contained drugs that were dangerous, although people at that time did not fully understand how dangerous.) Ask students to examine the labels closely and point out the names of any ingredients, including those that are harmful. Emphasize that knowledge about the effects of drugs has increased greatly since the 1800s. You may wish to send the Family Letter home at this time. You may want to assign Study Guide pages 326–327 for students to use independently as they read the lessons. The Study Guide can also be used as an extra chapter review. You might want to assign the activities in the Skills for Life Handbook on pages 353–355.

Strategies for Health Watch Notebook

After each student has reported, ask students what harmful drug effects have been noted and write their responses on the chalkboard.

Family Letter

Use the Family Letter (English or Spanish version) to introduce the subject matter of the chapter to the family and to suggest a way the family can become involved in the student's learning experience. This master may be reproduced from the Teacher's Resource Book.

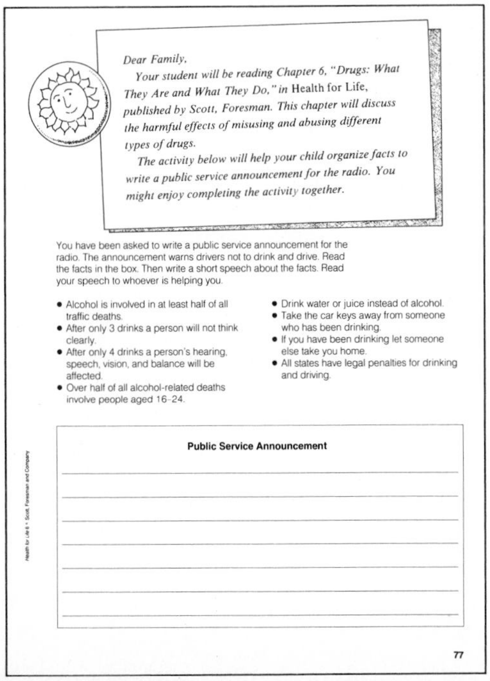

Dear Family,

Your student will be reading Chapter 6, "Drugs: What They Are and What They Do," in Health for Life, *published by Scott, Foresman. This chapter will discuss the harmful effects of misusing and abusing different types of drugs.*

The activity below will help your child organize facts to write a public service announcement for the radio. You might enjoy completing the activity together.

You have been asked to write a public service announcement for the radio. The announcement warns drivers not to drink and drive. Read the facts in the box. Then write a short speech about the facts. Read your speech to whoever is helping you.

- Alcohol is involved in at least half of all traffic deaths.
- After only 3 drinks a person will not think clearly.
- After only 4 drinks a person's hearing, speech, vision, and balance will be affected.
- Over half of all alcohol-related deaths involve people aged 16-24.
- Drink water or juice instead of alcohol.
- Take the car keys away from someone who has been drinking.
- If you have been drinking let someone else take you home.
- All states have legal penalties for drinking and driving.

Public Service Announcement

77

For High-Potential Students

Direct interested students to compose a song that has lyrics discouraging drug abuse. Students could write lyrics to fit the music of a popular song or compose both lyrics and music. As an alternative, students might do this activity in the form of a poem.

Teaching Plan

Lesson 1 pages 168–169

Lesson Objective
Define the word *drug* and list some common products that contain drugs.

Health Vocabulary
Drug

1 Motivate

Introducing the Lesson
Ask students for their definitions of the word *drug*. Lead the students to develop a definition they all agree upon. Write the definition on the chalkboard. Allow students to modify the definition after they read the chapter.

2 Teach

Strategies for Pages 168 and 169
• Direct students to read pages 168 and 169 to find out what drugs are. Ask students to compare the definition in the text with the class definition. • Ask students to name beverages that contain caffeine. (some kinds of coffee, tea, and soft drinks) • Ask students how caffeine affects the body. (stimulates the brain and nervous system, can make some people sleepless or nervous)

drug, any chemical substance that changes the way the body works. The physical changes might cause changes in emotions and behavior.

1 What Are Drugs?

Suppose that you, like the student shown in the picture, were asked to write a definition of *drug*. What would you write? Suppose, too, that you were asked to name some common products that have drugs in them. What would you name? Compare your ideas with the information on these two pages.

A **drug** is a chemical that changes the way the body works. The changes might be physical, such as the heart beating faster. The changes might also affect a person's emotions and behavior. Different drugs cause different changes. Medicines, for example, are drugs that produce changes in the body to prevent, treat, or cure an illness.

A mild drug called caffeine is in some teas, coffees, and soft drinks. The small amounts of caffeine in these drinks increase the activity of the brain and other parts of the nervous system. Too much caffeine can make a person sleepless and nervous. Most doctors recommend that young people limit drinks with caffeine. Many caffeine-free teas, coffees, and soft drinks are now available.

Alcohol is a drug that slows down the work of the nervous system. Alcohol can cause changes in the way a person thinks, feels, and acts. The kind of changes depend on how much alcohol is in the body.

Tobacco and tobacco smoke contain a drug called nicotine. This drug causes the blood vessels to narrow and the heart to beat faster. Other substances in tobacco and tobacco smoke irritate the nose, throat, and lungs.

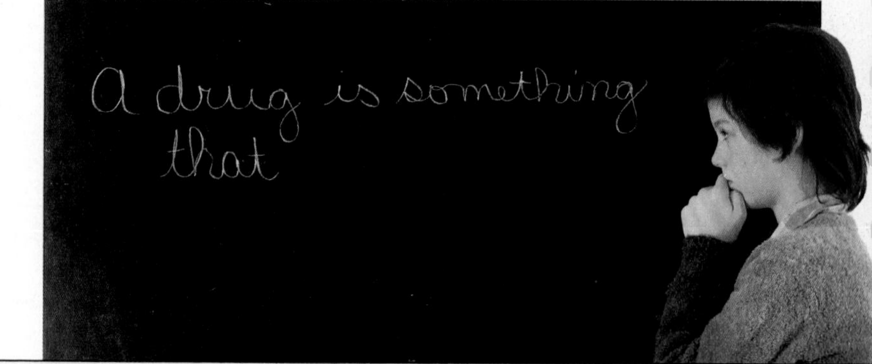

Teaching Options

Health Background

Many drugs that are commonly abused have legitimate medical uses. For example, morphine can be used as a pain killer for those who have serious ongoing medical problems, such as cancer. Often the drug is abused by those who desire its euphoric effects.

In recent years, the United States government has passed laws, created task forces, and negotiated with other countries to stop the growth of drug-producing plants, confiscate illegal drugs, and prosecute dealers and drug abusers.

Enrichment
Encourage students to find out about potions and salves that were once made or are now made from herbs or plants such as aloe. Let volunteers report their findings to the class.

Health and Social Studies
Ask students to find out about the drug laws in their state. Students should make a list of drugs that are illegal to use or possess. Ask students to include the possible sentences for use or possession of illegal drugs.

Reteaching
Encourage students to notice the warning labels on products that might be used as inhalants. Ask them to write down what the warnings say and to report their findings to the class.

You might be surprised to learn that the glue shown in the picture can have harmful, druglike effects on the body. The fumes from such products as glue, paint thinner, paints, and gasoline are poisonous. Inhaling these fumes can make a person feel dizzy and sick. The products are not intended to be used in ways that are harmful to health.

The items mentioned on these two pages are common products that you have probably seen in a store, at home, or in an advertisement. They are legal to use, although age restrictions might apply. Some drugs, however, are illegal to sell, buy, or use because of their extremely dangerous effects. Some illegal drugs can easily cause death, even in small amounts. You will learn more about the effects of these drugs later in the chapter.

All drugs, including medicines, can be harmful. People need to know the facts about drugs to make the wisest decisions about health.

Did You Know?
Most drugs are synthetic—made from chemicals in a laboratory. Other drugs come from bacteria, molds, minerals, and various parts of plants and animals.

Think Back • *Study on your own with Study Guide page 326.*

1. What is a drug?
2. What are some products that contain drugs?
3. What are some products that have druglike effects on the body if used in ways that are not intended?

Glues, paints, and thinners can be harmful if misused.

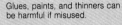

• Discuss how alcohol affects the body. (slows down the brain and nervous system) • Ask students how the drugs in tobacco and tobacco smoke affect the body. (They irritate the nose, throat, and lungs; can cause serious diseases.) • Direct students' attention to the picture on page 169 and ask them to name a product that is an inhalant. Make it clear that such products are not intended to be inhaled and that warnings on the labels of these products caution against breathing in the fumes. • Discuss with students how legal products can be harmful to health. (by being used in ways they were not intended to be used)

3 Assess

Expanding Student Thinking

Ask students to compare the effects of alcohol and caffeine on the body. (Both affect the nervous system; caffeine increases nervous system activity and alcohol slows it down.)

Thinking Skill Students are *organizing information.*

Answers to Think Back

1. A drug is a chemical that causes changes in the way the body works.
2. Answers might include some teas, coffees, and soft drinks; medicines, tobacco; and alcohol.
3. Answers might include glue, paint thinner, paints, and gasoline.

Teaching Plan

Lesson 2 pages 170–173

Lesson Objective
Define medicine and list the guidelines that one should follow to use medicines safely.

Health Vocabulary
Prescription medicine, over-the-counter medicine

1 Motivate

Introducing the Lesson
Ask students to describe advertisements for over-the-counter drugs. Encourage students to tell whether the advertisement encourages a person to take the drug safely.

2 Teach

Strategies for Pages 170 and 171
• Direct students to read pages 170 and 171 to find out about prescription and over-the-counter medicines.
• Ask students how people take most medicines (orally) and how the medicines get digested (stomach juices dissolve them). • Direct students to look at the pictures on page 170 and name other ways medicines get into the body. (by being injected, dropped in eyes, or rubbed on skin)

2 What Are Medicines and How Do People Use Them Safely?

Almost everyone has taken some kind of medicine at one time or another. During an illness, a doctor might have given you certain medicine to relieve pain or to help cure a disease. Medicines are drugs intended to be used for health reasons. Hundreds of medicines have been developed to prevent, treat, or cure many diseases.

How Do Medicines Get into the Body?

As the pictures show, medicines get into the body in different ways. Medicine for an eye infection might be a liquid dropped directly into the eyes. Medicine for a skin problem might be a lotion rubbed on the skin. Medicine for a nasal problem might be sprayed into the nose.

Sometimes a doctor or nurse injects medicine into the body through a hollow needle. Such shots are often given deep in the muscles of the upper arm. The muscle cells absorb the medicine, which then passes into the bloodstream. The blood carries the medicine to all parts of the body, including the part that is ailing. Sometimes medicine is injected directly into a vein.

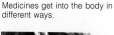

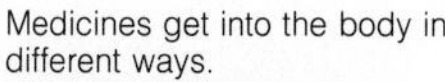

Medicines get into the body in different ways.

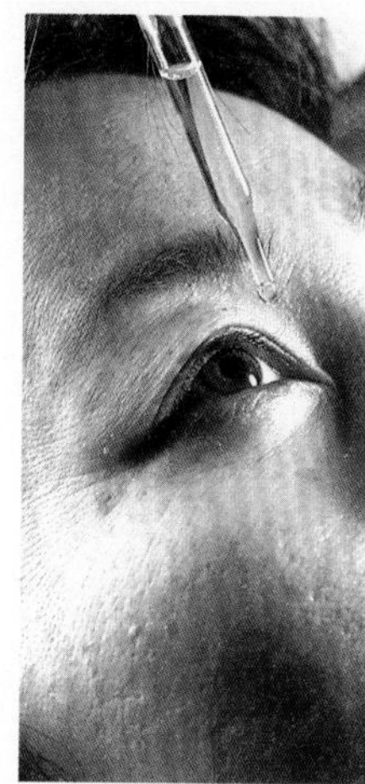

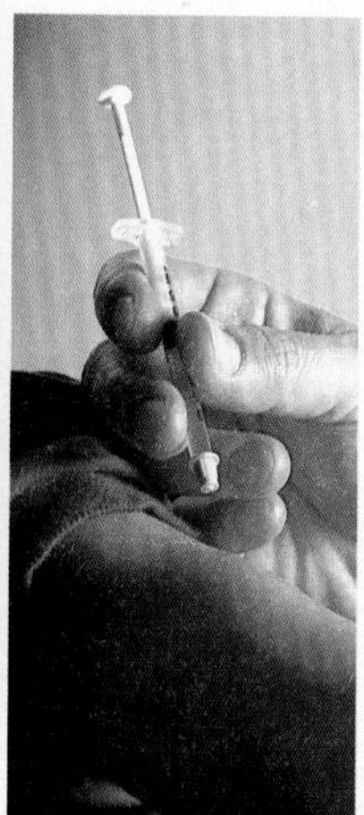

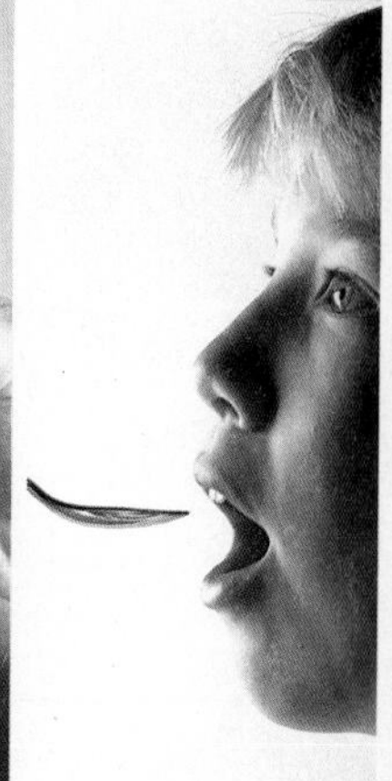

Teaching Options

Health Background

Medical researchers have developed new ways of taking certain medicines to reduce the possible side effects of medicines and the number of doses that must be taken. These medicines work on a time-release principle, slowly releasing medicine into the bloodstream over a period of several hours. Some devices have also been developed that release medicine slowly. For example, a transdermal patch can be worn on the skin to release medicine that controls motion sickness.

Enrichment
Encourage students to find out how quickly a medicine begins working if it is swallowed, if it is applied topically, and if it is injected. Students should find out why different medicines are administered differently. Suggest that students report their findings to the class.

Health and Science
Ask interested students to find out about the discovery of different kinds of medicines, such as vaccines and antibiotics.

Reteaching
Let students find out more about either prescription or over-the-counter medicines. Students could prepare a chart telling about the kind of medicines they researched, including uses, precautions, and possible side effects.

Special Education
Help learning-disabled students look through magazines for advertisements of over-the-counter drugs. Ask students to make a list of each type of OTC medicine, and the reason it is taken.

More often than not, people take medicine orally—through the mouth. Such medicine might be in the form of a pill, capsule, or liquid. Once the medicine is swallowed, it travels to the stomach within a few seconds. Stomach juices might dissolve the medicine. Then it can pass through the walls of the stomach and small intestine into the bloodstream. The blood carries the medicine to all parts of the body, including the part that needs it.

What Are Prescription and OTC Medicines?

Some medicines can be bought only with a prescription—a doctor's order for a specific medicine. These medicines are **prescription medicines**—Rx medicines. Notice the prescription shown here. It includes the kind and amount of medicine and directions for safe use. A pharmacist follows the doctor's order in preparing the medicine.

Buying **over-the-counter medicines**—OTC medicines—does not require a prescription. Aspirin, some cough syrup, and cold tablets are some OTC medicines usually found on store shelves. OTC medicines are intended only for occasional, short-term use. Although OTC medicines are generally not as powerful as prescription medicines, they can be dangerous if not used correctly.

prescription (pri skrip′ shən) **medicine,** a drug that can be purchased only with an order from a doctor.

over-the-counter medicine, a drug that can be purchased without a doctor's order.

What information is on this prescription?

• Discuss how medicine gets to the part of the body that needs it. (applied directly or carried through the blood) • Explain that medicine that is carried through the blood goes to every part of the body, which helps explain some of the side effects of taking medicine. • Ask students how prescription medicines are prepared. (by a pharmacist, according to a doctor's orders) • Encourage students to explain why over-the-counter medicines do not require prescriptions. (They are intended only for occasional, short-term use; they are usually not as powerful as prescription medicines.) • Ask students why medicines must be taken according to directions. (They can be harmful if misused.)

Teaching Plan

Lesson 2 continued

2 Teach

Strategies for Pages 172 and 173

• Direct students to read pages 172 and 173 to find out how people can use medicines safely. • Ask students how to tell how medicine should be used. (by reading the label) • Ask students to describe the information on a prescription label. (the name of the doctor, pharmacy, and patient; directions about how to take the medication; special warnings; directions for storage) • Direct students to look at the picture on page 172 and tell what other information they can find on a prescription label. • Ask students what information is contained on the label of over-the-counter medicines. (the purpose of the medicine, the correct amount to take, warnings about the length of use and possible side effects) • Discuss how a person can find out the possible side effects of a prescription drug. (If they are not on the label, a person can get the information from a doctor or pharmacist.) • Ask students what drug misuse involves. (taking too much medicine or taking it too often, combining medicines, or taking medicine prescribed for someone else)

Did You Know?
The oldest known prescriptions were written about four thousand years ago on the clay tablet shown below. The tablet contains about fifteen prescriptions calling for the use of plant materials.

How Can People Use Medicines Safely?

Like all drugs, medicines cause changes in your body. Therefore, medicines must be used with caution. The labels on medicine containers help you to use medicine safely.

Notice the label of the prescription medicine below. It lists the name of the doctor, pharmacy, and patient. The patient listed is the only person who should take that medicine. The label also includes directions about how much medicine to take and how often to take it. Special warnings and directions for safe storage might be included. All these directions should be followed exactly. What other information can you find on the prescription label?

Directions for safe use are on OTC medicines too, as the label to the right shows. These labels tell the purpose of the medicine, how much medicine to take, and any special warnings. Always read a warning carefully. Some people might not be able to use some OTC drugs if they have certain health problems or are currently taking other medicines.

What important information is on Rx and OTC medicine labels?

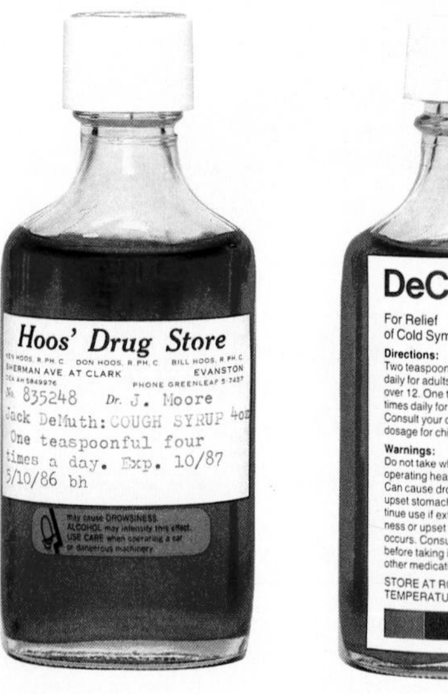

172

Teaching Options

Anecdote

Some time-release devices are implanted in a patient's body. One type of implant is a small pump that delivers medicine to a specific part of the body, rather than having the medicine travel to the entire body through the bloodstream. Such a device is used to release cancer-killing medicine to certain types of cancer cells.

Enrichment

Ask students to write a paragraph telling why it is not a good idea to use a regular spoon instead of a measuring spoon to measure medicine dosages. (The sizes of household spoons vary greatly.)

Health and Home Economics

Encourage students to find out about medicines that should not be taken in combination with certain foods; for example, dairy products interfere with the effectiveness of tetracycline—an antibiotic.

Reteaching

Direct students to write a paragraph about safety with medicines. Students might tell how to avoid drug misuse, and what to do if a side effect occurs.

Notice that the label on the OTC medicine also describes possible side effects—unwanted effects of the medicine. Headache, stomach upset, and drowsiness are common side effects of OTC and prescription medicines. Prescription medicine labels do not always list possible side effects. This information must come from your doctor or pharmacist. Be sure you are aware of the possible side effects before taking any medicine.

The chart lists safety guidelines to follow when using medicine. Taking medicine without following these guidelines is **drug misuse**—incorrectly using a medicine in a way that could harm health. Examples of drug misuse include taking more medicine than directed, taking two or more medicines at the same time without a doctor's permission, or taking medicine prescribed for someone else. You can prevent most drug misuse by reading and following the information on medicine labels.

drug misuse, incorrect use of a medicine in a way that can harm health.

Think Back • *Study on your own with Study Guide page 326.*

1. What is a medicine?
2. What happens to medicine after it is swallowed?
3. How do prescription and over-the-counter medicines differ?
4. What guidelines should people follow for using medicines safely?

Safety Guidelines for Using Medicine

- Do not take medicine without the permission of a doctor, parent, or other responsible adult.
- Read and follow all directions and warnings on the label.
- When the doctor prescribes a medicine, ask him or her what side effects you might expect.
- If an OTC medicine has a harmful or unexpected side effect, stop taking it immediately. Tell an adult member of your family about the side effect. If a prescription medicine has an unexpected side effect, call the doctor immediately.
- Do not use a medicine for every minor ailment. Occasional sleeplessness, headache, and slight cold can often be relieved with rest and relaxation.
- Keep medicine in its original container.
- Never take a medicine prescribed for someone else.
- Keep all medicines in places where young children cannot reach them.
- Take a prescription medicine for as long as the doctor directed, even if you feel well before then.

- Direct students to look at the chart on page 173 and tell how drug misuse can be prevented. (Answers should include the guidelines on the safety chart.)

3 Assess

Expanding Student Thinking

Ask students to explain why knowing the possible side effects of a drug before taking it is important. (Answers might include: a person could avoid activities that would be made dangerous by drowsiness; a person would not worry about minor side effects; a person would know what side effects were dangerous.)

Thinking Skills When students explain the importance of knowing a medicine's possible side effects, they are *interpreting information* and *drawing conclusions*.

Answers to Think Back

1. A medicine is a drug intended to be used for health reasons.

2. Medicine travels to the stomach, dissolves, and passes into the bloodstream, which carries it to all parts of the body.

3. Prescription medicine can be purchased only with a doctor's order, but over-the-counter medicines do not require one. Prescription medicines are generally more powerful than over-the-counter medicines.

4. Answers should include several of the guidelines shown on page 173.

Teaching Plan

Lesson 3 pages 174–179

Lesson Objective
Briefly describe the harmful effects of abusing different kinds of drugs.

Health Vocabulary
Dependence, depressant, drug abuse, hallucinogen, inhalant, narcotic, overdose, stimulant, tolerance, withdrawal

1 Motivate

Introducing the Lesson
Ask students why they think some people might take drugs for reasons other than their health. (peer pressure, desire to escape from problems) Discuss why drugs are not a good solution to these problems. (They do not enhance friendships; they do not solve problems; they only make matters worse; drugs can cause permanent health problems.)

2 Teach

Strategies for Pages 174 and 175
• Direct students to read pages 174 and 175 to find out the dangers of drug abuse. • Ask students to explain the difference between drug misuse and drug abuse.

drug abuse, the intentional use of drugs for reasons other than health.

tolerance, a condition in which the body gets used to the presence of a drug and needs larger amounts of that drug to produce the same effects.

3 What Are the Dangers of Drug Abuse?

The proper use of medicine helps millions of people around the world every day. Some people, however, use medicines and other drugs in harmful, dangerous ways. The intentional use of drugs for reasons other than health is **drug abuse.**

The abuse of drugs can produce many harmful effects. Some of these effects are immediate. They occur within a few minutes or hours after taking the drug. A sick feeling in the stomach is one common immediate effect of drug abuse. Others include headache, sleeplessness, high blood pressure, vomiting, and even death if a person takes too much of the drug.

Some dangerous effects of drug abuse occur after a period of continued abuse. These long-term effects include tolerance and dependence.

Tolerance occurs when a person's body gets used to a drug. The abuser must use more and more of the drug to get the same effect. For example, suppose a person starts the bad habit of taking a sleeping pill every night to fall asleep. That person's body will soon build tolerance to the sleeping pill. Then two pills might be needed to make the person sleepy. As tolerance continues to build, the person might need three or four pills each night to fall asleep.

This person needed emergency medical help to recover from an overdose.

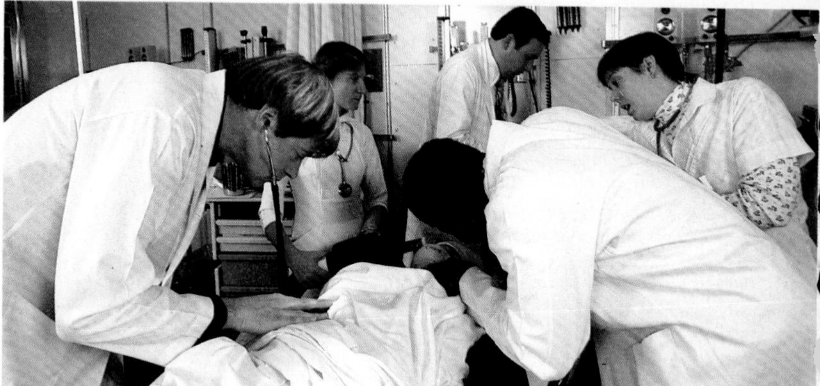

174

Teaching Options

Health Background
Physical dependence upon a drug occurs when an alteration in the physiological make-up or cellular state of the body exists. To maintain the altered states, the body acquires a need for the drug.

Enrichment
If possible, invite a professional drug-abuse counselor to visit the class and discuss the kind of help that is available to drug abusers in the community.

Health and Language Arts
Ask students to create an advertising campaign to warn the public about the dangers of drug abuse. Students could create bumper stickers, slogans, buttons, posters, and radio and TV commercials with antidrug themes.

Reteaching
Ask students how withdrawal symptoms might help keep a drug abuser physically dependent. (They make the person want to take the drug to avoid the symptoms.)

These larger amounts of sleeping pills might lead to an **overdose**—an amount of a drug too large for the body to use. An overdose can cause serious health problems. The patient shown on page 174 suffered from a drug overdose. The emergency team was able to save this person's life, but many other people die from overdoses.

Dependence is the need for a drug. The need might be mental or physical. A mentally dependent person *thinks* he or she needs the drug to function or make it through the day. With physical dependence, a person's body needs the drug to avoid feeling sick. A person can be both mentally and physically dependent on a drug.

Sometimes a person who is physically dependent on a drug stops taking it. The person might then suffer from a sickness called **withdrawal.** The symptoms of withdrawal can vary, depending on the drug that had been used. Withdrawal symptoms can be unpleasant and dangerous. Usually the person becomes nervous, depressed, or panicky. Other symptoms include chills, fever, vomiting, and severe aches and pains. People withdrawing from certain drugs often need to be hospitalized for a short time.

Usually, after a short withdrawal period, the body learns to function without the drug. Physical dependence stops. Mental dependence, on the other hand, is often more difficult to stop. A person can overcome dependence, but he or she must be willing to get proper help and find healthier, more constructive ways to deal with problems.

The picture shows one way of dealing with drug-related problems. A person who wants help is talking with someone who has special training and experience in helping others with their problems. Some organizations in your community probably provide such counseling.

What Are the Most Commonly Abused Drugs?

The most commonly abused drugs can be placed into five groups. They are depressants, stimulants, narcotics, hallucinogens, and inhalants. The charts on the next few pages describe these groups of drugs.

overdose, an amount of a drug that is too large for the body and can cause a dangerous reaction.

dependence (di pen′ dəns), the need for a drug. This need might be mental, physical, or both.

withdrawal (with drô′ əl), the symptoms that occur when a person who is physically dependent on a drug stops taking it.

Talking about drug-related problems helps.

• (Misuse is the incorrect use of a medicine that is taken for health. Abuse is the intentional use of a drug for reasons other than health.) • Encourage students to describe the two kinds of dangers of drug abuse. (immediate and long-term) • Ask students to name some of the immediate harmful effects of drug abuse (sick feeling, vomiting, headache, sleeplessness, high blood pressure, death) and some of the long-term effects (tolerance and dependence). • Discuss how tolerance can lead to an overdose. (A person's body gets used to the drug, and he or she must take more of it to get the desired effects. • Direct students to look at the picture on page 174 and tell what happens to a person who takes an overdose. (The person becomes ill. Sometimes he or she dies.) • Encourage students to describe the two kinds of dependence. (physical and mental) • Discuss with students how withdrawal occurs. (A person who becomes physically dependent on a drug tries to stop taking it, and then experiences negative symptoms.) • Ask students to name withdrawal symptoms. (nervousness, depression, panic, chills, fever, vomiting, severe aches and pains, and sometimes convulsions or death) • Ask students how a person ends a physical dependence on a drug. (by going through withdrawal and letting the body learn to feel normal again without the drug)

Teaching Plan

Lesson 3 continued

2 Teach

Strategies for Pages 176 and 177

• Direct students to read page 176 to find out about stimulants and depressants. • Discuss the difference between stimulants and depressants. (Stimulants speed up the nervous system, and depressants slow it down.) • Discuss how stimulants make a person feel. (They can make a person feel more awake and energetic, or can cause nervousness, sleeplessness, hallucinations, and loss of appetite.) • Encourage students to explain what can happen to a person who uses amphetamines heavily. (The person might become anxious or confused.) • Discuss the results of continual use of stimulants. (malnutrition, mental disorders, tolerance, mental dependence, and, in the case of cocaine, death) • Encourage students to name some depressants (alcohol, tranquilizers, barbiturates) and tell what they do (lower blood pressure, relax people, help people sleep, relieve nervousness). • Ask students why people mistakenly think barbiturates are safe. (because doctors sometimes prescribe them)

stimulant (stim′ yə lənt), a drug that speeds up the work of the nervous system.

depressant (di pres′ nt), a drug that slows down the work of the nervous system.

Did You Know?
"Designer drugs" are drugs made illegally in laboratories. These drugs resemble commonly abused narcotics, stimulants, depressants, and hallucinogens, but their "recipes" have been changed slightly. These recipe changes often make the drugs less expensive to produce or stronger but also make the drugs unpredictable and extremely dangerous. One such designer drug is called MDMA, or "Ecstasy." Impure batches of Ecstasy have been known to leave many people with the symptoms of Parkinson's disease—a disease of the nervous system that causes tremors, weakness, and paralysis.

Stimulants

What They Are: **Stimulants** are drugs that speed up the work of the nervous system. Stimulants can cause a feeling of being more awake or having more energy than usual. Strong stimulants include amphetamines, crank, "ice," cocaine, and crack. Amphetamines are illegal without a prescription. Crank, "ice," cocaine, and crack are illegal.

Harmful Effects: Misuse of amphetamines can cause a person to feel anxious or confused. The person might have trouble sleeping, become irritable, and lose his or her appetite. Also, heavy doses can dangerously increase the heart rate. Crank and "ice" cause extreme fear, anger, and violence and can damage the brain, heart, lungs, and kidneys. Cocaine is a strong stimulant that increases the heart rate and blood pressure. Crack is an especially potent form of cocaine. Cocaine and crack act upon the nervous system and cause a feeling of excitement that soon wears off. Then the user is likely to feel depressed. Other effects of cocaine and crack use include sleeplessness and hallucinations—seeing or hearing things that are not really there. Tolerance and dependence can develop from the use of amphetamines and cocaine. Crack, crank, and "ice" users develop tolerance and dependence very rapidly. An overdose of stimulants can cause death.

Depressants

What They Are: **Depressants** are drugs that slow down the work of the nervous system. The brain and nerves work more slowly, muscles relax, and the body takes longer to react. Alcohol, tranquilizers, and barbiturates are depressants. Doctors sometimes prescribe mild depressants, such as minor tranquilizers, to calm people or to help them sleep. Such prescriptions are for short-term use. Doctors might prescribe barbiturates to relax patients before surgery. Alcohol is illegal for sale to minors. Tranquilizers and barbiturates are illegal without a prescription.

Harmful Effects: Because doctors prescribe tranquilizers and barbiturates at times, some people think such drugs are safe to use as they choose. This idea is a mistake. Depressants often cause such symptoms as confusion, slurred speech, and staggering. A person who takes heavy doses of barbiturates usually has difficulty thinking and working effectively. As a result, that person might not remember how many doses he or she has taken and might accidentally take an overdose. Then the person's breathing and heart rate will slow down so much that the person might pass out, go into a coma, or die. People can develop tolerance and mental and physical dependence for depressants.

Teaching Options

Anecdote

Current United States government figures estimate that Americans spend 18 billion dollars a year for cocaine, and 44 billion for marijuana. The markup in price from dealer to user is estimated at as much as 200 percent.

Enrichment

Invite a representative from a local hospital or drug rehabilitation center to speak to the class about how drug abusers can overcome addiction.

Health and History

Encourage interested students to find out about the medical and legal history of narcotics. One source is an article about the opium poppy in *National Geographic,* February, 1985.

Reteaching

Direct students to make three columns on a sheet of paper. In the first colmnn students should list the groups of commonly abused drugs listed on pages 176 and 177. In the second column, students should write down all the dangerous physical effects of the drugs in each drug group. In the third column, students should list all the negative mental effects of the drugs in each drug group.

Narcotics

What They Are: **Narcotics** is a term for a group of depressant drugs that are made from opium or from a substance like opium. Narcotics include morphine, codeine, and heroin. Narcotics, like other depressants, slow down the work of the nervous system. Narcotics also stop the brain from feeling pain. Doctors use codeine and morphine to produce sleep and to relieve pain in operations and serious illnesses. However, doctors use these drugs with great care. As soon as they can, doctors stop giving these drugs. Morphine and codeine are illegal without a prescription. Heroin is not used medically in the United States and is illegal.

Harmful Effects: Narcotics are especially dangerous because they can produce physical and mental dependence quickly. Even people who want to give up taking a narcotic might find that they cannot. Withdrawal symptoms can be severe and usually include chills, fever, and stomach pains. Other health problems occur when people abuse a narcotic. They often spend so much time using or thinking about the drug that they neglect other body needs. Many narcotic abusers become malnourished. Infections, such as hepatitis and AIDS, can result from unsterile needles that abusers use to inject heroin.

Hallucinogens

What They Are: **Hallucinogens** are drugs that cause changes in the senses. A person who uses a hallucinogen might see, hear, smell, or feel things that are not really there. Hallucinogens change the messages carried by the nerves to the brain. Therefore, a whisper might sound like a shout. Time might appear to pass very slowly. Hallucinogens include LSD and PCP. All hallucinogens are illegal.

Harmful Effects: Hallucinogens increase the heart rate and blood pressure. Feet and hands might feel numb, and the stomach might become upset. Some hallucinogens affect people's moods. Hallucinogens are very unpredictable. Even in the same person, the effects of a hallucinogen can change each time the drug is used. Some users become violent or frightened. Some people injure themselves because they are not aware of danger. In some cases, users have gone into a coma and died. Continual use of hallucinogens can lead to mental problems and permanent brain damage.

narcotic (när kot′ ik), a legal term for a drug made from opium or from a substance like opium that is produced artificially.

hallucinogen (hə lü′ sn ə jen), a drug that causes changes in the senses, often making a person see, hear, smell, or feel things that are not really there.

Did You Know?
Some young people use anabolic steroids, a group of drugs similar to a male hormone. Some young people use steroids to build muscle quickly. They mistakenly believe that these drugs have no harmful effects. However, anabolic steroids are known to cause dangerous side effects, including severe liver damage, mental problems, skin problems, and the appearance of male characteristics in female users. Because they are so dangerous, the use of anabolic steroids is illegal in most athletic competitions.

• Discuss the harmful effects of heavy doses of depressants. (confusion, slurred speech, staggering, difficulties thinking and working, accidental overdose, tolerance, physical and mental dependence) • Ask students how a person could accidentally take an overdose of depressants, and what might happen if a person takes an overdose. (The person might forget how many doses he or she has taken, and then take too many. Then the heart rate and breathing slow down so much that the person might go into a coma or die.) • Direct students to read page 177 to find out about narcotics and hallucinogens. • Encourage students to explain how narcotics are different from other depressants. (They are made from opium or substances like opium, and they stop the brain from feeling pain.) • Ask students why doctors use narcotics as sparingly as possible. (because the drugs quickly produce physical and mental dependence and severe withdrawal symptoms) • Discuss the harmful effects of hallucinogens. (The effects are unpredictable. A person may become violent, frightened, or unaware of danger. Continual use can lead to mental problems.)

Source for Did You Know?

Sedative-Hypnotics. National Institute on Drug Abuse, 1983.

Teaching Plan

Lesson 3 continued

2 Teach

Strategies for Pages 178 and 179

• Direct students to read page 178 to find out about the effects of inhalants. • Encourage students to name some inhalants. (gasoline, airplane glue, nail polish remover, and other sprays and solvents that give off fumes) • Discuss how inhalants make a person feel. (They cause increased energy, followed by irritability, dizziness, vomiting, headaches, nosebleeds, loss of memory, and loss of consciousness.) • Ask students to name some of the harmful effects of inhalants. (permanent damage to the nose, throat, lungs, brain, liver, and kidneys) • Direct students to look at the picture on page 178 and describe how a person can use sprays and solvents safely. (by using them in a well-ventilated area) • Ask students to read page 179 and tell how drug abuse affects society. (increases crime; costs to arrest, try, and imprison abusers; and increases the number of accidents that result in injuries and deaths to others)

inhalant (in hā′ lənt), a substance that gives off fumes, which could produce druglike effects when breathed deeply into the body.

Inhalants

What They Are: **Inhalants** are substances that give off fum which could produce druglike effects when breathed deeply into the body. Dangerous inhalants include the fumes from lighter fluid, cleaning fluid, gasoline, paint thinner, airplane glue, nail polish remover, pesticides, and oven cleaners. The picture shows a safe way to use some of these household products. People who abuse these substances breathe the fumes deeply into the body. Then changes occur in the boc similar to changes caused when drugs are taken.

Harmful Effects: At first a person who inhales fumes might think that he or she has more energy. However, this feeling does not last long. Soon other effects take place. A person might feel irritable or dizzy. He or she might have trouble speaking clearly. Vomiting might occur. Headaches, nosebleeds, and loss of memory are common. A person might become drowsy or pass out. Constant or deep sniffing of fumes can permanently damage the nose, throat, lungs, brain, liver, and kidneys. Inhalants can cause death by stopping the heartbeat or breathing.

How is this person using the paints and thinner safely?

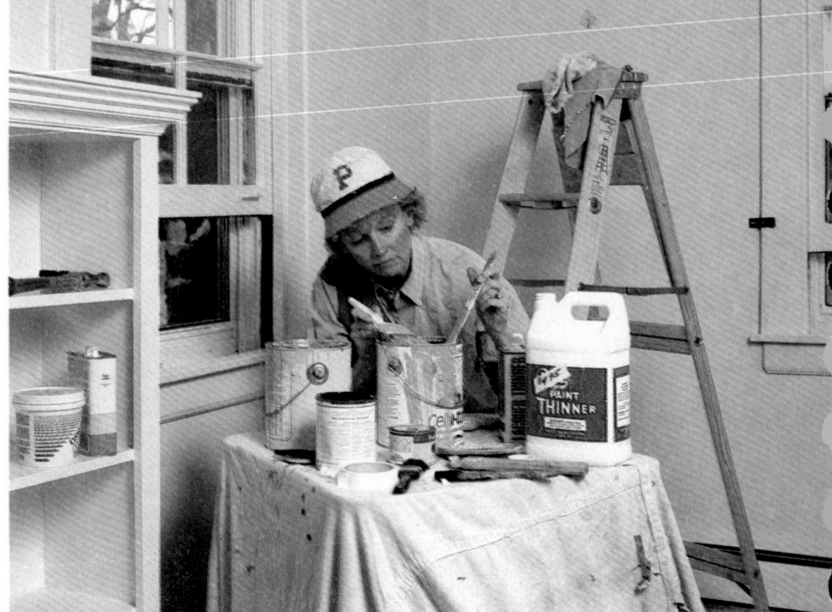

178

Teaching Options

Enrichment

Encourage interested students to find out which types of industrial jobs require that a worker wear a filtering device over the nose.

Special Education

Bring to class several empty containers of common household products that are inhalants. Direct students to read the warning labels on the products and tell how to use each product safely.

Reteaching

Discuss how a person would know if he or she were using sprays or solvents in a room that was not well enough ventilated. (strong fumes, dizziness, nausea)

How Does Drug Abuse Affect Society?

Drug abuse affects society as well as the person taking the drug. As the picture suggests, one effect of drug abuse on society is increased crime. Many people who abuse drugs obtain them illegally. Because the price of illegal drugs is often high, abusers often steal to pay for them. Abusers obviously cause harm to theft victims and sometimes police officers. Also, the arresting, trying, and imprisoning of abusers costs society millions of dollars.

People who abuse drugs affect society in another way. Drug abusers cause many accidents resulting in injuries or death to themselves or others. More than half of all motor vehicle accidents involve someone who has abused a drug.

Think Back • *Study on your own with Study Guide page 326.*

1. What is one possible long-term effect of drug abuse?
2. How can stimulants damage the body?
3. What are some harmful effects of depressants?
4. Why are the changes caused by hallucinogens dangerous?
5. What are some products that give off fumes that could be harmful unless the products are used properly?
6. How does drug abuse affect society?

Did You Know?

Society is affected by drug use in ways other than crime and accidents. Society loses when students do not learn or drop out of school because of drug use. Society also loses when workers miss work, work slowly, or make mistakes at work because of drug use. Society also loses when the babies born to alcoholic or drug-addicted mothers are born sick and brain damaged. These babies may never be able to develop into persons who can care for themselves. Therefore, they may have to be supported by society throughout their lives.

How does drug abuse lead to an increase in crime?

3 Assess

Expanding Student Thinking

Ask students to explain what stimulants and depressants have in common. (Both affect the nervous system, and both are dangerous when abused.)

Thinking Skill When students explain what stimulants and depressants have in common, they are *organizing information.*

Answers to Think Back

1. Answers should include tolerance or dependence.

2. Stimulants can increase the heart rate and blood pressure; lead to malnutrition and mental disorders; and cause tolerance, mental dependence, and illness through overdose.

3. Answers should include confusion, slurred speech, and staggering, as well as tolerance, dependence, and overdose.

4. Answers should refer to the unpredictability of hallucinogens, mental problems they can cause, and the risk of death.

5. Answers might include lighter fluid, cleaning fluid, gasoline, paint thinner, glue, and nail polish remover.

6. Answers should refer to crime caused by the need to get drugs, the financial burden of arresting and trying abusers, and the motor vehicle accidents that abusers cause.

Teaching Plan

Lesson 4 pages 180–181

Lesson Objective
State the harmful effects of marijuana on health.

1 Motivate

Introducing the Lesson
Encourage volunteers to describe a time they came close to being in a traffic accident. Ask students how the outcome might have been different if the driver's reaction time had been worse or if the driver had not been paying attention. Relate these incidents to the fact that marijuana use can greatly slow reaction time.

2 Teach

Strategies for Pages 180 and 181
• Direct students to read pages 180 and 181 to find out how marijuana affects health. • Discuss the effects of marijuana. (speeds the heart and can cause nervousness and excitability, slows coordination and timing)
• Direct students to look at the pictures on page 180 to learn about the effects of marijuana. • Ask students how marijuana damages health. (It harms the respiratory system and reduces resistance to disease.)

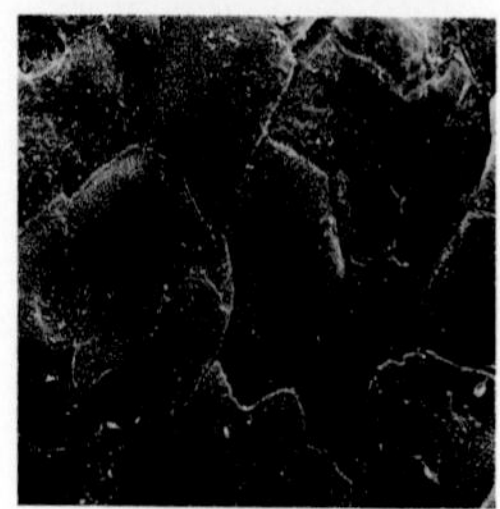

Cilia in healthy lungs

Cilia are destroyed by marijuana smoke.

4 How Does Marijuana Affect Health?

Marijuana is a drug that comes from the hemp plant. Marijuana cigarettes contain the dried leaves and stems of the plant. Scientists have been studying marijuana for over twenty years. Their findings show that using this drug harms health in many ways.

Marijuana contains more than four hundred chemicals—some of which can be harmful to the body. Like all drugs, marijuana can cause changes in the way the body works. It can also change the user's moods and actions.

The main mind-altering chemical in marijuana is called THC. When marijuana is smoked, the THC is absorbed by many body tissues and organs. The greater the amount of THC in the marijuana, the greater the effects will be on the user. Tests show that the THC from just one cigarette can stay in the body for about a month. Therefore, THC easily builds up in the body of a marijuana user.

When marijuana is smoked, the heartbeat speeds up. Blood vessels behind the eyes might become irritated. However, scientists think the most damaging physical effects of marijuana occur in the lungs. Marijuana smoke inflames the lining of the lungs and prevents them from working properly. The first picture above shows that air passages in healthy lungs are lined with hairlike cilia that sweep particles away from the lungs. Notice in the second picture that the cilia in a marijuana smoker have been completely destroyed. Chemicals in marijuana smoke can help cause lung cancer and other serious diseases of the lungs. In addition, evidence indicates that long-term marijuana use reduces the body's ability to resist diseases in general.

Use of marijuana can affect a person's timing and coordination. As a result, driving a bicycle or a car can be dangerous. Many traffic accidents are caused by people who use marijuana. Notice in the chart on the next page other driving skills affected by the use of marijuana. Think about how each skill is important to traffic safety. How does driving become dangerous if that skill is weakened?

180

Teaching Options

Health Background

The chemical name for THC, which is the main mind-altering chemical in marijuana, is tetrahydrocannabinol. THC enters the blood and is carried throughout the body. It is temporarily stored in body tissues and can remain in the body for about one month. Hashish is a stronger form of marijuana because it contains more THC. Hashish is made from the dark brown or black resin on the tops of the hemp plant *(Cannabis sativa).*

Enrichment
Encourage interested students to find out how marijuana is smuggled into the country and how law enforcement groups work to try to stop it.

Health and Language Arts
Direct students to write a short story about a friendship that suffers when one of the two friends begins smoking marijuana regularly. Suggest that students write the story from the point of view of the friend who does not smoke marijuana, but accept all stories that show an understanding of the effects of marijuana.

Reteaching
Discuss how marijuana might affect family life if one member of the family were a continual user of the drug.

Marijuana use can also affect a person's mood. Some users find that marijuana makes them feel nervous. Others say it makes them irritable. Some users become loud and talkative. Marijuana affects the moods of different people differently. It can also affect the same person differently at different times.

The use of marijuana is especially damaging to young people. It interferes with physical, emotional, and mental growth. For example, studies show that marijuana use might decrease the levels of certain hormones during puberty. This action slows the rate at which a young person matures. Also, young people who use marijuana to escape their problems might not learn the skills necessary to deal with everyday problems of growing up.

Many young people who use marijuana notice that their school grades drop, partially because marijuana can interfere with a person's ability to learn. The drug affects memory and thinking skills. Also, as a marijuana user becomes more interested in the drug, he or she often becomes less interested in school, activities, and friends.

Because of its danger to health, there are laws against growing, selling, and possessing marijuana.

Did You Know?
Marijuana can harm the reproductive system. As young people go through puberty, proper amounts of the male and female hormones are essential for normal growth. Marijuana has been shown to change the amount of these hormones. These changes can result in abnormal sexual development.

Think Back • *Study on your own with Study Guide page 327.*

1. How can marijuana use affect the body?
2. How might the use of marijuana lead to driving accidents?
3. How can marijuana affect a user's mood?
4. Why can the use of marijuana be especially harmful to young people?

Driving Skills that Marijuana Weakens

- Coordination
- Reaction time
- Ability to follow a moving object
- Perception of flashing lights
- Ability to adjust quickly to a sudden bright light

- Direct students to look at the chart on page 181 and tell how accidents might be caused by marijuana use. (Marijuana use affects coordination, reaction time, and perception.)
- Discuss how marijuana can interfere with a young person's mental and emotional growth. (by decreasing the levels of certain hormones and by allowing a person to put off problems instead of facing them and maturing)

3 Assess

Expanding Student Thinking

Ask students to write a paragraph explaining how the side effects of marijuana can cause bicycle and pedestrian accidents.

Thinking Skills Students are *drawing conclusions* and *communicating.*

Answers to Think Back

1. Answers should refer to marijuana's effects upon the respiratory and cardiovascular systems and on a person's physical, mental, and emotional growth.

2. The use of marijuana weakens driving skills such as coordination, reaction time, and perception.

3. The user might become nervous, irritable, or loud and talkative.

4. The use of marijuana interferes with young people's growth. It also interferes with school, activities, and friendships.

Teaching Plan

Lesson 5 pages 182–185

Lesson Objective
Describe the short-term and long-term effects of alcohol abuse, and tell where people who abuse alcohol can obtain help.

Health Vocabulary
Alcoholism, cirrhosis

1 Motivate

Introducing the Lesson
Encourage students to describe alcohol advertisements and the images they present of alcoholic beverages. Discuss whether alcohol really provides any of the qualities the advertisements seem to promise.

2 Teach

Strategies for Pages 182 and 183
• Direct students to read pages 182 and 183 to find out the immediate effects of alcohol. • Ask students what kind of drug alcohol is. (depressant) • Direct students to look at the chart on page 182 and tell how different levels of blood alcohol affect behavior.

On Your Own
Use the chart on this page to answer the following questions on a sheet of paper.
• At what percentage level of blood alcohol content does risk of accidents increase? Why?
• How does the risk of accidents change as the percentage increases? Why?

5 How Does Alcohol Affect Health?

Alcohol is a depressant drug. It is probably the most abused drug in the United States today. Alcohol is illegal for people under a certain age. This drug is found in such beverages as whiskey, beer, and wine.

Alcohol does not break down in the body the same way other foods do. It is absorbed right into the bloodstream from the stomach and the small intestine. Within two minutes after a person drinks alcohol, that alcohol starts to enter the bloodstream. The blood carries the alcohol to every part of the body.

What Are the Immediate Effects of Alcohol?

Because alcohol is a depressant, it slows down the activity of the brain, which slows other parts of the body. Like many drugs, alcohol can change a person's mood, emotions, or actions.

The degree to which alcohol affects a person depends on the blood alcohol level—the percentage of alcohol in the person's blood. The chart shows the effects of different blood alcohol levels on a person's bodily functions and behavior. Note that the higher the blood alcohol level, the more severe the effects of alcohol on the person. However, even a low level of alcohol can interfere with a person's ability to perform.

Effects of Blood Alcohol Level

Blood Alcohol Level (percent)	Examples of Effects
0.01-0.04	Blood circulates more rapidly; inhibitions lessened; user feels dizzy; ability to think clearly decreases; coordination lessens; judgment and memory are weakened; risk of accidents increases.
0.05-0.09	Unable to think clearly; behavior changes; judgment and reasoning become unreliable; coordination impaired; risk of accidents much higher.
0.10	Vision, hearing, speech, and balance are impaired; coordination poor; considered intoxicated by law in most states; risk of accidents very high.
0.20	Most behaviors are affected; standing and walking are difficult; user might lose bladder control; risk of accidents extremely high.
0.30 and up	Vomiting might alternate with unconsciousness; deep coma; death.
0.40-0.50	Usually causes death.

182

Teaching Options

Health Background
Researchers report that about 10 million Americans have an alcohol problem. In 1935, Alcoholics Anonymous was founded to help individuals with drinking problems. Currently AA has about 28,000 local groups in 92 countries.

Enrichment
Direct interested students to find out about the laws in your state regarding the legal drinking age and drunk driving. Encourage students to report their findings to the class.

Direct interested students to devise a campaign against drunk driving based on the effects alcohol has on the body.

Health and Science
Direct students to find out how the body gets rid of alcohol. Students could prepare a chart listing each step of the process.

Reteaching
Direct students to look again at the chart on page 183. Ask students which effects of alcohol would be likely to contribute to the high accident rate for drunk drivers.

A person's weight affects the blood alcohol level. A smaller person has a higher blood alcohol level than a larger person if both drink the same amount of alcohol. A smaller person has less body fluids, which dilute the alcohol. Why do you think young people would feel the effects of alcohol faster and more strongly than adults? Other things affect the blood alcohol level. The level rises quickly if a person drinks many drinks in a short period of time or if the stomach is empty. Also, each person's body chemistry is different and reacts to alcohol differently.

As the blood alcohol level increases, people lose their coordination. They lose their ability to walk, talk, and see properly. They lose memory and alertness, and they can lose self-control. They might do things that would be embarrassing to them if they were sober. Some people might argue, fight, or act in a silly way. The higher the alcohol level, the greater its effects. As the chart shows, a person with high levels might vomit or lose consciousness and could even die. The dangers are especially great among young people because alcohol affects them very quickly and severely.

Notice the facts in the chart below. Some of these figures might surprise you. They highlight one of the most disastrous effects of alcohol—accidents caused by drunk drivers.

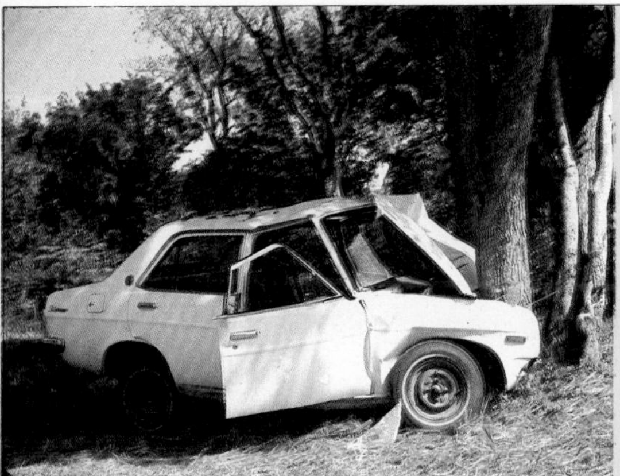

Some Facts About Drunk Driving in the United States

- About 26,000 people are killed in drunk driving accidents every year.
- Nearly 70 people are killed in drunk driving accidents every day.
- About 750,000 people suffer crippling and other serious injuries every year in drunk driving accidents.
- On an average weekend night, one out of ten drivers on the road is drunk.

- Ask students what factors affect blood alcohol level. (the size of the person, how much alcohol is consumed and how quickly, whether the stomach is empty, a person's body chemistry) • Discuss why alcohol usually affects young people more strongly and more quickly than adults. (Young people are smaller and therefore have less body fluids with which to dilute the alcohol.)
- Encourage students to name the effects of a high blood alcohol level. (loss of coordination; impaired memory, alertness, and self-control) • Ask students to name the effects of heavy alcohol consumption. (vomiting; inability to walk, talk, and see properly; loss of consciousness; sometimes death)

Using On Your Own

Risk of accidents increases at the lowest blood alcohol level—0.01 to 0.04—because coordination lessens and judgment weakens. The risk of accidents increases as the percentage of alcohol increases because coordination becomes more impaired and judgment becomes unreliable.

Thinking Skill When students analyze the blood alcohol chart, they are *interpreting information.*

Overhead Transparency Master

Use this blackline master to make a labeled overhead transparency or to make an unlabeled student worksheet. This blackline master may be reproduced from the Teacher's Resource Book.

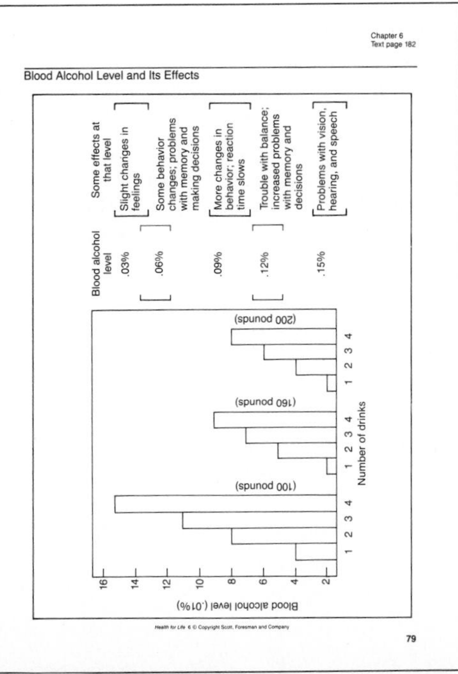

Teaching Plan

Lesson 5 continued

2 Teach

Strategies for Pages 184 and 185

• Direct students to read pages 184 and 185 to find out the long-term effects of alcohol. • Ask students why many people who abuse alcohol suffer from malnutrition. (because alcohol has little nutritional value and people who drink alcohol lose their appetites) • Encourage students to name some other long-term effects of alcohol. (cirrhosis of the liver, ulcers, brain damage, nerve damage, physical and mental dependence) • Direct students to look at the pictures on page 184 and compare the healthy liver to the damaged liver. • Ask students to describe the characteristics of alcoholics. (Alcoholics cannot control their heavy drinking. They drink so heavily and so often that drinking interferes with everyday life.) • Discuss some daily problems an alcoholic might have. (He or she might be unable to do school work, hold a job, or maintain family relationships.) • Encourage students to name some ways an alcoholic can get help. (by going to a physician or psychologist, or by becoming a member of Alcoholics Anonymous or a similar organization.)

cirrhosis (sə rō′sis), a disease of the liver that is often caused by heavy, long-term use of alcohol.

alcoholism (al′kə hô liz′əm), a disease in which a person cannot control his or her use of alcohol.

What Are the Long-Term Effects of Alcohol?

People who drink alcohol heavily over long periods of time suffer certain long-term effects. A common long-term effect of drinking alcohol is **cirrhosis,** a disease of the liver that can result in death. Notice in the picture how the diseased liver differs from the healthy liver. Alcohol can also cause brain damage, nerve damage, and ulcers—sores in the lining of the stomach. Many people who drink alcohol over a long period of time suffer from malnutrition. Although it provides Calories, alcohol contains none of the vitamins, minerals, or proteins that are needed for growth and health. In addition, many people who are long-time, heavy users of alcohol lose their appetites and do not eat nourishing meals.

Another long-term effect of drinking alcohol is physical and mental dependence. A person who develops such dependence on alcohol suffers from a progressive disease called **alcoholism.** An alcoholic cannot control his or her heavy drinking.

An alcoholic often drinks so heavily and so often that drinking interferes with everyday life. The alcoholic might be unable to do school work or hold a job. Family relationships are often ruined as alcohol becomes the most important thing in the person's life.

Healthy liver

Liver with cirrhosis

184

Teaching Options

Anecdote

Alcohol abuse is the nation's leading youth drug problem. More than half of all adolescent suicides are alcohol related.

Enrichment

If possible, invite a local representative from Alateen to visit the class and talk about the program.

Encourage interested students to find out how Alcoholics Anonymous got its start in this country and why it is still the most successful treatment program for alcoholics.

Health and Social Studies

Encourage students to discuss why age limitations exist for the purchase and consumption of alcohol. Points in the discussion should include the effects of alcohol on young people and the social and mental maturity levels of young people compared to those of adults.

Reteaching

Ask students to make a list of the long-term effects of alcohol. Help students note whether each effect harms physical health, mental health, or emotional health.

Health and Language Arts

Ask students to write a paragraph explaining how talking about a problem with people who have similar problems can help.

An alcoholic needs treatment. The disease can be controlled with proper help. However, the alcoholic must want help before he or she can be helped. A physician or a psychologist might provide counseling and treatment for the alcoholic.

One organization that helps many alcoholics stop drinking is Alcoholics Anonymous, or AA. Special branches of AA help family members of alcoholics. The branch for husbands, wives, other relatives, and friends is called Al-Anon. The branch for sons and daughters from age twelve to eighteen is Alateen, and the branch for sons and daughters who are under twelve is Alatots. The picture shows an Al-Anon meeting in session. Here, family and friends of alcoholics help each other by sharing their experiences and discussing ways to help solve their problems.

Think Back • *Study on your own with Study Guide page 327.*

1. Why does alcohol affect the body so quickly?
2. What are some immediate effects of alcohol?
3. What diseases can long-term alcohol abuse cause?
4. What can be done to help alcoholics?

Help is available for friends and families of alcoholics.

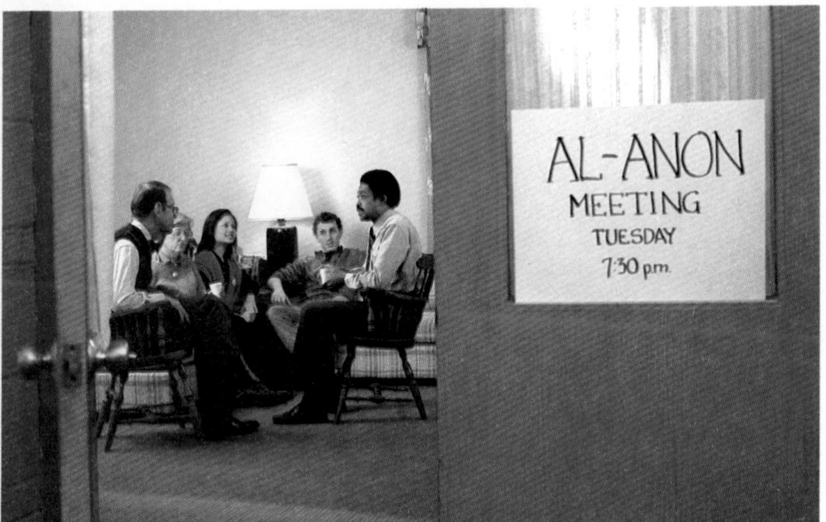

• Stress that alcholism is a treatable disease. • Ask students where the families of alcoholics can get help in coping with their relative's or friend's disease. (Al-Anon, Alateen, Alatots)

3 Assess

Expanding Student Thinking

Tell students that most experts agree that an alcoholic whose drinking has been controlled cannot have even an occasional drink. Ask students to give reasons why this is so. (Alcoholism is a disease that causes physical and mental dependence; a person could lose self-control again and begin drinking heavily.)

Thinking Skill When students tell why most experts agree that recovering alcoholics cannot have an occasional drink, they are *generalizing.*

Answers to Think Back

1. Alcohol affects the body quickly because it enters the bloodstream quickly. It is not digested.

2. Answers might include lack of coordination, shaking, lack of self-control, vomiting, an inability to see properly, and unconsciousness.

3. Long-term effects of alcohol include cirrhosis of the liver, ulcers, brain damage, nerve damage, malnutrition, and alcoholism.

4. Alcoholics can get treatment from a physician, a psychologist, or an organization such as AA.

Life Skills

Use this worksheet for practice in reading about a group that helps the families and friends of problem drinkers. This master may be reproduced from the Teacher's Resource Book and is located on page 21 of the Student's Workbook. Use with Chapter 6: pages 182–185.

Thinking Skill: **By answering questions about the passage, students are interpreting information.**

Name ____________________ Life Skills

Use with Chapter 6: pages 182–185.

Reading About Al-Anon

Read the paragraphs. Then answer the questions.

Al-Anon is a group that helps the families and friends of people who have problems with alcohol. Members of Al-Anon learn the facts about alcohol. They also come to meetings and talk about ways to help someone who drinks too much. Anyone is welcome at Al-Anon meetings. A person does not have to tell his or her name. Al-Anon does not cost anything to join.

Children and young friends of problem drinkers can belong to another group called Alateen. This group has meetings that are run by teenagers. Alateen can help young people understand the drinking problems of their parents or friends.

To find out more about Al-Anon or Alateen, contact the Al-Anon Information Service in your area.

1. What is Al-Anon? **Al-Anon is a group that helps the families and friends of problem drinkers.**
2. What do Al-Anon members do? **They learn the facts about alcohol. They also come to meetings to discuss ways to help problem drinkers.**
3. Who can come to Al-Anon meetings? **Anyone can come to Al-Anon meetings.**
4. Who can belong to Alateen? **Children and young friends of problem drinkers**
5. Who runs Alateen meetings? **Teenagers**
6. How does Alateen help its members? **It helps them to understand their parents' or friends' drinking.**

Extension Idea: **Ask students to write a paragraph about why Alateen is run by teenagers.**

81

Teaching Plan

Lesson 6 pages 186–189

Lesson Objective
Describe how tobacco affects the health of both the user and the non-user.

1 Motivate

Introducing the Lesson
Ask students what they think influences a person's decision about whether or not to smoke. Point out that increased awareness of the danger of cigarette smoking has caused the number of smokers to decrease in recent years in the United States.

2 Teach

Strategies for Pages 186 and 187
• Direct students to read page 186 to find out what happens when a cigarette is smoked. • Ask students to name the three most damaging substances in cigarette smoke. (nicotine, carbon monoxide, tars) • Ask students to describe nicotine. (a stimulant that speeds up the heart and can cause dependency) • Ask students what happens when a smoker breathes cigarette tar. (It stays in the lungs and cools to a brown, sticky mass that can cause lung cancer.)

6 How Does Tobacco Affect Health?

Every pack of cigarettes and all cigarette advertisements must carry one of the statements shown to the left. In addition, cigarettes cannot be advertised on radio or TV, and it is illegal for young people to buy cigarettes. The government has made these laws because of the dangers of tobacco.

What Happens When Cigarettes Are Smoked?

When a cigarette is puffed, smoke passes into the lungs. In this smoke is a mixture of particles, gases, and other chemicals. Almost all the harmful substances that are inhaled stay in the body. The three most damaging substances are nicotine, carbon monoxide, and tars.

Nicotine is a stimulant drug. It speeds up the heartbeat and can cause dependency.

Carbon monoxide is a poisonous gas. It replaces some of the oxygen in the blood. Then the smoker has to breathe faster to take in enough oxygen.

Tar is a yellow or brown substance with hundreds of chemicals in it. As the tars cool in the smoker's lungs, they form a brown, sticky mass. The picture demonstrates how tar accumulates in the lungs. The tar irritates the lungs and the lining of air passages. Tar in the lungs can cause lung cancer.

Did You Know?
Scientists estimate that a two-pack-a-day smoker shortens his or her life by about eight years.

What does this smoking demonstration show?

Teaching Options

Health Background

The amount of nicotine found in tobacco varies depending on the position of the leaf on the stalk, how the tobacco is treated, and where it is grown. The amount of nicotine absorbed in the body also varies depending on how much a person smokes and how deeply he or she inhales.

Enrichment

Ask students to bring in advertisements for cigarettes and smokeless tobacco. Discuss how advertisements try to convince people to use tobacco, and contrast the projected image of smoking with the actual risks of smoking.

Health and Science

Ask students to draw a picture of the lungs and label the major parts. Ask students to write a paragraph about how smoking can damage the different parts of the lung.

Reteaching

Explain to students that they are going to do an experiment that will give them an idea of what it is like to have emphysema. Instruct students to hold the nose closed with one hand. Then ask students to breathe through a cocktail straw or a plastic stir stick. Let students describe the experience. Be sure students are sitting while doing this activity. Do not prolong the activity as dizziness may result.

What Are the Long-Term Effects of Cigarette Smoking?

When a person first starts smoking cigarettes, he or she might feel sick. Sometimes the person might cough a lot or feel dizzy. If a person continues to smoke, the body develops tolerance. The person no longer feels uncomfortable. However, the person becomes dependent on the nicotine in tobacco. Dependent people feel nervous or jittery if they cannot smoke a cigarette.

Other clues that show a person has been smoking for a long time are shown in the chart. Perhaps you know someone who has been affected in one or more of these ways.

Besides causing unattractive traits and dependence on nicotine, smoking for several years can cause certain diseases. For example, long-term smoking can increase the risk of developing high blood pressure. The chances of having a heart attack or a stroke are greater in a smoker. Smoking can also cause lung cancer.

Emphysema is another disease that can be caused by cigarette smoking. In emphysema, tiny air sacs in the lungs are weakened and destroyed. People with this disease have trouble breathing. Sometimes they have to carry a supply of oxygen with them wherever they go. Emphysema cannot be cured.

Chronic bronchitis is still another disease caused by cigarette smoking. People with chronic bronchitis develop irritating coughs and have difficulty breathing.

On Your Own
Write a paragraph discussing why the following advice on smoking is a healthy idea: "The best tip is not to start."

Clues that a Person Is a Smoker

- The tars in cigarette smoke can stain a smoker's teeth.
- The odor of stale smoke clings to a smoker's clothes.
- A smoker's fingertips can be stained yellow or brown from holding cigarettes.
- A smoker might have bad breath.
- A smoker might develop a brown or black fur-like coating on the tongue.

• Discuss the effect of breathing in carbon monoxide. (It replaces oxygen that the body needs and makes it necessary for the smoker to breathe faster.) • Direct students' attention to the lung demonstration shown in the picture. Ask them to state what the brown or yellow stains represent. (tars) • Direct students to read page 187 to find out the long-term effects of smoking. • Encourage students to tell why a person might be jittery when he or she cannot smoke. (The person is probably dependent on tobacco.) • Encourage students to name some long-term risks of smoking. (heart disease, lung cancer, emphysema, chronic bronchitis) Tell students that smokers develop a smoker's cough because the body is trying to get rid of mucus and other material collecting in the lungs. Smoking destroys lung tissue, so the lungs lose much of their natural ability to clean themselves.

Using On Your Own
Encourage students to use supporting evidence from the lesson in writing the paragraph.
Thinking Skills When students tell why a person should not start smoking, they are *interpreting information* and *generalizing*.

Health and Art
Use this worksheet for practice in drawing advertisements against smoking. This master may be reproduced from the Teacher's Resource Book and is located on page 24 of the Student's Workbook. Use with Chapter 6: pages 186–189.

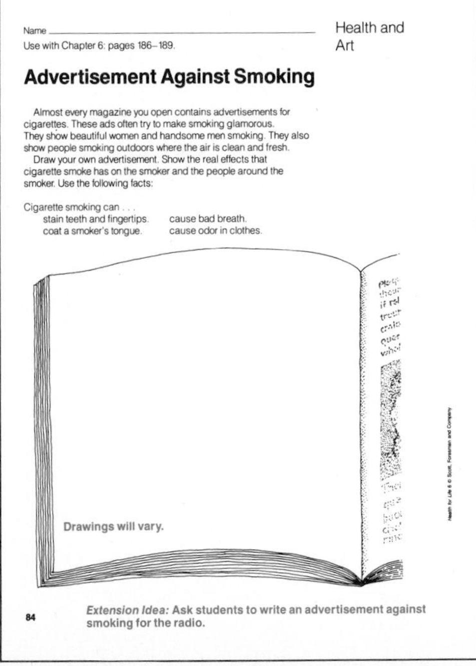

Name ____________________ Health and Art
Use with Chapter 6: pages 186–189.

Advertisement Against Smoking

Almost every magazine you open contains advertisements for cigarettes. These ads often try to make smoking glamorous. They show beautiful women and handsome men smoking. They also show people smoking outdoors where the air is clean and fresh.

Draw your own advertisement. Show the real effects that cigarette smoke has on the smoker and the people around the smoker. Use the following facts:

Cigarette smoking can . . .
stain teeth and fingertips. cause bad breath.
coat a smoker's tongue. cause odor in clothes.

Drawings will vary.

84

Extension Idea: Ask students to write an advertisement against smoking for the radio.

Teaching Plan

Lesson 6 continued

2 Teach

Strategies for Pages 188 and 189

• Direct students to read page 188 to find out how second-hand smoke affects health. • Ask students why sidestream smoke is more dangerous than mainstream smoke. (Sidestream smoke contains twice as much tar and nicotine and five times as much carbon monoxide as mainstream smoke.) • Discuss why many communities and businesses are putting up signs prohibiting smoking. (to protect nonsmokers, especially those with asthema, allergies, and lung diseases) • Ask students if they agree that public places should have no-smoking areas, and if some public places should not allow any smoking. • Direct students to read page 189 to find out how smokeless tobacco affects health. • Ask students what snuff is made of. (ground tobacco leaves and stems) • Ask students how smokeless tobacco can harm health. (can lead to mouth and throat cancer, gum diseases, and high blood pressure)

How Does Second-Hand Smoke Affect Health?

Today, more and more people say, "Yes, I *do* mind if you smoke." Being in the same room with a smoker exposes nonsmokers to second-hand smoke. Second-hand smoke comes from someone else's cigarette.

Second-hand smoke is of two kinds and has two sources. Sidestream smoke comes from the end of a burning cigarette. Mainstream smoke is exhaled by the smoker. Sidestream smoke is more dangerous than mainstream smoke. Sidestream smoke contains twice as much tar and nicotine and five times as much carbon monoxide as mainstream smoke does. Second-hand smoke can be especially dangerous for people who have allergies, asthma, other lung diseases, or heart disease.

More and more restaurants and public places have sections for nonsmokers. Some communities have passed laws requiring this. Also, an increasing number of signs are appearing in stores and other places suggesting that people not smoke there. Where have you seen signs like the one shown below?

Why are non-smoking areas important to public health?

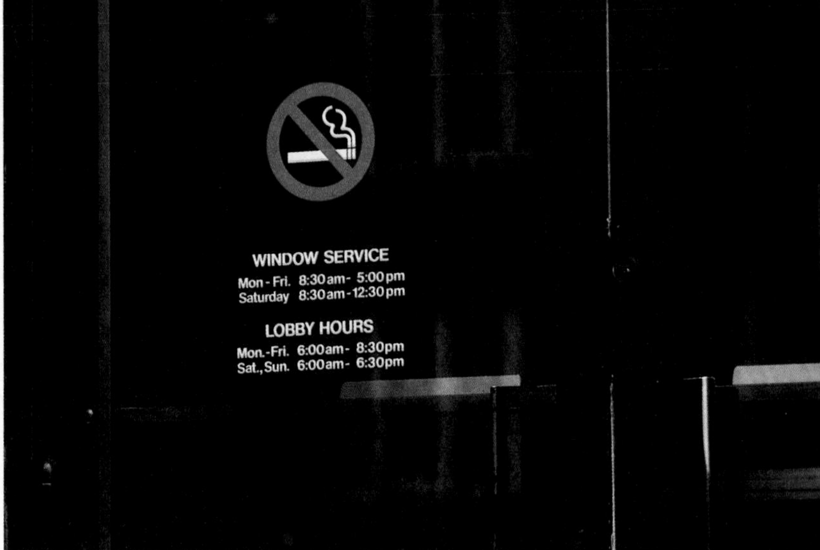

Teaching Options

Anecdote

Within sixty seconds of inhaling cigarette smoke, the blood vessels constrict, the heart pumps harder, and the temperature of the fingers and toes drops as much as 10° F. ("Sneaky Addiction." *Current Health.* January 1982, page 22.)

Enrichment

Encourage interested students to use magazine and newspaper articles to research the controversy and legal battles that have surrounded the movement toward designating nonsmoking areas.

Health and Art

Direct students to make posters that encourage other students not to start smoking. Students can draw their posters, use pictures from newspapers and magazines, or combine methods.

Reteaching

Direct students to draw or write about the effects smoking has on a person's appearance and health. Ask students to present their essays or drawings to the class.

How Does Smokeless Tobacco Affect Health?

In addition to being smoked, tobacco is sometimes used in the form of chewing tobacco and snuff. Chewing tobacco is coarsely ground tobacco leaves. Snuff is a powder made from grinding tobacco leaves and stems. It is usually sniffed through the nose.

Many young people mistakenly believe that smokeless tobacco is safe to use. Using chewing tobacco or snuff, like cigarette smoking, is very harmful to a person's health. Cancers of the mouth and throat, gum diseases, high blood pressure, and stomach trouble can quickly develop among people who use smokeless tobacco. Users also have bad breath and discolored teeth. What message does the poster give about smokeless tobacco?

Think Back • *Study on your own with Study Guide page 327.*

1. What are the three main harmful substances in cigarette smoke?
2. How do these substances affect the body?
3. What health hazards do smokers risk?
4. How is smoking dangerous to nonsmokers?

What is the message here?

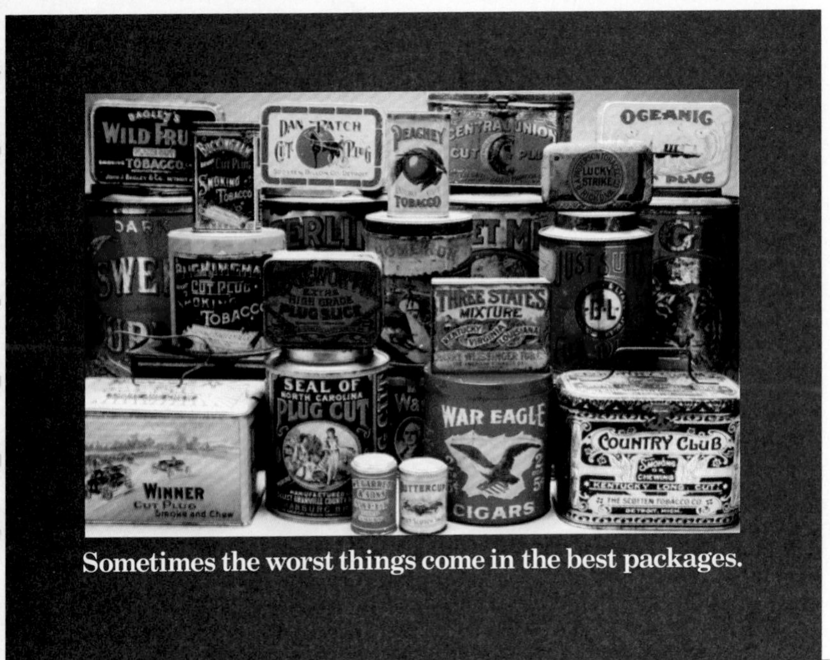

Sometimes the worst things come in the best packages.

3 Assess

Expanding Student Thinking

Explain to students that muscles need oxygen to work. When a person is exercising, the muscles need an increased supply of oxygen to do the extra work. Then ask students what effects cigarettes might have on athletic performance. (Students might answer that since carbon monoxide replaces needed oxygen, a smoker has to breathe faster and the heart has to beat more often to supply oxygen to the body. During exercise, the average smoker will be short of breath and have less endurance than a nonsmoker.)

Thinking Skills When students explain the effects of smoking on athletic performance, they are *interpreting information* and *drawing conclusions*.

Answers to Think Back

1. The three main harmful substances in tobacco are nicotine, carbon monoxide, and tars.

2. Nicotine speeds up the heart and can cause dependency. Carbon monoxide replaces oxygen in the blood. Tars cause lung cancer.

3. Smokers risk an increased chance of heart disease, stroke, lung cancer, emphysema, and chronic bronchitis.

4. Nonsmokers often breathe in second-hand smoke, which contains nicotine, carbon monoxide, and tars.

Activity Plan

Health Activities Workshop pages 190–191

Materials
Activity 3 newspaper and magazine clippings about accidents

Activity 1 Strategies
You might want to direct students to compare the cost of cigarettes at a drug store, a gas station, and in a vending machine. Students could calculate costs using the average price. Encourage students to think about the lifetime cost of smoking.
Thinking Skills When they investigate the cost of cigarette smoking and compute the amount of money a smoker spends, students are *collecting* and *interpreting information.*

Activity 2 Strategies
If possible, suggest other books about the history of smoking that are available in your school library. Encourage students to give oral reports to the class.
Thinking Skills When students investigate how smoking started and report on the topic, they are *collecting information* and *communicating.*

Activity 3 Strategies
You might want students to work in groups for this activity. Try to provide enough newspaper clippings so that each student or group of students has several. Ask each student or group to summarize the articles in a report to the class.
Thinking Skills When students read clippings about accidents to find out how many result from use of alcohol, they are *interpreting information* and *classifying.*

Activity 4 Strategies
The information on over-the-counter drugs is required through regulations developed by the Food and Drug Administration.
Thinking Skill When students answer questions about the information on over-the-counter medicine, they are *interpreting information.*

Health Activities Workshop

Learning More About the Harmful Effects of Drugs

1. Investigate the cost of smoking cigarettes. Find out what one pack of a certain brand costs. Suppose a person smokes a pack a day. How much money will he or she spend in a week? in a year?

2. Investigate and make a report on the topic "How Did Smoking Start?" A helpful book that might be in the library is *Smoking and You* by Arnold Madison.

3. Bring in clippings from the newspaper about accidents during a one-week period. Make a special note of articles that mention accidents as a result of the use of alcohol by car drivers or pedestrians.

4. Look at the information on the bottle of aspirin shown here. Then answer these questions.

- What is the adult dose?
- What cautions must be taken in the use of this medicine?

5. Design and make a poster that might prevent someone your age from using drugs. Be sure to include both a statement and a picture to get your message across.

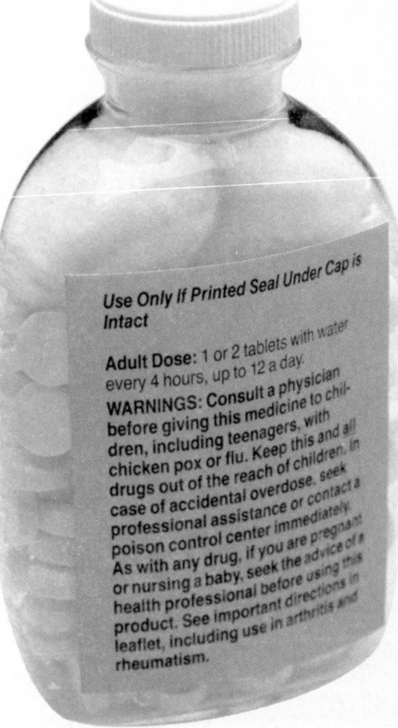

Use Only If Printed Seal Under Cap is Intact
Adult Dose: 1 or 2 tablets with water every 4 hours, up to 12 a day.
WARNINGS: Consult a physician before giving this medicine to children, including teenagers, with chicken pox or flu. Keep this and all drugs out of the reach of children. In case of accidental overdose, seek professional assistance or contact a poison control center immediately. As with any drug, if you are pregnant or nursing a baby, seek the advice of a health professional before using this product. See important directions in leaflet, including use in arthritis and rheumatism.

190

Looking at Careers

6. Many people who have a health-related job work in factories where medicines are made. **Pharmaceutical plant workers** help make and package most of the medicines found in stores. These workers perform many different jobs. Some people mix substances following careful procedures and directions to produce tablets, capsules, or solutions. Others might weigh pills to make sure they include the right amount of medicine. Some workers operate machines that fill bottles of liquid medicine.

Other pharmaceutical plant workers work in the maintenance department. They repair equipment and keep the plant clean. Workers in the shipping department are responsible for delivering the medicines to hospitals and stores on time.

Chemists also work at a pharmaceutical plant. Some chemists are involved with research. They try to find ways to improve medicines or develop new ones. Other chemists, called quality control chemists, make sure the medicine made in the plant is being produced properly.

Use an encyclopedia or science book to find out what other kinds of chemists do. Describe your findings in a paragraph or two.

For more information write to the Pharmaceutical Manufacturing Association, 1155 Fifteenth St. N.W., Washington, DC 20005.

Activity 5 Strategies

You might want students to work in small groups for this activity. Possible themes include the support of friends or the value of hobbies. Students could draw or use pictures from magazines and newspapers.

Thinking Skills When students design and make a poster to discourage people from using drugs, they are *suggesting alternatives* and *communicating*.

Activity 6 Strategies

Discuss the variety of jobs available in a pharmaceutical plant. Direct interested students to investigate the amount of education needed for different positions in a plant. The roles of chemists outside the pharmaceutical field would include a variety of jobs. Students might mention research in the fields of geology, genetics, biology, and specific kinds of companies that employ chemists, such as paint companies.

Thinking Skills When students investigate other roles of chemists and write for information about jobs in a pharmaceutical plant, they are *communicating* and *collecting information*.

Teaching Plan

Lesson 7 pages 192–193

Lesson Objective

Identify factors that contribute to alcohol, tobacco, marijuana, and other drug abuse. Describe the kind of information that would help someone decide not to abuse drugs, including knowing how to resist peer pressure.

1 Motivate

Introducing the Lesson

Ask students whether they were ever pressured by their peers to do something they did not want to do. Discuss ways to say no to peer pressure.

2 Teach

Strategies for Pages 192 and 193

• Direct students to read page 192 to learn how to resist pressure from others to use drugs. • Encourage a discussion of how people are sometimes pressured, however subtly, to do something they know is dangerous or wrong. • Discuss ways to say no to pressure from a friend. (just say no; say you have something else to do; walk away) • Discuss with students the decision-making process diagrammed on page 193.

7 How Can People Make Healthy Decisions About Drugs?

Many people make decisions not to abuse drugs. Such people know the harmful effects certain drugs have on those who misuse or abuse them. These people also realize that certain drugs are illegal.

Even though people know the dangers of drug abuse, sometimes they are tempted to try a drug because of the influence of a friend. These people might be afraid they will lose the friend if they say no. If this should ever happen to you, ask yourself if this person really is a friend. Would a true friend want you to do something that could harm you?

The best way to refuse drugs is to learn to say no. You could just say "No, thanks," or say you have something else to do. If the person continues to pressure you, you could just walk away. You do not have to let people tease or push you into something you do not want to do.

Another way to resist pressure to abuse drugs is to keep busy with activities you enjoy doing. You might want to develop a skill, such as writing or painting. You could try participating in team sports, or activities such as swimming and bicycling. You could develop a hobby such as collecting stamps or coins. The pictures suggest some activities you might enjoy.

If you are in a situation where you need to make a decision about drugs, follow the five steps to making healthy decisions. The following example shows how a healthy decision about drugs might be made.

Barbara had a week to finish a report comparing two books. She was telling her friend Kathy that she had only read one book and might have to stay up late each night to finish the report. Kathy offered her some amphetamine pills to help her stay awake. Barbara used a decision chart like the one on the next page and made a wise decision not to use the drug. Read the chart to find out how she arrived at her decision.

People who enjoy hobbies or other activities usually have no desire to try drugs.

Teaching Options

Health Background

Wise decisions about drugs may involve consideration of parents' wishes, religious beliefs, scientific facts, the opinions of experts, and personal goals such as maturation, social responsibility, and self-control. Self respect is an effective deterrent to drug misuse and drug abuse. Students who want to avoid drug misuse and drug abuse should examine alternative activities that satisfy their individual needs.

Enrichment

Suggest that a group of students produce a skit that shows how peer pressure can be a powerful factor in a person's decision about drugs. The skit should include ways to resist this pressure.

Health and Art

Suggest that students make posters showing different ways of saying *No* to drugs. Students might also make posters that celebrate the positive aspects of a drug-free life.

Reteaching

Encourage students to make a decision-making diagram like the one in the text, but based on a different situation involving drugs.

Barbara was able to make the right decision because she knew the dangers of drug abuse. She also knew how to make decisions through a five-step process. Barbara found out she could resist pressure from a friend and that drugs are not a solution to a problem.

Think Back • *Study on your own with Study Guide page 327.*

1. What might influence a person to abuse drugs?
2. What information about drugs helps people decide not to abuse them?
3. What are some ways to resist pressure from friends to abuse drugs?

Barbara's Decision-Making Chart

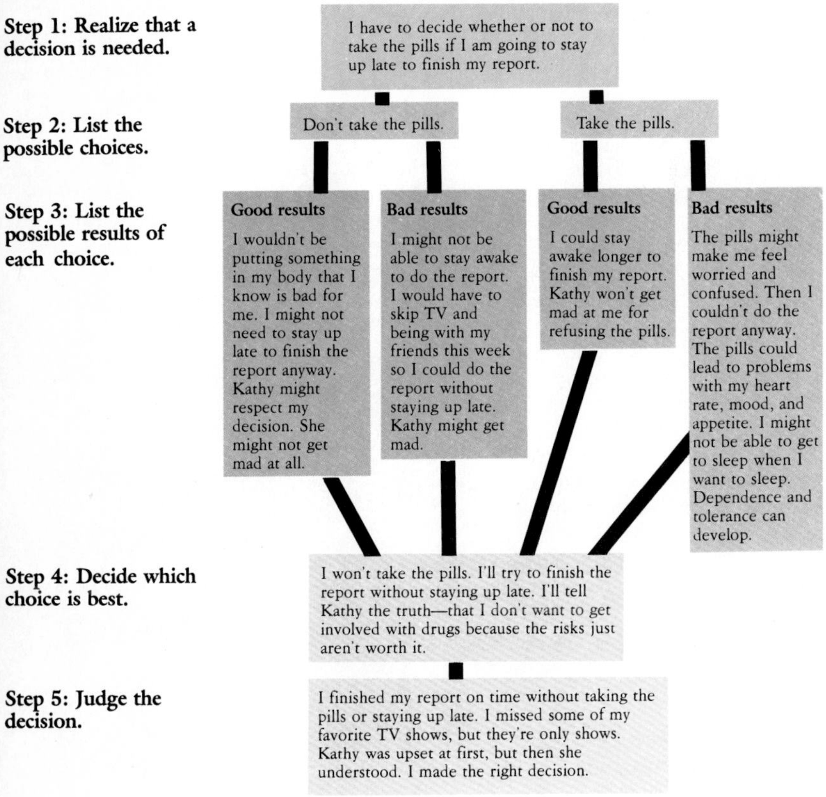

Step 1: Realize that a decision is needed.

I have to decide whether or not to take the pills if I am going to stay up late to finish my report.

Step 2: List the possible choices.

Don't take the pills. | Take the pills.

Step 3: List the possible results of each choice.

Don't take the pills: Good results	Don't take the pills: Bad results	Take the pills: Good results	Take the pills: Bad results
I wouldn't be putting something in my body that I know is bad for me. I might not need to stay up late to finish the report anyway. Kathy might respect my decision. She might not get mad at all.	I might not be able to stay awake to do the report. I would have to skip TV and being with my friends this week so I could do the report without staying up late. Kathy might get mad.	I could stay awake longer to finish my report. Kathy won't get mad at me for refusing the pills.	The pills might make me feel worried and confused. Then I couldn't do the report anyway. The pills could lead to problems with my heart rate, mood, and appetite. I might not be able to get to sleep when I want to sleep. Dependence and tolerance can develop.

Step 4: Decide which choice is best.

I won't take the pills. I'll try to finish the report without staying up late. I'll tell Kathy the truth—that I don't want to get involved with drugs because the risks just aren't worth it.

Step 5: Judge the decision.

I finished my report on time without taking the pills or staying up late. I missed some of my favorite TV shows, but they're only shows. Kathy was upset at first, but then she understood. I made the right decision.

• Ask students to name the five steps to making a wise decision about drugs. (Students should name the steps listed on page 193.) • Go through the example on page 193.

3 Assess

Expanding Student Thinking
Ask students why they think people sometimes try to pressure others into doing the same things they do, such as taking a drug or acting in a particular way; and why giving in to peer pressure can lead to unwise decisions. (Sometimes the person may feel more like "part of the crowd" if he or she knows that others are participating in similar activities. Peer pressure can lead to unwise decisions because it can keep people from deciding what is best for them as individuals.)

Thinking Skill Students are *drawing conclusions.*

Answers to Think Back

1. Peer pressure might influence a person to abuse drugs.

2. Information about the harmful effects of drugs, the illegality of drugs, how to say no to drugs, and how to enjoy life without drugs helps people decide not to abuse drugs.

3. Answers include learning to say no, walking away, keeping busy with other activities, and using the decision-making process.

Teaching Plan

Health Focus page 194

Discussion

Make sure that students understand that teens must be drug—and alcohol-free in order to join Kids Saving Kids. Ask students why Kids Saving Kids was formed. (to reach young people before they get the wrong idea that drugs are OK; to provide young people with an alternative group to join) Encourage students to tell how members of Kids Saving Kids might reach an audience. (through teaching, performing skits, or leading discussions) Ask students to create their own skits about why using drugs is not a wise thing to do.

Answers to Talk About It

1. The teens in Kids Saving Kids communicate accurate information about drugs and provide an alternative group for young people.
Thinking Skill Students are *recalling information.*
2. Students might suggest skits about marijuana use, tobacco use, or other forms of drug misuse or abuse.
Thinking Skill Students are *suggesting alternatives.*

Health Focus

Kids Saving Kids

"We think we can help young people live drug-free lives," says sixteen-year-old Peter True about the Kids Saving Kids program. Peter is actively involved in this program, in which high-school students talk to fifth- and sixth-graders about the dangers of drug and alcohol abuse. Peter is one of about thirty teens in the Hempfield School District in Pennsylvania who serve as positive role models.

The first requirement to join Kids Saving Kids is to be able to stand up and say, "I am drug and alcohol free." Then the teens go through a two-day training session and correctly answer 138 questions about drugs and how they affect the body. Once accepted, the teens are further trained by someone from the National Federation of Parents for Drug Free Youth.

Although becoming part of Kids Saving Kids involves work, the teens use fun to reach their audience. The teens perform skits to get their point across. One skit is called "Keggers." In this skit some teens want to have a beer party. Others want to be alert for skiing the next day. The "keggers" get so sick they cannot enjoy the skiing. Other skits are about tobacco, marijuana, and other drugs.

Throughout the skits, the teens include facts about the harm caused by drugs. "The point at the end is that 'Drugs are stupid, drugs are bad,'" says Peter. Then each teen leads a small group in a discussion.

"The most important thing is to reach young people before they get the wrong idea that drugs are OK," says Peter. "The biggest problem is pressure from friends and others in school," he adds. "The teens in Kids Saving Kids provide an alternative group for the young people to turn to."

Talk About It

1. What do the teens in Kids Saving Kids do to help prevent drug abuse?
2. Besides the one mentioned above, what other situation would make a good skit for the Kids Saving Kids program?

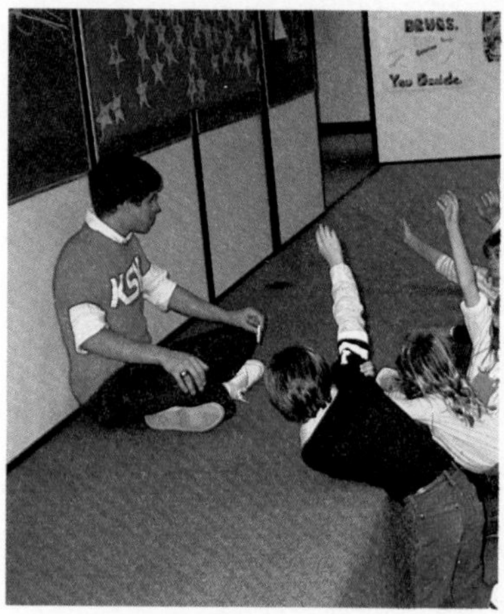

194

Teaching Options

Vocabulary

Use this worksheet for practice in reviewing chapter vocabulary words. This master may be reproduced from the Teacher's Resource Book and is located on page 22 of the Student's Workbook. Use with Chapter 6: pages 166–197.

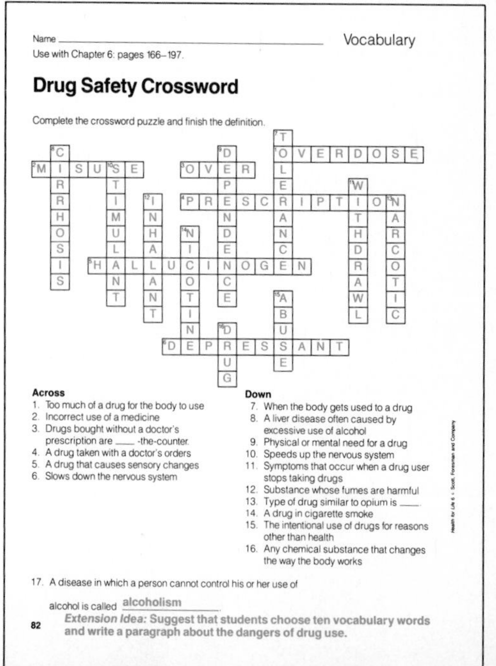

Name ______________________ Vocabulary

Use with Chapter 6: pages 166–197.

Drug Safety Crossword

Complete the crossword puzzle and finish the definition.

Across: 1 OVERDOSE, 2 MISUSE, 3 OVER, 4 PRESCRIPTION, 5 HALLUCINOGEN, 6 DEPRESSANT
Down: 7 TOLERANCE, 8 CIRRHOSIS, 9 DEPENDENCE, 10 STIMULANT, 11 WITHDRAWAL, 12 INHALANT, 13 NARCOTIC, 14 NICOTINE, 15 ABUSE, 16 DRUG

Across
1. Too much of a drug for the body to use
2. Incorrect use of a medicine
3. Drugs bought without a doctor's prescription are ____ -the-counter.
4. A drug taken with a doctor's orders
5. A drug that causes sensory changes
6. Slows down the nervous system

Down
7. When the body gets used to a drug
8. A liver disease often caused by excessive use of alcohol
9. Physical or mental need for a drug
10. Speeds up the nervous system
11. Symptoms that occur when a drug user stops taking drugs
12. Substance whose fumes are harmful
13. Type of drug similar to opium is ____.
14. A drug in cigarette smoke
15. The intentional use of drugs for reasons other than health
16. Any chemical substance that changes the way the body works

17. A disease in which a person cannot control his or her use of alcohol is called alcoholism.

82

Extension Idea: **Suggest that students choose ten vocabulary words and write a paragraph about the dangers of drug use.**

Health at Home

Checking the Home for Drug Safety

Your parents and other family members are likely to be very interested in what you have learned about drugs at school. Think over some of the ideas you might share with them. What can you tell them about drugs?

You might also join some family members at home in a medicine safety check. Here are some things to look for in your home.

- Is old medicine thrown away? If not, it should be. Old medicine can lose strength or get stronger. Check the expiration date on the label. If the date has expired, flush the medicine down the toilet. Throw empty containers in the garbage. If you are not sure if a medicine is still fresh, you could ask a pharmacist.
- Is medicine kept where small children cannot get it? Is it in child-proof containers? Is it in a locked cabinet?
- Do members of the family avoid calling any medicine "candy"? Young children might look for the "candy" and take dangerous doses of medicine.

Reading at Home

Drug Use and Drug Abuse by Geraldine Woods. Watts, 1979. Find out the medical uses of various drugs and the effects of drug abuse.

Over-the-Counter Drugs by Ann E. Weiss. Watts, 1984. Learn about how over-the-counter drugs can be helpful and harmful.

195

Health at Home

page 195

Strategies

Direct students to read page 197. Ask students what information about drugs a young person might want to discuss with parents. Make sure students know that medicines should be well marked and kept separate from other household chemicals. Explain that when a person is discarding old medicines, he or she should make sure that contents are flushed down the toilet and containers are rinsed before they are thrown away.

More Reading at Home

Drug Use and Drug Abuse. (Grades 4–6)

Over-the-Counter Drugs. (Grades 6–8)

Hyde, Margaret O. *Know About Smoking.* McGraw-Hill, 1983. By acting out situations, students learn how to refuse a cigarette or ask someone nearby to quit smoking in their presence. (Grades 4–6)

Study and Review

Use this worksheet for practice in reviewing drugs and their harmful effects on the body. This master may be reproduced from the Teacher's Resource Book and is located on page 23 of the Student's Workbook. Use with Chapter 6: pages 166–197.

Name ____________________ Study and Review

Use with Chapter 6: pages 166–197.

Making a Drug Abuse Chart

Joe is presenting a science fair project on drug abuse. He wants to make a chart showing reasons not to abuse drugs. The chart will show the harmful effects these drugs have on the body. Complete Joe's chart below.

Drug Abuse Chart

Type of Drug	Examples	Harmful Effects on the Body
1. Stimulant	Coffee; tea; cola drinks; cocaine	2. Nervousness; anxiety; sleeplessness; violence; death
Depressant	3. Alcohol; tranquilizers; barbiturates	4. Confusion; staggering; slurred speech; coma; death
5. Narcotic	Morphine; codeine; heroin	6. Malnutrition; physical dependence; infections
7. Hallucinogen	LSD; PCP	8. Unpredictable effects; coma; death; mental problems
9. Inhalant	10. Airplane glue; lighter fluid gasoline	Damage to nose, throat, lungs, brain, liver, and kidney; death

Extension Idea: **Ask students to design a poster showing ways to say no to drug use.**

83

Review Plan

Chapter 6 Review

pages 196–197

Answers to Reviewing Lesson Objectives

Use this section for guided study or for oral review. Objective numbers match lesson numbers.

1. Drugs are chemicals that cause changes in the way the body works. Products might include some teas, coffees, and soft drinks; cigarettes; and alcoholic beverages.

2. The guidelines should include some of those listed on page 173.

3. The harmful effects of abusing drugs are listed on pages 176–179.

4. Answers should refer to the dangerous effects of marijuana on the respiratory system, circulatory system, on growth, and on driving skills.

5. Short-term effects include lack of coordination, lack of self-control, vomiting, and unconsciousness. Long-term effects include problems with relationships at home, work, and school; and an increased risk of health problems such as brain and nerve damage, cirrhosis, ulcers, and malnutrition. Abusers can get help from a physician, a psychologist, or an organization such as Alcoholics Anonymous.

6. Users and nonusers breathe in tobacco smoke, which can lead to heart disease, lung cancer, emphysema, and chronic bronchitis.

7. Following the suggestion of a friend, rather than risking making the friend angry, is one reason for drug abuse. Information about the harmful effects of drugs, the illegality of drugs, how to say no to drugs, how to enjoy life without drugs, and how to use the five-step decision-making process would help someone decide not to abuse drugs. Ways to resist pressure to use drugs include learning to say no, walking away, keeping busy with activities, and using the decision-making process.

Answers to Checking Health Vocabulary

Use the vocabulary check as a review or as a test.

1. l	**7.** f	**13.** c
2. m	**8.** n	**14.** e
3. o	**9.** h	**15.** a
4. p	**10.** d	**16.** b
5. g	**11.** j	
6. k	**12.** i	

Chapter 6 Review

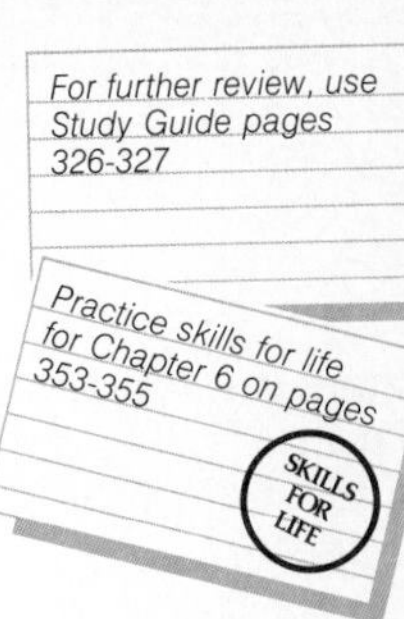

For further review, use Study Guide pages 326-327
Practice skills for life for Chapter 6 on pages 353-355
SKILLS FOR LIFE

Reviewing Lesson Objectives

1. Explain what drugs are, and list some common products that contain drugs. (pages 168–169)
2. List the guidelines for using medicines safely. (pages 170–173)
3. State the harmful effects of abusing each major kind of drug. (pages 174–179)
4. State the harmful effects of marijuana. (pages 180–181)
5. Describe the short- and long-term effects of alcohol abuse. Tell where alcohol abusers can get help. (pages 182–185)
6. Explain how tobacco can harm the health of users and nonusers. (pages 186–189)
7. Identify factors that contribute to alcohol, tobacco, marijuana, and other drug use. Describe some ways to resist pressure to abuse drugs. (pages 192–193)

Checking Health Vocabulary

Number your paper from 1–16. Match each definition in Column I with the correct word or words in Column II.

Column I

1. an amount of a drug that is too large for the body to use
2. a drug that can be used only with a doctor's order
3. a condition in which the body gets used to a drug
4. the symptoms that occur when a person who is physically dependent on a drug stops taking it
5. the incorrect use of medicine in a way that could harm health
6. a drug that can be purchased without a doctor's order
7. the intentional use of drugs for reasons other than health
8. a drug that speeds up the work of the nervous system
9. a drug that causes changes in the senses, often making a person see, hear, or feel things that are not really there
10. a drug that slows down the work of the nervous system
11. a drug made from opium or opiumlike substances
12. a substance that gives off fumes, which could produce druglike effects when breathed deeply into the body
13. the physical or mental need for a drug
14. any chemical substance that causes changes in a person's emotions, behavior, or the way the body works
15. a disease in which a person cannot control his or her use of alcohol
16. a disease of the liver that is often caused by heavy, long-term use of alcohol

Column II

a. alcoholism
b. cirrhosis
c. dependence
d. depressant
e. drug
f. drug abuse
g. drug misuse
h. hallucinogen
i. inhalant
j. narcotic
k. over-the-counter medicine
l. overdose
m. prescription medicine
n. stimulant
o. tolerance
p. withdrawal

196

Chapter 6 Tests Use Test A or Test B to assess students' mastery of the health concepts in Chapter 6. These tests are located on pages 49–56 in the Test Book.

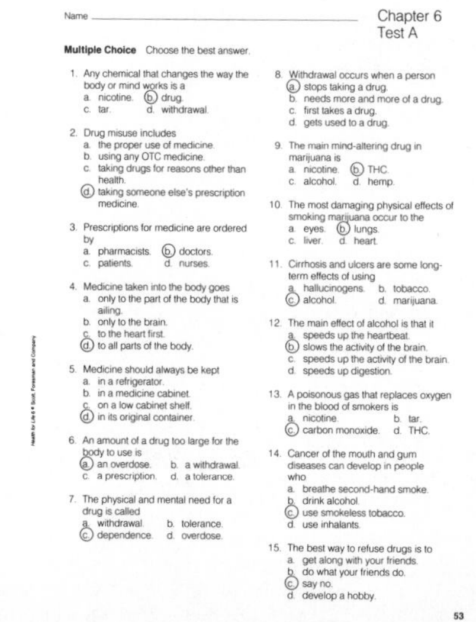

Name ______________________ Chapter 6 Test A

Multiple Choice Choose the best answer.

1. Any chemical that changes the way the body or mind works is a
   a. nicotine. (b.) drug. c. tar. d. withdrawal.
2. Drug misuse includes
   a. the proper use of medicine.
   b. using any OTC medicine.
   c. taking drugs for reasons other than health.
   (d.) taking someone else's prescription medicine.
3. Prescriptions for medicine are ordered by
   a. pharmacists. (b.) doctors. c. patients. d. nurses.
4. Medicine taken into the body goes
   a. only to the part of the body that is ailing.
   b. only to the brain.
   c. to the heart first.
   (d.) to all parts of the body.
5. Medicine should always be kept
   a. in a refrigerator.
   b. in a medicine cabinet.
   c. on a low cabinet shelf.
   (d.) in its original container.
6. An amount of a drug too large for the body to use is
   (a.) an overdose. b. a withdrawal. c. a prescription. d. a tolerance.
7. The physical and mental need for a drug is called
   a. withdrawal. b. tolerance. (c.) dependence. d. overdose.
8. Withdrawal occurs when a person
   (a.) stops taking a drug.
   b. needs more and more of a drug.
   c. first takes a drug.
   d. gets used to a drug.
9. The main mind-altering drug in marijuana is
   a. nicotine. (b.) THC. c. alcohol. d. hemp.
10. The most damaging physical effects of smoking marijuana occur to the
    a. eyes. (b.) lungs. c. liver. d. heart.
11. Cirrhosis and ulcers are some long-term effects of using
    a. hallucinogens. b. tobacco. (c.) alcohol. d. marijuana.
12. The main effect of alcohol is that it
    a. speeds up the heartbeat.
    (b.) slows the activity of the brain.
    c. speeds up the activity of the brain.
    d. speeds up digestion.
13. A poisonous gas that replaces oxygen in the blood of smokers is
    a. nicotine. b. tar. (c.) carbon monoxide. d. THC.
14. Cancer of the mouth and gum diseases can develop in people who
    a. breathe second-hand smoke.
    b. drink alcohol.
    (c.) use smokeless tobacco.
    d. use inhalants.
15. The best way to refuse drugs is to
    a. get along with your friends.
    b. do what your friends do.
    (c.) say no.
    d. develop a hobby.

Health for Life 6 © Scott, Foresman and Company

53

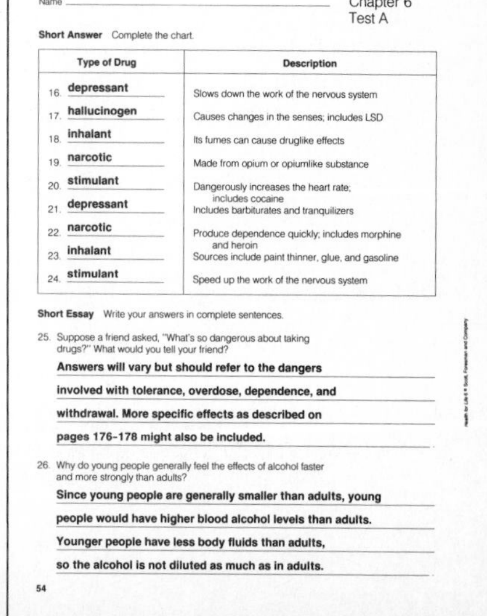

Name ______________________ Chapter 6 Test A

Short Answer Complete the chart.

Type of Drug	Description
16. **depressant**	Slows down the work of the nervous system
17. **hallucinogen**	Causes changes in the senses; includes LSD
18. **inhalant**	Its fumes can cause druglike effects
19. **narcotic**	Made from opium or opiumlike substance
20. **stimulant**	Dangerously increases the heart rate; includes cocaine
21. **depressant**	Includes barbiturates and tranquilizers
22. **narcotic**	Produce dependence quickly; includes morphine and heroin
23. **inhalant**	Sources include paint thinner, glue, and gasoline
24. **stimulant**	Speed up the work of the nervous system

Short Essay Write your answers in complete sentences.

25. Suppose a friend asked, "What's so dangerous about taking drugs?" What would you tell your friend?
    Answers will vary but should refer to the dangers involved with tolerance, overdose, dependence, and withdrawal. More specific effects as described on pages 176-178 might also be included.
26. Why do young people generally feel the effects of alcohol faster and more strongly than adults?
    Since young people are generally smaller than adults, young people would have higher blood alcohol levels than adults. Younger people have less body fluids than adults, so the alcohol is not diluted as much as in adults.

Health for Life 6 © Scott, Foresman and Company

54

Reviewing Health Ideas

Number your paper from 1–15. Next to each number write the word or words that best complete the sentence.

1. Some teas, coffees, and soft drinks contain a mild drug called ____.
2. Medicine that enters the body is carried by ____ to all parts of the body.
3. The name of a doctor, pharmacy, and patient would be found on a ____ medicine label.
4. Taking medicine prescribed for someone else is an example of drug ____.
5. Tolerance for a drug can lead a person to take an ____ of the drug.
6. A person who is ____ dependent on a drug *thinks* he or she needs it.
7. Two strong stimulants are amphetamines and ____.
8. Tranquilizers and barbiturates belong to the group of drugs called ____.
9. Inhalants can cause death by stopping the ____ or breathing.
10. The use of marijuana can lead to ____ cancer.
11. Studies show that the use of marijuana might decrease the levels of certain ____ during puberty.
12. Cirrhosis and ulcers are some long-term effects of abusing ____.
13. Carbon monoxide from tobacco smoke replaces ____ in the blood.
14. Gum diseases and cancers of the mouth and throat can develop from using ____ tobacco.
15. The best way to refuse drugs is to learn to say ____.

Understanding Health Ideas

Number your paper from 16–25. Next to each number write the word or words that best answer the question.

16. What are three kinds of information found on OTC medicine labels?
17. How do stimulants generally affect the body?
18. What depressant drugs are especially dangerous because they produce quick dependence and severe withdrawal symptoms?
19. What is the main mind-altering chemical in marijuana?
20. How long can the THC from one marijuana cigarette stay in the body?
21. What factors might influence a person to abuse drugs?
22. What is a blood alcohol level?
23. What is Alcoholics Anonymous?
24. What are the three most damaging substances in cigarette smoke?
25. What diseases can long-term smoking help cause?

Thinking Critically

Write the answers on your paper. Use complete sentences.

1. Suppose you have an earache. You remember that your father had an earache a month ago, and the doctor gave him a prescription medicine. Since you know where this medicine is, should you take it? Explain your answer.
2. Suppose you see a friend smoking marijuana. You advise your friend not to use the substance but he or she replies, "Why not? What's wrong with it?" What would you tell your friend?

Cooperative Learning Use the STAD Format described on page T24 to have four- to five-member teams study Chapter 6 Review together before completing Chapter 6 Test.

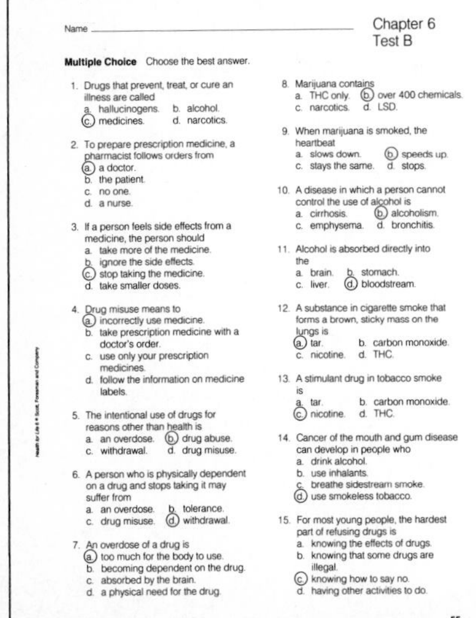

Name ____ Chapter 6 Test B

Multiple Choice Choose the best answer.

1. Drugs that prevent, treat, or cure an illness are called
   a. hallucinogens. b. alcohol. (c.) medicines. d. narcotics.
2. To prepare prescription medicine, a pharmacist follows orders from
   (a.) a doctor. b. the patient. c. no one. d. a nurse.
3. If a person feels side effects from a medicine, the person should
   a. take more of the medicine. b. ignore the side effects. (c.) stop taking the medicine. d. take smaller doses.
4. Drug misuse means to
   (a.) incorrectly use medicine. b. take prescription medicine with a doctor's order. c. use only your prescription medicines. d. follow the information on medicine labels.
5. The intentional use of drugs for reasons other than health is
   a. an overdose. (b.) drug abuse. c. withdrawal. d. drug misuse.
6. A person who is physically dependent on a drug and stops taking it may suffer from
   a. an overdose. b. tolerance. c. drug misuse. (d.) withdrawal.
7. An overdose of a drug is
   (a.) too much for the body to use. b. becoming dependent on the drug. c. absorbed by the brain. d. a physical need for the drug.
8. Marijuana contains
   a. THC only. (b.) over 400 chemicals. c. narcotics. d. LSD.
9. When marijuana is smoked, the heartbeat
   a. slows down. (b.) speeds up. c. stays the same. d. stops.
10. A disease in which a person cannot control the use of alcohol is
    a. cirrhosis. (b.) alcoholism. c. emphysema. d. bronchitis.
11. Alcohol is absorbed directly into the
    a. brain. b. stomach. c. liver. (d.) bloodstream.
12. A substance in cigarette smoke that forms a brown, sticky mass on the lungs is
    (a.) tar. b. carbon monoxide. c. nicotine. d. THC.
13. A stimulant drug in tobacco smoke is
    a. tar. b. carbon monoxide. (c.) nicotine. d. THC.
14. Cancer of the mouth and gum disease can develop in people who
    a. drink alcohol. b. use inhalants. c. breathe sidestream smoke. (d.) use smokeless tobacco.
15. For most young people, the hardest part of refusing drugs is
    a. knowing the effects of drugs. b. knowing that some drugs are illegal. (c.) knowing how to say no. d. having other activities to do.

55

Name ____ Chapter 6 Test B

Short Answer Complete the chart.

Type of Drug	Description
16. **depressant**	Includes tranquilizers and barbiturates
17. **narcotic**	Its use often causes malnutrition; produces dependence quickly
18. **hallucinogen**	Immediate effects are very unpredictable; includes PCP
19. **inhalant**	Includes the fumes of glue and paint
20. **hallucinogen**	Causes changes in the senses; includes LSD
21. **stimulant**	Speeds up the work of the nervous system
22. **stimulant**	Includes cocaine and amphetamines
23. **depressant**	Slows down the work of the nervous system
24. **narcotic**	Includes codeine, morphine, and heroin

Short Essay Write your answers in complete sentences.

25. What can a person do to resist pressure from others to use drugs?
    Answers might include: just say no, walk away, use the decision-making steps, do something else.
26. How are cigarettes a threat to people's health?
    Cigarettes are a threat to the health of both smokers and non-smokers. Smokers can develop heart disease, lung cancer, and emphysema. Second-hand smoke is dangerous for non-smokers since it still contains tar, nicotine, and carbon monoxide.

56

Answers to Reviewing Health Ideas

1. caffeine
2. blood
3. prescription
4. misuse
5. overdose
6. mentally
7. cocaine or crack
8. depressants
9. heartbeat
10. lung
11. hormones
12. alcohol
13. oxygen
14. chewing
15. no

Answers to Understanding Health Ideas

16. directions for safe use, warnings, purpose, side effects, and dosage
17. speed up the work of the nervous system
18. narcotics
19. THC
20. about one month
21. peer pressure, tolerance, dependence
22. the percentage of fluid in the bloodstream that is alcohol
23. an organization that helps alcoholics stop drinking
24. nicotine, carbon monoxide, and tars
25. lung cancer, emphysema, and chronic bronchitis

Answers to Thinking Critically

1. No, because a person should never use a medicine that is prescribed for someone else. Also, even though the symptoms might seem the same, the condition might be different, calling for a different medicine or no medicine at all.

Thinking Skills When students tell whether or not they should use the medicine, they are *interpreting information* and *drawing conclusions*.

2. Answers will vary but should include facts from this chapter about the harmful physical, mental, and social effects of smoking marijuana and the illegality of marijuana.

Thinking Skills When students tell what advice they would give to a friend who is smoking marijuana, they are *generalizing* and *communicating*.

Pupil Edition	Activities	Enrichment	Assessment	Independent Study
Chapter 7 Fighting Against Disease, pp. 198–233	Health Watch Notebook, p. 198	Health Focus, p. 230 Health at Home, p. 231	Chapter 7 Review, pp. 232–233	Study Guide, pp. 328–329 Skills for Life Handbook, pp. 356–358
Lesson 1 What Causes Communicable Diseases? pp. 200–203		Did You Know? p. 201	Think Back, p. 203	On Your Own, p. 202 Study Guide, p. 328
Lesson 2 How Does Your Body Fight Communicable Diseases? pp. 204–209		Did You Know? pp. 205, 208	Think Back, p. 209	Study Guide, p. 328
Lesson 3 What Are Some Diseases of the Respiratory System? pp. 210–215	Health Activities Workshop, pp. 216–217	Did You Know? pp. 211, 212, 214	Think Back, p. 215	Study Guide, p. 328
Lesson 4 What Causes Noncommunicable Diseases? pp. 218–223		Did You Know? p. 220	Think Back, p. 223	On Your Own, p. 222 Study Guide, p. 329
Lesson 5 What Is an Allergy? pp. 224–227			Think Back, p. 227	Study Guide, p. 329
Lesson 6 How Can a Healthy Lifestyle Help Prevent Disease? pp. 228–229		Did You Know? p. 228	Think Back, p. 229	Study Guide, p. 329

Teacher Resources

Jr. Medical Detective. Children's Better Health Institute. Introduces readers to the world of medical investigation through articles and activities that help students learn about health and solve the health mysteries and puzzles included in the magazine.

Nourse, Alan E. *Your Immune System.* Watts, 1982. Describes the body's immune system and what happens when this system functions perfectly, too vigorously, or not at all.

Read, Donald A., and Green, Walter H. *Creative Teaching in Health.* Macmillan, 1980. Includes chapters on health care, disease control, and other health-related topics.

Audio-Visual Resources

See page T43 for addresses of Audio-Visual Sources.

Before using any audio-visual materials, preview them for appropriateness for your students.

Body Defenses Against Disease, Britannica, film, 14 minutes. Provides viewers with a rare glimpse of disease-causing organisms. Emphasizes the importance of immunization in disease prevention and control.

Germs and What They Do, Coronet Films and Video, film. Examines germs and how they affect health.

The Human Body: What Can Go Wrong? Series I, Focus Media, Inc., filmstrips with cassettes. Examines different blood diseases, and explains how transfusions can save lives.

What Is AIDS?, MTI Film and Video, 16 minutes. Uses analogies and dramatizations to explain AIDS and how the AIDS virus destroys the immune system.

Protection Against Infection: The Inside Story of the Immune System and AIDS, Agency for Instructional Technology, film or video, 14½ minutes. Discusses the details of the immune system and the difference between risky and non-risky behaviors as they relate to AIDS.

Computer Software

Microbe. Synergistic. Presents a simulated situation in which students travel through the body in a miniaturized submarine as they learn about human anatomy.

	Teacher's Edition	Teacher's Resource Book	Test Book
Enrichment	Suggestions for each lesson: L. 1—pp. 200, 202 L. 2—pp. 204, 206, 208 L. 3—pp. 210, 212, 214 L. 4—pp. 218, 220, 222 L. 5—pp. 224, 226 L. 6—p. 228	Family Letter, p. 89 * Life Skills, p. 93 * Health and Language Arts, p. 96	
Reteaching	Suggestions for each lesson: L. 1—pp. 200, 202 L. 2—pp. 204, 206, 208 L. 3—pp. 210, 212, 214 L. 4—pp. 218, 220, 222 L. 5—pp. 224, 226 L. 6—p. 228	Transparency Masters, pp. 91-92 * Vocabulary, p. 94 * Study and Review, p. 95	
Assessment	Expanding Student Thinking: one assessment question per lesson that develops higher-order thinking skills—pp. 203, 209, 215, 223, 227, 229		Chapter 7 Test, Form A, pp. 57-58 Chapter 7 Test, Form B, pp. 59-60

* Also available in Workbook format (Student Edition and Teacher's Edition)

Chapter 7 Poster
A set of posters is available in a separate package. It provides a teaching poster for every chapter, including discussion and activity suggestions on the back. The poster for Chapter 7 is titled "How does the use of technology help fight disease?"

Overhead Transparencies
A set of color overhead transparencies is available for Grade 6. You may wish to use Transparency 18 to help teach about the AIDS virus.

Bulletin Board
Encourage students to bring to class newspaper or magazine articles about disease prevention. Cut out magazine pictures or draw pictures that show ways people can help prevent disease. Ask students to explain how a healthy lifestyle can help prevent disease.

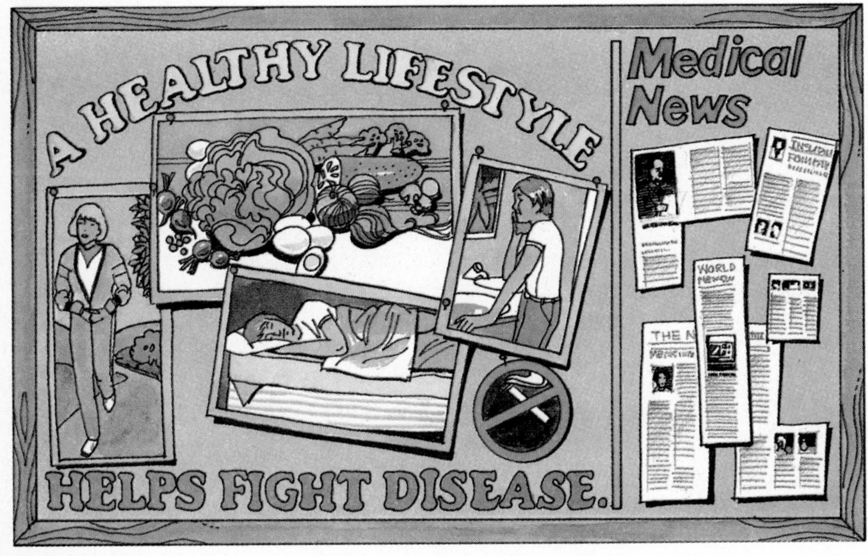

Teaching Plan

Chapter 7 pages 198–233

Chapter Main Idea
Healthy decisions and practices can control or prevent many human diseases.

Chapter Goals
• Show interest in personal medical history, particularly concerning vaccinations.
• Assume greater responsibility for proper treatment of oneself during a cold or other minor illness.
• Demonstrate an interest in new developments in medicine.

Lifetime Goal
Adopt health practices that help prevent disease.

Health Vocabulary
Allergen, antibiotic, antibody, atherosclerosis, cancer, cardiovascular disease, communicable disease, hypertension, immunity, noncommunicable disease, plaque, sinusitis, tumor

Chapter 7

Fighting Against Disease

What is unusual about this human heart? Look at the two large arteries that supply blood to the heart. The yellow spots show material that has built up inside the arteries. Material that builds up in arteries can lead to several diseases.

This chapter discusses these diseases and a wide range of others—from the common cold to cancer. You will discover how your body fights disease every day of your life and how your health practices can help prevent disease now and in the future.

Health Watch Notebook

Each day, write in your notebook activities you do to prevent disease. For each activity, explain how it helps keep you healthy.

1 What Causes Communicable Diseases?
2 How Does Your Body Fight Communicable Diseases?
3 What Are Some Diseases of the Respiratory System?
4 What Causes Noncommunicable Diseases?
5 What Is an Allergy?
6 How Can a Healthy Lifestyle Help Prevent Disease?

198

Teaching Options

Modeling Health Vocabulary
Use this technique to introduce new words as you teach each lesson in this chapter. First, introduce the word. Present the word in two sentences that serve to clearly define the word. For example, one sentence you might use to introduce the word *antibiotic* is the following: *An antibiotic is a medicine that can weaken or destroy harmful bacteria.* Either read the sentences to the students or write them on the chalkboard. Ask the students to generate two meaningful sentences using the word. Additional successful techniques for introducing new words can be found on page T23.

Cooperative Learning
Jigsaw Format (See page T24.)
Assign the following topics at random to your cooperative learning teams.

Topic A: Describe differences between bacteria and viruses and explain how a virus invades a cell.
Topic B: Describe three ways that white blood cells fight disease.
Topic C: Name two noncommunicable diseases and tell how you can help prevent them.
Topic D: Define the word allergen and list as many allergens as you can.

Have students search for information on their topic as they read the chapter. Then let all students with the same topic meet in an expert group to discuss the information. When students return to their teams, they may take turns presenting their topics to the team. Then give students a test covering all topics to complete individually (Chapter 7 test A or B in the Test Book). Award Superteam certificates to teams whose average test scores exceed 90%, and Greatteam certificates to teams whose average test scores exceed 80%.

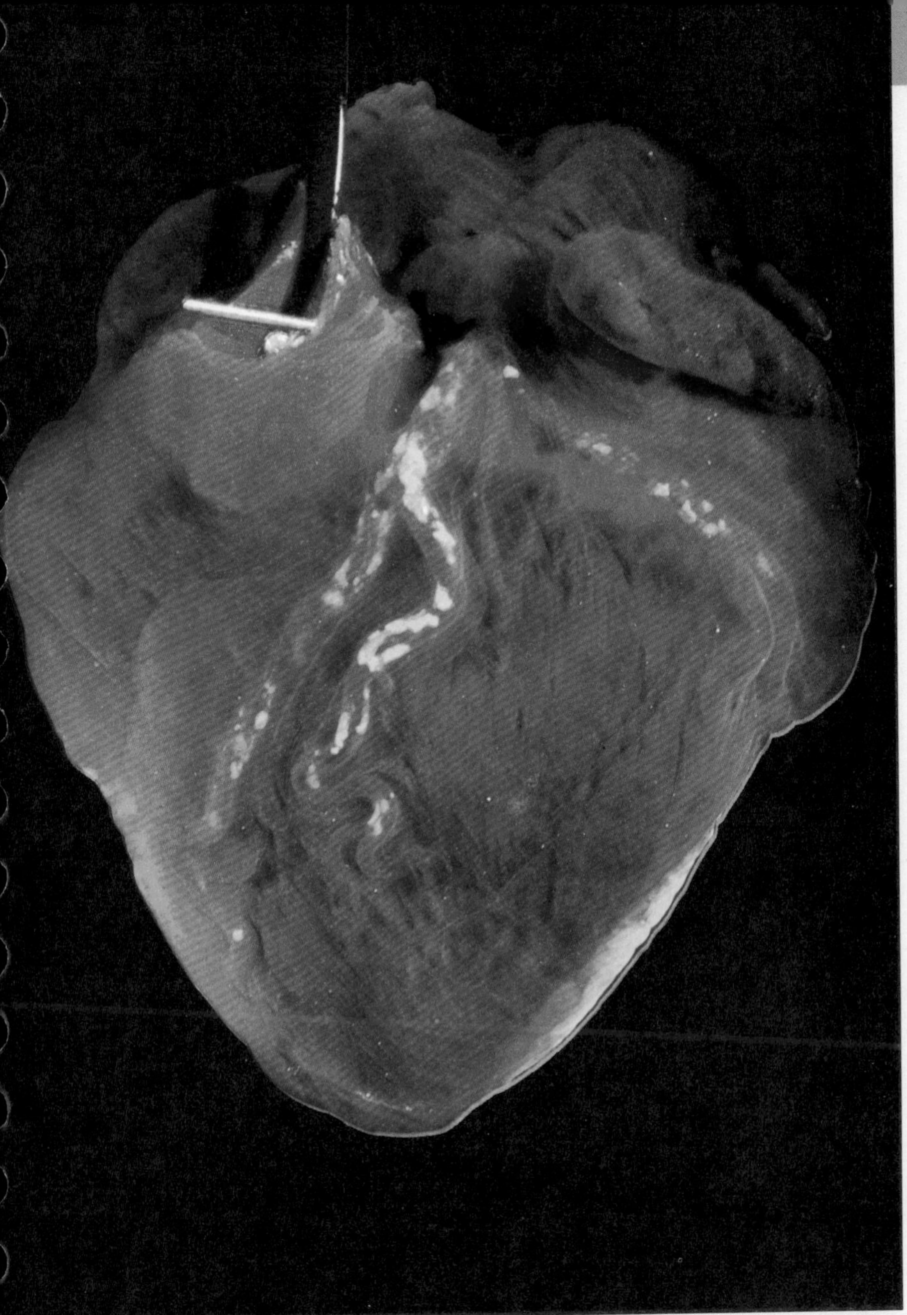

Words to Preteach

Allergy, bacteria, cell, cholesterol, cilia, contagious, disease germ, electron microscope, environment, heredity, lifestyle, microscopic, mucus, organism, penicillin, pneumonia, vaccine, virus, white blood cell

Introducing the Chapter

Ask the students to look at the picture and read page 198. Explain that the photograph shows a buildup of plaque (fatty substances) in the coronary arteries. Tell students that the main component of plaque is cholesterol. Explain that plaque buildup in the arteries can lead to a disease called atherosclerosis. Write the word on the chalkboard. Atherosclerosis is also referred to as hardening of the arteries. You may wish to send the Family Letter home at this time. You may want to assign Study Guide pages 328–329 for students to use independently as they read the lessons. The Study Guide can also be used as an extra chapter review. You might want to assign the activities in the Skills for Life Handbook on pages 356–358.

Stategies for Health Watch Notebook

Before students begin making entries in their notebooks, discuss with students things they can do to help prevent disease. Make sure students understand how each recommended activity helps keep them healthy.

Family Letter

Use the Family Letter (English or Spanish version) to introduce the subject matter of the chapter to the family and to suggest a way the family can become involved in the student's learning experience. This master may be reproduced from the Teacher's Resource Book.

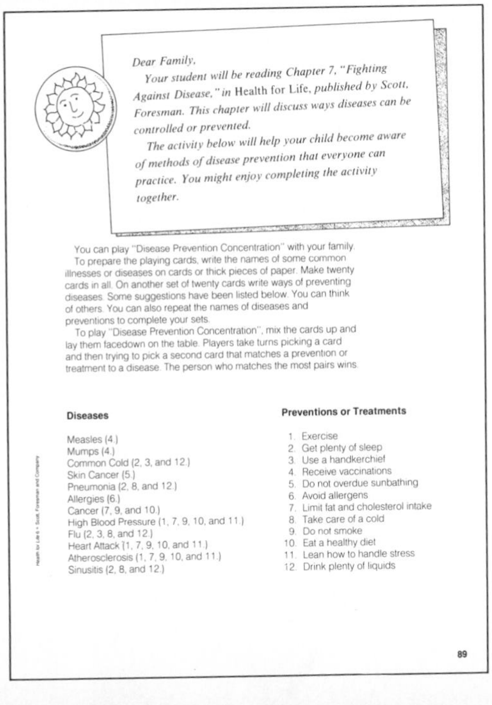

Dear Family,

Your student will be reading Chapter 7, "Fighting Against Disease," in Health for Life, *published by Scott, Foresman. This chapter will discuss ways diseases can be controlled or prevented.*

The activity below will help your child become aware of methods of disease prevention that everyone can practice. You might enjoy completing the activity together.

You can play "Disease Prevention Concentration" with your family.

To prepare the playing cards, write the names of some common illnesses or diseases on cards or thick pieces of paper. Make twenty cards in all. On another set of twenty cards write ways of preventing diseases. Some suggestions have been listed below. You can think of others. You can also repeat the names of diseases and preventions to complete your sets.

To play "Disease Prevention Concentration", mix the cards up and lay them facedown on the table. Players take turns picking a card and then trying to pick a second card that matches a prevention or treatment to a disease. The person who matches the most pairs wins.

Diseases

Measles (4.)
Mumps (4.)
Common Cold (2, 3, and 12.)
Skin Cancer (5.)
Pneumonia (2, 8, and 12.)
Allergies (6.)
Cancer (7, 9, and 10.)
High Blood Pressure (1, 7, 9, 10, and 11.)
Flu (2, 3, 8, and 12.)
Heart Attack (1, 7, 9, 10, and 11.)
Atherosclerosis (1, 7, 9, 10, and 11.)
Sinusitis (2, 8, and 12.)

Preventions or Treatments

1. Exercise
2. Get plenty of sleep
3. Use a handkerchief
4. Receive vaccinations
5. Do not overdue sunbathing
6. Avoid allergens
7. Limit fat and cholesterol intake
8. Take care of a cold
9. Do not smoke
10. Eat a healthy diet
11. Lean how to handle stress
12. Drink plenty of liquids

89

For High-Potential Students

Help students create a board game about how the body fights communicable and noncommunicable diseases. Guide students to design a game board, game cards, and tokens. Help students list rules for the game. Allow other students to play the game. Let them evaluate the game by listing the qualities of a good board game and then stating whether or not this game has those qualities.

Teaching Plan

Lesson 1 pages 200–203

Lesson Objective
Describe some major kinds of disease germs that cause communicable diseases.

Health Vocabulary
Communicable disease

1 Motivate

Introducing the Lesson
Ask volunteers to tell what kinds of illnesses they have had in the last year. List these illnesses on the chalkboard. Then ask if anyone else in the family also had these illnesses at about the same time. Help students identify which illnesses seemed to spread from one person to another.

communicable (kə myü′nə kə bəl) **disease,** a disease that can spread, usually from one person to another.

1 What Causes Communicable Diseases?

Try to think of the last time you had a cold or the flu. Was anybody else in your family sick at about the same time? Perhaps you had a cold just as your mother was getting over hers. A few days later your brother or sister might have started coughing and sneezing. Sometimes a disease seems to pass from one family member to the next.

Diseases that can spread from one person to another are called **communicable diseases.** Tiny organisms or substances called disease germs cause these diseases. Bacteria and viruses are two of the most common kinds of disease germs.

How Do Certain Kinds of Bacteria Harm Your Body?

Bacteria are the most numerous kinds of organisms. They exist in the air, ground, water, and your body. Bacteria are so tiny that millions of them could fit on a pinhead. The pictures show the various shapes of different kinds of bacteria seen through a microscope.

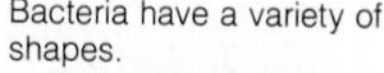
Bacteria have a variety of shapes.

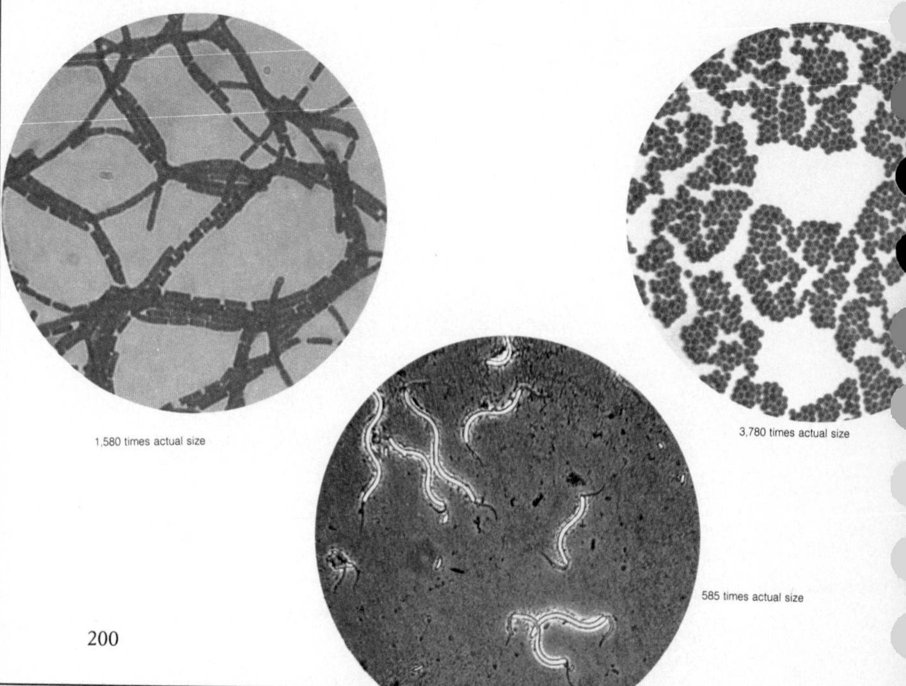
1,580 times actual size

3,780 times actual size

585 times actual size

200

Teaching Options

Health Background

Pathogens are disease-causing agents such as some bacteria, viruses, fungi, and protozoa. Pathogens injure specific kinds of body cells. For example, the poliomyelitis virus attacks nerve cells, while the typhoid bacillus injures lymphoid cells in the intestine. Pathogens enter the body through a body opening, a break in the skin, or through irritated tissue. Pathogens eventually cause their own destruction either by destroying the host or by stimulating the production of antibodies in the host.

Enrichment
If possible, ask the school nurse to visit the classroom and explain the technique used to take a throat culture. Explain that throat cultures are taken to find out if an infection is caused by bacteria and, if so, what kind. Once the doctor knows what is causing the infection, he or she can treat it properly.

Health and Social Studies
Ask students to find out how bubonic plague affected life in Europe in the mid-1600s. You might suggest that students read passages from the book, *1665: Story of the Plague Year* by Daniel Defoe. Students might want to research other diseases, such as polio, that have affected society.

Reteaching
Ask students to write a paragraph explaining what bacteria are, where they can live, how they grow, and how they can affect people.

Some kinds of bacteria are harmless, and many are helpful. A few kinds of bacteria, however, are harmful to humans and cause diseases. Such bacteria grow in your body and harm you by giving off wastes that are harmful to your cells.

A small number of harmful bacteria are not enough to make you sick. Bacteria, however, grow and reproduce very quickly. They grow best in warm, dark, moist places. The human body offers many such growing places for bacteria. The pictures show how quickly bacteria can reproduce and increase their numbers. Bacteria give off some wastes that act like poisons. A large number of harmful bacteria can produce enough poisonous wastes to make you sick.

Some diseases can be caused by different bacteria, and the same bacteria can sometimes cause different diseases. For example, several different kinds of bacteria can cause pneumonia. The bacteria that cause pneumonia can also cause sore throats, ear infections, and sinus infections. Bacteria that usually cause strep throat can also cause skin or sinus infections.

Did You Know?
In the mid-1300s a disease called bubonic plague spread throughout Europe. This disease killed more than a third of the European people in only two years. The bacteria that caused the plague came to Europe from Asia. The bacteria were carried by rats on board a ship. Fleas picked up the bacteria from the rats. The fleas helped spread the bacteria to other rats and to the people in Europe.

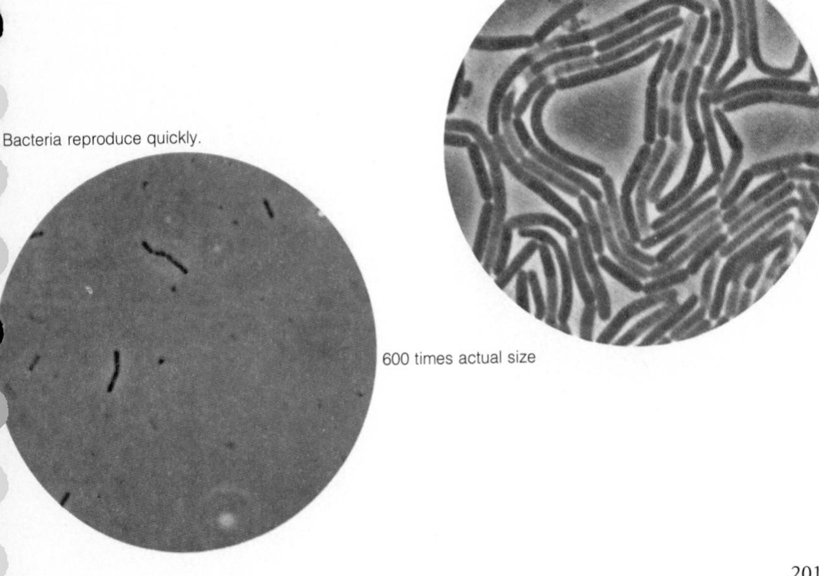

Bacteria reproduce quickly.

600 times actual size

2 Teach

Strategies for Pages 200 and 201

• Direct students to read page 200 to find out what causes communicable diseases. Then call on a student to define the term *communicable disease.* (a disease that can spread, usually from one person to another) • Ask students to name the two most common kinds of disease germs. (bacteria and viruses) • Direct students' attention to the pictures on page 200 and ask them to describe the differences in the bacteria shown. (different shapes: round, rod-shaped, and spiral) • Then let students read page 201 to find out how some bacteria are harmful to people. Point out that bacteria are important in the production of cheese, buttermilk, yogurt, sauerkraut, and vinegar. • Ask where bacteria grow best. (in warm, dark, moist places) Discuss how bacteria harm the body. (They produce wastes that are poisonous to the body's cells.) • Encourage students to name some diseases that are caused by bacteria. (some types of pneumonia, strep throat, tuberculosis)

Teaching Plan

Lesson 1 continued

2 Teach

Strategies for Pages 202 and 203

• Ask the students to read page 202 to find out how viruses harm the body. (They invade and damage body cells.) Direct the students to look at the picture on page 202 to see how viruses invade a cell. • Ask students to name some diseases caused by viruses (measles, colds, flu, mumps, and chicken pox) Emphasize that each kind of virus causes only one disease. • Then direct students to read page 203 to discover how the electron microscope helps scientists learn about viruses. (Because viruses are so small, scientists can only study them using an electron microscope.)

Using On Your Own

Answers might include washing; using separate utensils, glasses, and towels; covering the mouth and nose when sneezing and coughing; not rubbing one's eyes; disposing of garbage properly.

Thinking Skills By thinking of ways to prevent the spread of disease germs, students are *generalizing* and *suggesting alternatives.*

On Your Own
List some ways you can help prevent the spread of disease germs.

How Do Viruses Harm Your Body?

Viruses are even smaller than bacteria. They cause more illness than any other kind of disease germ. Viruses harm your body by entering and damaging body cells. The picture shows a virus invading a cell. Inside the cell the outer coat of the virus breaks down, and the virus reproduces rapidly. The new viruses use the cell's energy and crowd the inside of the cell, keeping it from working properly. The cell dies when the viruses break out of it. Then the viruses invade other cells. As with other kinds of disease germs, small numbers of viruses are not harmful. If the viruses reproduce, however, they can damage so many cells that you become sick.

In the last fifty years, scientists have identified hundreds of different kinds of viruses. Each kind of virus causes only one disease. For example, the virus that causes measles does not cause any other disease. A virus that causes a cold cannot cause any other disease. Flu, mumps, and chicken pox are also each caused by a certain kind of virus.

Viruses invade cells, use the cells' energy to reproduce, and break out to invade other cells.

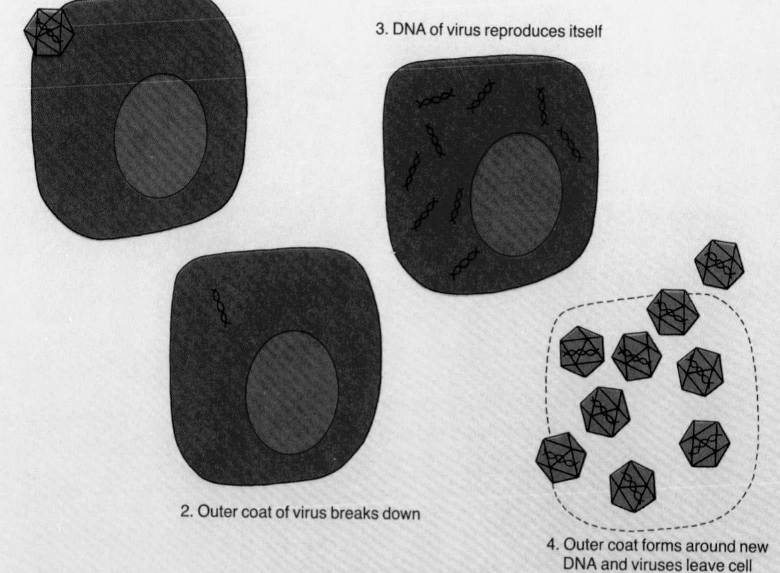
1. Virus enters cell
2. Outer coat of virus breaks down
3. DNA of virus reproduces itself
4. Outer coat forms around new DNA and viruses leave cell

Teaching Options

Anecdote

Bacteria have a rapid rate of reproduction. Some bacteria reproduce every twenty minutes. Under ideal conditions, a single bacterial cell could produce a mass of cells four thousand times as heavy as the earth in forty-eight hours. However, bacterial growth is quickly limited by environmental factors such as the availability of food. (*The Encyclopedia of Health and the Human Body*. Watts, 1977.)

Enrichment

Suggest that students use a life-science text or an enclyclopedia to find out why viruses are not considered organisms. (A virus is not a cell, nor is it made up of cells. Also, a virus does not carry on life processes—such as reproduction, respiration, and growth—by itself. A virus does reproduce, however, after it enters a cell, using the cell's material to carry on this life process.)

Health and Social Studies

Encourage interested students to find out about communicable diseases that are common in other countries. Suggest students find out how these diseases spread and report their findings to the class.

Reteaching

Let interested students find out more about diseases caused by bacteria and viruses. Tell them to find out which germ causes each disease and what the symptoms are.

Viruses can be seen only by using an electron microscope, like the one in the picture. This important tool helps scientists compare, identify, and study the activities of viruses. This microscope can magnify a virus up to two million times its actual size. An electron microscope enlarged the viruses shown here. Notice the variety of shapes and sizes.

Think Back • *Study on your own with Study Guide page 328.*

1. What is a communicable disease?
2. What are the two most common kinds of disease germs and how does each cause disease?
3. Can a virus that causes flu also cause mumps? Explain your answer.

685,880 times actual size

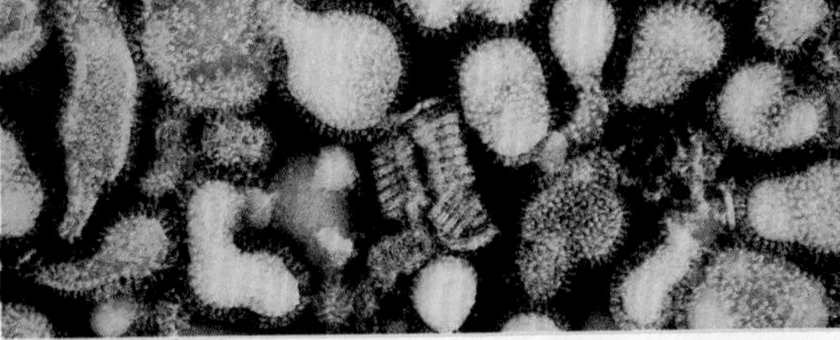

164,480 times actual size

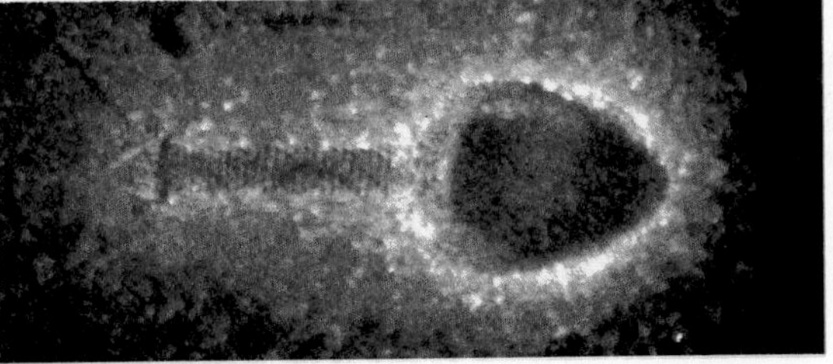

357,150 times actual size

What instrument enables scientists to see these viruses so clearly?

3 Assess

Expanding Student Thinking

Ask students to compare and contrast harmful bacteria and viruses. (Harmful bacteria and viruses are two major kinds of disease germs. Small numbers of the bacteria or viruses are not harmful, but both kinds of germs multiply and can then cause disease. Harmful bacteria give off wastes that are poisonous to cells. Viruses cause damage by entering the cells. Some kinds of bacteria can cause more than one disease, but each kind of virus can cause only one disease. Viruses are smaller than bacteria.)

Thinking Skill By comparing and contrasting bacteria and viruses, students are *organizing information.*

Answers to Think Back

1. A communicable disease is one that can spread, usually from one person to another.

2. Bacteria and viruses are the most common disease germs. Some bacteria produce poisonous wastes. Viruses enter cells, reproduce rapidly, crowd the inside of the cells, and prevent them from working properly. Also, viruses damage the cells when they break out.

3. No, each kind of virus can cause only one disease.

Teaching Plan

Lesson 2 pages 204–209

Lesson Objective
Describe the first-, second-, and third-line defenses against communicable disease. Explain what occurs when a person becomes infected with the AIDS virus.

Health Vocabulary
Antibody, immunity

1 Motivate

Introducing the Lesson
Ask students what they think a person should do for a cut or scrape. (Make sure the cut or scrape is washed well and covered.) Ask them to suggest reasons for doing this. (to remove disease germs, to prevent disease germs from entering the body)

2 How Does Your Body Fight Communicable Diseases?

Disease germs exist everywhere. In fact, the air you are breathing right now contains disease germs. You might wonder, then, why you do not get sick more often than you do.

What Are Your First-Line Defenses?

Your body has three major ways to defend itself against disease germs. Your first-line defenses work to keep disease germs out of your body's tissues and bloodstream.

The most noticeable defense is your skin. Most disease germs cannot enter the body through unbroken skin. However, disease germs can enter your body easily through such openings as your mouth and nose. There the germs are likely to be trapped in mucus—a sticky liquid that lines your nose, mouth, throat, windpipe, and lungs. Thousands of tiny hairlike structures, or cilia, are in the nose and sweep mucus and disease germs to the throat. Then the material can be coughed up or swallowed. Stomach acids usually kill the germs swallowed with mucus.

Some white blood cells destroy disease germs.

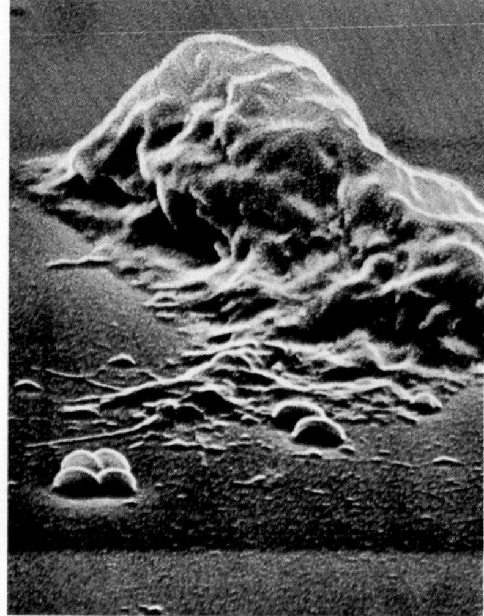

3,291 times actual size

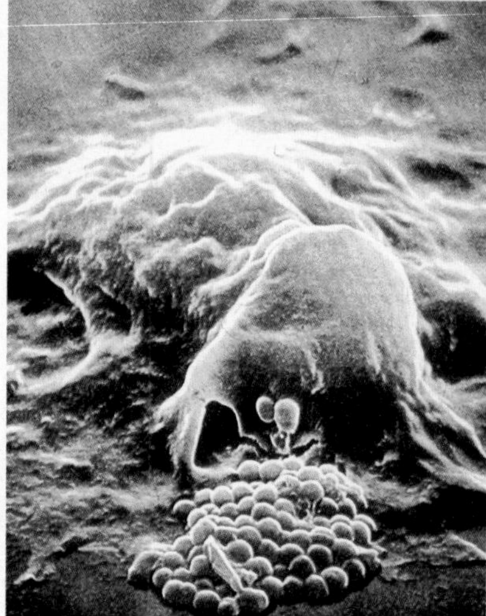

4,743 times actual size

204

Teaching Options

Health Background

In general, viruses and bacteria do not enter the body through unbroken skin. However, some other kinds of pathogens can do so. Hookworms, for example, can enter through the skin on the bottom of the feet. Fungi, such as those which cause ringworm and athlete's foot, grow on and within the skin.

The AIDS virus enters the body of an uninfected person when his or her blood or other body fluids become mixed with the body fluids of an infected person. For more background information on AIDS, see pages T38–T39.

Enrichment

Direct students to look in the *Readers' Guide to Periodical Literature* to find articles with information about interferon. Ask students to read some articles and report their findings to the class. (Interferon is an antiviral substance that is produced by cells exposed to a viral infection.)

Health and Social Studies

Ask students to contact the local Board of Health or a travel agent to find out what vaccinations are required for people from the United States who travel to Asia, South America, Europe, and Africa.

Reteaching

Help students draw an outline of a body. Then ask them to add and label the body's first and second lines of defense against disease germs.

Dust particles and disease germs can enter your body through the openings around your eyes. Your body responds by producing tears. The tears clean your eyes and contain a substance that kills some disease germs.

Some germs might enter your body with your food. The saliva in your mouth might kill or weaken many of these germs. Others die when they mix with the strong acids in your stomach.

What Is Your Second Line of Defense?

Sometimes your first-line defenses cannot prevent all disease germs from entering your body. Some might enter your bloodstream and other body tissues. Then your second line of defense goes to work.

Certain parts of your body produce white blood cells. Some of these cells circulate throughout your body. They surround and destroy disease germs, as shown in the pictures on these two pages. The first picture shows a white blood cell approaching a colony of bacteria, shown in green. In the second picture, the white blood cell has surrounded most of the colony. The colony has become a harmless jellylike mass inside the blood cell in the third picture.

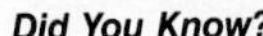

Did You Know?
Instead of circulating in your bloodstream, some white blood cells stay in one place, such as your liver, spleen, or tonsils. White blood cells filter out disease germs as the blood passes through these organs.

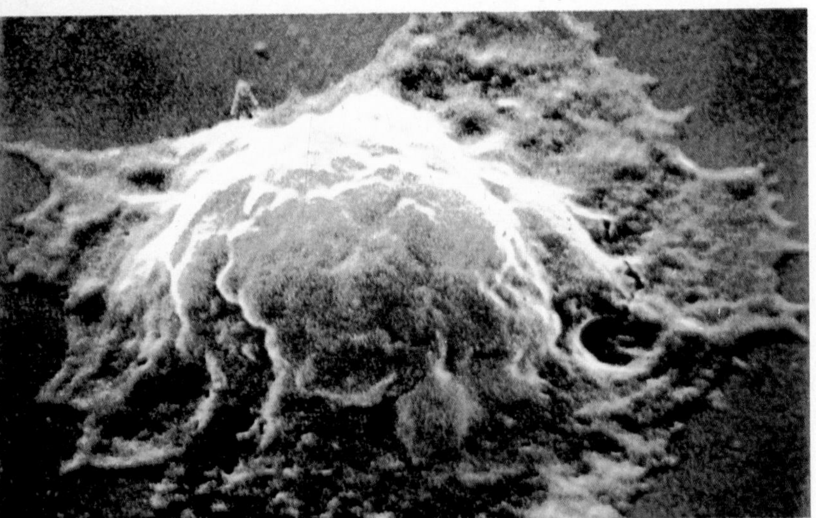

2 Teach

Strategies for Pages 204 and 205

• As students read through the lesson, help them list the body's first-, second-, and third-line defenses against communicable diseases.
• Direct the students to read page 204 to find out the function of the body's first-line defenses. • Ask students to name the body's first-line defenses against disease germs. (skin, mucus, tears, saliva, stomach acid) • Ask where mucus is found in the body. (lining of the nose, mouth, throat, windpipe, and lungs) • Ask students why covering the mouth and nose when sneezing or coughing is important. (Disease germs can enter the air when someone who is ill coughs or sneezes.) Explain that sneezing or coughing is one way the body tries to rid itself of germs. • Ask students to read page 205 and name the body's second line of defense against disease germs. (white blood cells) • Encourage students to look at the pictures and to explain how white blood cells protect the body. (They surround and destroy disease germs.) Explain that the third picture shows that the bacteria have been reduced to a harmless, jellylike mass.

Health and Language Arts

Use this worksheet for practice in learning the meanings of word parts found in health terms. This master may be reproduced from the Teacher's Resource Book and is located on page 28 of the Student's Workbook. Use with Chapter 7: pages 204–209.

Name ________________
Use with Chapter 7: pages 204–209.

Health and Language Arts

Identifying Disease Word Parts

Many diseases and their treatments have long names. You can use the chart below to help you understand some of these terms.

Word or word part	Meaning
bronchus	a tube leading to the lungs
cardio	heart
colon	large intestine
ectomy	the surgical removal of
encephalo	brain
itis	an inflammation (heat, redness, pain, and swelling might be present)
pneum	lung
tonsil	a mass of lymph tissue
vascular	blood vessels

Part I. Use the chart to help you divide each word into two parts.

1. Pneumonia **Pneum onia**
2. Tonsillectomy **Tonsil lectomy**
3. Cardiovascular **Cardio vascular**
4. Encephalitis **Encephal itis**
5. Bronchitis **Bronch itis**
6. Colitis **Col itis**

Part II. Use the chart to help you answer the questions.

1. Which body part does pneumonia affect? **Lungs**
2. What is a tonsillectomy? **The surgical removal of the tonsils**
3. Which two body parts are affected by cardiovascular disease? **Heart and blood vessels**
4. What is encephalitis? **An inflammation of the brain**
5. Which body part does colitis affect? **Colon or large intestine**
6. What is bronchitis? **An inflammation of the tube leading to the lungs**

96 ***Extension Idea:*** **Ask students to write their own definitions for five new terms and then compare their definitions to the dictionary.**

Teaching Plan

Lesson 2 continued

2 Teach

Strategies for Pages 206 and 207

• Direct the students to read page 206 to find out what the body's third line of defense is. (antibodies) Write the word *antibody* on the chalkboard and let students give the definition. (a tiny substance, made by certain white blood cells, that attaches to a disease germ, making it harmless) • Explain to students that the body has several kinds of white blood cells. Those that make antibodies are called lymphocytes, and those that surround and destroy disease germs are called phagocytes. • Encourage students to explain what is shown in the picture on page 206. (Antibodies are attaching to a disease germ, making it harmless, and a white blood cell is destroying a disease germ.)

antibody (an′ti bod′ē), a tiny substance made by white blood cells that attaches to a disease germ, making it harmless.

immunity (i myü′nə tē), the body's resistance to a disease through the presence of antibodies.

What Is Your Third Line of Defense?

Sometimes disease germs reproduce so quickly that white blood cells cannot destroy them fast enough. Then your third line of defense—**antibodies**—helps your body fight off disease germs.

Antibodies are tiny substances produced by some white blood cells. The antibodies attach themselves to disease germs. The drawing shows that antibodies attach themselves to the germs and make them harmless. Later, other white blood cells can destroy the germs.

Each kind of antibody can attack only a specific kind of disease germ. For example, antibodies that attack the flu germ cannot harm the germ that causes any other disease. If a different kind of disease germ invades your body, your white blood cells must make a different kind of antibody.

Antibodies can do more than help fight off disease germs. Antibodies can also prevent you from getting a disease. For example, suppose you get chicken pox. Some of your white blood cells will form antibodies that can fight off the chicken pox germs. Some other white blood cells do not make antibodies right away. These white blood cells act as memory cells that "remember" to make the correct antibodies in the future. Long after you are cured, the memory cells will stay in your blood. If chicken pox germs enter your body again, these memory cells can quickly make the antibodies that can attack the germs. The antibodies will be made so quickly that the disease germs will not have a chance to make you sick. Therefore, if you have had chicken pox once, you will probably never get it again. You have an **immunity** to this disease. Measles, mumps, and polio each provide lifelong immunity once you have had the disease.

Teaching Options

Anecdote

No one today needs to have a smallpox vaccination because a successful vaccination program by the World Health Organization eradicated the disease.

Enrichment

Let interested students find out about the kinds of vaccines that are available for domesticated animals. Students may want to contact a veterinarian. Ask students to present their information to the class.

Encourage interested students to find out how the World Health Organization successfully eliminated smallpox in the early 1980s.

Health and Science

Ask students to use the library or interview a health care professional to find out about developments in vaccines, such as the Hib vaccine, for certain types of flu.

Reteaching

Help students prepare a vaccination-checklist poster showing some diseases and indicating which have vaccines available.

How Do Vaccines Give You Immunity?

Having a disease can be a dangerous and painful way of building immunity. Today you can build immunity to certain diseases without having to get sick. Your body can be made to produce its own protection against certain disease germs. Preparations such as vaccines can be injected into the body. Or, in the case of polio vaccine, it can be taken into the body in syrup or on a sugar cube.

Vaccines give immunity against certain diseases.

The girl shown here is receiving a vaccine that will give her immunity against mumps. A vaccine is a small dose of killed or weakened disease germs. These germs are not strong enough to make the girl feel sick. However, the germs do cause some of her white blood cells to make antibodies against mumps. Some other white blood cells become memory cells for mumps. If she is exposed to the germs that cause mumps, the memory cells will produce the correct antibodies quickly. These antibodies will attack only germs that cause mumps. She must have other vaccines to get immunity against other diseases.

The chart shows the vaccines you should receive. Notice that some vaccinations must be repeated in order to give you complete immunity to that disease.

Recommended Vaccines

Disease	First doses	Later doses
Diphtheria Whooping cough (pertussis) tetanus	2 months, 4 months, 6 months, 18 months	DPT vaccine at 4 to 6 years then only tetanus-diptheria vaccine once every ten years
German measles (rubella)	1 year to early teens	None
Measles	15 months to adult	None, unless first dose was given before 12 months
Mumps	1 year to adult	None
Polio	2 months, 4 months, 18 months	4 to 6 years

• Let students explain how a person might become immune to a disease. (When a person gets a disease, the body's white blood cells produce antibodies to fight the disease germ. After the person recovers, some of these white blood cells stay in the bloodstream. In the future, they can quickly produce the same antibodies to fight off the disease germs before the germs have a chance to make the person sick again.) • Ask students to read page 207 to find out about another way to get immunity to certain diseases. (vaccines) • Call on students to explain how a vaccine works. (It causes white blood cells to make antibodies against a specific disease.) Ask students to look at the chart and name the vaccines that are listed. (vaccines for diphtheria, whooping cough, tetanus, German measles, mumps, and polio) Point out that immunity does not prevent disease germs from entering the body, but it prevents certain ones that do get in from doing harm.

Teaching Plan

Lesson 2 continued

2 Teach

Strategies for Pages 208 and 209

• Direct the students to read page 208 to find out how antibiotics help the body. (They kill many kinds of bacteria.) • Write the word *antibiotic* on the chalkboard. Refer students to the picture on page 208 showing how an antibiotic can kill bacteria. • Call on students to explain why antibiotics cannot be used to cure a cold or the flu. (because colds and the flu are caused by viruses) • Point out that many once-fatal diseases, such as tuberculosis, rarely cause death today because they can be treated with antibiotics. • Direct students to read page 209 to learn about AIDS. Ask students how AIDS is spread (by sharing needles used to inject illegal drugs; mothers transmitting the disease to babies during birth; sexual contact). Emphasize that AIDS patients can die of any of a number of different diseases because AIDS causes the immune system to break down.

antibiotic (an′ti bī ot′ik), a medicine that destroys or weakens bacteria.

Did You Know?
The first major use of penicillin was for treating infected wounds of soldiers during World War II.

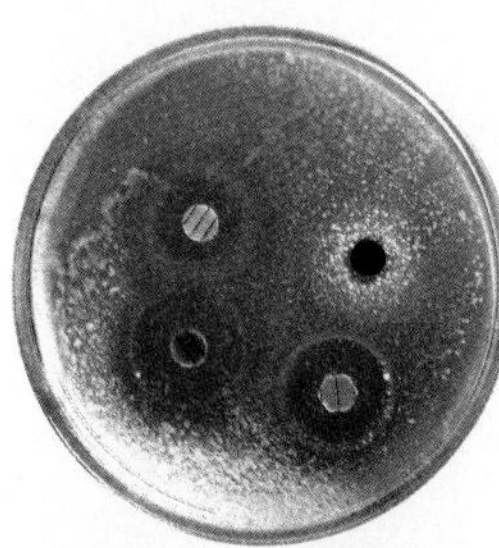

Antibiotics can kill some kinds of bacteria.

Penicillium forming on orange.

What Else Helps Fight Communicable Diseases?

Vaccinations do not exist for every communicable disease. Also, your body's own defenses are not always enough to prevent or cure a disease. You might need medicines to help your body destroy certain disease germs.

Antibiotics are medicines that can kill many kinds of bacteria. Antibiotics are only helpful in treating diseases caused by bacteria. This type of medicine cannot kill viruses and, therefore, cannot help cure a cold or flu.

The picture to the left shows the effectiveness of some antibiotics. Bacteria are growing in the liquid in the disk. The four colored disks contain different antibiotics. The clear areas around three of the disks show that the antibiotic has killed the bacteria near the disks. The one disk with bacteria growing around it shows that some antibiotics cannot destroy certain kinds of bacteria.

The most familiar antibiotic is penicillin. It is used to help cure strep throat, some types of pneumonia, and other diseases. The discovery of penicillin was made accidentally. In 1928, a Scottish scientist, Sir Alexander Fleming, was searching for a substance that would kill harmful bacteria. To perform his experiments, he grew bacteria in special dishes. One day Fleming noticed spots of green, fuzzy mold in the dishes of bacteria. On further study, he noticed that the bacteria around the mold had died. The mold, *Penicillium,* made a substance that could kill bacteria. Fleming named this substance penicillin. The picture shows the kind of mold that produces penicillin.

What is AIDS?

You probably have heard of a disease called acquired immune deficiency syndrome, or AIDS. AIDS is a preventable disease caused by a virus. The AIDS virus destroys the body's defense system against disease germs. This virus enters and destroys special white blood cells that signal the release of antibodies. Without these white blood cells, antibodies are not made to fight off disease germs.

208

Teaching Options

Anecdote

The bronchial tubes in the lungs are lined with cilia like the cilia in the nose. The cough reflex is triggered by particles of dirt and other foreign material trapped in mucus moving over the cilia.

Enrichment

Ask students to use the library to find out the names of several antibiotics, and how the drugs are used.

Health and Science

Guide interested students to look in books about scientific discoveries to find out more about how penicillin was discovered.

Reteaching

Let students make a chart showing some diseases that can and cannot be treated with antibiotics.

The AIDS virus does not spread easily. It cannot spread by casual contact, such as sharing a room or touching. It does not spread through air, water, food, or by mosquitos. People can become infected with the AIDS virus if they get body fluids from an infected person into their bloodstream. One way people can become infected is by sharing needles used to inject illegal drugs. Another way the AIDS virus can spread is by sexual contact with an infected person. Also, mothers with the virus can transmit it to their babies during or after birth. Before 1985, some people became infected after receiving blood transfusions. Now, blood banks and hospitals test blood for the presence of the virus.

Most people who have become infected with the AIDS virus are not aware that they have been exposed to the disease. A person might look and feel well for many years after being infected. During this period, however, he or she can transmit the virus to others. In time, people with the virus might develop infections or diseases that they would not normally get if their defense system worked properly. They can get a rare form of pneumonia, a cancer called Kaposi's sarcoma, or other diseases that their bodies cannot fight off. Eventually, people with AIDS die of these diseases.

AIDS is a serious health problem. There is no cure for AIDS; however, scientists all over the world are working to find a cure and a vaccine. Although AIDS is mainly an adult disease, people of all ages should know how to protect themselves from the AIDS virus.

Think Back • *Study on your own with Study Guide page 328.*

1. How do skin, mucus, and tears each protect against communicable diseases?
2. How do white blood cells help fight against disease?
3. How do antibodies help provide immunity against some diseases?
4. Would antibodies help cure a disease caused by viruses? Why or why not?
5. What is AIDS? How does it cause illness in infected people?

Did You Know?
Diseases that are spread by sexual contact are called sexually transmitted diseases, or STDs. AIDS is an STD that has no cure and can cause death. Other STDs can harm the body in other ways. Chlamydia, gonorrhea, and syphilis are STDs caused by bacteria. They can be cured with antibiotics, but they can damage the reproductive organs and other parts of the body if untreated. Gonorrhea and syphilis can lead to death. Genital herpes is caused by a virus and produces blisters in the genital area. Medicines can relieve the symptoms but cannot cure the disease.

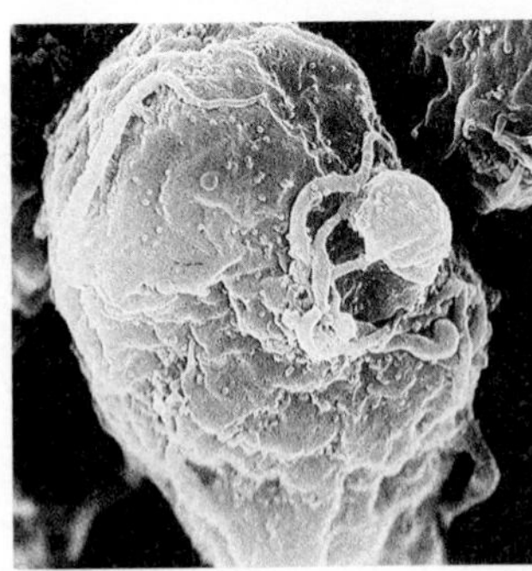

The AIDS virus

3 Assess

Expanding Student Thinking

Ask students to explain which of the things that help fight communicable diseases they think is most important. (Accept any answers students can defend.)

Thinking Skill By explaining which is the most important thing that helps fight diseases, students are *judging and evaluating.*

Answers to Think Back

1. Skin prevents disease germs from entering the body. Mucus traps germs that enter your nose, mouth, throat, and windpipe. Tears wash away and kill some germs that enter the body through the openings around the eyes.

2. Some white blood cells destroy disease germs. Some white blood cells produce antibodies, which make germs harmless.

3. Antibodies against certain disease germs can be produced quickly by memory cells if those kinds of germs have in the past caused white blood cells to make antibodies.

4. No, antibiotics work only against diseases caused by bacteria.

5. AIDS is a disease caused by a virus. It makes the body unable to fight infections properly, so that affected people become ill.

Teaching Plan

Lesson 3 pages 210–215

Lesson Objective
Describe the major causes, symptoms, and treatment of some of the common communicable respiratory diseases.

Health Vocabulary
Sinusitis

1 Motivate

Introducing the Lesson
Ask for four volunteers to play a board game in front of the class. Ask the rest of the students to observe the players' actions and identify ways cold viruses could be passed on during the course of the game if one of the players had a cold. (Specify which player has a cold.)

3 What Are Some Diseases of the Respiratory System?

Almost everyone is familiar with the cough, sore throat, watery eyes, and runny nose of a cold.

Disease germs affect parts of the respiratory system and cause a cold. Your respiratory system includes your nasal passages, throat, windpipe, and lungs. The box shows some of the microscopic air passages and other structures in the lungs. All these organs work together to help you get oxygen from the air you breathe and to get rid of the carbon dioxide your body produces. Check the drawing as you read how colds and other communicable diseases affect the respiratory system.

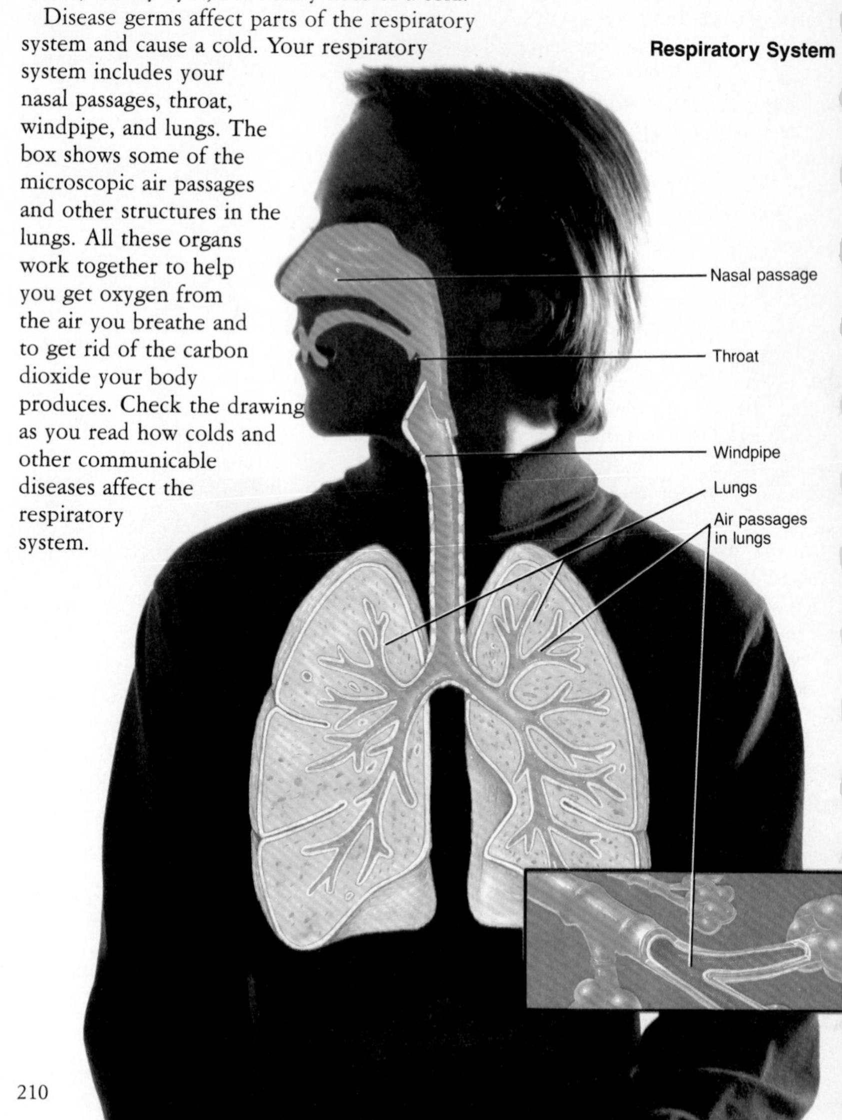

210

Teaching Options

Health Background

Sore throat can be a symptom of a cold or it can be caused by a bacterial infection. A strep throat is a bacterial infection that requires medical treatment. Without treatment, it can lead to rheumatic fever—a disease in which the heart valves can be damaged.

Enrichment
Encourage students to read about research that has been done to find a cure for the common cold. Allow students to report their findings to the class.

Health and Social Studies
Ask interested students to find statistics on the number of working days lost when people have colds and flu. How might this affect business and industry?

Reteaching
Ask students to visit a pharmacy to find out what types of medicines are available to treat cold and flu symptoms.

Special Education
Help learning-disabled students list the symptoms they have when they have a cold. Next to each symptom, let the students list something they can do to feel better.

What Causes a Cold?

The most common disease in the United States is the cold. Most people catch at least one cold a year. Many people your age catch four or five colds a year.

Many different kinds of viruses cause colds. Two kinds of cold viruses are shown in the pictures. Cold viruses in the air can enter your nasal passages and throat easily when you inhale. Cold viruses on your skin can enter your body if you touch your hand to your mouth, nose, or eyes. The viruses reproduce quickly inside the respiratory system. One or two days later the growing viruses cause the familiar symptoms of the common cold.

The early stage of a cold usually lasts three or four days. During this time viruses continue to multiply in your nasal passages and throat. The tissue that lines your nasal passages produces extra mucus, and you get a runny nose. The tissue might also swell, making your nose stuffy. Other symptoms might include coughing, sore throat, sneezing, watery eyes, mild fever, and a loss of appetite. You might experience all of these symptoms or only a few of them during the early stage of a cold. The cold viruses can be passed on to others during this stage. Therefore, doctors suggest you stay at home during this time.

About a week later your body's defenses destroy the viruses. During this stage a person can no longer pass the viruses to others. The cold symptoms, however, continue for a few days.

You have probably heard that no cure exists for the common cold. More than 150 kinds of viruses cause colds, and scientists have not yet developed a vaccine that is effective against all of them. Antibiotics kill only bacteria, not viruses. Products such as cough syrup and cold tablets might make you feel better when you have a cold. However, these products treat only the symptoms, not the disease itself.

Your body's defenses can fight off the invading viruses. To help your body's own defenses, doctors recommend that you get plenty of rest and drink more fluids than usual. You should also avoid other people as much as possible so you do not spread the cold viruses.

Did You Know?
Colds are more common during cold winter months when people spend more time indoors. People are closer together indoors and, therefore, more likely to catch colds from each other.

49,000 times actual size

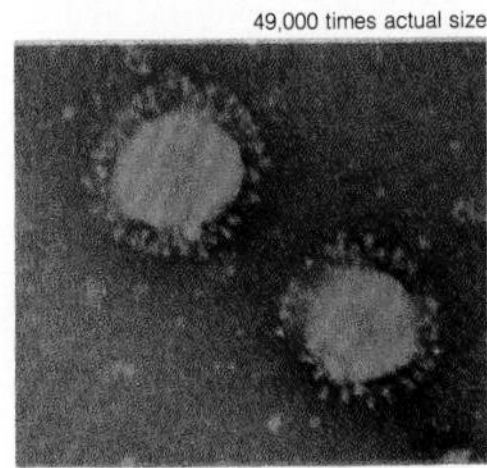

47,840 times actual size

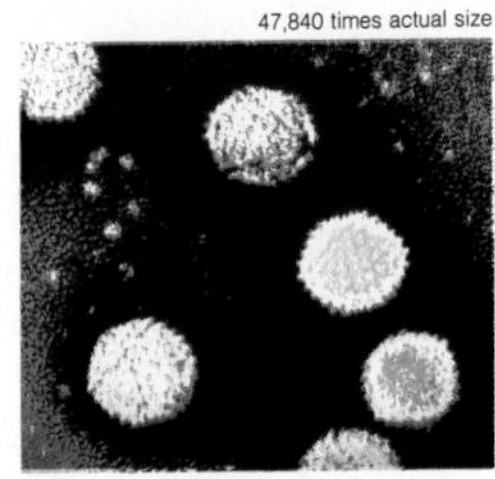

Two of the more than one hundred kinds of viruses that cause colds.

2 Teach

Strategies for Pages 210 and 211

• Write the lesson title question on the chalkboard. As students read through the lesson, list the diseases that are discussed. • Direct students to read page 210 and describe some symptoms of a cold. Write a list on the chalkboard. (sore throat, watery eyes, runny nose) • Then ask students to refer to the picture and name the body parts that make up the respiratory system. (nasal passages, throat, windpipe, lungs) • Let students read page 211 to find out what causes colds. (viruses) Ask how cold viruses can enter your body. (through the nasal passages, mouth, and openings around the eyes) • Help students add to their list of the symptoms of a cold. (runny or stuffy nose, sore throat, cough, sneezing, watery eyes, mild fever, loss of appetite) • Call on students to explain what causes a runny nose. (As viruses multiply, the tissue lining the nasal passages produces extra mucus.) • Ask if cough syrup or cold tablets can cure a cold. (No, they only treat the symptoms.) • Ask what a person can do to help the body's defenses fight off cold viruses. (rest, plenty of fluids) • Ask why a person with a cold should stay home for a few days. (to rest and to avoid spreading the cold to others)

Overhead Transparency Master

Use this blackline master to make a labeled overhead transparency or to make an unlabeled student worksheet. This blackline master may be reproduced from the Teacher's Resource Book.

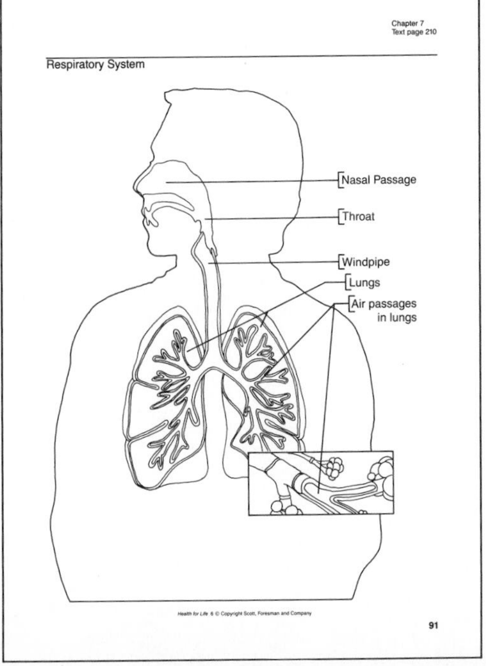

Teaching Plan

Lesson 3 continued

2 Teach

Strategies for Pages 212 and 213

• Write the word *sinusitis* on the chalkboard. • Direct students to read page 212 to learn what causes sinusitis. (Cold viruses cause the lining of the sinuses to swell and to produce more mucus than normal, blocking the sinus openings.) Encourage students to compare the two pictures of sinuses. (One shows normal conditions and the other shows the swelling due to sinusitis.) • Ask what treatment is available for a bad case of sinusitis. (Antibiotics can help reduce the number of bacteria present.)
• Let students explain how to avoid severe sinusitis. (by taking care of themselves when they have a cold)
• Ask students to read page 213 to find out some of the symptoms of the flu. (fever, chills, aching muscles, weakness, headache, dizziness, sore throat, and coughing) Ask which of these symptoms the students have experienced during the flu. Discuss what causes the flu. (flu viruses)

sinusitis (sī′nə sī′tis), a disease in which the sinus openings become blocked.

Did You Know?
Smoke can cause sinusitis. Smoke particles from cigarettes or bonfires can irritate the sinuses and make them swell. The lining of the sinuses makes extra mucus to wash away the particles. The extra mucus can block the sinus openings.

When Does Sinusitis Occur?

The bones of your head and face have spaces within them called sinuses. The white arrows in the first picture show how these sinuses connect with the nasal passages. Mucus usually drains through the sinus openings into the nose and throat. If these openings become blocked, you can get **sinusitis.**

Sinusitis often occurs immediately after a cold. The same kind of tissue that lines the nose also lines the sinuses. The lining of the sinuses swells and produces more mucus than usual. Tissue around the sinus openings might swell and close off the openings. The mucus might thicken so that it blocks the openings. Then mucus accumulates in the sinuses, as shown in the second picture. The thick mucus might back up into your throat, making you cough.

Most cases of sinusitis are mild. However, certain bacteria can grow in the thickening mucus and make the sinusitis worse, especially if the openings of the sinuses are blocked. This blockage might result in headaches or a feeling of pressure behind your eyes. Antibiotics can help reduce the number of bacteria.

You can usually avoid a severe case of sinusitis by taking care of yourself when you have a cold. This care includes getting rest, drinking fluids, and taking medicines if they are suggested by your doctor.

Clear and blocked sinuses

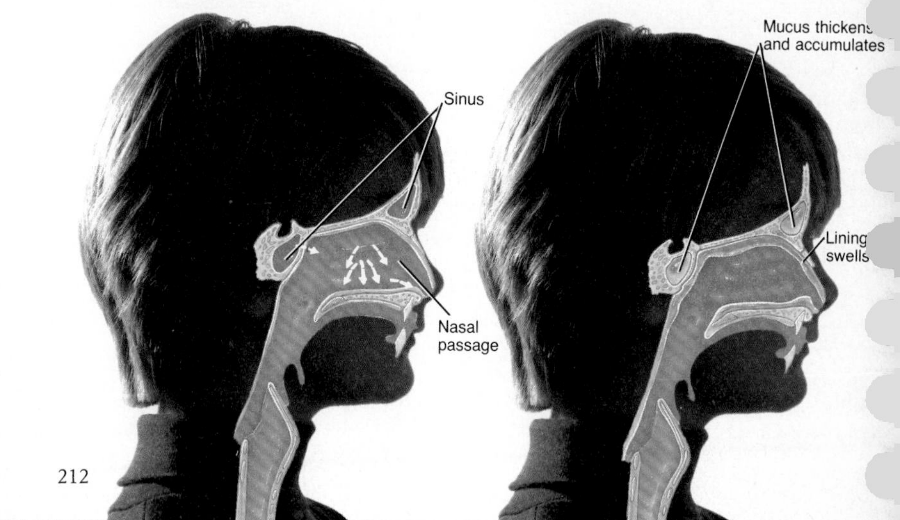

212

Teaching Options

Anecdote

Cold epidemics have long plagued the U.S. Army. In the 1960s researchers found out that two viruses were primarily responsible. Vaccines were made for the viruses, and the incidence of colds in the Army was reduced by 50 percent. Effective vaccines for colds are still unavailable on a larger scale due to the number of possible cold viruses.

Enrichment

Ask students to use library sources to find out how flu vaccines are developed and what groups of people doctors recommend the vaccines for.

Health and Social Studies

Ask students to look in books or magazine articles to find out about the flu epidemic of 1918 in the United States and Europe.

Reteaching

Let students make health posters by listing the symptoms and treatment of sinusitis and flu.

How Do You Get Influenza?

The flu—influenza—is similar to a cold in many ways. Like a cold, different kinds of viruses cause the flu. Flu viruses, like the one shown, invade the same parts of the body as cold viruses—the nose, throat, and air passages. Flu symptoms are similar to those of a cold, but much more severe. A person with the flu usually has fever, chills, aching muscles, and a general feeling of weakness. Other symptoms include headache, dizziness, sore throat, and coughing.

You can treat the flu as you do a cold. You should stay home for a few days to rest and to avoid spreading the disease germs to others. Flu is very easily spread. In fact, sometimes flu epidemics occur. The disease spreads so quickly that many people have it at the same time. With proper care, the flu usually lasts about four or five days.

As with a cold, no medicine can cure the flu or prevent you from getting the flu. No single vaccine can guard you against every kind of flu virus. Sometimes, however, scientists can predict what kinds of viruses will affect a population in a certain year. Then they can make a vaccine for those viruses.

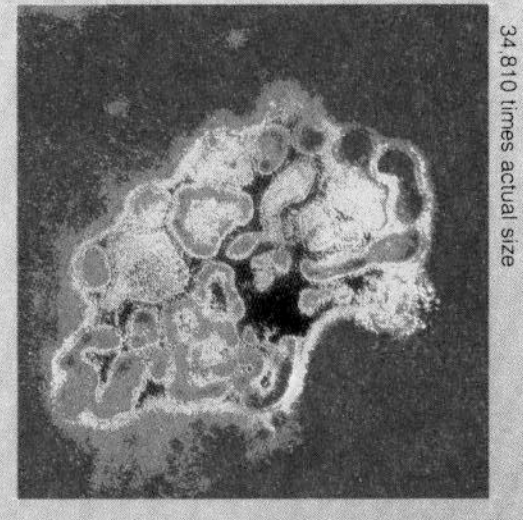

34 810 times actual size

Computer image of one kind of flu virus.

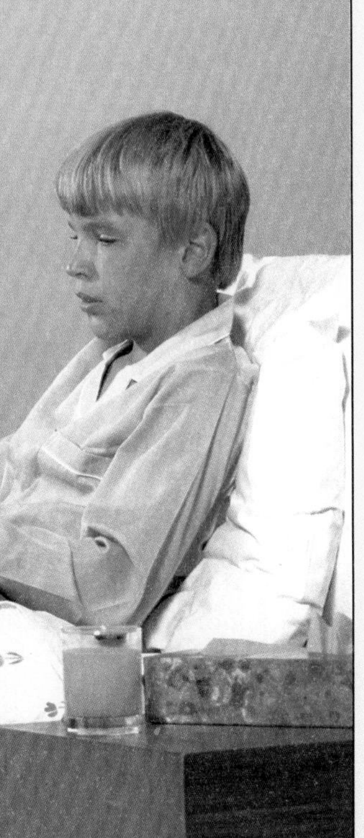

213

• Let students explain how to treat the flu. (rest at home, drink fluids) Ask if a vaccine can prevent the flu. (No single vaccine can prevent every kind of flu, but sometimes scientists can develop a vaccine against several kinds of flu.) • Explain to students that most doctors do not recommend that everyone receive a flu vaccine every year.

Life Skills

Use this worksheet for practice in classifying facts and opinions about respiratory diseases. This master may be reproduced from the Teacher's Resource Book and is located on page 25 of the Student's Workbook. Use with Chapter 7: pages 210–215.

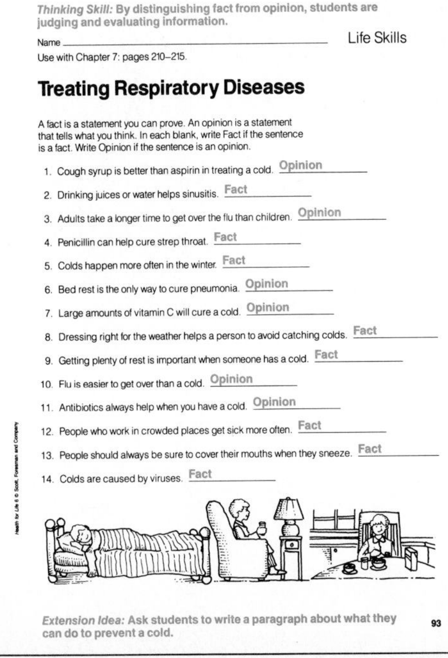

Thinking Skill: **By distinguishing fact from opinion, students are judging and evaluating information.**

Name ________________ Life Skills

Use with Chapter 7: pages 210–215.

Treating Respiratory Diseases

A fact is a statement you can prove. An opinion is a statement that tells what you think. In each blank, write Fact if the sentence is a fact. Write Opinion if the sentence is an opinion.

1. Cough syrup is better than aspirin in treating a cold. Opinion
2. Drinking juices or water helps sinusitis. Fact
3. Adults take a longer time to get over the flu than children. Opinion
4. Penicillin can help cure strep throat. Fact
5. Colds happen more often in the winter. Fact
6. Bed rest is the only way to cure pneumonia. Opinion
7. Large amounts of vitamin C will cure a cold. Opinion
8. Dressing right for the weather helps a person to avoid catching colds. Fact
9. Getting plenty of rest is important when someone has a cold. Fact
10. Flu is easier to get over than a cold. Opinion
11. Antibiotics always help when you have a cold. Opinion
12. People who work in crowded places get sick more often. Fact
13. People should always be sure to cover their mouths when they sneeze. Fact
14. Colds are caused by viruses. Fact

Extension Idea: **Ask students to write a paragraph about what they can do to prevent a cold.**

93

Teaching Plan

Lesson 3 continued

2 Teach

Strategies for Pages 214 and 215

• Write the word *pneumonia* on the chalkboard. Explain that *pneumon* means "lung" in Greek. • Direct students to read the first two paragraphs on page 214 and describe the symptoms of pneumonia. (coughing, fever, chest pain, noisy breathing) • Ask why viral pneumonia is more dangerous than bacterial pneumonia. (Viral pneumonia does not respond to treatment with antibiotics.) • Let students read the remainder of page 214 and page 215 to find out what can cause a sore throat. (respiratory disease, strep throat) • Ask what the tonsils are. (small oval-shaped masses of tissue on either side of the tongue) Discuss how disease germs can affect them. (make them red and swollen) • Call on students to explain the symptoms and treatment of strep throat. (severe sore throat; antibiotics, such as penicillin)

Did You Know?
Pneumonia sometimes occurs while a person has another disease and the body is in a weakened condition. A flu epidemic in 1918 became a worldwide disaster when many people with flu also developed pneumonia. A certain kind of bacteria caused this pneumonia. Antibiotics had not yet been developed, and millions of people in the United States and Europe died from the epidemic.

What Is Pneumonia?

Pneumonia is an inflammation of the lungs. Most kinds are infectious and are caused by bacteria and viruses which begin growing in the nose and throat and then move to the lungs. The disease germs cause the tissue in the lungs to swell. Thick mucus collects in the lungs and interferes with breathing. Notice the X-ray picture of healthy lungs and a lung with pneumonia. The arrow points to the swollen tissue.

Symptoms of pneumonia include coughing, fever, chest pain, and noisy breathing. The treatment for this disease depends on what caused it. If bacteria caused the disease, antibiotics can help. If a virus caused the disease, the doctor might simply recommend bed rest and plenty of fluids.

What Can Cause a Sore Throat?

Disease germs that grow in your respiratory system usually affect your throat. Therefore, a sore throat is a common symptom of many mild respiratory diseases, such as a cold or flu.

The X ray to the right clearly shows pneumonia in the lung.

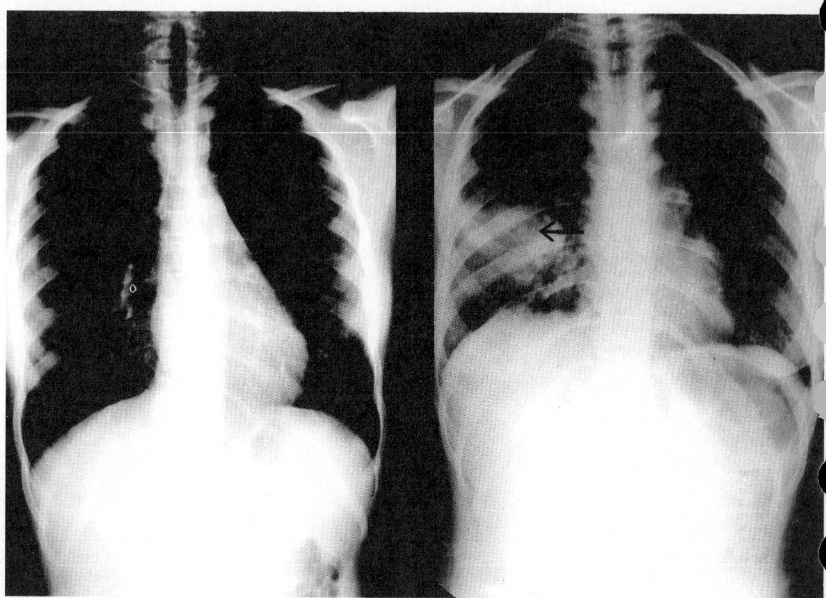

214

Teaching Options

Enrichment
If left untreated, strep throat can lead to a condition called rheumatic fever. Ask students to find out the cause, symptoms, and treatment of rheumatic fever.

Health and Science
Ask students to use the library to find information on another disease of the respiratory system, such as pleurisy. Tell students to find out what causes the disease and how it is treated.

Reteaching
Ask students to look in an encyclopedia or science book to find out which germ causes strep throat and what the germ looks like. Ask students to draw the germ.

When you have a sore throat, you might notice a change in your tonsils. Notice in the first picture that tonsils are small, oval-shaped clumps of tissue on either side of the tongue. Disease germs can make the tonsils red and swollen, as shown in the second picture. The swollen tonsils make the throat sore.

If you get a severe sore throat, you might have strep throat. This disease can be serious if it is not identified and treated by a doctor. A certain kind of bacteria causes strep throat. An antibiotic, such as penicillin, is usually effective in treating strep throat.

By taking care of your respiratory system, you might be able to prevent some diseases. The box to the right lists some ways to care for your respiratory system. Even with proper care, you might get a few respiratory infections each year. The symptoms do cause discomfort, but you can recover quickly if you take care of yourself properly.

Care of the Respiratory System
- Avoid exposure to people with respiratory infections.
- Help your body resist infection by eating a balanced diet and getting proper rest.
- Exercise regularly to keep your chest muscles strong.
- Do not smoke.
- Avoid breathing indoor pollutants such as sidestream smoke and aerosol sprays.

Think Back • *Study on your own with Study Guide page 328.*
1. What causes a cold and flu? What do doctors recommend for treating these diseases?
2. How can the sinuses become blocked?
3. What are some symptoms of pneumonia?
4. What respiratory diseases can be treated successfully with antibiotics?
5. How can you care for your respiratory system?

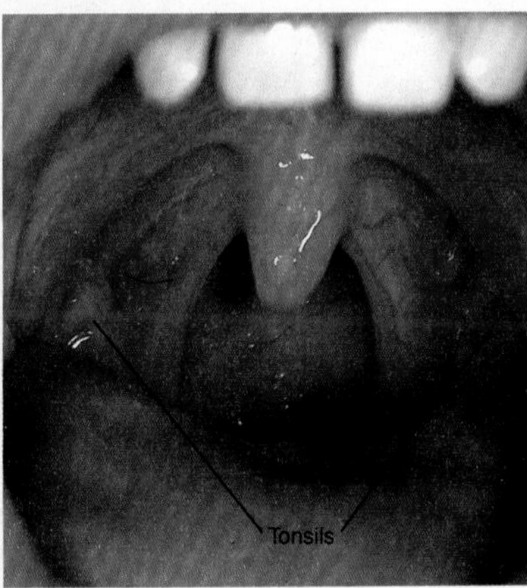

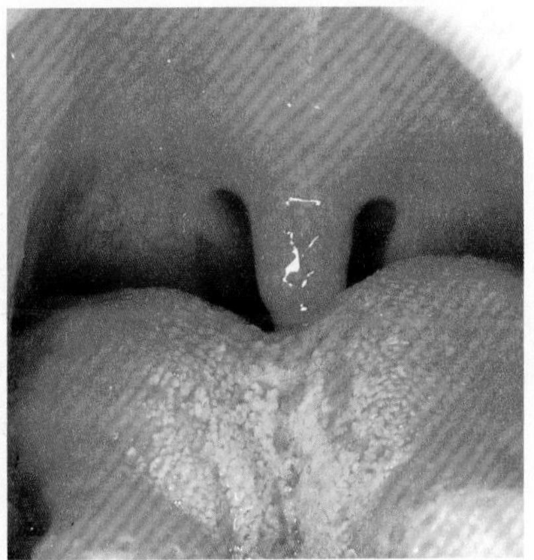

Healthy and swollen tonsils

3 Assess

Expanding Student Thinking

Ask students to list symptoms common to many respiratory diseases. (sore throat, stuffy nose, coughing, fever)

Thinking Skill By listing symptoms common to many respiratory diseases, students are *organizing information.*

Answers to Think Back

1. Viruses cause colds and the flu. Doctors recommend plenty of rest, drinking fluids, and staying away from others when possible to avoid spreading the disease.

2. Viruses might cause the tissue around the sinuses to swell, blocking the sinus openings. The mucus might thicken so that it blocks the sinus openings.

3. Symptoms of pneumonia include coughing, fever, chest pain, and noisy breathing.

4. Respiratory diseases caused by bacteria can be treated with antibiotics. These include sinusitis, pneumonia, and strep throat.

5. To care for your respiratory system, avoid exposure to people with infections, eat a balanced diet, get proper rest and exercise, avoid smoking, and try not to breathe indoor pollutants.

Activity Plan

Health Activities Workshop pages 216–217

Activity 1 Strategies
Guide students in looking up *-itis* in the dictionary. (*-itis* means "inflammation of") Let students list the names of some diseases that end with this suffix. (tonsillitis, meningitis, arthritis, bronchitis, and so on)
Thinking Skill By finding out the meaning of a suffix, students are *collecting information.*

Activity 2 Strategies
You might want students to work in small groups for this activity. Try to provide enough magazines and newspapers so that all groups will have access to materials for their scrapbooks. If students need help summarizing the articles they have found, suggest that they first try to answer questions that use the following cues: Who? What? When? Where? Why? How?
Thinking Skills By collecting and summarizing articles, students are *collecting* and *organizing information.*

Activity 3 Strategies
Ask students to name what is shown in the cartoon. (tears, white blood cells, antibodies, and a disease germ) Students' paragraphs should explain that the cartoon shows that the body has many defenses against disease germs.
Thinking Skill By explaining the idea the cartoon shows, students are *interpreting information.*

Health Activities Workshop

Learning More About Communicable Disease

1. You might have noticed that many names of diseases end with *-itis*. Use a dictionary to find out what this suffix means.

2. Collect articles from current magazines and newspapers about new developments in fighting disease. Put the articles in a scrapbook. Along with each article, include one or two paragraphs that summarize the article. Share the information you have gathered with your class.

3. Look at the cartoon. Then write a paragraph describing what idea the cartoon shows.

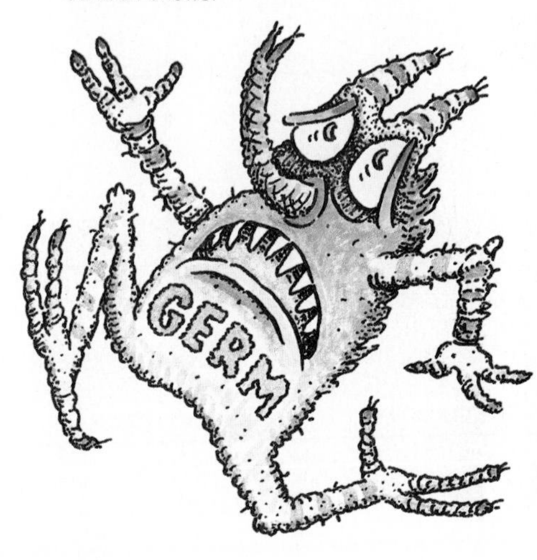

216

Looking at Careers

4. "Get this to the lab right away." "We'll know more when we get the lab results." "Well, according to the lab report, . . ."

If you have ever spent time in a hospital or watched a medical program on television, you might have heard such statements. Before deciding upon the proper treatment for a patient, a doctor often needs to order laboratory tests. A sample of a patient's blood, urine, saliva, or body tissue is sent to the lab. Then a medical laboratory worker analyzes the sample. The doctor interprets the analysis and decides upon the best treatment for the patient. A laboratory employs several kinds of medical workers.

Medical technologists perform complicated tests and analyses. The technologist shown here is analyzing bacteria from a patient to determine the type of bacteria that is causing the patient's disease. By knowing the type of bacteria, the patient's doctor can decide how to treat the disease.

Medical laboratory technicians perform some of the same tests, usually under the guidance of a technologist.

Medical laboratory assistants assist technologists and technicians. Assistants perform some of the simpler tasks in the laboratory. For example, they might clean and sterilize equipment, store supplies, and prepare chemical solutions.

Each kind of laboratory worker needs a different amount of education. Technologists must have at least four years of college education. Technicians must have two years of college. Assistants must have taken a one-year course that includes laboratory training.

What school subjects do you think would be helpful in preparing someone for a career as a medical laboratory worker? Why would these subjects be helpful for this career?

For more information write to the American Society for Medical Technology, 330 Meadowfern Drive, Houston, TX 77067.

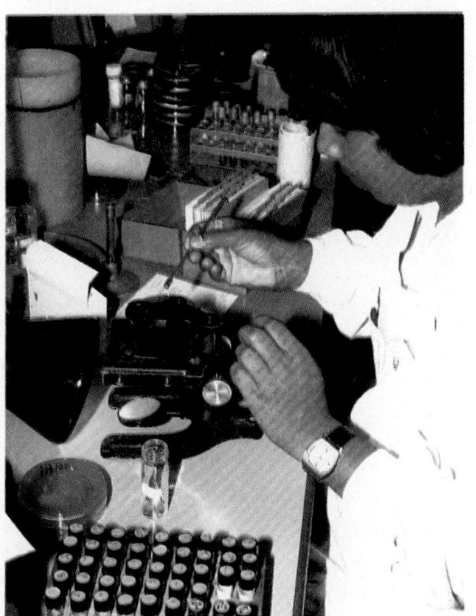

Activity 4 Strategies
If possible, invite a medical laboratory worker to visit the class and explain his or her work. School subjects that are helpful to a medical laboratory worker include science, especially biology and chemistry, for learning about medicine and chemicals and for learning good scientific skills such as observation, record keeping, and analysis. English would help in improving communication skills. Mathematics would help in dealing with the calculations that laboratory workers make.

Thinking Skills By naming school subjects helpful to a medical laboratory worker, students are *generalizing* and *drawing conclusions*.

Teaching Plan

Lesson 4 pages 218–223

Lesson Objective
Explain the causes and prevention of such noncommunicable diseases as cardiovascular diseases and cancer. Describe how to care for the cardiovascular system.

Health Vocabulary
Atherosclerosis, cancer, cardiovascular disease, hypertension, noncommunicable disease, plaque, tumor

1 Motivate

Introducing the Lesson
List several examples of noncommunicable diseases. (cancer, heart disease, muscular dystrophy, and so on) Discuss why these diseases have become more of a health concern today than they were years ago. (Years ago people died at an earlier age, before symptoms of some of these diseases appeared. People also did more physical work and this activity helped prevent some types of noncommunicable diseases. Society's current demands put more stress on people. Today's diets consist of more foods that include high fat and sugar content.)

noncommunicable (non′kə myü′nə kə bəl) **disease,** a disease that is not caused by germs and that does not spread.

4 What Causes Noncommunicable Diseases?

At the beginning of this century in the United States, communicable diseases were the most deadly ones. Today, antibiotics, better health care, and better sanitary conditions make these diseases much less dangerous. The diseases that now account for the most deaths in the United States are **noncommunicable diseases.**

Disease germs do not cause noncommunicable diseases, such as heart disease and cancer. These diseases cannot spread from one person to another. Also, noncommunicable diseases often take years to develop in the body and might last a lifetime.

The known causes of noncommunicable disease can be placed into two main groups: heredity and environment. Heredity involves the passing of genes from parents to children. A person might inherit genes that cause a certain disease. For example, muscular dystrophy is an inherited disease of the muscles.

The environment includes your surroundings. You cannot control heredity, but you usually have some control over environmental causes of disease. Cigarette smoking, for example, is a cause of cancer that people have some control over.

How does plaque buildup in arteries affect health?

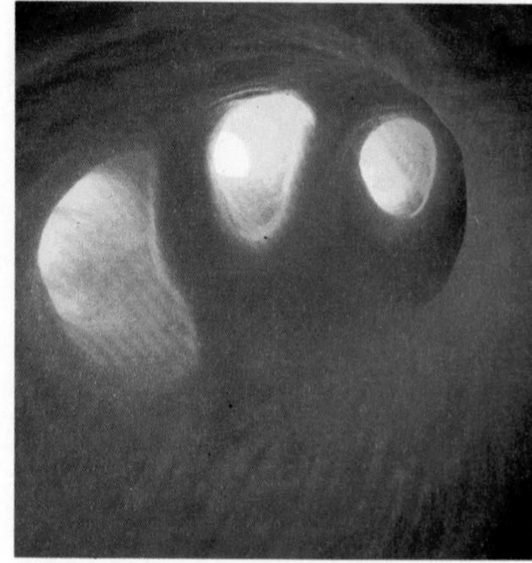

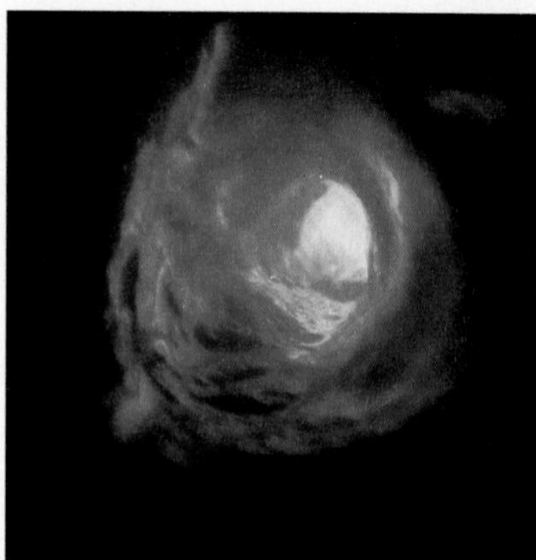

218

Teaching Options

Health Background

Heredity, environment, or a combination of both can contribute to noncommunicable diseases. Some diseases, such as hemophilia and Tay-Sachs disease, are caused by heredity. For other diseases, people inherit a tendency to get the disease, but they may or may not develop the disease. Heart diseases, some cancers, and diabetes mellitus are examples of diseases for which people might inherit a tendency. Environmental risk factors that can lead to disease include radiation, chemicals, smoking, and a high-cholesterol diet.

Enrichment
Ask students to find out and compare the death rates due to various types of cancer and cardiovascular diseases among several countries. Suggest that they contact the local heart association and cancer society for information. Let students speculate about the reasons for the differences they find. (For example, few Japanese develop cancer of the colon, possibly because their diet is high in fiber.)

Health and Math
Help students find statistics about various diseases to learn which age groups the diseases most often affect. Students can make a chart of their findings.

Reteaching
Ask students to write a paragraph on how plaque can cause a heart attack. (Plaque buildup can block arteries and keep the heart from getting needed blood.)

Special Education
To make material on cardiovascular diseases more concrete, you may wish to review with learning-disabled students the structure and functions of the parts of the circulatory system. If possible, use models of the heart and blood vessels.

Heredity and environment usually act together to cause a noncommunicable disease. For example, heredity might make a person more likely than other people to have a heart attack. If the person smokes, however, his or her chances of having a heart attack become even greater.

What Are Cardiovascular Diseases?

Cardiovascular diseases are diseases of the heart and blood vessels. The first three pictures show the insides of blood vessels called arteries. **Plaque**—a fatty substance—has built up on the inside walls of some of the arteries. This buildup of plaque is called **atherosclerosis.** As plaque continues to build up, the hollow part of the blood vessel becomes narrow.

The first picture shows the clear passageway through a healthy artery. Notice the smooth walls. The second picture shows a buildup of plaque on the artery walls. The heart has to pump harder to keep the blood flowing because the passageway through the artery is narrower. In the third picture, the passageway is even more blocked. The yellow spots in the fourth picture show another view of plaque buildup in arteries.

Atherosclerosis is serious because the buildup of plaque can prevent the body cells from getting oxygen and other materials that the blood usually brings. This buildup of plaque can cause other problems too.

cardiovascular (kär′dē ō vas′kyə lər) **disease,** a disease of the heart or blood vessels.

plaque (plak), a fatty substance that builds up along the inside walls of an artery.

atherosclerosis (ath′ər ō sklə rō′sis), a cardiovascular disease in which material builds up inside the arteries.

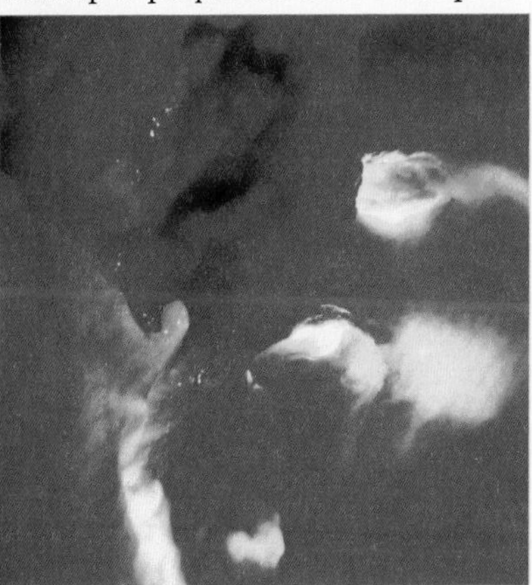

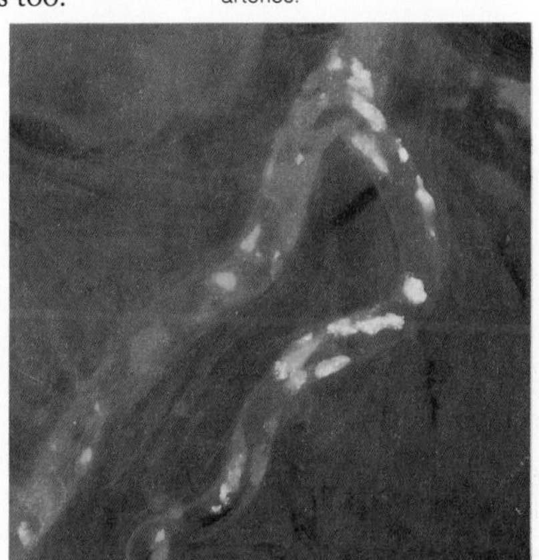

Yellow spots show plaque in arteries.

2 Teach

Strategies for Pages 218 and 219

• Direct the students to read page 218 to find out how noncommunicable diseases differ from communicable diseases. (Noncommunicable diseases are not caused by disease germs and do not spread from one person to another.) • Ask students to name two causes of noncommunicable diseases. (heredity and environment) • Ask students to name a disease caused by heredity (muscular dystrophy) and one that can be caused by environment (cancer).
• Tell students to read page 219 to find out what cardiovascular diseases are. • Ask what plaque is. (a fatty substance that builds up inside the walls of blood vessels) Discuss how it affects the heart and the body's cells. (Plaque blocks the blood vessels and causes the heart to pump harder. Plaque can prevent the cells from getting oxygen and nutrients.) Remind students that plaque that forms in blood vessels is not the same as plaque that forms on teeth.

Teaching Plan

Lesson 4 continued

2 Teach

Strategies for Pages 220 and 221

• Direct students to read page 220 to find out how atherosclerosis can lead to other diseases. (By blocking the arteries, atherosclerosis can lead to hypertension, heart attack, and stroke.) • Write the word *hypertension* on the chalkboard and ask students to define it. (high blood pressure) • Compare high blood pressure with the kinds of pressure water exerts against the inside wall of a hose, and how this pressure can be felt against the thumb when it partially blocks the flow of water out of the hose. • Be sure students understand the difference between a heart attack and a stroke. (In a heart attack, an artery leading to the heart is blocked and part of the heart is damaged. In a stroke, an artery leading to the brain is blocked and part of the brain is damaged.) • Ask students to read page 221 and then list ways to reduce the risk of heart problems. (Limit foods high in fat and cholesterol; exercise; do not smoke; learn to deal with stress.)

hypertension (hī′pər ten′shən), high blood pressure.

Did You Know?
During coronary artery bypass surgery, a piece of blood vessel, usually taken from the leg, can be connected to the heart so that the flow of blood to the heart bypasses, or goes around, the blocked artery.
As an alternative to surgery, some patients choose angioplasty. With this method, a tiny tube with a small, strong balloon at the end is inserted into the narrowed artery. The balloon is inflated, pressing the plaque against the artery wall. This action reopens the passageway.

What Other Diseases Can Atherosclerosis Lead To?

Atherosclerosis is often associated with **hypertension**—high blood pressure. Hypertension can cause artery walls to weaken, balloon out, and break, especially when the walls are already weakened by the buildup of plaque.

Atherosclerosis can also lead to a heart attack or a stroke. If an artery that supplies blood to the heart becomes blocked, part of the heart is damaged. The damage of part of the heart is a heart attack.

If an artery leading to the brain becomes blocked, part of the brain is damaged, and a stroke occurs. Part of the brain becomes damaged because it cannot get oxygen and other nutrients it needs. The inch-long (2.5 cm) piece of plaque in the picture caused a stroke. The drawing shows where the plaque built up in the neck. A stroke can also be caused by hypertension. The high blood pressure can cause an artery in the brain to weaken and burst.

How Can You Help Prevent Cardiovascular Diseases?

Cardiovascular diseases are more common in adults than in people your age. However, good health practices begun at an early age can help prevent these diseases from occurring later in life. You can care for your cardiovascular system by eating properly, exercising, not smoking, and handling stress in healthy ways.

This plaque built up in an artery in the neck and caused a stroke.

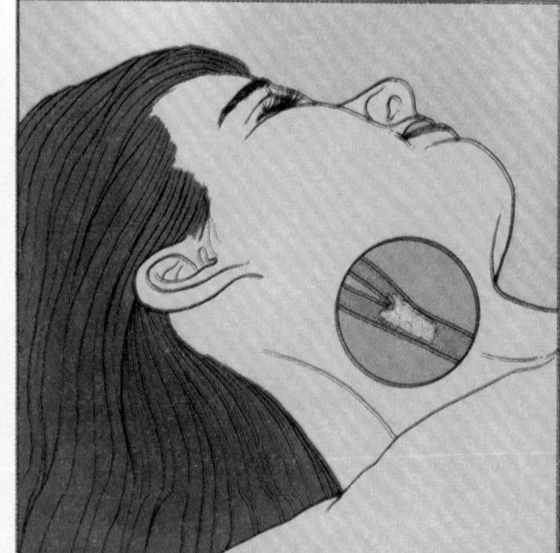

220

Teaching Options

Anecdote

Cardiovascular diseases are the leading cause of death in the United States. These diseases kill more than one million people each year.

Enrichment

Ask students to use an encyclopedia or book on nutrition to find out which foods are low in fat and cholesterol. Students could make a list of these foods for reference in planning a healthy diet that is low in fat and cholesterol.

Health and Math

Help students find information regarding annual death rates due to heart attacks over the past fifteen years in the United States. The local chapter of the American Heart Association can provide data. Help students graph the results of their research and look for trends. (In recent years deaths from heart attacks have decreased.)

Reteaching

Suggest that students list and describe three diseases that atherosclerosis can lead to. (high blood pressure—blood pushes with greater force than usual against the walls of the arteries; heart attack—the heart is damaged by a blocked artery; stroke—part of the brain is damaged due to a blocked artery)

By reducing the amount of fat and cholesterol you eat, you can reduce the chance of building up plaque in your blood vessels. Cholesterol is a fatlike substance that makes up part of plaque. Food such as hot dogs, hamburgers, egg yolks, and butter are high in fat or cholesterol. These foods do not have to be eliminated, but they should be only a small part of your diet.

Exercise is an effective way to reduce the risks of heart disease. Exercise makes the heart larger and stronger. A stronger heart does not have to work as hard to pump blood. Also, a stronger heart can pump more blood with each beat. Exercise also reduces the amount of fat in the blood. Then the chances of building up plaque are less. Cycling, running, walking, and swimming are particularly helpful kinds of exercise.

Not smoking is one of the most effective ways to reduce the risk of heart attack and stroke. The nicotine in smoke narrows the blood vessels. Then the openings of the vessels become smaller, and blood pressure increases. Not smoking keeps the openings of the blood vessels as large as possible to keep blood flowing properly. Notice in the chart how smoking increases the risk of having a heart attack. What other factors, shown in the chart, increase the risk of having a heart attack?

Blood vessels also narrow when you are under stress. By learning to handle stress calmly, you can help keep your blood vessels healthy.

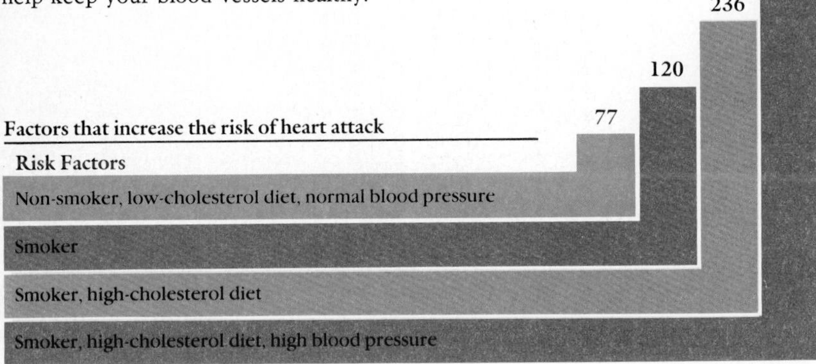

• Encourage students to think of stressful situations that might cause hypertension and suggest healthy ways a person might reduce the stress. (job interview—be prepared, be on time; traffic jam—leave for destination early to allow extra time)

• Direct students to read page 222 to find out what cancer is. (uncontrolled growth of abnormal body cells) Write the word *tumor* on the chalkboard. Tell students that it takes approximately one billion cells to make up a tumor that is noticeable to the touch. Point out that not all tumors are cancerous. Explain that noncancerous tumors are called *benign* tumors. Cancerous tumors are called *malignant* tumors.

Teaching Plan

Lesson 4 continued

2 Teach

Strategies for Pages 222 and 223

• Be sure students understand why cancerous tumors are dangerous. (They grow rapidly and invade the surrounding tissue. They damage healthy cells and interfere with the normal functions of the body. They may also invade other areas of the body.) • Help students list some environmental causes of certain kinds of cancer. (smoking, sun's radiation, high-fat diet) • Let students read page 223 to discover ways that various kinds of cancer are treated. (surgery, radiation, drugs) • Direct students' attention to the chart. Call on students to read aloud the ways to help prevent cancer.

Using On Your Own

People might put off seeing a doctor because they are afraid of cancer and would rather not know they have the disease. Some people might mistakenly assume that all cancer is untreatable.

Thinking Skill By writing about why people might put off seeing a doctor for cancer, students are *suggesting alternatives*.

cancer (kan′sər), the uncontrolled growth of abnormal body cells.

tumor (tü′mər), a clump of useless tissue caused by the buildup of abnormal cells.

On Your Own

People often recognize possible signs of cancer in their bodies long before they see a doctor. Write a paragraph explaining why you think some people might put off seeing a doctor about such a serious illness.

What Is Cancer?

People can get many different kinds of cancer. However, all cancers are alike in some ways. In all cancers certain body cells begin to grow and spread abnormally. The uncontrolled growth of abnormal body cells is called **cancer.** In some types of cancer, abnormal cells continue to grow and reproduce until they form a clump of tissue called a **tumor.** The drawing shows how a tumor forms. Tumors can form in the brain, lung, stomach, or other organs.

Not all tumors are cancerous. Sometimes cells clump and form fairly harmless tumors. They grow slowly, stay in one part of the body, and can usually be completely removed by surgery.

Cancer tumors are more dangerous. They grow rapidly and invade the surrounding tissue. Some cancer cells might break away from the tumor, travel through the bloodstream, and begin to grow in other parts of the body. Cancer cells damage healthy cells and interfere with the normal functions of the body.

Heredity plays a role in causing some cancers. However, many factors in the environment increase the chances of someone getting cancer. Cigarette smoking can lead to lung cancer in some people. Overexposure to the sun and to other kinds of radiation can cause skin cancer. A diet high in fat might contribute to other types of cancer.

Abnormal cells grow in an unorganized way to form a tumor.

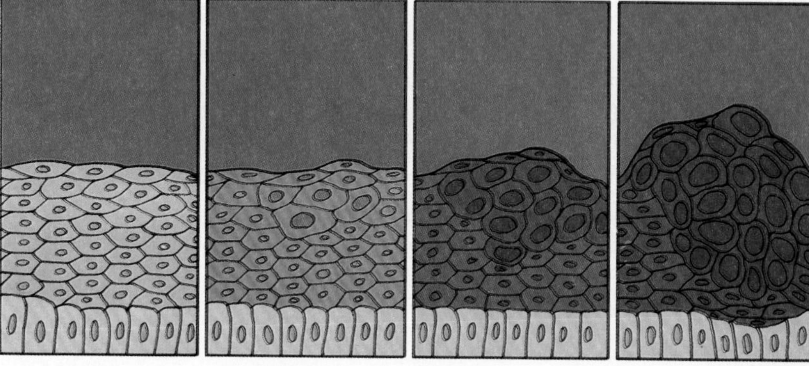

222

Teaching Options

Enrichment

Ask students to find magazine articles about people who have had cancer. Let students report on the medical developments that have helped these people readjust to daily life and the types of adjustments they have had to make. Articles about Norman Cousins might be especially interesting and enriching.

Health and Science

Encourage students to find out more about the latest technological advances made in treating cancer.

Reteaching

Ask students to write a one-page report explaining how following the eight practices in the chart can lead to a healthier life in ways other than helping to prevent cancer.

Ask students to list three environmental factors that can increase their chances of getting cancer. (cigarette smoking, overexposure to the sun, and a high fat diet)

How Can Cancer Be Treated and Prevented?

Several treatments can help cancer patients live longer lives. The three major treatments include using surgery to remove tumors, using radiation to kill cancer cells, and using drugs to kill cancer cells. The kind of treatment used depends on the type of cancer. Often, a combination of treatments gives the best results. Some kinds of cancer can be cured if they are found in early stages. At early stages cancer cells are less likely to have spread in the body. Because of this, it is important to be aware of the warning signs of cancer, shown below in No. 7. If you notice any of these signs, notify your doctor.

Scientists have recently made much progress in treating cancer. However, the best way to fight this disease is to try to prevent it from occurring. The chart shows how you can help reduce the risks of developing cancer. You might notice that many of these health practices also help prevent other diseases.

Think Back • *Study on your own with Study Guide page 329.*

1. What are the two main causes of noncommunicable diseases?
2. How can atherosclerosis cause a heart attack?
3. What is the difference between cancerous tumors and noncancerous tumors?
4. How can a person reduce the risks of getting cancer or cardiovascular diseases?

How to decrease the risk of developing cancer

1 Do not smoke.	2 Limit the amount of fat and cholesterol in your diet.	3 Eat more poultry and fish and less red meat, such as beef.	4 Eat more fruits and vegetables.
5 Do not sunbathe, especially between 11:00 A.M. and 2:00 P.M. when the sun's rays can do the most harm. When in the sun, wear a protective sunscreen.	6 Avoid unnecessary drugs.	7 Be aware of the warning signs of cancer. These signs include a lump in the breast or elsewhere, a sore that does not heal, unusual bleeding, and changes in size or color of a wart or mole.	8 Seek medical help if you feel you might have cancer. Many cancers can be treated successfully if discovered early enough.

3 Assess

Expanding Student Thinking

Ask students to write a paragraph describing a healthy lifestyle that could reduce the risk of developing cardiovascular diseases and some kinds of cancer. (Accept all answers that reflect an understanding of the lesson content.)

Thinking Skill By describing a lifestyle that could reduce the risk of developing cardiovascular diseases or cancer, students are *drawing conclusions*.

Answers to Think Back

1. Heredity and environment are the two main causes of noncommunicable diseases.

2. If atherosclerosis occurs in an artery leading to the heart, the artery could become completely blocked. This blockage stops the flow of blood to the heart tissue, causing a heart attack.

3. Tumors that are not cancerous are fairly harmless, grow slowly, stay in one place, and can be removed surgically. Tumors that are cancerous are more dangerous, grow more rapidly, and invade other areas of the body.

4. Preventive practices include eating a well-balanced diet, not smoking, not overexposing skin to the sun, checking for early warning signs, and seeking professional help as early as possible.

Teaching Plan

Lesson 5 pages 224-227

Lesson Objective
Describe the symptoms and causes of several kinds of allergies.

Health Vocabulary
Allergen

1 Motivate

Introducing the Lesson
Ask if any of the students have allergies. Let volunteers share their experiences with the symptoms and treatment of their allergies.

allergen (al′ər jən), a substance in the environment that causes an allergy.

5 What Is an Allergy?

Rain had fallen earlier in the day, but by afternoon the countryside was bathed in the warmth of the sun. Signs of spring were everywhere. Light-green leaves dotted the trees, and wildflowers lent a splash of color to the meadows. Gentle breezes carried nature's fragrances to the nearby farms.

For many people the spring day described above might be one of the most pleasant days of the year. For others, however, this day might be one of the most miserable. The flowers and breezes of spring often lead to sneezing, watery eyes, and other symptoms of allergies.

An allergy is a harmful reaction in some people's bodies to certain substances. An allergic reaction often resembles the symptoms of a cold. Something that causes an allergy is an **allergen.** Flowering plants, like those shown below, produce one of the most common allergens—pollen. Winds easily blow tiny pollen grains into the air. Then the pollen gets into the eyes, nose, and throat and causes a variety of reactions in millions of allergy sufferers.

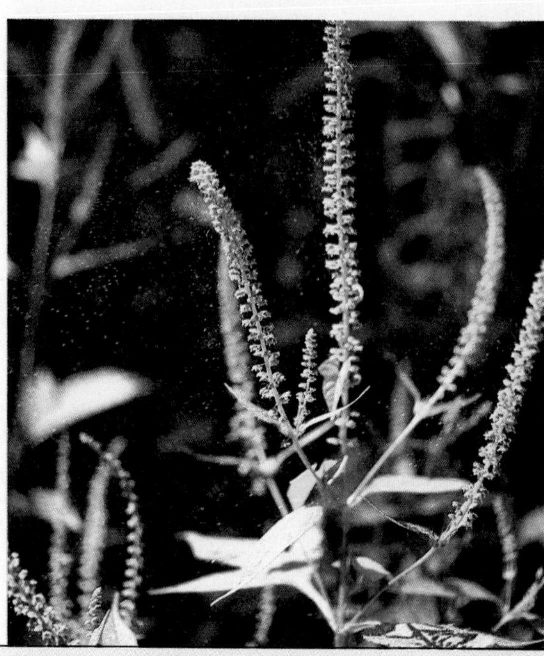

Wind blows pollen from plants.

224

Teaching Options

Health Background

An allergy is an unusual reaction to a substance in the environment. An allergy is usually caused by an inherited tendency combined with something in the environment. The symptoms that allergic persons have when they come in contact with the allergen are called allergic reactions. Common allergic reactions are sneezing, stuffy nose, runny nose, headache, skin rash, upset stomach, and difficult breathing. Asthma often becomes worse when a person experiences stress. About one-tenth of the population suffers from allergies.

Enrichment

Ask students to find out how doctors can test people for allergies. (Small amounts of the allergen are put under the skin or under the tongue to see if an allergic reaction develops.)

Students might want to find out the names of common plant allergens and at which seasons these allergens are usually most troublesome.

Health and Science

Let students use an encyclopedia to find out about some of the drugs that are used to treat asthma and hay fever. Students can write a report about how these drugs work.

Reteaching

Ask students to divide their papers into two columns labeled *Hayfever* and *Asthma.* Under each column, students should list how a person with that particular allergic condition might respond to allergens.

What Are the Symptoms of Hay Fever and Asthma?

Hay fever and asthma are two of the most common allergies. When a person has hay fever, the tissue that lines the nasal passage becomes swollen. The swollen tissue makes breathing through the nose difficult. Other symptoms include sneezing, a runny or itchy nose, and red, itchy eyes.

Asthma often involves more serious symptoms. The lining of the air passages in the lungs becomes swollen. Mucus builds up in these passages, as shown. Tiny air passages in the lungs tighten. Breathing becomes very difficult. The person's breathing can cause whistling or wheezing sounds as air forces its way out through the narrowed passages.

The most common allergens of hay fever and asthma are materials that people inhale, such as pollen, dust, fur, and smoke.

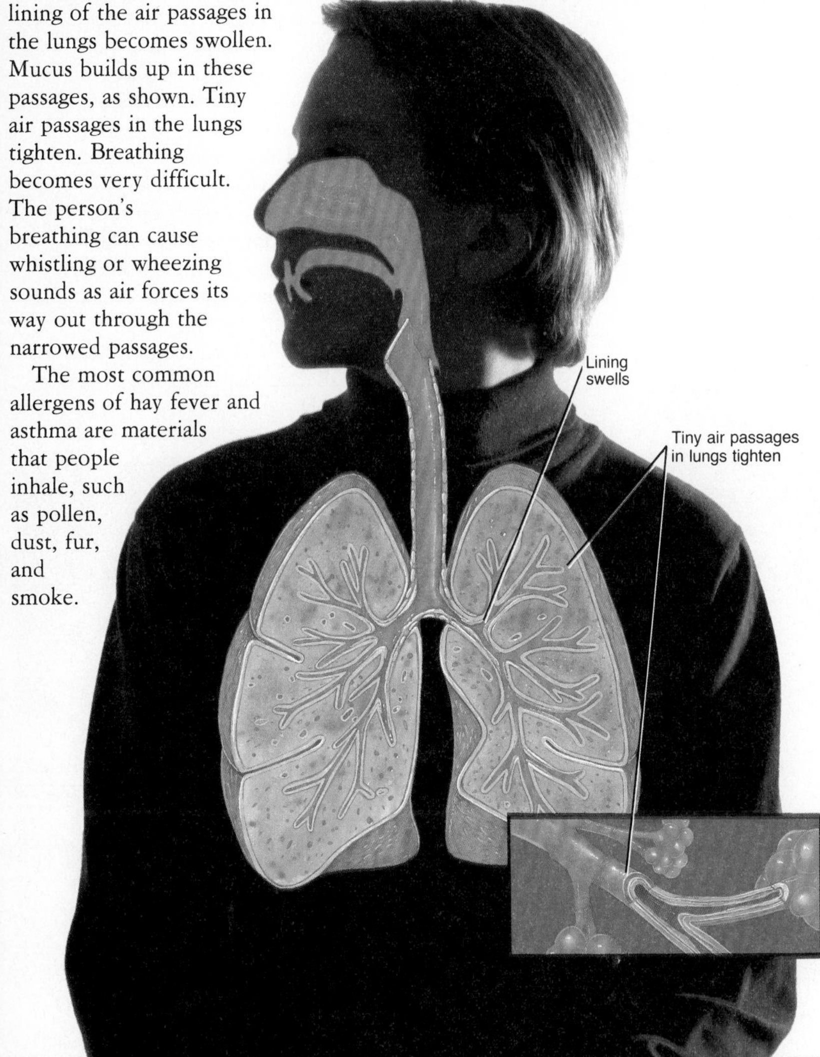

Air passages become swollen during asthma.

2 Teach

Strategies for Pages 224 and 225

• Write the lesson title question on the chalkboard. Let students read page 224 to find the answer. (An allergy is a harmful reaction in some people's bodies to certain substances, or allergens.) • Direct students to read page 225 to find out the symptoms of hay fever (sneezing, runny or itchy nose, red or itchy eyes) and asthma (swollen air passages to the lungs, difficulty breathing). Ask what common allergens cause hay fever and asthma. (pollen, dust, animal fur, smoke) • Make sure students understand that the symptoms of an allergy appear only if a person comes in contact with the allergen.

Teaching Plan

Lesson 5 continued

2 Teach

Strategies for Pages 226 and 227

• Ask students to read page 226 and list some common allergens. (medicines, clothing materials, foods, insect stings and so on) • Ask students to name some common symptoms of allergic reactions. (itchy skin, rash, difficult breathing, weakness, dizziness) You might want to explain that an extreme allergic reaction is known as anaphylactic shock. It is characterized by difficulty in breathing, vomiting, cramps, and diarrhea. If no medical attention is available, a person can die from anaphylactic shock within fifteen minutes. • Let students read page 227 to find out about how allergies can be treated. (avoid the allergen, take medicine to relieve the symptoms, take a series of shots to become less sensitive to the allergen)

What Are Some Other Kinds of Allergies?

About 35 million people in the United States have some sort of allergy. In fact, you could name any substance and chances are good that someone is allergic to it.

Some people are allergic to certain medicines, such as penicillin. This allergy might cause itchy skin, fever, or more serious effects. Other people are allergic to certain clothing material, such as wool. This allergy usually causes red, itchy rashes. Substances that cause an allergic reaction are called allergens. Nuts, milk, grains, chocolate, and shellfish are some common food allergens that can cause itchy skin rashes or the symptoms of hay fever and asthma.

The picture shows another common allergen. The stings of bees, wasps, and other insects cause discomfort for almost everyone. Some people, however, have allergic reactions to these stings. A rash might occur. The person might have a feeling of heat all over the skin. Later, he or she might feel weak and dizzy and have difficulty breathing. A person who has such allergic responses should get medical help immediately.

Insect stings are common allergens.

Teaching Options

Anecdote

Any food can be an allergen, but nuts cause about half of the food-related allergic reactions. Eggs and milk are responsible for a fifth of the allergic reactions from foods.

Enrichment

Help students find out more about how shots can make a person less sensitive to an allergen.

Health and Art

Suggest that students make a scrapbook showing common allergens. They can draw the pictures or use pictures cut from magazines. They can also use snapshots they took themselves. Students could refer to an encyclopedia or other reference book to find a more complete list of allergens.

Reteaching

Ask students to suggest ways a person might deal with a food allergy. (Avoid the food. Replace it with another food that provides the same nutritional value.)

What Can You Do About Allergies?

The first step in treating an allergy is to discover the allergens—the substances that cause the allergy. Quite often you can be the detective who figures out that you have an allergic reaction whenever you are in contact with a certain substance. Sometimes, however, a person has no idea what might be causing his or her allergy. The nurse in the picture is testing several substances on a patient to find out which ones cause an allergy.

If you have an allergy, the best way to treat it is to avoid the allergens. For example, a person might have to avoid certain foods or not keep a pet. Such allergens as pollen and dust are difficult to avoid. People who are allergic to these substances can take medicines to relieve the symptoms. Many people who have allergies take a series of shots. The shots gradually make the patient less sensitive to the allergen.

Think Back • *Study on your own with Study Guide page 329.*

1. What are some common allergens?
2. How does hay fever differ from asthma?
3. In addition to trouble with breathing, what other symptoms do people with allergies experience?
4. How can allergies be treated?

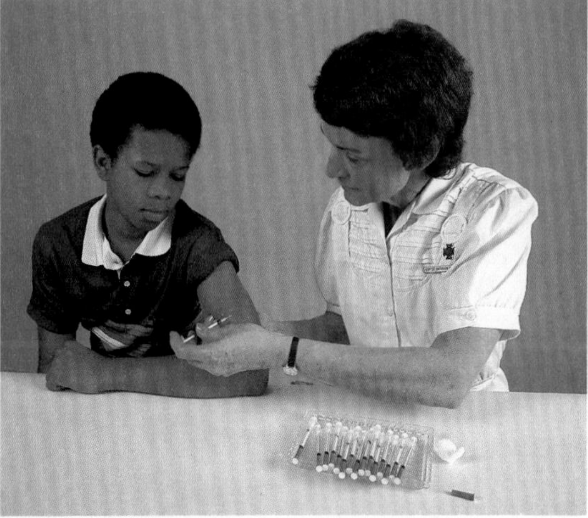

Searching for the allergens

3 Assess

Expanding Student Thinking

Ask students why they think doctors are very cautious when prescribing medicines for people who have hay fever or asthma. (People with allergies to food, plants, and other substances might also be allergic to certain medicines.)

Thinking Skill By telling why doctors are cautious in prescribing medicines for allergy sufferers, students are *drawing conclusions*.

Answers to Think Back

1. Common allergens include pollen, fur, dust, smoke, certain foods, clothing materials, medicines, and insect stings.

2. With hay fever, the tissue that lines the nasal passages becomes swollen. With asthma, the air passages leading to the lungs become swollen. Asthma is more serious than hay fever and more critically affects the person's ability to breathe.

3. Other symptoms include a runny nose, sneezing, itchy eyes, itchy skin rashes, dizziness, and stomach cramps.

4. Allergies can best be treated by avoiding the allergens. Other treatments include medicines to relieve the symptoms and a series of shots that gradually make the patient less sensitive to the allergen.

Teaching Plan

Lesson 6 pages 228–229

Lesson Objective
List health practices that help prevent and control disease.

1 Motivate

Introducing the Lesson
Review with students what they have learned about communicable and noncommunicable diseases in Lessons 1 through 5. Focus on some ways to prevent each of these types of diseases. (cleanliness, healthy diet, exercise, and dealing with stress in healthy ways)

2 Teach

Strategies for Pages 228 and 229
• Let students read pages 228 and 229 to find out what a healthy lifestyle involves. (doing things that will help you stay well) • Ask students why staying physically fit is important to their health. (The body's defenses against disease work best if the body is in good physical condition. • Ask students to suggest ways they could make their own lifestyles healthier. (Answers should reflect a knowledge of what makes a healthy lifestyle.)

Did You Know?
Medical experts believe that up to a third of all cancers—including cancers of the esophagus, breast, liver, lungs, and stomach—could be prevented if people were to adopt a healthy lifestyle. By not smoking, eating a low-fat diet, and limiting alcohol consumption, for example, people greatly reduce the risk of developing cancers of these organs.

6 How Can a Healthy Lifestyle Help Prevent Disease?

The scene below is a common sight in any park. If you were to sit on a park bench for an hour, you would probably see dozens of people walking, running, skating, or bicycling past you. Today more and more people are adopting healthier lifestyles. They are taking better care of themselves by exercising, eating healthy foods, and giving up unhealthy habits.

Having a healthy lifestyle means doing things that will help you stay well. Staying physically fit is one part of a healthy lifestyle. Your body's defenses against disease work best if your body is in good physical condition. Regular exercise helps you keep fit, helps maintain proper body weight, and reduces the chances of getting cardiovascular diseases.

A healthy lifestyle also includes eating foods that are low in fat, sugar, salt, and cholesterol. Making wise decisions about tobacco, alcohol, and other harmful drugs is another part of a healthy lifestyle.

A healthy lifestyle includes exercise.

228

Teaching Options

Health Background

Many organizations and agencies help monitor and protect public health. One of these organizations is the federal Department of Health and Human Services (HHS). Divisions of the HHS support and conduct research into the causes and prevention of diseases, publish health information, and deal with community health programs. These agencies collect information on health and suggest ways people can maintain or improve their health, including beneficial changes in lifestyle.

Enrichment

Direct students to use the *Readers' Guide to Periodical Literature* to survey the content of recent health magazines for articles relating to teenagers' health. Ask them to read a few articles and write short summaries to share with the class.

Health and Physical Education

Ask students to plan a schedule for doing physical activities at least three times a week, for fifteen minutes in each exercise session. Students should schedule time for activities that can improve cardiovascular fitness. Refer students to Chapter 4 to help them make their plans.

Reteaching

Let students list physical activities that they enjoy, and tell how these activities might be part of a healthy lifestyle and help prevent disease.

The picture on this page gives you a clue about another important part of a healthy lifestyle—keeping clean. Regular showering or bathing keeps harmful bacteria off your body. Brushing and flossing prevent the growth of bacteria on your teeth. Many people catch colds by spreading viruses from their hands to their eyes, nose, or mouth. Therefore, you should wash your hands frequently, especially when someone in the house has a cold.

A healthy lifestyle includes dealing with stress in healthy ways, such as facing your problems and trying to solve or accept them. Research studies show that your body's defenses work better if you deal with stress in calm ways.

A healthy lifestyle will not prevent you from ever getting sick. It will, however, greatly improve your body's ability to fight against harmful germs and to resist all kinds of disease.

Think Back • *Study on your own with Study Guide page 329.*

1. What practices does a healthy lifestyle include?
2. How does keeping clean help you stay healthy?

A healthy lifestyle includes keeping clean.

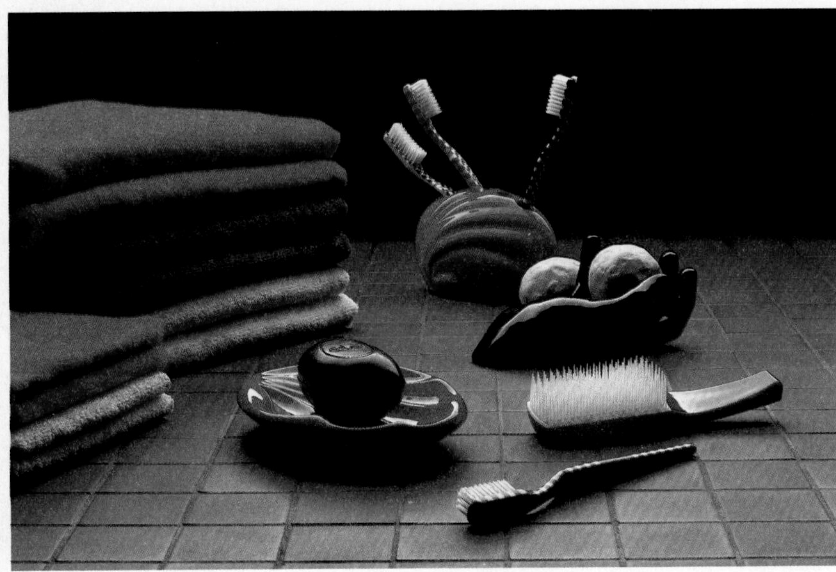

• Encourage students to list some causes of stress they feel at school. (having to give a speech, taking a test, and so on) Help students think of healthy ways to deal with each of these causes.

3 Assess

Expanding Student Thinking

Ask students to make a series of drawings or find several magazine pictures that show health practices that can help prevent or control diseases. (Accept all drawings that show an understanding of lesson content.)

Thinking Skills By making drawings or finding pictures that show ways to promote health practices, students are *organizing information* and *communicating.*

Answers to Think Back

1. A healthy lifestyle includes staying physically fit, eating nutritious foods, making wise decisions about drugs, keeping clean, and dealing with stress in healthy ways.

2. Keeping clean keeps bacteria and other disease germs off your body.

Teaching Plan

Health Focus page 230

Discussion

After students have read page 230, ask them to explain how Jenner's vaccine worked. (The cowpox vaccine cause the boy's body to produce antibodies to fight off the disease germs that also cause smallpox. The boy became immune to smallpox.) Discuss the importance of this discovery.

Answers to Talk About It

1. Jenner discovered that smallpox could be prevented by purposely exposing people to cowpox, a less dangerous disease.
Thinking Skill Students are *recalling information.*
2. Material from the cowpox sore contained cowpox viruses, which were actually weakened forms of smallpox viruses. The cowpox viruses caused white blood cells to make antibodies against the viruses. Some of the white blood cells that could make these antibodies stayed in the body and could make more antibodies quickly if smallpox viruses entered the body.
Thinking Skill Students are *making analogies.*

Edward Jenner's Great Discovery

In 1796 George Washington was President of the United States. In that same year Edward Jenner, an English scientist, made a discovery that was a first step toward wiping out one of the most dreaded diseases in history—smallpox.

This disease got its name because of the little scars, called pockmarks, that formed on the face and body. Smallpox was very contagious. Sometimes whole families or villages died from it.

Dr. Jenner noticed that people did not get smallpox if they already had gotten cowpox. This disease was like smallpox, but much milder. Dr. Jenner thought that if people got cowpox on purpose, they would never get smallpox.

Dr. Jenner tested this idea in 1796 after many years of studying both diseases. He took material from a cowpox sore on a woman's hand. Then he rubbed this material into a scratch that he made on the arm of James Phipps, a healthy eight-year-old boy. The painting shows this historic vaccination.

The boy got cowpox, as Dr. Jenner expected. This disease gave James Phipps only a sore arm and a headache for a couple of days. Then, several weeks later, Dr. Jenner scratched the boy's arm again. This time he rubbed material from a smallpox sore into the scratch. James Phipps did not get smallpox. Dr. Jenner had discovered how people could be protected from this disease for the rest of their lives!

Edward Jenner discovered and developed the first successful vaccine. As a result of Dr. Jenner's discovery and a worldwide vaccination effort, in recent years smallpox has been eliminated throughout the world.

Talk About It

1. What was Edward Jenner's great discovery?
2. How was material from a cowpox sore able to provide immunity from smallpox?

Teaching Options

Vocabulary

Use this worksheet for practice in reviewing chapter vocabulary words. This master may be reproduced from the Teacher's Resource Book and is located on page 26 of the Student's Workbook. Use with Chapter 7: pages 198–233.

Name ______________________ Vocabulary
Use with Chapter 7: pages 198–233.

Disease Wordsearch

Mark each sentence **True** or **False**. The puzzle has numbers from 1–12 that go with the numbered true or false sentences. You will find the answer to the riddle below if you shade in the numbers of only the true sentences.

False 1. Everything that causes cancer has been discovered.
True 2. Mucus can be found in your nose, mouth, throat, windpipe, and lungs.
True 3. Antibodies can help make disease germs harmless.
True 4. AIDS is caused by a virus.
True 5. A noncommunicable disease does not spread to others.
False 6. All tumors are cancerous.
False 7. Plaques help blood flow through your blood vessels.
True 8. The AIDS virus can spread through contact with infected blood.
False 9. Hypertension is low blood pressure.
True 10. Dust and smoke are allergens to some people.
False 11. Pneumonia is a noncommunicable disease.
True 12. A vaccine can stop a person from getting a disease.

10	4	3	9	6	11	11	2	6	7	9	11	10	2	3	11	4	10	12	1	10	12	12	11	8	12	10	7	11	5	12	5	11	6	7	9	2	11	1	11	6
5	1	2	7	1	9	10	7	12	1	7	1	12	9	10	9	7	2	6	11	8	7	9	1	5	1	2	11	7	7	10	1	7	1	11	10	7	12	7	9	11
3	5	12	11	7	5	12	2	10	8	11	6	8	6	11	1	6	5	7	1	3	2	11	7	2	4	3	9	6	11	8	6	11	6	5	12	2	10	8	6	1
12	6	4	1	4	6	7	11	6	6	5	1	10	7	3	9	11	8	9	6	5	1	6	11	10	6	5	11	1	9	5	9	7	4	11	1	6	11	1	5	7
2	3	10	6	3	9	1	7	9	11	4	7	12	5	2	6	9	3	11	7	4	2	3	9	10	7	11	12	7	3	3	2	7	3	9	11	9	7	6	4	9

These are so small that over one thousand of them can fit on the point of a pencil.

What are they? Bacteria

94 *Extension Idea:* **Ask students to rewrite the false sentences to make true statements.**

Controlling the Spread of Disease Germs

Disease germs spread easily from one person to another, especially among people living in the same place. You can help control the spread of disease germs at home in many ways.

You can stop some germs from spreading by covering your nose or mouth when you sneeze or cough. A sneeze or cough releases many dust particles and droplets of moisture into the air. These particles and droplets contain millions of disease germs. Other people inhale the germs.

You can stop the spread of many disease germs by washing your hands after you sneeze, cough, or blow your nose. Germs on your hands can spread to every doorknob, light switch, and other object you touch. Washing is especially important before eating, setting the table, or preparing meals.

Disposing of garbage properly is another way you and your family can control the spread of disease germs. Hungry animals easily overturn garbage cans with loose-fitting lids. Disease germs, which grow quickly in garbage, spread to racoons, dogs, rats, and other animals that eat the garbage. These animals can spread the germs by biting or just being near other animals and people. How is the girl in the picture disposing of garbage properly?

Share the information on this page with your family. Try to make these practices part of your everyday life. They will help keep you, your family, and your community healthy.

Reading at Home

Germs by Dorothy Hinshaw Patent. Holiday House, 1983. Learn how germs were discovered, how they affect you, and what exciting research is taking place concerning the control of germs.

Medicine: The Body and Healing by Gordon Jackson. Watts, 1984. Explore the function of the major body systems, some of the main causes of illness, and how the body deals with infection.

Health at Home

page 231

Strategies

Let students read page 231. Then discuss some of the ways disease germs are spread. (coughing, sneezing, hands, garbage) Review ways of controlling the spread of disease germs at home. (covering a cough or sneeze, keeping hands clean, disposing of garbage properly) Point out that flies and fleas lay eggs in garbage and that they carry germs on their bodies. They can spread the germs just by landing on people or on food. Rats are also a health problem because they carry infected fleas. Some cities have campaigns to control rat populations by using strong poisons. Students might have seen signs posted warning of this use of poison.

More Reading at Home

Germs (Grades 4–6)

Medicine: The Body and Healing (Grades 5–6)

Winn, Marie. *The Sick Book*. Four Winds, 1976. Tells what happens to the body during many common illnesses and injuries. (Grades 4–7)

Study and Review

Use this worksheet for practice in reviewing types of diseases and allergies. This master may be reproduced from the Teacher's Resource Book and is located on page 27 of the Student's Workbook. Use with Chapter 7: pages 198–233.

Name ______________________

Use with Chapter 7: pages 198–233.

Study and Review

Fighting Diseases Review

Part I. Fill in the chart.

Disease	Communicable or Noncommunicable	Symptoms or causes	Treatment
Sinusitis	1. Communicable (usually)	2. Clogged sinuses, coughing	3. Antibiotics
Cancer	4. Noncommunicable	5. Uncontrolled growth of abnormal body cells	6. Surgery, radiation, drugs
Strep throat	7. Communicable	8. Severe sore throat	9. Antibiotics
Pneumonia	10. Communicable	11. Coughing, fever, chest pains, noisy breathing	12. Antibiotics, bed rest, fluids

Part II. Fill in the sentences below with these words.

allergy allergen asthma breathe dust fur hay fever

1. A certain reaction of the body to something in the environment is an allergy.
2. Something that causes an allergy is an allergen.
3. The two most common allergies are hay fever and asthma.
4. A person with an allergy might find it hard to breathe.
5. Two allergens that can be found in many places are fur and dust.

Extension Idea: **Ask students to extend the chart by adding a column labeled "Prevention."**

95

Chapter 7 Review

pages 232–233

Answers to Reviewing Lesson Objectives

Use this section for guided study or for oral review. Objective numbers match lesson numbers.

1. Answers should include information on bacteria and viruses.

2. The first line of defense includes the skin, mucus, tears, and other fluids that kill germs. The second line of defense includes white blood cells that destroy germs. The third line of defense includes antibodies and immunity to some diseases. When a person becomes infected with the AIDS virus, the immune system breaks down and the person is unable to fight off infections.

3. Causes include viruses for colds and influenza, and viruses or bacteria for sinusitis and pneumonia. Symptoms include coughing, sneezing, sore throat, fever, stuffy or runny nose, and noisy breathing. Treatment includes bed rest, drinking fluids, and antibiotics for bacterial infections.

4. Causes include heredity and environment. Preventive measures include good nutrition, exercising, handling stress wisely, and not smoking.

5. Symptoms of allergies often include sneezing, watery or itchy eyes, runny nose, and difficulty breathing. Causes involve heredity and a variety of environmental factors such as pollen, dust, fur, certain foods, and smoke.

6. Health practices that help prevent diseases include exercising; eating healthy foods; giving up unhealthy habits, such as smoking; keeping clean; and dealing with stress in healthy ways.

Answers to Checking Health Vocabulary

Use the vocabulary check as a review or as a test.

1. k	**8.** d	**15.** j
2. b	**9.** i	**16.** m
3. p	**10.** a	**17.** e
4. n	**11.** o	**18.** q
5. h	**12.** l	**19.** g
6. s	**13.** c	
7. f	**14.** r	

Chapter 7 Review

Reviewing Lesson Objectives

1. Describe some major kinds of disease germs that cause communicable diseases. (pages 200–203)
2. Describe the first-, second-, and third-line defenses against communicable diseases. Explain what occurs when a person becomes infected with AIDS. (pages 204–209)
3. Describe the major causes, symptoms, and treatment of some common respiratory diseases. (pages 210–215)
4. Explain some causes of and some ways to help prevent cardiovascular diseases and cancer. (pages 218–223)
5. Describe the symptoms and the causes of several kinds of allergies. (pages 224–227)
6. List health practices that help prevent and control diseases. (pages 228–229)

For further review, use Study Guide pages 328-329

Practice skills for life for Chapter 7 on pages 356-358

SKILLS FOR LIFE

Checking Health Vocabulary

Number your paper from 1–19. Match each definition in Column I with the correct word or words in Column II.

Column I

1. the body's resistance to a disease through the presence of antibodies
2. a harmful reaction of the body to a substance in the environment
3. a disease in which the sinus openings become blocked
4. a fatty substance that builds up in an artery
5. the general term for a disease that can spread
6. a cell that destroys disease germs
7. the uncontrolled growth of abnormal body cells
8. a substance that attaches to a germ and makes it harmless
9. a disease in which the body becomes unable to fight infection
10. a substance that causes an allergic response
11. a disease in which the lungs become inflamed
12. a sticky liquid that lines the mouth, nose, and windpipe
13. a medicine that destroys bacteria
14. a small dose of killed or weakened disease germs that provides immunity to a disease
15. high blood pressure
16. the general term for a disease that does not spread
17. a disease in which material builds up inside the arteries
18. a clump of useless tissue caused by the buildup of abnormal cells
19. a disease of the heart or blood vessels

Column II

a. allergen
b. allergy
c. antibiotic
d. antibody
e. atherosclerosis
f. cancer
g. cardiovascular disease
h. communicable disease
i. AIDS
j. hypertension
k. immunity
l. mucus
m. noncommunicable disease
n. plaque
o. pneumonia
p. sinusitis
q. tumor
r. vaccine
s. white blood cell

232

Chapter 7 Tests Use Test A or Test B to assess students' mastery of the health concepts in Chapter 7. These tests are located on pages 57–64 in the Test Book.

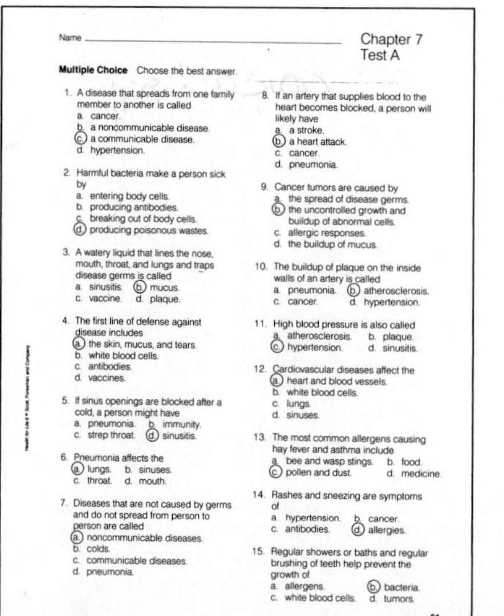

Name ______________________ Chapter 7 Test A

Multiple Choice Choose the best answer.

1. A disease that spreads from one family member to another is called
   a. cancer. b. a noncommunicable disease. (c.) a communicable disease. d. hypertension.
2. Harmful bacteria make a person sick by
   a. entering body cells. b. producing antibodies. c. breaking out of body cells. (d.) producing poisonous wastes.
3. A watery liquid that lines the nose, mouth, throat, and lungs and traps disease germs is called
   a. sinusitis. (b.) mucus. c. vaccine. d. plaque.
4. The first line of defense against disease includes
   (a.) the skin, mucus, and tears. b. white blood cells. c. antibodies. d. vaccines.
5. If sinus openings are blocked after a cold, a person might have
   a. pneumonia. b. immunity. c. strep throat. (d.) sinusitis.
6. Pneumonia affects the
   (a.) lungs. b. sinuses. c. throat. d. mouth.
7. Diseases that are not caused by germs and do not spread from person to person are called
   (a.) noncommunicable diseases. b. colds. c. communicable diseases. d. pneumonia.
8. If an artery that supplies blood to the heart becomes blocked, a person will likely have
   a. a stroke. (b.) a heart attack. c. cancer. d. pneumonia.
9. Cancer tumors are caused by
   a. the spread of disease germs. (b.) the uncontrolled growth and buildup of abnormal cells. c. allergic responses. d. the buildup of mucus.
10. The buildup of plaque on the inside walls of an artery is called
    a. pneumonia. (b.) atherosclerosis. c. cancer. d. hypertension.
11. High blood pressure is also called
    a. atherosclerosis. b. plaque. (c.) hypertension. d. sinusitis.
12. Cardiovascular diseases affect the
    (a.) heart and blood vessels. b. white blood cells. c. lungs. d. sinuses.
13. The most common allergens causing hay fever and asthma include
    a. bee and wasp stings. b. food. (c.) pollen and dust. d. medicine.
14. Rashes and sneezing are symptoms of
    a. hypertension. b. cancer. c. antibodies. (d.) allergies.
15. Regular showers or baths and regular brushing of teeth help prevent the growth of
    a. allergens. (b.) bacteria. c. white blood cells. d. tumors.

Health for Life 6 • Scott, Foresman and Company

61

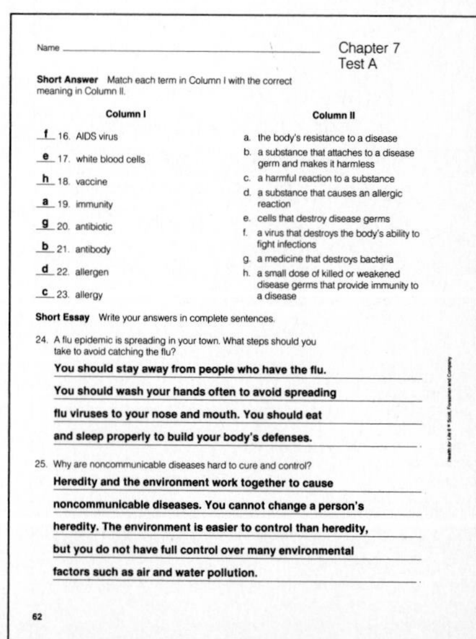

Name ______________________ Chapter 7 Test A

Short Answer Match each term in Column I with the correct meaning in Column II.

Column I

__f__ 16. AIDS virus
__e__ 17. white blood cells
__h__ 18. vaccine
__a__ 19. immunity
__g__ 20. antibiotic
__b__ 21. antibody
__d__ 22. allergen
__c__ 23. allergy

Column II

a. the body's resistance to a disease
b. a substance that attaches to a disease germ and makes it harmless
c. a harmful reaction to a substance
d. a substance that causes an allergic reaction
e. cells that destroy disease germs
f. a virus that destroys the body's ability to fight infections
g. a medicine that destroys bacteria
h. a small dose of killed or weakened disease germs that provide immunity to a disease

Short Essay Write your answers in complete sentences.

24. A flu epidemic is spreading in your town. What steps should you take to avoid catching the flu?
    You should stay away from people who have the flu. You should wash your hands often to avoid spreading flu viruses to your nose and mouth. You should eat and sleep properly to build your body's defenses.
25. Why are noncommunicable diseases hard to cure and control?
    Heredity and the environment work together to cause noncommunicable diseases. You cannot change a person's heredity. The environment is easier to control than heredity, but you do not have full control over many environmental factors such as air and water pollution.

Health for Life 6 • Scott, Foresman and Company

62

Reviewing Health Ideas

Number your paper from 1-17. Next to each number write the word or words that best complete the sentence.

1. Disease _____ cause communicable diseases.
2. Bacteria give off wastes that act like _____.
3. Each kind of _____ causes only one disease.
4. _____ attach themselves to disease germs and make them harmless.
5. A vaccine causes some _____ blood cells to make antibodies.
6. Antibiotics can kill only _____.
7. The respiratory system includes the nasal passages, throat, _____, and lungs.
8. When the sinus openings into the nose and throat become blocked, _____ can result.
9. AIDS cannot be spread by _____ contact.
10. Heart disease and cancer are examples of _____ diseases.
11. When an artery leading to the brain becomes blocked, the person will likely have a _____.
12. Fairly harmless tumors grow _____ and stay in one part of the body.
13. Cancer has the best chance of being cured if it is found in the _____ stages.
14. A substance that causes an _____ is an allergen.
15. _____ grains are among the most common allergens of hay fever.
16. Regular showering or bathing keeps harmful _____ off the body.
17. Brushing and _____ prevent the growth of bacteria on the teeth.

Understanding Health Ideas

Number your paper from 18–28. Next to each number write the word or words that best answer the question.

18. What kind of disease germ causes the most illnesses?
19. How many diseases does each kind of virus cause?
20. What is the body's second line of defense against disease germs?
21. What are two things a person with a cold can do to try to avoid a severe case of sinusitis?
22. What dietary changes can be made to reduce the chance of plaque building up in the blood vessels?
23. How does the nicotine in cigarette smoke affect the blood vessels?
24. What are the three major treatments for cancer?
25. What are two of the most common allergies?
26. What is the first step in treating an allergy?
27. What are two health benefits of regular exercise?
28. How can a person help prevent the spread of viruses from his or her hands?

Thinking Critically

Write the answers on your paper. Use complete sentences.

1. Does having measles give you immunity to mumps? Explain your answer.
2. Cardiovascular diseases are more common in adults than in people your age. Why should you be concerned about these diseases now?

233

Answers to Reviewing Health Ideas

1. germs
2. poisons
3. virus
4. antibodies
5. white
6. bacteria
7. windpipe
8. sinusitis
9. casual
10. noncommunicable
11. stroke
12. slowly
13. early
14. allergy
15. pollen
16. bacteria
17. flossing

Answers to Understanding Health Ideas

18. virus
19. one
20. white blood cells
21. get rest; drink fluids; take any prescribed medicines
22. reduce the amount of fat and cholesterol eaten
23. narrows blood vessels
24. surgery to remove tumors; radiation to kill cancer cells; drugs to kill cancer cells
25. hay fever and asthma
26. to discover the substances that cause the allergy
27. helps you keep fit; helps maintain proper body weight; reduces chances of getting cardiovascular diseases
28. by washing hands often

Answers to Thinking Critically

1. Having measles does not give immunity to mumps. When measles germs invade the body, white blood cells produce antibodies that attack measles germs. Each kind of antibody can attack only one kind of disease germ. Therefore, if mumps germs invade the body, white blood cells must make a different kind of antibody.

Thinking Skills By deciding whether one disease gives immunity to another, students are *making analogies* and *drawing conclusions*.

2. Students should be concerned now because the causes of these diseases involve poor health practices that often begin early in life. Healthy practices begun early in life can help prevent these diseases from occurring later in life.

Thinking Skills By explaining why they should be concerned about cardiovascular diseases now, students are *suggesting alternatives* and *drawing conclusions*.

Cooperative Learning Use the STAD Format described on page T24 to have four- to five-member teams study Chapter 7 Review together before completing Chapter 7 Test.

Name ______________________ Chapter 7 Test B

Multiple Choice Choose the best answer.

1. Viruses harm the body by
   a. producing poisonous wastes.
   (b.) invading body cells.
   c. producing bacteria.
   d. producing saliva.
2. Disease germs cause
   a. noncommunicable diseases.
   b. allergies.
   c. cancer.
   (d.) communicable diseases.
3. White blood cells
   a. produce germs. b. kill allergens.
   (c.) destroy germs. d. fight mucus.
4. A vaccine causes some white blood cells to
   a. die. (b.) make antibodies.
   c. multiply. d. fight allergens.
5. Antibodies
   a. destroy plaque.
   (b.) make disease germs harmless.
   c. spread diseases.
   d. cause noncommunicable diseases.
6. When your body has formed antibodies to fight off a disease, you have
   a. an allergy. b. an antibiotic.
   c. hypertension. (d.) an immunity.
7. Antibiotics help to
   (a.) destroy harmful bacteria.
   b. prevent cancer.
   c. destroy harmful viruses.
   d. produce blood.
8. Cold viruses are destroyed by
   a. bacteria.
   b. vaccines.
   c. aspirin.
   (d.) the body's own defenses.
9. Colds and the flu are caused by
   a. mucus. b. bacteria.
   (c.) viruses. d. antibodies.
10. Plaque is
    (a.) a fatty substance that builds up along the walls of arteries.
    b. the uncontrolled growth of cells.
    c. a substance that causes a communicable disease.
    d. a substance that causes allergies.
11. A stroke often results when a blockage occurs in an artery leading to the
    (a.) brain. b. lungs.
    c. heart. d. liver.
12. When abnormal cells grow and reproduce, they form a clump of tissue called
    a. plaque. b. an antibody.
    (c.) a tumor. d. a disease germ.
13. Allergies are caused by
    a. asthma. b. hay fever.
    (c.) allergens. d. antibodies.
14. During an attack of asthma,
    a. the skin becomes red.
    b. the skin itches.
    (c.) air passages become swollen.
    d. the skin becomes hot.
15. A healthy lifestyle will
    a. keep you from ever getting sick.
    b. solve all of your problems.
    (c.) improve your body's ability to fight harmful germs.
    d. make it harder for your body to fight harmful germs.

63

Name ______________________ Chapter 7 Test B

Short Answer Match each term in Column I with the correct meaning in Column II.

Column I	Column II
f 16. communicable disease	a. general term for a disease that does not spread from person to person
c 17. pneumonia	b. a disease that leaves the body unable to fight infections
b 18. AIDS	c. a disease in which mucus builds up in the lungs
a 19. noncommunicable disease	d. high blood pressure
d 20. hypertension	e. a disease in which material builds up inside the arteries
g 21. cardiovascular disease	f. general term for a disease that can spread from one person to another
h 22. cancer	g. a disease of the heart and blood vessels
e 23. atherosclerosis	h. the uncontrolled growth of abnormal body cells

Short Essay Write your answers in complete sentences.

24. Describe two defenses you have against disease.
    Answers will vary, may include: the skin, tears, and saliva which attack germs before they enter the body; white blood cells which destroy germs within the body; antibodies which attack specific kinds of disease germs; vaccines which help protect people from disease.
25. What can you do to prevent disease and stay well?
    Answers will vary, may include: staying physically fit; eating foods that are low in fat, salt, and cholesterol; deciding not to smoke, drink or use drugs; keeping clean; dealing with stress.

64

Pupil Edition	Activities	Enrichment	Assessment	Independent Study
Chapter 8 Daily Care for Good Health, pp. 234–255	Health Watch Notebook, p. 234	Health Focus, p. 252 Health at Home, p. 253	Chapter 8 Review, pp. 254–255	Study Guide, pp. 330–331 Skills for Life Handbook, pp. 359–361
Lesson 1 Why Is Good Posture Important to Your Health? pp. 236–237		Did You Know? p. 236	Think Back, p. 237	Study Guide, p. 330
Lesson 2 How Can You Take Care of Your Teeth? pp. 238–241			Think Back, p. 241	Study Guide, p. 330
Lesson 3 How Do Vision and Hearing Keep You Safe? pp. 242–243			Think Back, p. 243	Study Guide, p. 330
Lesson 4 Why Should You Take Care of Your Skin and Hair? pp. 244–245	Health Activities Workshop, pp. 246–247	Did You Know? p. 245	Think Back, p. 245	Study Guide, p. 331
Lesson 5 Why Are Sleep, Rest, and Recreation Important? pp. 248–251		Did You Know? p. 249	Think Back, p. 251	On Your Own, pp. 248, 251 Study Guide, p. 331

Teacher Resources

Halls, Dianne. *The Complete Book of Sleep.* Addison-Wesley, 1981. Introduces many aspects of sleep, and explains it importance to health.

The Journal of School Health. American School Health Association. Provides articles for teachers on various health-related issues.

Opening Your Eyes to the Health of Your Mouth. American Association of Orthodontists. Explains orthodontia and the role it can play in overall oral health.

Orthodontics: A Special Kind of Dentistry. American Association of Orthodontists. Answers questions about orthodontic treatment.

Audio-Visual Resources

See page T43 for addresses of Audio-Visual Sources.

Before using any audio-visual materials, preview them for appropriateness for your students.

Brushing and Flossing Techniques: Dentistry Today Series, Coronet Films and Video, film or video, 8 minutes. Demonstrates proper methods of brushing and flossing to remove food and plaque.

Posture: Thinking Tall. BFA Educational Media, film or video, 12 minutes. Demonstrates that posture contributes to a person's performance and well-being.

Your Health: It's Your Responsibility, Sunburst Communications, Inc., filmstrips with cassettes. Examines the relationship between various personal habits and long-term health problems.

Computer Software

Feeling Great, Educational Images. Helps students become aware of how lifestyle and environment can affect health.

Health and Our Bodies, Right On Program. Explains how the body works, and emphasizes the effects of good daily health habits.

MARCH 6-9

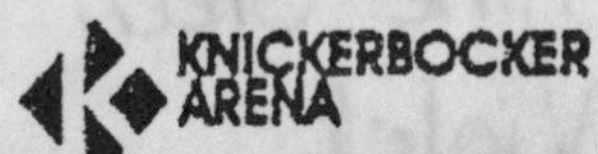

Ordinary Time - Green

Lent - Violet

Christmas Season - White

Advent - Violet

Easter Season - White

The Triduum → White/Red.

	Teacher's Edition	Teacher's Resource Book	Test Book
Enrichment	Suggestions for each lesson: L. 1—p. 236 L. 2—pp. 238, 240 L. 3—p. 242 L. 4—p. 244 L. 5—pp. 248, 250	Family Letter, p. 101 * Life Skills, p. 105 * Health and Mathematics, p. 108	
Reteaching	Suggestions for each lesson: L. 1—p. 236 L. 2—pp. 238, 240 L. 3—p. 242 L. 4—p. 244 L. 5—pp. 228, 250	Transparency Masters, pp. 103-104 * Vocabulary, p. 106 * Study and Review, p. 107	
Assessment	Expanding Student Thinking: one assessment question per lesson that develops higher-order thinking skills—pp. 237, 241, 243, 245, 251		Chapter 8 Test, Form A, pp. 65-66 Chapter 8 Test, Form B, pp. 67-68

* Also available in Workbook format (Student Edition and Teacher's Edition)

Chapter 8 Poster

A set of posters is available in a separate package. It provides a teaching poster for every chapter, including discussion and activity suggestions on the back. The poster for Chapter 8 is titled "What happens during sleep?"

Overhead Transparencies

A set of color overhead transparencies is available for Grade 6. You may wish to use Transparencies 8, 9, and 15 to help teach about brushing and flossing and the structure of eyes, ears, and skin.

Advance Preparation

You will need to prepare materials in advance for the following activities from the Health Activities Workshop.

Activity 1, page 246 Ask each student to bring to class a shampoo bottle with label.

Activity 2, page 246 Supply medicine droppers or straws, cooking oil, and shampoo.

Activity 5, page 246 Supply clay and cardboard or construction paper.

Bulletin Board

Draw outlines of the body that illustrate good posture and poor posture. Discuss how students can build good posture.

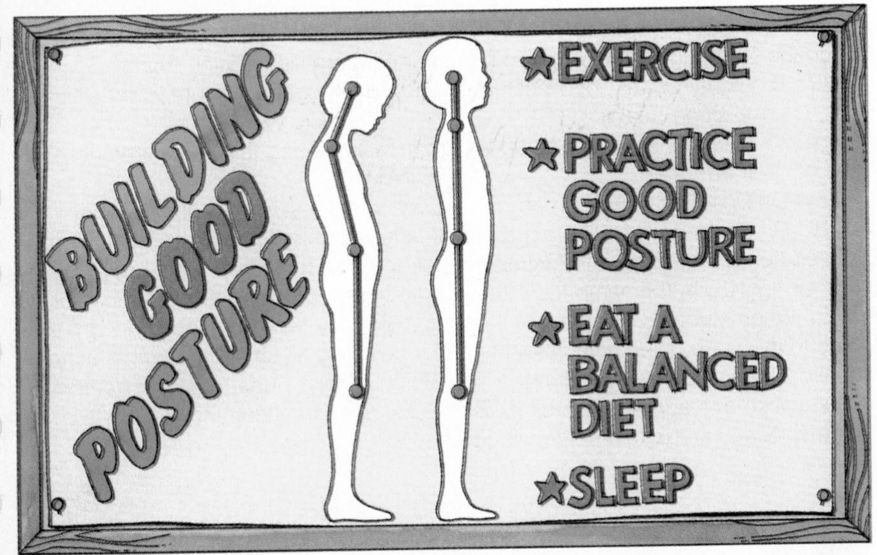

Teaching Plan

Chapter 8 pages 234–255

Chapter Main Idea
Health practices that should be observed each day include good posture, proper dental care, personal hygiene, and sufficient sleep.

Chapter Goals
• Appreciate the importance of good daily health practices.
• Demonstrate a desire to improve aspects of daily health such as posture, dental care, personal hygiene, and sleep habits.

Lifetime Goal
Appreciate the importance of maintaining good daily health practices throughout life.

Health Vocabulary
Cavity, fatigue, gum disease, oil gland, perspiration, plaque, posture, sweat gland

Words to Preteach
Acne, bacteria, carbon dioxide, dandruff, enamel, farsighted, puberty, nearsighted, scoliosis, tooth decay

Chapter **8**

Daily Care for Good Health

Do you like haircuts? Some people your age do. Others, like the boy in this picture, are not so sure. Taking care of your appearance can be a part of good health. There are many other things you can do to keep yourself healthy.

This chapter explains the importance of good daily health care. You will discover how you can improve your health and maintain good health every day of your life.

Health Watch Notebook

Make a daily care collage. Look in magazines or newspapers for pictures of people doing activities that promote good health. Paste these pictures in your notebook. Under your collage, write a paragraph describing how you take care of your health each day.

1 Why Is Good Posture Important to Your Health?
2 How Can You Take Care of Your Teeth?
3 How Do Vision and Hearing Keep You Safe?
4 Why Should You Take Care of Your Skin and Hair?
5 Why Are Sleep, Rest, and Recreation Important?

234

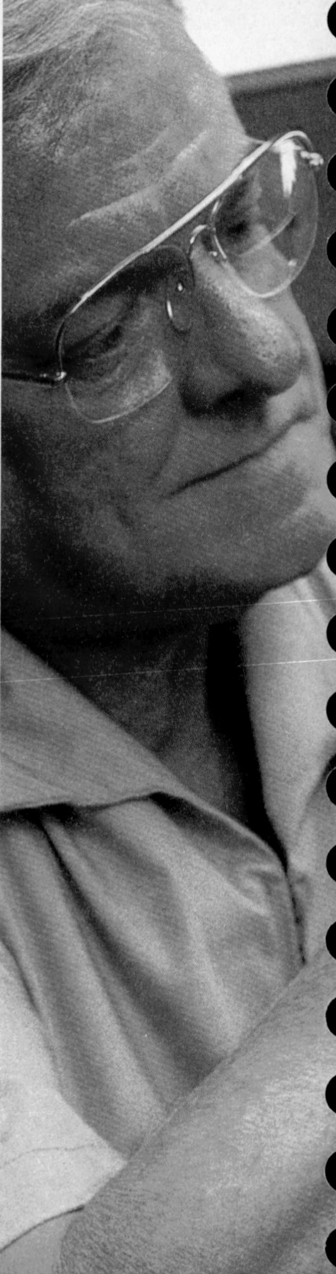

Teaching Options

Modeling Health Vocabulary
Use this technique to introduce new words as you teach each lesson in this chapter. First, introduce the word. Present the word in two sentences that serve to clearly define the word. One sentence you might use to introduce the word *plaque* is: *Plaque is a colorless film that builds up on teeth and gums.* Either read the sentences to the students or write them on the chalkboard. Ask the students to generate two meaningful sentences using the word. Additional successful techniques for introducing new words can be found on page T23.

Cooperative Learning
Jigsaw Format (See page T24.)
Assign the following topics at random to your cooperative learning teams.

Topic A: Explain what good posture is and tell why good posture is important to good health.
Topic B: Define the terms *plaque* and *gum disease* and tell how each can harm teeth.
Topic C: Describe how you can care for eyes, ears, skin, and hair.
Topic D: Describe two different types of fatigue and tell how to prevent them.

Have students search for information on their topic as they read the chapter. Then let all students with the same topic meet in an expert group to discuss the information. When students return to their teams, they may take turns presenting their topics to the team. Then give students a test covering all topics to complete individually (Chapter 8 test A or B in the Test Book). Award Superteam certificates to teams whose average test scores exceed 90%, and Greatteam certificates to teams whose average test scores exceed 80%.

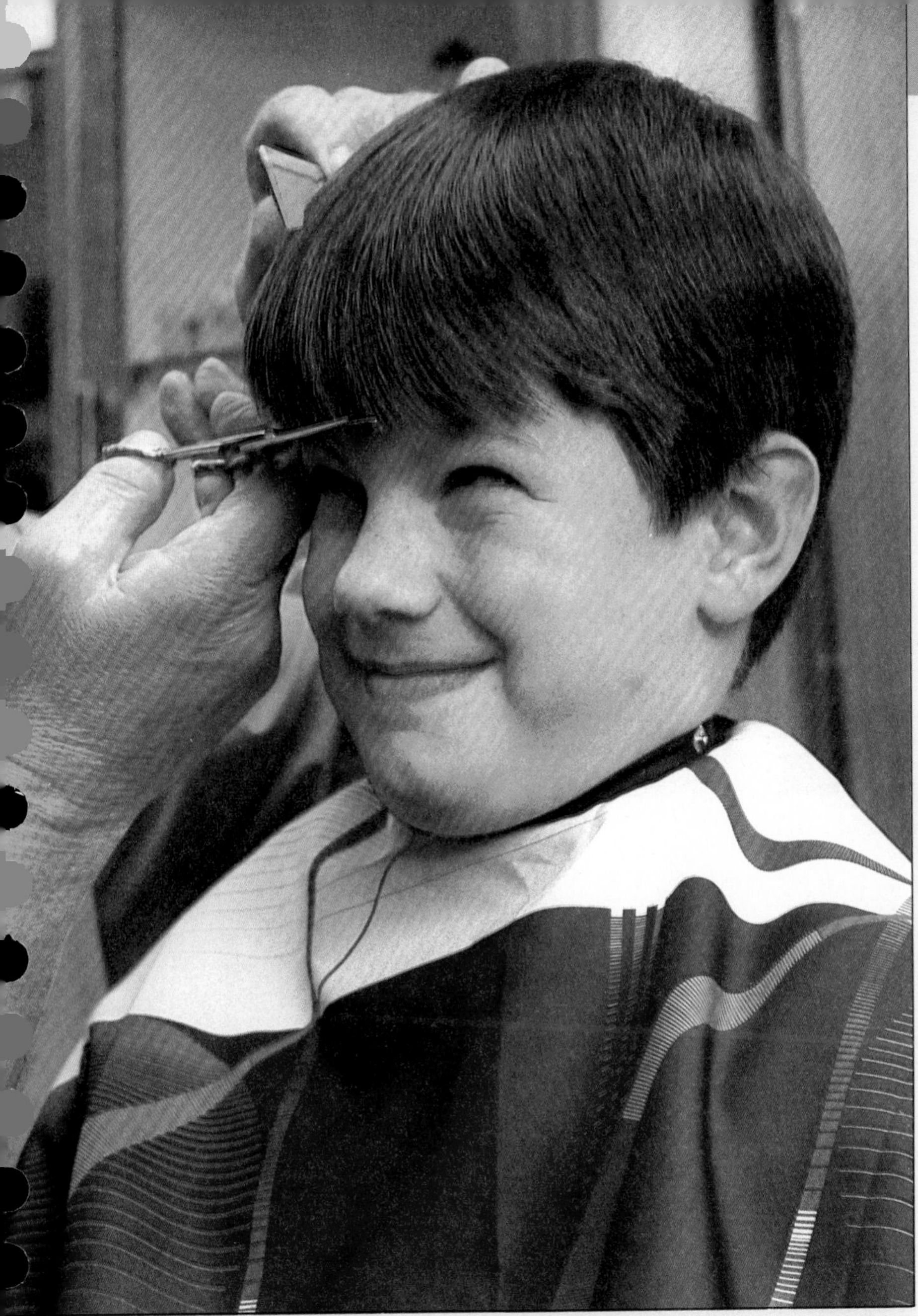

Introducing the Chapter

Discuss with students things that could be done each day to promote personal health. (Answers may include taking a shower, brushing and flossing teeth, eating a well-balanced diet, and so on.) Develop a class list of these things. You could ask students to add to the list as they study the lessons in this chapter. You may wish to send the Family Letter home at this time. You may want to assign Study Guide pages 330–331 for students to use independently as they read the lessons. The Study Guide can also be used as an extra chapter review. You might want to assign the activities in the Skills for Life Handbook on pages 359–361.

Strategies for Health Watch Notebook

Suggest to students that, as they gather pictures for their collages, they be on the lookout for health-promoting activities that they themselves do not practice. Suggest that students try to add such activities to their daily routine.

Family Letter

Use the Family Letter (English or Spanish version) to introduce the subject matter of the chapter to the family and to suggest a way the family can become involved in the student's learning experience. This master may be reproduced from the Teacher's Resource Book.

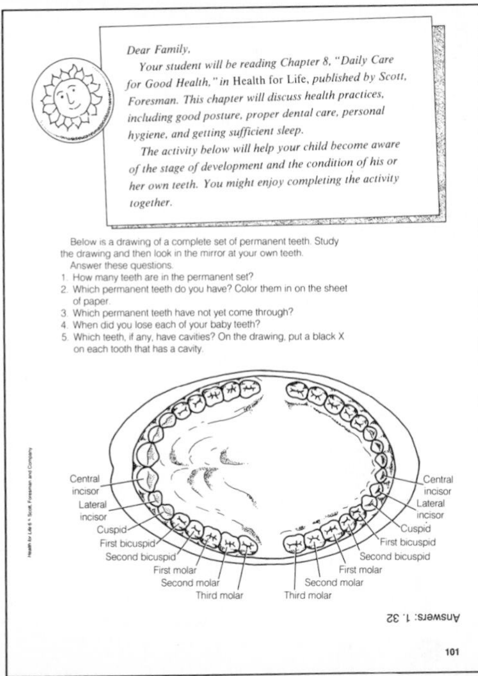

Dear Family,

Your student will be reading Chapter 8, "Daily Care for Good Health," in Health for Life, *published by Scott, Foresman. This chapter will discuss health practices, including good posture, proper dental care, personal hygiene, and getting sufficient sleep.*

The activity below will help your child become aware of the stage of development and the condition of his or her own teeth. You might enjoy completing the activity together.

Below is a drawing of a complete set of permanent teeth. Study the drawing and then look in the mirror at your own teeth.

Answer these questions.

1. How many teeth are in the permanent set?
2. Which permanent teeth do you have? Color them in on the sheet of paper.
3. Which permanent teeth have not yet come through?
4. When did you lose each of your baby teeth?
5. Which teeth, if any, have cavities? On the drawing, put a black X on each tooth that has a cavity.

Answers: 1. 32

101

For High-Potential Students

Help interested students design and carry out an experiment which tests the effectiveness of different methods of cleaning teeth (brushing manually versus using an electric toothbrush, flossing versus not flossing, or using a water brush, and so on). Effectiveness could be determined by using disclosing tablets of a solution of green food coloring to see how much plaque remains on teeth after using each method. The experiment should follow a simple four-step scientific method of stating the problem, forming the hypothesis, testing the hypothesis, and drawing conclusions. The results of the experiment could be presented as a written or oral report.

Teaching Plan

Lesson 1 pages 236-237

Lesson Objective
Explain why good posture is important to good health and how posture can be improved.

Health Vocabulary
Posture

1 Motivate

Introducing the Lesson
Ask students to write a simple explanation of what they think good standing posture involves. Save the papers so that students can compare them, at the end of the lesson, to what they have learned.

2 Teach

Strategies for Pages 236 and 237
• Write the lesson title question on the chalkboard. • Direct students to read page 236 to find the answer. (Good posture keeps bones and muscles in position to support the body without strain. Good posture helps prevent headaches, lower back pains, muscle soreness, and weariness.) • Discuss the drawing on page 236. Be sure students understand the difference between good and poor posture.

posture (pos′chər), the position of the body.

Did You Know?
Scoliosis (skō′lē ō′sis) is a condition in which the spine curves to the side, as shown in this X-ray photograph. Poor posture does not cause scoliosis. However, poor posture is sometimes a symptom of this condition. Scoliosis typically develops between the ages of eight and fifteen. Many schools have screening programs to find and help students who have developed scoliosis.

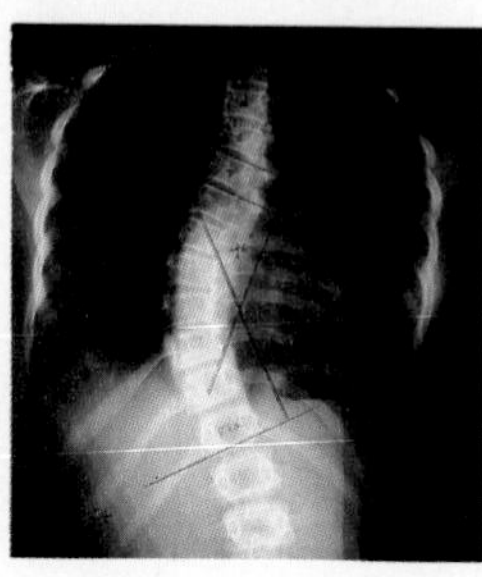

1 Why Is Good Posture Important to Your Health?

Think of the last time you stood in one place for a long period of time. Perhaps you were waiting in line to see a movie, or presenting a report in class. Did you quickly get tired of standing? Did your neck, back, or shoulders begin to ache? Such reactions might mean you could improve your **posture**—the way you hold your body.

The drawing shows how good posture keeps various parts of the body balanced in a straight column. Bones and muscles are in position to support the body weight properly. Now notice what happens when one part of the body, such as the head, moves out of line. Other parts of the body must move out of line to balance the body. This movement puts unnecessary strain on certain bones, muscles, and other body parts. Poor posture can cause headaches, lower back pains, and other muscle soreness.

Good posture helps prevent these aches and pains. Good posture also helps you stand, sit, or move about for long periods of time without getting tired. Then you can perform activities better. In addition, good posture improves the way you look.

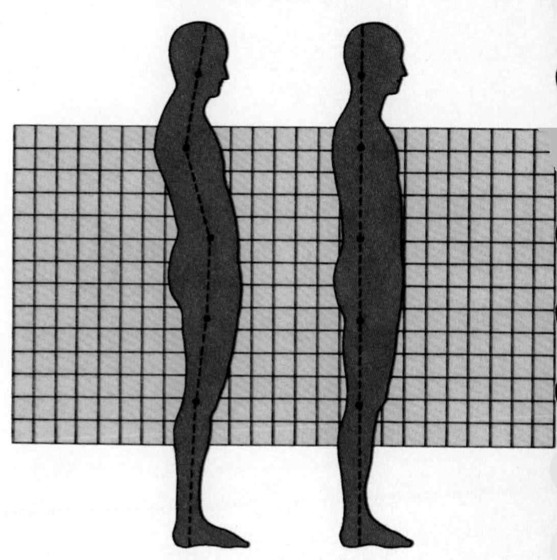

Good posture keeps the body balanced in a straight column.

236

Teaching Options

Health Background
Scoliosis is an abnormal lateral curvature of the spine. This disease affects 8 to 10 percent of young people as they go through their growth spurt. Scoliosis affects girls seven times more often than boys. Ninety percent of the cases have no known cause. During screening tests, an observer looks for such signs as one shoulder blade or hip higher than the other, a hump in the back near the ribcage or waist, or a leaning to one side. Treatment can include traction, casts, bracing, an exercise program, or surgery.

Enrichment
Suggest that students find out more about people for whom good posture is important in their work. (models, athletes, actors, and so on) Encourage students to write short reports on why good posture is important for these people.

Health and Art
Suggest students make health posters showing good posture while sitting or walking. If possible, display the posters on a bulletin board.

Reteaching
If possible, ask the physical education teacher or school nurse to visit the class and demonstrate other exercises that promote good posture.

How Can You Improve Your Posture?

Your posture depends greatly upon the rest of your health. Therefore, an important way to improve your posture is to keep your body strong and healthy. Eating a balanced diet and getting plenty of exercise help build the strong bones and muscles needed for good posture. Two simple exercises for improving posture are shown here. Be sure your teacher shows you how to do them correctly. You can also help improve your posture by getting enough sleep at night. If you are rested, you will be less likely to get tired and slouch during the day.

Another way to improve your posture is to practice good posture throughout the day. While sitting, keep your body far back on the chair. When standing or walking, keep your head centered over the rest of your body. Be aware of your posture throughout the day. If you find you are slumping in your chair, make an effort to sit up straight.

The posture you develop now will likely be the posture you have throughout your life. Therefore, developing good, healthy posture is an important part of your daily health practices.

Think Back • *Study on your own with Study Guide page 330.*
1. How is good posture important to good health?
2. How can posture be improved?

237

• Ask what problems bad posture can cause. (strain on bones, muscles, and other body parts; headaches, lower back pain, and muscle soreness) • Discuss scoliosis. Emphasize that poor posture does not cause scoliosis. • Ask students to read page 237 to learn ways to improve posture. (keep body strong and healthy, get enough sleep, practice good posture throughout the day, exercise)

3 Assess

Expanding Student Thinking
Ask students why they think it is important to develop good posture while they are still young. (Good posture is part of healthy growth; bad posture habits are difficult to break as one gets older.)

Thinking Skill When students tell why good posture is important while they are young, they are *interpreting information.*

Answers to Think Back
1. Good posture helps prevent muscle soreness; helps a person stand, sit, or move about without getting tired easily; improves one's ability to perform activities; and improves one's appearance.

2. Posture can be improved by improving other aspects of health such as fitness, diet, and sleep. Posture can also be improved by practicing good posture throughout the day and by doing certain exercises.

Life Skills
Use this worksheet for practice in improving personal health care. This matter may be reproduced from the Teacher's Resource Book and is located on page 29 of the Student's Workbook. Use with Chapter 8: pages 236–255.

Thinking Skill: By listing personal care activities, students are recalling information. By making a plan to fit these activities into their day, students are organizing information.

Name ____________ Life Skills

Use with Chapter 8: pages 236–255.

Making a Plan for Good Health

Personal care is important at all times. You can help keep yourself in good health by practicing good personal care. Make sure you know how to take care of your health every day. List what you can do in each of the areas below.

1. **Good Posture** Keep body strong and healthy, practice it by keeping head centered over body during the day
2. **Good Dental Care** Brush and floss teeth daily, choose food wisely, visit a dentist regularly
3. **Good Skin Care** Wash face and hands several times a day
4. **Good Hair Care** Shampoo hair often, being sure to rinse it well
5. **Relieve Fatigue** Change activity, get rest, food, exercise, or do something enjoyable
6. Make a plan to fit these personal care activities into each day. Write your plan in the space provided on the right.

My Plan for Good Health

Time	Activity
	Answers might vary.
7:30 a.m.	Brush teeth Wash face
8:00 a.m.	Eat healthy Breakfast
4:30 p.m.	Play hockey
9:00 p.m.	Go to sleep

Extension Idea: Encourage students to evaluate their personal care habits after one week and suggest improvements. 105

Teaching Plan

Lesson 2 pages 238–241

Lesson Objective
Describe aspects of correct dental care, including proper brushing and flossing methods, a proper diet, and regular dental checkups.

Health Vocabulary
Cavity, gum disease, plaque

1 Motivate

Introducing the Lesson
Ask the students to imagine what their lives would be like if they had no teeth. List the changes in lifestyle that would result. (garbled speech, unable to eat certain foods, changed physical appearance)

2 Teach

Strategies for Pages 238 and 239
• Write the lesson title question on the chalkboard. As students read the lesson, ask them to suggest answers.
• Tell students to read pages 238 and 239 to find out what causes most dental problems. (the buildup of plaque) Point out the bacteria in plaque shown in the picture on page 238.

plaque (plak), a sticky, colorless film, consisting largely of bacteria, that forms on teeth and gums.

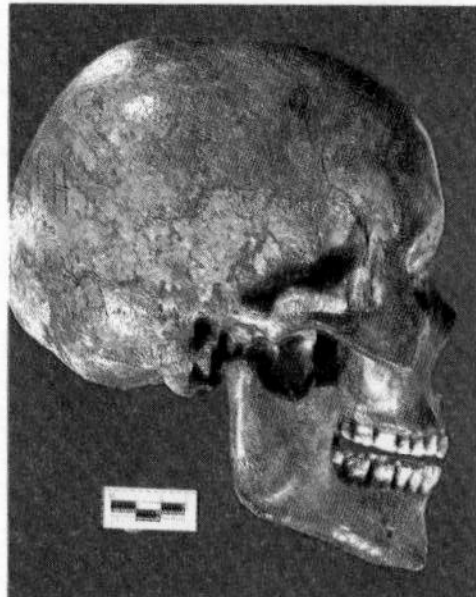

These teeth are thousands of years old.

2 How Can You Take Care of Your Teeth?

The skull in the picture is thousands of years old. Through the years, the bone has become very fragile and brittle. Yet the teeth appear to be as strong and solid as ever. Teeth are made of very hard material. In fact, they are often the only preserved parts of prehistoric animals. However, many of the foods people eat today can damage even the strongest teeth. Your teeth need proper daily care to stay as strong and useful as possible.

What Causes Most Dental Problems?

More than 65 percent of the young people in the United States have had some tooth decay by the time they become adults. If you have had tooth decay, you know that it can be painful. Sometimes decayed teeth need to be removed. Losing teeth can affect a person's speech, appearance, and ability to chew food.

Tooth decay is caused by **plaque**—a sticky, colorless film of bacteria. Plaque is always forming on your teeth and gums because bacteria are always present in your mouth. The picture shows a highly magnified view of plaque on a tooth. The rounded shapes are the bacteria in the plaque.

Bacteria on a tooth

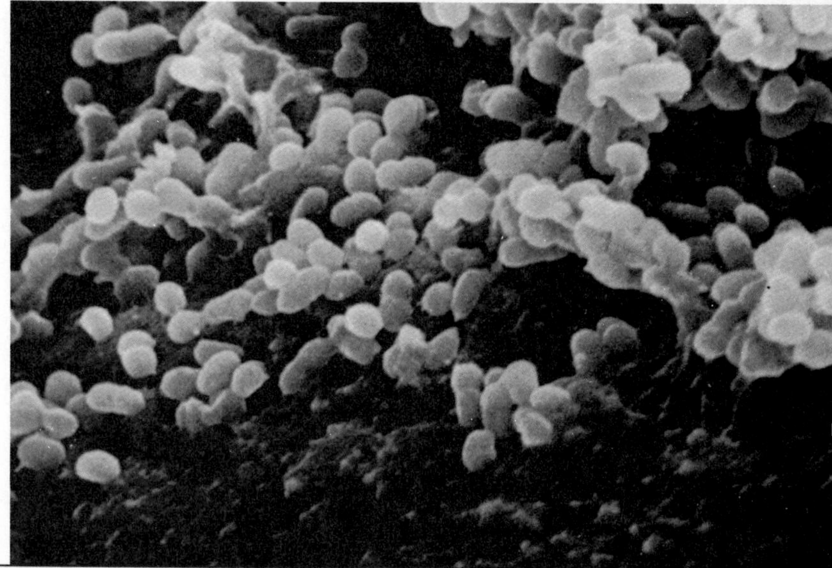

Teaching Options

Health Background

Tooth enamel is the hardest substance in the body. The bacteria in plaque use the sugar and other carbohydrates in food to form acids. These acids can erode the enamel and cause tooth decay. If decay is not treated, the bacteria can eventually penetrate the pulp of the tooth, thus increasing the likelihood that the tooth will die. Since children under twelve have enamel that is still developing, a dentist can apply flouride to their teeth each year to help prevent decay.

Enrichment

If possible, obtain a plastic model of a set of teeth and jaws. Let students do research and then use the model to point out the location and function of different kinds of teeth.

Health and Social Studies

Encourage students to research the history of dental care. Suggest they find out about early ways to clean teeth, first dental instruments, early false teeth, and so on. Ask students to prepare a brief oral report on their findings.

Reteaching

Encourage students to make drawings showing the stages of gum disease. (Bacteria in the plaque attack the gums; gums recede; small pockets form around the teeth and trap more bacteria; the bones supporting the teeth are affected; gums begin to shrink; teeth become loose and may fall out.)

Plaque by itself does not cause tooth decay. The bacteria in plaque use the sugars in food to produce acids. The acids destroy the enamel on teeth, leading to tooth decay. The pictures show how these acids can damage a tooth.

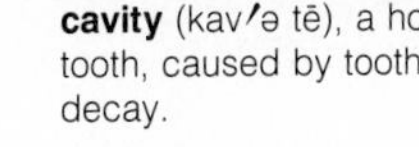

cavity (kav′ə tē), a hole in a tooth, caused by tooth decay.

Another common dental problem is **gum disease.** Plaque often builds up in tiny spaces between the teeth and under the gumline. If the plaque is not removed, it hardens, and is called calculus. The calculus irritates the gums. Then they might become swollen and bleed. In time, the gums pull away from the teeth as more layers of plaque build up. Pockets form in the gums and allow the bacteria to attack and weaken the bone that holds the teeth in place. Eventually, some teeth might become loose and even fall out.

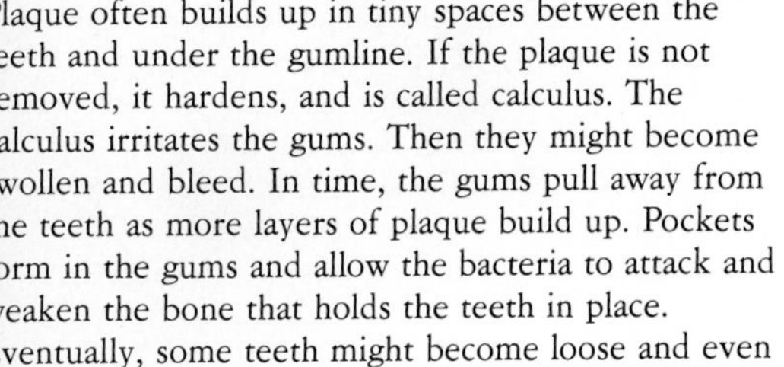

gum disease, a condition begun by plaque building up and hardening between the teeth and under the gumline. This buildup irritates the gums, eventually causing them to pull away from the teeth, and leaving pockets through which bacteria can attack bone.

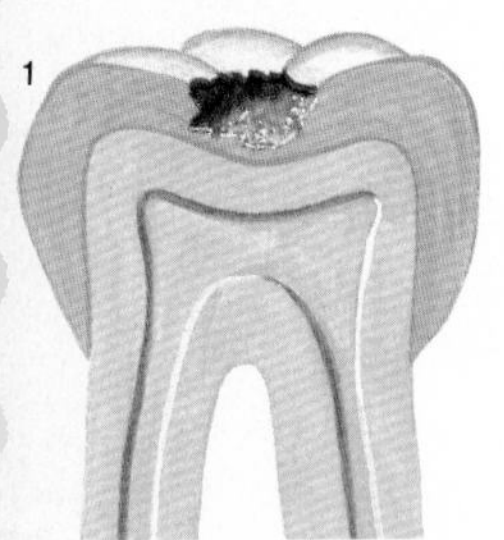

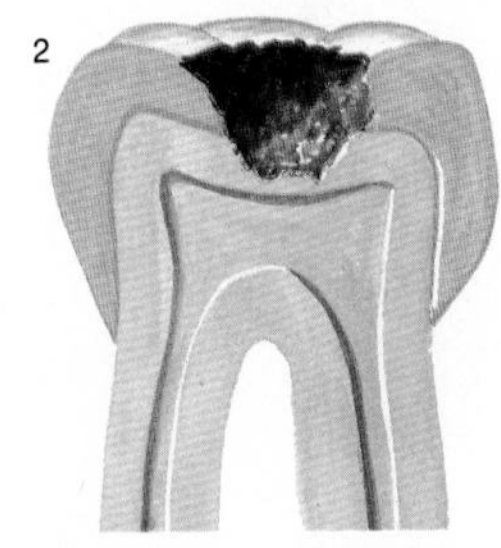

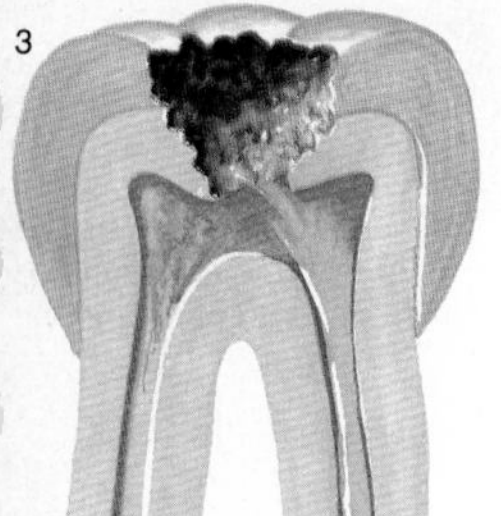

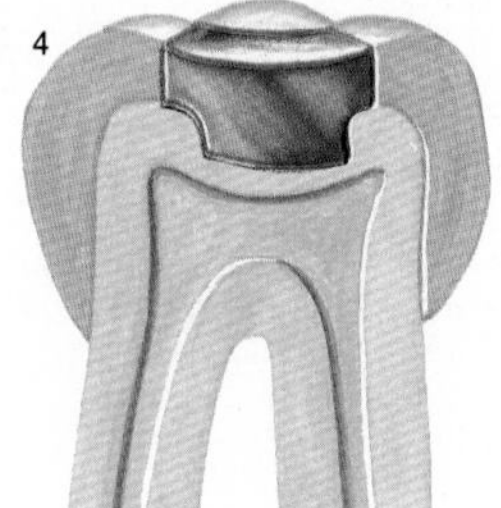

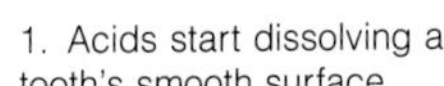

1. Acids start dissolving a tooth's smooth surface.
2. Eventually, decay spreads through the outer covering and makes a hole—**cavity**—in the tooth.
3. If the cavity is not treated, decay can spread deeper into the tooth, causing soreness and pain. Pus might form.
4. If treated in time, a dentist can clean out the decay and put in a filling. One common filling is silver amalgam—a mixture of silver, mercury, and tin. The dentist fills the cleaned cavity with this soft mixture. In a few minutes the silver amalgam hardens to form a solid filling.

- Ask students to name two common dental problems. (tooth decay and gum disease) • Let students explain how plaque can lead to cavities. (Bacteria in plaque use the carbohydrates in foods to produce acids that eat through the enamel on teeth.)
- Direct students' attention to the pictures on page 239 showing the formation of a cavity. Ask them to describe what each picture shows.
- Ask what can happen if cavities are not treated. (Decay can spread deeper into the tooth, causing a toothache.) • Discuss the causes of gum disease. (Plaque builds up between the teeth and under the gumline. Gums become irritated and swollen. Pockets form between the teeth and gums allowing bacteria to attack the bone that holds teeth in place.)

Teaching Plan

Lesson 2 continued

2 Teach

Strategies for Pages 240 and 241

• Ask students to read the first paragraph on page 240 to learn how brushing and flossing help prevent dental problems. (by removing plaque and bits of food from the surfaces of teeth and gums, from between teeth, and from under the gumline) • Direct the students to the pictures on pages 240 and 241. Call on students to read the captions aloud. • Emphasize that flossing is a skill that can be developed with a little practice and patience. • Discuss other tips for cleaning teeth. (replacing worn toothbrush, cleaning tongue with toothbrush to remove bacteria, rinsing mouth after eating sweets)
• Ask students to read the rest of page 241 to learn other ways to prevent dental problems. (choosing foods wisely, limiting snacks, having regular dental checkups) Make sure students understand that they can best prevent dental problems by brushing teeth after each meal and snack as well as flossing daily.

How Do Brushing and Flossing Help Prevent Dental Problems?

The most common dental problem of people your age is tooth decay. Gum disease is more common in adults, but people your age can also develop this problem. It often results from poor dental care during earlier years. You can help prevent both tooth decay and gum disease by cleaning your teeth daily. Brushing and flossing, shown here, are the best ways you can clean your teeth. Brushing removes plaque and bits of food from the surfaces of your teeth and gums. Flossing removes these substances from between your teeth and from under the gumline.

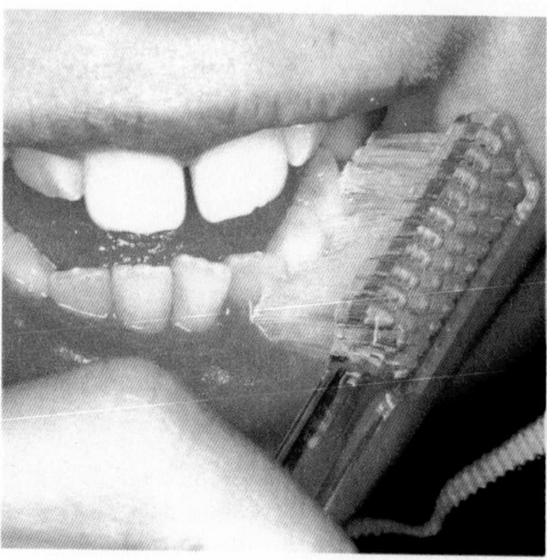

Proper way of brushing

Place the toothbrush bristles against the outside of the teeth, and angle the bristles against the gums. Move the brush back and forth using short, gentle strokes.

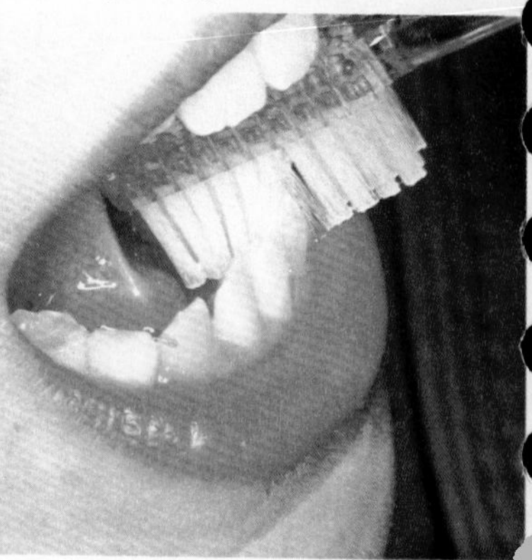

Brush the outsides and insides of all your teeth. Be sure to brush the chewing surfaces of the teeth too. Plaque and food can collect in the grooves on the chewing surfaces of teeth.

Use the front bristles to brush the insides of your front teeth.

240

Teaching Options

Anecdote

At one time false teeth were made of bone, ivory, wood, or even animals' teeth.

Enrichment

Let students research fluoride, plastic sealants, and vaccines used to fight tooth decay.

Encourage students to find out more about the kind of tools a dentist uses to remove plaque from the teeth.

Health and Science

Suggest students find out about X-rays and why they are often part of a dental checkup. (X-rays show cavities between the teeth, the position of teeth under the gums, and the beginnings of gum disease that may not be apparent otherwise.) If possible, obtain some dental X-rays so that students can compare normal and decayed teeth.

Reteaching

Ask a dentist or a dental hygienist to visit the class to demonstrate the proper way to brush and floss and to explain his or her work.

Arrange for your students to present a program on proper dental care to a group of younger students. The program could include posters, skits, and demonstrations of brushing and flossing techniques.

Special Education

Provide a model of a set of teeth to help learning-disabled students practice good brushing and flossing techniques.

How Can You Help Prevent Dental Problems?

In addition to visiting the dentist regularly, you can prevent dental problems by choosing foods wisely. Many foods contain some sugar. If you eat sweet snacks or desserts, the sugar settles on your teeth and gums. The bacteria in plaque use this sugar to make acids that attack your teeth. Limit the snacks you eat, and try to brush and floss your teeth after eating to remove sugar, food, and plaque.

Think Back • *Study on your own with Study Guide page 330.*

1. How does the combination of plaque and sugar lead to tooth decay?
2. What do brushing and flossing remove from teeth?
3. What does correct dental care include?

Proper way of flossing

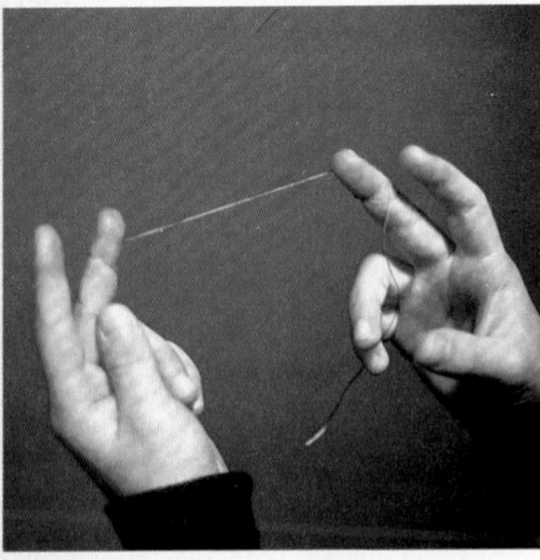

Break off about eighteen inches of floss, and wrap most of it loosely around one of your middle fingers. Hold the floss tightly between each thumb and forefinger.

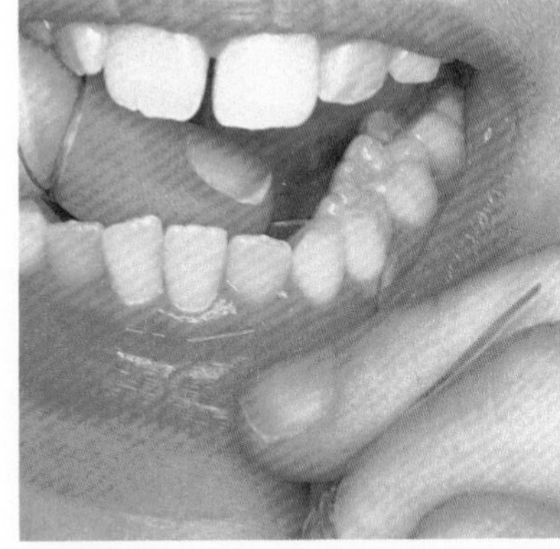

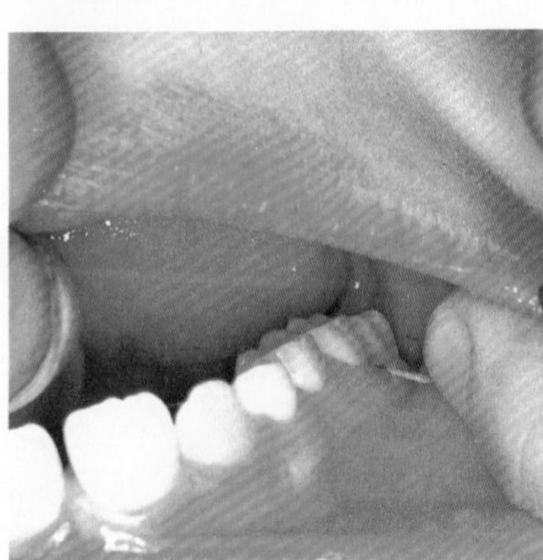

Use a sawing motion to slide the floss gently into the space between the gum and tooth. Curve the floss into a C shape after doing this.

Scrape the floss up and down gently against the side of each tooth. Use a clean part of the floss for each tooth.

3 Assess

Expanding Student Thinking

Ask students to explain why proper dental care now is important for a healthy future. (Proper care now can help prevent tooth loss and gum disease that often occur later in life.)

Thinking Skills When students explain the importance of dental care for a healthy future, they are *interpreting information* and *generalizing*.

Answers to Think Back

1. Bacteria in plaque use sugar to produce acids that eat away at tooth enamel, leading to decay.

2. Brushing and flossing remove plaque and bits of food from the teeth and from under the gumline.

3. Correct dental care includes brushing, flossing, limiting sweets, and visiting a dentist regularly.

Teaching Plan

Lesson 3 pages 242-243

Lesson Objective
Describe symptoms of vision and hearing problems.

1 Motivate

Introducing the Lesson
Ask students to name the five senses. (taste, touch, smell, hearing, and vision) Then discuss which of the senses is most important and why. (Answers will vary)

2 Teach

Strategies for Pages 242 and 243
• Direct students to read page 242 to learn how to protect their vision.
• Discuss with students the difference between nearsightedness and farsightedness. (Nearsighted people see nearby objects clearly, but far away objects are blurred; farsighted people see far away objects clearly, but nearby objects are blurred.) • Ask students to name other symptoms of eye disorders. (sore or itching eyes, headaches) • Direct students' attention to the chart on page 242. Call on students to take turns reading from the chart ways that they can protect their eyes.

Protecting Your Eyes
- If your doctor has prescribed glasses or contact lenses, wear them as directed.
- Always wear cover goggles when doing activities that could harm the eyes.
- Use good lighting and rest your eyes often when reading or doing close work.
- Avoid rubbing your eyes if something gets in them. Allow the flow of tears to cleanse the eye or seek the help of an adult.
- Do not use eyedrops unless they are prescribed by your doctor.
- Immediately notify a doctor if you notice a change in vision, eye pain, itching, or headaches.

3 How Do Vision and Hearing Keep You Safe?

Your five senses—vision, hearing, touch, taste, and smell—help you every day by giving you information about the world around you. Of the senses, vision and hearing are especially important. The eyes and ears help you as you work and play and can keep you out of danger. Can you imagine crossing a busy street without being able to see and hear? Your eyes tell you when the light is green and whether there is traffic. Your ears alert you to possible dangers from oncoming cars and allow you to hear sirens and horns. Together, the two senses help keep you safe.

Because the eyes and ears are so important, you need to know how to protect them. You also need to know the signs of vision and hearing problems.

What Are Some Common Problems with Vision?

The condition of nearsightedness is common in people your age. In this condition, a person can see objects that are close by, but objects far away appear blurred. Eyeglasses or contact lenses can correct this. A nearsighted person might need glasses to read the chalkboard at school, see a movie, or drive.

Another vision problem, more common in adults, is farsightedness. In this condition, a person can see faraway objects clearly, but close objects appear blurred. Like nearsightedness, farsightedness can be corrected with glasses. A farsighted person might need eyeglasses to read or do close work. The pictures show how objects close and far away might appear to people who are nearsighted and farsighted.

Nearsighted and farsighted people see different things clearly.

Teaching Options

Health Background

The eye functions much like a camera. Light from an object at a distance from the eye passes through the lens of the eye. The lens focuses the light on the eye's retina. The pattern of light falling on the retina creates impulses which are carried by the optic nerve to the brain where the impulses are interpreted as a picture. Not until the impulses have reached the brain does the eye actually "see."

Enrichment
Suggest that students research the differences in the various types of contact lenses (hard, soft, and extended-wear lenses) and report their findings to the class.

Discuss with students why, when a foreign object enters the eye, it is usually best to wait a few moments before seeking help. (Sometimes all that is needed is to give tears a chance to wash the object out of the eye.)

Health and Science
Ask students to find out why farsightedness is more common in adults than in young people and to report their findings to the class.

Reteaching
Ask an audiologist to visit the class and give students further information on what they can do to protect themselves against hearing loss.

It is important for you to notify an eye doctor if you notice any change in your ability to see objects up close and far away. Often, special eyeglasses will solve the problem. However, vision changes can also indicate a more serious eye disease or infection. Soreness or itching of the eyes and headaches are also clues that you need to see an eye doctor. The chart on page 242 lists some ways that you can protect your eyes.

What Are Some Hearing Problems?

Your ears, like your eyes, require care. You should wash the outer part of your ears with soap and water and dry them well each day. Never place any object, even a cotton-tipped swab, into your ear. Excess earwax should only be removed by your doctor. You should also avoid loud sounds, which can permanently damage the structures in the ear that allow you to hear. If you must be near loud sounds, wear protective ear coverings or plugs to prevent hearing loss.

Sometimes hearing problems occur despite good care. One ear problem that you might be familiar with is ear infection. Ear infections occur when germs, usually from a cold, are forced into the middle ear. The germs can be forced into the ear if you blow your nose too hard or hold your nose when you sneeze. It is important to gently blow your nose and to allow both nostrils to remain open during nose-blowing and sneezing. The nerves in the ear that allow hearing can become damaged if an ear infection is not treated. If you notice pain in your ears, it is very important to see a doctor at once.

Damage to nerves in the ear can also be caused by loud noises or ear injuries. When the nerves in the ears are damaged, hearing loss is permanent. The hearing of people with damaged nerves can often be improved with the use of hearing aids.

Hearing aids can help people who have nerve damage in their ears.

Think Back • *Study on your own with Study Guide page 331.*

1. What are four signs that indicate the need to see an eye doctor?
2. What are some ear problems that indicate the need to see a doctor?

243

• Ask students to read page 243 to learn about proper care of the ears.
• Ask students what occurs when an ear becomes infected. (Germs, usually from a cold, are forced into the middle ear.) Discuss what can happen if an ear infection is left untreated. (Nerves of the ear can become damaged, leading to loss of hearing.) Ask students to name other causes of damage to ear nerves. (loud noises and ear injuries) Emphasize that ear nerves, once damaged, cannot be repaired and that the only solution remaining is to wear a hearing aid.

3 Assess

Expanding Student Thinking

Ask students why the saying "Never put anything in your ear smaller than your elbow," is a wise saying as well as a humorous one. (Even though an elbow would never fit in an ear, the saying emphasizes the fact that a person should never put anything of any size in his or her ears.)

Thinking Skills By explaining why people should not put anything into the ears, students are *drawing conclusions* and *making analogies.*

Answers to Think Back

1. Change of vision, itching, pain, headaches

2. pain, loss of hearing

Teaching Plan

Lesson 4 pages 244–245

Lesson Objective
Explain the importance of washing regularly, in relation to skin and hair care.

Health Vocabulary
Oil glands, perspiration, sweat glands

1 Motivate

Introducing the Lesson
Discuss ways that appearance can contribute to good health. (Cleanliness can help remove disease-causing bacteria. Looking your best helps you feel good about yourself.)

2 Teach

Strategies for Pages 244 and 245
• Read the lesson title question aloud. • Direct students to read page 244 and the first two paragraphs on page 245 to learn the importance of cleaning the skin. (to remove dirt and bacteria; to prevent perspiration odor; to control excess oil and help prevent acne) • Help students locate the sweat and oil glands in the picture on page 244.

sweat glands, tiny structures in the skin that collect some body wastes and transfer them to the surface of the skin.

perspiration (pėr′spə rā′shən), the water, salt, heat, and other body wastes transferred by the sweat glands to the skin's surface.

4 Why Should You Take Care of Your Skin and Hair?

The most important way to care for your skin is to keep it clean. Tiny dirt particles and bacteria land on your skin constantly. Some of these bacteria can lead to illness when they get into your body. You can transfer the dirt and bacteria to others by shaking hands or touching an object that someone else touches. You can help prevent the transfer of bacteria to food by washing your hands before eating.

As you grow older, skin care becomes more important. Perspiration and oily skin increase your need for cleanliness.

Notice the **sweat glands** in the drawing of the skin. Sweat glands collect body wastes such as water, salt, and heat. The glands transfer these wastes, called **perspiration,** to the surface of the skin. Bacteria on your skin cause perspiration to develop an unpleasant odor, which can be most noticeable under your arms and on your feet.

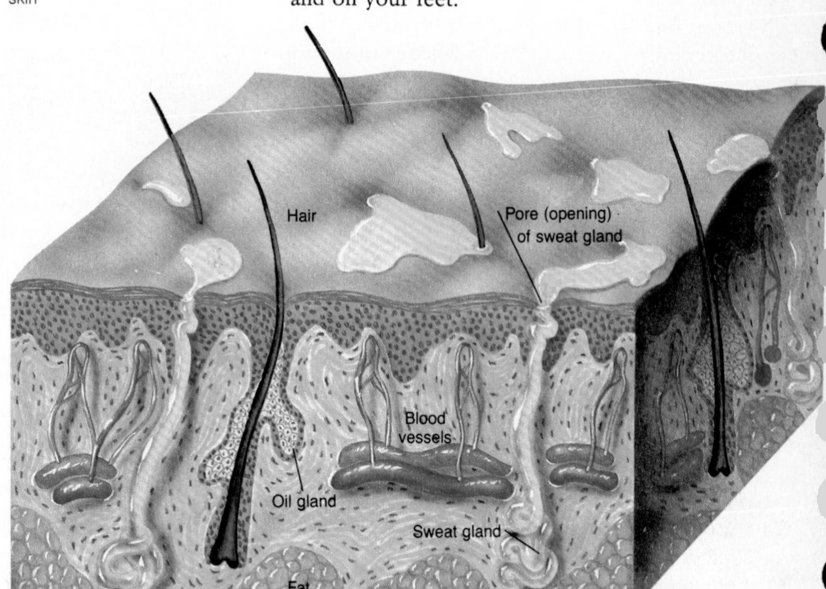

Sweat glands and oil glands in skin

Teaching Options

Health Background

Antiperspirants close the pores through which perspiration usually surfaces on the skin. Therefore, antiperspirants actually control sweating. Deodorants on the other hand do not prevent sweating. Rather, they reduce odors resulting from the action of bacteria in the perspiration. Some products contain both deodorants and antiperspirants.

Enrichment
Encourage students to list other ways to care for the skin. (eating healthy foods, limiting fried foods and chocolate and other sugary foods, which seem to affect the skin conditions of some people; washing towels and linens frequently so they are free of dirt and germs; keeping hands away from the face so bacteria cannot be transferred to the face)

Health and Physical Education
Discuss with students why athletes must be sure to drink water after practicing their sport or working out. (to replace some of the water lost through perspiration)

Reteaching
Discuss with students why people use deodorants and antiperspirants.

Special Education
Review in detail for learning-disabled students the steps for proper care of the hair and skin. You might also want to invite local hair and skin care professionals to visit the class to demonstrate some basic techniques and to stress the importance of cleanliness to good health.

In the next few years, during puberty, your sweat glands will become more active and you will perspire more. Frequent washing removes any buildup of perspiration and bacteria. Such products as antiperspirants and deodorants can help control perspiration odor.

Notice the **oil glands** in the drawing. These glands produce an oily substance that keeps your skin soft and smooth. Like the sweat glands, your oil glands will become more active in the next few years. You might notice the skin on your face becoming more oily. The extra oil can clog some of the openings in your skin. Then pimples and other kinds of acne might form. You can help control oily skin and acne by washing your face daily with soap and warm water.

Your scalp becomes oily for the same reason your face does. Oil glands beneath your scalp become more active. Extra oil might gather on your scalp and hair and might trap dirt.

You can use a shampoo to wash away the dirt and extra oil on your hair. Shampooing also helps control dandruff. Your scalp, like the rest of your skin, sheds dead skin cells constantly as new cells grow. Oil on the scalp makes the dead cells clump into flakes of dandruff. Any shampoo will cleanse your hair and scalp of dirt, oil, and loose dandruff flakes. You might want to use a special dandruff shampoo if you have a severe dandruff problem. When you shampoo, rinse your hair thoroughly. Shampoo left on your hair can dry and flake off, looking much like dandruff.

Proper skin and hair care should be part of your daily activities. By keeping clean, you help control the buildup of dirt and bacteria on your body. You also improve your appearance. Looking your best gives you greater confidence and improves the way you feel about yourself.

Think Back • *Study on your own with Study Guide page 331.*

1. What will happen to people your age in the next few years that makes proper skin and hair care more important?
2. Why is it important to wash the skin and hair regularly?

oil glands, tiny structures in the skin that produce an oily substance and transfer it to the surface of the skin.

Did You Know?

The hair that you can see on your body is made of dead cells. That is why you can cut your hair without feeling any pain. You do feel pain, however, if you pull your hair because you also pull on the living part of the hair beneath your skin's surface.

• Discuss why pimples form (Extra oil clogs openings in the skin.) and how to help control them. (Wash the face with soap and warm water daily.)
• Explain that the sweat and oil glands become more active during puberty because of the increase of hormones in the body. • Let students read the rest of page 245 and then explain how to care for the hair. (Shampoo to wash away dirt and extra oil; rinse the hair thoroughly.)

3 Assess

Expanding Student Thinking

Ask students what would happen if the body did not perspire. (Salt and other wastes would build up; since perspiration helps cool the body down when it becomes overheated, the body could overheat.)

Thinking Skills When students explain what would happen if the body did not perspire, they are *interpreting information* and *drawing conclusions.*

Answers to Think Back

1. Sweat glands and oil glands will become more active in the next few years, producing more perspiration, oily skin and hair, and possibly acne.

2. Regular washing of skin and hair controls the buildup of dirt and bacteria on the body. Regular washing also controls buildup of perspiration and oil on the skin. In addition, regular washing improves appearance and health.

Overhead Transparency Master

Use this blackline master to make a labeled overhead transparency or to make an unlabeled student worksheet. This blackline master may be reproduced from the Teacher's Resource Book.

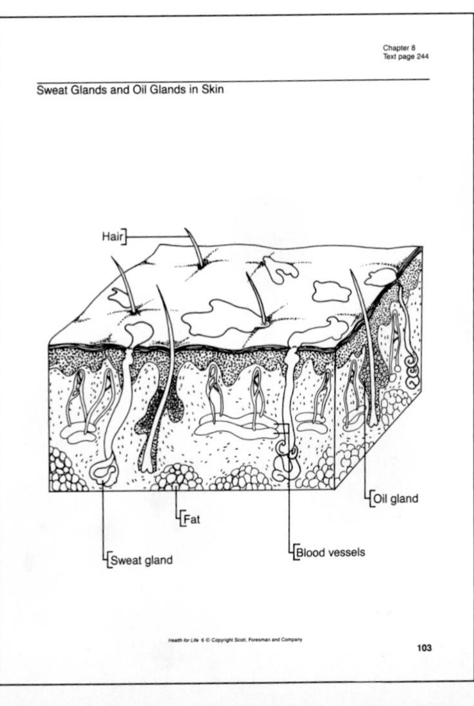

Health Activities Workshop pages 246–247

Materials
Activity 1 shampoo bottles with labels (Stress that students need not buy shampoo for this activity. Students can bring shampoo from home or copy the list of ingredients and bring that list to school.)
Activity 2 medicine droppers or straws, cooking oil, shampoo
Activity 5 clay, cardboard or construction paper

Activity 1 Strategies
Group the students so that each group has the same kind of shampoo (for oily hair, for dry hair, for normal hair, dandruff shampoo, or baby shampoo). Help students compare active ingredients such as soaps and antibacterial agents. The lists of ingredients will probably be similar. Explain that differences in shampoo ingredients might be due to color, fragrance, or a special purpose, such as treatment of oily hair or dry hair. These differences should be reflected in the lists of ingredients.
Thinking Skills When students compare shampoos, they are *organizing information* and *drawing conclusions.*

Activity 2 Strategies
The drop of oil should break up and dissolve in the soapy water.
Thinking Skills When students do the experiment, they are *collecting information* and *making analogies.*

Activity 3 Strategies
Some students may have crossed out almost every item on their lists. The activity shows them that by avoiding those foods they can greatly improve their dental health.
Thinking Skills When students review a list of snack foods, they are *classifying* and *drawing conclusions.*

Activity 4 Strategies
After doing the research, let students give short oral reports of their findings. The ADA-approved toothpastes all have flouride.
Thinking Skills When students compare toothpastes, they are *collecting information* and *drawing conclusions.*

Health Activities Workshop

Investigating Practices and Products of Personal Health

1. Bring a shampoo bottle to school. List the shampoo's ingredients. Form a group with three or four classmates and compare your lists. Circle the ingredients that are on all the lists in your group. Do you think any one of the shampoos does a better job of cleaning hair than the others? Explain your answer. List some of the differences among the shampoos.

2. Observe the effectiveness of shampoo. Use a medicine dropper or straw to place a drop of cooking oil in a cup of water. Notice what happens. Mix another cup of water with a small amount of shampoo, and place a drop of oil in this cup. What happens to the oil? What does this activity tell you about how shampoo cleans your hair?

3. Working with three or four classmates, make a list of all the kinds of snack foods you recall eating. Try to include at least fifteen items. Cross out the items that can most easily help cause tooth decay and gum disease. Which items are left? What does this activity tell you about how you can help prevent dental problems?

4. The American Dental Association (ADA) approves brands of toothpaste that meet the ADA's standards of quality. The picture shows how the ADA seal of approval appears on a toothpaste label. Check several brands of toothpaste at a grocery store or drugstore to find out which ones are approved by the ADA. Record and compare the lists of ingredients to find out what the approved toothpastes have in common.

5. Use information from an encyclopedia or other book to make a poster or model of a tooth. You can use clay, cardboard, construction paper, or other materials if you make a model. Use the words *crown, root, gum, enamel, dentin, pulp, bone,* and *cementum* to label the parts of the tooth and surrounding areas.

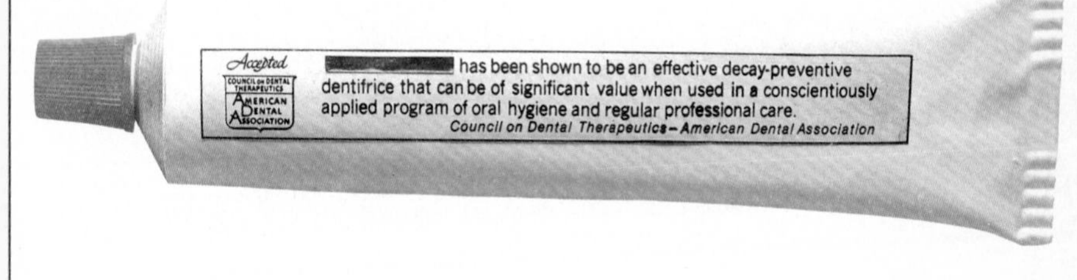

Accepted
COUNCIL on DENTAL THERAPEUTICS
AMERICAN DENTAL ASSOCIATION
has been shown to be an effective decay-preventive dentifrice that can be of significant value when used in a conscientiously applied program of oral hygiene and regular professional care.
Council on Dental Therapeutics—American Dental Association

Looking at Careers

6. Looking your best helps you feel good about yourself. **Hairstylists** wash, cut, and style hair to help men and women look their best. Hairstylists keep up with current trends in hairstyles. Customers sometimes request hairstyles similar to those worn by models in magazine photographs. Hairstylists use their skills to provide the wanted look.

People who want to become hairstylists attend special schools to learn about hair care. Since many hairstylists operate their own shops, they might also take business courses in high school and college.

Hairstylists work closely with their customers. Keeping this fact in mind, write down some special qualities you think a hairstylist should have.

For more information, write to Associated Master Barbers and Beauticians of America, 219 Greenwich Rd., P.O. Box 220782, Charlotte, NC 28222.

7. Good health and good posture are important to the people in the picture. They are professional **dancers.** Dancers practice daily for many hours so that their movements express the proper feelings and are pleasant to watch. Dancers practice good posture so they will be able to move and hold their bodies in various positions during a dance routine. Dancers also learn proper breathing methods so they will not become too tired during a performance. Many dancers study the human body and how it works. They apply this information to their own body movements in dance.

People who want to become dancers often attend classes at a dance studio or at a school of fine arts.

Look in an encyclopedia to find out about the many different kinds of dance. List and describe each kind.

For more information write to the American Dance Guild, 570 7th Ave., 20th Fl., New York, NY 10018. Enclose a stamped, self-addressed envelope.

Activity 5 Strategies
You may wish to have pupils work with partners for this activity. If possible, display the finished posters and models.
Thinking Skills When students make posters or models, they are *collecting information* and *communicating.*

Activity 6 Strategies
Special qualities a hair stylist should have include the ability to get along well with people. You may wish to invite a hair stylist to the classroom to discuss hair care as a profession.
Thinking Skill When students find out about a career as a hair stylist, they are *collecting information.*

Activity 7 Strategies
Ask volunteers to share with the class what they learned about different kinds of dance. If possible, invite a dance teacher to the classroom to talk about dancing as a career. Ask the speaker to stress the importance of physical fitness and good posture for a career in dance.
Thinking Skills When students learn about dance and write for information about dancing as a career, they are *collecting information* and *communicating.*

Teaching Plan

Lesson 5 pages 248–251

Lesson Objective
Explain the importance of sleep, rest, and recreation for maintaining good health and relieving fatigue.

Health Vocabulary
Fatigue

1 Motivate

Introducing the Lesson
Tell students that the human body has a daily need for rest and sleep. Ask students to write down the number of hours of sleep they usually get each night. Use the information to make a histogram on the chalkboard.

On Your Own
Think back to the last night you slept for a shorter period of time than is normal for you. In a paragraph, describe how you felt the next morning. Now, reread the third paragraph on this page. Do you notice any similarities between your description and the research findings described? List the similarities.

5 Why Are Sleep, Rest, and Recreation Important?

The boy in the picture is in a deep sleep. All appears peaceful . . . quiet . . . still. Yet, parts of his body are in a whirl of activity. His digestive system is busy breaking down the food he ate during dinner. New cells are forming to replace those worn out. Meanwhile, the feelings, sounds, and images of dreams pass through his mind.

Sleep is an important part of your life and your health. For example, your body produces most of your growth hormone while you sleep. During sleep your heart rate, breathing rate, and some of your other body processes slow down. Therefore, more energy is available to build or repair body cells. Sleep also gives some of your muscles and other body parts a chance to rest from the day's activities.

The importance of sleep is best understood when sleep is taken away. Research experiments show that people who do not sleep for a day or two often cannot perform simple tasks. They often have trouble concentrating and easily become angered. Their senses become unreliable, and sometimes they hear or see things that do not exist.

The amount of sleep a person needs depends largely on his or her age. Infants often need sixteen to twenty hours of sleep each day. Adults usually sleep seven or eight hours a night. Most people your age need nine or ten hours of sleep each night.

Sleep is an important part of your health.

Teaching Options

Health Background

Scientists have learned from brain wave patterns that sleep occurs in several stages. At each stage, sleep becomes deeper and the brain waves become larger and slower. Then, about ninety minutes after a person falls asleep, he or she enters REM (rapid eye movement) sleep. During this time the eyes move back and forth rapidly beneath the eyelids, and the brain waves show a burst of activity similar to the activity when the person is awake. Most dreams occur during REM sleep.

Enrichment
Let interested students find out more about sleep research and the different stages of sleep. Encourage students to report their findings to the class.

Health and Art
Paintings by Salvador Dali, René Magritte, and other surrealists show various perceptions of dreams. Display reproductions of several of such paintings, asking students to describe what they see. Discuss possible meanings of the images in the paintings.

Reteaching
Let students draw cartoons showing how they feel after a restless night or a night with little sleep.

A healthy night's sleep includes about an hour of dreaming. Everybody dreams. You do not always remember your dreams, but sleep experiments show that people usually dream four or five times each night. Each of these dream periods lasts from a few minutes to half an hour.

The woman shown here is participating in a sleep experiment. While she sleeps, electric signals from her brain travel through wires to a machine. The machine records the signals as waves on a sheet of paper. By observing the brain waves, scientists can tell when the woman is sleeping lightly, sleeping deeply, or dreaming.

Scientists do not know why people dream, but they do know dreaming is important to health. During some sleep experiments, people were awakened whenever they started dreaming. The next day they were tired and irritable, even though they slept for their normal amount of time. Dreaming seems to be almost as important to your health as sleep itself.

Did You Know?
Sleep experiments are helping scientists understand illnesses that used to be mysteries. For example, by observing brain waves during sleep, scientists can tell if a person has narcolepsy (när′ kə lep′ sē). This illness causes sudden attacks of deep sleep, which could occur even while a person is talking, driving, or playing. Once a person is known to have narcolepsy, that person can be helped.

Participating in a sleep experiment

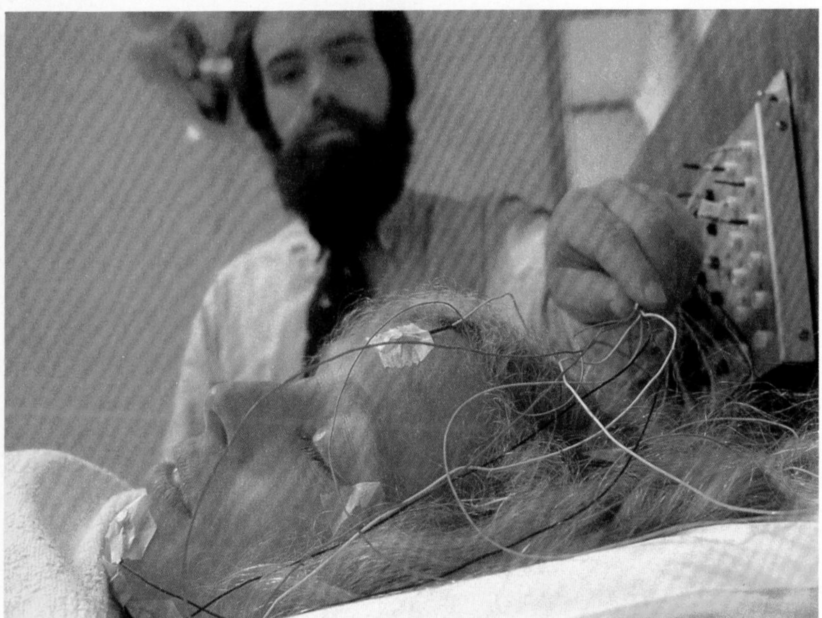

2 Teach

Strategies for Pages 248 and 249

• Direct students' attention to the picture on page 248. • Let students read page 248 to find why sleep is important. (During sleep, new cells form while others are repaired, heart rate, breathing, and some other body processes slow down; muscles and other body parts rest; growth hormone is produced.) • Discuss with students how much sleep people usually need. (Infants need sixteen to twenty hours; adults, seven to eight hours; sixth-graders, nine to ten hours. However, sleep needs vary somewhat among individuals.) • Tell the students to read page 249 to find out how dreaming is important to health. (People who are not allowed to dream are tired and irritable the following day, even though they have had enough sleep.)

Using On Your Own

Descriptions will vary depending on the students' experiences. The list of similarities might include an inability to perform simple tasks, trouble concentrating, easily becoming angered, senses becoming unreliable, and hearing or seeing things that do not exist.

Thinking Skills When students relate their experiences to research findings, they are *organizing information* and *making analogies*.

Health and Mathematics

Use this worksheet for practice in computing sleep time. This master may be reproduced from the Teacher's Resource Book and is located on page 32 of the Student's Workbook. Use with Chapter 8: pages 248–251.

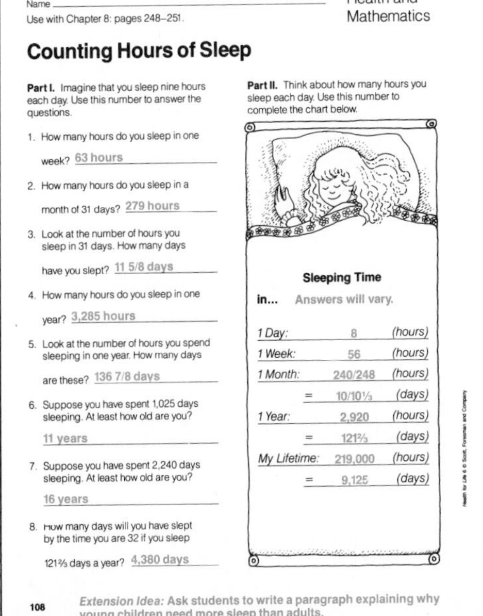

Name ____________________
Use with Chapter 8: pages 248–251.

Health and Mathematics

Counting Hours of Sleep

Part I. Imagine that you sleep nine hours each day. Use this number to answer the questions.

1. How many hours do you sleep in one week? 63 hours
2. How many hours do you sleep in a month of 31 days? 279 hours
3. Look at the number of hours you sleep in 31 days. How many days have you slept? 11 5/8 days
4. How many hours do you sleep in one year? 3,285 hours
5. Look at the number of hours you spend sleeping in one year. How many days are these? 136 7/8 days
6. Suppose you have spent 1,025 days sleeping. At least how old are you? 11 years
7. Suppose you have spent 2,240 days sleeping. At least how old are you? 16 years
8. How many days will you have slept by the time you are 32 if you sleep 121⅔ days a year? 4,380 days

Part II. Think about how many hours you sleep each day. Use this number to complete the chart below.

Sleeping Time

in... Answers will vary.

1 Day:	8	*(hours)*
1 Week:	56	*(hours)*
1 Month:	240/248	*(hours)*
=	10/10⅓	*(days)*
1 Year:	2,920	*(hours)*
=	121⅔	*(days)*
My Lifetime:	219,000	*(hours)*
=	9,125	*(days)*

Extension Idea: Ask students to write a paragraph explaining why young children need more sleep than adults.

Teaching Plan

Lesson 5 continued

2 Teach

Strategies for Pages 250 and 251

• Ask students to describe situations in which they felt tired even though they slept well the night before. (after physical exercise, after a test, during a boring movie, and so on) • Write the word *fatigue* on the chalkboard and explain that fatigue is weariness than can be caused by exercise, stress, hunger, or boredom. • Direct the students to read page 250 to find out what causes physical fatigue (During exercise wastes build up in the muscles, making the muscles tired and sore.) and how to relieve it (rest). • Let students read page 251 to learn about other kinds of fatigue (mental and emotional fatigue) and ways to relieve them (mental—exercise; emotional—doing something enjoyable). Ask students to explain how the people in the pictures are relieving fatigue. (doing enjoyable activities)

fatigue (fə tēg′), weariness caused by physical exercise, stress, concentration, boredom, or a lack of energy.

How Can You Reduce Fatigue?

Several times throughout the day you might feel **fatigue**—weariness—even though you slept well the night before. Sleep does not always relieve fatigue. For example, if you skipped breakfast today, your body probably lacks energy. You might feel fatigue. Sleep will not relieve the fatigue, but food will.

Fatigue can be relieved in different ways. The kind of relief depends on the kind of fatigue. The runner shown in the picture is experiencing physical fatigue. This kind of fatigue results when muscles are used a lot. During exercise, the body produces wastes, such as carbon dioxide. After much exercise, these wastes build up in the body, making the muscles tired and sore. A rest period gives the blood a chance to remove the wastes from the muscles. Then the fatigue goes away.

You probably rest several times a day to relieve physical fatigue. After pedaling your bicycle for a while, you might rest your leg muscles by coasting. After writing sentences for spelling class, you might put your pen down for a minute to relax your hand and wrist muscles.

What kind of fatigue is this runner feeling?

Teaching Options

Anecdote

Sleepwalking is more common among children than adults. It rarely occurs when a person is dreaming, but rather during a period of deep sleep.

Enrichment

Suggest students find out about battle fatigue, a kind of fatigue suffered by some soldiers during war. Encourage students to report their findings to the class.

Health and Mathematics

Ask students to perform a physical activity such as writing sentences until they experience physical fatigue. Have students note the time required for them to become fatigued and the time needed for them to recover. Then have students determine the ratio between the activity and the recovery time. Students might like to try other physical activities to see if the ratios remain the same.

Reteaching

Ask students to think of activities they do, other than those listed in the text, that cause physical fatigue. Discuss how they relieve the fatigue from each of these activities. Make a class list of students' suggestions for relieving mental or emotional fatigue.

Not all fatigue is physical. Mental fatigue often results when you concentrate on one task for a long time. For example, studying at home for two hours without a break might make you feel tired. Exercise, such as taking a walk or a bicycle ride, will help relieve this mental fatigue. The pictures show other activities you might enjoy while taking a break to relieve mental fatigue.

Stress can cause emotional fatigue. For example, you might take a test in the morning and spend the rest of the day worrying about how you did. On top of that, you might have an argument with a friend and feel angry the whole day. Such stressful situations can make you feel tired. Activities that you find relaxing or enjoyable might help relieve emotional fatigue.

Fatigue is one of your body's ways of telling you a change is needed. This change might involve rest, food, exercise, or an activity you find enjoyable.

On Your Own
Think of a time when strong emotions, such as anger, caused you to feel fatigue. On a sheet of paper, describe how you showed this emotional fatigue. Then, explain how you could have relieved your fatigue.

Think Back • *Study on your own with Study Guide page 331.*

1. How does sleep help the body?
2. How does rest relieve physical fatigue?
3. How could someone relieve emotional fatigue?

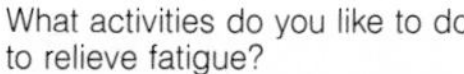
What activities do you like to do to relieve fatigue?

Using On Your Own
Answers will vary depending on the situations and the activities students choose to relieve emotional fatigue.
Thinking Skills By thinking about ways to relieve emotional fatigue, students are *suggesting alternatives* and *drawing conclusions.*

3 Assess

Expanding Student Thinking
Let students write a short letter to a friend who is sleeping well at night but feels fatigued at school each day. What would the students advise? (Eat properly, exercise, rest when necessary, do something you enjoy, and see a doctor if fatigue continues.)
Thinking Skill When students give advice about fatigue, they are *suggesting alternatives.*

Answers to Think Back

1. Sleep gives the body a chance to build or repair cells, and sleep gives the muscles a chance to rest from the day's activities.
2. Rest gives the blood a chance to remove wastes from muscles, making them able to work once again.
3. A person can relieve emotional fatigue by exercising, drawing, or doing some other enjoyable activity.

Teaching Plan

Health Focus page 252

Discussion

Review with students how plaque can lead to tooth decay. (Bacteria that form plaque use the sugar in foods to produce acids that can destroy enamel on teeth.) Relate how plaque can cause gum disease. (The acids produced by bacteria in the plaque destroy the tough, elastic fibers in the gum that support the teeth and hold them in place. Destruction of these fibers causes the formation of pockets in the gum that allow the entrance of more harmful bacteria.)

Answers to Talk About It

1. Answers should include removing hardened plaque below the gumline to control gum disease, advising physicians on the side effects of certain medicines, and teaching patients how to prevent gum disease.
Thinking Skill By telling how Dr. Adams helps her patients, students are *recalling information*.
2. Answers should include a description of the proper methods of brushing and flossing the teeth.
Thinking Skill When students answer what they would tell patients, they are *organizing information*.

Health Focus

Dr. Adams Keeps People Smiling

Healthy teeth are powerful cutting tools that you use every day. Because you use them so often, you might take your teeth for granted.

However, proper dental and gum care is a very important part of maintaining health according to Dr. Melba K. Adams. Dr. Adams is a periodontist—a dentist who specializes in treating gum disease. The treatment often involves cleaning the teeth below the gumline. Dr. Adams uses special tools to remove hardened plaque on the part of the teeth below the gums.

Dr. Adams also works with physicians in caring for her patients. Some of her patients take medicine for diseases such as epilepsy. Some of these medicines cause side effects, including damage to the gums. Dr. Adams talks with her patients' physicians about prescribing medicines that do not harm the mouth.

Helping patients prevent gum disease is another important part of Dr. Adams's work. She helps her patients learn how to brush and floss their teeth correctly. With Dr. Adams's help, her patients can keep their teeth as healthy as her own.

Talk About It

1. How does Dr. Adams help her patients achieve good health?
2. If you were Dr. Adams, how would you tell your patients they could prevent gum disease?

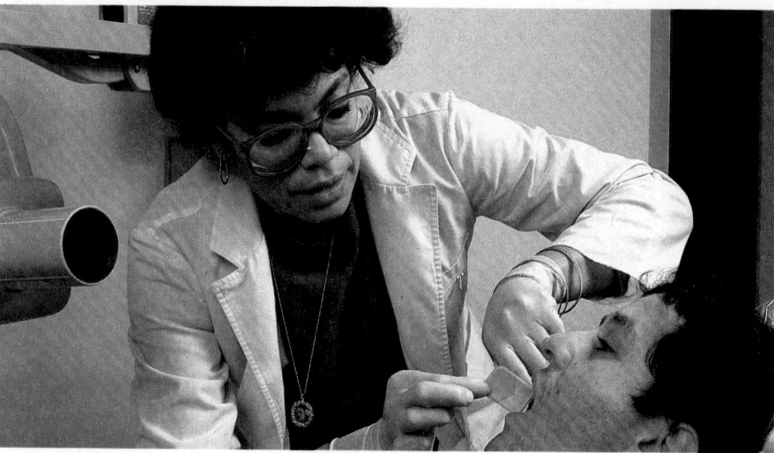

252

Teaching Options

Vocabulary

Use this worksheet for practice in reviewing chapter vocabulary words. This master may be reproduced from the Teacher's Resource Book and is located on page 30 of the Student's Workbook. Use with Chapter 8: pages 234-255.

Name ______________________ Vocabulary

Use with Chapter 8: pages 234–255.

Personal Care Word Scramble

Part I. Unscramble the vocabulary words below. Then write each unscrambled word on the line beside its meaning.

RSTAPEORNIPI ACYITV MGU ADISSEE EQLPUA
OSTREPU GETAUFI HNRIGSUB NSLSOGIF

CAVITY 1. A hole in a tooth.
BRUSHING 2. A method of removing plaque and bits of food from the surfaces of your teeth and gums.
PLAQUE 3. A thin, sticky, colorless film of bacteria.
FATIGUE 4. A weariness caused by physical exercise, stress, concentration, or a lack of sleep.
GUM DISEASE 5. A condition resulting in gums pulling away from the teeth, leaving pockets.
POSTURE 6. The way in which you stand, sit, and carry yourself.
PERSPIRATION 7. The water, salt, and other body wastes moved by the sweat glands to the skin's surface.
FLOSSING 8. A method of removing plaque and bits of food from between your teeth and gums.

Part II. Use the words from Part I and the pictures below to describe a good, daily health care routine.

Answers will vary.

106

Extension Idea: Suggest that students make a chart to record the health care practices they do each day.

Using the "Green Detective" to Find Plaque

Brushing and flossing help prevent the buildup of plaque on your teeth and gums. However, since plaque is colorless, you cannot always tell if you are cleaning your teeth well enough to remove all the plaque.

A small amount of green food coloring can help you discover how well you are cleaning your teeth. The food coloring stains plaque on your teeth and gums.

Clean your teeth as you usually do. Then mix two drops of green food coloring with about an inch (2.5 cm) of water in a cup, as shown. Swish the colored water in your mouth, and spit the water out into a sink. Then, examine your teeth in a mirror. Do you notice any stains from the food coloring like those in the picture? These stains show where plaque remains on the teeth and gums. Brush and floss again until all the stains are removed. The next time you clean your teeth, remember the extra brushing and flossing you needed to remove all the plaque.

Show members of your family how the "green detective" finds plaque. They might enjoy discovering how well they clean their teeth. You and your family can use food coloring every now and then to help improve your brushing and flossing skills.

Reading at Home

Is the Cat Dreaming Your Dream? by Margaret O. Hyde. McGraw-Hill, 1980. Find out about the hows and whys of dreaming as you explore the world of sleep.

Junior Body Machine by Dr. Christian Barnard, Consulting editor. Crown, 1983. Read about how the human body works and how to keep it in the best physical health through exercise and proper diet.

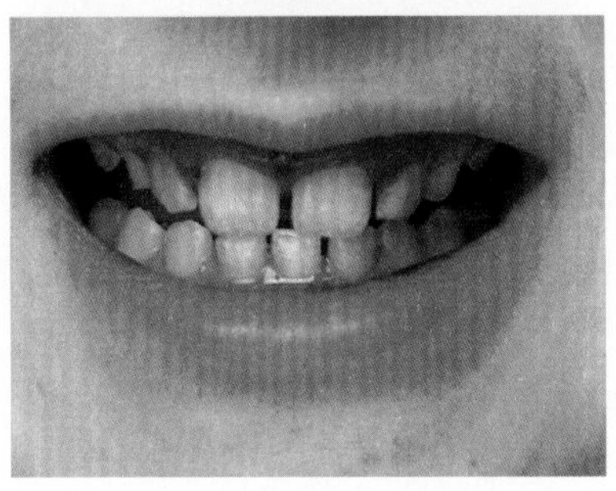

Health at Home
page 253

Strategies
Review with students the proper techniques for brushing and flossing. Refer to the pictures on pages 240 and 241 if necessary. Students may wish to make a chart for themselves to see how their brushing and flossing techniques have improved. They could test for plaque once a week and rate their cleaning technique as good, fair, or poor.

More Reading at Home
Is the Cat Dreaming Your Dream? (Grades 5–8)

Junior Body Machine (Grades 4–7)

Berry, Joy Wilt. *What to Do When Your Mom or Dad Says . . . "Stand Up Straight!"* Childrens Press, 1984. Explains how children can learn to acquire better posture. (Grades 4–7)

Study and Review
Use this worksheet for practice in reviewing tooth-brushing procedure. This master may be reproduced from the Teacher's Resource Book and is located on page 31 of the Student's Workbook. Use with Chapter 8: pages 234–255.

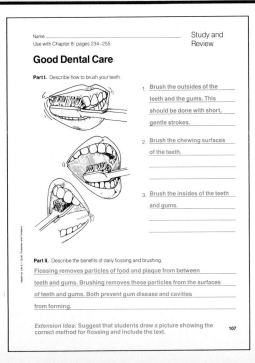

Name ______________________ Study and Review
Use with Chapter 8: pages 234–255.

Good Dental Care

Part I. Describe how to brush your teeth.

1. Brush the outsides of the teeth and the gums. This should be done with short, gentle strokes.
2. Brush the chewing surfaces of the teeth.
3. Brush the insides of the teeth and gums.

Part II. Describe the benefits of daily flossing and brushing.

Flossing removes particles of food and plaque from between teeth and gums. Brushing removes these particles from the surfaces of teeth and gums. Both prevent gum disease and cavities from forming.

Extension Idea: Suggest that students draw a picture showing the correct method for flossing and include the text.

107

Review Plan

Chapter 8 Review

pages 254–255

Answers to Reviewing Lesson Objectives

Use this section for guided study or for oral review. Objective numbers match lesson numbers.

1. Good posture is important because it prevents many kinds of muscle soreness, helps prevent a person from getting tired too easily during activities, helps a person perform activities better, and improves appearance.

2. Correct dental care includes cleaning the teeth properly, choosing foods wisely, and visiting a dentist regularly.

3. Symptoms of vision problems include changes in vision, soreness or itching of the eyes, and headache. Pain and loss of hearing are symptoms of hearing problems.

4. Washing regularly removes dirt, bacteria, and oil from the skin. Bacteria on the skin can lead to body odor and certain diseases. Excess oil on the skin and hair can lead to acne and dandruff.

5. Sleep gives the body a chance to rest from the day's activities and to build and repair body cells. Rest and recreation are important because they help relieve fatigue.

Answers to Checking Health Vocabulary

Use the vocabulary check as a review or as a test.

1. c
2. b
3. a
4. e
5. f
6. g
7. h
8. d
9. decay
10. plaque
11. sugar
12. enamel
13. cavity
14. gum disease
15. calculus
16. brush or floss
17. floss or brush

Chapter 8 Review

For further review, use Study Guide pages 330-331
Practice skills for life for Chapter 8 on pages 359-361
SKILLS FOR LIFE

Reviewing Lesson Objectives

1. State reasons why good posture is important to good health. (pages 236–237)
2. Describe what is included in correct dental care (pages 238–241)
3. Describe symptoms of vision and hearing problems. (pages 242–243)
4. Explain why washing regularly is important for proper skin
5. and hair care. (pages 244–245)
Explain how sleep, rest, and recreation are important for good health. (pages 248–251)

Checking Health Vocabulary

Number your paper from 1–8. Match each definition in Column I with the correct word or words in Column II.

Column 1	Column II
1. a dental problem which results in gums pulling away from the teeth, leaving pockets	a. cavity
2. a weariness that can be caused by physical exercise	b. fatigue
3. a hole in a tooth, caused by tooth decay	c. gum disease
4. the water, salt, heat, and other body wastes that are transferred to the skin's surface	d. oil gland
5. a sticky film of bacteria that forms on the teeth and gums	e. perspiration
6. the position of the body	f. plaque
7. a tiny structure in the skin that collects some body wastes and transfers the wastes to the surface of the skin	g. posture
8. a tiny structure in the skin that produces an oily substance and transfers the substance to the surface of the skin	h. sweat gland

Number your paper from 9–17. Next to each number write the word or words that correctly complete the sentences in the paragraph.

Tooth __(9)__ is the most common dental problem for young people. It is caused by the bacteria in __(10)__. The bacteria use __(11)__ in food to produce acids. The acids destroy the __(12)__ on teeth. Eventually the acids can form a hole or __(13)__ in the teeth. __(14)__ is a dental problem caused by plaque building up between the teeth and under the gum-line. As the plaque hardens it is called __(15)__. People can help prevent tooth decay and gum disease when they __(16)__ and __(17)__ their teeth.

Chapter 8 Tests Use Test A or Test B to assess students' mastery of the health concepts in Chapter 8. These tests are located on pages 65–72 in the Test Book.

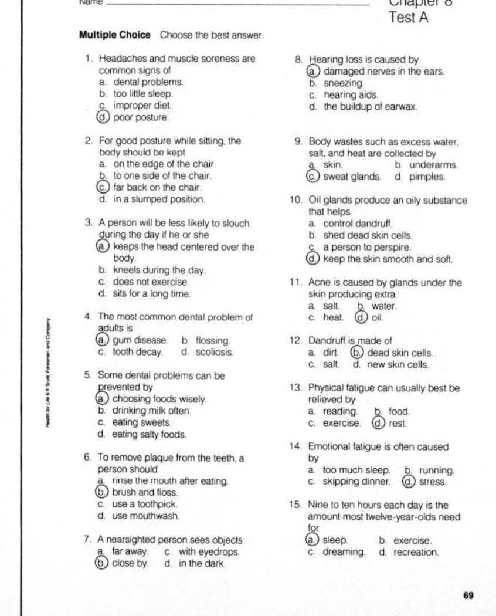
Name ______________ Chapter 8 Test A

Multiple Choice Choose the best answer.

1. Headaches and muscle soreness are common signs of
   a. dental problems. b. too little sleep. c. improper diet. **(d.)** poor posture.
2. For good posture while sitting, the body should be kept
   a. on the edge of the chair. b. to one side of the chair. **(c.)** far back on the chair. d. in a slumped position.
3. A person will be less likely to slouch during the day if he or she
   (a.) keeps the head centered over the body. b. kneels during the day. c. does not exercise. d. sits for a long time.
4. The most common dental problem of adults is
   (a.) gum disease. b. flossing. c. tooth decay. d. scoliosis.
5. Some dental problems can be prevented by
   (a.) choosing foods wisely. b. drinking milk often. c. eating sweets. d. eating salty foods.
6. To remove plaque from the teeth, a person should
   a. rinse the mouth after eating. **(b.)** brush and floss. c. use a toothpick. d. use mouthwash.
7. A nearsighted person sees objects
   a. far away. c. with eyedrops. **(b.)** close by. d. in the dark.
8. Hearing loss is caused by
   (a.) damaged nerves in the ears. b. sneezing. c. hearing aids. d. the buildup of earwax.
9. Body wastes such as excess water, salt, and heat are collected by
   a. skin. b. underarms. **(c.)** sweat glands. d. pimples.
10. Oil glands produce an oily substance that helps
   a. control dandruff. b. shed dead skin cells. c. a person to perspire. **(d.)** keep the skin smooth and soft.
11. Acne is caused by glands under the skin producing extra
   a. salt. b. water. c. heat. **(d.)** oil.
12. Dandruff is made of
   a. dirt. **(b.)** dead skin cells. c. salt. d. new skin cells.
13. Physical fatigue can usually best be relieved by
   a. reading. b. food. c. exercise. **(d.)** rest.
14. Emotional fatigue is often caused by
   a. too much sleep. b. running. c. skipping dinner. **(d.)** stress.
15. Nine to ten hours each day is the amount most twelve-year-olds need for
   (a.) sleep. b. exercise. c. dreaming. d. recreation.

69

Name ______________ Chapter 8 Test A

Short Answer Match each meaning in Column I with the correct word or words in Column II. Write the correct letter on the blank.

Column I	Column II
c 16. the position of body	a. cavity
f 17. a dental problem in which the gums pull away from the teeth	b. perspiration
e 18. a sticky film of bacteria that forms on teeth and gums	c. posture
a 19. a hole in a tooth, caused by tooth decay	d. fatigue
b 20. the wastes that sweat glands transfer to the skin's surface	e. plaque
d 21. a weariness that can be caused by physical exercise, stress, or a lack of energy	f. gum disease
g 22. a condition in which a person can see faraway objects clearly while close objects appear blurred	g. farsightedness
h 23. structures in the skin that produce an oily substance and transfer it to the skin's surface	h. oil glands

Short Essay Write your answers in complete sentences.

24. What good general health practices improve posture?
   Eating a well-balanced diet and getting plenty of exercise help build the strong bones and muscles needed for good posture. Getting the right amount of sleep helps prevent a person from getting tired and slouching during the day.
25. Why do you think tooth decay was not as common a few hundred years ago as it is today?
   Answers should refer to the fact that candy and other sweet foods eaten today were not available or so common a few hundred years ago. Answers should also refer to the way sugar can damage teeth by being used by bacteria to produce acids.

70

Reviewing Health Ideas

Number your paper from 1–15. Next to each number write the word or words that best complete the sentence.

1. Good posture enables bones and _____ to support the body weight correctly.
2. _____ posture puts unnecessary strain on other body parts.
3. Plaque is always forming because _____ are always in the mouth.
4. If pockets form in the gums, bacteria can attack the _____ that holds the teeth in place.
5. The most common dental problem of young people is _____.
6. Flossing removes plaque and bits of food from _____ the teeth.
7. To prevent dental problems, people should brush and floss their teeth at least _____ a day.
8. The longer a food stays in the mouth, the longer _____ have to form.
9. Only a dental-care professional can remove hardened _____ from teeth.
10. Frequent _____ removes the buildup of perspiration and bacteria.
11. Sweat glands and oil glands become more active during the stage of _____.
12. More _____ is available to build and repair cells when a person sleeps.
13. Experiments show that _____ is almost as important as sleep itself.
14. Physical _____ occurs when wastes such as carbon dioxide build up in the body.
15. Worrying and being angry can produce _____ fatigue.

Understanding Health Ideas

Number your paper from 16–28. Next to each number write the word or words that best answer the question.

16. Where is a person with poor posture likely to have pain?
17. What happens when one part of the body moves out of line?
18. What do bacteria in the mouth use to produce acids?
19. What is calculus?
20. What are the two best ways to clean teeth daily?
21. What are two signs of ear problems that indicate the need to see a doctor?
22. What kinds of foods are especially harmful to the teeth?
23. What glands transfer perspiration to the skin?
24. What causes perspiration to develop an odor?
25. When should a person see an eye doctor?
26. Is most of the growth hormone produced when a person is asleep or awake?
27. How many times does a person generally dream each night?

Thinking Critically

Write the answers on your paper. Use complete sentences.

1. Explain the meaning of the following equation: Plaque + Sugar = Decay
2. Suppose a friend seems fatigued even though he or she slept for nine hours last night. How might the friend relieve his or her fatigue?

255

Cooperative Learning Use the STAD Format described on page T24 to have four- to five-member teams study Chapter 8 Review together before completing Chapter 8 Test.

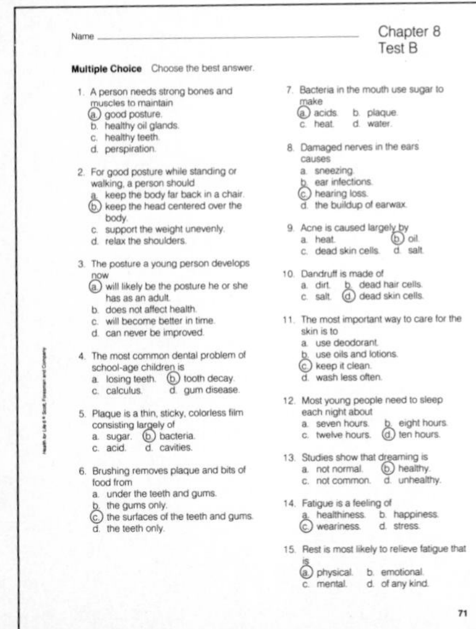

Name ______________________ Chapter 8 Test B

Multiple Choice Choose the best answer.

1. A person needs strong bones and muscles to maintain
   (a.) good posture.
   b. healthy oil glands.
   c. healthy teeth.
   d. perspiration.
2. For good posture while standing or walking, a person should
   a. keep the body far back in a chair.
   (b.) keep the head centered over the body.
   c. support the weight unevenly.
   d. relax the shoulders.
3. The posture a young person develops now
   (a.) will likely be the posture he or she has as an adult.
   b. does not affect health.
   c. will become better in time.
   d. can never be improved.
4. The most common dental problem of school-age children is
   a. losing teeth. (b.) tooth decay. c. calculus. d. gum disease.
5. Plaque is a thin, sticky, colorless film consisting largely of
   a. sugar. (b.) bacteria. c. acid. d. cavities.
6. Brushing removes plaque and bits of food from
   a. under the teeth and gums.
   b. the gums only.
   (c.) the surfaces of the teeth and gums.
   d. the teeth only.
7. Bacteria in the mouth use sugar to make
   (a.) acids. b. plaque. c. heat. d. water.
8. Damaged nerves in the ears causes
   a. sneezing.
   b. ear infections.
   (c.) hearing loss.
   d. the buildup of earwax.
9. Acne is caused largely by
   a. heat. (b.) oil. c. dead skin cells. d. salt.
10. Dandruff is made of
    a. dirt. b. dead hair cells. c. salt. (d.) dead skin cells.
11. The most important way to care for the skin is to
    a. use deodorant.
    b. use oils and lotions.
    (c.) keep it clean.
    d. wash less often.
12. Most young people need to sleep each night about
    a. seven hours. b. eight hours. c. twelve hours. (d.) ten hours.
13. Studies show that dreaming is
    a. not normal. (b.) healthy. c. not common. d. unhealthy.
14. Fatigue is a feeling of
    a. healthiness. b. happiness. (c.) weariness. d. stress.
15. Rest is most likely to relieve fatigue that is
    (a.) physical. b. emotional. c. mental. d. of any kind.

71

Name ______________________ Chapter 8 Test B

Short Answer Match the word or words in Column I with the correct meaning in Column II. Write the correct letter on the blank.

Column I	Column II
f 16. posture	a. the body wastes that sweat glands transfer to the skin's surface
e 17. cavity	b. a sticky film of bacteria that forms on teeth and gums
d 18. gum disease	c. a condition in which a person can clearly see only objects that are close by
b 19. plaque	d. a dental problem in which the gums pull away from the teeth
a 20. perspiration	e. a hole caused by tooth decay
c 21. nearsightedness	f. the positioning of parts of the body to support body weight
g 22. sweat glands	g. structures in the skin that collect body wastes and transfer them to the skin's surface
h 23. oil glands	h. structures in the skin that produce an oily substance and transfer it to the skin's surface

Short Essay Write your answers in complete sentences.

24. Why is it important to clean one's teeth after eating?
    Cleaning the teeth removes bits of food, including sugar, that contribute to tooth decay. Brushing and flossing also helps remove plaque from teeth and gums before the plaque hardens and leads to gum disease.
25. Why should you wash your hands before eating?
    Washing helps remove the dirt and bacteria that constantly land on the skin. These substances can easily be transferred to food if hands are not washed. Some of the bacteria can cause illness.

72

Answers to Reviewing Health Ideas

1. muscles
2. poor
3. bacteria
4. bone
5. tooth decay
6. between
7. once
8. acids
9. plaque
10. washing
11. puberty
12. energy
13. dreaming
14. fatique
15. emotional

Answers to Understanding Health Ideas

16. lower back or head
17. the rest of the body moves out of line, putting unnecessary strain on body parts
18. sugar
19. hardened plaque
20. brush and floss
21. pain, loss of hearing
22. sweets
23. sweat glands
24. bacteria on the skin
25. for vision change, pain or itching of eyes, or headaches
26. asleep
27. four or five

Answers to Thinking Critically

1. The equation means that the bacteria in plaque use sugar to produce acids. These acids eat away at teeth, causing tooth decay.
Thinking Skill By explaining the meaning of the equation students are *interpreting information.*
2. Answers will vary but should include finding out the possible cause of the friend's fatigue and then suggesting ways to relieve it, such as by eating properly, exercising, or doing some recreational activity.
Thinking Skills By suggesting ways to relieve fatigue, students are *drawing conclusions* and *suggesting alternatives.*

Pupil Edition	Activities	Enrichment	Assessment	Independent Study
Chapter 9 Your Decisions as a Health Consumer, pp. 256–283	Health Watch Notebook, p. 256	Health Focus, p. 280 Health at Home, p. 281	Chapter 9 Review, pp. 282–283	Study Guide, pp. 332–333 Skills for Life Handbook, pp. 362–364
Lesson 1 How Can You Become a Wise Health Consumer? pp. 258–261			Think Back, p. 261	Study Guide, p. 332
Lesson 2 How Can Advertising Influence You as a Consumer? pp. 262–267	Health Activities Workshop, pp. 268–269		Think Back, p. 267	On Your Own, p. 263 Study Guide, p. 332
Lesson 3 What Should You Consider When Choosing Health Products? pp. 270–274	Health Activities Workshop, p. 275	Did You Know? p. 270	Think Back, p. 274	On Your Own, p. 271 Study Guide, p. 333
Lesson 4 How Can You Benefit Most from a Health Checkup? pp. 276–279		Did You Know? p. 276	Think Back, p. 279	Study Guide, p. 333

Teacher Resources

Penny Power Magazine. Consumer Reports. Presents consumer issues that children can understand and relate to.

Stossel, John. *Shopping Smart.* Putnam, 1980. Contains specific chapters on health-related consumer issues.

Vogt, Thomas A. *Making Health Decisions: An Epidemiologic Perspective on Staying Well.* Nelson-Hall, 1983. Encourages a balance between openness to new ideas and healthy skepticism concerning health claims on TV or in the newspapers.

Audio-Visual Resources

See page T43 for addresses of Audio-Visual Sources.

Before using any audio-visual materials, preview them for appropriateness for your students.

Habits of Health: The Physical Examination, BFA Educational Media, film or video, 10 minutes. Acquaints young people with what a doctor does, and explains the purpose of a physical examination.

Math for the Young Consumer, Educational Activities, Inc., filmstrips with cassettes. Examines how to evaluate packaging and labeling when comparison shopping.

Over-the-Counter Drugs: Smooth Talk and Small Print, Barr Films, film or video, 22 minutes. Points out the sales tactics used by advertisers and the importance of consulting a pharmacist about over-the-counter drug purchases.

What About Food Additives? Food and Drug Administration, slides with cassette. Describes the FDA's role in regulating food additives and the consumer's responsibility in being aware of the additives contained in the food they buy.

Computer Software

Life Skills, Aquarius Software. Teaches basic living skills such as decision making, consumerism, and comparison shopping.

	Teacher's Edition	Teacher's Resource Book	Test Book
Enrichment	Suggestions for each lesson: L. 1—pp. 258, 260 L. 2—pp. 262, 264, 266 L. 3—pp. 270, 272, 274 L. 4—pp. 276, 278	Family Letter, p. 113 * Life Skills, p. 117 * Health and Language Arts, p. 120	
Reteaching	Suggestions for each lesson: L. 1—pp. 258, 260 L. 2—pp. 262, 264, 266 L. 3—pp. 270, 272, 274 L. 4—pp. 276, 278	Transparency Masters, pp. 115–116 * Vocabulary, p. 118 * Study and Review, p. 119	
Assessment	Expanding Student Thinking: one assessment question per lesson that develops higher-order thinking skills—pp. 261, 267, 274, 279		Chapter 9 Test, Form A, pp. 73–74 Chapter 9 Test, Form B, pp. 75–76

* Also available in Workbook format (Student Edition and Teacher's Edition)

Chapter 9 Poster
A set of posters is available in a separate package. It provides a teaching poster for every chapter, including discussion and activity suggestions on the back. The poster for Chapter 9 is titled "Which soup is the best buy?"

Overhead Transparencies
A set of color overhead transparencies is available for Grade 6. You may wish to use Transparency 20 to help teach about reading product labels.

Advance Preparation
You will need to prepare materials in advance for the following activity from the Health Activities Workshop.
Activity 1, page 268 Obtain newspapers and magazines for cutting out ads.

Bulletin Board
Draw ads or attach magazine ads for health products. Ask students to evaluate each ad.

Teaching Plan

Chapter 9 pages 256–283

Chapter Main Idea
People can become wise health consumers when they learn about the factors that influence their decisions.

Chapter Goals
- Develop an interest in becoming a wise health consumer.
- Decide to analyze advertising more carefully.
- Express an interest in getting the most benefit from a health examination.

Lifetime Goal
Develop and use consumer skills throughout life.

Health Vocabulary
Advertisement, fad, health consumer, logo, net weight, unit price

Words to Preteach
Allergies, blood pressure, guarantee, gum disease, immunization, plaque, tooth decay

Chapter 9

Your Decisions as a Health Consumer

"Which one should I choose?" Think about a time when you might ask yourself this question. The choices you make are important, especially when they concern your health. No matter what you are choosing, some basic guidelines can help you make the wisest decisions.

This chapter will show how you can make wise decisions about the health products and services you buy and use. You will learn how to get the best products and services available at the prices you can afford. The consumer skills you learn now can be used throughout your lifetime.

Health Watch Notebook
Collect magazine and newspaper advertisements and place them in your notebook. Under each ad, explain how it influences the consumer.

1 How Can You Become a Wise Health Consumer?
2 How Can Advertising Influence You as a Consumer?
3 What Should You Consider When Choosing Health Products?
4 How Can You Benefit Most from a Health Checkup?

Teaching Options

Modeling Health Vocabulary
Use this technique to introduce new words as you teach each lesson in this chapter. First, introduce the word. Present the word in two sentences that serve to clearly define the word. One sentence you might use to introduce the word *logo* is the following: *The logo was an eye-catching symbol that everyone remembered.* Either read the sentences to the students or write them on the chalkboard. Ask the students to generate two meaningful sentences using the word. Additional successful techniques for introducing new words can be found on page T23.

Cooperative Learning
Jigsaw Format (See page T24.)
Assign the following topics at random to your cooperative learning teams.

Topic A: What are some guidelines used by wise health consumers?
Topic B: What are some ways of evaluating ads?
Topic C: What things should a wise consumer consider when purchasing a health product?
Topic D: What are the advantages of regular health checkups?

Have students search for information on their topic as they read the chapter. Then let all students with the same topic meet in an expert group to discuss the information. When students return to their teams, they may take turns presenting their topics to the team. Then give students a test covering all topics to complete individually (Chapter 9 test A or B in the Test Book). Award Superteam certificates to teams whose average test scores exceed 90%, and Greatteam certificates to teams whose average test scores exceed 80%.

Introducing the Chapter

Ask students to think of something they or a family member bought recently that required choosing among similar products. As one example, suggest students think about choosing a pair of gym shoes. Ask students how they would choose among many pairs of gym shoes. Challenge the students to analyze their criteria for making consumer choices. Ask students to read page 256 and think about some of the choices they make when purchasing items. You may wish to send the Family Letter home at this time. You may want to assign Study Guide pages 332–333 for students to use independently as they read the lessons. The Study Guide can also be used as an extra chapter review. You might want to assign the activities in the Skills for Life Handbook on pages 362–364.

Strategies for Health Watch Notebook

Before students begin collecting advertisements, suggest that they look for ads with a variety of ways to appeal to consumers. When the ads have been collected, ask for volunteers to present some of their choices to the class. Ask students to present ads that they think have particularly strong appeal and to give their reasons for thinking so.

Family Letter

Use the Family Letter (English or Spanish version) to introduce the subject matter of the chapter to the family and to suggest a way the family can become involved in the student's learning experience. This master may be reproduced from the Teacher's Resource Book.

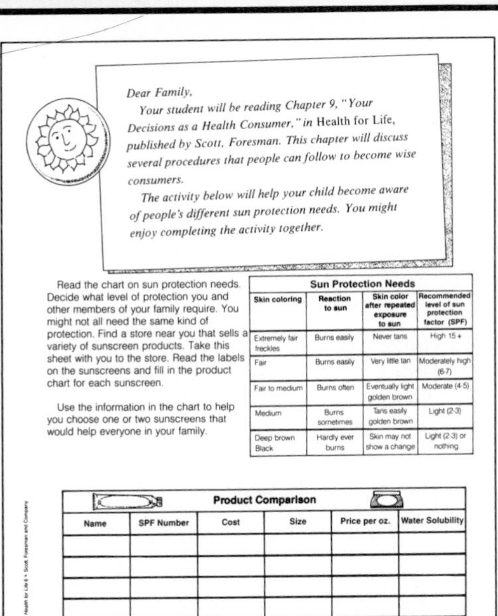

Dear Family,

Your student will be reading Chapter 9, "Your Decisions as a Health Consumer," in Health for Life, *published by Scott, Foresman. This chapter will discuss several procedures that people can follow to become wise consumers.*

The activity below will help your child become aware of people's different sun protection needs. You might enjoy completing the activity together.

Read the chart on sun protection needs. Decide what level of protection you and other members of your family require. You might not all need the same kind of protection. Find a store near you that sells a variety of sunscreen products. Take this sheet with you to the store. Read the labels on the sunscreens and fill in the product chart for each sunscreen.

Use the information in the chart to help you choose one or two sunscreens that would help everyone in your family.

Sun Protection Needs

Skin coloring	Reaction to sun	Skin color after repeated exposure to sun	Recommended level of sun protection factor (SPF)
Extremely fair freckles	Burns easily	Never tans	High 15 +
Fair	Burns easily	Very little tan	Moderately high (6-7)
Fair to medium	Burns often	Eventually light golden brown	Moderate (4-5)
Medium	Burns sometimes	Tans easily golden brown	Light (2-3)
Deep brown Black	Hardly ever burns	Skin may not show a change	Light (2-3) or nothing

Product Comparison

Name	SPF Number	Cost	Size	Price per oz.	Water Solubility

113

For High-Potential Students

Encourage interested students to devise a rating graph or chart that can be used to evaluate health products such as soaps, deodorants, toothpastes, and shampoos. First ask the students to decide criteria on which each group of products will be judged. Criteria might include cost, effectiveness, and packaging. Ask students to rate various brands of each kind of health product according to the criteria established. Encourage the students to share their graphs or charts with the class. Some students may wish to read *Consumer Reports* or a similar magazine to assist them in their evaluation.

Teaching Plan

Lesson 1 pages 258–261

Lesson Objective
List guidelines that can help people become wise consumers of health products.

Health Vocabulary
Health consumer

1 Motivate

Introducing the Lesson
Tell the students to imagine that they are in a store buying a loaf of bread. Discuss how they might go about making a decision on what brand or kind of bread to buy. (Among the factors influencing the decisions could be advertising, others' opinions, what they have tried in the past, and how much money they want to spend.)

health consumer, a person who buys or uses health products or services.

1 How Can You Become a Wise Health Consumer?

Who is a **health consumer?** You are. In fact, everyone is. A health consumer is anyone who buys or uses products and services that contribute to health. How do the products shown here contribute to health? As you grow older, you will find yourself making more decisions on your own about what health products and services to buy and use.

Perhaps you think there is nothing much to learn about buying. You just go into a store, pick out what you want, and pay for it. Wise shopping, however, is not always that simple. For one thing, most people have to budget their money very carefully. They want to save money whenever they can. Many people have learned, too, that the most costly products are not always the best ones. Even people with a lot of money do not want to spend it needlessly.

How does each item contribute to health?

Teaching Options

Health Background

A number of federal and local health agencies can assist the consumer in making wise health product purchases. Government agencies include the Food and Drug Administration, which approves new drugs and inspects facilities that manufacture or store health products, and the Federal Trade Commission, which is concerned about false or misleading advertising. The United States Postal Service protects the consumer by prosecuting those who sell fraudulent products and services through the mail.

Enrichment
Help students think of other questions they might ask themselves before buying a product. List their suggestions on the chalkboard.

Health and Language Arts
Suggest that students write a story about a wise and an unwise shopper. The story might answer some of the following questions: What did each shopper set out to buy? How did each determine what product to buy? Did either shopper go home with extra products? What happened after they got home?

Reteaching
Help the students make a bulletin board illustrating the Before-You-Buy Guidelines with pictures or original drawings.

Suggest that students think of a health product they would like to buy. Then ask them to apply the Before-You-Buy Guidelines to the product by writing appropriate answers to the guideline questions.

Special Education
Encourage special education students to develop a "store" of health care items. Ask all students in your class to bring in empty containers of health care products from home. Then help special education students evaluate each item.

Before you make any purchase, try doing what careful shoppers do. Ask yourself if you really need what you are about to buy. In other words, do you need the product or do you just want it? Sometimes people buy a product simply because their friends use it or because they think it will make them more popular.

Unwise shoppers often buy things impulsively. That is, they see something on a shelf or counter and are attracted by it. Without any careful thought, they quickly buy the product even though they do not need it. They usually do not even realize they want the product until they see it. Products bought impulsively are often displayed at checkout counters. What are some of these products?

The chart lists some questions to ask yourself before buying a product. Use these questions as guidelines for careful shopping.

Before-You-Buy-Guidelines

- Do I need it or do I just want it?
- If I buy it, will I really use it?
- Am I buying on impulse?
- Do I already have other products very much like this one?
- Can I afford it?
- Could I buy something better if I take more time to look and think about it?

2 Teach

Strategies for Pages 258 and 259

• Ask students to read page 258 to learn why making wise shopping decisions is important. • Direct the students' attention to the picture. Ask how the products contribute to their health. (The products are used to help keep people clean and free of germs, to prevent or treat illness and injury, or for food. All of the products shown can affect a person's health.) • Suggest that students read page 259 to find out what an impulsive buyer is and what questions to ask before buying a product. • Explain that many times products are put near the checkout counters to encourage impulsive buying. Then ask what some of these products are. (Accept any reasonable answers such as magazines, candy, small gadgets, and toys.) Stress that impulsive buying is not necessarily bad if the buyer uses the item bought and if it is not significantly less expensive elsewhere. • Direct the students to the chart listing Before-You-Buy Guidelines. Read each question to the class. After reading each one, ask volunteers to share shopping experiences that relate to the questions to ask before buying a product.

Life Skills

Use this worksheet for practice in learning about consumer protection agencies. This master may be reproduced from the Teacher's Resource Book and is located on page 33 of the Student's Workbook. Use with Chapter 9: pages 258–261.

Thinking Skill: By using information from the chart to answer questions, students are interpreting and analyzing information.

Name ______________________ Life Skills

Use with Chapter 9: pages 258–261.

Learning About Consumer Protection

Part I. Use the information on the chart to answer the questions.

Agency	Products Checked	Services
Consumer Product Safety Commission	Household products, including appliances, cleaning agents, and toys	Sets safety standards for these products; tests and approves products before they can be sold; removes dangerous products
Food and Drug Administration	Processed and prepared foods, medicines, cosmetics, and dishes and utensils used for food preparation	Sets standards for food purity and nutritional content; sets standards for purity, safety, and effectiveness of medicines; inspects food factories, researches food additives, checks accuracy of food and drug labels and advertisements
Agriculture Department	Fruits, vegetables, grains, poultry; meat, milk, and milk products	Checks conditions under which food animals and crops are raised; sets standards for and inspects food
National Bureau of Standards	Household furnishings, clothes, stoves, and construction materials	Sets standards for the resistance of these products to fire

1. List two services of the Consumer Product Safety Commission.
   Answers might include: sets safety standards for household products, removes dangerous products.
2. List two services of the Food and Drug Administration.
   Answers might include: sets purity and safety standards for foods and medicines, inspects food factories.

Part II. List the agency that is responsible for making sure that each product is safe to use.

1. Bananas Agriculture Department
2. Bicycle Consumer Product Safety Commission
3. Sweater National Bureau of Standards
4. Canned corn Food and Drug Administration

Extension Idea: Suggest that students choose a toy and describe ways the CPSC might test the toy for safety.

117

Teaching Plan

Lesson 1 continued

2 Teach

Strategies for Pages 260 and 261

• Let students read pages 260 and 261 to learn how others can help them become wise health consumers. • Discuss how family members influence health decisions. (Parents and older members of the family buy health products for younger ones. Family members might take children to the doctor or dentist.) • Emphasize that children can share new information with family members as they learn more about health products. • Ask students to name some health and cosmetic products that are popular among their age group. (Accept all reasonable answers.) • Direct the students to the picture on pages 260 and 261 and ask them to note the titles of the books, magazines, and pamphlets. • Emphasize that several of these publications are written especially for young people. • Ask students to name two sources, besides family and friends, for learning about health care products. (the library, the school nurse)

What Can Help You Become a Wise Health Consumer?

When you think about a purchase before making it, you might realize that you need some help. Older members of your family are good sources of help since they probably make many of your family's health decisions. For example, your older brother or sister might have bought the toothpaste for your family. Your grandmother might have taken you to the doctor for your last examination. Your mother or father might have chosen which foods the family ate for dinner last night.

Sometimes your friends are a good source of information. Before you follow a friend's advice, however, be sure that you really need the product. You should not buy a product just because your friend has it.

The school nurse, a pharmacist, and other health care professionals can give you some advice about health care products.

The next time you go for a health checkup, you might ask the doctor about buying certain health products. You also might start looking at the library for materials that can help you be a smart shopper. A large variety of up-to-date, dependable materials are shown below. At the library, notice that some magazines on consumer advice are especially written for young people.

Teaching Options

Anecdote

In the early 1900s, novelist Upton Sinclair's book, *The Jungle,* about the filthy conditions in meat-packing plants led to the creation of the Federal Food and Drug Act of 1906.

Enrichment

Encourage interested students to go to the library and find consumer reports or magazines written for young people. Ask them to prepare a brief report on a particular health product to share with the class.

Health and Math

Encourage students to compare the prices of different brands of pain relief tablets in a local store. Let students check labels to make sure the main ingredients and number and strength of tablets are the same. Ask them to find out if a popular name brand, less-known brand, or store brand is the least expensive.

Reteaching

Ask students to write a paragraph describing some health consumer decisions that a parent or other responsible adult could help students make wisely.

As you gain more experience in shopping wisely, you will find that you can make better decisions and purchases. You will also find that you can learn from your experiences. For example, suppose you buy a large can of deodorant. After using it for three days, you develop a rash. You stop using the deodorant. You also read the label. The next time you buy a deodorant, you might buy a smaller can that has slightly different ingredients. Then you will be less likely to develop a rash. Also, you will not have wasted as much money if the new deodorant causes a rash too. Judging the decisions you make will help you make wiser decisions in the future.

Think Back • *Study on your own with Study Guide page 332.*

1. What are six questions to keep in mind before you buy a product?
2. What are four major sources of health information?

The library has many sources of consumer information.

• Stress that part of becoming a wise consumer is learning from mistakes. Emphasize also that popular brand name products are not always better than less popular brands.

3 Assess

Expanding Student Thinking

Ask students to explain why, when a person is buying a product he or she has never tried before, buying the smallest size is usually the best. (So that if the product is not satisfactory, the person will not have spent a lot of money on a product he or she will not use.)

Thinking Skill When students think about why buying a small size of a new product is wise, they are *interpreting information.*

Answers to Think Back

1. The six questions are: Do I need it or just want it? If I buy it will I really use it? Am I buying on impulse? Do I already have products very much like this one? Can I afford it? Could I buy something better if I take more time to look and think about it?

2. Good sources of information include family members, friends, the school nurse, consumer magazines, and experience.

Teaching Plan

Lesson 2 pages 262–267

Lesson Objective
List several methods that advertisers use to promote the sale and use of products, and explain what to keep in mind when evaluating an ad before selecting a health product.

Health Vocabulary
Advertisement, logo

1 Motivate

Introducing the Lesson
Ask students which ads on TV they remember most. (Many students will mention ads that have catchy jingles, logos, or slogans.) Then ask them to think about why they remember these ads. Ask students to what extent they think they are influenced by advertisements they read, see, or hear. (Accept any reasonable answers.)

2 Teach

Strategies for Pages 262 and 263
• Tell students to read page 262 to learn how people are influenced by advertising. • Discuss the various types of advertising. (TV and radio commercials; ads in newspapers and magazines or on billboards)

advertisement, a public notice or announcement recommending a product or service.

2 How Can Advertising Influence You as a Consumer?

You decide to buy one kind of bandage when four other kinds are on the shelf. Why? You choose one kind of suntan lotion over another. Why? You want to buy a hamburger from one restaurant instead of another. Why?

Advertisements, or ads, often influence your decisions to buy. An ad is a recommendation for a product or service. Radio and television commercials are forms of advertisements. Printed advertisements appear in magazines and newspapers. Every day thousands of products and services are promoted through advertising.

Flattery
Some ads try to convince you to buy a product by complimenting you. The message is that the product is for you because you deserve the very best.

Free gift
Sometimes ads offer you something "free" if you buy a certain product. A prize in a cereal box is an example. Often, though, the prize offered is worthless or its price has been added to the price of the product.

Join the crowd
Such ads show people using a product and indicate that "everyone" likes and uses the product. The ads urge you not to be left out.

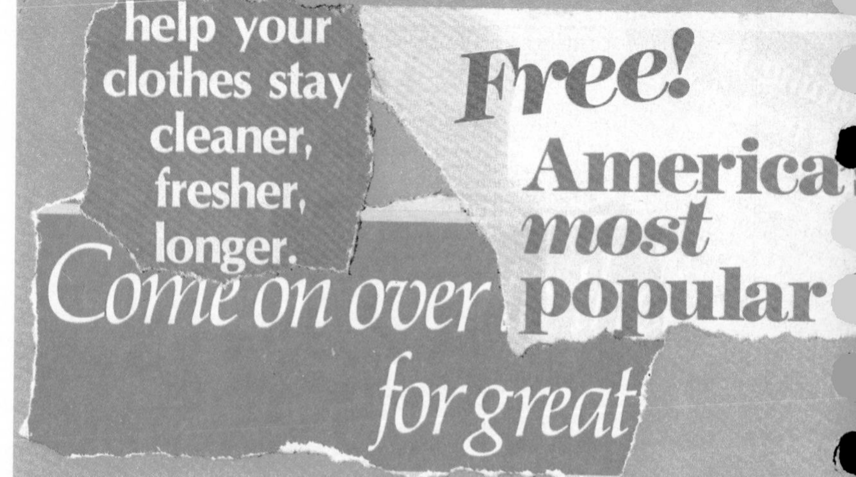

262

Teaching Options

Health Background

Some laws ensure truthful information on products themselves. The Fair Packaging and Labeling Act requires that the net weight of a package appear on the product label. The Wholesome Meat Act requires all states to have meat inspected by officials from the U.S. Department of Agriculture. The meat is then rated as to quality.

Enrichment

Suggest students keep a folder containing ads that depict various methods of advertising. Challenge students to find ads in magazines and newspapers that use other methods to influence buyers besides the six techniques mentioned in the text.

Let interested students research ads in magazines from the 1950s and 1960s to see what kinds of advertising were used then. Ask them to compare these ads with those used today. Let the students report their findings to the class.

Encourage students to compare ads for different brands of a similar product. Ask students to look for differences and similarities in advertising techniques.

Reteaching

List the six advertising techniques on the chalkboard. Then ask students to give examples of each.

Health and Language Arts

Ask students to write a helpful ad and a misleading ad for a health care product. Discuss with the class the differences between the two ads.

Advertisements are sources of information. They help make people aware of different products or services. Ads help make one product stand out from other products. Some ads also give helpful information about a product or service.

Not all ads, however, give you the helpful information you need and want. Many ads are planned just to make you want to buy a product. They use various methods that have little or nothing to do with giving you worthwhile information. Six advertising methods are described and shown on these two pages. Have you noticed any of these methods in ads?

Almost every product ad uses some recognizable selling method. The product may or may not be a good choice for you. Knowing how an ad is trying to convince you will help you make better choices.

On Your Own

Each statement below is an example of an advertising method described on these two pages. Write down each statement. Next to each example, write the name of the method. Then describe why that example fits in that category.

- "New and improved"
- "Five out of six doctors recommend"
- "Sure it's expensive, but aren't you worth it?"
- "Free coupon"
- "Millions use it"

Famous people like it
Some ads show famous people with a product. The ads want you to believe that if someone famous likes the product, you will like it too. Some people think if they use the product, they will be like the famous person.

Scientific claims
Some ads claim that experts and scientific information back the product. These ads want people to believe that the product is good simply because an expert says it is.

Unclear statements
Sometimes an ad includes a statement that is not explained or that can be interpreted in different ways. For example, "You can't buy a better product" might mean you could buy many products just as good.

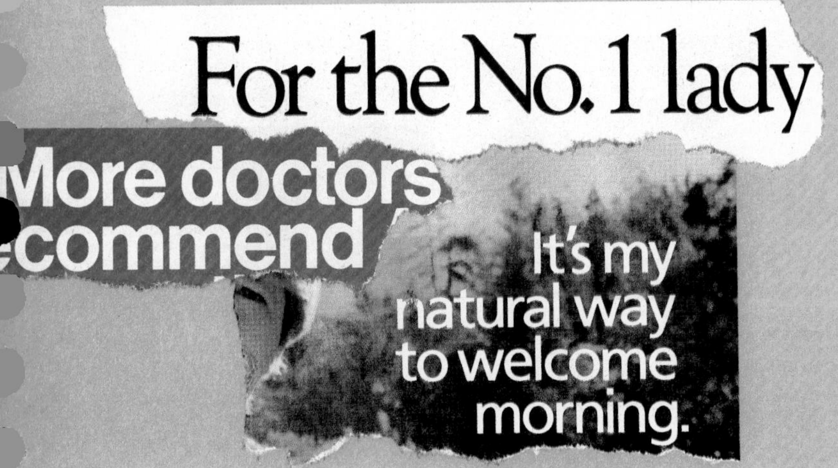
For the No. 1 lady
More doctors
commend
It's my
natural way
to welcome
morning.

• Be sure students understand that advertisers use various techniques to try to influence people to buy their product. • Call on volunteers to read aloud each of the advertising techniques on pages 262 and 263. Discuss each technique separately. Direct students to match each of the techniques with one of the ad lines shown in the pictures. Ask students if they have noticed any of these methods in ads. Let students tell about similar ads they have seen and the products that were being sold. • Then discuss why many of these techniques are misleading. (Accept any answers the students can explain.)

Using On Your Own

The advertising methods are: (1) *unclear statement*—the words do not tell you anything specific about the product, (2) *scientific claim*—doctors are said to recommend the product, (3) *flattery*—the statement says that you are worth spending a lot of money on, (4) *free gift*—the statement promises a bonus for buying the product, (5) *join the crowd*—the manufacturer wants you to believe that you should use the product because everybody else is using it.

Thinking Skill When students tell what techniques are being used in the ads, they are *classifying*.

Health and Language Arts

Use this worksheet for practice in writing a letter of complaint. This master may be reproduced from the Teacher's Resource Book and is located on page 36 of the Student's Workbook. Use with Chapter 9: pages 262–267.

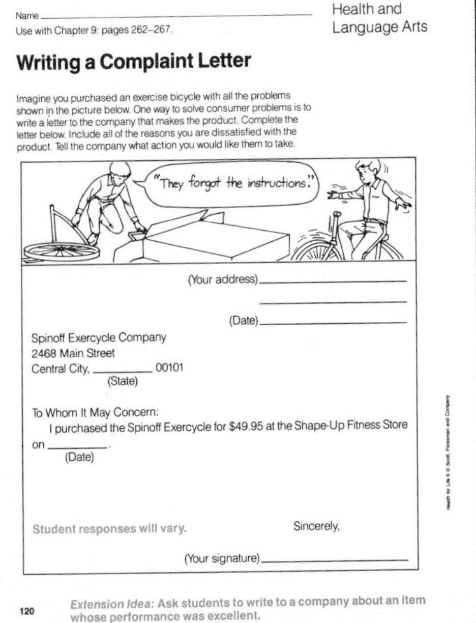

Name ______________________
Use with Chapter 9: pages 262–267.

Health and Language Arts

Writing a Complaint Letter

Imagine you purchased an exercise bicycle with all the problems shown in the picture below. One way to solve consumer problems is to write a letter to the company that makes the product. Complete the letter below. Include all of the reasons you are dissatisfied with the product. Tell the company what action you would like them to take.

"They forgot the instructions."

(Your address) ______________________
____
(Date) ______________________

Spinoff Exercycle Company
2468 Main Street
Central City, ________ 00101
(State)

To Whom It May Concern:
I purchased the Spinoff Exercycle for $49.95 at the Shape-Up Fitness Store on ________.
(Date)

Student responses will vary.

Sincerely,

(Your signature) ______________________

120

Extension Idea: Ask students to write to a company about an item whose performance was excellent.

Teaching Plan

Lesson 2 continued

2 Teach

Strategies for Pages 264 and 265

• Suggest that students read pages 264 and 265 to learn how jingles and logos influence decisions. • Discuss why advertisers use jingles. (They hope people will remember the tune and associate it with the product.) • Point out that while millions of dollars are spent each year on developing jingles, many people can remember a jingle but not the product. • Ask what a logo is (symbol that identifies a company or product) and why companies have them. (A logo is used on all company products. The advertiser hopes that people who like one of the company's products will try others if they recognize the logo.) • Ask students to give examples of popular logos. • Ask students to find the logo on the binding of this textbook.

How Do Jingles, Logos, and Packaging Influence Your Decisions?

Advertisements come in many forms. Not only can you read them, watch them, and hear them—but you can sing, hum, and whistle them as well. Advertisers spend millions of dollars each year developing catchy tunes, or jingles, to sell products. Some ads involve entire songs. Other ads just have one or two lines set to music. Either way, the advertisers hope that the jingle will help you remember the product. When you are in a store, you might hum the jingle, think about the product, and automatically buy it.

Advertisers also use **logos** to sell their products. A logo is a symbol that identifies a company. Some logos are simple shapes, such as a circle or rectangle. Other logos might be detailed drawings, the initials of the company, or the full name of the company designed in a special way.

What logos have you seen?

264

Teaching Options

Anecdote

The Federal Trade Commission reports that 36 cents of every dollar spent for the purchase of ten leading headache medicines goes toward advertising costs.

Enrichment

Let interested students try to think of a well-known company logo and draw it from memory. Tell the students to try to copy the style of the art as best they can.

Health and Music

Ask a group of volunteers to sing examples of popular advertising jingles.

Encourage interested students to make up a jingle for an imaginary health care product. The jingles can be music only or words set to music.

Reteaching

Ask students to bring in the empty containers of name brand health care products and generic containers of the same products. Then ask which containers impulse shoppers might reach for first, and why.

The advertisers hope that if you are happy with one of their products, you will be happy with any product that the company makes. They hope that whenever you see the logo, you will think of the company and buy one of their products. The logos shown here might be similar to ones you have seen. How might the colors and shapes of each logo influence your decision to buy a product from that company?

logo, a symbol used to identify something for advertising purposes.

Special packaging is another part of advertising. Advertisers hope that a fancy package will cause you to choose their product over another one in a plain package. For example, some shampoos come in very fancy or decorative bottles. Often the price of a shampoo is higher simply because it comes in a fancy container.

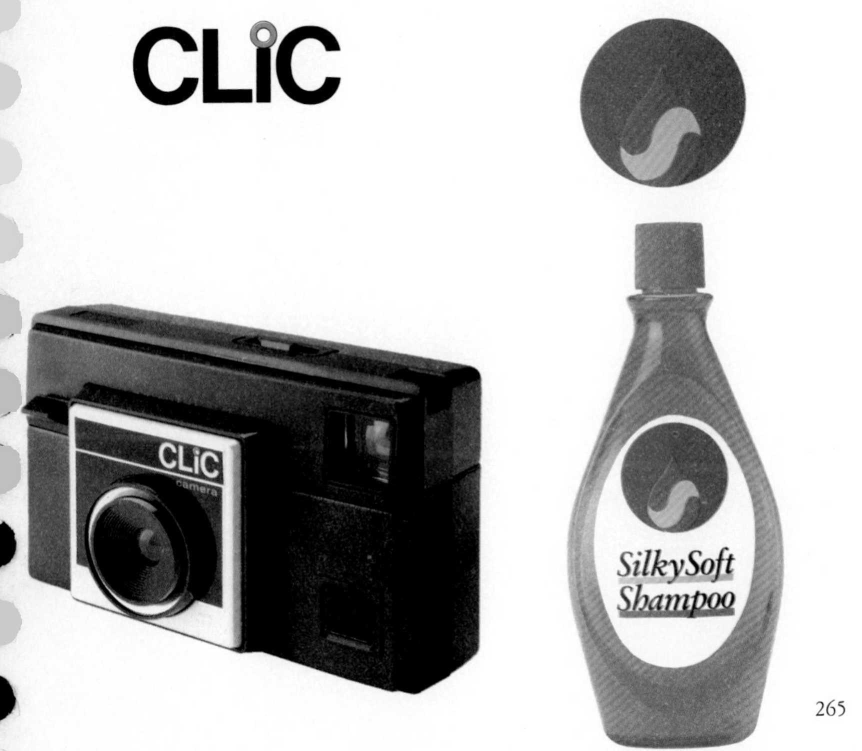

• Ask how the color and shape of the logo might make people think of a particular product or company. Discuss how the color and shape of a logo might influence a person's decision to buy a product. (A person who finds the color or logo pleasing might expect to also like the product.) Ask students what useful information they might find on a package. (manufacturer, price, volume, net weight of contents) • Point out that often the products with fancy packaging cost more simply because of the packaging. Such packaging is expensive for the manufacturer, and the price is passed to the consumer.

Teaching Plan

Lesson 2 continued

2 Teach

Strategies for Pages 266 and 267

• Ask the students to read pages 266 and 267 to learn more about evaluating advertisements. • Point out that to be a wise health consumer a person needs to know how to evaluate ads.
• Direct students' attention to the pictures and discuss what is being sold in each ad. (first ad: a service or idea; second ad: a product; third ad: a company's image) Ask what method the manufacturer is using to convince people to buy, and whether the ad presents useful facts. (Accept all reasonable answers that indicate that students are able to differentiate between advertising techniques and useful information. Only the ad about National Eye Care Week provides concrete, useful information.)
• Discuss how a person can become a wise health consumer. (by gaining experience in buying and judging purchases and by learning to evaluate advertisements)

How Can You Evaluate Ads?

To be a good health consumer, you need to become aware of ads and how to analyze them. When you see or hear an ad, be sure to first identify what is being sold. A product, service, idea, or image are the things to look for. Can you identify what is being sold in each ad shown here?

Next, ask yourself how the advertiser is trying to convince you to buy something. Remember the selling methods that advertisers often use in their ads. Notice the methods used in the ads on these pages.

Finally, decide if the ad contains useful facts. The more information you have, the more likely you will be able to make a wise consumer decision. What useful information do you see in these ads?

Evaluate these ads.

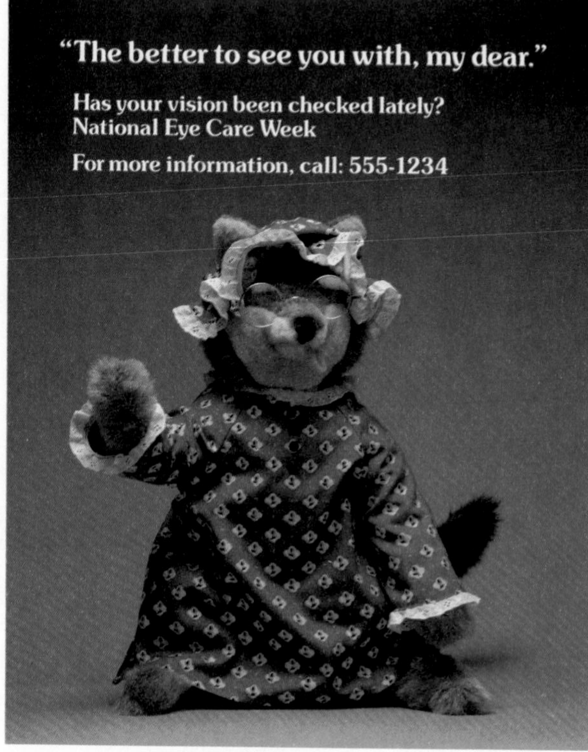

"The better to see you with, my dear."
Has your vision been checked lately?
National Eye Care Week
For more information, call: 555-1234

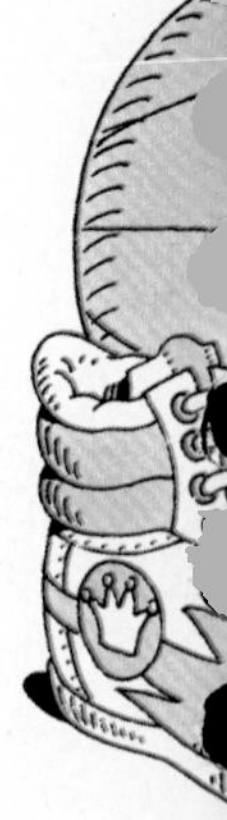

266

Teaching Options

Enrichment
Let interested students analyze TV ads according to the six advertising techniques explained in the textbook. Encourage them to share their findings with the class.

Reteaching
Suggest that students put together an advertising campaign recommending their school as the place to receive a good education and meet new people. The campaign could include a school logo, jingle, and slogan. Tape recordings and posters could also be utilized.

Special Education
To help teach learning-disabled students to be wise health consumers, write and cast your own TV commercial and let the students participate in presenting it. Then discuss with them techniques that were used to get people to buy the product.

You do not become a wise consumer overnight. It takes experience in buying, judging your purchases, and learning to evaluate ads. The more experience you get in evaluating ads, the better consumer you will become.

Think Back • *Study on your own with Study Guide page 332.*

1. What are six methods in which ads try to persuade people to buy a product?
2. How can jingles, logos, and packaging influence a consumer's decisions?
3. What should be kept in mind when trying to evaluate an ad?

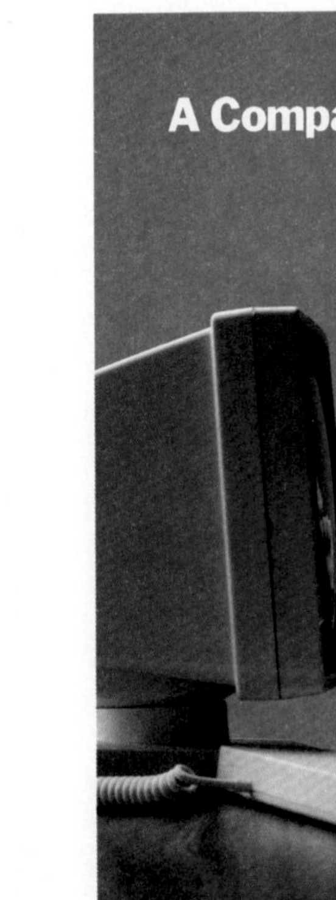

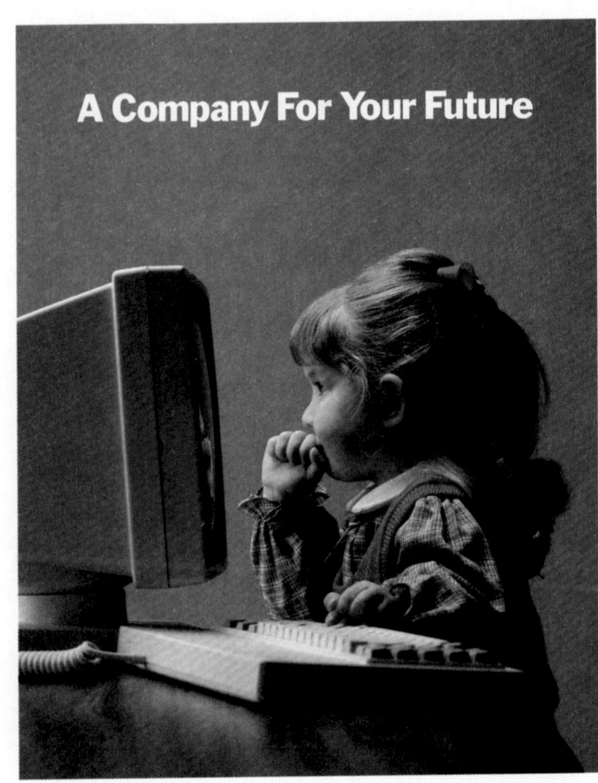

3 Assess

Expanding Student Thinking

Ask students why they think some companies might use several different ads to sell the same product. (The companies might want to try several different advertising techniques to see which works best, or they might want to appeal to different types of people.)

Thinking Skill When students tell why companies use different forms of advertising, they are *drawing conclusions*.

Answers to Think Back

1. The six methods are flattery, free gift, join the crowd, famous people like it, scientific claims, and unclear statements.

2. Jingles influence buying because catchy tunes stay in people's minds and cause them to think about a product and possibly buy it. Logos influence people by reminding people of a product, company, or family of products from a company they are familiar with. Fancy packaging can influence buying because it is attractive.

3. When evaluating ads, a person should keep in mind what is being sold, the method being used to sell it, and whether or not the ad contains any useful information.

Overhead Transparency Master

Use this blackline master to make a labeled overhead transparency or to make an unlabeled student worksheet. This blackline master may be reproduced from the Teacher's Resource Book.

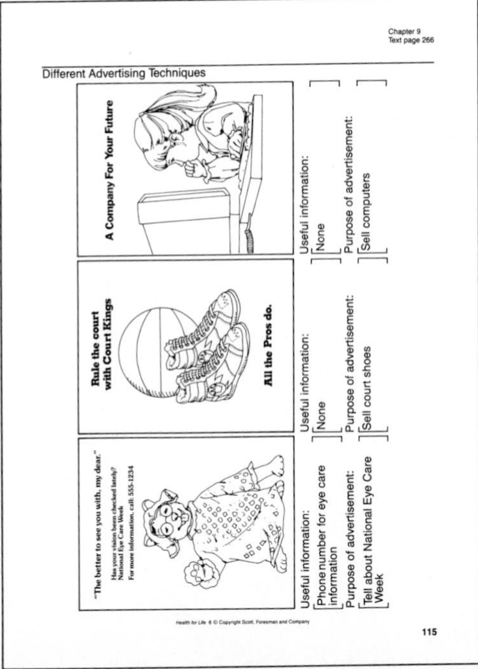
Chapter 9
Text page 266

Different Advertising Techniques

A Company For Your Future

Useful information: None

Purpose of advertisement: Sell computers

Rule the court with Court Kings

All the Pros do.

Useful information: None

Purpose of advertisement: Sell court shoes

"The better to see you with, my dear."

Useful information: Phone number for eye care information

Purpose of advertisement: Tell about National Eye Care Week

Health for Life 6 © Copyright Scott, Foresman and Company

115

Health Activities Workshop pages 268–269

Materials
Activity 1 magazines and newspapers.

Activity 1 Strategies
Answers will vary depending on the ads chosen, but should indicate that students understand the concepts presented in Lesson 2.
Thinking Skills When students evaluate the claims of ads, they are *collecting information* and *judging and evaluating.*

Activity 2 Strategies
Students can find jingles and slogans on TV, radio, and billboards; and in magazines and newspapers.
Thinking Skill When students identify jingles and slogans, they are *interpreting information.*

Activity 3 Strategies
Suggest that students use the advertising techniques on pages 262 and 263 to design ads that will influence people to buy their product. Some students may devise other techniques of their own. Discuss each advertisement, the sales method used, and whether the rest of the class would buy the product or not.
Thinking Skill When students design their own advertisements, they are *suggesting alternatives.*

Activity 4 Strategies
Some magazines that might be helpful include: *Current Consumer, Life Studies, FDA Consumer,* and *Penny Power.*
Thinking Skills By using consumer magazines to evaluate products, students are *collecting information* and *judging and evaluating.*

Evaluating Ads and Products

1. Make a collection of ads for health products from newspapers and magazines. Note the advertising methods used to get people to buy. Identify the useful information. Which ads are most appealing? Which of the advertised products would you consider using?

2. Think of as many advertising jingles and slogans as you can. Hum the jingles and read a list of the slogans to some of your classmates. How many products can you and your classmates identify from the jingles and slogans? Evaluate the effectiveness of each jingle and slogan.

3. Design an ad for a health product, as these students are doing. You can choose an existing product or make up one of your own. You might choose toothpaste, shampoo, or another health product that you are familiar with. Decide on a brand name. Draw a logo. Try to make your ad influence people through words and pictures. Share your ad with your classmates. Would they buy your product?

4. Think about a health product you use frequently. Do you know if you are making wise consumer choices about this product? To find out, go to the library and find a consumer publication. Look for information about the product. Be sure that the publication also contains information about competitor's products. Evaluate the different brands. Write down the benefits and drawbacks of each brand. Give reasons why you would choose one brand over another.

Looking at Careers

5. Do you enjoy drawing and doodling? Have people ever told you that you were creative? Do your teachers ever say that you write or talk with a great deal of imagination? If you can answer yes to any of these questions, you might want to consider a career as an **advertising copywriter.**

Advertising copywriters turn ideas into effective advertisements. They write material for the ads that appear in print and on radio and television. They often have to develop the ideas for artwork and jingles as well.

The education requirements are quite varied for advertising copywriters. Most copywriters have high-school diplomas. Many also have college degrees in advertising or communications. A music or art background also is useful for this career.

Choose an ad from radio, television, or magazines and decide how you might change the ad to make it better. For example, you might think of ways the ad could be more noticeable, more humorous, or more informative.

For more information write to the American Association of Advertising Agencies, 200 Park Ave., New York, NY 10017.

Activity 5 Strategies
Many school districts have a person in charge of publications or public relations. This person might have training as an advertising copywriter. If so, you might want to invite him or her to speak to the class.
Thinking Skill When students learn more about a career as an advertising copywriter, they are *collecting information.*

Teaching Plan

Lesson 3 pages 270–274

Lesson Objective
Explain why comparing unit prices, reading labels, and being aware of fads are important considerations for a health consumer.

Health Vocabulary
Fad, net weight, unit price

1 Motivate

Introducing the Lesson
Explain that comparison shopping means comparing similar products to find the best product for the best price. Then ask students if they have ever done comparison shopping before buying a product. Discuss what criteria might be used to compare products. (individual needs, price, availability, effectiveness)

Did You Know?
Body odor under the arms develops when bacteria on the skin interacts with perspiration. A deodorant controls body odor by slowing the growth of bacteria on the skin. An antiperspirant controls body odor by closing the pores of sweat glands, thereby reducing the amount of perspiration. Some products for controlling body odor are both deodorants and antiperspirants.

Why might one brand cost more?

3 What Should You Consider When Choosing Health Products?

Asking yourself if you do or do not need a health product is one way of becoming a careful health consumer. Once you decide that you need a health product, you must ask yourself which brand is the best buy. The girl shown here is examining two brands of deodorant. Both brands might be equally good at controlling body odor, yet one brand costs more. The price might be higher because the brand is advertised more often. The price might also be higher if a fancy container is used. However, the brand might cost more because it really is a better product. Consumer guides, pharmacists, and other dependable sources of information can help you find out if the brand really is better than most others.

Teaching Options

Health Background

One function of the Food and Drug Administration is to test each drug carefully in order to determine if it is safe before it is put on the market. Since 1976, manufacturers of cosmetics and toiletries have been required to list ingredients on their products in order of predominance. The FDA has been responsible for banning the use of certain harmful ingredients such as hexachlorophene in soap.

Enrichment
Ask students to go to a grocery store and find several examples of products that cost less to buy in a large size than a small size.

Health and Math
Suppose a box of mashed potato flakes costs 22 cents an ounce. If a serving consists of 3.5 ounces, how much does each serving of mashed potatoes cost? (77 cents per individual serving. Students should multiply 22 cents by 3.5 ounces.) If your family includes four people, what would be the cost of feeding the whole family mashed potatoes? (3.08. Students should multiply 77 cents by 4 people.)

Reteaching
Ask students to tell how to find the unit price of a product, and how knowing the unit price can make a person a wiser shopper.

What Is the Unit Price of a Health Product?

Not only are store shelves stocked with many brands of the same product, but also one brand might offer several sizes of the same product. Comparing the costs of products among so many brands and sizes might seem confusing.

An easy way to find the true cost of a product is to figure out the **unit price.** The unit price is the price of a product per ounce, gram, or some other unit of measure. You can figure out the unit price by dividing the full price of a product by its **net weight**—the weight of the contents, not including the container.

Study the picture below to find the unit price of each tube of toothpaste. Which one has the lowest unit price and gives you the most for your money?

unit price, the price of a product per ounce, gram, or other unit of measure.

net weight, the weight of the contents of a product, not including the container.

On Your Own

Suppose you are choosing between two cans of orange juice. Both cans are the same brand. One has a net weight of 6 ounces and costs 79¢. The other can has a net weight of 12 ounces and costs $1.47. What is the unit price of each product? Which product gives you more for your money?

Which product has the lowest unit price?

Personal
Net weight - 1.5 oz.
Price - 69¢
69¢ ÷ 1.5 oz. = 46¢ per ounce

Medium
Net weight - 3 oz.
Price - $1.05
$105 ÷ 3 oz. = 35¢ per ounce

Family
Net weight - 7 oz.
Price - $1.54
$1.54 ÷ 7 oz. = 22¢ per ounce

Super
Net weight - 9 oz.
Price - $1.89
$1.89 ÷ 9 oz. = 21¢ per ounce

2 Teach

Strategies for Pages 270 and 271

• Direct students to the picture and ask them what decision the girl is trying to make. (choosing between two deodorant products) • Then ask students to read pages 270 and 271 to find out why the girl is studying the two products. • Discuss what people should consider when choosing a health product. (need for the product, which product is the best buy) • Ask why one product might cost more than another. (advertised more often, fancier packaging, might be a better product) • Be sure students understand that the unit price of a product is the price per ounce, gram, or other unit. • Tell students to study the picture on page 271 and figure out which tube of toothpaste is the best buy for the money. (the super size, for 21 cents per ounce) • Point out that a larger size product can be cheaper in the long run because it often costs less per unit than a smaller size product.

Using On Your Own

Students should divide .79 by 6 (13 cents per ounce) and 1.47 by 12 (12 cents per ounce). The 12-ounce can gives you more for your money.
Thinking Skill By determining which size is a better buy, students are *judging and evaluating.*

Teaching Plan

Lesson 3 continued

2 Teach

Strategies for Pages 272 to 274

• Ask students to read pages 272 and 273 to find out how reading labels can make a person a better health consumer. Discuss with students the order in which ingredients are listed on a product label. (by weight) • Ask what the major ingredient in the creme rinse in the picture is. (water) • Ask why following directions when using a product is important. (to get the best results and to use a product safely) • Discuss what a guarantee is. (a promise by the manufacturer to replace or repair the product or give money back if a product proves unsatisfactory) • Let students tell where a person could write if he or she were not satisfied with the creme rinse in the picture. • Make sure students understand that, when necessary, health care products must carry warning signs. • Ask students what warnings appear on the products in the picture on page 273. • Discuss warning signs on products the students are familiar with. • Be sure students understand that the warning is there to protect the consumer from accidents.

How Can Reading Labels Make You a Better Consumer?

As a consumer, you need and have the right to know what a product is made of and what it will and will not do. Laws require labels on many products. Any claims that the label makes must be truthful.

One of the first things you notice on a label is a list of ingredients. The ingredients are listed in order by weight. Therefore, the first ingredient is the one in the greatest amount by weight. What is the major ingredient of the creme rinse shown here? Checking ingredients can be very important if you know you have certain allergies.

Health care products, also give directions for use. You might not get the best results if you do not follow all of the directions. For example, if you do not follow the directions for using this creme rinse, your hair might not look clean.

As a careful consumer, you should check to see if the label carries a guarantee. A guarantee is a promise by the manufacturer to replace, repair, or give money back for a product if it proves to be unsatisfactory. The name and address of the manufacturer are also listed on the label.

Why is reading labels important?

Creme Rinse

Directions: Use after every shampoo. Squeeze excess water from hair. Apply enough to cover hair from roots to ends and massage throughout hair. Rinse thoroughly.

Contains: Water, Cetyl Alcohol, Fragrance, Glutaral, FD&C Red #40 and FD&C Yellow #5

Guarantee: If you're not fully satisfied, send proof of purchase for a full cash refund to Clean Hair Company, Chicago, IL

Manufactured by Clean Hair Company, Chicago, IL

Teaching Options

Anecdote

More than 87 billion dollars a year is spent on advertising in the United States. (*The World Book Encyclopedia,* Vol. 1. World Book-Childcraft International. 1982.)

Enrichment

Let students compile a consumer record book that lists the guarantees, warnings, and three main ingredients of several health care products. Students should report their findings to the class.

Health and Social Studies

Encourage interested students to find out about the Federal Food, Drug, and Cosmetic Act. How does the law affect product labeling? Which government agency enforces the Act? Let students report their findings to the class.

Reteaching

Ask students to create their own product and product labels complete with guarantees, warnings, and lists of ingredients.

Some health care products must carry warnings by law. For example, a can of hair spray must warn the user not to let the spray get near the eyes. What other warnings are on the can of hair spray shown here?

Warnings on medicines are particularly common and helpful. Such warnings usually include information on dosage, storage, the limited usefulness of the medicine, and side effects.

As a consumer, you are responsible for reading the labels on all health products. Paying attention to the ingredients, directions, guarantees, and warnings can help you make wise consumer decisions.

What do these warnings say?

- Write the word *fad* on the chalkboard. Then ask students to read page 274 to find out about fads.
- Discuss what fads are. (products or practices that are very popular for a short time) • Ask students to give examples of fads while you list them on the chalkboard. (Accept all reasonable answers.) • Ask students to explain why following fads is not necessarily bad, but is limiting. (The fad products might be usable and worthwhile purchases at the time, but automatically following a fad can limit a buyer's choices, and fad products might become out of date quickly.)
- Guide students to understand that the plain shirts in the picture are considered less of a fad than the other shirts. • Discuss which fads can be dangerous. (unsafe diets that suggest eating only a few foods or long periods of eating no food)

Teaching Plan

Lesson 3 continued

3 Assess

Expanding Student Thinking

Ask the students to pretend they are in a situation where they must choose between two unfamiliar shampoos. Ask them to explain how they would go about making their choice. (Information that might help in choosing includes the manufacturer, unit price, ingredients, size of the products, product guarantees, and recommendations by others.

Thinking Skills Students are *interpreting information* and *making decisions*.

Answers to Think Back

1. The price might be higher for a certain brand because it is advertised more, has a fancier container, or is actually better.

2. The unit price of a product can be figured by dividing the cost of the product by the net weight.

3. Labels list ingredients, give directions, give warnings if necessary, and sometimes include guarantees.

4. A fad item might not really be needed and might go out of style before being used up.

fad, a product or practice that is popular only for a short time.

What Are Fads?

Try to recall a hairstyle or an item of clothing that everyone seemed to be wearing last year. Are many people wearing it this year, or has another product become popular? Products or practices that are very popular for a short time are **fads.** Fashions, dance steps, and certain games are often fads.

Smart shoppers think carefully before they buy products that are fads. For example, a smart shopper understands that a kind of fancy jacket that is very popular this year might be out of style next year. Someone who follows that fad might soon be left with a jacket that is not worn-out but suddenly looks odd or out of date. A smart shopper might choose a plainer jacket, which is likely to be useful for several years. Which of the T-shirts shown here do you think were fads?

Following some fads is not necessarily a bad practice, but it can be limiting. Eventually you might wish you had spent your money in a different way.

Think Back • *Study on your own with Study Guide page 333.*

1. Why might one brand of a health product cost more than another brand?
2. How can the unit price of a product be figured?
3. What information do health product labels have?
4. Why might the purchase of fad items be unwise?

Teaching Options

Enrichment

Ask students to bring to class items that are examples of fads and that they no longer or seldom use. Note how many students bring in similar items. You might want to contribute to such a collection also, and describe the items' former popularity.

Health and Social Studies

Ask students to find out about the clothing fads in the 1970s. (Clothing items that students might find out about include hip huggers, bell bottoms, miniskirts, maxiskirts, and differences in jacket and tie styles.) Point out that most people no longer wear these styles. Ask students to draw pictures of fad clothing and display the pictures in the classroom.

Reteaching

Ask students to write a paragraph explaining how following fads can end up costing a consumer extra money.

Buying Health Care Products Wisely

1. Suppose a store is having a "special" on a brand of soap. The "special" soap is packaged as two bars together and is priced at 38¢. Nearby, single bars of the same size and brand of soap are priced at 22¢ each. Is the "special" soap really a bargain? Why or why not?

2. Figure out the unit price of each can of adhesive bandages shown below. Which can gives you the most for your money?

100 Strips	60 Strips
$2.60	$1.99

Looking at Careers

3. Some stores employ people to work for them as **comparison shoppers.** The comparison shoppers go from store to store and check on various product prices as directed by the store manager. In this way the manager can be sure that the prices in his or her store are competitive—not much more than the prices at other stores nearby.

You might think of having a job like this as a part-time job in high school. Usually the stores train their own comparison shoppers. However, certain qualities might be helpful for such a job. What do you think some of these qualities might be? Why might a store manager want to make sure his or her prices are not much higher than prices at other stores?

For more information check with the owners or managers of stores in your neighborhood.

Activity Plan

Health Activities Workshop page 275

Activity 1 Strategies
The special soap is a bargain because the price of each bar is 19 cents. The regular price of a bar of soap is 22 cents.
Thinking Skill By determining whether the special soap is a bargain, students are *judging and evaluating.*

Activity 2 Strategies
The unit price for the smaller container of bandages is approximately 24 cents. The unit price for the larger container is approximately 22 cents. The larger container is cheaper.

Thinking Skills By deciding which product is the better buy, students are *judging and evaluating* and *making decisions.*

Activity 3 Strategies
Job qualities might include enjoying working with people, enjoying math, and liking to work in various locations. The manager of a store would want to make sure that his or her prices are not too high because higher prices might cause shoppers to buy from other stores.
Thinking Skills When students consider qualities needed for a job as a comparison shopper, they are *collecting information* and *generalizing.*

Teaching Plan

Lesson 4 pages 276–279

Lesson Objective
State the responsibilities consumers have in getting the most out of their health checkups, and describe what takes place during a health checkup.

1 Motivate

Introducing the Lesson
Ask the students what kinds of health problems people can take care of without going to the doctor. (Students will probably say colds, flu, and some cuts and bruises.) Then ask volunteers to share information about times when they went to the doctor.

Did You Know?
People should not hesitate to get a second doctor's opinion about a troublesome health problem. In fact, many insurance companies will not pay for certain medical services until the person gets a second opinion.

4 How Can You Benefit Most from a Health Checkup?

Besides being a consumer of health products, you are also a consumer of health services. Like the boy in the picture, you have probably used the services of a doctor during a health checkup.

How long ago was your last health checkup? Doctors think young people should have a checkup every two or three years. However, in some cases more frequent checkups are advised. For example, a young person should have a health checkup before trying out for a competitive sport, such as swimming or basketball.

When the doctor sees you regularly, he or she can check your continued growth and development. The doctor keeps a record of your health during past visits. By knowing your health history, the doctor is better able to help you if you get sick. If a doctor finds a minor problem during a checkup, the problem can be corrected before it gets worse.

During a health checkup, you get a chance to know the doctor better. You have a chance to ask any questions you might have about your health. Be open and honest with your doctor. Be sure to tell the doctor about any health problems that concern you. For example, you might have had some headaches lately. Perhaps you have had trouble seeing the writing on the chalkboard or hearing the teacher talk. The more your doctor knows about you, the easier it will be for him or her to help you.

During a health checkup, the doctor might find a problem that needs further study. For example, you might have a temperature of 101°F (38.3°C). Normal body temperature is about 98.6°F (37°C). Your higher temperature might indicate the beginning of some illness or the presence of an infection. The doctor might ask that someone take your temperature the next day and call him or her. Also, the doctor might instruct you to stay home from school and rest and drink plenty of fluids. If the doctor's instructions sound complicated, you might write them down.

Teaching Options

Health Background

Four basic procedures are generally used during a physical examination. The first is observation of the area under study (such as the eyes, ears, or lungs). The second procedure is feeling various parts of the body to detect unusual masses, swelling, or enlargement. The third involves tapping body parts, such as the chest or lungs, to produce sound, which can help reveal thickening of lung tissue, or fluid in the air spaces of the lung. For the fourth procedure, a physician uses a stethoscope to listen to organs as they function.

Enrichment

Help students make a record of their own health history. Suggest they record information such as dates of childhood diseases, any broken bones or sprains, hospital stays, medications taken, shots received (with dates), and any unusual health problems. Students might want to interview a parent to complete this information. Stress that a health history is a personal matter between family and doctor. Students do not need to show their health histories to their classmates.

Reteaching

Ask students to make a list of ways people can be wise consumers of health services.

Health and Language Arts

Ask students to write a short story in which a person has a routine health checkup that helps prevent a serious disease.

Suppose the doctor prescribes some medicine, but after a couple of days of taking the medicine, you get no relief. Be sure you or someone else calls your doctor. You should also make sure someone calls your doctor if you get any unpleasant or unexpected side effects from the medicine. Do not wait for your next checkup.

As a wise health consumer, you should talk with your doctor about any treatment plans that are suggested. You have the right to know what is going to be done for you and why.

How often should you have a health checkup?

2 Teach

Strategies for Pages 276 and 277

• Ask students to read pages 276 and 277 to learn about health checkups. • Discuss why checkups are important for young people. (The doctor can check a person's continued growth and development and can detect health problems before they get serious.) • Point out that a person should have a checkup before starting a competitive sport. A doctor could tell if the physical strain of the sport would be too much for the person. The doctor could also give advice on how to prepare the body for the sport—how to get fit enough to play the sport safely. • Discuss questions a student might want to ask the doctor. (current health concerns, methods of treatment, medications, costs of treatment, and possible side effects) • Stress that cooperation and communication are the keys to getting the most out of a physical examination. • Tell students that the more a doctor knows about a person the more he or she can help that person.

Teaching Plan

Lesson 4 continued

2 Teach

Strategies for Pages 278 and 279

• Ask a volunteer to read the first paragraph of page 278. • Stress that being a wise health consumer is the responsibility of the patient. • Call on volunteers to read each caption as the rest of the class looks at the pictures. • Ask why the doctor notes posture. (gives clues to general health) • Ask what the doctor is looking for when he or she checks the eyes, ears, nose, and throat. (signs of disease or infection) • Discuss why blood samples are sent to the laboratory for tests. (to be sure the number of red and white blood cells falls within a normal range) • Discuss the importance of keeping a record of immunization shots. (so the doctor will know if a person is properly protected against certain diseases) • Encourage volunteers to discuss which of the tests and procedures were done during their medical checkups.

What Happens During a Health Checkup?

The pictures on these two pages show some of the common procedures a doctor follows during a health checkup. You might recognize some of these procedures from your own checkups. When you go for a checkup, be sure to ask the doctor about any procedure you wonder about.

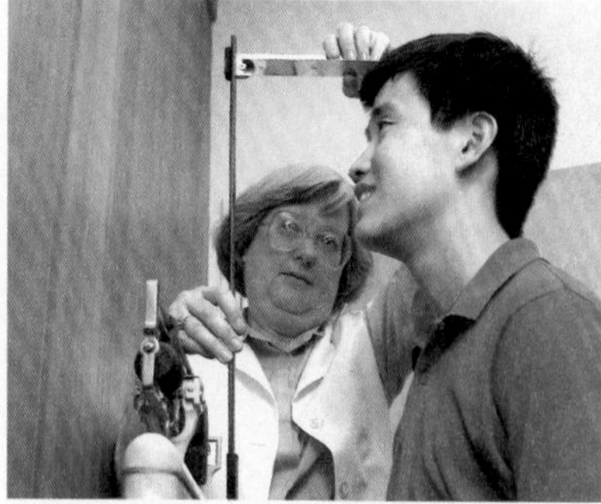

The doctor or nurse checks height and weight to determine whether you are growing in the way that is right for you.

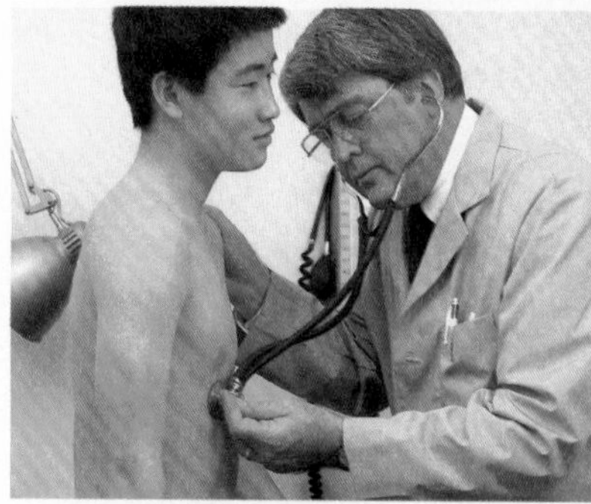

Using a stethoscope, the doctor listens to the heart to make sure its beat is steady. The doctor can also tell if the valves of the heart are opening and closing properly.

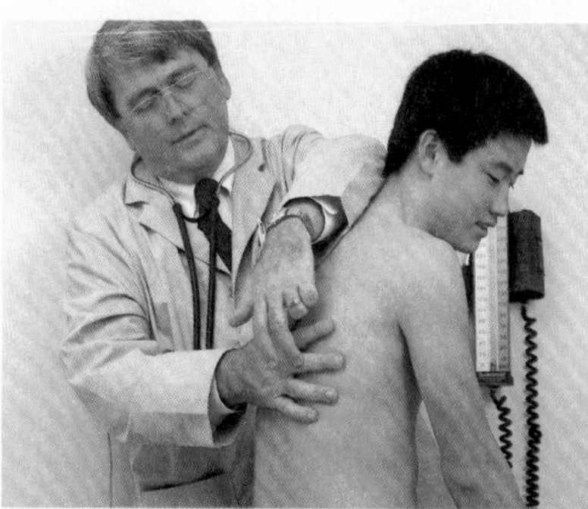

The doctor also uses the stethoscope to listen to the sounds the air makes in the lungs. The doctor can then tell if air is getting to all parts of the lungs. Tapping the back is another method the doctor uses to listen to the sounds in the lungs.

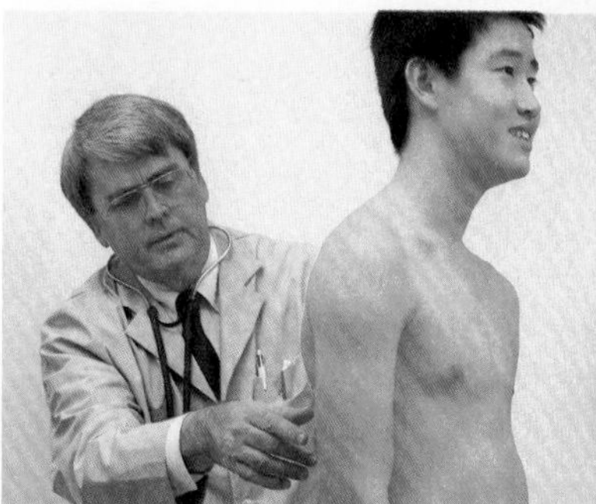

The doctor or nurse notes posture, since it gives some clues about general health. He or she searches, in the event of poor posture, for possible causes such as poor nutrition, lack of proper sleep or exercise, or bone deformities.

278

Teaching Options

Anecdote

Currently there are more than 300,000 physicians in the United States. Approximately 7 percent of these are women.

Enrichment

Invite a local doctor, nurse, or other health care professional to discuss with students the procedures of a health examination.

Health and Science

Ask interested students to find out about diseases, such as polio or tetanus, for which vaccines are available. Encourage them to find out where the diseases are most common and when vaccines were developed to prevent the diseases. Let the students report their findings to the class.

Reteaching

Ask students to make posters that list what the doctor might check (such as height, weight, eyes, ears, and so on) during an office visit. Let students draw or cut out pictures to display on their posters.

Think Back • *Study on your own with Study Guide page 333.*

1. About how often do young people your age need a health checkup?
2. What are your responsibilities as a wise consumer of a doctor's health care services?
3. List eight procedures that a doctor follows in a checkup.

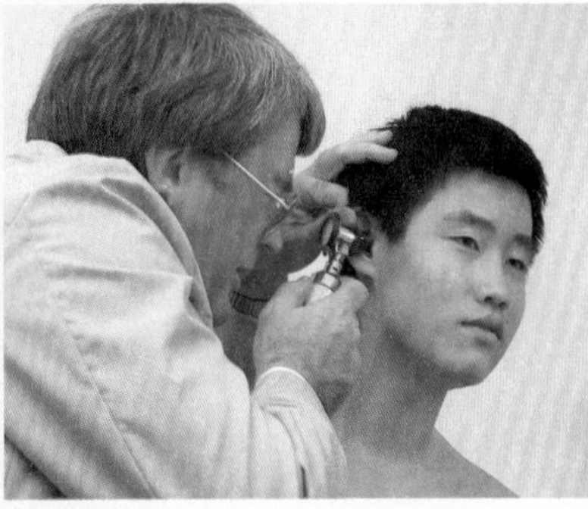

The doctor looks for signs of disease or infection in the eyes, ears, nose, and throat. He or she also checks to see if the eardrums are unbroken and to see if any accumulations of wax need to be removed.

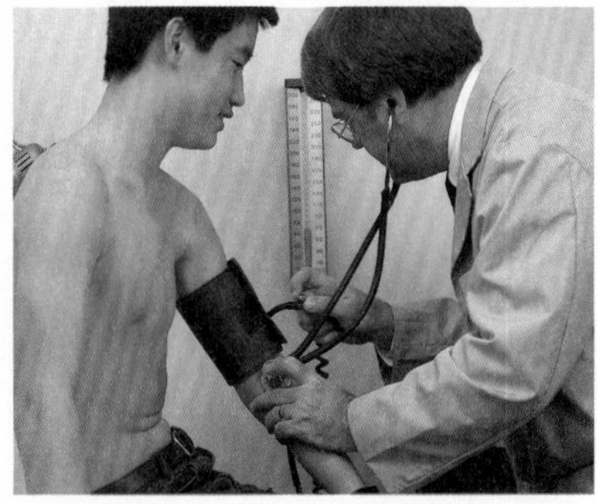

The doctor or nurse checks the blood pressure at full force of the heart's beating and at the time the heart is filling up with blood to see if these pressures are within normal ranges.

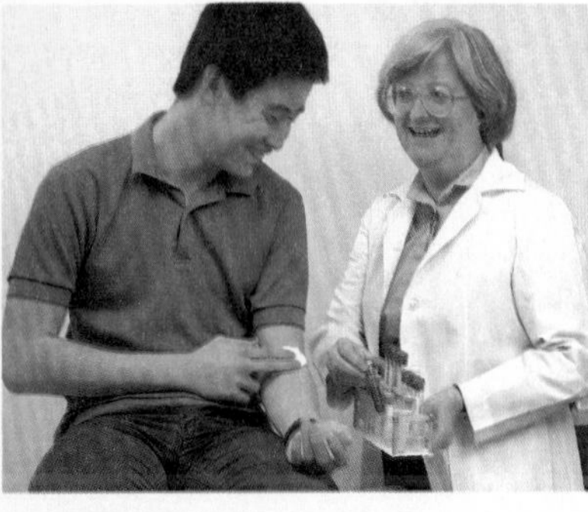

The doctor or nurse takes a blood sample and sends it to a laboratory for tests. One of the tests reveals if a sufficient number of red blood cells are in the blood. A sample of urine is also sent to a laboratory. From the urine test results, the doctor notes how well the kidneys are working.

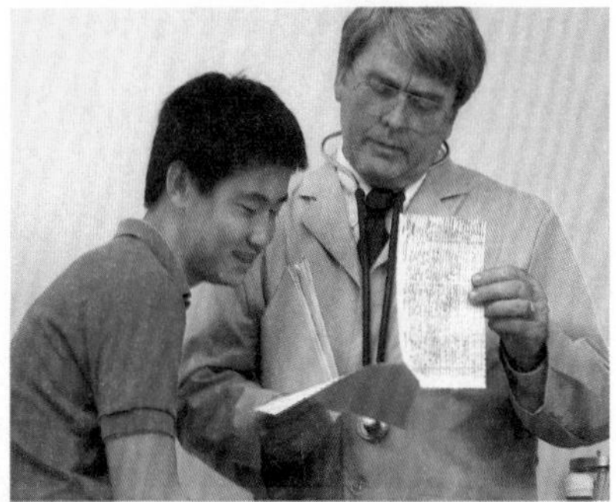

The doctor checks your vaccination record to be sure you are properly protected against such diseases as tetanus, polio, measles, mumps, German measles, and diphtheria.

3 Assess

Expanding Student Thinking

Ask students how frequent health checkups might reduce the probability of getting a serious illness. (Immunizations can be given to prevent certain diseases. Blood and urine tests and examinations of the eyes, ears, nose, throat, heart, lungs, and other parts of the body can detect many diseases.)

Thinking Skills When students explain how health checkups can reduce the chances of getting serious diseases, they are *drawing conclusions* and *generalizing*.

Answers to Think Back

1. Young people need to have checkups every two to three years.

2. A wise health consumer's responsibilities include being honest with the doctor, understanding procedures and following through on treatment, and calling the doctor if there is no improvement or if medication produces side effects.

3. Eight procedures a doctor follows during a routine checkup are: checking height, weight, and physical development; heart and lungs; posture; eyes, ears, nose, and throat; blood pressure; blood; urine; and immunizations.

Teaching Plan

Health Focus page 280

Discussion

Esther Peterson encouraged food companies to display unit prices. Unit pricing involves advertising the price per unit weight for a product. Discuss with the students how unit pricing aids comparison shopping.

Ask students to look for the unit prices of health care products at a pharmacy or supermarket. Let students report back to the class about choosing health care products by using unit prices.

Answers to Talk About It

1. Esther Peterson helped pass laws that require fair packaging and labeling. These laws require that companies present simple, direct, clear information on packages and labels.
Thinking Skill By telling how Esther Peterson helped consumers, students are *recalling information.*

2. Accept any answer that shows students have evaluated product information when making decisions.
Thinking Skill By explaining how they have used information to decide which product to buy, students are *judging and evaluating.*

Health Focus

Esther Peterson: Protecting the Consumer

Esther Peterson used to have a lot of complaints when she came home from shopping for her family. At the supermarket she had to decide between "giant" pint packages and just plain pint packages. She had to figure out whether to buy king-sized boxes or jumbo-sized boxes. "Cents off" sales caught her eye, but she could not tell how much money she was saving.

Esther Peterson complained that a person needed to be an expert in mathematics to figure out the best buys.

She complained that advertisements and packages were designed to confuse the consumer. However, Esther Peterson was an adviser on consumer affairs to both President Johnson and President Carter. Therefore, perhaps more than others, she was able to do something about problems that plagued shoppers.

Working for laws that ensured fair packaging and labeling was one way Esther Peterson helped make shopping easier. These laws require simple, direct information about a product to appear clearly on each container. The shape of a container must not mislead shoppers as to the product's size. The label must not give false or useless information.

Esther Peterson has also advised different companies about how to help consumers. Next time you go shopping, notice all the information given on food packages, clothes labels, and even on signs on shelves in the stores. Thanks to the work of Esther Peterson and others, you have the information you need to become a wise consumer.

Talk About It

1. How has Esther Peterson helped consumers?
2. How have you used information on packages or labels to decide which product to buy?

280

Teaching Options

Vocabulary

Use this worksheet for practice in reviewing chapter vocabulary words. This master may be reproduced from the Teacher's Resource Book and is located on page 34 of the Student's Workbook. Use with Chapter 9: pages 256–283.

Name ______________________ Vocabulary

Use with Chapter 9: pages 256–283.

Advertising Vocabulary

Part I. Define each term listed below.

1. Advertisement— **Public notice offering product or service**
2. Logo— **A symbol used to identify something**
3. Health Consumer— **A person who buys or uses a health product or service**
4. Net weight— **Weight of product contents**
5. Unit price— **Product's cost divided by its net weight**

Part II. Circle and label the four terms listed above on the picture below.

Part III. In the space below describe how the unit price of Shine shampoo was determined. Show your work.

Answers should include the following information: the purchase price, $2.49, was divided by the net weight, 12 oz.

$$\begin{array}{r} .207 \\ 12\overline{)2.490} \\ 2\,4 \\ \hline 90 \\ 84 \\ \hline 6 \end{array}$$

118 ***Extension Idea:*** **Ask students to identify and describe the advertising technique used in the illustration.**

Becoming a Careful Health Consumer

You can help all the members of your family become better health consumers. Just practice some of the ideas and suggestions you have learned in this chapter.

The next time your family goes shopping, ask to go along. Offer to help make the shopping list. At the store be a smart shopper. Read the labels and find out the unit prices of the items that you want to buy. Some stores post the unit price of an item right on the shelf.

Be sure to read the labels on all health products carefully. Examine the ingredients. Be sure that your family needs the product. Remember not to be fooled by advertising techniques and special packaging.

When you follow some of these practices, you and your family members are being careful health consumers. You can save money and feel good about yourself as well.

Reading at Home

Body Sense, Body Nonsense by Seymour Simon. Lippincott, 1981. Find out about human health through folk sayings about the human body.

Health Care for the Wongs: Health Insurance, Choosing a Doctor by Marilyn Thypin and Lynn Glasner. EMC, 1980. Learn how one particular family found out about medical clinics, how to obtain health insurance, and how to select a family doctor.

Health at Home
page 281

Strategies
Encourage students to accompany parents on shopping trips for food and other health products. Remind them to read labels and figure unit prices. Suggest that, when visiting the family doctor, students prepare a list of questions in advance.

More Reading at Home
Body Sense, Body Nonsense (Grades 3–6)

Health Care for the Wongs: Health Insurance, Choosing a Doctor (Grades 5–6)

Kyte, Kathy S. *The Kids' Complete Guide to Money*. Knopf, 1984. Describes ways to make wise product choices and get the most for your money. (Grades 4–6)

Study and Review
Use this worksheet for practice in reviewing advertising techniques. This master may be reproduced from the Teacher's Resource Book and is located on page 35 of the Student's Workbook. Use with Chapter 9: pages 256–283.

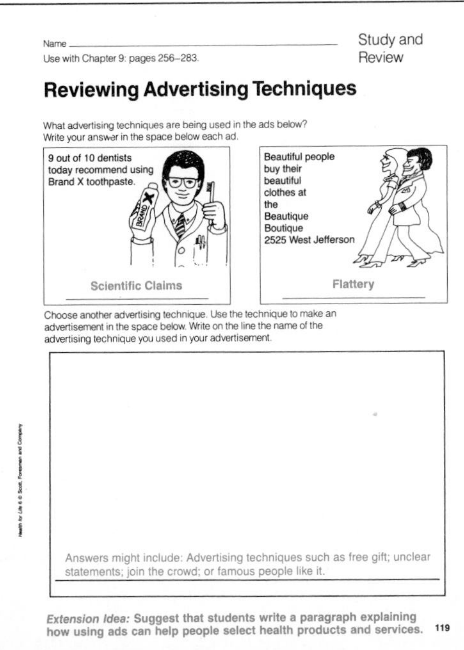

Name ______________________ Study and Review

Use with Chapter 9: pages 256–283.

Reviewing Advertising Techniques

What advertising techniques are being used in the ads below? Write your answer in the space below each ad.

9 out of 10 dentists today recommend using Brand X toothpaste.
BRAND X
Beautiful people buy their beautiful clothes at the Beautique Boutique 2525 West Jefferson

Scientific Claims

Flattery

Choose another advertising technique. Use the technique to make an advertisement in the space below. Write on the line the name of the advertising technique you used in your advertisement.

Answers might include: Advertising techniques such as free gift; unclear statements; join the crowd; or famous people like it.

Extension Idea: **Suggest that students write a paragraph explaining how using ads can help people select health products and services.** 119

Review Plan

Chapter 9 Review

pages 282–283

Answers to Reviewing Lesson Objectives

Use this section for guided study or for oral review. Objective numbers match lesson numbers.

1. Guidelines in the form of questions are: Do I need it?, Will I use it?, Am I acting on impulse?, Do I already have a product like it?, and Could I afford something better?

2. Methods include flattery, free gifts, join the crowd, famous people, scientific claims, and unclear statements. When evaluating an ad, a person should keep in mind what is being sold, the method being used to sell it, and whether or not the ad contains any useful information.

3. Unit price gives the true cost of the product. Reading labels gives the consumer useful information such as name and address of the manufacturer, ingredients, directions for use, guarantees, and warnings. Being aware of fads helps the consumer evaluate the true need and long-term usefulness of an item.

4. Responsibilities include being honest with the doctor; asking for answers to any questions one has, the treatment prescribed, expenses, and effects of medication; following the doctor's instructions; and calling the doctor if unexpected side effects occur. The procedures should include some of those described on pages 278–279.

Answers to Checking Health Vocabulary

Use the vocabulary check as a review or as a test.

1. f
2. a
3. e
4. c
5. d
6. b
7.–15. Answers will vary but should reflect students' understanding of the meaning of the words as used in the text.

Chapter 9 Review

For further review, use Study Guide pages 332-333

Practice skills for life for Chapter 9 on pages 362-364

SKILLS FOR LIFE

Reviewing Lesson Objectives

1. List some guidelines that can help people become wise consumers of health products. (pages 258–261)
2. List several methods that advertisers use to promote the sale and use of products. Explain what to keep in mind when evaluating an ad before selecting a health product. (pages 262–267)
3. Explain why a consumer should compare unit prices, read labels, and be aware of fads when choosing health products. (pages 270–274)
4. State the responsibilities that consumers have in getting the most out of their health checkups. Describe some of the procedures a doctor follows during a health checkup. (pages 276–279)

Checking Health Vocabulary

Number your paper from 1–6. Match each definition in Column I with the correct word or words in Column II.

Column I	*Column II*
1. the cost of a product per ounce, gram, or some other unit of measurement	a. advertisement
2. a public notice or announcement recommending a product or service	b. fad
3. the weight of the contents of a product, not including the container	c. health consumer
4. a person who buys or uses a health product	d. logo
5. a symbol used to identify something for advertising purposes	e. net weight
6. a product or practice that is popular only for a short time	f. unit price

Number your paper from 7–15. Next to each number write a sentence using each word or group of words.

7. consumer guide
8. guarantee
9. health checkup
10. health service
11. impulse
12. label
13. selling method
14. smart shopper
15. stethoscope

Chapter 9 Tests Use Test A or Test B to assess students' mastery of the health concepts in Chapter 9. These tests are located on pages 73–80 in the Test Book.

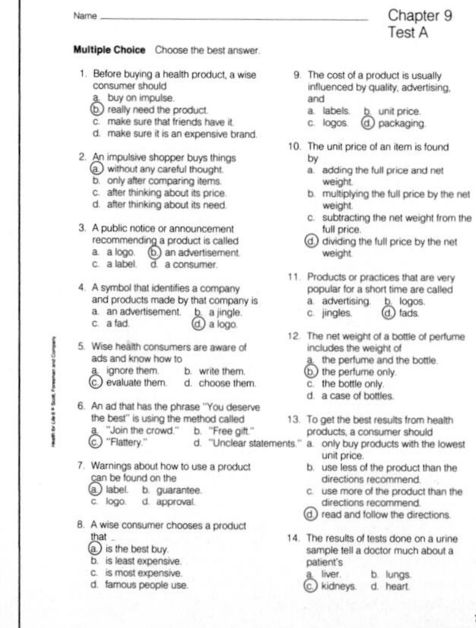

Name ______________ Chapter 9 Test A

Multiple Choice Choose the best answer.

1. Before buying a health product, a wise consumer should
   a. buy on impulse.
   (b.) really need the product.
   c. make sure that friends have it.
   d. make sure it is an expensive brand.
2. An impulsive shopper buys things
   (a.) without any careful thought.
   b. only after comparing items.
   c. after thinking about its price.
   d. after thinking about its need.
3. A public notice or announcement recommending a product is called
   a. a logo. (b.) an advertisement.
   c. a label. d. a consumer.
4. A symbol that identifies a company and products made by that company is
   a. an advertisement. b. a jingle.
   c. a fad. (d.) a logo.
5. Wise health consumers are aware of ads and know how to
   a. ignore them. b. write them.
   (c.) evaluate them. d. choose them.
6. An ad that has the phrase "You deserve the best" is using the method called
   a. "Join the crowd." b. "Free gift."
   (c.) "Flattery." d. "Unclear statements."
7. Warnings about how to use a product can be found on the
   (a.) label. b. guarantee.
   c. logo. d. approval.
8. A wise consumer chooses a product that
   (a.) is the best buy.
   b. is least expensive.
   c. is most expensive.
   d. famous people use.
9. The cost of a product is usually influenced by quality, advertising, and
   a. labels. b. unit price.
   c. logos. (d.) packaging.
10. The unit price of an item is found by
    a. adding the full price and net weight.
    b. multiplying the full price by the net weight.
    c. subtracting the net weight from the full price.
    (d.) dividing the full price by the net weight.
11. Products or practices that are very popular for a short time are called
    a. advertising. b. logos.
    c. jingles. (d.) fads.
12. The net weight of a bottle of perfume includes the weight of
    a. the perfume and the bottle.
    (b.) the perfume only.
    c. the bottle only.
    d. a case of bottles.
13. To get the best results from health products, a consumer should
    a. only buy products with the lowest unit price.
    b. use less of the product than the directions recommend.
    c. use more of the product than the directions recommend.
    (d.) read and follow the directions.
14. The results of tests done on a urine sample tell a doctor much about a patient's
    a. liver. b. lungs.
    (c.) kidneys. d. heart.

77

Name ______________ Chapter 9 Test A

Short Answer Match each meaning in Column I with the correct word or words in Column II. Write the correct letter on the blank.

Column I	**Column II**
e 15. a person who buys or uses a health product or service	a. fad
f 16. a public notice or announcement recommending a product or service	b. unit price
d 17. a symbol used to identify something for advertising purposes	c. net weight
a 18. a product or practice that is popular only for a short time	d. logo
c 19. the weight of the contents of a product, not including the container	e. health consumer
b 20. the cost of a product divided by the net weight	f. advertisement

Short Essay Write your answers in complete sentences.

21. An advertisement reads: "Be the first of your friends to own one." How is the ad trying to appeal to consumers?

    This ad is trying to appeal to many people's desire to be the first to own something. The message is given that you are better than your friends if you buy this product before they do.

22. Why should a boy trying out for the football team have a health examination?

    Sports require a great deal of energy and physical stress. Anyone playing sports should make sure that they are healthy. A health checkup might uncover a problem that needs treatment.

78

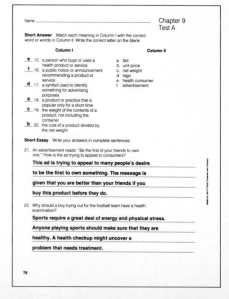

Reviewing Health Ideas

Number your paper from 1–13. Next to each number write the word that best completes the sentence.

1. A health ____ buys or uses health products or services.
2. A basic question to ask before buying a product is "Do I ____ it or do I just want it?"
3. Advertisements can be sources of useful ____.
4. Some ads try to convince people to buy a product by showing a ____ person who uses it.
5. A catchy jingle helps consumers to ____ a certain product.
6. A ____ is a symbol that identifies a company.
7. A product in a fancy package will probably cost ____ than the same kind of product in a simple package.
8. A product's net weight includes the weight of the product but not the weight of the ____.
9. Ingredients on labels are listed in order by ____.
10. A ____ is a promise by the manufacturer to replace, repair, or give money back for a product that is unsatisfactory to the consumer.
11. A person should tell a doctor about any unexpected side ____ from a prescribed medicine.
12. Noting posture gives a doctor some clues about a patient's general ____.
13. The results from a urine test let a doctor know how well a patient's ____ are performing their work of removing wastes from the body.

Understanding Health Ideas

Number your paper from 14–22. Next to each number write the word or words that best answer the question.

14. What are three possible sources of information about health products?
15. How is the statement, "You can't buy a better product" an example of an unclear statement in ads?
16. What is a logo?
17. How can a person figure out the unit price of a product?
18. What are four kinds of information found on the labels of health products?
19. What is a fad?
20. How often do doctors recommend that young people have health checkups?
21. What does a doctor usually check for when he or she looks in a patient's ears during a checkup?
22. What are three diseases for which people usually get vaccinations?

Thinking Critically

Write the answers on your paper. Use complete sentences.

1. How can you benefit most from a health checkup?
2. What would you conclude about a product whose ads do not seem to give any useful information?
3. Why might a wise consumer decide to buy a product that has a higher unit price than a similar product with a lower unit price?

283

Answers to Reviewing Health Ideas

1. consumer
2. need
3. information
4. famous
5. remember
6. logo
7. more
8. container
9. weight
10. guarantee
11. effects
12. health
13. kidneys

Answers to Understanding Health Ideas

14. family members, friends, school nurse, consumer magazines and books, experience
15. can mean you could buy several products that are just as good
16. a symbol used to identify something for advertising purposes
17. Divide price by net weight.
18. ingredients, directions for use, a guarantee, and warnings
19. a product or practice that is popular only for a short time
20. every two or three years
21. for signs of disease or infection, to see if the eardrums are unbroken, and to see if any accumulations of wax need to be removed.
22. tetanus, polio, measles, mumps, German measles, and diphtheria

Answers to Thinking Critically

1. By asking questions, being open and honest with the doctor, writing down and following the doctor's instructions, and discussing treatment plans.
Thinking Skill By telling how a person can benefit from a health checkup, students are *drawing conclusions.*
2. Answers will vary but should mention that perhaps the product is not really better than others.
Thinking Skill By analyzing ads that do not give useful information, students are *drawing conclusions.*
3. Answers might suggest that a consumer might buy a product with a higher unit price because the product is a smaller size and the consumer would not use all of a larger size, or because the consumer has never tried the product before.
Thinking Skill By thinking about why a consumer might buy a product with a higher unit price, students are *generalizing.*

Cooperative Learning Use the STAD Format described on page T24 to have four- to five-member teams study Chapter 9 Review together before completing Chapter 9 Test.

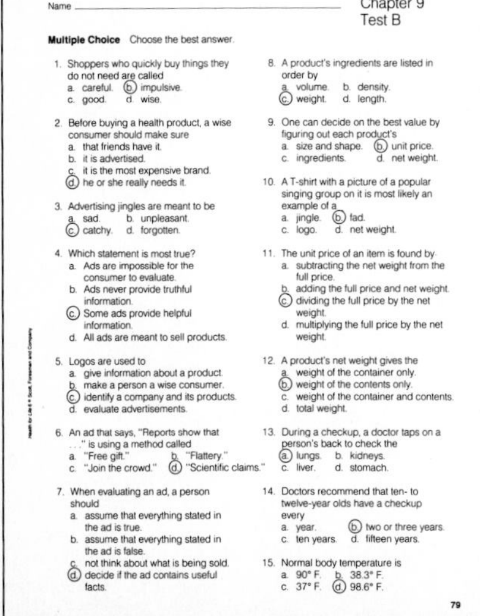

Name ____________ Chapter 9 Test B

Multiple Choice Choose the best answer.

1. Shoppers who quickly buy things they do not need are called
a. careful. (b.) impulsive. c. good. d. wise.
2. Before buying a health product, a wise consumer should make sure
a. that friends have it.
b. it is advertised.
c. it is the most expensive brand.
(d.) he or she really needs it.
3. Advertising jingles are meant to be
a. sad. b. unpleasant. (c.) catchy. d. forgotten.
4. Which statement is most true?
a. Ads are impossible for the consumer to evaluate.
b. Ads never provide truthful information.
(c.) Some ads provide helpful information.
d. All ads are meant to sell products.
5. Logos are used to
a. give information about a product.
b. make a person a wise consumer.
(c.) identify a company and its products.
d. evaluate advertisements.
6. An ad that says, "Reports show that . . ." is using a method called
a. "Free gift." b. "Flattery." c. "Join the crowd." (d.) "Scientific claims."
7. When evaluating an ad, a person should
a. assume that everything stated in the ad is true.
b. assume that everything stated in the ad is false.
c. not think about what is being sold.
(d.) decide if the ad contains useful facts.
8. A product's ingredients are listed in order by
a. volume. b. density. (c.) weight. d. length.
9. One can decide on the best value by figuring out each product's
a. size and shape. (b.) unit price. c. ingredients. d. net weight.
10. A T-shirt with a picture of a popular singing group on it is most likely an example of a
a. jingle. (b.) fad. c. logo. d. net weight.
11. The unit price of an item is found by
a. subtracting the net weight from the full price.
b. adding the full price and net weight.
(c.) dividing the full price by the net weight.
d. multiplying the full price by the net weight.
12. A product's net weight gives the
a. weight of the container only.
(b.) weight of the contents only.
c. weight of the container and contents.
d. total weight.
13. During a checkup, a doctor taps on a person's back to check the
(a.) lungs. b. kidneys. c. liver. d. stomach.
14. Doctors recommend that ten- to twelve-year olds have a checkup every
a. year. (b.) two or three years. c. ten years. d. fifteen years.
15. Normal body temperature is
a. 90° F. b. 38.3° F. c. 37° F. (d.) 98.6° F.

79

Name ____________ Chapter 9 Test B

Short Answer Match each meaning in Column I with the correct word or words in Column II. Write the correct letter on the blank.

Column I	Column II
d 16. a person who buys or uses a health product or service	a. advertisement
f 17. a symbol used to identify something for advertising purposes	b. unit price
a 18. a public notice or announcement recommending a product or service	c. guarantee
b 19. the cost of a product divided by the net weight	d. health consumer
c 20. a promise by the maker to replace or repair an unsatisfactory product	e. net weight
e 21. the weight of the contents of a product, not including the container	f. logo

Short Essay Write your answers in complete sentences.

22. Which of the following two advertisements is the best source of consumer information? Why?

Ad #1 This toothpaste gives you a brighter smile!	Ad #2 This toothpaste contains fluoride and is approved by the American Dental Association.

Ad #2 is the best because it gives the most information. It gives you specific information about the toothpaste's ingredients and approval.

23. John's doctor recommended Brand A aspirin, but the unit price of Brand B is lower. Which should John probably buy? Why?

John should probably buy Brand A because of his doctor's recommendation. Some brands cost more because they are higher in quality.

80

CHAPTER 10 PLANNING GUIDE **Pupil Edition**

Pupil Edition	Activities	Enrichment	Assessment	Independent Study
Chapter 10 Working for a Healthy Community, pp. 284–313	Health Watch Notebook, p. 284	Health Focus, p. 310 Health at Home, p. 311	Chapter 10 Review, pp. 312–313	Study Guide, pp. 334–335 Skills for Life Handbook, pp. 365–367
Lesson 1 What Health Services Do People Provide for the Community? pp. 286–291		Did You Know? p. 287	Think Back, p. 291	Study Guide, p. 334
Lesson 2 How Do People Help Provide for a Clean Environment? pp. 292–297		Did You Know? pp. 293, 297	Think Back, p. 297	Study Guide, p. 334
Lesson 3 How Can People Dispose of Garbage More Safely? pp. 298–299	Health Activities Workshop, pp. 300–301	Did You Know? p. 299	Think Back, p. 299	Study Guide, p. 335
Lesson 4 How Does a Community Reduce Noise? pp. 302–303		Did You Know? p. 303	Think Back, p. 303	Study Guide, p. 335
Lesson 5 What Recreational Opportunities Does a Community Provide? pp. 304–307			Think Back, p. 307	On Your Own, p. 306 Study Guide, p. 335
Lesson 6 How Can You Help Keep Your Community Healthy? pp. 308–309		Did You Know? p. 308	Think Back, p. 309	Study Guide, p. 335

Teacher Resources

Air Pollution Primer. American Lung Association. Discusses the sources and effects of air pollution.

Calabrese, Edward J., and Dorsey, Michael W. *Healthy Living in an Unhealthy World.* Simon and Schuster, 1984. Presents a guide to the chemical hazards in the environment, and tells how they can be avoided or minimized.

Dorfman, John; Kitzinger, Sheila; and Schuchman, Herman. *Well-Being: An Introduction to Health.* Scott, Foresman, 1980. Explores the importance of a healthy life-style and a healthy community.

Miller, G. Tyler, Jr. *Living in the Environment: Concepts, Problems, and Alternatives.* 4th ed. Wadsworth, 1985. Discusses the problems that exist in the environment, and explains how these problems can have an effect on people's health.

Audio-Visual Resources

See page T43 for addresses of Audio-Visual Sources.

Before using any audio-visual materials, preview them for appropriateness for your students.

Health: Past, Present, Future, BFA Educational Media, filmstrips with cassettes. Examines ways in which government agencies and medical professionals are working to improve health services.

Noise, BFA Educational Media, film or video, 10 minutes. Discusses the growing problem of noise pollution, and suggests how to limit it.

Pollution: Problems and Prospects, National Geographic Society, filmstrips with cassettes. Shows community efforts to reduce pollution, and examines various ways to meet human needs while protecting the environment.

That Horrible Noise, AIMS Media, film or video, 11 minutes. Looks at the detrimental physiological and psychological effects of noise pollution.

	Teacher's Edition	Teacher's Resource Book	Test Book
Enrichment	Suggestions for each lesson: L. 1—pp. 286, 288, 290 L. 2—pp. 292, 294, 296 L. 3—p. 298 L. 4—p. 302 L. 5—pp. 304, 306 L. 6—p. 308	Family Letter, p. 125 * Life Skills, p. 129 * Health and Language Arts, p. 132	
Reteaching	Suggestions for each lesson: L. 1—pp. 286, 288, 290 L. 2—pp. 292, 294, 296 L. 3—p. 298 L. 4—p. 302 L. 5—pp. 304, 306 L. 6—p. 308	Transparency Masters, pp. 127–128 * Vocabulary, p. 130 * Study and Review, p. 131	
Assessment	Expanding Student Thinking: one assessment question per lesson that develops higher-order thinking skills—pp. 291, 297, 299, 303, 307, 309		Chapter 10 Test, Form A, pp. 81–82 Chapter 10 Test, Form B, pp. 83–84

* Also available in Workbook format (Student Edition and Teacher's Edition)

Chapter 10 Poster

A set of posters is available in a separate package. It provides a teaching poster for every chapter, including discussion and activity suggestions on the back. The poster for Chapter 10 is titled "Which of these can be recycled?"

Overhead Transparencies

A set of color overhead transparencies is available for Grade 6. You may wish to use Transparency 19 to help teach about groundwater pollution.

Advance Preparation

You will need to prepare materials in advance for the following activity from the Health Activities Workshop.

Activity 1, page 300 Obtain dirt, two small jars, a plastic bottle, cotton, pebbles, and sand for each student or group of students.

Bulletin Board

Draw two scenes from a city. One scene should show pollution, the other a cleaner city environment. Ask students to compare and contrast the two environments.

Teaching Plan

Chapter 10 pages 284–313

Chapter Main Idea
People provide a variety of services that contribute to the health of an entire community.

Chapter Goals
• Express a responsible attitude toward community health by not littering or otherwise polluting the environment.
• Realize that loud, continuous noise harms the body, and attempt to reduce excessive noise in school, at home, and in the community.
• Discover and take advantage of the variety of recreational facilities provided in the community.

Lifetime Goal
Be aware of community health problems and work to help solve or deal with them.

Health Vocabulary
Acid rain, carbon monoxide, decibel, environment, epidemiologist, pollution, recycling, sanitarian, sanitary landfill, scrubber, smog

Chapter **10**

Working for a Healthy Community

Have you ever seen a building like the large, flat one in the picture? It is a water treatment plant. Here, water is cleaned and made safer to drink for the community. Providing clean water is an important health service. This chapter describes the many health services the people in your community share. You will also discover ways you can help improve your community's health now and in the future.

Health Watch Notebook

Contact your local health officials, recreation department, or department of sanitation to find out about the services they offer your community. Report your findings in your notebook.

1 What Health Services Do People Provide for the Community?
2 How Do People Help Provide a Clean Environment?
3 How Can People Dispose of Garbage More Safely?
4 How Does a Community Reduce Noise?
5 What Recreational Opportunities Does a Community Provide?
6 How Can You Help Keep Your Community Healthy?

Teaching Options

Modeling Health Vocabulary
Use this technique to introduce new words as you teach each lesson in this chapter. First, introduce the word. Present the word in two sentences that serve to clearly define the word. One sentence you might use to introduce the word *decibel* is the following: *A decibel is a unit for measuring the loudness of sound.* Either read the sentences to the students or write them on the chalkboard. Ask the students to generate two meaningful sentences using the word. Additional successful techniques for introducing new words can be found on page T23.

Cooperative Learning
Jigsaw Format (See page T24.)
Assign the following topics at random to your cooperative learning teams.
Topic A: List some of the services provided by community volunteers.
Topic B: How do communities reduce air and water pollution?
Topic C: How do communities reduce land and noise pollution?
Topic D: What recreational facilities do communities provide for their inhabitants?
Have students search for information on their topic as they read the chapter. Then let all students with the same topic meet in an expert group to discuss the information. When students return to their teams, they may take turns presenting their topics to the team. Then give students a test covering all topics to complete individually (Chapter 10 test A or B in the Test Book). Award Superteam certificates to teams whose average test scores exceed 90%, and Greatteam certificates to teams whose average test scores exceed 80%.

Words to Preteach

Aquarium, arboretum, bacteria, communicable disease, community, groundwater, incinerator, planetarium, respiratory system, stress, vaccination, virus, volunteer

Introducing the Chapter

Ask the students when they first used a community health service. (Answers will vary but might include at birth and for vaccinations.) Let students read page 284. Then ask how the people who operate the water treatment plant shown are providing an important community health service. You may wish to send the Family Letter home at this time. You may want to assign Study Guide pages 334–335 for students to use independently as they read the lessons. The Study Guide can also be used as an extra chapter review. You might want to assign the activities in the Skills for Life Handbook on pages 365–367.

Strategies for Health Watch Notebook

You may want to divide the class into teams and have each team contact a different department. You may wish to arrange to have the students visit the facility, or have a representative visit your classroom.

Family Letter

Use the Family Letter (English or Spanish version) to introduce the subject matter of the chapter to the family and to suggest a way the family can become involved in the student's learning experience. This master may be reproduced from the Teacher's Resource Book.

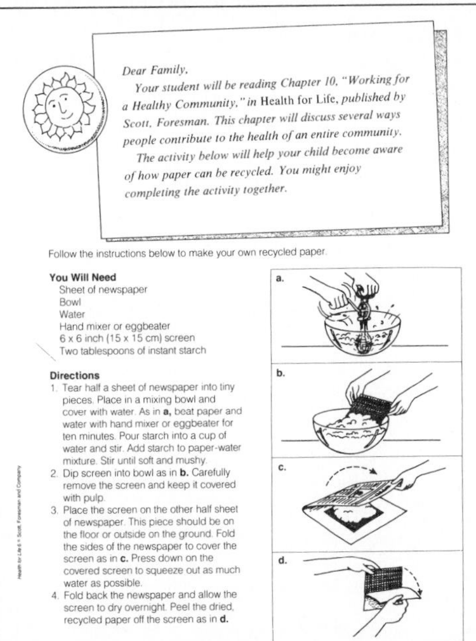

Dear Family,

Your student will be reading Chapter 10, "Working for a Healthy Community," in Health for Life, *published by Scott, Foresman. This chapter will discuss several ways people contribute to the health of an entire community.*

The activity below will help your child become aware of how paper can be recycled. You might enjoy completing the activity together.

Follow the instructions below to make your own recycled paper.

You Will Need

Sheet of newspaper
Bowl
Water
Hand mixer or eggbeater
6 x 6 inch (15 x 15 cm) screen
Two tablespoons of instant starch

Directions

1. Tear half a sheet of newspaper into tiny pieces. Place in a mixing bowl and cover with water. As in **a,** beat paper and water with hand mixer or eggbeater for ten minutes. Pour starch into a cup of water and stir. Add starch to paper-water mixture. Stir until soft and mushy.
2. Dip screen into bowl as in **b.** Carefully remove the screen and keep it covered with pulp.
3. Place the screen on the other half sheet of newspaper. This piece should be on the floor or outside on the ground. Fold the sides of the newspaper to cover the screen as in **c.** Press down on the covered screen to squeeze out as much water as possible.
4. Fold back the newspaper and allow the screen to dry overnight. Peel the dried, recycled paper off the screen as in **d.**

For High-Potential Students

Help interested students build mobiles that depict five important factors influencing the health of the community. These might include air pollution, water pollution, garbage, adequacy of recreational facilities, and noise. Ask the students to build the mobile in such a way that every negative influence is balanced by a positive influence, such as a person or organization working to improve the health of the community.

Teaching Plan

Lesson 1 pages 286-291

Lesson Objective
Describe how health departments, hospitals, and volunteers meet the needs of the community.

Health Vocabulary
Epidemiologist, sanitarian

1 Motivate

Introducing the Lesson
Explain that refrigerators were not common around the turn of the century and that food often spoiled. Point out that unsanitary conditions often existed in meat-packing factories, dairies, and restaurants and that these conditons caused serious diseases. Then encourage students to think of other ways that health conditions have improved over the last one hundred years. (Accept all reasonable answers that the students can explain.)

epidemiologist (ep′ə dē′mē ol′ə jist), a physician or research scientist who studies the occurrence and causes of diseases.

sanitarian (san′ə ter′ē ən), an environmental health specialist who works to ensure the safe quality of food, water, or air for the public health.

1 What Health Services Do People Provide for the Community?

Every time you wash your hands or bandage a cut, you are performing a health service for yourself. You can provide for some of your own health needs. Your family and your doctor provide for other health needs. Some of your health needs, however, require the services of other people in the community.

How Do Health Departments Serve the Community?

People in the health department perform very different jobs. However, they all work together for the public health, especially when a health problem occurs. For example, suppose an outbreak of food poisoning occurs in a community. The pictures show how some people in the health department might respond to solve this problem.

Epidemiologists search for the source of the food poisoning.

The contaminated food is found to all come from one restaurant. Sanitarians close the restaurant and inspect it.

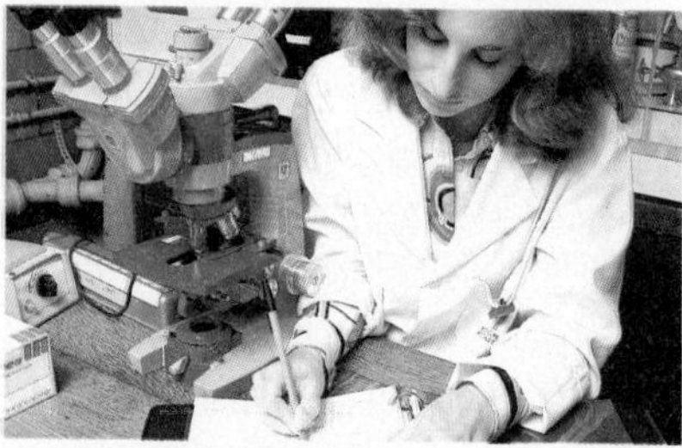
Laboratory technicians test samples of the victims' blood or leftover food and discover that a harmful kind of bacteria contaminated the food.

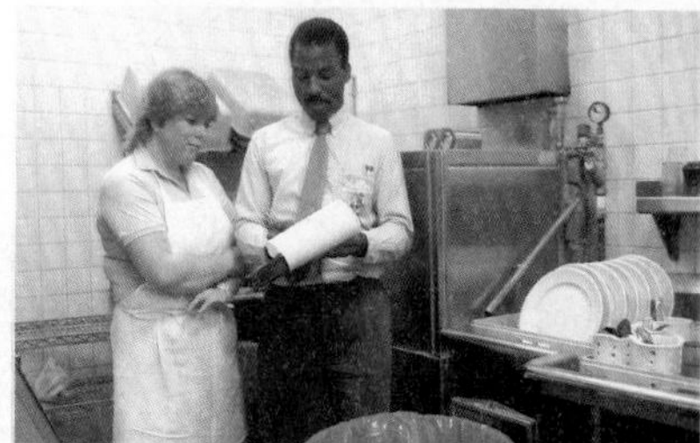
After discovering how the bacteria got into the food, a sanitarian shows the restaurant owner how to prevent the problem from happening again.

286

Teaching Options

Health Background

Health services in the United States are provided on three main levels: federal, state, and local. Local health departments include the municipal or county health departments. Depending on the size of the population served, the health department is staffed by some or all of the following health specialists: physicians, epidemiologists, laboratory technicians, dentists, nurses, sanitarians, engineers, educators, conselors, and vision and hearing technicians.

Enrichment
Ask students to investigate the services provided by the county health department and to compare these services with the ones provided by the nearest municipal health department.

Health and Social Studies
Suggest that interested students find out about kosher food preparation and how it can help keep food safe. Let students report their findings to the class.

Reteaching
Let students make a list of health department workers and describe how they serve the community.

A local health department serves the community in many other ways. The goal of these services is to protect the community from disease. Some sanitarians check the quality of the water in a community, as shown. They might test drinking water to make sure it is safe to use. They might also test water from lakes, rivers, and swimming pools.

Public health nurses make home visits to help families learn how to take care of sick family members. The nurses might also advise families about nutrition and child care. Some health departments operate clinics that provide vaccinations against diseases. Other clinics provide care for people with high blood pressure and other health problems.

Some health department workers help control the spread of disease by spraying insect killer where certain insects are likely to breed. The workers also help control the populations of rats and other pests that spread disease.

Health departments keep records of all births, deaths, marriages, and cases of certain communicable diseases in the community. This information is valuable when planning for new health facilities or when trying to find the cause of certain epidemics.

Did You Know?
A sanitarian checks the cleanliness of forks, spoons, and other eating utensils in restaurants. First, the sanitarian rubs a cotton swab over the utensil. Then, the cotton swab is placed in a germ-free container and sent to a laboratory. There, workers can determine the number of bacteria on the swab. A high bacteria count indicates that the utensil was not properly cleaned.

How is this public health worker serving the community?

2 Teach

Strategies for Pages 286 and 287

• Write the lesson title question on the chalkboard. • Ask students to read pages 286 and 287 to find out how health departments serve the community. • Ask students to name some of the different workers in the health department. (epidemiologists, nurses, sanitarians, laboratory technicians) Call on students to describe the role of each of these health workers. (Epidemiologists study the spread and causes of diseases; public health nurses make home visits to solve health problems; sanitarians ensure the safe quality of food, water, and air for public health; and laboratory technicians run tests of substances for suspected contamination.) • Discuss how each of these workers would respond to an outbreak of food poisoning in the community. • Emphasize that each job is important and that all the workers have to work as a team in order to solve health problems. • Ask students how spraying insect killer where mosquitoes are likely to breed helps the community. (Mosquitoes can carry diseases and transmit them to people. Killing mosquitoes helps prevent diseases.) • Be sure students understand that the goal of most of these services is to protect the community from disease.

Life Skills

Use this worksheet for practice in reading comprehension and learning to eliminate a health menace. This master may be reproduced from the Teacher's Resource Book and is located on page 37 of the Student's Workbook. Use with Chapter 10: pages 286–291.

Name ____________________ Life Skills

Use with Chapter 10: pages 286–291.

Eliminating a Health Hazard

Read the article on flies. Then answer the questions.

Flies are a health menace. Flies use tiny, sticky hairs on their legs to gather and deposit disease germs wherever they land. Germs are easily caught in these hairs and then rubbed off.

Flies also leave disease germs wherever they eat. They dissolve food with their saliva since they cannot eat solid food. Then flies suck up the liquid. Flies often suck up and spit out the same solution many times causing germs from the flies' saliva to spread to the food source.

Fly's leg Magnified

1. How is the fly able to carry disease germs?
   Disease germs are carried on sticky hairs on the fly's legs.
2. Why are flies a health menace?
   They spread disease germs.
3. How do flies eat solid food?
   Flies dissolve solid food with their saliva and then suck up the solution.
4. In what ways do flies spread disease germs?
   They carry germs in the hairs covering their legs and feet; they suck up and spit out liquid solutions of food containing germs.
5. On the lines below, list ways you can prevent flies from spreading disease germs.
   Answers might include: keep food covered, place trash in covered bins, and keep countertops clean.

Extension Idea: Ask students to list other health menaces and describe ways to prevent each menace from spreading disease.

129

Teaching Plan

Lesson 1 continued

2 Teach

Strategies for Pages 288 and 289

• Call on volunteers to name health professionals who work in a hospital. (Accept all reasonable answers.) You may wish to make a list on the chalkboard. • Then suggest that students read pages 288 and 289 to learn more about how hospital workers serve the community. • Discuss the workers who helped Ann while she was in the hospital. Call on volunteers to describe what is happening in each picture. • If possible, get an X-ray of a broken bone and show it to the class on an overhead projector.

How Do Hospitals Serve the Community?

If someone asked you to describe what happens in a hospital, you might reply "Doctors and nurses help sick people get well." This answer is true, but incomplete. The following pictures will help you answer this question more completely. They show some of the people who helped Ann while she was in the hospital. Ann had a bad fall and broke her leg. Notice the variety of health professionals who work at a hospital to serve the community's health needs.

Emergency medical technicians gave Ann first aid and brought her and her parents to the emergency room of the hospital.

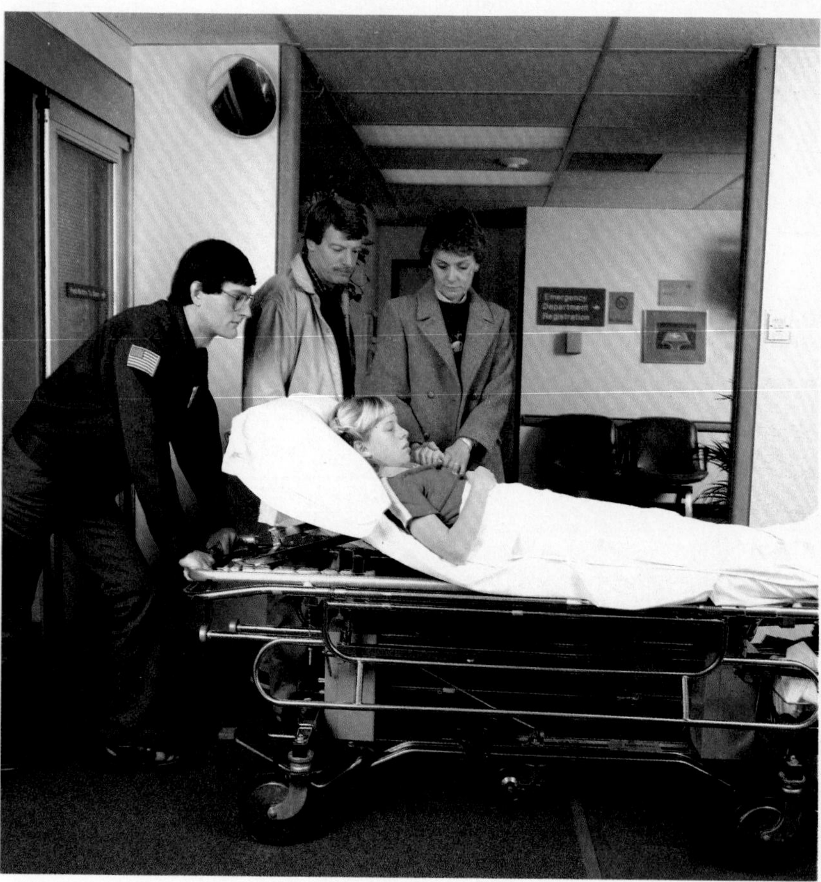

Teaching Options

Anecdote

Proprietary hospitals—hospitals owned by an individual or a corporation and operated for profit—are increasing in number in the United States. Today, proprietary hospitals account for approximately 15 percent of all community hospitals.

Enrichment

Invite a hospital administrator or other hospital worker to visit the class to discuss his or her work. Students should prepare questions in advance of the visit.

Health and Social Studies

Ask the students to mark the locations of your community's hospitals on a map. Help the students determine the population of the community, and then ask if new hospitals are needed. (Answers will vary but students should attempt to relate available hospital services to the population of the area.)

Reteaching

Let students play the following game to review the jobs of hospital workers. Write a list of hospital workers on the chalkboard. The list might include emergency medical technicians, doctors, nurses, admissions office workers, X-ray technicians, laboratory technicians, surgical nurses, physical therapists, nurses' aides, pharmacists, record keepers, and administrators. Divide the class into two teams. Name a task performed by one of the hospital workers and ask students to name the worker or workers who perform this task. The first team to respond with the correct answer wins a point. The team with the most points at the end of the game wins.

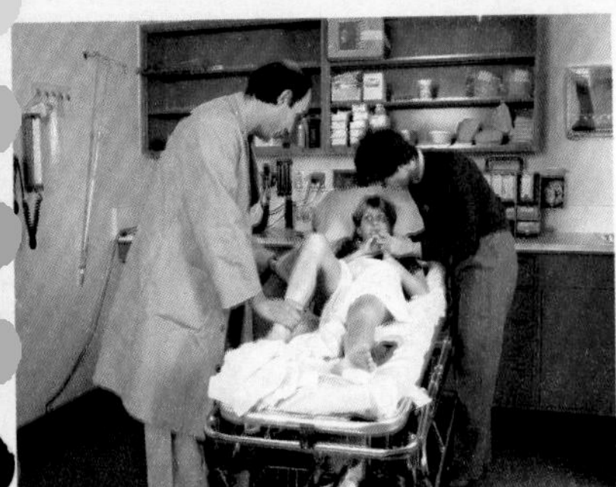
A doctor examined her injury.

One of Ann's parents stopped at the admissions office to give some information for the records.

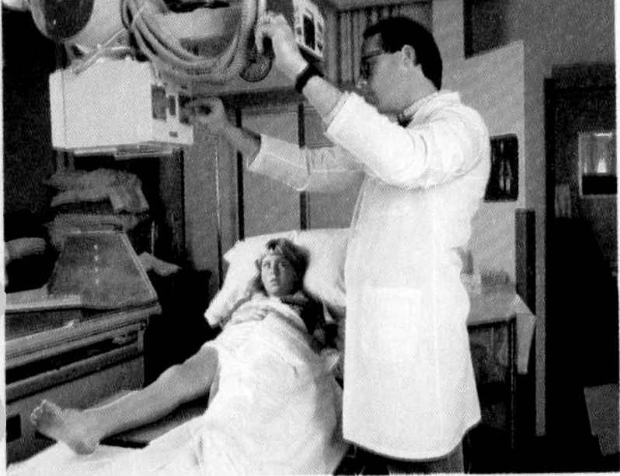
A technician took X-ray pictures of Ann's leg. The pictures showed bits of broken bone in her leg. She needed surgery to remove the bits of bone and repair torn muscles.

A laboratory technician tested samples of Ann's blood to check for the presence of certain diseases. The results helped doctors plan for the surgery.

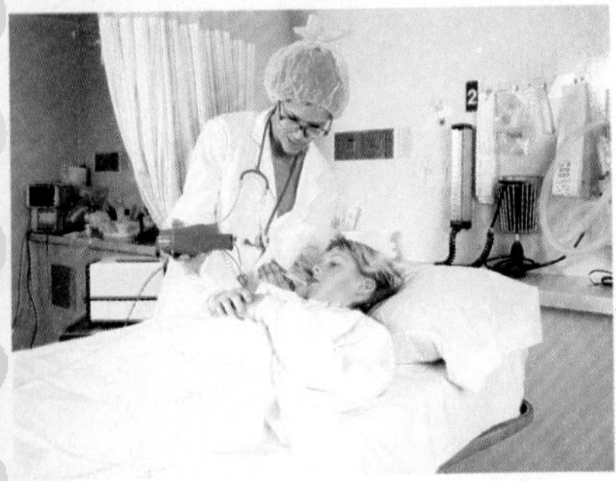
After surgery Ann was taken to the recovery room. Nurses watched her closely in case any problems resulted from the surgery.

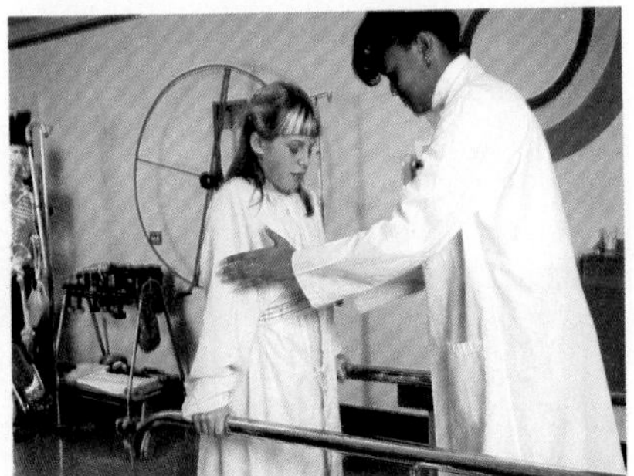
The day after surgery, Ann worked with a physical therapist to learn how to use crutches.

• Ask why Ann was taken to a recovery room after surgery. (to watch for any problems that might result from the surgery) • Ask students why a hospital has procedures for dealing with emergencies. (Answers may vary but students should understand that research and experience have helped hospital workers know the most effective way of dealing with a particular emergency.)

Teaching Plan

Lesson 1 continued

2 Teach

Strategies for Pages 290 and 291

• Ask students to suggest some hospital workers that Ann did not see. (Accept all reasonable answers.)
• Then suggest students read page 290 to find out more about Ann's stay in the hospital. • Discuss what behind-the-scenes hospital workers do. (The pharmacist prepares medicine; the administrator plans and directs the hospital programs.) • Discuss what the physical therapist did. (helped Ann with exercises to help her regain strength in her leg) • Ask students what other workers are in a hospital. (dietitians, cooks, maintenance workers, housekeepers)

• Ask students to read page 291 to find out how volunteers help the community. • Be sure students understand that volunteers are people who offer their time and help without getting paid. • Discuss what some volunteers might do. (visit people who are sick at home, deliver hot meals, drive people who need a ride, work at the hospital information desk, answer telephone hot lines) • Point out to students that people their age can do certain types of volunteer work.

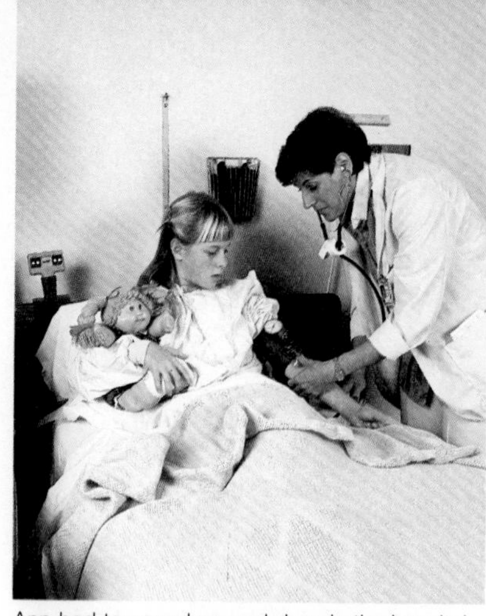

Ann had to spend several days in the hospital. Nurses provided the day-to-day care and emotional support that she needed. Nurses also performed treatments and gave Ann medications that the doctor ordered.

Ann did not see all the people in the hospital who helped her get well. Some of these people were the pharmacists. They prepared the medicine she needed.

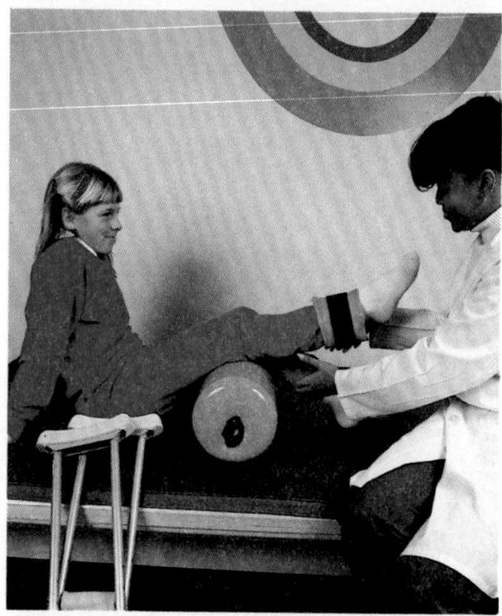

Ann left the hospital about a week after surgery. However, she needed to return for more physical therapy about two months later to regain strength in her leg.

All the health services that helped Ann were the responsibility of the hospital administrators. They plan and direct hospital services based on the community's needs.

Teaching Options

Enrichment

Encourage students to volunteer for a community health event or to offer to do volunteer work at a community health facility. After a period of time, ask students to describe the benefits they think they derived from the community service.

Health and Language Arts

Ask students to write a paragraph explaining how they feel when they help another person. Then ask students to write a paragraph explaining how they feel when another person helps them.

Reteaching

Ask students who have been in hospitals to tell how various hospital workers have helped them.

How Do Volunteers Serve the Community?

Some people work in communities as volunteers. They offer their time and services without getting paid. The picture shows a volunteer called a candy striper. This person helps hospital patients under the direction of a nurse or other staff member. Other volunteers work in a hospital at the information desk.

Volunteers might help ill people at home by shopping or housecleaning for them. They also deliver hot meals to people who live alone and cannot shop or cook for themselves. Other volunteers might drive handicapped people to and from work. The work of volunteers is an important part of a community's health.

Think Back • *Study on your own with Study Guide page 334.*

1. How does a local health department improve the health of a community?
2. How do doctors, nurses, laboratory technicians, and pharmacists in hospitals each contribute to the health of patients?
3. In what ways do volunteers serve a community?

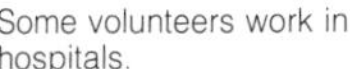
Some volunteers work in hospitals.

• Ask students why they think volunteers do what they do. (Answers might include to get experience, a desire to help, a feeling of doing something worthwhile.)

3 Assess

Expanding Student Thinking

Ask students to explain the importance of taking X rays when a bone is broken. (The doctor needs to determine how bad the injury is, the location of the break, and whether or not the bone has been chipped.)

Thinking Skill Students are *suggesting alternatives*.

Answers to Think Back

1. Answers might refer to the health department's role in protecting the community from disease or to specific activities. A local health department uses sanitarians to prevent food and water contamination and epidemiologists to study the spread and control of diseases. Public health nurses make home visits and advise families about nutrition. Other workers keep track of births, deaths, and marriages.

2. Accept all applicable job descriptions listed on pages 288–290.

3. Volunteers offer their time and service free to help other people. These services might include helping people who are ill at home, driving people who need a ride, and helping with hospital services.

Teaching Plan

Lesson 2 pages 292–297

Lesson Objective
Describe some causes of water and air pollution, and describe how communities reduce water and air pollution.

Health Vocabulary
Acid rain, carbon monoxide, environment, pollution, scrubber, smog

1 Motivate
Introducing the Lesson
Tell students that people who live in a large city are more likely to have respiratory problems than those who live in a rural area. Ask students to suggest reasons for this. (Large cities have more cars and factories, which pollute the air, than do rural areas.)

environment (en vī′rən mənt), all the living and nonliving surroundings that affect living things.

pollution (pə lü′shən), a change in the environment that is harmful or undesirable to living things.

2 How Do People Help Provide a Clean Environment?

Look around you. Notice everything you see, indoors and outdoors. Listen closely for any sounds. Do you detect any odors? All of the sights, sounds, and odors are part of your **environment.** Your environment is all of the living and nonliving things that surround and affect you. The water you drink, the air you breathe, the sounds you hear, and the ground you walk on are all part of your environment.

The actions of people often cause harmful or undesirable changes in the environment. Any such change is **pollution.** Most pollution comes from wastes that people add to the environment. Sewage, engine exhaust, and garbage are some wastes that pollute the water, air, and land. Many people in your community work to reduce the problems of pollution. They try to provide a clean, healthy environment for everyone.

What Is Sewage?

Sewage, or wastewater, from factories, houses, and other buildings threatens the safety of the drinking water supply. Sewage from your home might include human wastes, bits of food that go down the kitchen drain, and water you use to wash your hands. Factory sewage, like that shown in the river, often includes oil, grease, and poisonous chemicals. All sewage usually contains bacteria and viruses, which can cause disease. Sewage also contains sticks, rags, and other large objects that drain into sewers from city streets.

What does sewage contain?

292

Teaching Options

Health Background
As technology advances, more substances are produced that are hazardous to the environment. Air pollutants include lead, carbon monoxide, and asbestos. Water can be contaminated by untreated sewage, thermal pollution, and pesticides. Land pollution usually refers to the surface accumulation of substances that are not biodegradable.

Enrichment
Ask students to visit the local sewage or water treatment plant. Help them prepare in advance questions about how the plant works.

Encourage students to bring to class newspaper articles about pollution problems.

Health and Social Studies
Suggest that students use library sources to find out how people disposed of sewage and other wastes in European towns during the Middle Ages or in American cities during the early nineteenth century. Interested students might want to explore how these waste disposal methods led to the spread of disease.

Reteaching
Show students a map of the local area. Ask them to locate what they think are high pollution areas and tell why they think these areas are polluted.

How Do Treatment Plants Improve a Community's Water?

To reduce the amount of water pollution, most communities in the United States pipe their sewage to wastewater treatment plants, commonly called sewage treatment plants. Many factories have their own sewage treatment plants. The drawing shows how some harmful substances are removed from sewage at such a plant, although not all plants use all these processes. First, sewage is piped through screens that remove sticks and other large objects. Next, the sewage moves into settling tanks where small, solid materials settle out. The remaining sewage then might go to aeration tanks. Bacteria in the tanks feed on the sewage. Air is pumped into the aeration tanks to keep the bacteria alive. In another settling tank, the bacteria clump together and settle out. Next, chlorine gas is added to kill harmful bacteria and some viruses. Finally, the treated sewage is pumped to a nearby river, lake, or other body of water.

Notice the difference between the sewage that enters the treatment plant and the sewage that leaves it. The treated wastewater is clean enough to send to a river or lake, but, of course, the water is still not safe to drink. Many harmful substances remain, even if you cannot see them. Also, the water might have an unpleasant color, taste, and smell.

To make water safe and pleasant for drinking, communities use water treatment plants. These plants help to clean water from rivers or lakes. The water passes through a series of screens, settling tanks, and filters. Chlorine is added to kill harmful bacteria. In some communities, the water is then sprayed into the air. This process adds oxygen to the water to make it taste better. The clean water then is piped to homes and other places in the community.

Did You Know?

Communities that get their water from wells do not use water treatment plants. Instead, the community water department usually treats the well water at the site of the well.

Sewage after and before treatment

Sewage is cleaned at a sewage treatment plant

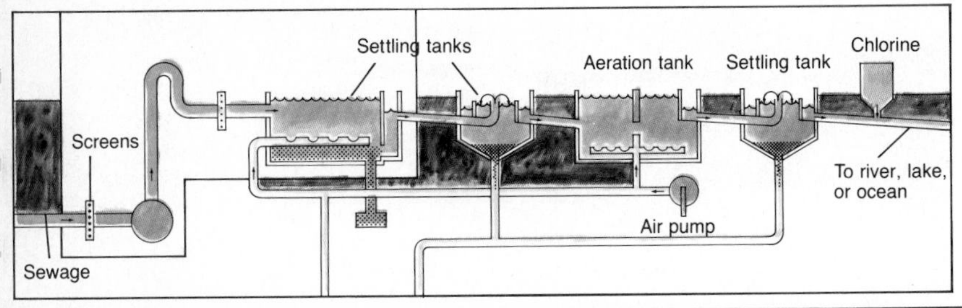

2 Teach

Strategies for Pages 292 and 293

• Make sure students understand that their environment includes all the living and nonliving surroundings that affect them. • Discuss positive aspects of an environment. (lakes, parks, well-kept homes, recreational facilities.) Discuss negative aspects. (litter, dirty water, noise) • Point out that people often cause harmful changes in the environment. • Then ask students to read pages 292 and 293 to find out more about pollution problems. • Discuss what is found in sewage and why sewage is harmful.
• Be sure students understand that sewage treatment and waste treatment are synonymous terms. • Ask how sewage treatment and water treatment plants improve a community's water. (Sewage treatment plants filter and treat sewage to reduce harmful substances. Water treatment plants filter and treat water to make the water safe for drinking.) • Students might wonder why the untreated sewage shown on page 293 is not darker or muckier. Explain that sewage entering a treatment plant contains a variety of chemicals and much water—all of which give raw sewage a cloudy, gray appearance.

Health and Language Arts

Use this worksheet for practice in making a health cartoon. This master may be reproduced from the Teacher's Resource Book and is located on page 40 of the Student's Workbook. Use with Chapter 10: pages 292–297.

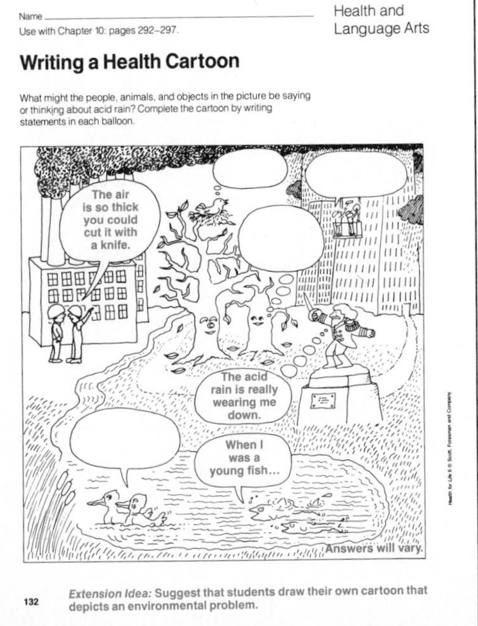

Name ____________________

Use with Chapter 10: pages 292–297.

Health and Language Arts

Writing a Health Cartoon

What might the people, animals, and objects in the picture be saying or thinking about acid rain? Complete the cartoon by writing statements in each balloon.

The air is so thick you could cut it with a knife.
The acid rain is really wearing me down.
When I was a young fish...
Answers will vary.

Extension Idea: Suggest that students draw their own cartoon that depicts an environmental problem.

132

Teaching Plan

Lesson 2 continued

2 Teach

Strategies for Pages 294 and 295

• Call on volunteers to read page 294 aloud to learn about groundwater pollution. • Discuss the causes of groundwater pollution. (waste and other substances leaking from underground pipes, storage tanks, and drums; leaks from landfills and dumps) Be sure students understand that groundwater is water that collects underground between bits of soil and rocks and in the cracks of large rock formations. Explain that the upper limit of this groundwater is called the water table. • Lead students to understand that the most dangerous sources of groundwater pollution are the billions of gallons of chemical wastes produced each year and stored in drums, buried, or left in open dumps. • Discuss some problems caused by chemical wastes. (Accept all answers students can justify.) Make it clear that the diagram shows examples of how pollution in one area can affect many other areas.

• Ask students to read page 295 to find out the dangers of air pollution.

Why Is Groundwater Pollution Dangerous?

One of the greatest dangers that faces the environment is groundwater pollution. About half the people in the United States get their drinking water from the ground. The drawing shows how wastes and other substances can leak from underground pipes and from storage tanks and drums. Notice how this pollution can spread throughout the groundwater and enter wells and streams.

Perhaps the most dangerous sources of groundwater pollution are the billions of gallons of poisonous chemical wastes produced in the United States each year. Some of these wastes are made harmless by burning them at high temperatures or changing them in other ways. Most poisonous—or toxic—wastes, however, are stored in drums and left in open dumps or buried. People in some communities have had to move because chemicals from leaking drums have contaminated the water supply.

New laws, improved storage, and clean-up efforts have helped prevent or improve some cases of groundwater pollution. However, much remains to be done to solve this problem.

What causes groundwater pollution?

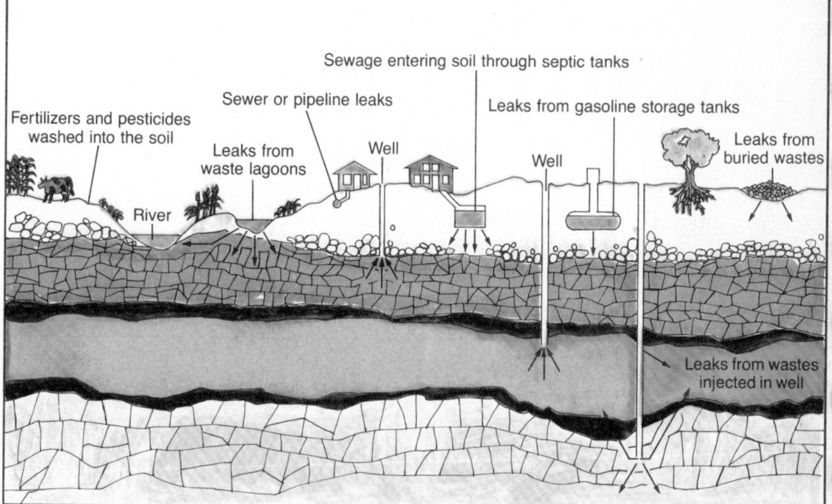

294

Teaching Options

Anecdote

During the 1960s, many experts feared Lake Erie would soon contain no fish and would be unusable for humans. But pollution control methods have reduced the pollutants entering Lake Erie by over 60 percent. Commercial fishing is making a comeback and beaches that had been closed for thirty years were reopened in the 1970s and 1980s.

Enrichment

Many weather reports on radio and television include smog alerts, ozone warnings, and other pollution information in their forecasts. Ask students to listen to such reports and use an encyclopedia to research the weather conditions that promote high levels of air pollution. (The presence of pollution warnings on forecasts varies with the area and time of year.)

Health and Science

Ask students to look in science periodicals to find out what effect scientists think air pollution might have on the earth's climate. Let students report their findings to the class.

Reteaching

Invite students to collect particles that are part of air pollution. Cover several glass slides with a thin film of petroleum jelly and suspend the slides at various locations around the school or neighborhood for 48 hours. After that time, examine the slides under a microscope. Challenge students to compare the slides and explain any differences in the amount of particles on the slides.

What Are Some Problems Caused by Air Pollution?

No matter where you live, the air is probably polluted to some amount. Most air pollution results from the burning of such materials as coal, oil, and gasoline. This burning produces waste gases and particles.

The pie graph shows that cars cause most of the air pollution in the United States. Car exhaust contains many harmful gases. One gas is **carbon monoxide.** It deprives the body of oxygen and can cause dizziness and headaches. Sunlight causes other gases in car exhaust to combine and form **smog.** You can imagine how the smog in the picture irritates the eyes and throat. Smog can also make breathing difficult, especially for babies, older people, and people with respiratory problems.

Notice the other sources of air pollution on the pie graph. Factories and power plants burn great amounts of coal and oil, producing smoke. The smoke contains harmful gases and tiny bits of coal, oil, lead, and other substances. The smoke irritates the eyes and respiratory system.

However, air pollution can be more than just irritating. In the last forty years, thousands of people have become ill or died from unusually heavy levels of air pollution. For example, in 1948 an industrial town in Pennsylvania experienced three windless days of heavy, deadly pollution. Smoke hung over the valley town, turning the sky dark gray. Twenty people died and thousands became ill. A similar incident killed four thousand people in London in 1952. These and other disasters have increased people's efforts to develop ways to reduce air pollution.

carbon monoxide (kär′bən mo nok′sīd), a colorless, odorless, and poisonous gas in the exhausts of motor vehicles.

smog (smog), pollution caused by engine exhaust gases reacting with other gases in the presence of sunlight.

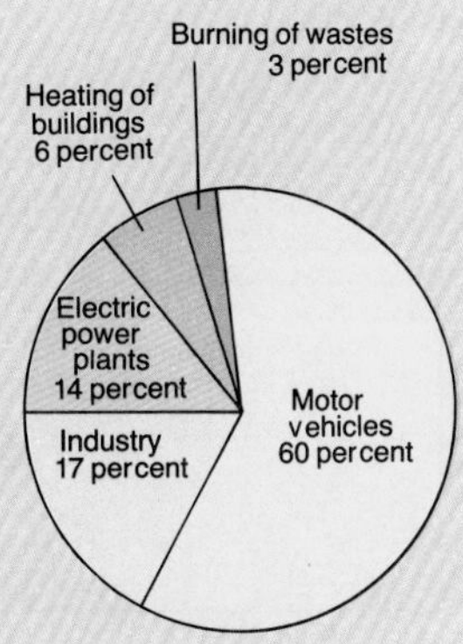

Air Pollution Sources

• Write the terms *carbon monoxide* and *smog* on the chalkboard. Call on volunteers to define the two terms. (Carbon monoxide is a poisonous gas found in engine exhaust. Smog is pollution caused by gases from engine exhaust reacting with other gases in the air in the presence of sunlight.) Point out that the smog referred to in the text is photochemical smog, common in cities with warm, dry air and a sunny climate, such as Los Angeles and Mexico City. Industrial smog is pollution caused by gases from smokestacks and chimneys reacting with moisture in the air. Particles of ash, coal, and oil are also part of industrial smog.

• Ask students to explain the problems caused by carbon monoxide and smog. (Carbon monoxide in the air deprives the body of oxygen and can cause dizziness and headaches. Smog can cause the eyes and throat to become irritated, and makes breathing difficult.)

• Encourage students to study the pie graph. Be sure students understand that cars cause the major portion of air pollution.

Overhead Transparency Master

Use this blackline master to make a labeled overhead transparency or to make an unlabeled student worksheet. This blackline master may be reproduced from the Teacher's Resource Book.

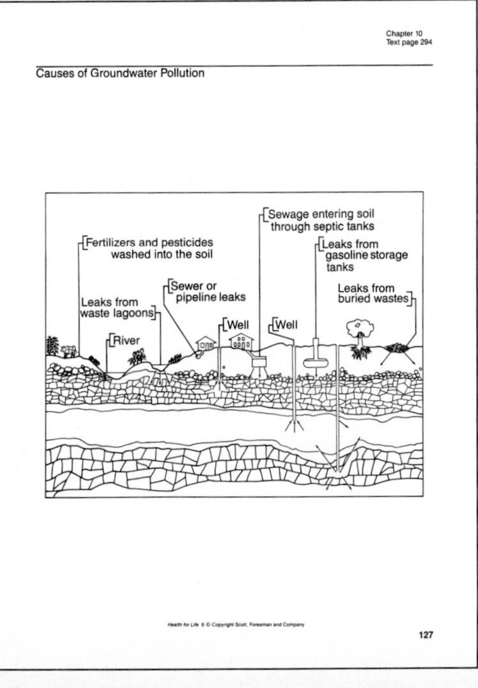
Chapter 10
Text page 294

Causes of Groundwater Pollution

127

Teaching Plan

Lesson 2 continued

2 Teach

Strategies for Pages 296 and 297

• Write the term *acid rain* on the chalkboard. Then ask the students to read page 296 to find out the effects of acid rain. • Ask what causes acid rain. (the burning of coal and oil that contains sulfur) • Discuss why acid rain is a problem. (Smoke from factories reacts with moisture in the air to produce drops of acid. Rain mixed with this acid falls to earth as acid rain and damages crops, trees, and fish.) • Be sure students understand that acid rain is thought to be only indirectly harmful to people. • Suggest that students read page 297 to learn how people are reducing air pollution. • Discuss how air pollution is being controlled. (Cars have devices that reduce the amount of carbon monoxide in automobile exhaust; factories use scrubbers which remove harmful gases and particles from smoke; aircraft have antipollution devices; people use fuels that burn cleaner, such as lead-free gas and low-sulfur coal; electrical motors are substituted for fuel-burning engines.

acid rain, rain that contains a higher than normal amount of acids. These acids are caused by certain gases released into the air.

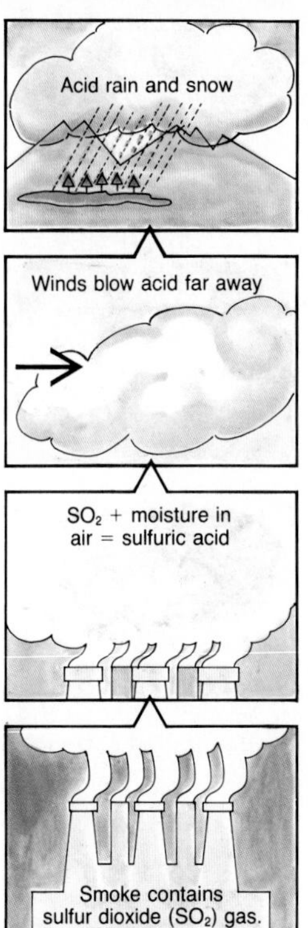

Formation of acid rain

What Are the Effects of Acid Rain?

Sometimes the solution to one problem causes another problem. For example, some power plants use extremely tall smokestacks to release smoke high enough into the air so that it does not cause air pollution for the towns nearby. While winds carry the smoke away, certain gases in the smoke react with moisture in the air to make tiny drops of acids. Raindrops mix with these acids and fall to the ground as **acid rain.**

Acid rain is caused largely by the burning of coal and oil that contain much sulfur. The drawing shows how the burning of fuels with sulfur leads to acid rain. Notice that acid rain often falls on rivers, lakes, and forests hundreds of miles from the cities or factories that caused it.

Although acid rain does not seem to hurt humans directly, it can be very harmful to crops, trees, and fish. This pollution destroys millions of dollars of crops in the United States each year. Some lakes in the northeastern United States, as well as in Norway and Sweden, are almost lifeless due to the acid rain. Some of these lakes are being restored by adding lime to the water, as shown. The lime cancels the effect of the acid. Then the lake can be restocked with fish. Many people think, however, that the best solution is to reduce the amount of air pollution that causes acid rain in the first place.

Lakes damaged by acid rain can sometimes be restored.

296

Teaching Options

Enrichment

Ask students to prepare diagrams explaining the way various pollution-control devices work. Students might describe catalytic converters and some devices attached to smokestacks, such as electrostatic precipitators, baghouse filters, cyclone separators, and scrubbers.

Health and Social Studies

Encourage interested students to use the periodical section of a library to research the public attitude toward pollution in the 1960s and 1970s.

Reteaching

Ask students to suggest ways they could help reduce air pollution.

How Are People Reducing Air Pollution?

In recent years much progress has been made in reducing some kinds of air pollution. Antipollution devices on cars have greatly reduced the amount of carbon monoxide in automobile exhaust. Aircraft also use antipollution devices. Many factories use machines, such as the ones shown to the right, that remove most of the particles from smoke before it goes up the smokestack. Other devices, called **scrubbers,** remove much harmful gas, as well as particles, from smoke. These devices are expensive, but they work.

People are reducing air pollution by using fuels that burn more cleanly. Newer cars use lead-free gasoline. These cars do not pollute the air with bits of lead. In addition, engineers are improving engines that use electricity and other energy sources instead of gasoline. Some industries use coal that contains less sulfur. Low-sulfur coal burns more cleanly than high-sulfur coal and reduces acid rain. Scientists have developed ways to remove up to 40 percent of the sulfur from coal.

Perhaps the simplest way to reduce air pollution is to cut down on the use of cars and other machines that burn fuel. Some communities encourage car pooling, in which people share rides to work. Using public transportation also cuts down on the number of cars on the road. In some large cities, cars are not allowed in the downtown areas. How does this practice reduce pollution?

Think Back • *Study on your own with Study Guide page 334.*

1. What harmful substances are found in sewage?
2. How do sewage treatment plants reduce water pollution?
3. What is one way groundwater can become polluted?
4. How does acid rain form?
5. What are some ways people are reducing air pollution?

scrubber, a device attached to a factory smokestack that removes much of the harmful gas and most of the particles from smoke.

Special machines remove most particles from smoke.

Did You Know?
Acid rain slowly eats away at rock and metal, damaging buildings and statues, including the Statue of Liberty and other famous monuments. For example, acid rain and other kinds of pollution have caused more damage to the famous Greek Parthenon in the last fifty years than all causes did in its first two thousand years.

3 Assess

Expanding Student Thinking

Ask students to describe the conditions that probably existed during the Pennsylvania and London disasters described on page 295. (Answers should show that students understand that conditions probably included heavy burning of fuel and little wind to blow the pollution away.)

Thinking Skills Students are *drawing conclusions* and *generalizing.*

Answers to Think Back

1. Harmful substances in sewage include viruses, bacteria, and poisonous chemicals.

2. A sewage treatment plant sends sewage through a series of screens, settling tanks, and chemical treatments to reduce water pollution.

3. Groundwater can become polluted from sewage, oil, toxic wastes, and other substances leaked into the environment through the sources described on page 294.

4. When coal or oil that contains sulfur is burned, certain gases in the smoke react with moisture in the air to make tiny drops of acids. Raindrops mix with these acids and fall to earth as acid rain.

5. Ways of reducing pollution involve the use of scrubbers on smokestacks, antipollution devices on cars and aircraft, lead-free gasoline, low-sulfur coal, reduced use of cars and machines, and carpooling.

Teaching Plan

Lesson 3 pages 298–299

Lesson Objective
Describe how communities can dispose of solid wastes safely. Recognize that people need to protect the environment in order to protect people's health.

Health Vocabulary
Recyclying, sanitary landfill

1 Motivate

Introducing the Lesson
Ask the students to list items that make up typical household garbage. (Answers will include such items as bottles, cans, paper, and fruit peels.) Then ask them to think of ways in which some of these items can be reused. (Students will probably suggest recycling of cans, glass, and paper.) Explain that in some cities household garbage is burned to produce electricity.

2 Teach

Strategies for Pages 298 and 299
• Suggest that students read pages 298 and 299 to learn how people can dispose of garbage more safely.

sanitary landfill, an area of land where garbage is buried in such a way as to minimize water pollution, air pollution, and the spread of disease.

recycling, changing a waste product so that it can be used again.

Glass can be recycled.

3 How Can People Dispose of Garbage Mo[re] Safely?

Disposing of garbage is a major problem for many large cities. Garbage has to go somewhere. In the past, "somewhere" was usually a street, river, or open dump on the edge of town. These methods of garbage disposal were extremely unhealthy. The garbage attracted rats and other animals that carried diseases. The trash was often burned at the dump, but this burning caused much air pollution.

Today many communities dispose of garbage in ways that pollute as little as possible. One way is by using a **sanitary landfill.** Bulldozers smash the garbage together, as shown. Then a tractor covers the garbage with a layer of dirt. The next day, another layer of garbage is compacted and covered with dirt. This process is repeated with each day's garbage. Sanitary landfills reduce some kinds of pollution, but they must be checked constantly for leaks. Some landfills leak dangerous chemicals into the soil and groundwater. Another problem with sanitary landfills is that they use up a lot of land, and many communities are running out of land for them.

Another way to deal with the garbage problem is b[y] **recycling**—changing waste products so they can be used again. The glass bottles in the picture, for example, will be separated according to their color. The glass will be crushed, melted, and made into new bottles. Paper, aluminum, and rubber are some other materials that can be recycled.

How is garbage buried at a sanitary landfill?

298

Teaching Options

Health Background

Currently about 82 percent of urban solid waste is buried in landfills, 8 pecent is burned in municipal incinerators, and 10 percent is recycled. Some municipal incinerators are called waste-to-energy plants or resource recovery plants. They have facilities for sorting recyclable materials and using the heat from incineration to produce steam, which in turn is used to heat buildings, operate machines, or run a generator to produce electricity. Noncombustible materials and ashes from the incinerator may be stored in a sanitary landfill.

Enrichment

Encourage interested students to find out more about the disposal of garbage in the community. Ask them to write or call the local health department for information.

Invite a sanitary engineer to visit the class and discuss garbage control in the community.

Health and Math

Studies have found that the average person produces 4.5 pounds (about 2 kg) of garbage each day. Ask the students how much each person produces in a week, a month, and a year. Then let them figure out how much garbage the class produces in a year.

Reteaching

Suggest that students make a chart listing the different ways to dispose of garbage. Students should include the advantages and disadvantages of each disposal method.

Some communities burn garbage in large furnaces called incinerators. Trucks empty the garbage into a huge pit, like the one shown. A crane lifts the garbage and drops it down a chute that leads to an incinerator. Many incinerators have scrubbers or other devices to remove many of the materials from the smoke.

Disposing of wastes without polluting improves the quality of life in a community. Clean water, air, and land provide what a community needs for good health.

Think Back • *Study on your own with Study Guide page 335.*

1. What are the advantages and disadvantages of using sanitary landfills to dispose of garbage?
2. How do recycling and incineration help communities deal with garbage disposal?

Did You Know?
Some hospitals and large apartment buildings in Sweden use one of the most advanced garbage-disposal systems in the world. Trash is dumped into chutes and is sucked through a vacuum-powered pipeline to a central incinerator. The heat from the burning garbage generates electricity, warms buildings, and melts ice on roads during the winter.

Some communities burn garbage in large incinerators.

299

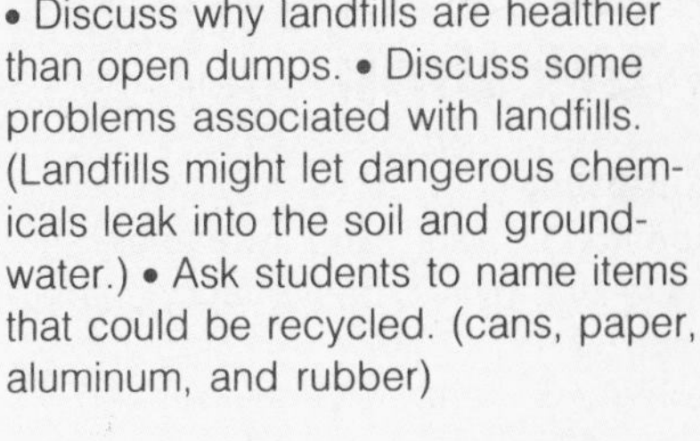

• Discuss why landfills are healthier than open dumps. • Discuss some problems associated with landfills. (Landfills might let dangerous chemicals leak into the soil and groundwater.) • Ask students to name items that could be recycled. (cans, paper, aluminum, and rubber)

Source for Did You Know?
Miller, G. Tyler, Jr. *Living in the Environment.* Wadsworth, 1985.

3 Assess

Expanding Student Thinking

Ask students to pretend they are head of the sanitation department for the community. Explain that their job is to decide how to dispose of waste. Ask them to decide which method they would use and why. (Methods might include burning in an incinerator, landfills, recycling.)

Thinking Skill Students are *making decisions.*

Answers to Think Back

1. Sanitary landfills reduce some kinds of pollution and do not attract rats and other carriers of disease. Sometimes landfills leak dangerous chemicals into soil and groundwater. They require lots of land.

2. Recycling changes waste products so they can be used again. Incinerators with scrubbers or other antipollution devices burn garbage with reduced air pollution.

Activity Plan

Health Activities Workshop pages 300–301

Materials
Activity 1 dirt, sand, two small glass jars, plastic bottle, tape, cotton, pebbles
Activity 2 encyclopedia or earth science textbook

Activity 1 Strategies
As a way of getting the filtered water cleaner, students might suggest pouring the water through the filter again, pouring it through a different filter, or letting the dirt settle out and pouring off the cleaner water. You might want to have the bottoms of the plastic bottles cut off and taped before the class begins this activity.
Thinking Skills By making a water filter and studying how it works, students are *collecting information* and *making analogies*.

Activity 2 Strategies
In the condition known as temperature inversion, a cool layer of air is trapped underneath a warm layer of air. Normally, heated air near the earth's surface expands and rises, carrying pollutants away with it. In a temperature inversion the cool layer of air near the ground cannot rise, and pollutants accumulate within this cool layer.
Thinking Skill By researching how a temperature inversion affects air pollution, students are *interpreting information.*

Activity 3 Strategies
Encourage interested students to ask the health department about the extent of rat and other pest problems in your community. Find out if rats tend to gather at such places as beaches, parks, amusement parks, or other places where littering may be heavy.
Thinking Skills By researching and reporting on methods of garbage disposal, students are *collecting information* and *communicating.*

Health Activities Workshop

Discovering How Your Community Fights Pollution

1. You can get an idea of how part of the water treatment process works by making a water filter. First, mix some dirt in a small jar of water to make the water dirty. Then, cut off the bottom of a plastic bottle and cover any sharp edges with tape. Close the narrow opening of the bottle with cotton. Next, arrange layers of pebbles and sand in the bottle, as shown. Now, hold the filter over a jar and pour the dirty water into the filter. The water will take a few minutes to go through the filter.

   Compare the dirty water with the filtered water. Remove some of the cotton and examine it. What could you do to get the filtered water cleaner? *CAUTION: Do not drink the filtered water at any time. It is still not clean enough to be safe.*

2. Use an earth science textbook or an encyclopedia to find out how a condition called a temperature inversion can affect air pollution.

3. Find out what happens to garbage after it is picked up from your home. You might find the information you need by talking with an adult at home. You could also talk with someone at the local Department of Streets and Sanitation, health department, or the company that collects your garbage. Write a report on how the garbage is disposed of and share the information with the class.

4. Talk with an older adult, such as a grandparent or family friend, about pollution problems in the past. How did pollution affect life in the past? Have different kinds of pollution increased or decreased over the years?

Looking at Careers

5. Many people use their education and skills to help fight pollution. Some **sanitary engineers,** for example, work with architects to design sewage treatment plants, water treatment plants, incineration plants, or sanitary landfills. They make sure the plant or landfill is being built properly so that it will serve its purpose safely.

300

Once the structure is built, other kinds of sanitary engineers, sometimes called operation engineers or control engineers, oversee the day-to-day operation of the plant or landfill. Like all engineers, sanitary engineers need at least four years of college education.

Find the nearest sewage or water treatment plant or incineration plant in your area. Then call or write to see if group tours are available.

For more information write to the Engineer's Council for Professional Development, 345 E. 47th St., New York, NY 10017.

6. If you enjoy the beauty of the outdoors and want others to enjoy it, you might consider a career as a **landscape architect.** These architects design outdoor open areas such as parks, community gardens, tree-lined medians along highways, and the parklike property around office buildings.

Before designing any property, a landscape architect needs to consider the purpose of the property. For example, is the space supposed to be used for playing sports, for picnicking, or for just walking through? Often a large park is supposed to provide all these and other kinds of spaces.

Keeping the purpose in mind, the architect looks at the land—its shape, the way sunlight hits it, the kind of plants on it, the makeup of the soil, and the buildings or land around it. Then the architect is ready to draw up plans. The plans might include ideas of where to plant certain trees, flowers, and shrubs; where to enlarge or make a pond; where to put sidewalks, fountains, and benches; and what materials to use.

Many colleges across the country offer four- or five-year programs for people wanting to be landscape architects.

Look around your home, school, or neighborhood for a place you think could be improved by a landscape architect. Describe the improvements you would make.

For more information write to the American Society of Landscape Architecture, Inc., 1900 M St. NW, Washington, DC 20036.

Activity 4 Strategies
Be sure students ask the adults if they think pollution problems are worse today and, if so, why. Let students share their discussions with the class. Some students might be able to record their interviews on tape and play them for the class.
Thinking Skill By interviewing someone about pollution, students are *collecting information.*

Activity 5 Strategies
When contacting the incineration or treatment facility, you might wish to make the writing of the letter a language arts activity. The entire class could help draft the letter while you write it on the chalkboard. Then a student could write the letter on paper to mail. You might wish to have a student type the letter using a computer.
Thinking Skills By contacting an incineration or treatment facility, students are *communicating* and *collecting information.*

Activity 6 Strategies
Ask students to give reasons for the changes they would make to improve the area they chose.
Thinking Skill By describing environmental improvements they would make around home, school, or the neighborhood, students are *suggesting alternatives.*

Teaching Plan

Lesson 4 pages 302-303

Lesson Objective
Explain how noise pollution affects people and how noise levels can be reduced. Recognize that communities need to protect the environment in order to protect people's health.

Health Vocabulary
Decibel

1 Motivate

Introducing the Lesson
During a time when the students are working quietly, clap your hands or make some other sudden noise. Ask the students to describe their reactions. Explain that many people react to loud noises, even expected ones, as if they were in danger.

2 Teach

Strategies for Pages 302 and 303
• Ask students to read pages 302 and 303 to learn how a community reduces noise. • Ask how the jet in the picture is polluting the environment. (The jet produces harmful noise and fumes.)

4 How Does a Community Reduce Noise?

How is the jet in the picture polluting the environment? Fumes from the engines certainly pollute the air. The engines of this jet cause another harmful or undesirable change in the environment—noise.

Noise pollution is nothing new. In the 1700s Benjamin Franklin moved across Philadelphia to escape the noise of a nearby market. In 1906 a woman led a campaign to ban tugboat whistles at night in the New York harbor. Today, however, noise pollution is a much more serious problem. Machines—from hair dryers to jets—cause noise that can have harmful effects on people's health.

Too much noise can be annoying and interrupt activities. It makes some people nervous or tired. Continuous loud noise narrows blood vessels, making the heart work harder. Blood pressure might increase. In addition, loud noise over a period of time causes hearing loss. About twenty million people in the United States suffer some permanent hearing loss because of too much noise in their environment. Such hearing loss often comes from loud, continuous noise at factories and other work places. Increasingly common causes of hearing loss include the use of stereo headphones and the loud, continuous sounds from radios held too close to the ear.

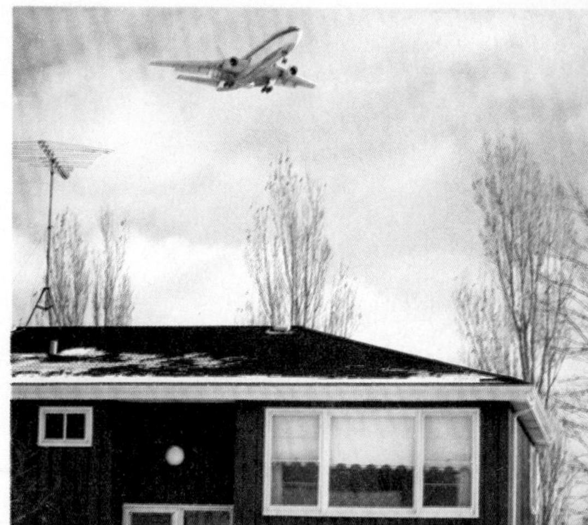

How is the jet polluting the environment?

302

Teaching Options

Health Background

Noise is measured in units called *decibels*. The decibel scale is a logarithmic scale. Each increase of ten decibels means a tenfold increase in the strength of a sound. A decibel rise from thirty to sixty, for example, represents a thousandfold increase in loudness. Besides loudness, the decibel chart on page 303 takes into consideration the pitch of sounds. High-pitched sounds are more annoying than low-pitched sounds. The amount of hearing injury depends on exposure time and individual susceptibility, as well as loudness and pitch.

Enrichment

Suggest that interested students find out how noise pollution in the home can be reduced by the use of special building materials and furnishings that absorb sound. Then ask students to draw a picture of a room that is fairly soundproof. Let students explain the soundproofing features they have included in their drawing.

Health and Science

Ask students to find out what makes sounds (vibrations) and how loud sounds differ from soft sounds (difference in amplitude of vibrations).

Reteaching

Ask students to predict the sound levels of various areas of the school. Then ask an environmental sanitarian from the health department to walk through various areas of the school to measure noise. Use the results to pinpoint areas where noise reaches harmful levels and suggest ways such noise can be reduced.

Special Education

Encourage hearing-impaired students to explain how vibrations help them detect sounds.

The chart shows some of the noise levels that people experience. Notice that noise is measured in units called **decibels.** Over a period of time, noise levels of eighty decibels or more can cause ear damage. Think about the noises that you experience. Compare them to the examples in the chart.

Since the early 1970s, laws have led to the design of quieter motors and engines. Trucks, airplanes, factories, and some appliances are less noisy than they once were. Subway trains in some cities use rubberized wheels. These wheels do not screech as steel wheels do. In Europe, construction workers sometimes work inside small sheds or tents to reduce noise for the community.

The picture shows one way people protect themselves from noise pollution in a noisy environment. What other kinds of workers might wear headsets to shield out noise?

decibel (des′ə bəl), a unit for measuring the loudness of sound.

Did You Know?
Studies have shown that people who live in quiet places for a long time generally have better hearing than those who live in noisy places.

Some workers have to protect their hearing.

Think Back • *Study on your own with Study Guide page 335.*

1. How does noise pollution affect people in a community?
2. What are some sources of noise that can be unhealthy?
3. How can noise pollution be reduced?

Decibels	Source	Effect on hearing
150	Jet take-off less than 100 feet away	Possible eardrum rupture
140	Shotgun blast, aircraft carrier deck	
130 Painful	Jet take-off 300 feet away, earphone at loud level	
120	Firecrackers, loud thunder, siren nearby	
110 Uncomfortable	Radio held close to ear, steel mill, car horn at 3 feet	
100	Subway train, power lawn mower, jackhammer	Permanent hearing damage (8 hours of continuous exposure)
90 Loud	Heavy city traffic, food blender	Temporary hearing damage
80	Garbage disposal, freight train 60 feet away	Possible temporary hearing damage
70 Annoying	Automobile at 50 mph 50 feet away, party	
60	Typewriter, window air conditioner	
50 Quiet	Singing birds, normal conversation	
40	Library, refrigerator, soft background music	
30	Dripping faucet, rural area at night	
20 Very quiet	Light rainfall, rustling leaves, whisper	
10 Just able to be heard	Breathing	

• Discuss how too much noise affects a person. • Suggest that students look at the chart on page 303 to find out more about decibels and to learn which noises pose a threat to hearing. Be sure students understand that a decibel is a unit for measuring the loudness of sound. • Discuss various noise levels.

3 Assess

Expanding Student Thinking

Let students list the machines in their homes that did not exist one hundred year ago. Then ask students how their lists help explain why noise pollution is a more serious problem today than it was in the past. (Many more machines that produce noise exist today.)

Thinking Skills Students are *classifying* and *drawing conclusions.*

Answers to Think Back

1. Noise pollution can make people nervous and tired, constrict the blood vessels, make the heart work harder, cause high blood pressure, and cause hearing loss.

2. Unhealthy sources of noise include jet take offs, loud music, sirens, power tools, and heavy city traffic.

3. Noise pollution can be reduced by designing quieter engines and motors, using rubber wheels on some trains, shielding the community from construction noises, and lowering the volume on TVs and stereos.

Teaching Plan

Lesson 5 pages 304-307

Lesson Objective
List and describe some recreational facilities and activities that a community provides for its members and explain how they meet the health needs of people.

1 Motivate

Introducing the Lesson
Help students to prepare a list of recreational facilities and community activities in your area. Discuss which facilities and activities the students like best and why. Ask students which activities they like to do during their free time that involve the use of a community area or facility.

5 What Recreational Opportunities Does a Community Provide?

In the mid-1850s the poet William Cullen Bryant was concerned about the rapid growth of New York City. He feared that buildings and streets would soon replace all the fields and wooded areas on Manhattan Island. Bryant called for ". . . a range of parks and public gardens along the central part of the island . . . for the refreshment and recreation of the citizens. . . " A few years later, the city established one of the largest city parks in the world—Central Park.

Communities provide parks of all kinds. Some, like Central Park shown here, have places where people can play sports, row a boat, have a picnic, or stroll along paths. All these activities are forms of recreation. Other forms of recreation include attending a concert, visiting a zoo, drawing, and other activities you might enjoy in your spare time. Recreation gives you a chance to relax, exercise, and relieve stress. Some amount of recreation is important for good mental and physical health. A community can provide places for all kinds of recreation.

Central Park—an important recreational area for New York

Teaching Options

Health Background
Recreational areas and opportunities are important to a community's mental, social, and physical health. Not only are they often aesthetically pleasing, but they offer places for social interaction and provide facilities and areas that encourage physical fitness activities.

Enrichment
If possible, arrange a trip to an aquarium, planetarium, or other local cultural center. Ask the center to provide a guide who can explain the kind of activities provided and tell how the center is funded.

Ask interested students to find out why Frederick Law Olmstead was an important person in the development of recreational areas. (Olmstead, along with Calvert Vaux, designed New York City's Central Park. He designed parks in New York, as well as in Montreal, Philadelphia, Detroit, Chicago, and other cities. He also worked to preserve the area that is now Yosemite National Park in California.)

Reteaching
Ask each student to make a poster promoting the mental, social, and physical health benefits of a recreational facility in their community. Posters might be displayed in school hallways so students in other classes can see them.

Health and Language Arts
Encourage students to write a paragraph telling which of the following recreational facilities they would most like to visit: a science and technology museum, an art museum, an historical museum, a planetarium, or an aquarium. Encourage them to first read about the facility they have chosen and list what exhibits they would most like to see.

Many people enjoy visiting a museum to relax, have fun, and learn about the world around them. Museums are exciting and fascinating places to explore. The museum in the picture has a collection of famous aircraft and spacecraft. Here you can see these machines and learn about the people who flew them. You might find some similar items at a museum of science and technology, where you can discover the wonders and uses of science through displays and activities. Art museums contain masterpieces from famous artists all over the world. Museums of natural history let you explore ancient civilizations or look at dinosaur fossils. Historical museums offer glimpses of your community's past.

Other recreational facilities include planetariums and aquariums. Notice the round roof of the planetarium in the picture. Inside, the ceiling becomes a night sky, showing you images of stars and planets. You can take an imaginary journey through space.

An aquarium takes you on a different journey—to the depths of streams, lakes, and oceans. At the aquarium shown, visitors can observe the rich, colorful variety of life that inhabits the waters of the world. Which of these facilities have you visited?

Planetarium

Aquarium

Museums are exciting places to explore.

2 Teach

Strategies for Pages 304 and 305

• Ask students to read pages 304 and 305 to learn some of the recreational areas and opportunities a community provides. • Ask why recreation is important. (Recreation gives people a chance to relax, exercise, and reduce stress.) • Discuss various kinds of recreational activities. (parks, zoos, museums, art galleries, planetariums, and acquariums) • Be sure to point out any museums, art galleries, or cultural activities that might be of interest to your students. Explain that many parks offer opportunities for physical activities such as boating, camping, hiking, and swimming.

• Point out that some state and national parks are open in winter and provide an opportunity for people to participate in winter activities such as sledding, skiing, and ice skating.

• Discuss the importance of year-round exercise for good health.

• Encourage students to visit and explore local recreational areas they are not already familiar with.

Teaching Plan

Lesson 5 continued

2 Teach

Strategies for Pages 306 and 307

• Encourage students to read pages 306 and 307 to learn about outdoor facilities provided by communities. • Ask students who have visited a nature center to describe their experiences there. • Discuss how nature centers provide good health. (Nature centers provide an opportunity to be outdoors, relax, and get exercise. They also provide enjoyable, educational experiences.) • Call on a volunteer to define an arboretum. (a recreational area featuring various types of trees and shrubs) • Discuss with students why communities maintain arboretums. (provide recreation and an opportunity to learn more about trees and nature) • Let students identify other community recreational areas and activities. (playgrounds, beaches, swimming pools, sports, exercise classes, art classes, camping, and field trips)

On Your Own
Parks and forested areas provide places for recreation. Write a paragraph explaining why else these areas are important to a community.

What Outdoor Areas Do Communities Provide?

Most communities—whether they be towns, cities, or counties—have set aside large areas of land where people can enjoy nature. Such areas might be called parks, woods, groves, or forest preserves. These places usually have picnic facilities as well as hiking and biking trails.

Many cities and towns have nature centers located nearby. Nature centers give people the opportunity to learn about wildlife while enjoying the outdoors. Wildlife managers talk to visitors about the kinds of animals they might see on the trails.

Another kind of outdoor recreational area is an arboretum. An arboretum is actually a living tree museum. The arboretum in the picture is beautifully landscaped with trees from all over the world. Each kind of tree is identified so that visitors can learn more about nature as they walk along the paths.

Teaching Options

Anecdote

More than a third of the 294 parks, seashores, lakeshores, and scenic riverways managed by the National Park Sevice are surrounded by or adjacent to urban areas, making many recreational areas easily accessible to much of the population. (*Urban Open Spaces*, Smithsonian Institution, Rizzoli International Publications, 1981.)

Enrichment

Form a volunteer group to help clean up litter in a local park. Arrange in advance for supervision and permission from park authorities.

Health and Social Studies

Ask students to write a report on one of the national parks. Reports should tell where the park is located, when it was established, and the kinds of facilities and recreational activities offered. Students might also like to include maps, pictures, or drawings of the park in their report.

Reteaching

Have students write a letter to a community recreation facility such as the YMCA or a museum. The letter should thank the agency for the services it provides and tell why it helps the community stay healthy.

Special Education

Encourage orthopedically handicapped students to tell the class what special accommodations (ramps, wider doors, special parking places) have been provided in order to make access to community recreational facilities easier for people in wheelchairs. If no special accommodations have been provided, students might point out specific areas that could be improved.

What Other Recreational Opportunities Do Communities Offer?

Playgrounds, beaches, swimming pools, and gymnasiums are a few other places of recreation your community might have. In addition, many organizations in your community probably offer a wide range of activities. The Girl Scouts, Boy Scouts, YWCA, YMCA, local park districts, and other community organizations have programs that include sports, exercise classes, art classes, camping, field trips, and many other activities.

Your community might provide many opportunities for you and others to relax, explore, learn, and have fun. Recreation is an important part of good health.

Think Back • *Study on your own with Study Guide page 335.*

1. How is recreation important to good health?
2. What are some opportunities for recreation that communities might provide?
3. What would be found in a planetarium? in an aquarium? in an arboretum?

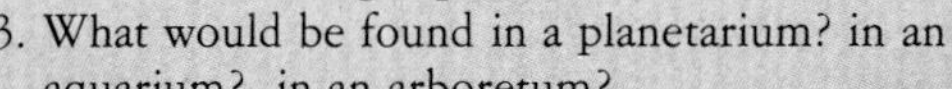

Using On Your Own

Answers may stress the conservation aspects of these areas, such as the homes they provide for wildlife. Answers might also point to the aesthetic value of such places. Accept other reasonable answers.

Thinking Skills Students are *generalizing* and *communicating*.

3 Assess

Expanding Student Thinking

Suggest that students look at a community map and decide if the community needs more recreational areas. If so, let the students suggest what kind of recreational areas they would provide and where they would put them.

Thinking Skills Students are *interpreting information* and *making decisions*.

Answers to Think Back

1. Recreation lets a person relax, exercise, and relieve stress.

2. Answers might include parks, museums, planetariums, aquariums, arboretums, nature centers, gymnasiums, and opportunities for sports, exercise classes, art classes, and camping.

3. A planetarium displays images of stars and planets. An aquarium shows the variety of life that inhabits streams, lakes, and oceans. An arboretum grows various trees and shrubs for study and recreation.

Teaching Plan

Lesson 6 pages 308–309

Lesson Objective
List several ways an individual can help improve the environment and health of a community.

1 Motivate

Introducing the Lesson
Ask the students to think about types of pollution they observe as they walk or ride to and from school. Encourage them to recall specific examples, such as litter and factory smoke.

2 Teach

Strategies for Pages 308 and 309
• Call on volunteers to read pages 308 and 309 aloud. • Discuss how the students can fight pollution in the community. (by not littering; by recycling glass, paper, and other materials; by using cars less often; by turning down radios, TV, and stereos to reduce noise) • Ask students why they think people litter. (Accept any answers students can explain.) List the reasons on the chalkboard and call on volunteers to suggest ways to improve the littering problem. (set an example for others, remind family and friends not to litter, put up signs)

Did You Know?
Some grocery stores have recycling machines, such as the one shown. They operate like vending machines in reverse. A person puts empty aluminum cans in the machine, and money for the cans comes out.

Everybody can help fight pollution.

6 How Can You Help Keep Your Community Healthy?

So far, you have read about how people in the community help improve your health. You can help improve the community's health too.

One of the best ways to help your community is to fight pollution. Notice the litter in the picture. This pollution was not caused by car exhaust or factory sewage. It was caused by individuals who did not bother to use the trash cans. Such land pollution makes a community unhealthy and unsightly. Try not to litter. Even gum wrappers pollute the landscape. Parks and sidewalks often have trash cans. Use them. If a trash can is not nearby, save the trash until you can throw it away properly.

Recycling helps reduce the amount of garbage your community must deal with. Many communities have recycling centers where aluminum, paper, glass, and other materials are collected. The materials are then made into new products. Recycling makes a lot of sense. It saves much of the energy, money, and natural resources that would have gone into making a totally new product. Recycling also reduces some of the air, water, and noise pollution that would have resulted from making a new product.

308

Teaching Options

Health Background

Recycling is an important way that students and adults alike can improve community health. Many people dispose of recyclable materials in separate containers. For example, one bag might be just for paper, another for glass, and another for metals. This separated waste can then be brought to recycling centers. More than 250 cities in the United States provide curbside pickup for separated wastes that are then brought to recycling centers.

Enrichment
If possible, arrange for a recycling day so that members of the community can bring paper or aluminum cans to a site at the school. Help students take the collection to a recycling center.

Health and Language Arts
Read several editorials from the local newspaper to the class. Explain that editorials attempt to persuade people to accept the writer's opinion. Ask students to write an editorial about a community health problem. Make sure they understand that they should express an opinion about the problem and use facts to try to persuade others to accept their opinion.

Reteaching
Let students list various kinds of pollution and things they can do to reduce each kind.

People can further reduce air pollution by using cars less often. Think about the times you asked someone to drive you somewhere. Could you have walked or ridden a bicycle instead?

You can help reduce noise pollution by lowering the volume of radios, televisions, and record players. Loud music from radios outdoors can be especially annoying to others in the community.

A problem cannot be solved unless people know the problem exists. Make an effort to find out about local health problems by reading newspapers and listening to newscasts. What health problem is this girl reading about?

All of these suggestions show how your actions can affect the health of others. Perhaps you can think of other ways you could help keep your community healthy. You are an important part of your community. Try to make it as healthy and pleasant a place as possible.

Think Back • *Study on your own with Study Guide page 335.*

1. How can people help keep their community healthy?
2. What are the advantages of recycling certain materials instead of throwing them away?

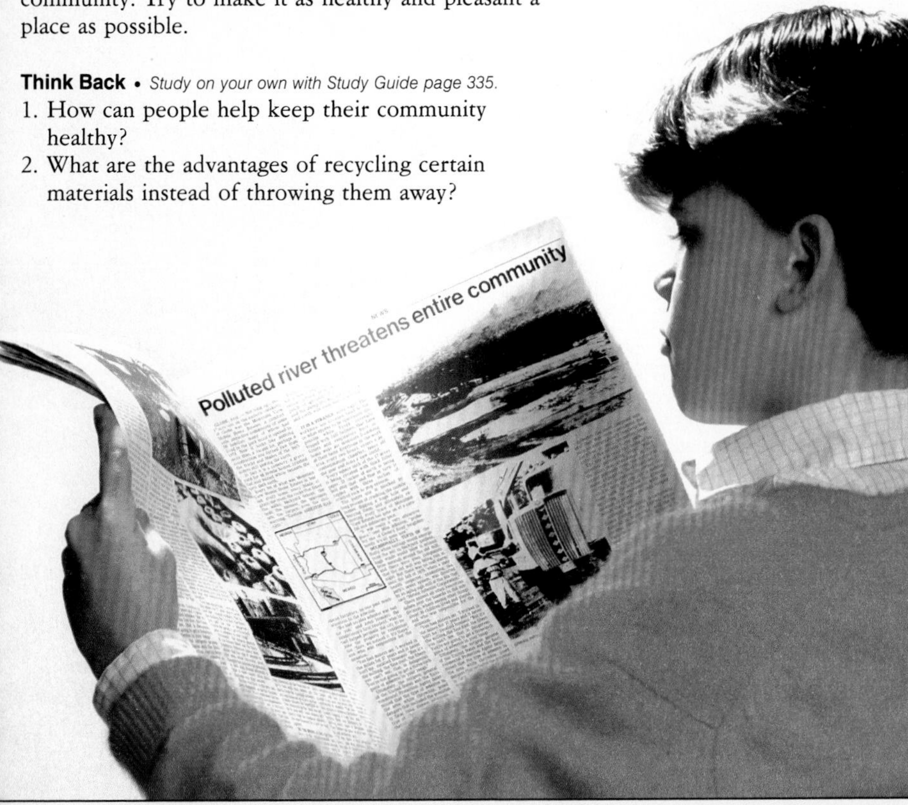
Polluted river threatens entire community

Learning about health problems is the first step to solving them.

• Ask why recycling is healthy for a community. (Recycling reduces the amount of garbage and saves energy, money, and natural resources.) Suggest that students look at the picture and tell what health problem the girl is reading about. • Discuss the importance of keeping informed of health problems in the community. (A problem cannot be solved unless people know it exists.)

3 Assess

Expanding Student Thinking

Discuss safety slogans with the class. Such slogans might include *Only you can prevent forest fires, Buckle up for safety,* or *The life you save may be your own.* Then encourage students to write their own slogans that will help discourage pollution. (Accept all reasonable slogans that indicate that people cause pollution.)

Thinking Skill By writing a slogan that helps discourage pollution, students are *communicating* and *suggesting alternatives.*

Answers to Think Back

1. People can help keep their community healthy by not polluting the air, water, or land; by reducing noise pollution; and by becoming informed about health problems.

2. Recycling reduces pollution and saves energy, money, and natural resources.

Teaching Plan

Health Focus page 310

Discussion

Besides planting the community garden, people have beautified the neighborhood by planting flowers in window boxes and planters. Discuss with students other ways people can beautify their neighborhood. (planting individual gardens, planting trees, training vines along a fence, picking up litter, and painting houses and fences) Discuss ways, other than beautification, that people can improve their feelings about their neighborhood. (cooperating in crime watches; assisting in general clean-ups; working to improve maintenance of parks and other public areas)

Answers to Talk About It

1. The neighborhood beautified an empty lot by planting a community garden.
Thinking Skill Students are *recalling information.*
2. Fixing up an empty lot keeps the empty lot from becoming an unsafe place and makes it more attractive. Improving the lot can make it an enjoyable meeting place and a source of community pride.
Thinking Skill Students are *generalizing.*

Health Focus

A Community Grows a Paradise

In any city or town, a building might be torn down from time to time. Often the resulting empty lot becomes a temporary parking lot or junkyard. It also might become an unsafe place for children to play.

Empty lots, however, do not need to become eyesores. In fact, in one neighborhood in Chicago, community members have turned an empty lot into a place of enchantment.

After a corner building was torn down, some people got permission to make a garden that everyone in the community could enjoy. They cleared the land of rubble and garbage, put up a fence, and began to plan the garden. Part of their garden was to be planted with flowers. People could sit on benches in this part of the garden and talk, rest, and just enjoy their surroundings. The other part of the garden was used to grow vegetables. Here, members of the community could grow their own food.

With the plans set, the gardeners of the neighborhood got to work. They laid down woodchip paths, prepared the soil, planted flowers, shrubs, and vegetables, and painted a sign. People in the neighborhood and local businesses donated plants and materials. Adults and children worked together to keep the garden growing.

The garden was so beautiful, the community named it "El Paraiso," which means The Paradise. People in this Chicago neighborhood are proud of their planted paradise.

Talk About It

1. What is included in "El Paraiso?"
2. What are some community benefits of fixing up empty lots?

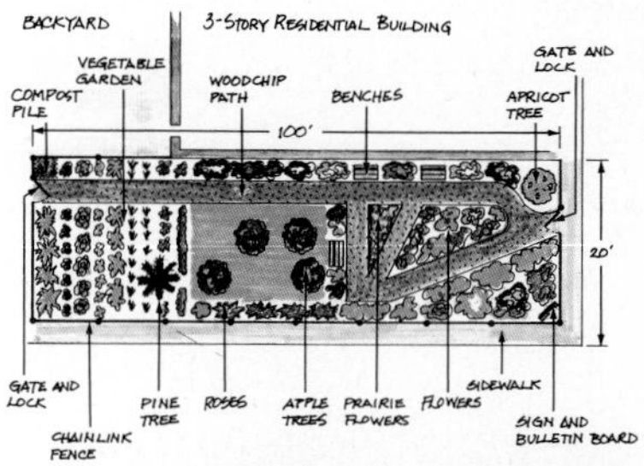

310

Teaching Options

Vocabulary

Use this worksheet for practice in reviewing chapter vocabulary words. This master may be reproduced from the Teacher's Resource Book and is located on page 38 of the Student's Workbook. Use with Chapter 10: pages 284–313.

Name ______________________ Vocabulary
Use with Chapter 10: pages 284–313.

Community Health Acrostic

Part I. Write sentences that contain the words below. Use the letters in OUR COMMUNITY as starters. The first sentence has been done for you.

Acid rain	Carbon monoxide	Decibel	Environment
Epidemiologist	Pollution	Recreation	Recycling
Sanitarian	Sanitary landfill	Scrubber	Smog

1. **O**ld bottles can be used again after they go to the **recycling** center.
2. **U**______
3. **R**______
4. **C**______
5. **O**______
6. **M**______
7. **M**______
8. **U**______
9. **N** Answers might include:
10. **I**n sanitary landfills, garbage is buried so it causes little harm.
11. **T**he living and nonliving things that affect you are your environment.
12. **Y**______

Part II. On the lines below describe three ways you can reduce pollution in and around your school.

Answers might include: not littering, speaking quietly, and putting books and games away.

RECYCLING CENTER

130 *Extension Idea:* Suggest that students use the vocabulary words to make their own crossword puzzles.

Improving Your Home Environment

In this chapter, you have learned about different kinds of pollution and how you can reduce pollution in your community. Below are some additional ways to keep your home environment as healthy and pleasant as possible.

Cooperate with members of your family to reduce noise pollution at home. For example, suppose someone is watching television in the living room and it is interfering with the music from your radio in the bedroom. Instead of turning up the volume on the radio, ask the person to turn down the volume on the television. Look for other sources of noise at home. Talk with your family about ways to reduce the noise.

The family members shown here are working together to improve their home's appearance. Take a look around the outside of your home and decide how you could improve it. Every day pick up litter that might have blown near your home. Encourage the rest of your family to do the same.

Reading at Home

The Hospital Book by James Howe. Crown, 1981. Learn more about what happens in the various parts of a hospital.

Safeguarding the Land by Gloria Skurznski. Harcourt, 1981. Read about careers in public land management, such as ranger and conservationist.

Health at Home
page 311

Strategies

Ask students to describe how the family in the picture is working together to improve their environment at home. Then ask the students to read the page. Discuss ways they could encourage their families to reduce noise and other pollution around the home. (Answers might include washing windows, keeping the yard free of litter, using the car less, and disposing of garbage properly.) Help the students make a one-week diary with a page devoted to each day. Some students might wish to decorate the diary cover. Encourage the students to use the diary to record the activities their families performed to improve their home environments. Activities can be major projects, such as cleaning the attic or yard, or small ones, such as turning down the volume on the TV or radio.

More Reading Home

The Hospital Book (Grades 4–6)

Safeguarding the Land (Grades 4–8)

Pringle, Laurence. *Water: The Next Great Resource Battle.* Macmillan, 1982. Explains the importance of water as a resource, and tells how water is wasted or becomes unfit to use. (Grades 6–8)

Study and Review

Use this worksheet for practice in studying and reviewing the water treatment process. This master may be reproduced from the Teacher's Resource Book and is located on page 39 of the Student's Workbook. Use with Chapter 10: pages 284–313.

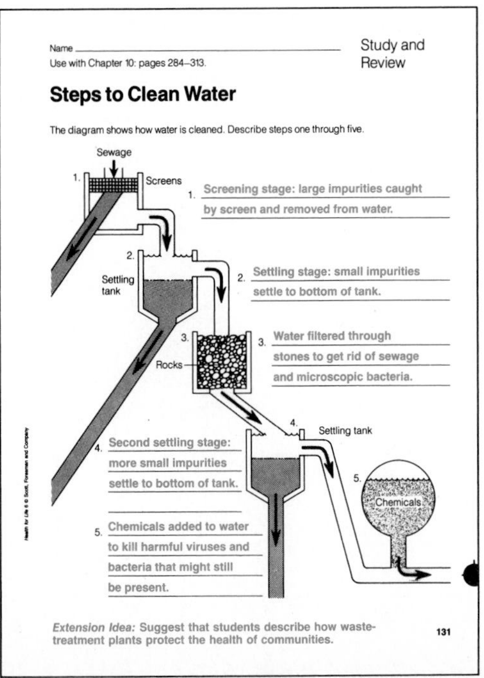

Name ____________ Study and Review

Use with Chapter 10: pages 284–313.

Steps to Clean Water

The diagram shows how water is cleaned. Describe steps one through five.

1. Screening stage: large impurities caught by screen and removed from water.
2. Settling stage: small impurities settle to bottom of tank.
3. Water filtered through stones to get rid of sewage and microscopic bacteria.
4. Second settling stage: more small impurities settle to bottom of tank.
5. Chemicals added to water to kill harmful viruses and bacteria that might still be present.

Extension Idea: Suggest that students describe how waste-treatment plants protect the health of communities.

131

Review Plan

Chapter 10 Review

pages 312–313

Answers to Reviewing Lesson Objectives

Use this section for guided study or for oral review. Objective numbers match lesson numbers.

1. Health departments make inspections, inform the public about health problems, and run clinics and treatment centers. Health workers in hospitals work to prevent and treat disease. Health volunteers help patients with cleaning, cooking, and shopping, and provide handicapped people with transportation.

2. Causes of water and air pollution include industrial wastes, sewage, car exhaust, and smoke from power plants. Water and sewage treatment plants reduce water pollution. Air pollution is reduced through the use of anti-pollution devices, lead-free gasoline, low-sulfur coal, machines that require less fuel, carpooling, and public transportation.

3. Communities can dispose of solid wastes by using sanitary landfills, by recycling, and by burning garbage in furnaces equipped with antipollution devices.

4. Noise pollution can make people nervous and tired, affect the blood vessels and heart rate, and cause high blood pressure, and hearing loss. Noise pollution can be reduced by designing quieter engines and motors; by shielding the community from loud noises; and by encouraging people to lower the volume on TVs and stereos.

5. Communities might provide parks, museums, nature centers, arboretums, cultural activities, swimming pools, and gymnasiums. These help people to relax, exercise, and relieve stress.

6. Individuals can help improve the environment and health of the community by not polluting the air, water, or land; by reducing noise pollution; and by being informed about community health problems.

Answers to Checking Health Vocabulary

Use the vocabulary check as a review or as a test.

1. h	**4.** d	**7.** g	**10.** k
2. i	**5.** j	**8.** b	**11.** a
3. c	**6.** f	**9.** e	

Chapter 10 Review

For further review, use
Study Guide pages
334-335
Practice skills for life
for Chapter 10 on pages
365-367
SKILLS FOR LIFE

Reviewing Lesson Objectives

1. Describe how health departments, hospitals, and volunteers each contribute to meet the needs of the community. (pages 286–291)
2. State some causes of water pollution and air pollution. Describe how communities reduce water and air pollution. (pages 292–297)
3. Describe how communities can dispose of solid wastes more safely. (pages 298–299)
4. Explain how noise pollution affects the people in a community. Describe how noise levels can be reduced. (pages 302–303)
5. List and describe some recreational facilities and activities that a community provides for its members and explain how they meet the health needs of people. (pages 304–307)
6. List several ways an individual can help improve the environment and health of a community. (pages 308–309)

Checking Health Vocabulary

Number your paper from 1–11. Match each definition in Column I with the correct word or words in Column II.

Column I

1. a person who works to ensure the quality of food, water, and air for the public health
2. an area of land where garbage is buried in such a way as to minimize pollution
3. a unit for measuring the loudness of sound
4. all the living and nonliving surroundings that affect living things
5. a device attached to factory smokestacks that removes harmful gases and particles from smoke
6. a change in the environment that is harmful or undesirable to living things
7. changing a waste product so that it can be used again
8. a colorless, odorless, and poisonous gas that is part of motor vehicle exhaust
9. a physician or research scientist who studies the occurrence and causes of disease
10. pollution caused by engine exhaust gases reacting with other gases in the presence of sunlight
11. a kind of pollution caused when certain gases mix with moisture in the air

Column II

a. acid rain
b. carbon monoxide
c. decibel
d. environment
e. epidemiologist
f. pollution
g. recycling
h. sanitarian
i. sanitary landfill
j. scrubber
k. smog

Chapter 10 Tests Use Test A or Test B to assess students' mastery of the health concepts in Chapter 10. These tests are located on pages 81–88 in the Test Book.

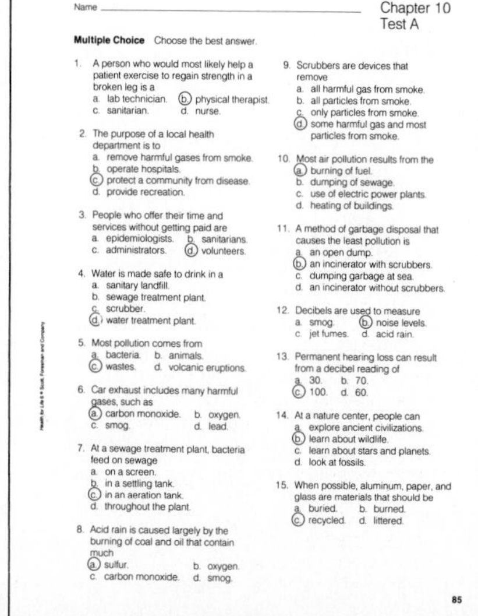
Name ____________ Chapter 10 Test A

Multiple Choice Choose the best answer.

1. A person who would most likely help a patient exercise to regain strength in a broken leg is a
   a. lab technician. (b.) physical therapist. c. sanitarian. d. nurse.
2. The purpose of a local health department is to
   a. remove harmful gases from smoke. b. operate hospitals. (c.) protect a community from disease. d. provide recreation.
3. People who offer their time and services without getting paid are
   a. epidemiologists. b. sanitarians. c. administrators. (d.) volunteers.
4. Water is made safe to drink in a
   a. sanitary landfill. b. sewage treatment plant. c. scrubber. (d.) water treatment plant.
5. Most pollution comes from
   a. bacteria. b. animals. (c.) wastes. d. volcanic eruptions.
6. Car exhaust includes many harmful gases, such as
   (a.) carbon monoxide. b. oxygen. c. smog. d. lead.
7. At a sewage treatment plant, bacteria feed on sewage
   a. on a screen. b. in a settling tank. (c.) in an aeration tank. d. throughout the plant.
8. Acid rain is caused largely by the burning of coal and oil that contain much
   (a.) sulfur. b. oxygen. c. carbon monoxide. d. smog.
9. Scrubbers are devices that remove
   a. all harmful gas from smoke. b. all particles from smoke. c. only particles from smoke. (d.) some harmful gas and most particles from smoke.
10. Most air pollution results from the
   (a.) burning of fuel. b. dumping of sewage. c. use of electric power plants. d. heating of buildings.
11. A method of garbage disposal that causes the least pollution is
   a. an open dump. (b.) an incinerator with scrubbers. c. dumping garbage at sea. d. an incinerator without scrubbers.
12. Decibels are used to measure
   a. smog. (b.) noise levels. c. jet fumes. d. acid rain.
13. Permanent hearing loss can result from a decibel reading of
   a. 30. b. 70. (c.) 100. d. 60.
14. At a nature center, people can
   a. explore ancient civilizations. (b.) learn about wildlife. c. learn about stars and planets. d. look at fossils.
15. When possible, aluminum, paper, and glass are materials that should be
   a. buried. b. burned. (c.) recycled. d. littered.

85

Name ____________ Chapter 10 Test A

Short Answer Match each meaning in Column I with the correct word or words in Column II. Write the correct letter on the blank.

Column I

b 16. a doctor who studies the spread of communicable disease
a 17. a person who works to ensure the safe quality of food, water, or air for the public health
d 18. the living and nonliving surroundings that affect living things
e 19. a device attached to factory smokestacks that removes harmful gases and particles from smoke
c 20. the changing of a product or resource so that it can be used again

Column II

a. sanitarian
b. epidemiologist
c. recycling
d. environment
e. scrubber

Short Essay Write your answers in complete sentences.

21. Several people became ill after eating a meal at a particular restaurant. What steps might the community take in response?
Answers might include: temporarily closing the restaurant, inspecting food and water at the restaurant, sending food or water samples to a lab to determine the cause of the illness, treating the ill people at clinics and hospitals, conferring with the restaurant owners to correct the problem and make sure it doesn't happen again.

22. Suppose a company is building a large factory along a river or lake in your community. What would you want the company to do to control pollution from the factory?
Answers should refer to water pollution controls, such as the use of sewage treatment; the use of anti-air pollution devices such as scrubbers; and noise pollution controls.

86

Reviewing Health Ideas

Number your paper from 1–15. Next to each number write the missing word or words that complete the sentence.

1. A ____ inspects restaurants and other places to make sure food is safe to eat.
2. The medicines that people use in a hospital are prepared by ____.
3. Most pollution comes from ____ that people add to the environment.
4. Water is made safe to drink at a ____ treatment plant.
5. Chlorine is added to sewage or drinking water to kill harmful ____.
6. In some places, toxic wastes have leaked into the ground and contaminated the ____.
7. Most air pollution results from the ____ of coal, oil, and gasoline.
8. Carbon monoxide, which is part of car exhaust, deprives the body of ____.
9. Some gases in factory smoke react with moisture in the air to make ____ rain.
10. Scrubbers remove much of the harmful gas and many of the ____ from smoke.
11. Many factories reduce air pollution by using coal that contains less ____.
12. Glass, paper, aluminum, and rubber are materials that can be ____ and used again.
13. Loud continuous noise narrows blood ____.
14. An arboretum is a living ____ museum.
15. A person must know about a health problem before helping to ____ that problem.

Understanding Health Ideas

Number your paper from 16–25. Next to each number write the word or words that best answer the question.

16. What is the purpose of a recovery room in a hospital?
17. What kind of information do local health departments keep on record?
18. What might sewage contain?
19. What are settling tanks used for at sewage and water treatment plants?
20. What is one source of groundwater pollution?
21. What is one effect of acid rain?
22. How is garbage disposed of at a sanitary landfill?
23. What is one source of noise that can damage hearing permanently?
24. What could be seen at a museum of natural history?
25. What is one way a person can improve the health of the community?

Thinking Critically

Write the answers on your paper. Use complete sentences.

1. Describe an example of a community health problem in which epidemiologists, public health nurses, and sanitarians help solve the problem.
2. Suppose a company wants to build a large factory in your community. What questions would you ask the company before they build the factory?
3. How could air pollution or water pollution in one part of the country affect people in other parts of the country?

Cooperative Learning Use the STAD Format described on page T24 to have four- to five-member teams study Chapter 10 Review together before completing Chapter 10 Test.

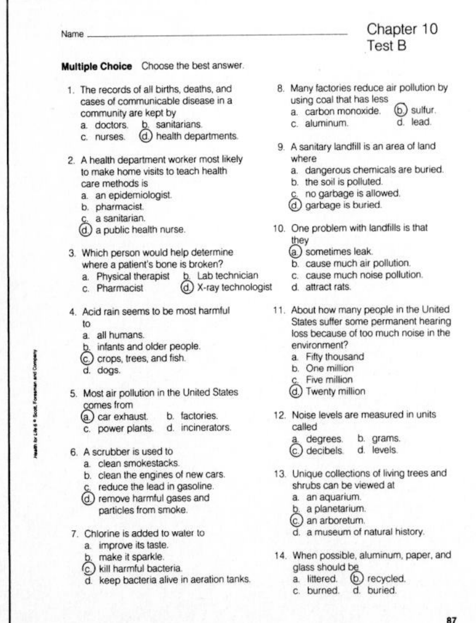

Name ____________ Chapter 10 Test B

Multiple Choice Choose the best answer.

1. The records of all births, deaths, and cases of communicable disease in a community are kept by
   a. doctors. b. sanitarians. c. nurses. (d.) health departments.
2. A health department worker most likely to make home visits to teach health care methods is
   a. an epidemiologist. b. pharmacist. c. a sanitarian. (d.) a public health nurse.
3. Which person would help determine where a patient's bone is broken?
   a. Physical therapist b. Lab technician c. Pharmacist (d.) X-ray technologist
4. Acid rain seems to be most harmful to
   a. all humans. b. infants and older people. (c.) crops, trees, and fish. d. dogs.
5. Most air pollution in the United States comes from
   (a.) car exhaust. b. factories. c. power plants. d. incinerators.
6. A scrubber is used to
   a. clean smokestacks. b. clean the engines of new cars. c. reduce the lead in gasoline. (d.) remove harmful gases and particles from smoke.
7. Chlorine is added to water to
   a. improve its taste. b. make it sparkle. (c.) kill harmful bacteria. d. keep bacteria alive in aeration tanks.
8. Many factories reduce air pollution by using coal that has less
   a. carbon monoxide. (b.) sulfur. c. aluminum. d. lead.
9. A sanitary landfill is an area of land where
   a. dangerous chemicals are buried. b. the soil is polluted. c. no garbage is allowed. (d.) garbage is buried.
10. One problem with landfills is that they
    (a.) sometimes leak. b. cause much air pollution. c. cause much noise pollution. d. attract rats.
11. About how many people in the United States suffer some permanent hearing loss because of too much noise in the environment?
    a. Fifty thousand b. One million c. Five million (d.) Twenty million
12. Noise levels are measured in units called
    a. degrees. b. grams. (c.) decibels. d. levels.
13. Unique collections of living trees and shrubs can be viewed at
    a. an aquarium. b. a planetarium. (c.) an arboretum. d. a museum of natural history.
14. When possible, aluminum, paper, and glass should be
    a. littered. (b.) recycled. c. burned. d. buried.

Health for Life 6 © Scott, Foresman and Company

87

Name ____________ Chapter 10 Test B

Short Answer Match each meaning in Column I with the correct word or words in Column II. Write the correct letter on the blank.

Column I

c 15. a change in the environment that is harmful or unpleasant to living things
e 16. the total surroundings that affect living things
a 17. pollution caused by engine exhaust gases reacting with other gases in the presence of sunlight
b 18. a colorless, odorless, and poisonous gas that is part of automobile exhaust
d 19. part of a sewage treatment plant in which bacteria feed on sewage

Column II

a. smog
b. carbon monoxide
c. pollution
d. aeration tank
e. environment

Short Essay Write your answers in complete sentences.

20. Suppose you break an arm and must go to the hospital immediately. Describe how some of the workers at the hospital might help you.
    Answers might refer to an emergency room team of doctors and nurses to provide immediate care, an X-ray technologist to take X rays of the arm, an operating team of doctors and nurses if an operation is necessary, a pharmacist to prepare medicine if it's necessary, and possibly a physical therapist to show exercises to do to regain strength in the arm.
21. Suppose a company wants to build a sanitary landfill on farmland near your community. What questions would you want answered before giving permission for the landfill?
    Answers might include: What materials will be buried? What are the chances of the landfill leaking? If it leaks, wil our drinking water supply be endangered? How long before the landfill is filled?

Health for Life 6 © Scott, Foresman and Company

88

Answers to Reviewing Health Ideas

1. sanitarian
2. pharmacists
3. wastes
4. water
5. bacteria
6. groundwater
7. burning
8. oxygen
9. acid
10. particles
11. sulfur
12. recycled
13. vessels
14. tree
15. solve

Answers to Understanding Health Ideas

16. to provide care for patient right after surgery
17. records of births, deaths, marriges, and certain diseases
18. human wastes, food, waste water, bacteria, viruses, oil, grease, poisonous chemicals, rags, and sticks
19. to allow solid particles to settle out of the sewage or water
20. chemical wastes, and leaks from sewage pipes, gasoline tanks, landfill, and septic systems
21. harms plants and fish
22. smashed together and covered with a layer of dirt
23. loud, continuous noise at work places; stereo headphones; or loud, continuous noise from radios held close to the ear
24. dinosaur fossils and information about ancient civilizations
25. by helping fight pollution

Answers to Thinking Critically

1. Answers might include examples of epidemics or food poisonings in which epidemiologists find the cause of the problem, public health nurses help give health care and advice, and sanitarians inspect food preparation facilities and water supplies.
Thinking Skills Students are *organizing information and making analogies.*
2. Answers might include the size of the factory, what it will make, what pollution could result, and how pollution will be minimized.
Thinking Skills When students think of questions to ask about a new factory, they are *suggesting alternatives* and *making analogies.*
3. Answers should refer to winds or water carrying pollution.
Thinking Skill When students tell how pollution in one part of the country could affect other places, they are *drawing conclusions.*

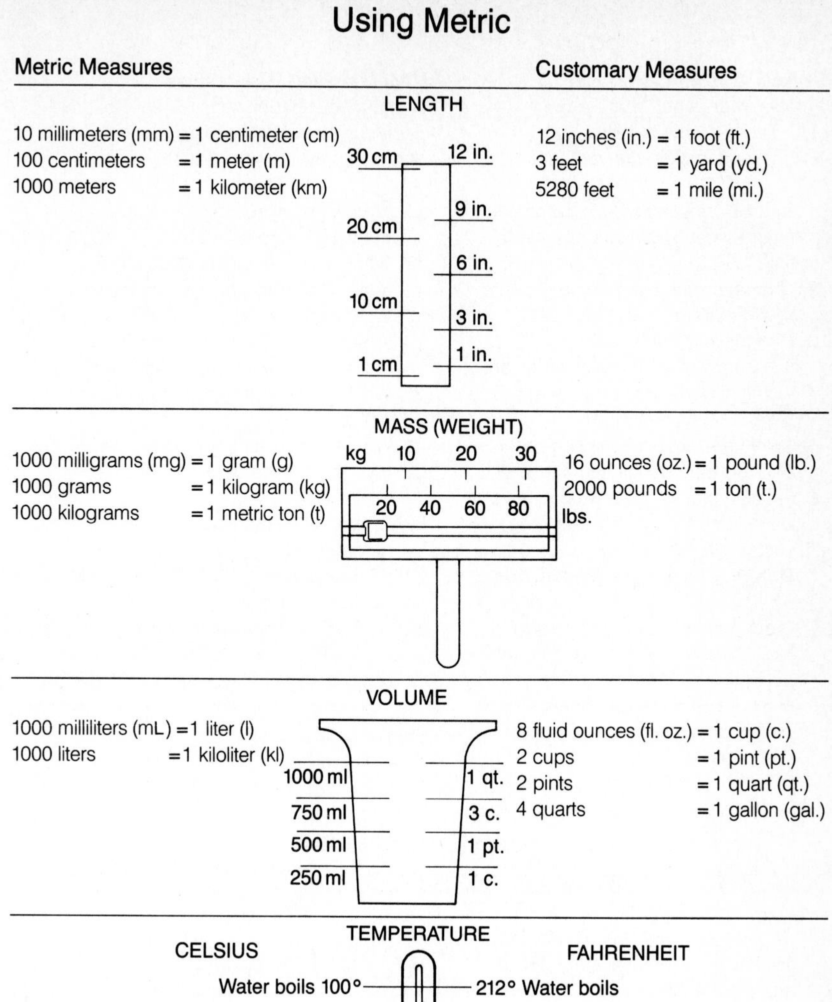

Using Metric

Metric Measures | **Customary Measures**

LENGTH

10 millimeters (mm) = 1 centimeter (cm)
100 centimeters = 1 meter (m)
1000 meters = 1 kilometer (km)

12 inches (in.) = 1 foot (ft.)
3 feet = 1 yard (yd.)
5280 feet = 1 mile (mi.)

MASS (WEIGHT)

1000 milligrams (mg) = 1 gram (g)
1000 grams = 1 kilogram (kg)
1000 kilograms = 1 metric ton (t)

16 ounces (oz.) = 1 pound (lb.)
2000 pounds = 1 ton (t.)

VOLUME

1000 milliliters (mL) = 1 liter (l)
1000 liters = 1 kiloliter (kl)

8 fluid ounces (fl. oz.) = 1 cup (c.)
2 cups = 1 pint (pt.)
2 pints = 1 quart (qt.)
4 quarts = 1 gallon (gal.)

TEMPERATURE

Independent Study Guide

Use the *Independent Study Guide* to review the lessons in each chapter. After you read each lesson, answer the questions to find out what you remember. Answering the questions will help you learn the important ideas in each lesson. You can also use the study guide to help you review for the chapter test.

Chapter 1 Study Guide pages 316–317

Answers to Study Guide

Lesson 1

1. self-image
2. good
3. confidence
4. accept
5. a way of thinking about yourself
6. nobody
7. weaknesses
8. strengths
9. mistakes
10. learn
11. improve

Lesson 2

1. relationship
2. along
3. the way they would like to be treated
4. problems
5. some of the same interests, activities, and attitudes
6. angry
7. unhappy
8. admit
9. Once angry feelings are gone, people can deal with the problem that made them angry.
10. anger
11. ride a bicycle, walk, or do some other physical activity
12. a family member, friend, or teacher

Chapter 1 Study Guide

On a separate sheet of paper write the word or words that best complete the sentence or answer the question.

Lesson 1 pages 20–23

1. _____ is the way a person feels about herself or himself.
2. People who have a _____ self-image generally feel good about themselves.
3. Having _____ is a characteristic of someone with a good self-image.
4. People can often get along with others when they _____ differences in other people.
5. What is an attitude?
6. Everyone is special because _____ is exactly like anyone else.
7. People should recognize and accept their _____ but not dwell on them.
8. People can help to overcome their weaknesses if they think more about their _____.
9. Making _____ is a part of life.
10. When a person makes a mistake, he or she should try to _____ from it.
11. The way a person reacts to a disappointment can either _____ or hurt the person's self-image.

Lesson 2 pages 26–29

1. A _____ is a connection between persons or groups.
2. Getting _____ with others does not mean always doing what other people do.
3. How should people treat other people?
4. Friends can talk to each other about their _____.
5. What do friends usually share?
6. Many people feel _____ when they think they have been treated unfairly, or notice other people being treated unfairly.
7. Keeping angry feelings inside can make a person feel _____.
8. People can deal with anger when they first _____ that they are angry.
9. Why is it important to get rid of angry feelings?
10. Keeping the mind busy can often help a person get rid of _____.
11. What are two ways to work off angry feelings?
12. Whom might a person talk to if feelings of anger will not go away?

316

Lesson **3** pages 30–35

1. ____ is the body's physical and mental reactions to demanding situations.
2. ____ events as well as upsetting or dangerous events can cause stress.
3. What are seven common effects of stress?
4. When first dealing with problems that cause stress, people should realize that they are ____.
5. When several problems are bothering someone, it is best to work on ____ at a time.
6. Some problems cannot be solved and must simply be ____.
7. Describe a breathing exercise that helps a person relax.
8. Besides doing breathing exercises, how else might a person relax?
9. Getting the mind off a problem is not the same as ____ a problem.
10. What are the five basic steps of decision-making?

Lesson **4** pages 36–41

1. How is a long-term goal different from a short-term goal?
2. People can set ____ goals when they have abilities that help them reach their goals.
3. A realistic goal is not too hard and not too ____.
4. What do people gain as they reach their goals?
5. When people try new activities, they often discover that they have ____ that they did not know they had.
6. What should a plan for reaching a goal include?
7. Why is it important to check your progress while trying to reach a goal?
8. Goals are easier to reach when they are divided into ____ parts.
9. People often have an easier time reaching a goal when they set aside a special ____ to work on that goal.

Lesson 3

1. stress
2. exciting
3. headaches, sleeplessness, upset stomachs, nervous feelings, getting angry easily, losing an appetite, eating too much
4. upset
5. one
6. accepted
7. breathe out completely, breathe in deeply through nose and hold breath for four counts, breathe out through mouth for eight counts
8. by playing sports or doing any other kind of enjoyable physical exercise
9. avoiding
10. Realize that a decision is needed. List the possible choices. List the possible results of each choice. Decide which choice is best. Judge your decision.

Lesson 4

1. Long-term goals take a long time to be reached. Short-term goals can be reached in a short period of time.
2. realistic
3. easy
4. self-confidence
5. abilities
6. a list of tasks to be completed to reach the goal, a list of possible problems in reaching the goal, and possible solutions to those problems
7. When people check their progress, they can be encouraged if the plan is working or they can change the plan if it is not working well.
8. smaller
9. time

Chapter 2 Study Guide pages 318–319

Answers to Study Guide

Lesson 1

1. spurt
2. two to three years
3. girls
4. ages nine to thirteen
5. ages eleven to fifteen
6. different
7. adult

Lesson 2

1. hormones
2. pituitary gland
3. A person stops growing and reaches adult height.
4. pituitary gland
5. testes
6. ovaries
7. hormones
8. a period of time when the body develops adultlike qualities and is able to reproduce

Lesson 3

1. inherited
2. generation
3. inside the nucleus of a cell
4. a spiraling ladder
5. DNA
6. a portion of DNA that affects only one trait
7. forty-six chromosomes
8. twenty-three chromosomes
9. sex
10. egg
11. Y
12. same
13. heredity

Chapter 2 Study Guide

On a separate sheet of paper write the word or words that best complete the sentence or answer the question.

Lesson 1 pages 50–52

1. The stage of rapid growth that usually begins between the ages of nine and fifteen is called the growth ____.
2. How long does the growth spurt usually last?
3. Who usually begins their growth spurts first, girls or boys?
4. At what ages do girls usually begin their growth spurt?
5. When do boys usually experience rapid changes in growth?
6. Different parts of the body grow at ____ rates during the growth spurt.
7. The timing of the growth spurt does not affect ____ size.

Lesson 2 pages 54–55

1. Endocrine glands make chemicals called ____.
2. Which pea-sized gland produces the growth hormone?
3. What happens when the pituitary gland stops making a lot of growth hormone?
4. Which gland produces hormones that cause the reproductive glands to become more active?
5. The ____ produce sperm cells.
6. Egg cells are produced in the ____.
7. ____ from the ovaries and testes cause the body to develop adultlike features.
8. What is puberty?

Lesson 3 pages 56–61

1. A mother and a father share in giving a child ____ traits.
2. Traits are passed on from one ____ to the next.
3. Where are chromosomes found?
4. What does the structure of DNA look like?
5. The chemical structure of ____ determines a person's heredity.
6. What is a gene?
7. How many chromosomes are in each body cell?
8. How many chromosomes are in each reproductive cell?
9. Chromosomes that determine a person's sex are called ____ chromosomes.
10. An ____ cell always contains an X chromosome.
11. A sperm cell can have an X or ____ chromosome.
12. Children in a family received forty-six chromosomes from their parents, but not the ____ forty-six chromosomes.
13. What influences how fast a person grows during the growth spurt?

318

Lesson 4
pages 64–65

1. Heredity, endocrine glands, and health ____ affect a person's growth.
2. People cannot control the actions of their ____ and their endocrine glands.
3. Heredity sets ____ for a person's growth.
4. People can give themselves the materials they need for growth by eating a ____ of foods.
5. What can give a person control over weight, body shape, and muscle development?
6. Strong muscles can help a person hold the body correctly, giving the person good ____.
7. Muscles can develop only if a person ____ them.
8. How many hours of sleep do eleven- to twelve-year-olds need each night?
9. When does the body usually build new cells?
10. What hormone is produced mainly when a person sleeps?
11. List three wise health decisions that can help a person grow properly.

Lesson 5
pages 66–67

1. How might changes during the growth spurt make a person feel?
2. Changes in height and weight can lead to ____ changes.
3. Mood swings, unhappy feelings, and worrying about the way you look are a normal part of ____.
4. During the growth spurt, friendships with people of the same ____ often become more important.
5. Friendships often change as people develop new ____.

Lesson 6
pages 68–69

1. If you have a good self-image, you will probably have a greater ____ in yourself.
2. Accepting ____ can help a person develop a strong self-image.
3. New responsibilities come with new ____.
4. List four people a person could talk to about feelings concerning growth.
5. During the growth spurt, your friends might grow slower or ____ than you grow.
6. Your own pattern of growth makes you a ____ person.

319

Lesson 4
1. decisions
2. heredity
3. limits
4. variety
5. exercise
6. posture
7. exercises
8. nine to ten hours
9. when a person sleeps
10. growth hormone
11. eating right, exercising, and getting enough sleep

Lesson 5
1. uncomfortable or clumsy
2. emotional
3. growing
4. age
5. interests

Lesson 6
1. confidence
2. responsibility
3. privileges or freedoms
4. a friend, parent, older brother or sister, or other relative
5. faster
6. special

Chapter 3 Study Guide pages 320–321

Answers to Study Guide

Lesson 1

1. food
2. sugar, starch, fiber
3. sugar and starch
4. fiber
5. sugar
6. fats
7. overweight, high blood pressure, heart disease
8. proteins
9. protein
10. bones, muscles, skin, hair
11. fat
12. variety
13. milk
14. They help to give people healthy red blood cells.
15. water

Lesson 2

1. nutrients
2. three
3. two
4. day
5. People should limit sugar, fat, cholesterol, and salt.
6. half
7. fat
8. heart
9. high

Chapter 3 Study Guide

On a separate sheet of paper write the word or words that best complete the sentence or answer the question.

Lesson **1** pages 76–81

1. People get their energy from ____.
2. List three major kinds of carbohydrates.
3. Which two carbohydrates provide most of the energy that the body uses?
4. ____ provides almost no energy but helps to move materials through the body.
5. Eating too much ____ can lead to tooth decay and overweight.
6. Which group of nutrients supplies energy and carries important nutrients to the body cells?
7. List three problems that too much fat in the diet can lead to.
8. Which group of nutrients builds and repairs cells?
9. Dried beans, peas, eggs, and fish are good sources of ____.
10. List four parts of the body that are made mainly of proteins.
11. Most animal sources of food contain more ____ than protein.
12. People generally do not need to take vitamin pills if they eat a ____ of food.
13. Which food is a good source of calcium and phosphorus?
14. How do the minerals iron and copper help the body?
15. The body is mainly made up of the nutrient called ____.

Lesson **2** pages 82–87

1. No single food can supply all the ____ that the body needs every day.
2. How many daily servings do children need from the milk-cheese group?
3. ____ daily servings are recommended from the meat-fish-poultry-bean group.
4. People should eat foods from each food group every ____.
5. Which four foods do nutrition experts think that people should limit?
6. Most sweetened breakfast cereals contain one ____ sugar.
7. Fried foods should be limited because they contain a lot of ____.
8. Too much cholesterol can lead to diseases of the ____ and blood vessels.
9. Too much salt can lead to ____ blood pressure.

320

Lesson 3 pages 90–95

1. State one reason why grocery stores have a greater variety of foods today than they did one hundred years ago.
2. Washing, cutting, mixing, cooking, drying, canning, and freezing foods are examples of food ____.
3. Drying removes water from food so that ____ cannot grow in the food and spoil it.
4. List two foods that have been dried.
5. How is freeze-drying different from drying?
6. Which two food-processing methods reduce the size and weight of food?
7. How are canned and frozen foods convenient?
8. Canned foods are sealed airtight to prevent ____ from entering them.
9. How does freezing foods prevent bacterial growth?
10. Many processed foods are high in ____.
11. Fresh foods lose some of their ____ between the time they are picked and the time they are eaten.
12. ____ foods keep nearly all their nutrients unless they have been completely precooked.
13. A food labeled *fortified* or *enriched* has ____ added to it.
14. What is milk usually fortified with?
15. Any substance added to food is called an ____.
16. What is a preservative?
17. What does the Food and Drug Administration do if it discovers a harmful additive?
18. Vegetables that are cooked until ____ have lost much of their vitamins.

Lesson 4 pages 96–98

1. A wise consumer reads and compares food ____ to find foods with the most nutrition at the best price.
2. If a food label lists the ingredients "sugar, barley, dried skim milk, and honey," then that food contains mostly ____.
3. List three kinds of nutrition information that might be found on a food label.
4. How might the name of the food manufacturer be important to a food consumer?
5. Many restaurants serve foods that are high in ____, sugar, and salt.
6. A person can avoid ____ at a restaurant by taking leftover food home.

321

Lesson 3

1. because people have discovered how to use basic foods to make new food products
2. processing
3. bacteria
4. Answers might include raisins, dry cereals, pudding mixes, and macaroni.
5. Drying removes water from food. Freeze-drying removes water from food while the food is frozen.
6. drying and freeze-drying
7. Canned and frozen foods can be stored for a long time and do not take long to prepare.
8. bacteria
9. Bacteria cannot live at such low temperatures.
10. salt
11. nutrients
12. frozen
13. nutrients
14. vitamin D
15. additive
16. an additive that helps keep food from spoiling
17. limits or stops the use of the additive
18. soft

Lesson 4

1. labels
2. sugar
3. Answers might include the amount of protein, vitamins, minerals, and other nutrients per serving, as well as the amount of fat, salt, and cholesterol.
4. If a person is dissatisfied, he or she can write to the manufacturer.
5. fats
6. overeating

Chapter 4 Study Guide pages 322–323

Answers to Study Guide

Lesson 1

1. by relieving stress and improving self-image
2. communication and cooperation
3. It carries oxygen and nutrients to the cells and carbon dioxide and other wastes away from cells.
4. rests
5. A fit heart is able to supply the body with the extra blood needed to exercise.
6. arteries
7. The fit person breathes more deeply and less often.
8. endurance
9. health

Lesson 2

1. health
2. energy
3. under the skin and around the organs and muscles
4. a calipers
5. 10 to 15 percent of the total body weight
6. Calorie
7. two thousand to three thousand Calories
8. more
9. Choose foods from the basic four food groups in the daily food guide and exercise regularly.
10. weighs

Lesson 3

1. skills
2. the ability to change the body position quickly and to control the movement of the whole body
3. power
4. reaction

Chapter 4 Study Guide

On a separate sheet of paper write the word or words that best complete the sentence or answer the question.

Lesson 1 pages 106–111

1. How can exercise improve mental health?
2. What two important social skills do team sports help develop?
3. What substances does the cardiovascular system carry to the cells and away from the cells?
4. A strong heart ____ longer between beats than a weaker heart.
5. Why is a fit heart important when a person exercises?
6. Regular exercise helps keep the ____ clear of fatty material.
7. How does the breathing of a fit person differ from the breathing of an unfit person?
8. Exercise can improve muscular strength, flexibility, and ____.
9. Muscular strength and flexibility are two parts of physical fitness called ____ fitness.

Lesson 2 pages 112–115

1. Body fatness is a part of ____ fitness.
2. Body fat is stored ____.
3. Where is body fat found?
4. What tool can be used to measure body fat?
5. How much body fat should an eleven- to twelve-year-old have?
6. A ____ is the unit used to measure the energy in food.
7. Generally, how many Calories does an eleven- to twelve-year-old need to take in every day?
8. People gain weight if they take in ____ Calories than they use.
9. What is the best way to take in the right amount of Calories and nutrients every day?
10. The number of Calories a person uses depends on how much a person ____ and how long an activity is done without stopping.

Lesson 3 pages 116–117

1. ____ fitness is the ability to perform well in activities that require certain skills.
2. What is agility?
3. What part of skills fitness is the ability to quickly do activities that require strength?
4. The amount of time it takes a person to move once he or she observes the need to move is called ____ time.

322

Lesson **4** pages 120–125

1. People can build fitness by setting fitness ____.
2. It is important to determine a person's needs, interests, and ____ before setting fitness goals.
3. Some people have a body type that makes it easy for them to gain body ____.
4. Running in place can help a person measure ____ fitness.
5. What part of health fitness can push-ups measure?
6. What test can a person do to measure his or her flexibility?
7. The backward hop can be used to test the part of skills fitness called ____.
8. What test can measure coordination?
9. A good way to test speed is to ____ in place.

Lesson **5** pages 126–129

1. Choosing activities that improve certain parts of fitness can help a person achieve fitness ____.
2. People should not stop doing an ____ just because it does not improve a certain part of fitness.
3. What parts of health fitness is soccer excellent for developing?
4. What parts of skills fitness is baseball excellent for developing?
5. To build and maintain fitness, a person should exercise at least ____ times a week.
6. While a person is exercising, the heart should beat at a rate of ____ beats per minutes.
7. How can a person keep track of how hard the heart is working while exercising?
8. Why is it important to warm up before exercising?
9. List three exercises that are good for warming up.
10. Why are comfortable shoes and loose clothing important for exercising?
11. After doing highly active exercise, a person should do ____ exercises.
12. How do cooling down exercises help the body?
13. A person who has not exercised for a long time should start slowly and ____ build up the amount of exercise done.

Lesson 4

1. goals
2. abilities
3. fat
4. cardiovascular
5. muscular strength
6. two-hand ankle grab
7. balance
8. double ball bounce
9. run

Lesson 5

1. goals
2. enjoyable
3. cardiovascular fitness and control of body fatness
4. coordination, reaction time, and power
5. three
6. 135 to 155
7. by taking the pulse
8. Warming up prevents muscle injury and helps get the heart ready for more active exercise.
9. Answers might include the side stretch, toe reach, jumping jack, slow walking, and slow jog.
10. Comfortable shoes support and protect the feet, and loose clothing allows for free movement.
11. gentle
12. Cooling down prevents soreness and helps the heart rate come back to normal slowly.
13. gradually

Chapter 5 Study Guide pages 324–325

Answers to Study Guide

Lesson 1

1. caused

2. risks

2. crosswalks

4. Answers might include no swimming when lifeguard is off duty, no skating, or no running in the halls.

5. safety

Lesson 2

1. falls

2. rubber backing

3. a substance that is harmful if it gets inside the body

4. Answers might include cleaning fluids, bleaches, detergents, and paint thinners.

5. children

6. warnings

7. fire

8. covered

9. water

10. The screen can prevent sparks and small pieces of burning wood from falling onto material that can burn.

11. fire

12. dampened

13. say that the person cannot talk or come to the door right now and to call or come back later

14. alone

15. adult

16. several

Chapter 5 Study Guide

On a separate sheet of paper write the word or words that best complete the sentence or answer the question.

Lesson 1 pages 142–143

1. Accidents do not just happen; they are ___.
2. Many people cause accidents because they take unnecessary ___.
3. People should cross streets only at ___.
4. What are two safety rules that help protect people from harm?
5. It is important to wear a ___ belt while riding in a car.

Lesson 2 pages 144–149

1. ___ are the most common kind of accident in the home.
2. What can people put on the back of a rug to prevent others from slipping?
3. What is a poison?
4. List three common household items that are poisonous.
5. All poisons, including medicines, should be kept out of reach of young ___.
6. Poisonous substances bought in a store have ___ written on their labels.
7. Plugging too many appliances into one outlet can cause a ___.
8. Unused outlets should be ___, especially if young children are around.
9. People should never use electrical appliances in or near ___.
10. How can putting a screen around a fireplace prevent a fire?
11. Unlike a fall or poisoning, a ___ often harms more than one person.
12. Before throwing away a burnt-out match, it should be ___.
13. If a stranger asks to see or talk to someone who is not home, what should a person do?
14. A person should never let a stranger know he or she is home ___.
15. Rather than giving directions to a stranger, a young person could tell a stranger to ask an ___.
16. If a person chooses to give directions to a stranger, he or she should stay ___ feet away from the car.

324

Lesson **3** pages 152–155

1. What is an emergency?
2. People can have the best chances of reacting correctly and safely to an emergency if they are ___.
3. List three kinds of telephone numbers that should be listed near the telephone.
4. Some communities use the number ___ as a special emergency telephone number.
5. A smoke ___ makes a loud, shrill noise when smoke reaches it.
6. What can a person use to put out a small fire?
7. If a large fire occurs, a person should leave the building ___.
8. List four items that a home first-aid kit should contain.

Lesson **4** pages 156–161

1. Immediate medical care is called ___.
2. First aid requires ___ thinking and quick actions.
3. What should a person do as quickly as possible if an emergency occurs?
4. Moving an injured person can often make the injury ___.
5. When giving first aid, a person should not do more than he or she ___ how to do.
6. What should a person do if someone is trying to cough up an object?
7. First aid for a person who has stopped breathing is called artificial ___.
8. Most people suffer brain damage or die after four to ___ minutes without oxygen.
9. What position should the victim be in for artificial respiration?
10. What is the general treatment for a first-degree or second-degree burn?
11. What is the correct first-aid procedure for a third-degree burn?
12. Shock occurs when the heart, lungs, brain, and other organs do not get enough ___.
13. What can cause a person to go into shock?
14. First aid for shock includes laying the person down and keeping the person ___.
15. If a person has a leg, chest, or ___ injury, do not raise the legs to improve circulation.

Lesson 3

1. a sudden need for quick action
2. prepared
3. Answers might include the police department, fire department, doctor's office, hospital, poison control center, several nearby friends, and family work numbers.
4. 911
5. alarm
6. a fire extinguisher
7. immediately
8. Answers might include bandages, gauze, cotton, scissors, tweezers, soap, and an antiseptic.

Lesson 4

1. first-aid
2. clear
3. send for help
4. worse
5. knows
6. not interfere
7. respiration
8. six
9. on the back with the head tilted back
10. apply cool water and cover with a sterile cloth or bandage
11. get immediate medical attention and cover with a sterile dressing
12. blood
13. an accident or serious illness
14. warm
15. head

Chapter 6 Study Guide pages 326–327

Answers to Study Guide

Lesson 1

1. drug
2. caffeine
3. slows down the way it works
4. nicotine
5. Answers might include glue, paint thinner, paints, and gasoline.

Lesson 2

1. Answers might include dropped directly into the eye, rubbed on the skin, sprayed in the nose, injected into a muscle, injected into a vein, or taken orally.
2. a pharmacist
3. prescription
4. Answers might include the name of the doctor, pharmacy, patient, directions on the use of the medicine, special warnings, and directions for safe storage.
5. Answers might include headache, upset stomach, and drowsiness.
6. misuse

Lesson 3

1. the intentional use of a drug for reasons other than health reasons
2. tolerance
3. A person with a mental dependence thinks he or she needs the drug. The body of a person with a physical dependence needs the drug to avoid feeling sick.
4. when a person who is physically dependent on a drug stops taking it
5. depressants, stimulants, narcotics, hallucinogens, and inhalants
6. stimulants
7. hallucinations
8. depressants
9. illegal
10. narcotics
11. heroin
12. hallucinogens
13. Inhalants can cause the body to stop breathing or the heart to stop beating.
14. society
15. half

Chapter 6 Study Guide

On a separate sheet of paper write the word or words that best complete the sentence or answer the question.

Lesson **1** pages 168–169

1. A ____ is a chemical that changes the way the body works.
2. Certain teas, coffees, and soft drinks contain ____, which can increase the activity of the nervous system.
3. How does alcohol affect the nervous system?
4. Tobacco and tobacco smoke contain the drug ____.
5. List three products that can produce harmful fumes.

Lesson **2** pages 170–173

1. List three ways medicines can get into the body.
2. What kind of health professional can prepare a prescription medicine?
3. An over-the-counter medicine can be bought without a ____.
4. List four kinds of information that can be found on a prescription label.
5. What are two common side effects that might be listed on the label of an OTC medicine?
6. Taking two or more medicines at the same time without a doctor's permission is called drug ____.

Lesson **3** pages 174–179

1. What is drug abuse?
2. ____ occurs when a drug user must use more and more of a drug to get the same effect.
3. How is mental dependence different from physical dependence?
4. When does withdrawal occur?
5. What are the five main groups of drugs?
6. Which group of drugs speeds up the nervous system?
7. Taking cocaine can cause ____—seeing or hearing things that are not really there.
8. Which group of drugs slows down the nervous system?
9. Tranquilizers and barbiturates are ____ without a prescription.
10. ____ are drugs made from opium or opiumlike substances.
11. ____ is a narcotic that is illegal and not used medically in the United States.
12. ____ are drugs that change the messages carried by the nerves to the brain.
13. How can inhalants cause death?
14. Drug abuse affects ____ by causing an increase in crime.
15. More than ____ of all motor vehicle accidents involve someone who has abused a drug.

326

Lesson 4 pages 180–181

1. Marijuana contains about ___ chemicals.
2. Which main mind-altering chemical easily builds up in the body of a marijuana user?
3. The THC from one marijuana cigarette can stay in the body for a ___.
4. The most damaging effects of marijuana occur in the ___.
5. What are two driving skills that the use of marijuana weakens?
6. Marijuana is especially dangerous to young people because it can interfere with their physical, ___, and mental growth.
7. It is ___ to grow, buy, sell, or use marijuana.

Lesson 5 pages 182–185

1. Alcohol is a ___ drug.
2. How quickly can alcohol enter the bloodstream?
3. If a large person and a smaller person drink the same amount of alcohol, which person has the higher blood alcohol level?
4. What are two effects of drinking a large amount of alcohol?
5. ___ is a disease of the liver which can be caused by the long-term use of alcohol.
6. Physical and mental dependence on alcohol is called ___.
7. Alcoholism can be controlled with proper help only if the alcoholic ___ the help.
8. List three special branches of Alcoholics Anonymous and state which part of the family each branch helps.

Lesson 6 pages 186–189

1. Smokers have to breathe faster than others because of the carbon ___ in cigarette smoke.
2. When ___ from cigarette smoke cool on a smoker's lungs, they form a brown, sticky mass.
3. A cigarette smoker becomes ___ on the nicotine in tobacco.
4. What are three diseases that smoking can cause?
5. ___ smoke comes from someone else's cigarette.
6. How is sidestream smoke different from mainstream smoke?
7. How is snuff different from chewing tobacco?
8. List three harmful effects from using chewing tobacco or snuff.

Lesson 7 pages 192–193

1. ___ pressure leads some people to abuse drugs.
2. What can a person say if she or he is pressured to use drugs?
3. State an activity that a person can do to resist the pressure of abusing drugs.
4. What are five important steps in making a decision?

327

Lesson 4

1. four hundred
2. THC
3. month
4. lungs
5. Answers might include timing, coordination, and reaction time.
6. emotional
7. illegal

Lesson 5

1. depressant
2. within two minutes after a person drinks alcohol
3. the smaller person
4. Answers might include loss of consciousness, stopping of breathing or heartbeat, and death.
5. cirrhosis
6. alcoholism
7. wants
8. Al-Anon helps husbands, wives, and other relatives. Alateen helps sons and daughters aged twelve to eighteen. Alatot helps sons and daughters under twelve years of age.

Lesson 6

1. monoxide
2. tars
3. dependent
4. Answers might include heart disease, lung cancer, emphysema, and chronic bronchitis.
5. second-hand
6. Sidestream smoke comes from the end of a burning cigarette, and mainstream smoke is exhaled by the smoker. Side-stream smoke is more dangerous than mainstream smoke.
7. Snuff is the powder made by grinding tobacco leaves and stems. Chewing tobacco is coarsely ground tobacco leaves.
8. Answers might include bad breath, discolored teeth, stomach trouble, mouth and throat cancers, gum disease, and high blood pressure.

Lesson 7

1. peer
2. "No, thanks." or "I have something else to do."
3. Answers might include writing, painting, playing team sports, developing hobbies, and working on arts and crafts.
4. Realize that a decision is needed. List the possible choices. List the possible results of each choice. Decide which choice is best. Judge the decision.

Chapter 7 Study Guide pages 328–329

Answers to Study Guide

Lesson 1

1. communicable
2. bacteria
3. warm, dark, moist places
4. sore throats, ear infections, sinus infections
5. damaging
6. by using an electron microscope

Lesson 2

1. bloodstream
2. Answers should include any three of the following: skin, mucus, stomach acids, tears, saliva.
3. white blood
4. Stomach acids usually kill the germs swallowed with mucus or food.
5. antibodies
6. one
7. Answers should include any three of the following: measles, mumps, polio, chicken pox.
8. by getting a vaccine for each of those diseases
9. Casual
10. Answers should include any two of the following: sharing needles used for illegal drugs, infected blood transfusions, during or after childbirth, or sexual contact.

Lesson 3

1. the cold
2. The tissue lining the nasal passages produces extra mucus.
3. the first stage
4. Sinuses are spaces within the bones of the head and face.
5. Antibiotics can help reduce the number of bacteria that are growing in the thickening mucus.
6. breathing
7. tonsils
8. strep

Chapter 7 Study Guide

On a separate sheet of paper write the word or words that best complete the sentence or answer the question.

Lesson 1 pages 200–203

1. Disease germs cause ____ diseases.
2. What are the most numerous kinds of organisms?
3. Describe the kind of place in which bacteria grow best.
4. Name three other diseases that can be caused by the bacteria that cause pneumonia.
5. Viruses harm the body by entering and ____ body cells.
6. How can viruses be seen?

Lesson 2 pages 204–209

1. The body's first-line defenses work to keep disease germs out of the body's tissues and ____.
2. List three first-line defenses against disease.
3. ____ ____ cells surround and destroy disease germs.
4. How do stomach acids play a role in the body's first line of defense against disease germs?
5. What is the third line of defense against disease germs?
6. How many kinds of disease germs can each kind of antibody attack?
7. List three diseases each of which provides lifelong immunity once a person has had the disease.
8. How can a person build immunity to certain diseases without getting those diseases?
9. The AIDS virus does not spread by ____ contact.
10. What are two ways people can become infected with the AIDS virus?

Lesson 3 pages 210–215

1. What is the most common disease in the United States?
2. What causes a runny nose during the early stage of a cold?
3. During what stage of a cold can a person pass the cold viruses to others?
4. What are sinuses?
5. How can antibiotics help a person with sinusitis?
6. When a person has pneumonia, thick mucus collects in the lungs and interferes with ____.
7. Disease germs can make the ____ red and swollen, causing a sore throat.
8. A severe sore throat might mean that the person has a disease called ____ throat.

328

Lesson **4** pages 218–223

1. Why are communicable diseases less dangerous today than they were in the beginning of this century?
2. Disease germs do not cause ____ diseases.
3. ____ involves the passing of genes from parents to children.
4. Cigarette smoking greatly increases the chances of getting cardiovascular diseases and lung ____.
5. Heredity and ____ usually act together to cause a noncommunicable disease.
6. Cardiovascular diseases are diseases of the ____ and blood vessels.
7. How can hypertension affect the artery walls?
8. What happens when an artery that supplies blood to the heart becomes blocked?
9. What are two causes of strokes?
10. How does exercise reduce the risks of heart disease?
11. How does stress affect the blood vessels?
12. What are three environmental factors that increase the chances of getting cancer?

Lesson **5** pages 224–227

1. An ____ is a harmful reaction in some people's bodies to certain substances.
2. What disease does an allergic reaction often resemble?
3. Why can breathing be difficult for a person with asthma?
4. What are two symptoms that might result from an allergic reaction to an insect sting?
5. Other than avoiding allergens, how can allergies be treated?

Lesson **6** pages 228–229

1. Why is it important to have a healthy lifestyle?
2. The body's ____ against disease work best if the body is in good physical condition.
3. A healthy lifestyle includes eating foods low in fat, sugar, salt, and ____.
4. A healthy lifestyle includes making wise decisions about tobacco, alcohol, and other harmful ____.
5. How does bathing regularly help prevent diseases?
6. The body's defenses work better when a person deals with ____ in healthy ways.

329

Lesson 4

1. because of antibiotics, better health care, and better sanitary conditions
2. noncommunicable
3. heredity
4. cancer
5. environment
6. heart
7. Hypertension can cause artery walls to weaken, balloon out, and break.
8. Part of the heart dies—this is called a heart attack.
9. atherosclerosis and hypertension
10. Exercise makes the heart larger and stronger, so it does not have to work as hard; it also reduces the amount of fat in the blood, thereby reducing the chances of plaque building up.
11. Stress narrows the blood vessels.
12. cigarette smoking; overexposure to the sun and to other kinds of radiation; a diet high in fat

Lesson 5

1. allergy
2. a cold
3. Air passages leading into the lungs become swollen and build up with mucus.
4. Answers should include any two of the following: a rash, a feeling of heat all over the skin, feeling weak and dizzy, difficulty breathing.
5. take medicines to relieve symptoms; take shots

Lesson 6

1. to help you stay well
2. defenses
3. cholesterol
4. drugs
5. Bathing regularly keeps harmful bacteria off the body.
6. stress

Chapter 8 Study Guide pages 330–331

Answers to Study Guide

Lesson 1

1. tired
2. balanced
3. headaches, lower back pains, and other muscle soreness
4. health
5. The body should be far back in the chair.
6. head
7. The posture is likely to be the same.

Lesson 2

1. more than 65 percent
2. speech, appearance, and the ability to chew food
3. Plaque is the sticky, colorless film of bacteria that is always forming on the teeth and gums.
4. acids
5. enamel
6. The decay can spread deeper into the tooth causing soreness and pain.
7. calculus
8. The gums become swollen and bleed and pull away from teeth.
9. decay
10. by flossing
11. at least once a day
12. Sticky sweets stay on teeth a long time, allowing acids to form.
13. rinse the mouth with water

Lesson 3

1. nearsighted
2. farsighted
3. doctor
4. germs
5. Answers may include any two of the following: loud noises, ear injuries, ear infections, nerve damage.

Chapter 8 Study Guide

On a separate sheet of paper write the word or words that best complete the sentence or answer the question.

Lesson **1** pages 236–237

1. Good posture helps a person move about for long periods of time without getting ____.
2. Good posture keeps parts of the body ____ in a straight column.
3. List three problems that poor posture can cause.
4. Posture depends on the rest of a person's ____.
5. What is the correct way to sit in a chair?
6. When people stand or walk, the ____ should be centered over the body.
7. How does the posture people have as adults usually compare to the posture they had as young people?

Lesson **2** pages 238–241

1. What percentage of young people have tooth decay by the time they become adults?
2. List three things that the loss of teeth can affect.
3. What is plaque?
4. The bacteria in plaque use sugar in food to produce ____.
5. Acids destroy ____ on teeth and lead to tooth decay.
6. What can happen if a cavity is not treated?
7. Hardened plaque is called ____.
8. What happens to gums in gum disease?
9. The most common dental problem of eleven- to twelve-year-olds is tooth ____.
10. How can people remove plaque and bits of food between their teeth and under their gumline?
11. How often do people need to brush and floss?
12. Why are sticky sweets especially harmful to teeth?

Lesson **3** pages 242–243

1. If a person is ____, he or she can see objects close by, but objects far away appear blurred.
2. A vision problem that is more common in adults than children is ____.
3. Whom should you notify if you have eye pain, itching, headaches, or trouble seeing?
4. Ear infections occur when ____ get into the middle ear.
5. What are two things that can damage a person's hearing?

330

Lesson **4** pages 244–245

1. What is the most important way to care for the skin?
2. Tiny dirt particles and ____ land on the skin constantly.
3. How can people prevent the transfer of bacteria to food?
4. Oily skin and ____ increase the need for cleanliness.
5. What are three body wastes the sweat glands collect?
6. What causes perspiration to change to an unpleasant odor?
7. At what stage in life do sweat glands get more active?
8. What products can people use to control perspiration and body odor?
9. Which glands help to keep the skin soft and smooth?
10. Extra oil on the skin can clog openings and produce ____ and other forms of acne.
11. How can people control oily skin and acne?
12. What is dandruff?
13. What can look like dandruff if it is not rinsed completely out of the hair?

Lesson **5** pages 248–251

1. What kind of hormone is produced mainly when people sleep?
2. List two body functions that slow down during sleep.
3. During sleep, more ____ is available to build and repair cells.
4. List three problems that can occur when people miss a day or two of sleep.
5. ____ often need sixteen to twenty hours of sleep each day.
6. How many hours of sleep does a typical eleven- to twelve-year-old need each night?
7. How long does a person usually dream during a healthy night's sleep?
8. How long does a typical period of dreaming last?
9. During sleep experiments, how can scientists tell if a person is sleeping lightly, deeply, or dreaming?
10. Sleep does not always relieve ____.
11. What are three kinds of fatigue?
12. What is the best way to relieve physical fatigue?
13. What can cause emotional fatigue?
14. Fatigue is a sign that the body needs a ____.

Lesson 4

1. keep it clean
2. bacteria
3. wash the hands before eating
4. perspiration
5. water, salt, and heat
6. bacteria on the skin
7. puberty
8. antiperspirants and deodorants
9. oil glands
10. pimples or acne
11. by washing the face with soap and warm water every day.
12. dead skin cells that combine with oil on the scalp
13. shampoo

Lesson 5

1. growth hormone
2. heart rate and breathing rate
3. energy
4. People can have trouble concentrating; they might become angry easily; the senses can become unreliable.
5. infants
6. nine to ten hours
7. about an hour
8. from a few minutes to a half hour
9. They observe brain waves.
10. fatigue
11. physical, mental, and emotional
12. rest
13. stress
14. change

Chapter 9 Study Guide pages 332–333

Answers to Study Guide

Lesson 1

1. a person who buys or uses products and services that contribute to health

2. best

3. Careful shoppers ask if they really need the product.

4. impulsive

5. family

6. Do not buy the product just because the friend has it.

7. library

8. experience

9. judge

Lesson 2

1. a recommendation for a product or service

2. Answers might include radio and television commercials and printed ads in magazines and newspapers.

3. information

4. Free gifts are often worthless, and the cost of the gift is often reflected in the product cost.

5. People often hum jingles, which makes them think about the product and then automatically buy the product.

6. logos

7. higher

8. methods

Chapter 9 Study Guide

On a separate sheet of paper write the word or words that best complete the sentence or answer the question.

Lesson 1 pages 258–261

1. What is a health consumer?
2. A wise shopper knows that the most costly products are not always the ___ products.
3. What do careful shoppers ask themselves before they buy a product?
4. ___ shoppers quickly buy a product when they see it even though they do not need it.
5. ___ members are often good sources of information when it comes to making health decisions.
6. What should a person remember before he or she follows a friend's recommendation?
7. The ___ has good, dependable materials about becoming a wise health consumer.
8. As people gain ___ in shopping wisely, they often find that they can make better decisions and purchases.
9. When people ___ the decisions they make, they can make wiser decisions in the future.

Lesson 2 pages 262–267

1. What is an advertisement?
2. List two forms of advertisements.
3. Some ads are planned just to make a person buy a product, and offer little or no helpful ___.
4. List two reasons why the advertising method that uses free gifts is often deceiving.
5. How are jingles effective forms of advertisements?
6. Advertisers use ___ to identify their company.
7. The cost of a product in a fancy package is often ___ than another product in a simpler package.
8. Evaluating advertisements can sometimes be tricky because advertisers often use several ___ in one ad.

Lesson **3** pages 270–274

1. List three reasons why one brand of a product might cost more than another brand.
2. The ____ price of a product is the cost of the product divided by the net weight.
3. The net weight is the weight of the contents, not including the ____.
4. Any claim that a label makes must be ____.
5. How are the ingredients listed on a label?
6. What is a guarantee?
7. Some health products, such as hair spray, must carry ____ by law.
8. When people follow ____, they often wish they had spent their money in a different way.

Lesson **4** pages 276–279

1. How often do doctors think young people should generally have health checkups?
2. It is very important to be ____ with the doctor.
3. The more the doctor knows about a person, the more she or he can ____ the person.
4. What might a temperature higher than 98.6°F (37°C) indicate?
5. What should a person do if the doctor's instructions seem very complicated?
6. What should a person do if he or she has an unpleasant side effect from a medicine?
7. What does a doctor check to determine if a person is growing in a way that is correct for that person?
8. What instrument does the doctor use to check the heart and lungs?
9. What might poor posture indicate?
10. The doctor tests the blood ____ to see if it is in the normal ranges.
11. What is one thing that can be learned from a blood test?
12. A ____ test can help a doctor determine how well the kidneys are working.
13. List five diseases that people get vaccinations for.

333

Lesson 3

1. One product might be advertised more; one might come in a fancier container; one really might be a better product.
2. unit
3. container
4. truthful
5. in order by weight
6. a promise to replace, repair, or give the money back if the product is unsatisfactory
7. warnings
8. fads

Lesson 4

1. every two or three years
2. honest
3. help
4. the beginning of some illness or the presence of an infection
5. write them down
6. call the doctor rather than waiting for the next checkup
7. a person's height and weight
8. stethoscope
9. inadequate nutrition, lack of proper sleep or exercise, or bone deformities
10. pressure
11. if a sufficient number of red blood cells are in the blood
12. urine
13. Answers might include tetanus, polio, measles, mumps, rubella (German measles), and diphtheria.

Chapter 10 Study Guide pages 334–335

Answers to Study Guide

Lesson 1

1. public
2. sanitarian
3. to protect the community from disease
4. public health nurse
5. emergency room
6. physical therapist
7. volunteers

Lesson 2

1. environment
2. a change in the environment that is harmful or undesirable to living things
3. sewage
4. chlorine
5. water
6. Answers might include septic systems, sewer and pipe leaks, waste dumps, animal wastes, and leaks from gasoline storage tanks.
7. poisonous chemical wastes
8. burning
9. the use of cars
10. It deprives the body of oxygen and can cause dizziness and headaches.
11. respiratory
12. sulfur
13. crops, trees, and fish
14. gas
15. Answers might include car pools, public transportation, walking, and riding bicycles.

Chapter 10 Study Guide

On a separate sheet of paper write the word or words that best complete the sentence or answer the question.

Lesson **1** pages 286–291

1. People in a health department perform different jobs but work together for _____ health.
2. What kind of health worker would inspect a restaurant to check on safety methods?
3. What is the goal of the public health department?
4. What kind of health worker makes home visits and instructs families on health, child care, and nutrition?
5. To which hospital area would a person be brought if he or she has suffered an injury?
6. What kind of hospital worker would help a patient learn to walk with crutches?
7. People called _____ offer their time and services without getting paid.

Lesson **2** pages 292–297

1. The living and nonliving things that surround and affect you make up your _____.
2. What is pollution?
3. To prevent some water pollution, sewage is partly cleaned at a _____ treatment plant.
4. What kind of gas is added to sewage to kill harmful bacteria and some viruses?
5. To make water safe for drinking, communities use _____ treatment plants.
6. What are three sources of groundwater pollution?
7. What is the most dangerous source of groundwater pollution?
8. Most air pollution results from the _____ of coal, oil, and gasoline.
9. What causes most air pollution in the United States?
10. How does carbon monoxide affect the body?
11. Smoke and smog irritate the _____ system.
12. Acid rain is caused largely by burning coal and oil that contain large amounts of _____.
13. What are three things toward which acid rain is directly harmful?
14. Devices called scrubbers remove much harmful _____ as well as particles from factory smoke.
15. List two ways people can cut down on the use of cars.

Lesson **3** pages 298–299	1. In the past, what kinds of problems were caused when people threw their garbage in the street, river, or in an open dump? 2. Garbage is compacted, layered, and covered with dirt at a sanitary ____. 3. List two disadvantages of a sanitary landfill. 4. What are four kinds of materials that can be recycled? 5. Some communities burn their garbage in large furnaces called ____.
Lesson **4** pages 302–303	1. What are three health effects of too much noise? 2. How many people in the United States suffer permanent hearing loss because of too much noise in the environment? 3. Noise is measured in units called ____. 4. A noise level of ____ decibels or more can cause ear damage over a period of time. 5. Motors and engines are ____ than they once were. 6. Some subway trains use ____ wheels to reduce noise.
Lesson **5** pages 304–307	1. Recreation can give people a chance to relax, exercise, and relieve ____. 2. What kind of museum would likely contain fossils and other signs of the past? 3. What would a person see in a planetarium? 4. What can people learn about at an aquarium? 5. What is one place people can learn about wildlife as they enjoy the outdoors? 6. List three community organizations that might offer recreational activities.
Lesson **6** pages 308–309	1. What is one of the best ways people can help their community? 2. What should people do with litter when a trash can is unavailable? 3. List three things that recycling can save. 4. When people walk or ride a bicycle, they can reduce ____ pollution. 5. How can people find out about local health problems?

Lesson 3

1. The garbage attracted rats and other animals that carried disease. Burning of the trash caused air pollution.
2. landfill
3. It can leak chemicals into the soil and groundwater and uses a lot of land.
4. glass, paper, aluminum, and rubber
5. incinerators

Lesson 4

1. It can make a person nervous, it narrows blood vessels and makes the heart work harder, it increases blood pressure, and it can cause hearing loss.
2. about twenty million people
3. decibels
4. eighty
5. quieter
6. rubberized

Lesson 5

1. stress
2. a museum of natural history
3. images of stars and planets
4. life that is found in water
5. a nature center
6. Answers might include Girl Scouts, Boy Scouts, YMCA, YWCA, and the local park district.

Lesson 6

1. fight pollution
2. save it until it can be thrown away properly
3. energy, money, and natural resources
4. air
5. read newspapers and listen to newscasts

Teaching Plan

Skills for Life Handbook

pages 336–337

Strategies
The Skills for Life Handbook will help teachers relate information in each chapter to skills and situations that students will use in real life. The activities help students build life management skills through practice. Each chapter has a decision-making activity and one to three others to build the following skills: self-esteem building skills; goal-setting skills; coping skills; social and communication skills; refusal skills; and consumer skills. Background information on each of these skills can be found on pages T36–T37. Strategies for how to incorporate these activities into *Health for Life* are suggested below.

The activities in the Handbook are intended to be used for independent learning and practice, but teachers can use the activities for class discussions or adapt them to develop skits. The activities are written in the third person so that students can evaluate appropriate behavior objectively. Some of the life skills activities provide the beginning of a situation, and students must decide the best way to handle it. In other cases, it is more appropriate to model behavior and ask students to evaluate it. For example, when a situation involves the use of harmful drugs, the scenario demonstrates how students make a responsible decision not to use the drugs. Teachers can then use more open-ended situations if they wish to provide more decision-making practice. For all the life skills activities, students will examine and practice how to handle themselves in healthful ways.

Deciding What To Do These activities extend the application of the decision-making steps and guidelines presented in Lesson 3 of Chapter 1 (page 35). The Handbook allows students to practice using the five-step process for making decisions and evaluating choices for every chapter. As students do these activities, make sure they go through each step and use the guidelines as an integral part of this process to help eliminate unwise and unhealthy choices. The decision-making chart referred to in these activities can be reproduced from page 134 of the Teacher's Resource Book.

Skills for Life Handbook

Use the activities in this handbook to develop skills for life—skills that will help you deal with events in your life in positive, healthful ways. Read stories about how people your age deal with some difficult situations. Then answer the questions to tell what these people should do or to evaluate what they have done.

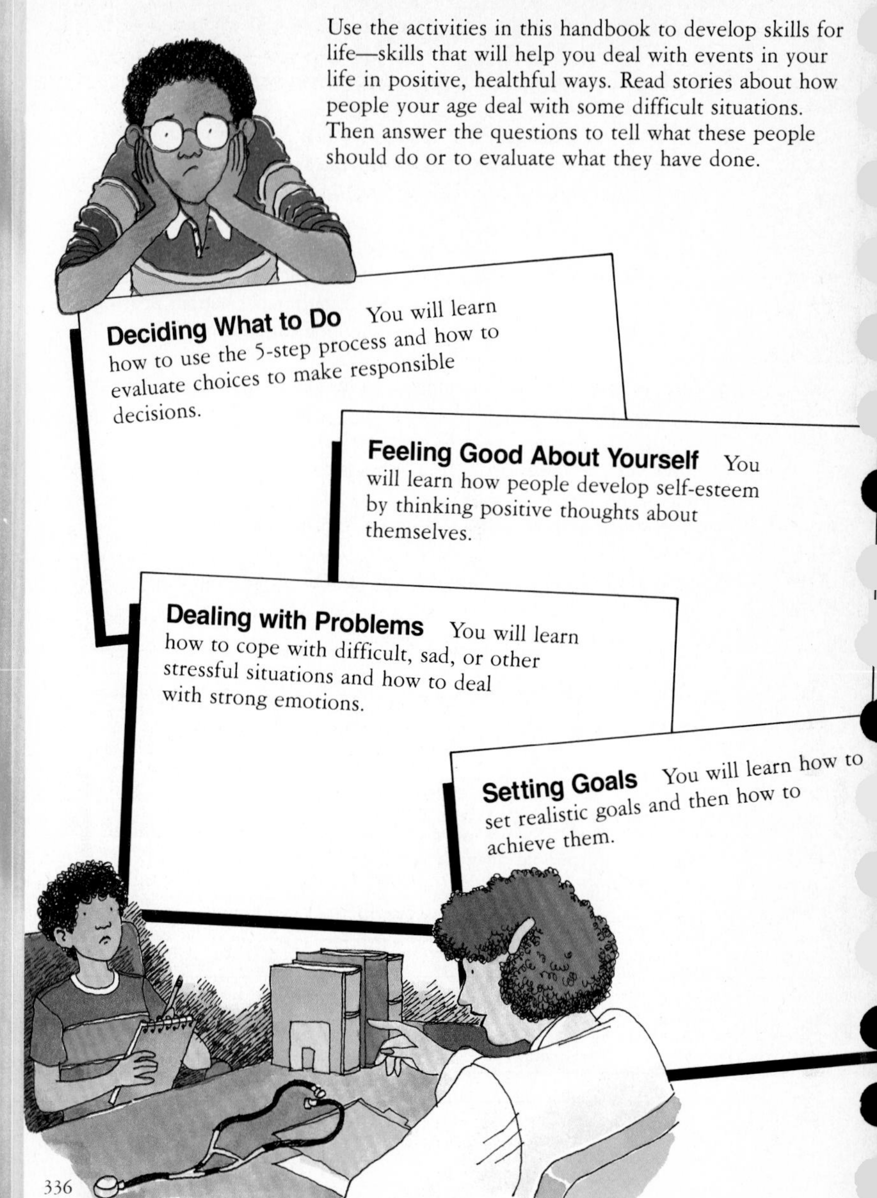

Deciding What to Do You will learn how to use the 5-step process and how to evaluate choices to make responsible decisions.

Feeling Good About Yourself You will learn how people develop self-esteem by thinking positive thoughts about themselves.

Dealing with Problems You will learn how to cope with difficult, sad, or other stressful situations and how to deal with strong emotions.

Setting Goals You will learn how to set realistic goals and then how to achieve them.

336

Setting Goals These activities focus on one or several of the aspects of setting appropriate goals. Goals should be realistic (not too hard or too easy); goals should be specific and measurable; a plan for achieving the goal should be developed that includes steps towards attainment and a time table.

Explain to students that a goal is something a person wants to do or achieve. Then tell them that there are many things people can do to help reach their goals. You may want to discuss only the aspect(s) of goal setting mentioned in the activity or include a discussion of all the aspects mentioned above. Emphasize that working to reach a goal is just as important as actually attaining it.

Feeling Good About Yourself These activities teach students the skills to build their self-esteem by recognizing the negative thoughts they have about themselves and to learn to change them to more positive, realistic thoughts. Negative thoughts about oneself ("I'm so stupid") and about one's potential ("I'll never understand this math") are very self-defeating and lower self-esteem. Realistic thinking ("Math is hard for me, but if I study hard I can pass the test") and positive thinking ("I can learn math") can help raise self-esteem. Explain that everyone has negative thoughts about themselves at times, but thinking in more positive and realistic ways is a skill to use throughout their lives.

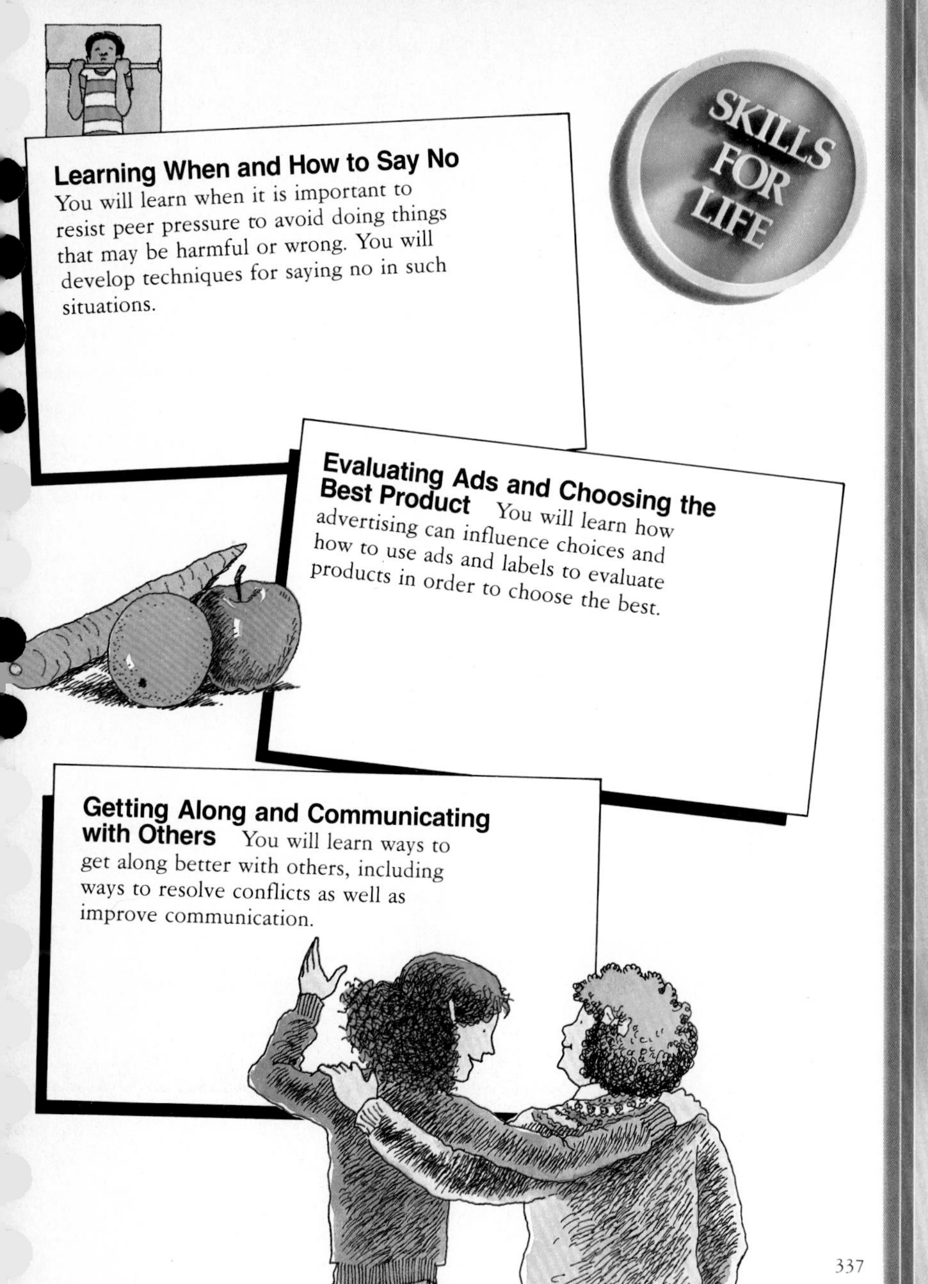

Learning When and How to Say No You will learn when it is important to resist peer pressure to avoid doing things that may be harmful or wrong. You will develop techniques for saying no in such situations.

Evaluating Ads and Choosing the Best Product You will learn how advertising can influence choices and how to use ads and labels to evaluate products in order to choose the best.

Getting Along and Communicating with Others You will learn ways to get along better with others, including ways to resolve conflicts as well as improve communication.

337

Overhead Transparencies

The following overhead transparencies are available in a package for Grades 4–6 to help teach some of the life skills:

Transparency 1: Making Good Decisions
Transparency 2: Characteristics of a Good Goal
Transparency 3: Ways to Say No
Transparency 4: Coping with Stress

Dealing With Problems These activities give students a way to admit that certain problems exist and learn ways to cope with them. Situations include children facing problems that upset them or that they cannot control. Explain that nervous, upset, or angry feelings may be accompanied by a "knot" in the stomach, sweaty palms, or tense neck muscles. Mention that adults have these same feelings. Ways to deal with these feelings include talking to someone you trust, practicing deep breathing exercises, and doing another activity (such as exercise) to get your mind off the problem. You may want to expand the activities in the Handbook to discuss other situations in which these strategies can help.

Getting Along with Others and **Communicating Well** These activities help students understand the cues and barriers to good communication. Explain that the tone of a person's voice, the look on a person's face, and the way a person stands are all part of communication. Discuss how paying attention to these cues can improve communication and help people get along better. Discuss how communicating well and getting along can help people feel better about themselves.

Learning When and How to Say No These activities teach students refusal skills necessary to deal with negative peer pressure. Basic techniques students can use to "say no" include: (1) Just say no (or other phrases that mean the same thing). (2) Ignore the person's suggestion. (3) Invite the person to do something else. (4) Have comeback lines ready. (5) Leave the scene in a confident manner.

You may want to mention all of these techniques in a discussion before or after the Handbook activity. Also, these techniques could be rehearsed aloud for more practice after the activity.

Evaluating Ads and **Choosing the Best Product** These activities help students practice being wise consumers of health care products and services. Explain that advertisers use many techniques to get people to buy their products. For example, they use fancy packaging or feature famous people in their ads. Before beginning the activities, you may want to discuss how ads or labels can influence a consumer, or what information is important or helpful when choosing different products.

Chapter 1 Skills for Life

pages 338–340

Life Management Skill
Decision Making

Answers
Sylvia's choices are to take her friend's diet pills or not take them. Students should use the decision-making steps and guidelines to determine that Sylvia should not take any of Jeannette's pills. Accept any reasonable answers for the possible outcomes of each choice. Reasons for advising Sylvia not to take the diet pills may include: people should not take someone else's pills, diet pills are not safe, Sylvia's parents would not approve of her taking diet pills, she may not get the proper amount of nutrients from food if she took diet pills.

Thinking Skills: By evaluating Sylvia's decision, students are *judging and evaluating* and *making decisions.*

Deciding What to Do

Sylvia and her friend Jeannette made plans to meet for lunch on Saturday at a local fast-food restaurant. When they arrive, they each order their meals and sit at a table. Sylvia notices that Jeannette has ordered only a soft drink, and comments on this to her friend. Jeannette confides that she has not been hungry since her sister gave her some diet pills that she obtained from her doctor. Jeannette points out that Sylvia, too, could avoid being hungry. She offers to share her diet pills with Sylvia.

Sylvia knows that it is dangerous to use medicines prescribed for someone else. She also knows that diet pills can be harmful. She points out to Jeannette that the best way to lose weight is to follow a sensible diet and exercise more. Jeannette continues to urge Sylvia to take the diet pills.

On a separate sheet of paper or the *Health for Life* decision-making chart, examine this situation. Use the five-step decision-making process to decide the choices that Sylvia has and the possible outcome of each choice. Ask yourself whether each choice fits the following guidelines for a good decision:
• The choice is safe and promotes good health.
• The choice is legal.
• Sylvia's parents would approve of the choice.
• The choice shows respect for Sylvia and others.

What would you advise Sylvia to do? Why?

Feeling Good About Yourself

While leaving the lunch line, Lucy tripped and spilled her tray on the cafeteria floor. Students nearby clapped, and Lucy felt very embarrassed.

Like everyone, Lucy has a "voice" inside her head that tells her about herself. This "voice" is really positive or negative thoughts that Lucy has about herself. Often, Lucy finds herself having negative thoughts when she could substitute more positive thinking. These thoughts make Lucy feel bad about herself. After tripping in the cafeteria, Lucy finds herself thinking negative thoughts about herself, even though she knows that spilling her tray does not make her a bad person. She is uncomfortable with this negative thinking, but is also embarrassed that she spilled her lunch tray.

Answer the following questions on a separate sheet of paper.

1. What negative thoughts might Lucy have after tripping? Write at least five negative things that Lucy might think.
2. For every negative thought that Lucy might have about herself, what is one positive thing that she could substitute? Write one positive thought for each negative thought that Lucy could have.

Chapter 1 Skills for Life
continued

Life Management Skill
Self-Esteem Building

Answers
Answers will vary. Samples of acceptable answers are provided. (Each of the letters (a–e) in Question #1 relate to the same letter in Question #2)

1. Negative thoughts:
a. I'm so clumsy.
b. Everyone is staring at me.
c. Boy, am I stupid.
d. I can never do anything right.
e. I always make a mess of things.

2. Positive thoughts:
a. Everyone trips sometimes. I'll just be more careful next time.
b. Everyone who is looking at me is probably remembering a time when he or she tripped and felt silly. Everyone understands how it feels to be embarrassed.
c. It's not stupid to trip; it's just an accident.
d. I do a lot of things well. Tripping and spilling my tray does not reflect my abilities at all.
e. I've made a mess just now. I'll help clean it up and be more careful with the next tray.

Thinking Skill: When students create positive and negative thoughts Lucy might have about herself, they are *suggesting alternatives.*

Chapter 1
Skills for Life
continued

Life Management Skill
Coping

Answers
Answers will vary. Samples are provided. (Each of the letters in Question #1 (a–c) relate to the same letters in Questions #2 and #3.)

1. Causes:
a. oversleeping
b. rushing to catch the bus
c. forgetting books, homework, and lunch

2. Solutions:
a. using alarm clock; responding to mother's reminders
b. get up a little earlier each day; leave the house earlier
c. put books in a special place each evening; keep books in a bookbag by the door; put lunch in bookbag every morning

3. Consequences:
a. having more time in the morning; mother not annoyed
b. more time in the morning; more time to get to bus
c. having a special place will help form a habit of picking up books; a special bag for books and lunch is easy to see and is a daily reminder

4. One of the suggestions made in the "solutions" column should be circled.

Thinking Skills: By analyzing Jackie's problem, students are *suggesting alternatives* and *drawing conclusions.*

Dealing with Problems

Jackie has been feeling a lot of stress lately. She has overslept almost every day this week, and has had to rush to catch the school bus every morning. She has not had time to eat a healthy breakfast all week, and has forgotten her lunch three times. She also has forgotten her books and homework several times. Jackie's mother is annoyed with her because she needs constant reminders to get out of bed in the morning. She also is not doing her morning chores.

Jackie knows that she has a problem that she needs to work on. She realizes that several factors are causing her to feel stress. She would like to identify these problem areas and decide what to do about them to relieve her stress.

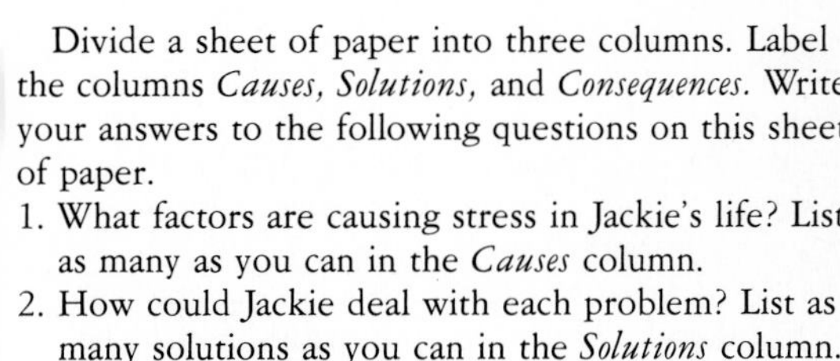

Divide a sheet of paper into three columns. Label the columns *Causes, Solutions,* and *Consequences.* Write your answers to the following questions on this sheet of paper.

1. What factors are causing stress in Jackie's life? List as many as you can in the *Causes* column.
2. How could Jackie deal with each problem? List as many solutions as you can in the *Solutions* column.
3. What are some possible consequences of each suggestion? List as many as you can in the *Consequences* column.
4. What do you think is the best solution for each problem? For each cause, circle the solution that you would advise Jackie to use.

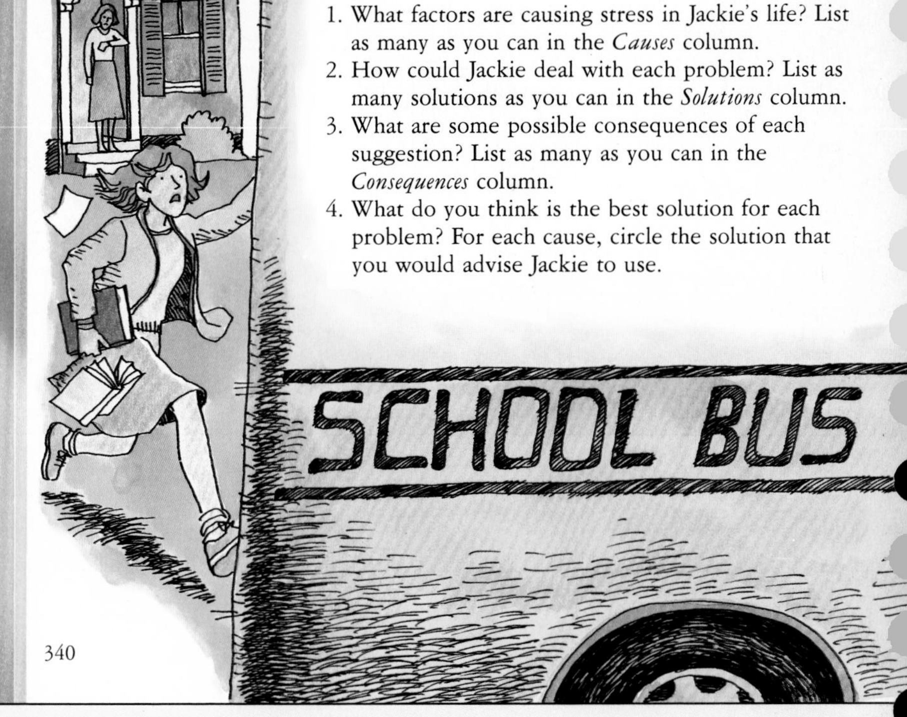

Deciding What to Do

Paul has just finished reading Chapter 2, "Growing and Changing." He knows that both heredity and good health decisions affect his growth. He has been invited to go on a weekend campout with his best friend's family. Having just gotten over a bout with the flu, Paul still does not feel completely well. He is still quite tired, and needs more rest than usual. Paul also has a lot of schoolwork to catch up on. He has a test on Monday morning that he needs to study for. He also knows that next week will be especially busy.

Paul knows that he needs rest in order to recover from his illness and remain healthy. He does not want to put his health in danger. On the other hand, he very much wants to go camping with his friend's family. He knows that they would have a good time fishing, hiking, and sleeping in tents. Paul also knows that he will not have a chance to go camping again until next year.

On a separate sheet of paper or the *Health for Life* decision-making chart, examine this situation. Use the five-step decision-making process and what you learned in Chapter 2 to decide what Paul should do.

Chapter 2 Skills for Life

pages 341–343

Life Management Skill
Decision Making

Answers
Accept all reasonable answers that show Paul using the decision-making steps to decide that he should not go camping for the weekend. Reasons that students give may include: he can better recover from the flu, he will have time to catch up on his homework and study for his test, his parents would approve of this decision, staying home shows respect for himself and others.

Thinking Skills: When students determine what Paul should do about going camping with his friends, they are *organizing information* and *making decisions*.

Chapter 2 Skills for Life
continued

Life Management Skill
Refusal

Answers
Answers will vary. Accept all reasonable answers. Possible student answers might include the following:

a. Ways to say no:

1. "No, I don't want to smoke cigarettes."

2. Sarah could ignore Lisa's suggestion.

3. "I'm going to try this shirt on."

4. "True friends don't push each other to do things they don't want to do."

5. Sarah could leave.

b. Consequences of each method: (Each number (1–5) correlates to suggestions from above)

1. Sarah's friends may make fun of her, continue to pressure her, or may accept her refusal.

2. Lisa might not realize that Sarah is refusing her suggestion and may continue to pressure Sarah.

3. An alternative temporarily removes Sarah from the situation, but she may be pressured later on.

4. Sarah's friends may stop pressuring her, but they might become angry also.

5. Sarah's friends might become angry, but Sarah would no longer be present.

Thinking Skills: By suggesting ways that Sarah can say no to smoking and evaluating the consequences of Sarah's actions, students are *suggesting alternatives* and *judging and evaluating.*

Learning When and How to Say No

While spending the afternoon with her friends at the shopping mall, Sarah is offered a cigarette by Lisa. Sarah knows that smoking can affect her growth and health, but does not want to lose her friends.

Sarah has learned that when her friends try to get her to do something, it is called *peer pressure.* She knows that peer pressure can be positive, such as when her friends encouraged her to try out for the school play. She also knows that peer pressure can be negative. When her friends encourage her to smoke cigarettes, it is negative peer pressure.

Learning how to say no to negative peer pressure is an important part of growing up. There are several ways to say no without losing friends. These methods include:

1. Just saying no.
2. Ignoring the friend's suggestions.
3. Changing the subject or suggesting another activity.
4. Explaining that true friends do not push each other to do things that they don't want to do.
5. Leaving the situation.

Divide a sheet of paper into two columns. On the left side of the paper, list five different ways that Sarah could say no to Lisa. Use the five methods above as a guide. In the right-hand column, write the possible consequences of each method. Which suggestion would you advise Sarah to follow?

Dealing with Problems

Jorge is upset with his family. His parents always expect Jorge to participate in family activities, even though Jorge would rather be with his friends. His older sister often embarrasses Jorge by telling his friends stories about what Jorge did when he was little. Worst of all, Jorge has to share a bedroom with Felipe, his little brother, who is always trying to tag along whenever Jorge is with his friends. Jorge is at his wit's end. He loves his family, but he feels pressured to spend too much time with them. He would like to have more time for himself and his friends. He feels that he has no privacy. He wishes that he did not have to share a room with Felipe. He finds himself getting angry with his family members easily, and this makes him uncomfortable.

Answer the following questions on a separate sheet of paper.

1. Why is Jorge upset?
2. What would you advise Jorge to do to help him cope with his feelings?
3. How will your suggestion in question #2 help Jorge?

Chapter 2 Skills for Life

continued

Life Management Skill

Coping

Answers

Answers will vary. Samples are provided.

1. Reasons Jorge is upset may include: he would like to spend more time with his friends instead of with his family, his sister embarrasses Jorge with her stories about him, he has to share a bedroom with his brother and take him places when he is with his friends.

2. Jorge could talk over his feelings with his family, do something else when he is feeling angry, or practice deep breathing exercises when he feels angry.

3. Jorge can get his feelings out in the open, calm down, and start to deal with his problem.

Thinking Skills: When students analyze Jorge's feelings and suggest ways that he can deal with his problems, they are *drawing conclusions* and *judging and evaluating.*

Chapter 3 Skills for Life

pages 344–346

Life Management Skill
Decision Making

Answers
Susan's choices are to follow the advice of her doctor and mother to gain weight or not change her eating habits.

1. Gaining 5 to 10 pounds would be safe and promote health for Susan since she has not been eating properly and has been feeling very tired. If Susan does not change her eating habits, it would not promote health.

2. Susan's parents would approve of her decision to follow her doctor's advice and gain weight. They would not approve of a decision to do nothing to change her eating habits.

3. If Susan began eating a more healthy and balanced diet and gained some weight, it would show respect for herself. If she does not change her eating habits, it would not show respect for herself.

Students should advise Susan to listen to her doctor and her mother.

Thinking Skills: By evaluating Susan's choices, students are *judging and evaluating* and *making decisions.*

Deciding What to Do

Susan's mother is concerned because Susan has been very tired lately. The doctor has told Susan that she is below the average weight for her height. He is concerned that she is not taking in enough nutrients to stay healthy. Susan thinks that she looks fine at her current weight. She is very active and does not eat many Calories each day. Susan is not certain that she wants to gain weight. She really does not want to become overweight, but she knows that the doctor would like her to gain 5 to 10 pounds. She admits to herself, though, that she *has* been unusually tired lately.

On a separate sheet of paper, list the choices Susan has in this situation. Evaluate each choice by asking the following questions.

1. Is Susan's choice safe? Does it promote good health?
2. Would Susan's parents and doctor approve of her decision?
3. Does the choice show respect for Susan and others?

What would you advise Susan to do?

Getting Along with Others

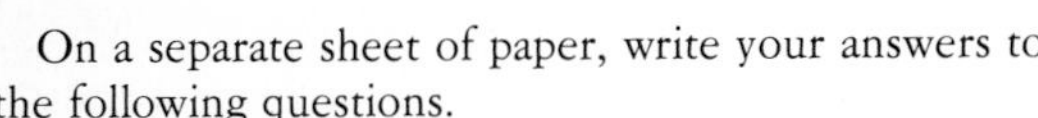

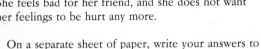

Mary Ann's best friend, Jane, is overweight for her height. Mary Ann knows that Jane is self-conscious about her weight and is trying to lose a few pounds. The other girls in Mary Ann's group, though, often make fun of Jane's weight, even when she can hear them. Mary Ann does not join in when her friends criticize Jane, but she does not say anything to stop them from being hurtful. Mary Ann knows that Jane is very discouraged and feels left out by the group. She feels bad for her friend, and she does not want her feelings to be hurt any more.

On a separate sheet of paper, write your answers to the following questions.

1. What could Mary Ann tell Jane to show that she respects her feelings?
2. What are three things that Mary Ann could say to her friends to discourage them from making fun of Jane?
3. What might be the consequences of each suggestion in question 2?
4. Which suggestion would you choose?

Chapter 3 Skills for Life

continued

Life Management Skill
Social and Communication

Answers
Accept all reasonable answers. Samples are provided.

1. "It must hurt when others say that you're too heavy." or "I know you're trying to lose weight, and I think that's great. Don't give up!"

2. **a.** Mary Ann could say that Jane's feelings are hurt by their comments.
b. She could explain that Jane is trying to lose weight and is discouraged. Mary Ann could point out that the group could *help* Jane.
c. She could point out Jane's positive points to help the others be more accepting.

3. (Answers in a–c refer to points made in Question #2)
a. The other girls might try to be nicer to Jane, or they might not.
b. The other girls might stop criticizing Jane and start to encourage her to lose weight.
c. The group might become more accepting of Jane.

4. Answers will vary depending on the responses given for Questions #2 and #3. Accept any reasonable answers.

Thinking Skills: When students analyze this situation, where Mary Ann is trying to help Jane get along with their other friends, they are *interpreting information, suggesting alternatives,* and *judging and evaluating.*

Chapter 3 Skills for Life

continued

Life Management Skill
Consumer

Answers
Students' answers will vary, but might include the following:
1. spaghetti, ground beef, tomato sauce or ingredients needed to make it from scratch, lettuce, vegetables for salad, dressing, milk, fruit.
2. Factors Steven should consider: whether the foods contain necessary nutrients, how the foods are processed, whether the foods are high in cholesterol or salt, whether the foods contain unnecessary preservatives or additives.
3. Reading food labels will give Steven a list of ingredients, nutritional information, the weight, date, name of the manufacturer, and storage information. By reading labels, Steven can pick the foods and brands that are the most nutritious for his family.

Thinking Skills: When students determine what Steven should consider when buying food products to prepare a meal, they are *interpreting information* and *drawing conclusions*.

Choosing the Best Products

Steven's health class has just finished reading Chapter 3 in his health book. Steven is eager to share what he has learned with his family. After discussing good nutrition with his parents and sister, Steven asks if he can plan and prepare a meal for them. His parents agree to help him select a menu, make a shopping list, and shop for and prepare a healthy dinner. Together, they decide to have spaghetti with meat sauce, salad, bread, milk, and fruit.

On a separate sheet of paper, write your answers to the following questions.

1. Using the menu for their dinner, what items will be on Steven's shopping list? (List as many as you can.)
2. When shopping for the items on his list, what should Steven keep in mind? Use what you learned in Chapter 3 to list as many factors as you can to help Steven choose the most nutritious foods.
3. How can reading food labels help Steven evaluate products and decide which brands to buy?

Deciding What to Do

While practicing the shuttle run for the President's Physical Fitness Test, Jim twisted his ankle. It is not bruised, but it is swollen and does hurt a little to walk or run. The school nurse gave Jim an ice pack and told him to rest the ankle for a day to allow the swelling to go down. She advised him to notify his doctor if the pain increased or the swelling did not improve within a day.

Jim is disappointed because he had planned to play in an important Little League game tonight. He knows that his teammates are depending on him to pitch, and he does not want to let them down. He also is scheduled to be tested on the shuttle run tomorrow during PE class. He has been practicing this event and is impatient to be tested. On the other hand, Jim knows that an injury can get worse if it is not taken care of. If this were to occur, he knows that he might be prevented from participating in his favorite activities for longer than a day.

On a separate sheet of paper or the *Health for Life* decision-making chart, examine this situation. Use the five-step decision-making process and what you learned in Chapter 4 to determine what choices Jim has and which he should choose.

Chapter 4 Skills for Life

pages 347–349

Life Management Skill
Decision Making

Answers
Accept all reasonable answers that show students using the five-step decision-making process and incorporate the guidelines for making good decisions. The best choice is for Jim to decide to rest his ankle for the day.

Thinking Skill: When students determine what Jim should do about his sore ankle, they are *making decisions*.

Chapter 4 Skills for Life
continued

Life Management Skill
Self-Esteem Building

Answers
Answers will vary. Samples are provided.

a. Negative thoughts:

1. No one likes me.

2. I'm not being picked because I'm clumsy.

3. I'm so short/fat/tall/ugly/clumsy.

4. I've never been good at team sports.

5. The teacher hates me.

b. Positive thoughts:(Each of the answers (1–5) refers to the corresponding negative thought from above.)

1. I haven't been picked because the team captains aren't sure of my skills. They'll be happy to see that I've improved.

2. No one is good at every sport. I'm trying hard, and my skills are improving. I'm not clumsy.

3. My appearance is not important in this sport. When I'm picked, I'll try my best for the team.

4. When I'm picked, I'll try my best. I know I've improved since last time.

5. The teacher might not understand how hard it is waiting to be picked. I'll talk with her and maybe she'll let me be a team captain soon.

Thinking Skills: By developing negative and positive thoughts Laura might have about herself, students are *suggesting alternatives*.

Feeling Good About Yourself

Laura is very discouraged. Every time a team captain chooses players in PE class, she is the last to be chosen. She knows that she is not the best athlete in the class, but she has become more skillful and coordinated this year.

Like everyone else, Laura has a "voice" in her head telling her about herself. When Laura has negative thoughts, she hears the voice telling her negative things about herself. When she has positive thoughts, she tells herself good things. When teams are being chosen in PE class, Laura finds herself having negative thoughts. She doubts her skills and abilities, and wonders whether she will have friends if she does not play ball well.

Divide a sheet of paper into two columns by folding it in half lengthwise. On the left side of the paper, list five examples of negative thinking that Laura might have when teams are being chosen. In the right-hand column, write a positive thought that Laura could substitute for each negative thought.

Setting Goals

An important part of growing up and learning about yourself is developing the ability to recognize what you are good at and in what areas you need improvement. When you have identified these areas, it becomes possible to form goals for yourself and work to achieve your goals.

Physical fitness is essential to overall health. Exercise can improve both physical and mental well-being. Because of this, it is important for you to include exercise in your daily activities. You can develop an exercise plan by identifying your fitness strengths and weaknesses. You can then develop goals for yourself.

On a separate sheet of paper, use what you learned in Chapter 4 to answer the following questions.

1. What are your fitness strengths? In what areas would you like to improve?
2. What are three fitness goals that you would like to achieve?
3. How will you measure whether you have reached your fitness goals? If you cannot measure one of your goals, revise it so that it becomes measurable.

Chapter 4 Skills for Life

continued

Life Management Skill
Goal Setting

Answers

1. Answers will vary but should focus on parts of health fitness and skills fitness that students want to improve.

2. Answers will vary. Goals should be measurable.

3. Answers will vary.

Thinking Skill: When students write about their fitness strengths and goals for improving fitness, they are *judging and evaluating.*

Chapter 5 Skills for Life

pages 350-352

Life Management Skill
Decision Making

Answers
Jake's choices are to let the man inside the house to make an emergency telephone call, not let him in, or make the call for the man without letting him inside. Students should use the decision-making steps to decide that Jake should not let the man inside the house because it might not be safe and would not be approved by his parents. However, it would be safe and acceptable to make the emergency call while the man waits outside. Making the call for the man would be helpful and also show respect. It would also protect them from potential harm from the man in case there is really no emergency.

Thinking Skills: By evaluating what Jake should do about the man at the door, students are *judging and evaluating* and *making decisions.*

Deciding What to Do

Because both of his parents have to work today, Jake is home alone with his six-year-old sister, Laura. His parents have left instructions not to have any visitors or allow anyone into the house while they are gone. They have also left telephone numbers where they can be reached and the telephone numbers of the neighbors, police department, and fire department.

The day is passing smoothly. As Jake works on a science project, Laura plays with her building set. Later, both Laura and Jake hear a knock at the door. As he checks through the peephole, Jake asks, "Who is it?" A man answers that he needs to use the phone for an emergency. Jake does not know the man, but recognizes him from the neighborhood. Jake knows that he is not supposed to open the door for strangers, but wants to help the man.

On a separate sheet of paper or the *Health for Life* decision-making chart, examine this situation. Use the five-step decision-making process and what you learned in Chapter 5 to determine Jake's choices. Evaluate each choice by asking whether it is safe and whether Jake's parents would approve of his decision. What would you advise Jake to do?

Learning When and How to Say No

SKILLS FOR LIFE

Carlos and his neighbor Kurt have spent the afternoon ice skating. The sun is beginning to go down, and the temperature is dropping. Both boys are supposed to be home before it is dark. Although Carlos and Kurt only live a few blocks away from the skating rink, they are too tired and cold to walk home. They also know that they will not make it home before it is dark. Both boys' parents are still at work, so they cannot call home for a ride. None of their friends are at the rink, either, so they cannot get a ride home with someone they know. Kurt suggests that he and Carlos hitch-hike home. He urges that there is no need to worry since they live so close to the skating rink. Carlos knows that hitch-hiking can be very dangerous. He decides that he would rather be cold and tired and arrive home late than put himself in a dangerous situation. He does not want to go along with Kurt's plan to hitch-hike home.

Fold a piece of paper in half lengthwise to make two columns. In the left column, list five ways that Carlos could say no to Kurt. In the right-hand column, write the possible consequences of each method. Which suggestion do you think is best?

Chapter 5 Skills for Life

continued

Life Management Skill
Refusal

Answers
Students' answers will vary. Possible answers include the following:

a. Ways to say no:

1. "No, hitch-hiking is dangerous."
2. "Let's wait until my mother gets home. She'll come and get us."
3. "If you were my friend, you wouldn't want to make me hitch-hike if I didn't want to."
4. Ignore Kurt's suggestion.
5. Carlos could leave and walk home by himself.

b. Consequences of each method: (Each number (1–5) corresponds to the method mentioned above.)

1. Does not solve problem of how to get home, Kurt might continue pressuring him
2. Solves problem of getting home, not likely to anger Kurt
3. Might anger Kurt, might convince Kurt to try to find another way home
4. Doesn't solve problem of getting home, probably would not stop Kurt from pressuring Carlos to hitch-hike
5. Might convince Kurt to walk home with him

c. Students will probably indicate that they would advise Carlos to wait and call his mother. However, answers may vary. Accept reasonable responses.

Thinking Skills: When students describe ways that Kurt can say no to Carlos about hitch-hiking and evaluate how Carlos may react to Kurt's actions, they are *suggesting alternatives* and *judging and evaluating.*

Chapter 5 Skills for Life

continued

Life Management Skill
Social and Communication

Answers

1. Robert's words say that he is not hurt, but his actions indicate that he is in pain.
2. Katy can observe Robert's body language and examine the area of injury to decide if she thinks he is really hurt.
3. Communication is confused because Robert is saying one thing and doing another.
4. Katy could point out that Robert's body language shows that he is in pain. She could emphasize that he needs first aid for his injuries.

Thinking Skills: By evaluating Robert's communication, students are *interpreting information* and *suggesting alternatives.*

Communicating Well

Katy and Robert were riding their bicycles in the park when Robert fell off his bike. He landed hard, striking his elbow on the pavement. His shirt was torn and his elbow was scraped. Small pieces of gravel were on Robert's skin, and he was bleeding a little. The elbow appeared to be very bruised, and it hurt Robert to bend it. Katy told Robert that he should go home to wash the elbow, apply ice, and have an adult check the injury. Robert protested that he was not hurt. Katy pointed out that he might need to see a doctor, but Robert argued that he was not injured badly enough to cut their bicycle ride short. He cradled his elbow in his other hand, and winced when he moved his arm.

On a separate sheet of paper, write your answers to the following questions.

1. In what ways are Robert's words different from his actions?
2. How can Katy tell if Robert is hurt or not?
3. How is communication confused in this situation?
4. What can Katy say to Robert to convince him to get first aid?

Deciding What to Do

It is Saturday, and Erin is home alone for the day. Her mother had to go to work, and her father went to visit Erin's uncle, who is in a hospital several miles away. When Erin's mother calls, she suggests that Erin ask Patty, her fourteen-year-old cousin, to come over for the afternoon.

Shortly after Patty arrives, she and Erin decide to make lunch. While Erin is making sandwiches, Patty removes a pack of cigarettes from her purse and lights one. After taking a puff, she offers the lit cigarette to Erin and encourages her to share it.

Erin knows that cigarettes contain many harmful substances, and that they are habit-forming. She does not want to harm her body or develop a dangerous habit. She also thinks that smoking is an ugly habit. She does not want to smell like smoke or have stained teeth. On the other hand, Erin is grateful that Patty has come to keep her company. She does not want her older cousin to think that she is a baby. She wonders if smoking just once would really be a problem.

On a separate sheet of paper, list the choices that Erin has. Evaluate each choice by asking the following questions.

1. Is the choice safe? Does it promote good health?
2. Is the choice legal?
3. Would Erin's parents approve of her choice?
4. Does the choice show respect for Erin and others?

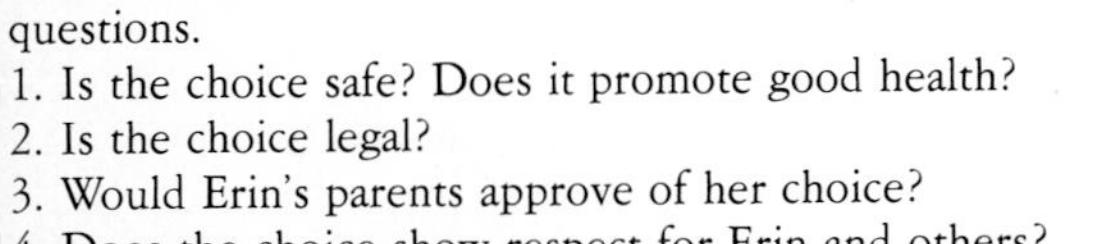

Which choice would you advise Erin to make? Why?

Chapter 6 Skills for Life

pages 353–355

Life Management Skill
Decision Making

Answers
Erin's choices are to smoke a cigarette with her cousin or not smoke.

1. Smoking is not safe and does not promote health. Refusing the cigarette is both safe and promotes health.
2. It is not legal for a person Erin's age to smoke. Refusing the cigarette would be legal.
3. Erin's parents would approve if she refused the cigarette. They would not approve of her smoking.
4. If Erin smokes, it would not show respect for herself. By refusing to smoke, it would show respect for herself.

Students should advise Erin not to smoke. They should explain that this choice is healthy, legal, acceptable to her parents, and shows respect for herself.

Thinking Skills: By evaluating Erin's choices, students are *judging and evaluating* and *making decisions.*

Chapter 6 Skills for Life

continued

Life Management Skill
Refusal

Answers
Answers will vary. Possible responses may include the following:
1. "No, I don't want any."
2. Gerald could ignore Larry's suggestion.
3. "Let's play basketball instead."
4. "True friends don't push others to do things they don't want to do."
5. Gerald could walk away.

Thinking Skill: When students propose ways that Gerald can refuse alcohol, they are *suggesting alternatives*.

Learning When and How to Say No

Gerald and Larry are neighbors and have been close friends since they were very young. Because they live so close to each other and enjoy being with each other, they often walk home from school together.

One day while walking home from school, Larry pulls a bottle of liquor from his backpack. He tells Gerald that he took it from his older brother, and that no one will ever know that it is missing. After taking a drink from the bottle, he offers it to Gerald and encourages his friend to share it with him.

Gerald knows that alcohol is illegal and dangerous for him to use. He does not want to use anything that will harm his body or cause a dangerous habit to form. He is certain that he does not want to drink any of Larry's liquor. Larry continues to insist that he try the liquor.

On a separate sheet of paper, write five ways that Gerald can say no to Larry.

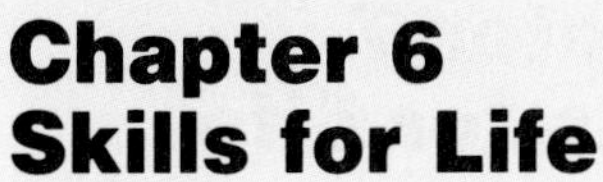

Dealing with Problems

SKILLS FOR LIFE

Danny has always been taught that smoking is harmful to the body. Neither of his parents smoke, nor do his friends. Danny knows that tobacco contains nicotine, an addictive drug. Lately, some of his friends have been encouraging Danny to try smokeless tobacco. They say that it is not harmful like smoking because it does not cause lung cancer. Danny knows that smokeless tobacco can cause a number of serious health problems, including oral cancer, and he will not try it. He does not want to develop a destructive addiction, and firmly tells his friends that he is not interested in trying smokeless tobacco. His friends, though, tell Danny that if he will not chew with them, he cannot do anything with them. This does not change Danny's mind about using smokeless tobacco, but going against his friends' wishes does make him uncomfortable. He feels sad and hurt to be left out of his group.

On a separate sheet of paper, write five suggestions to help Danny cope with the feelings created by peer pressure. Which suggestion would you encourage Danny to follow?

Chapter 6 Skills for Life

continued

Life Management Skill
Coping

Answers

Accept all reasonable answers. Sample answers are provided.

1. Danny can remind himself of the harmful effects of tobacco and feel proud of making the right decision.

2. Danny could confront his friends and point out that true friends do not expect each other to do things they don't want to do.

3. Danny could find new friends who do not use tobacco.

4. Danny could reward himself for making a healthy decision.

5. Danny could talk over his feelings with a parent, family member, or another friend.

Thinking Skill: When students suggest ways that Danny can cope with peer pressure, they are *suggesting alternatives.*

Chapter 7 Skills for Life

pages 356–358

Life Management Skill
Decision Making

Answers
Students should use the decision-making steps to determine that Wendy's choices are to go to the slumber party with a sore throat or stay home.
Students' answers to the questions may be as follows:
1. Staying home is safe and promotes health. Going to the party may not be safe or promote health because Wendy could become sicker or spread her germs to the other girls.
2. Wendy's parents would approve if she stayed home. They would not approve of her going to the slumber party with a sore throat.
3. Staying home would show respect for the health of herself and others. Going to the party would be fun, but would not show respect for herself or others.

Students should realize that staying home would be the best decision.

Thinking Skills: By evaluating Wendy's decision, students are *judging and evaluating* and *making decisions.*

Deciding What to Do

Wendy has been invited to a slumber party for her friend's birthday, and she has been looking forward to it all week. The morning of the party, Wendy's throat feels scratchy. She does not feel too ill, but knows that her mother would not let her go to the party if she knew about Wendy's sore throat. Although she does not want to miss the party, Wendy is worried that her sore throat will get worse during the night, and that one of her friends will catch it from her.

On a separate sheet of paper or your *Health For Life* decision-making chart, examine this situation. Use the five decision-making steps and what you learned in the chapter on fighting disease to determine what Wendy should do. Evaluate her options by asking:

1. Is the choice safe? Does it promote good health?
2. Would Wendy's parents and friends approve of her decision?
3. Does the choice show respect for herself and others?

What decision would you make?

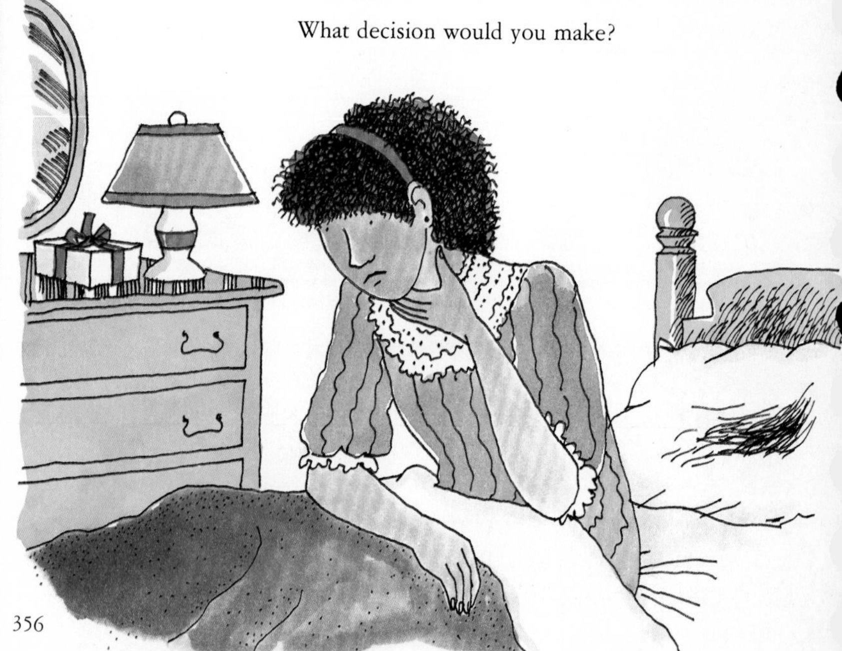

Choosing the Best Advertisement

The job of advertisers is to influence consumers to buy their products. Advertisers know that people who do not feel well are especially likely to purchase health products that promise to help them feel better. Their advertisements aim to convince consumers that their products will relieve the symptoms of illness better than the competitors' products. Consumers spend a great deal of money on health products, many of which are not effective.

Divide a sheet of paper into three columns by folding it into thirds lengthwise. Label the columns *A*, *B*, and *C*. Along the left margin, number from 1 to 6. Look at the advertisements for products *A*, *B*, and *C* shown below. Use what you learned in Chapter 7 to compare the products by answering the following questions for each. Write your answers in the appropriate column on your paper.

1. What product is the advertisement trying to sell?
2. What symptoms does the advertisement claim that the product will help?
3. What does the advertisement promise the consumer?
4. How does the advertisement attempt to draw the consumer away from the competitors?
5. What helpful information does the advertisement give?
6. Which product would you be most likely to buy?

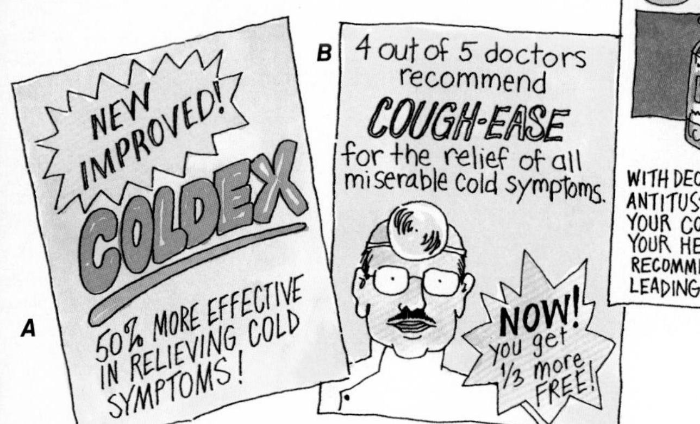

357

Chapter 7 Skills for Life
continued

Life Management Skill
Consumer

Answers
Ad A:
1. Coldex, a cold remedy
2. symptoms of the common cold
3. more effective in relieving cold symptoms
4. new and improved product, 50% more effective
5. relieves symptoms of the common cold

Ad B:
1. Cough-ease, a cold remedy
2. all miserable cold symptoms
3. 1/3 more free, relief of all cold symptoms
4. 4 out of 5 doctors recommend it, 1/3 more free
5. relief of cold symptoms, 4 of 5 doctors recommend

Ad C:
1. Cold-Ban, cold remedy
2. cough and stuffy head
3. decongestant and antitussive medicine, relief from cough and stuffy head
4. Most often recommended by pediatricians, costs less than others
5. contains decongestant and antitussive, treats cough and stuffy head, costs less than competitors

6. Answers may vary, but students are likely to indicate that Ad C gives the most information and that they would be most likely to buy this product.

Thinking Skills: By analyzing the advertisements, students are *interpreting information* and *judging and evaluating*.

Chapter 7 Skills for Life

continued

Life Management Skill
Social and Communication

Answers

1. The doctor needs to know Wallace's symptoms and how long he has had these symptoms.
2. Wallace can make a list of information that the doctor will need. He can answer the doctor's questions carefully.
3. Wallace can ask questions to make sure he understands the doctor's instructions.
4. Wallace can write down the instructions to be sure that he remembers them.

Thinking Skill: By determining how Wallace can best communicate with the doctor, students are *suggesting alternatives.*

Communicating Well

Wallace has stayed home from school because he has a bad headache and sore throat. His mother was unable to take the day off from work, but has made an appointment for him at the doctor's office. A neighbor will take Wallace to the doctor on her way to the store and will give him a ride home. For the first time, however, Wallace must see the doctor alone. He is a little nervous that he might forget to tell the doctor something important, and he wants to communicate clearly during his appointment. Wallace decides that it would be a good idea to make a list of things that he would like to remember to tell the doctor. He writes his symptoms and some questions he has for the doctor in a notebook.

On a separate sheet of paper, write your answers to the following questions.

1. What information will the doctor need to know?
2. How can Wallace be sure that he gives the doctor the necessary information?
3. How can Wallace make certain that he understands the doctor's instructions?
4. How can Wallace be sure that he remembers what the doctor instructs him to do?

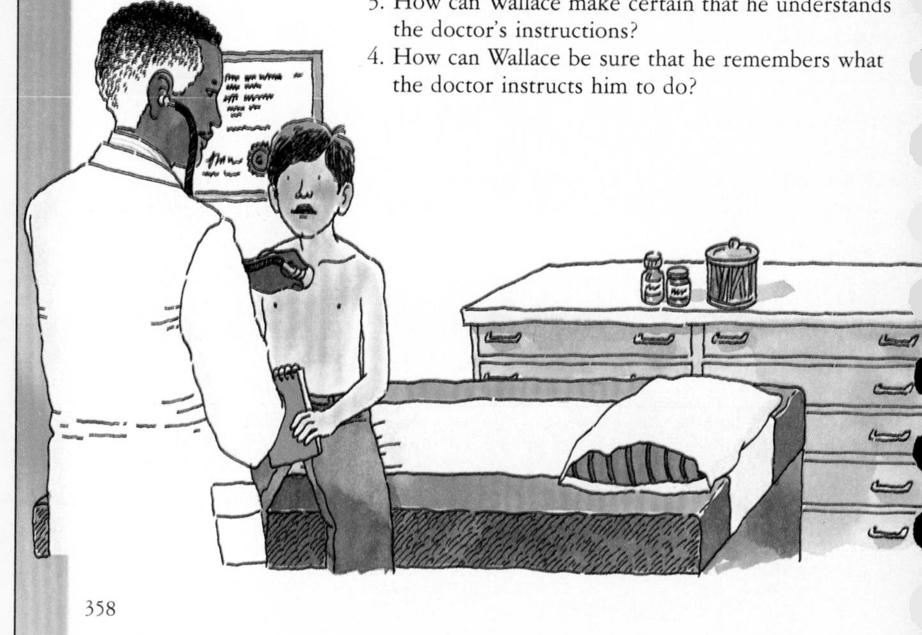

Deciding What to Do

SKILLS FOR LIFE

After wearing them for three years, Abigail has just had her braces removed. The orthodontist has given her a retainer, a device to keep her teeth in the proper position. Abigail is supposed to wear her retainer all day and night. Abigail is relieved to have her braces off after waiting for so long, and she enjoys the compliments that people give her new smile. She is also glad that no one can call her names like "Metal Mouth" any more.

Abigail does not like to wear her retainer because she finds it to be uncomfortable. The retainer also makes her feel self-conscious because she lisps a little when wearing it. Because she is uncomfortable with it, Abigail would prefer not to wear her retainer all of the time. On the other hand, she wants her teeth to remain in the correct position so that she does not have to wear braces again.

On a separate sheet of paper or the *Health for Life* decision-making chart, evaluate this situation. Use the five-step decision-making process and what you learned in this chapter to determine the options that Abigail has. What would you advise Abigail to do?

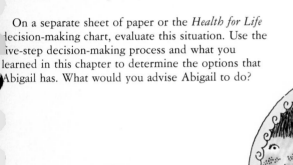

Chapter 8 Skills for Life

pages 359–361

Life Management Skill
Decision Making

Answers
Accept all reasonable answers. Students should determine that Abigail's choices are to always, sometimes, or never wear her retainer. They should use the five-step decision-making process to determine that the best choice is for Abigail to always wear her retainer. Students should advise Abigail to wear her retainer because it is the healthiest choice, will help her teeth remain in position, would be approved by her parents and dentist, and shows respect for herself and others. Even though it may be uncomfortable sometimes, students should realize that the positive consequences outweigh the negative consequences.

Thinking Skills: By determining what Abigail should do about wearing her retainer, students are *judging and evaluating* and *making decisions.*

Chapter 8 Skills for Life

continued

Life Management Skill
Self-Esteem Building

Answers
Answers will vary.

1. Negative thoughts:
  a. I'm so ugly.
  b. I feel like a freak.
  c. Everyone stares at me.

2. Positive thoughts: (Each of the letters (a–c) corresponds to the response with the same letter from above.)
  a. This brace is bulky, but I will only have to wear it for a few months. Even if it's not attractive, it will help my appearance and health in the long run.
  b. None of my classmates has a brace like this, but some wear braces on their teeth. I'm not a freak, I just have a condition to be treated.
  c. When people look at my brace, it is probably because they are curious. They are not staring at me.

Thinking Skill: By describing negative and positive thoughts Josie might have about herself, students are *suggesting alternatives*.

Feeling Good About Yourself

Josie has just found out that she has scoliosis, a condition that causes her spine to bend to the side. Her doctor has explained that Josie must wear a special brace for several months to straighten her spine and improve the condition. The brace is bulky, and shows through Josie's clothes. It also prevents Josie from moving in certain ways. She is self-conscious because she appears different from her classmates and cannot always participate in their activities. Sometimes, other kids make fun of Josie, which makes her feel even more uncomfortable around everyone else.

Fold a sheet of paper in half lengthwise to divide it into two columns. Label one column *Negative Thoughts* and the other *Positive Thoughts.* Write your answers to the following questions on this sheet of paper.

1. What negative thoughts might Josie have as a result of having scoliosis? Write your answers in the *Negative Thoughts* column.
2. For each negative thought that Josie might have about herself, write a positive thought that she could substitute in the *Positive Thoughts* column.

Dealing with Problems

SKILLS FOR LIFE

William is feeling very anxious. His parents are getting divorced, and his mother expects him to look after his little sister after school and start dinner for the family each evening. William misses being able to play with his friends. He does not like the responsibility of caring for his sister. His schoolwork is suffering because his chores often prevent him from finishing his homework until late in the evening. He is often very tired during the school day and has even fallen asleep during class. He only sees his father on weekends and his mother is very tired at the end of the day. Therefore, no one is available to help William with his homework.

William knows that he is under stress. He realizes that a lack of rest and recreation can affect his health. He wants to identify the problem areas and determine what to do about them.

Divide a sheet of paper into three columns. Label the columns *Causes, Solutions,* and *Consequences.*

1. What factors in William's life are causing him to feel stress? List as many problems as you can in the *Causes* column.
2. How could William deal with each problem? List as many options as you can in the *Solutions* column.
3. What are some possible outcomes of each solution? List each outcome in the *Consequences* column next to the solution.
4. For each problem, circle the solution that you would advise William to use to reduce his stress.

Chapter 8 Skills for Life

continued

Life Management Skill
Coping

Answers
Students' answers may include the following. (The letters (a–c) in Question #1 refer to the same letters for Questions #2 and #3.)

1. Causes:
   a. parents getting divorced
   b. babysitting for sister
   c. schoolwork suffering
2. Solutions:
   a. William cannot change this.
   b. talk to mother about getting help babysitting, such as hiring a babysitter, arranging for sister to go to a friend's house, or do other activities some afternoons
   c. arrange for tutor, arrange with mother to reschedule chores so that homework gets done earlier
3. Consequences:
   a. ______
   b. more time for schoolwork and friends, ease pressure from mother
   c. more time to complete assignments, schoolwork done before William gets too tired
4. Students should circle one of the solutions identified in #2.

Thinking Skills: By determining what William can do to relieve his stress, students are *suggesting alternatives* and *judging and evaluating.*

Chapter 9 Skills for Life

pages 362–364

Life Management Skill
Decision Making

Answers
Accept reasonable answers from students that use the decision-making steps and guidelines to explain why Olivia made the right decision. Students should explain that by waiting to take any medicine, she was being safe since she was not sure of what the warnings on the bottles meant. Her action would be acceptable to her parents because she knows that she should not take medicines without the supervision of adults. Even though she may not feel better as quickly, Olivia made the safe and wise decision.

Thinking Skills: When students examine Olivia's choices, they are *judging and evaluating* and *making decisions*.

Deciding What to Do

Olivia stayed home from school today because she ha[s] a cold, sore throat, and cough. Because both of her parents work, she is home alone. As the day goes on, she finds that her sore throat is getting worse. Olivia finds a cough medicine and a cold remedy in the medicine cabinet. One bottle tells her that the product will relieve the symptoms of a cold and sore throat but does not mention anything about a cough. The other product promises to relieve the symptoms of a sore throat and cough. Both bottles list warnings about using the medicine.

Olivia is not certain which, if any, medicine she should take. She is not sure if the warnings on the labels apply to her. She does not want to harm her body. She decides to not take any medicine until her mother comes home.

On a separate sheet of paper or the *Health for Life* decision-making chart, examine this situation. Use the five-step decision-making process to evaluate why Olivia made the right decision. Evaluate each choice by asking whether it fits the guidelines for a good decision.

Choosing the Best Advertisement

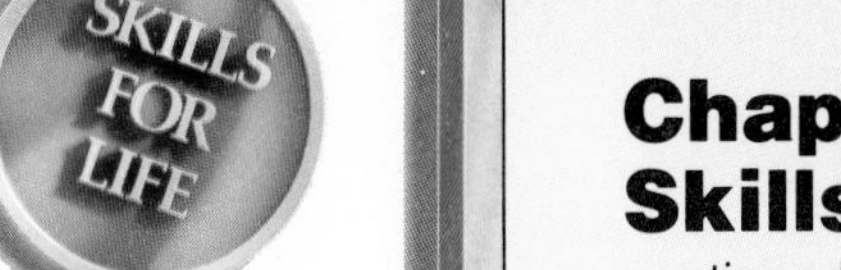

Larry and his younger brother, Steven, are watching television on Saturday morning. Larry notices that every time a commercial comes on the screen, his brother says, "I want that." He knows that television advertisers try to influence consumers to purchase their products by making promises about the products. Larry also knows that these commercials often do not present accurate or useful information to consumers, especially young viewers like Steven.

Larry decides to analyze the cereal ads that he and his brother see that morning and to observe the influence of these commercials on Steven. The advertisement for one cereal, Super Crunchees, features a cowboy who promises "the best crunch in the west." Another cereal, Sweet Nuggets, offers a golden ring in each box and promises the sweetest taste. A third brand of cereal, Oat Toasties, promises 100% of the United States RDA for the essential vitamins and minerals. Larry noted that his brother responded most to the advertisement for Sweet Nuggets.

On a separate sheet of paper, write your answers to the following questions.

1. What did each cereal advertisement promise the consumer?
2. What useful information about the product did each advertisement give the viewer?
3. Why do you think that the Sweet Nuggets commercial appealed the most to Steven?
4. Using what you learned in Chapter 9, which cereal would you choose, and why?

Chapter 9 Skills for Life

continued

Life Management Skill

Consumer

Answers

1. Super Crunchees: the best crunch in the west; Sweet Nuggets: a golden ring, sweetest taste; Oak Toasties: 100% US RDA for vitamins and minerals

2. Super Crunchees: no useful information; Sweet Nuggets: no useful information; Oak Toasties: 100% US RDA for vitamins and minerals

3. Sweet Nuggets offers a gold ring in each box and the sweetest taste. Both of these would appeal to a young child.

4. Oat Toasties, because the ad gave useful information about the vitamin and mineral content and would be the most nutritious.

Thinking Skills: When students analyze the cereal advertisements, they are *interpreting information* and *drawing conclusions*.

Chapter 9 Skills for Life

continued

Life Management Skill
Social and Communication

Answers

1. Hector should actively listen to the doctor. He can take notes.
2. Hector should ask questions to make sure he understands what the doctor is saying.
3. Hector can write down the doctor's instructions to make sure he remembers them.

Thinking Skill: When students evaluate how Hector can best communicate with his doctor, they are *suggesting alternatives*.

Communicating Well

Hector has recently learned that he has diabetes, a disease in which the body is not able to absorb the proper amount of sugar and starch. He has found out that people with diabetes must carefully monitor their diet and exercise so that they do not become ill. Hector will need to follow a special food and activity plan each day. In addition, many people with diabetes must take a medicine called *insulin.* The doctor is explaining to Hector that he must take a certain amount of insulin at specific times each day. Hector becomes a little confused, because the doctor is giving him a lot of instructions. He is not sure that he understands everything that he is being told, nor is he certain that he will remember everything that he needs to do to stay healthy.

On a separate sheet of paper, write your answers to the following questions.

1. What should Hector do as he listens to the doctor?
2. How can Hector be certain that he understands what the doctor is saying?
3. How can Hector be sure that he remembers the information that the doctor gives him?

Deciding What to Do

Leroy's mother has asked him to go to the grocery store to buy a large container of laundry detergent. She instructed him to select the brand with the best price. Once there, Leroy finds four brands that cost the same amount. One brand, packaged in a plastic jug, contains phosphates, an ingredient that Leroy has heard is unhealthy for the environment. Another brand, in a cardboard box, contains artificial colors. A third brand, in a cardboard box, is labeled *biodegradable,* a term that tells Leroy that the detergent breaks down into a harmless form in the environment. A fourth brand, in a plastic jug, is also labeled *biodegradable.* Leroy knows that he must select one of these detergents, but he is not sure which to choose. He decides to make his choice by evaluating each detergent's effects on the environment.

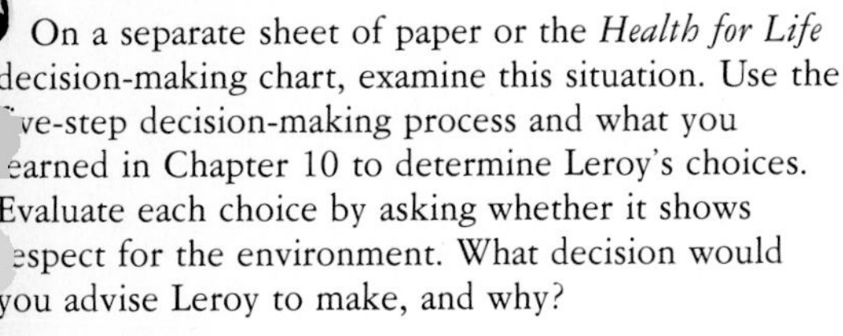

On a separate sheet of paper or the *Health for Life* decision-making chart, examine this situation. Use the five-step decision-making process and what you learned in Chapter 10 to determine Leroy's choices. Evaluate each choice by asking whether it shows respect for the environment. What decision would you advise Leroy to make, and why?

Chapter 10 Skills for Life

pages 365–367

Life Management Skill
Decision Making

Answers
Students should use the decision-making steps to determine that detergent #3 is the best choice. Each of the choices have a good price. However, brand #1 is in a plastic jug that is not biodegradable and contains phosphates that harm the environment. Brand #2 is in a cardboard box that is biodegradable, but it contains artificial colors that could harm the environment. The detergent in the fourth brand is biodegradable, but the plastic jug it comes in is not. In terms of protecting the environment, brand #3 is the best because both the detergent and container are biodegradable and it has a good price.

Thinking Skills: When students evaluate Leroy's decision, they are *organizing information* and *making decisions.*

Chapter 10 Skills for Life

continued

Life Management Skill
Goal Setting

Answers
Accept all reasonable answers. Samples are provided.
1. Divide the goal into smaller parts. Perhaps the goal is not realistic, and the class should adjust their goal for the number of cans they plan to donate each week. This can help students feel that they are accomplishing what they set out to do.
2. Remind students of what they hope to accomplish, and how good they will feel if they succeed. By thinking of the new microscope, students might increase their efforts.
3. Promise a reward. Increase student interest by holding a weekly contest to see who can collect the most cans and newspapers.
4. Have students try to think about goals they have reached in the past.
5. Students could set specific times to work on their goal to help insure that it is reached.

Thinking Skill: By identifying ways to help Lisa's class reach their goal, students are *suggesting alternatives*.

Setting Goals

Lisa's class is trying to earn enough money to buy three new microscopes for their science lab. When investigating money-making activities, they discover that they can collect money from the local recycling center by turning in used aluminum cans and old newspapers. They are excited that they can earn money while improving their community, and decide to collect these items from their neighbors. Their goal is for each student to collect one bag of cans and twenty newspapers each week. Every Saturday, their science teacher will take two volunteers from the class to the recycling center to turn in their cans and papers. The class determines that by the end of two months, they will have enough money to buy the microscopes.

For the first few weeks, the project goes smoothly. The class is eager, and each student contributes at least one bag of cans and twenty newspapers each week. Soon, however, the students begin to lose interest, and fewer contributions are made. The students become discouraged.

On a separate sheet of paper, list five ways to help the class continue to work toward their goal.

Choosing the Best Place to Live

People choose the places where they live for a variety of reasons. These reasons may include what the community has to offer each resident. Many people consider parks, beaches, other recreation facilities, schools, and hospitals to be very important factors in their choice of a place to live.

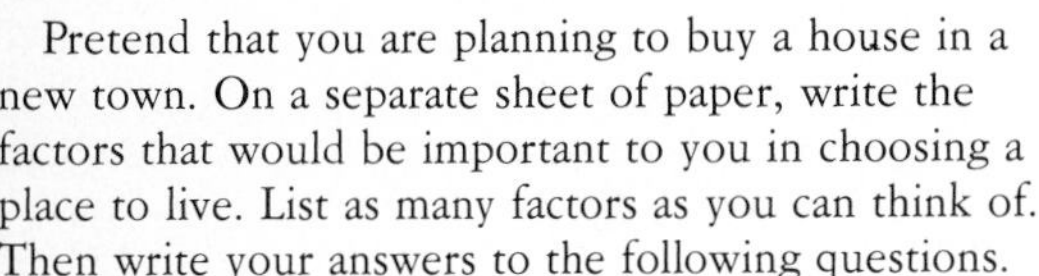

Pretend that you are planning to buy a house in a new town. On a separate sheet of paper, write the factors that would be important to you in choosing a place to live. List as many factors as you can think of. Then write your answers to the following questions.

1. Which factors are most important to you as a consumer?
2. If you were buying a home, would the community in which you now live meet your requirements?
3. If your community does not meet your requirements, what changes would need to be made before you would choose to buy a home there?
4. How could you help make the necessary changes in your community?

Chapter 10 Skills for Life

continued

Life Management Skill
Consumer

Answers

1. Answers will vary, but might include parks, recreation facilities, schools, hospitals, shopping areas, etc.
2. Answers will vary.
3. Answers will vary.
4. Answers will vary.

Thinking Skills: By identifying factors to consider when choosing a place to live, students are *generalizing* and *suggesting alternatives*.

Glossary

Pronunciation Key

The pronunciation of each word is shown just after the word, in this way: **ab bre vi ate** (ə brē/vē āt). The letters and signs used are pronounced as in the words below. The mark / is placed after a syllable with primary or heavy accent, as in the example above. The mark / after a syllable shows a secondary or lighter accent, as in **ab bre vi a tion** (ə brē/vē ā/shən).

a	hat, cap
ā	age, face
ä	father, far
b	bad, rob
ch	child, much
d	did, red
e	let, best
ē	equal, be
ėr	term, learn
f	fat, if
g	go, bag
h	he, how
i	it, pin
ī	ice, five
j	jam, enjoy
k	kind, seek
l	land, coal
m	me, am
n	no, in
ng	long, bring
o	hot, rock
ō	open, go
ô	order, all
oi	oil, voice
ou	house, out
p	paper, cup
r	run, try
s	say, yes
sh	she, rush
t	tell, it
th	thin, both
ŦH	then, smooth
u	cup, butter
u̇	full, put
ü	rule, move
v	very, save
w	will, woman
y	young, yet
z	zero, breeze
zh	measure, seizure
ə	represents:
a	in about
e	in taken
i	in pencil
o	in lemon
u	in circus

368

A

abdomen (ab′dō mən), the lower part of the body of humans and other mammals, containing the digestive organs, such as the stomach and intestines.
acid rain, rain that contains a higher than normal amount of acids. These acids are caused by certain gases released into the air.
acne (ak′nē), a skin disease in which the oil glands become clogged and inflamed, often causing pimples.
additive (ad′ə tiv), any substance added to food for a particular purpose.
advertisement, a public notice or announcement recommending a product or service.
agility (ə jil′ə tē), the ability to change the position of the body quickly and to control body movements.
alcoholism (al′kə hô liz′əm), a disease in which a person cannot control his or her use of alcohol.
allergen (al′ər jən), a substance in the environment that causes an allergy.
allergy (al′ər jē), a harmful reaction of the body to a substance in the environment.
antibiotic (an′ti bī ot′ik), a medicine that destroys or weakens bacteria.
antibody (an′ti bod′ē), a tiny substance made by the white blood cells that attaches to a disease germ, making it harmless.
antiperspirant (an′ti per′spər ənt), a chemical preparation that controls body odor by closing the pores of sweat glands.
aquarium (ə kwer′ē əm), a place where living fish and water plants are collected and shown.
arboretum (är′bə rē′təm), a place where trees and shrubs are grown and exhibited for scientific and educational purposes.
artery (är′tər ē), a blood vessel that carries blood from the heart to other parts of the body.
artificial respiration (är′tə fish′əl res′pə rā′shən), a method of first aid that forces air into the lungs.
atherosclerosis (ath′ər ō sklə rō′sis), a cardiovascular disease in which material builds up inside the arteries.
attitude (at′ə tüd), a way of thinking about a particular idea, situation, or person.

B

bacteria (bak tir′ē ə), a group of organisms that can usually be seen only with a microscope. Some bacteria are harmful, causing disease and tooth decay.
blood alcohol level, the percentage of fluids in the bloodstream that is alcohol.
body fatness, the amount of a person's weight that is body fat.

C

caffeine (ka fēn′), a mild stimulant drug found in some coffees, teas, soft drinks, and chocolate.
calipers (kal′ə pərz), an instrument used to measure the thickness of something. Calipers can be used to measure the thickness of body fat under the skin.
Calorie (kal′ər ē), a unit used to measure the amount of energy a food can produce in the body and the amount of energy the body uses during activity.
cancer (kan′sər), the uncontrolled growth of abnormal body cells.
carbohydrates (kär′bō hī′drātz), a group of nutrients that supplies energy and includes sugar, starch, and fiber.
carbon dioxide (dī ok′sīd), a colorless, odorless gas produced as a body waste in humans and other animals.
carbon monoxide (kär′bən mo nok′sīd), a colorless, odorless, and poisonous gas in the exhausts of motor vehicles.
cardiovascular (kär′dē ō vas′kyə lər) **disease,** a disease of the heart or blood vessels.
cardiovascular (kär′dē ō vas′kyə lər) **system,** the body system made up of the heart, blood, and blood vessels. This system moves oxygen and nutrients to body cells and removes cell wastes.

cavity (kav′ə tē), a hole in a tooth, caused by tooth decay.
cell (sel), the basic unit of living matter.
chlorine (klôr′ēn′), a chemical added to sewage and to drinking water to kill bacteria.
cholesterol (kə les′tə rol′), a fatlike substance that is made naturally in the body and is present in foods from animal sources.
chromosome (krō′mə sōm), a strand of matter in the nucleus of a cell that contains the information for a person's heredity.
cilia (sil′ē ə), hairlike projections that line parts of the respiratory system.
circulation (sėr′kyə lā′shən), the flow of the blood from the heart through the arteries and veins back to the heart.
cirrhosis (sə rō′sis), a disease of the liver that is often caused by heavy, long-term use of alcohol.
clinic (klin′ik), a place where people can receive medical treatment, often free or at low cost.
communicable (kə myü′nə kə bəl) **disease,** a disease that can spread, usually from one person to another.
community (kə myü′nə tē), a group of people living in the same area.
contagious (kən tā′jəs), able to be spread from one person to another.
coordination (kō ôrd′n ā′shən), the ability to use the senses together with body parts or to use two or more body parts together.

D

dandruff, clumps of dead skin cells that form on the scalp.
decibel (des′ə bəl), a unit for measuring the loudness of sound.
deodorant (dē ō′dər ənt), a chemical preparation that controls body odor by slowing the growth of bacteria on the skin.
dependence, the need for a drug. This need might be mental, physical, or both.
depressant (di pres′nt), a drug that slows down the work of the nervous system.
diet, a general term for the kind of food and drink a person consumes daily.
dietitian (dī′ə tish′ən), an expert on how the body uses nutrients and what nutrients are necessary for good health.
disease germ, an organism or substance that causes a communicable disease.
DNA, a chemical substance that makes up chromosomes and determines inherited traits.
drug, any chemical substance that changes the way the body works. The physical changes might cause changes in emotions and behavior.
drug abuse, the intentional use of drugs for reasons other than health.
drug misuse, incorrect use of a medicine in a way that can harm health.

E

egg cell, the female reproductive cell.
electron microscope, an instrument that enables people to view viruses and other tiny substances up to two million times their actual sizes.
emergency, a sudden need for quick action.
enamel (i nam′əl), the smooth, hard, outer layer of a tooth.
endocrine (en′dō krən) **gland,** an organ that produces chemicals and releases them directly into the blood.
energy, the ability to do work. The body gets energy from food to do all the work that keeps the body alive and healthy.
enriched, having had nutrients, such as vitamins and minerals, added.
environment (en vī′rən mənt), all the living and nonliving surroundings that affect living things.
epidemiologist (ep′ə dē′mē ol′ə jist), a physician or research scientist who studies the occurrence and causes of diseases.

F

fad, a product or practice that is popular only for a short time.
fatigue (fə tēg′), weariness caused by physical exercise, stress, concentration, boredom, or a lack of energy.

fats, a group of nutrients that provides energy and carries certain vitamins through the body.
fiber (fī′bər), a carbohydrate that helps move food and wastes through the body.
first aid, immediate medical care given to someone who is injured or suddenly ill.
flexibility (flek′sə bil′ə tē), the ability to move the joints fully and to move body parts easily.
food consumer, a person who buys or uses food. Everyone is a food consumer.
food processing, the changing of food before it is eaten.
fortified (fôr′tə fīd), enriched with vitamins and minerals.

G

gene (jēn), a small part of a chromosome that influences a specific inherited trait.
goal (gōl), something a person wants to do or achieve.
groundwater, water in the ground, near the earth's surface. Groundwater is usually located in the soil and in the cracks of rock beneath the surface.
growth spurt, a period of rapid growth. A growth spurt usually begins between the ages of nine and fifteen.
guarantee (gar′ən tē′), a promise by a manufacturer to replace, repair, or give money back for a product if it proves to be unsatisfactory.
gum disease, a condition begun by plaque building up and hardening between the teeth and under the gumline. This buildup irritates the gums, eventually causing them to pull away from the teeth, and leaving pockets through which bacteria can attack bone.

H

hallucinogen (hə lü′sn ə jen), a drug that causes changes in the senses, often making a person see, hear, smell, or feel things that are not really there.
health consumer, a person who buys or uses health products or services.
health fitness, the kind of fitness that helps a person look and feel his or her best and reduces the risk of disease.
heredity (hə red′ə tē), the passing of traits from parents to children.
hormone (hôr′mōn), a chemical, made by an endocrine gland, that affects how body cells work.
hypertension (hī′pər ten′shən), high blood pressure.

I

immunity (i myü′nə tē), the body's resistance to a disease through the presence of antibodies.
infection (in fek′shən), the presence of disease germs in the body.
inhalant (in hā′lənt), a substance that gives off fumes, which could produce druglike effects when breathed deeply into the body.

L

lifestyle, the way a person lives his or her life. A person's lifestyle includes that person's daily or usual actions that affect his or her health.
logo (lō′gō), a symbol used to identify something for advertising purposes.

M

mainstream smoke, smoke that is exhaled by the smoker.
marijuana (mar′ə wä′nə), the dried leaves and stems of a hemp plant used illegally as a mind-altering drug.
medicine, a drug that produces changes in the body to prevent, treat, or cure an illness.
minerals, a group of nutrients needed to provide healthy teeth, bones, muscles, and blood cells.

371

mucus (myü′kəs), a watery and somewhat sticky liquid that lines the mouth, nose, throat, windpipe, and lungs.
muscular endurance (en dyür′əns), the ability of muscles to work for long periods of time without getting tired.

N

narcotic (när kot′ik), a legal term for a drug made from opium or from a substance like opium that is produced artificially.
net weight, the weight of the contents of a product, not including the container.
nicotine (nik′ə tēn′), a stimulant drug found in cigarette smoke.
noncommunicable (non′kə myü′nə kə bəl) **disease,** a disease that is not caused by germs and that does not spread.
nucleus (nü′klē əs), the part of a cell that controls the cell's activities.
nutrient (nü′trē ənt), a substance found in food that your body needs to stay healthy.
nutrition (nü trish′ən), the study of nutrients and how the body uses them. Also, food or nourishment.

O

oil glands, tiny structures in the skin that produce an oily substance and transfer it to the surface of the skin.
organ, a structure made of living tissues that perform a specific function. For example, each endocrine gland is an organ.
organism (ôr′gə niz′əm), an individual living thing.
ovaries (ō′vər ēz), female reproductive glands.
overdose, an amount of a drug that is too large for the body and can cause a dangerous reaction.
over-the-counter medicine, a drug that can be purchased without a doctor's order.
oxygen (ok′sə jən), a colorless, odorless, and tasteless gas that humans, other animals, and plants need to live.

P

penicillin (pen′ə sil′ən), an antibiotic that cures many bacterial diseases.
perspiration (pėr′spə rā′shən), the water, salt, heat, and other body wastes transferred by the sweat glands to the skin's surface.
pharmacist (fär′mə sist), a person licensed to fill prescriptions.
physical fitness, the ability to exercise, play, and work without tiring easily and without a high risk of injury.
pituitary (pə tü′ə ter′ē) **gland,** the endocrine gland that makes growth hormone and other hormones that control the activities of other endocrine glands.
planetarium (plan′ə tər′ē əm), a building or room where the movements of the sun, moon, planets, and stars can be shown on the inside of a dome.
plaque (plak), a fatty substance that builds up along the inside walls of an artery. Also, a thin, sticky, colorless film, consisting largely of bacteria, that forms on teeth and gums.
pneumonia (nü mō′nyə), a respiratory disease in which a lung becomes inflamed, often accompanied by chills, a pain in the chest, cough, and fever.
poison, a substance that is harmful if it gets inside the body.
pollution (pə lü′shən), a change in the environment that is harmful or unpleasant to living things.
posture (pos′chər), the position of the body.
prescription (pri skrip′shən) **medicine,** a drug that can be purchased only with an order from a doctor.
preservative (pri zėr′və tiv), an additive that helps keep food from spoiling.
proteins (prō′tēnz′), the group of nutrients that builds, repairs, and maintains body cells.
puberty (pyü′bər tē), a period of time when the body develops more adultlike qualities, including the ability to reproduce.

R

recreation (rek′rē ā′shən), activity, such as exercise or a hobby, that provides relaxation during leisure time.

recycling, changing a waste product so that it can be used again.

reflexes, automatic body reactions.

relationship (ri lā′shən ship), a connection or condition that exists between two or more people.

reproduce (rē′prə düs′), produce offspring.

reproductive cell, a cell that gives a male or female the ability to reproduce. The male reproductive cells are sperm cells, and the female reproductive cells are egg cells.

reproductive gland, a gland that develops reproductive cells, giving a male or female the ability to reproduce. The male reproductive glands are testes, and the female reproductive glands are ovaries.

respiratory (res′pər ə tôr′ē) **system,** the body system that includes the nose, air passages, and lungs. This system helps bring oxygen to the body and remove carbon dioxide from the body.

rickets (rik′its), a childhood disease in which the bones do not develop properly; caused by a lack of vitamin D and calcium.

S

sanitarian (san′ə ter′ē ən), an environmental health specialist who works to ensure the safe quality of food, water, or air for the public health.

sanitary landfill, an area of land where garbage is buried in such a way as to minimize water pollution, air pollution, and the spread of disease.

scoliosis (skō′lē ō′sis), a condition in which the spine curves to the side.

scrubber, a device attached to a factory smokestack that removes much of the harmful gas and most of the particles from smoke.

scurvy (skėr′vē), a disease characterized by bleeding gums, bruises on the skin, and extreme weakness; caused by a lack of vitamin C.

self-image, the way a person feels about himself or herself.

sewage (sü′ij), the waste material carried through sewers and drains, also called wastewater.

sewage treatment plant, a facility where sewage is partially cleaned before being sent to a river, lake, or ocean; also called wastewater treatment plant.

shock, a condition that occurs when the body fails to circulate blood adequately, causing body functions to slow down.

sidestream smoke, smoke that comes from the end of a burning cigarette.

sinusitis (sī′nə sī′tis), a disease in which the sinus openings become blocked.

skills fitness, the kind of fitness that helps a person perform physical skills.

smog (smog), pollution caused by engine exhaust gases reacting with other gases in the presence of sunlight.

snuff, a powder made from grinding tobacco leaves and stems. It is usually sniffed through the nose.

sodium (sō′dē əm), a soft silver-white element, which is the main component of salt.

sperm (spėrm) **cell,** the male reproductive cell.

stimulant (stim′yə lənt), a drug that speeds up the work of the nervous system.

stress, the body's physical and mental reactions to demanding situations.

sulfur dioxide (sul′fər dī ok′sīd), a major component of air pollution. Sulfur dioxide reacts with moisture in the air to form acid rain.

sweat glands, tiny structures in the skin that collect some body wastes and transfer them to the surface of the skin.

symptom (simp′təm), a sign or indication of a disease.

T

tar, a yellow or brown substance in the smoke of cigarettes. Tars form a brown, sticky mass in smokers' lungs.
testes (tes′tēz) *sing.* **testis** (tes′tis), male reproductive glands.
THC, the main mind-altering chemical in marijuana.
tolerance, a condition in which the body gets used to the presence of a drug and needs larger amounts of that drug to produce the same effects.
tooth decay, a condition in which acids destroy the enamel of teeth.
toxic, poisonous.
trait (trāt), a feature or quality of a person or thing.
tumor (tü′mər), a clump of useless tissue caused by the buildup of abnormal cells.

U

unit price, the price of a product per ounce, gram, or other unit of measure.
unnecessary risk, an action that is not necessary to perform and that greatly increases the threat to a person's safety.

V

vaccine (vak′sēn), a small dose of killed or weakened disease germs that prevents a person from getting a disease.
vein (vān), a blood vessel that carries blood back to the heart.
virus (vī′rəs), a group of tiny, disease-causing substances.
vitamins (vī′tə mənz), a group of nutrients needed in small amounts to keep the body working properly.
volunteer (vol′ən tir′), a person who offers services without pay.

W

water treatment plant, a facility where water from a river or lake is cleaned to make it safe and pleasant for drinking; also called water purification plant.
white blood cell, a blood cell that destroys disease germs.
withdrawal, the symptoms that occur when a person who is physically dependent on a drug stops taking it.

Index

*A **bold-faced** number indicates a page with a picture about the topic.*

A

B

375

376

D

E

377

F

G

H

379

I-J

L

M

N

381

R

S

383

Acknowledgments

Page **162:** From "She Knew What to Do" from CHILD LIFE magazine. Copyright © 1981 by Benjamin Franklin Literary & Medical Society, Inc., Indianapolis, Indiana. Adapted by permission of the publisher.

Page **310:** Figure by Josephine Bellalta-Moriarty from "Local Garden Helps Pilsen Bloom" by Rebecca Severson, THE NEIGHBORHOOD WORKS, April 1985. Reprinted by permission of Josephine Bellalta-Moriarty.

Picture Credits

Page **18–19:** © Photri/Marilyn Gartman Agency
Page **26(l):** © Donald Smetzer/Click/Chicago
Page **27(l):** © Donald Dietz/Stock Boston
Page **31:** Courtesy Daniel L. Feicht/Cedar Point, Inc.
Page **44:** Photo courtesy of WTTW, Chicago
Page **58:** © Ed Reschke
Page **59: (b)** Courtesy of Genetics Department, Children's Memorial Hospital, Chicago, IL.
Page **63:** © Plantek 1985/Photo Researchers
Page **74–75:** © 1983 Mark Wexler
Page **76:** © Rice Sumner Wagner
Page **81:** Jim and Mary Whitmer
Page **90:** Courtesy The Manning Brothers Historical Collection
Page **91:** Jim and Mary Whitmer
Page **92:** Edith G. Haun/Stock Boston
Page **100:** Courtesy Parke-Davis, Division of Warner Lambert Company
Page **104–105:** © David Brownell 1983
Page **106:** Jim Whitmer/Nawrocki Stock Photo
Page **110(l):** © Joseph Nettis 1983/Photo Researchers
(r): Focus West
Page **111:** Bill Ross/West Light
Page **116(l):** Jim Whitmer/Nawrocki Stock Photo
(c): Joseph A. DiChello, Jr.
Page **117(c):** Click/Chicago
Page **119:** John J. Lopinot
Page **120(r):** © Dave Black 1986
Page **136:** John J. Lopinot
Page **143(tr):** Courtesy Speciality Vehicle Institute of America
Page **162:** Reprinted with permission from THE SATURDAY EVENING POST Company © 1981
Page **166–167:** Warshaw Collection. Smithsonian Institution.
Page **172:** © University Museum. University of Pennsylvania
Page **174:** Larry Mulvehill/Photo Researchers
Page **179:** © Russ Kinne 1978/Photo Researchers
Page **180(t,b):** Courtesy Dr. Donald T. Tashkin, M.D., University of California Los Angeles
Page **183:** Ira Kirschenbaum/Stock Boston
Page **184(l):** Martin K. Rotker/Taurus
(r): © 1985 James E. Eisman/Journalism Services/Nawrocki Stock Photo
Page **191:** Cameramann International
Page **198–199:** Lou Lainey/© DISCOVER PUBLICATIONS, INC.
Page **200(l):** Jonathon D. Eisenback/Phototake
(c): Eric Gravé/Phototake
(r): L.J. LeBeau, University of Illinois Hospital/Biological Photo Service
Page **201(l,r):** Gene Cox/Micro Colour, England
Page **203(tl):** Omikron/Photo Researchers
(cl): Dr. R. Dourmashkin/SPL/Photo Researchers
(bl): T. R. Broker/Phototake
(r): Dick Luria/Photo Researchers
Page **204–205:** Lennart Nilsson, from *Behold Man*, Courtesy Little, Brown and Company, Boston. Used with permission.
Page **208(t):** Courtesy Centers for Disease Control
Page **209:** Prof. Luc Montagnier/Institut Pasteur/CNRI/Science Photo Laboratory/Photo Res.
Page **211(t):** Dr. R. Dourmashkin/SPL/Photo Researchers
(b): T. R. Broker/Phototake
Page **213(t):** Ray Simon/Photo Researchers
Page **215(r):** © 1985 Martin M. Rotker/Taurus
Page **217:** Dr. Rob Stepney/SPL/Photo Researchers
Page **218(l):** Lennart Nilsson, from *Behold Man*, Courtesy Little, Brown and Company, Boston. Used with permission.
Page **218(r):** Photograph by Dr. Lennart Nilsson
Page **219(l):** Photograph by Dr. Lennart Nilsson
Page **219(r):** Lou Lainey/© DISCOVER PUBLICATIONS, INC.
Page **220(l):** Warren Uzzle/© DISCOVER PUBLICATIONS INC.
Page **224:** Marty Cooper/Peter Arnold Inc.
Page **226:** Hans Pfletschinger/Peter Arnold Inc.
Page **230:** Courtesy Parke-Davis, Division of Warner-Lambert Company
Page **236:** Susan Leavines/Photo Researchers
Page **238(t):** Courtesy Cleveland Museum of Natural History
(b): Z. Skobe, Forsyth Dental Center/Biological Photo Service
Page **240–241:** Copyright by the American Dental Association. Reprinted by permission.
Page **247:** Robert Lightfoot/Nawrocki Stock Photo
Page **249:** © 1986 Christopher Springman. All rights reserved.
Page **250:** Joseph A. DiChello, Jr.
Page **252:** Photo by John E. Gilmore for Scott, Foresma
Page **280:** Courtesy National Archives
Page **284–285:** Cameramann International
Page **286(tl):** © Ed Bock 1985
(tr): Tom Pantages
Page **287:** Ann McQueen/Stock Boston
Page **291:** Brent Jones
Page **292:** © Michael Philip Manheim/Marilyn Gartman Agency
Page **295:** Cameramann International/Marilyn Gartman Agency
Page **296:** Ted Spiegel/Black Star
Page **296:** Ted Spiegel/Black Star
Page **299:** © Ovak Arslanian
Page **302:** Ray Hillstrom/Hillstrom Stock Photo
Page **303:** Coco McCoy/Rainbow
Page **304:** Tom Hollyman/Photo Researchers
Page **305(t):** Courtesy Adler Planetarium, Chicago
(c): Gerald Corsi/Tom Stack
(b): Nathan Benn/Woodfin Camp & Assoc.
Page **310:** Rebecca Severson/Chicago Botanic Garden

All photographs not credited are the property of Scott, Foresman and Company. These include photographs taken by the following photographers:

James L. Ballard: Pages 20–21, 28–29 (all), 30, 32–33, 36, 42, 48–49, 50–51, 53, 64–65 (all), 66–67 (all), 68, 69, 70, 71, 92 (b), 107, 116 (r), 137, 143 (l), 145, 148 (all), 149, 150, 152, 156, 163, 175, 178, 185, 195, 22 234–235, 256–257, 260–261, 264–265 (all), 266 (l), 26 (r), 268, 272, 277–279 (all), 281, 286 (br), 306–307, 31
Ralph Cowan: Pages 130–135 (all)
Michael Goss: Pages 24–25, 77, 78, 79, 83 (all), 84–85, 86–87, 95, 153, 154–155 (b), 170 (all), 171, 192 (all),
Edward Hughes: Pages 181, 188, 189
Glen D. Phelan: Pages 61 (b), 297
Diana O. Rasche: Pages 143 (br), 288–290 (all)
Ryan Roessler: Pages 96–97 (b), 140–141, 157 (all), 158–159 (all), 169, 190, 258–259, 269, 273, 298 (l)

384